EUROP

D0866014

EUROPE by EURAIL
HOW TO TOUR EUROPE BY TRAIN

Nineteenth Edition

written by
George Wright Ferguson

edited by
LaVerne Ferguson and Christian Martin

A Voyager Book

The Globe Pequot Press

OLD SAYBROOK, CONNECTICUT

TO THE MEMORY OF
JACK WATSON
FRIEND, CORRESPONDENT,
AND RAIL NOMAD EXTRAORDINAIRE

Library of Congress Catalog Card Number: 87-658136
ISBN: 1–56440–501–X

Manufactured in the United States of America
Nineteenth Edition/First Printing

THE FERGUSON TEAM

George Wright Ferguson was born in Philadelphia twenty minutes after his mother was taken from a Washington–New York express train. He grew up alongside the Baldwin Locomotive Works on the "Pennsy" main line, and trains have continued to play an important role in his life.

A graduate of Penn State, George served in Europe during World War II as a test pilot and engineering officer with the Eighth Air Force. His first European train ride was aboard a vintage 1918 "40-and-8" freight car between Munich and Antwerp, a trip that lasted four days and four nights!

After a stint as editor, and later publisher, of a farm-equipment magazine, George was recalled to active military duty with assignments in Korea, Japan, and Vietnam and at the Pentagon in Washington, D.C. George retired from the Air Force in 1967 with more than 5,000 flying hours in his log book. As a senior Air Force logistician, he was commended by Defense Secretary Robert McNamara for his study of the Air Force's worldwide-movement capabilities.

George's international experiences continued with his position as an international coordinator for the Battelle Memorial Institute, the world's largest sponsored-research organization, headquartered in Columbus, Ohio. His work included assignments in Germany, Thailand, Iran, and South America. George met the other member of his team, LaVerne, at Battelle.

LaVerne first discovered her love for travel in a third-grade geography class. Determined to "see the world," she has collected brochures and information about various countries for many years. LaVerne majored in social studies and English at Ohio State University. She also completed courses in library search and business communications. LaVerne contributes her experience as an executive secretary and technical writer to the Ferguson team.

In addition to researching and writing rail guidebooks and articles, the Fergusons also own Rail Pass Express, Inc., a rail-only sales agency in Columbus, Ohio. Their trained staff members are experts in all aspects of European rail travel. George and LaVerne welcome comments and suggestions. You can write to them at Rail Pass Express, Inc., 2737 Sawbury Boulevard, Columbus, OH 43235–4583; or call toll-free (800) 722–7151.

5

CONTENTS

APPENDIXES

INTRODUCTION

"To travel by train," wrote Agatha Christie, "is to see nature and human beings, towns and churches and rivers, in fact, to see life." This book has been written to assist you in seeing all that is life in Europe in the best possible way—by train.

Europe by Eurail is a train-travel guide that brings European-train-related information to its readers in a direct, pragmatic manner. It is not a hotel guide, but it tells how to locate them. A restaurant occasionally gains mention, especially if it adds to the graciousness and enjoyment of a train trip or a stay in a city. *Europe by Eurail* deals with the necessities of train travel in Europe and offers guidance for appreciating the educational and cultural sites that abound along the right of way of the Continent's magnificent rail system, Eurail.

We welcome you aboard and wish you a very pleasant journey!

Base City–Day Excursion Concept

In 1976, *Europe by Eurail* launched a new concept for comfortable, hassle-free train travel by combining the economy of a Eurailpass with the Fergusons' "Base City–Day Excursion" method of touring Europe. *Europe by Eurail* has proved to be a most useful traveling companion for travelers using any of the rail passes that access the Eurail system. It identifies base cities throughout Europe in which you can stay in comfort and from which you can make numerous day excursions to interesting places yet return each night to the same hotel room. You can eliminate the hassles of daily packing and unpacking. This relaxed approach to rail travel is not only an enjoyable way to visit Europe's great cities, but it also produces an astonishing and delightful variety of things to see and do *outside* the cities.

Those who would doubt that a rail system could reach remote places as well as major points within a country—or series of countries, as is the case in Europe—should consider that the system in Europe followed a well-developed plan of roadways and waterways. It spread like a series of connecting "webs" between major cities and, consequently, differs from the "linear" type of railroad construction found on the North American continent. Thus, Europe's "weblike" rail structure provides the perfect opportunity to utilize the most comfortable do-it-yourself touring mode available—the "Base City–Day Excursion" method.

With a Eurailpass and a current copy of *Europe by Eurail,* you become your own tour guide, packing and moving on only when *you* want to. For the experienced traveler, or the novice, it's the only *real* way to go!

World's Finest Rail System

The rail system in Western Europe today is, without reservation, the finest in the world—and it's getting better. Many trains in Europe run at speeds in excess of one hundred miles per hour; and the French TGV (*train à grande vitesse*) Atlantique, currently the holder of the world's speed record at 317 miles per hour, runs at speeds up to 186 miles per hour (300 kilometers) in regular passenger service.

Each of the Atlantique TGVs features public phones, a nursery, special facilities for handicapped travelers, and even salons for business meetings. Each train set is capable of transporting 485 passengers—a 30 percent increase over the original Paris-Lyon TGVs—and when coupled together in tandem for 970 passengers, they outclass jumbo-jet performance over point-to-point distances between the major cities in France.

TGV service also operates between Paris and Geneva, Lausanne, and Berne. The TGV North system connects Paris with Brussels and Amsterdam to the north as well as with London via the English Channel tunnel (Chunnel). Presently, the fastest rail-hovercraft connection between Paris and London takes five hours, thirty minutes; via the Chunnel, the total time is reduced to only three hours.

Similar modernization programs are underway in other European countries. For example, Germany has improved its trackage to allow speeds up to 165 miles per hour for its InterCity Express (ICE) service. Departures are hourly throughout the business week to every major city within Germany. If changing trains en route is required, with typical German efficiency the train you are transferring to will be standing immediately across the platform from the train you are arriving in. Comfort is being emphasized, too. Both first- and second-class coaches have increased leg room, and the seats now recline farther for those who wish to take a nap.

Switzerland continues with its major rail-line modifications to speed up traffic in both east-west and north-south directions. Hourly and sometimes half-hourly service between major Swiss cities is now available. The sparkling modern rail stations at the Swiss airports in Geneva and Zurich operate with Swiss-watch efficiency, speeding arriving and departing air passengers on their way.

RENFE, the Spainsh rail system, has its own version of the high-speed French TGV called the AVE (Alta Velocidad Expanola). It was inaugurated for the opening of EXPO '92 in Seville, Spain. Like the TGV, AVE trains cruise at 186 miles per hour. These sleek white trains have navy and gray stripes along the sides and boast airline-type amenities, such as headsets with music channels and television monitors. Unlike other Spanish trains, AVE fares are calculated according to class of travel (Club, Preference, or Coach) and time of day rather than distance traveled. Consequently, rail pass holders must pay a supplement of 15 to 40 percent, depending on class, to ride the AVEs. Reservations are, of course, required.

The basis for high-speed rail traffic is a flawless rail bed. Europe's rails sing as trains move smoothly enough to permit dining without fear that the next curve might slosh your coffee. Most rail lines throughout western Europe today are equipped with endless, welded track. The old "clickety-clack" of the track, regardless of its nostalgic value, is gone forever.

"See Europe by train" has been the favorite slogan of Europe's railways for decades. But it has never been as full of meaning as it is today. Rail travel, too fast now for any chance of boredom, is still leisurely enough for full enjoyment of the constantly changing scenes of hills and hamlets, farms and forests, and cities and countrysides that make the European landscape fascinating. Every country has its own special attractions to offer rail travelers as they speed by, ensconced in comfort and free from worry or distraction. To the pleasure of the passing scene is added the opportunity of taking meals and refreshments at leisure in ideal surroundings and chatting with your fellow passengers—the very kinds of people you hoped to meet.

Airport and Ferry Connections

The number of European cities where the airport is connected by rail to the central station is growing. Such facilities already exist in the following base cities: Amsterdam, Barcelona, Berlin, Brussels, Munich, Paris, Rome, Vienna, and Berne (through Zurich). GermanRail has hourly InterCity service from the Frankfurt Airport to more than forty cities in Germany, Austria, and the Netherlands. The Swiss Federal Railways have a "welcome" service for arriving air passengers to forward their baggage by rail.

Ferry and catamaran connections play an important role in those areas of Europe where large bodies of water separate the land masses. On some of the major ferry connections, the rail coaches are actually loaded aboard ship. In Denmark, the fleet of rail ferries plying between Korsor-Nyborg on the great belt line connecting Copenhagen with Germany has been expanded from four to seven vessels. (Details begin on page 611.)

The Chunnel and Eurostar Services

In 1888, Louis Figuier proclaimed that "linking France and England will meet one of the present day needs of civilization." On May 6, 1994, England's Queen Elizabeth II and France's President François Mitterand inaugurated a new era in European train travel by witnessing the linking of England and France via a tunnel that runs underground and under the English Channel. More than 17 million tons of earth were moved to build the two rail tunnels (one for northbound and one for southbound traffic) and one service tunnel.

The project cost more than $13 billion and took seven years to complete.

Plagued by delays and billions of dollars in cost overruns, the Chunnel has proven to be one of the world's largest undertakings. Not since the Ice Age has France and England been joined. Napoleon's engineer, Albert Mathieu, planned the first tunnel in 1802, incorporating an underground passage with ventilation chimneys above the waves. For obvious reasons the British were nervous. Later, in 1880, the first real attempt at a tunnel was undertaken by Colonel Beaumont, who bored 2,000 meters into the earth before abandoning the project. When work on another tunnel began in 1974, the Beaumont tunnel was found to be in good condition. Construction of the current tunnels began in 1987. They are 38 kilometers in length undersea and have an average depth of 40 meters under the seabed.

At press time, limited "discovery" passenger service was expected to begin November 14, 1994, with full service scheduled to begin in June 1995. Operated by British Rail, the French (SNCF) and Belgium (SNCB) railways, the Eurotunnel will provide different types of service between England and the Continent. Eurostar will provide passenger service, and Le Shuttle will provide automobile, coach, and lorry service between Folkstone and Calais. International rail freight rounds out the list.

Eurostar service will be offered from London's new Waterloo International Eurostar Terminal to Paris' Gare du Nord or Brussels Midi stations. Travel times from London to Paris will be reduced from more than seven hours to three hours; Brussels is only three hours and fifteen minutes away, thus making a European Capitals tour nothing more than a day excursion. *Eurailpass will not be accepted for service through the Chunnel.* The sleek Eurostar trains (*Trans Mache Super Trains*) each carry 794 passengers (210 in first class and 584 in second class) and reach speeds of 200 miles per hour in France and 100 miles per hour in England, with speeds through the Chunnel of 80 miles per hour. The trains are accessible to handicapped passengers. In the next few years international service will continue to expand, providing day and evening trains to various destinations.

The EuroCity System

Like the icing on a cake, we have saved the best part for last—it's called EuroCity. Introduced in 1987, the EuroCity system consists of seventy-four pairs of fast, air-conditioned, international day trains, all with food services and many with public telephones aboard. The system is augmented by eight EuroNight trains offering couchette and sleeping cars. EuroCity trains haul both first- and second-class cars. Some of the trains require a special fare supplement and seat-reservation fees. Eurailpass holders, however, are not required to pay the supplement, but for certain trains the seat-reservation payment will be necessary.

Now the best international trains in Europe, the EuroCity network serves more than 200 cities in fifteen countries. The trains have been selected on the basis of high-speed performance; their minimum speed on all trips is ninety kilometers per hour, including stops. The nine pairs of overnight (EuroNight) trains match the speed of the EuroCity day trains and consist wholly of sleeping cars with berths and, in some cases, couchettes.

Eurailpass

For economy, versatility, and convenience, the "king" of all rail passes is the Eurailpass. The popular pass entitles a traveler to unlimited, first-class rail travel, free of any fast-train surcharge (except on Spain's AVE trains), throughout seventeen European countries: Austria, Belgium, Denmark, Finland, France, Germany, Greece, Hungary, Ireland, Italy, Luxembourg, Netherlands, Norway, Portugal, Spain, Sweden, and Switzerland. It also gives access to many steamers, ferries, and buses, either entirely free or at reduced fares. You go as you please, stopping where and when you want. It is still one of the finest transportation values available today. To complement the length of your trip, you can choose from five categories of Eurailpass: fifteen days, twenty-one days, one month, two months, or three months.

As a rule of thumb, if your itinerary includes two or more countries, you probably need a Eurailpass or Europass. We have listed point-to-point fares between base cities on page 626 to aid in your decision-making process. If you are visiting one country only, you may want to investigate that country's "national rail pass." Eligibility requirements and pass-use regulations vary with each country, so you should write or telephone the national tourist office (beginning on page 633) of the country in which you plan to travel.

Eurail Youthpass

If you are under twenty-six years of age, you are eligible to purchase the Eurail Youthpass. It entitles you to the same privileges as the first-class Eurailpass. You must travel in second class, however, as do most Europeans. If your budget is limited but you want to see as much of Europe as possible and your passport (which never lies about age) records that you've not yet reached your twenty-sixth birthday, then consider a fifteen-day, one- or two-month Eurail Youthpass.

Eurail Saverpass

Three or more people traveling together may take advantage of the Eurail Saverpass, valid for fifteen consecutive days of unlimited, first-class rail travel in the same countries honoring, and with the same privileges as, Eurailpass. From October 1 through March 31, the fifteen-day, twenty-one-day, and one-month Eurail Saverpass are also available for two people traveling together.

Eurail Flexipass and Youth Flexipass

The Eurail Flexipass provides exactly what its name implies—flexibility. You can choose from three categories of Flexipass: any five, ten, or fifteen days unlimited first-class rail travel to be used within a two-month period. The flexibility of the pass lies in the fact that the days need not be consecutive, as is the case with other types of Eurailpasses. It can be used *any* days within the validity period. After validation and before boarding the first train or ship each day, the traveler must enter the date of use where indicated on the pass.

The Youth Flexipass (for persons under age twenty-six) provides unlimited second-class rail travel for *any* five, ten, or fifteen days within two months.

Europass

If your Eurail travel will be limited to Germany, France, Italy, Spain and/or Switzerland, you may want to consider a Europass. You can purchase from five to fifteen travel days that can be used within a two-month period in three, four, or all five of the aforementioned countries. The countries you wish to visit must be selected at the time of purchase, and they must be adjacent to each other. Use of this pass takes more advance planning than some of the others. As with the Eurail Flexipass, the travel days need not be consecutive.

Eurailpass Validation

From the date of purchase, you have six months to begin using your Eurailpass. Prior to boarding your first train in Europe, present your pass for validation at the rail station from which you intend to start your Eurail journey. The European rail official validating your pass will enter the starting and ending date of the pass, together with your passport number. *Do not* make any entries (such as filling in your passport number) prior to validation. Be certain that your pass is validated before you entrain; otherwise, you may have to pay a penalty. Check the validation dates before accepting the pass from the validating official. If an error has been made in either the dates or your passport number, have it corrected *immediately*.

Allow for a little extra time validating your pass. The information window may be crowded. Once your pass is validated, however, that ends standing in line to buy another ticket—a convenience you'll like.

How to Order Rail Passes

Current rates for European rail passes including Eurailpass and Eurail Youthpass, Saverpass, Flexipass and Europass begin on page 627. To order any of these super rail bargains, call the toll-free order number: (800) 722–7151. MasterCard and Visa are accepted. Your rail pass will be delivered to you *within two business days*. You will also receive a free Eurail timetable and a free copy of the Eurail Travelers Guide booklet with a fold-out Eurail network map.

Why Eurail?

Many visitors to Europe fail to realize that the European rail system (Eurail) can take you to practically every nook and cranny of the Continent, so they insist on renting a car. At first glance, those European fly-drive packages appear enticing. But the more you investigate them, the less appealing they become. Annually, European road traffic has four times the number of fatal accidents North America has, and watching the road ahead is not what most folks go to Europe to do. That four-passenger economy car never could carry four passengers *and* their luggage—so bring on the Mercedes at three times the price and double the gas. Prepare yourself for another shock—the price of gasoline in Europe is about three times that in the United States.

Another very important facet of a fly-drive package is the VAT (value added tax), which currently ranges from 6 to 33 percent in European countries. In some countries, foreign tourists are eligible for refunds on certain purchases, but there are no VAT refunds on car rentals. Reference to the VAT is either tactfully avoided in car-rental information or hidden in the fine print of the terms. Whether or not it's hidden, after determining the low, low cost of a rental car with unlimited mileage privileges (which also includes the privilege of buying the gas), don't forget to multiply the bottom line by the VAT value of the country for the true cost of your intended auto excursion.

Another item overlooked frequently is insurance. To assure yourself of the *minimum* personal-insurance protection, plan to add at least $8.00 a day for that coverage. By now, you will begin to realize why Europeans are parking their cars and riding the trains.

One of the real reasons for going to Europe is to mingle with the Europeans you came to Europe to meet. Traveling about Europe day after day in a motor coach filled with other American tourists or riding for hours in a small rental car with the spouse and kids crammed in with the suitcases are not, in our opinion, the ways to accomplish this.

On the trains of Europe, Europeans will be sitting next to you or across from you in the diner. You will be sharing the same experiences, so conversation will come easily. It's a great way to make new friends and the kids can eat, get a drink, or go to the bathroom just as often as their little hearts desire.

Trains have an aura of romance about them that cannot be found in any other mode of transportation. For example, the mere mention of the Orient Express sparks visions of intrigue, mystery—and sumptuous dining. Along with the original Orient Express, the famous name trains such as Mistral and Train Bleu are gone. They've been replaced by efficient, modern, high-speed international express trains. But the thrill of rail travel is still there. Travel by rail in Europe is a unique and pleasurable experience. We urge you to try it— and take your imagination with you.

1   EURAIL TRIP PLANNING

Careful planning is the main key to success in just about everything we do. Planning a Eurail vacation is no exception. The following information is presented as a planning guide for those considering such an adventure.

How Much?

Perhaps the most important consideration of any vacation is its cost. Can you afford it? How much will it *actually* cost—including all the extras that seem to creep into a vacation regardless of how well it was planned. Many a vacation has turned into a financial nightmare owing to these "unknown" costs. The way to reduce them to a minimum is to maximize the "known" costs.

The three basic elements of any vacation are transportation, accommodations, and food. A European motor-coach tour is no doubt an ideal way of stabilizing all three, for each is usually included in the tour "package." Nevertheless, the rigors of staying at a different hotel almost every night, accompanied by the wasteful exercise of constant packing and unpacking, become less enchanting to more tourists every year. Speaking of packing, and recalling our admonition to take as little as possible with you, we know of some people who have purchased so many new clothes "to wear on the trip" that they couldn't afford the trip. Unlike a motor-coach tour, the beauty of a Eurail tour is that you will not be seeing the same people day after day. Consequently, a simple wardrobe will do.

Properly planned, a Eurail tour can maximize the "known" costs yet, at the same time, provide the individual with complete mobility and freedom. Contrary to rental-car tours, where the farther you go the more it costs, traveling on the European rail system with a Eurailpass works in an inverted progress—*the more miles traveled, the less the average cost per mile*. The Eurail system is so extensive that about the only additional transportation costs you encounter will probably be for an occasional bus, taxi, or a ticket for a local tour. Speaking of taxis, use them sparingly, since they are the most expensive means of transportation. Arriving in a base city burdened with luggage, you may feel justified in hailing a cab. Once rid of that excess weight, however, public transportation is the *only* way to go.

If you plan to go sightseeing within a base city, investigate the availability of multiple-ride tickets on the city's public-transportation systems. The cost is inexpensive, and there's a surprising number of sights you can see on your own. Coupled with your air-transportation ticket, purchasing a Eurailpass nails down total transportation costs long before your trip begins.

What about the other two basic elements—accommodations and food? How can they be stabilized on a Eurail vacation?

Accommodations

There are several means by which you can regulate accommodations costs. One, of course, is the budget. So much for a night's lodging and no more. This hard, firm line is about the only way a person on the move can make it with no fixed itinerary and no knowledge (or care) of where they might be tomorrow. The Eurailpass is invaluable to such a traveler. If you are unable to find lodging that suits your budget within the city center, use your pass to board the next train to the suburbs, where lower rates and more vacancies usually exist. Train systems, such as the S-Bahn of Munich (see page 416), offer a wide selection of housing options in the suburbs and countryside surrounding the city. Their frequent commuter service simplifies return to the central train station for city sightseeing or day-excursion departures.

While on the subject of budgeting, the staff of the city tourist information offices are well aware that most tourists have financial limitations. Consequently, don't be shy about it. Time after time, we have witnessed the same scenario: The tourist asks about the availability of hotel rooms in the city. The clerk assures them that vacancies exist, then asks, "How much do you want to pay?" The visitor usually responds by saying, "As little as possible." To the visitor's embarrassment, the clerk then produces the hostel listing—which is not what the visitor had in mind.

Remedy the situation and avoid the embarrassment by determining what your hotel budget per night equates to in local currency—and tell the clerk that when you are asked, "How much do you want to pay?" With your budget figure at hand, it will be no time at all until you are en route to your lodgings.

Confirmed and assured hotel reservations, made prior to departure for Europe by using the toll-free "800" telephone services listed on page 636, are an excellent means of ensuring that a room will be waiting for you on arrival and that the price quoted will remain fixed.

Accommodations Options

Another option is to have your local travel agency arrange the entire trip for you, including your air ticket and hotel reservations. The price tag is the total you will pay for the entire package. If you ask your travel consultants to book you into the "lower cost" European hotels, you may have to pay a surcharge (usually all travel services are free) for the additional costs incurred for fax messages, international airmail correspondence, and foreign-currency exchange. Oddly enough, the "lower cost" hotel is rapidly disappearing in Europe. In most European cities, the rate difference between first-class and standard hotels is no more than $10 to $20.

A plan we often follow during our frequent trips to Europe is to make confirmed reservations only in the arrival city. Following our arrival, we present the balance of our itinerary to the hotel concierge and ask him or her to arrange our subsequent reservations. A tip is expected, but consider it well spent. By the way, you can advise the concierge regarding the maximum room charge your budget will allow, and he will adhere to it without fail.

Should the title "concierge" baffle you, welcome to the amenities of European hostelry, where the art of conducing comfort and convenience for guests has been practiced for centuries. The domain of the concierge is found nearby—but never in—the registration and cashier areas of the hotel. The concierge is multilingual, arranges for your luggage and mail, makes reservations, and suggests things to do and places to see in the city. The concierge will even know the shortest route to the closest McDonald's or Wendy's.

Budgets and Hostels

For the strict-budget traveler, we suggest writing well in advance of departure to the appropriate European tourist offices in North America listed in the Appendix, which begins on page 633. Inform them of your intended itinerary while in their countries and ask to be provided with information about budget accommodations. The responses will amaze you, what with the plenitude of modestly priced lodgings and inexpensive restaurants in existence, even in Europe's "most expensive" cities.

For those who are interested in international hostels, you must join the American Youth Hostels. A junior (age seventeen and under) membership is $10; adult (age eighteen to fifty-four) is $25; senior citizen (age fifty-five and over) is $15. For information or a membership application, write to Rail Pass Express, 2737 Sawbury Boulevard, Columbus, OH 43235, or call (800) 722–7151.

Not by Bread Alone

Turning to the last of the basic vacation elements, food, we come to the most variable of the three. Personal preferences, varying appetites, and so forth make the difference. Oddly enough, the reader who exists on hamburgers and milk shakes back home will find such a diet extremely expensive to maintain in Europe, except at one of the American-style fast-food outlets that are in most of Europe's major cities. Such "culinary delights" are less in demand, more difficult to find, and more expensive to purchase.

Europe abounds in good, wholesome food. Practically every major railway station has a cafeteria, where the food is displayed along with the prices. "Order the spaghetti Bolognese," was the advice of one tourist official in Switzerland. "You can't go wrong," he declared. He was right—and it's become one of our favorites! Many of the railway stations have dining-room facilities, in addition to cafeteria service, where you may employ the help of the waiter or waitress in deciphering the menu.

Most European restaurants offer a tourist menu at a fixed cost. Look for the "menu" sign, posted outside, showing the prices and the food selections.

If you are puzzled, as we sometimes are, by the contents of a foreign menu, take heart. Many European restaurants also have menus that have been translated into your language. Although that might take some of the "adventure" out of eating in a foreign country, it also might save an embarrassing moment—such as ordering the *poulet* which you recognize as chicken, and ending up with a whole roasted chicken!

To help hold the food price line, insist that the cost of your lodgings include breakfast. In this way, you are left only with the variables of the other two meals—lunch and dinner. With few exceptions, unless you are staying in one of the American-style chain hotels, your breakfast is included, but it pays to check.

On day excursions, pack a lunch basket. Bread, cheese, pastry, cold cuts, fruits, soft drinks, and beer or wine—all are available from local shops. If you will give the concierge advance notice, he can arrange for the hotel to prepare a basket lunch.

Meals served aboard the trains are, quite naturally, on the expensive side. In many cases, though, the food is excellent and well worth the premium you pay for enjoying it as you speed along through the scenic countryside. Many European trains provide buffet and cafeteria service, and you can usually count on a food vendor's being aboard to sell drinks and sandwiches from a cart he pushes from car to car. One fact remains: The least expensive food you can find aboard a train is that which you have brought with you. Again, plan ahead and save.

How Long?

How long should your Eurail tour be? Answer that question and you have completed at least 50 percent of the planning. There are many factors bearing on this determination, the most important being the individual. How much annual vacation time do you have? How do you take it? All at one time or in two or more segments? Travel magazines and the travel sections of the Sunday newspapers are usually loaded with one-week trips to almost anywhere—Europe included. Based on our own experience, however, we can state categorically that going to Europe for any period of less than two weeks is a waste of time and money.

A look at the logistics involved in a European visit supports our thesis. Aircraft departures from North America usually begin in the evening and arrive in Europe the following morning. During the flight time of from seven to eight hours crossing the Atlantic, you will be subjected to a cocktail hour, a dinner, a break for an after-dinner drink, and a full-length feature movie. In the morning, you'll be awakened and served breakfast.

Add up the time consumed by all the scheduled events en route and you'll quickly determine that your night aloft over the Atlantic consisted of many things—except sleep. Theoretically, even if you slept through the entire trip, instead of eating, drinking, and watching movies, your body and all its functions will be arriving in Europe a few hours after midnight by North American time. It will crave adjustment to a phenomenon known as "jet lag," which will be trying its best to interrupt your plans for a carefree vacation.

In other words, if you take two days for travel and at least one day for adjusting properly to the time change, the balance left in a one-week vacation hardly seems worth the trip. Upon your return home, you'll probably be a living example of the old adage, "A person who looks like he needs a vacation usually has just returned from one."

Another consideration to be taken into account when deciding how long your Eurail vacation should be is the type of airline ticket to purchase. Most of the economical fares for transatlantic air travel evolve around day fourteen, meaning that your minimum time to be spent in Europe after departing from North America must be 14 days in order to qualify for the APEX (advanced purchase excursion) fares. Consequently, in consideration of both time and money, your stay in Europe should be at least two full weeks.

If possible, plan your departure for a Thursday. It makes sense when you consider that you will be gaining an additional weekend before having to return to work. Also consider that APEX fares are higher for eastward departures on weekends. So, "go for it"—on Thursday.

How to Get There

Transatlantic air traffic is so frequent and varied today that no description of it—short of an entire book—could do it justice. Excursion fares are still available in a multitudinous variety. Charter flights are still available, and they are still mostly money savers. But some APEX excursion fares could mean further savings over charters. Make inquiries and then compare. You can start with the toll-free numbers on page 636. It's not uncommon even on a regular, scheduled airliner winging its way to Europe to find that every passenger in your row of seats paid a different fare for the same flight on the same schedule with the same service. The more that the air transportation industry is deregulated, the more there are variations.

We refer readers to their travel agents for airline information. But there has been a tremendous erosion of such information in travel agencies, brought about in general by the proliferation of air fares. The agencies face the almost impossible task of keeping tabs on the airline industry. Let's put it this way, if you've dealt with a reputable travel agency over the years, contact them the moment you've decided to do Europe by Eurail and ask the agency to come up with some air-excursion-fare options. Don't get miffed at your travel agency when they state one fare and then you spot a lower one in the newspaper. Even in the computer age, things like this will happen. Unfortunately, their computers don't read the newspapers . . . yet.

In the 1990s, the adage "there's nothing more constant than change" certainly applies to the air carriers providing transatlantic passenger service. We've listed a few toll-free airline numbers for those airlines *currently* providing transatlantic services on page 636 in the Appendix. You may also dial 800 directory information at (800) 555–1212.

What to Take

Obviously, the answer to this question is "as little as possible!" The tourist's tendency is to pack everything one conceivably might use during a vacation, lug it everywhere, use it very little, and return with longer arms. In these days of wash-and-wear fabrics (and of deodorants), this is no longer necessary, particularly on a Eurail vacation. (See our previous comments on this subject appearing on page 16.) May we suggest a rule of thumb? Take one medium-size suitcase. Nothing else, except perhaps a shoulder bag. Hold to this rule and you'll enjoy your trip.

How to Pack

Samsonite, one of the major manufacturers of quality luggage, has published an interesting booklet on the subject of suitcases and travel. With the catchy title *Lightening the Travel Load—Travel Tips and Tricks,* it is crammed with helpful tips running from the analysis of luggage needs and the basic points of safeguarding luggage to packing for a trip. Helpful hints on carry-on luggage, how to tip, how to clear customs, and how to stay healthy while on your trip are also included in the booklet. For a free copy, write to Samsonite Traveler Advisory Service, P.O. Box 39603, Denver, CO 80239. Be certain to include a self-addressed business envelope with postage affixed for two ounces first-class U.S. postage.

Take a Timetable

We recommend the *Thomas Cook European Timetable* as a part of your Eurail trip planning. An invaluable aid, it contains complete timetables covering every major rail route in the seventeen countries honoring the Eurailpass. In addition, it contains plans of the major rail terminals throughout Europe and a wealth of other information, such as monthly temperature and rainfall statistics for each base city. We suggest that you purchase a copy before departing on your Eurail trip and that you take it with you. It may be a bit bulky, but you'll find yourself delving constantly between its covers.

The timetable is published on the first day of each month. The June through

September issues contain the summer train schedules; the issues from October to May contain the winter schedules. To assist in planning summer rail tours, the issues from February through May contain an advance summer-service supplement.

When you purchase your Eurailpass from Rail Pass Express's toll-free number (800) 722–7151, you will receive, free of charge, a current *Eurail Timetable* of major rail connections.

Traveling Companions

Europe by Eurail is an excellent companion to the *Thomas Cook European Timetable*. The train schedules listed in each base-city description of *Europe by Eurail* refer to specific tables appearing in Cook's *European Timetable*. If you want to travel to a base city at a time other than those given in *Europe by Eurail*, Cook's lists the complete twenty-four-hour train service. Most of the day-excursion descriptions in this edition of *Europe by Eurail* bear a reference to a specific table in the *European Timetable*. *Europe by Eurail* generally lists day-excursion trains for outbound trips in the morning and return trips in the late afternoon or early evening, in accordance with our "base city–day excursion" concept. The Thomas Cook publication, however, provides a complete selection of train services. Each publication complements the other. Again, we suggest you carry both with you during your Eurail trip.

In the United States and Canada, copies of the *Thomas Cook European Timetable* can be purchased from many bookstores or from the U.S. distributor: Forsyth Travel Library, P.O. Box 2975, Dept. ER, Shawnee Mission, KS 66201. Elsewhere in the world, write to: Thomas Cook Ltd., Timetable Publishing Office, Box 36, Dept. ER, Peterborough, PE3 6SB, England. In Europe, the *Thomas Cook European Timetable* can be purchased only at the company's main offices in major cities.

Rail-Station Timetables

In most European rail stations, poster timetables, available in the foyer of the station and on the train platforms, show departure and arrival times as well as the platform numbers. These timetables can be recognized easily by the color of their background. As a rule, departure timetables are printed on a yellow background; arrival timetables have a white background.

All trains on these timetables are listed chronologically from 0001 to 2400. Fast trains are shown in red instead of black. Next to the departure or arrival time, you will find the name and number of the train, its routing to final destination, and the most important intermediate stops along the route, together with the track and platform number at which the train departs or arrives. Free train schedules also are readily available at most of the rail stations.

Jet Lag

We mentioned jet lag earlier in this chapter. It can seriously affect your European trip unless you understand it and know the means of dealing with it. The following explanation of what jet lag is, and some of the means of combating it, should prove helpful to any traveler planning a trip involving four or more hours of time change.

The human body has numerous rhythms. That for sleep is one of them. Even without sunlight, as in a cave, the body will still maintain a twenty-four-hour awake-asleep cycle. The heart rate has another cycle, one that falls to a very low ebb in the early hours of the morning. Body temperature, which affects the mental processes, also drops during this time. Thus, if a traveler were transported rapidly to a location five or six time zones (hours) removed from the point of departure, even though it may be eight or nine o'clock in the morning at the arrival point, the traveler's body functions would be at a low ebb. Consequently, the traveler would feel subpar, and this feeling can persist for as long as three days or so unless something is done to correct it.

What to Do about It

To cope effectively with jet lag, start varying your normal sleep-eat-work pattern a week or so before your departure. If you are normally up by 7:00 A.M. and in bed around 11:00 P.M. or so, start getting up earlier and going to bed later for a few days. Then reverse the procedure by sleeping in a bit in the morning and going to bed ahead of your normal time. Vary your meal times, possibly putting off breakfast until you can combine it with brunch at noon. What this erratic life style will do is to condition your body to begin accepting changes in its normal routine. In turn, when the big transatlantic change comes, it won't be as much of a shock to your system.

To lessen the effects of jet lag during your trip, avoid excessive drinking and eating en route to Europe. Set your watch to local time at your destination as you depart on your flight. When you do this, your eyes will begin to tell your body functions that there is something new going on, and you'll accelerate your adjustment to the new time zone. Exercise on the first day you arrive in Europe by taking a vigorous stroll; then take a long nap. Rest and relax through the balance of that day. Then on the second day, begin doing everything you normally do back home—but on European time. Above all, don't keep your watch set at the time back home. (How many times have you looked at your watch and then realized that you were hungry?) Respect jet lag and take these precautions in order to enjoy your Eurail vacation to its fullest.

Trip Tips

Here are some tips to help you enjoy your Eurail trip to the fullest:

Don't carry more cash than you can afford to lose; use traveler's checks. Whenever possible, cash your traveler's checks at the currency-exchange offices in the railway stations and airports. These offices are government-supervised and pay the official exchange rates at all times. Banks will often charge an additional fee for cashing traveler's checks; hotels and stores seldom give you the full exchange value.

Take a credit card with you. It usually proves to be an important adjunct to your finances en route. American Express is a popular card to carry. The privilege of cashing personal checks at American Express offices is invaluable. Card members may cash personal checks up to $1,000 ($200 in local currency and $800 in traveler's checks). Visa and MasterCard have gained popularity in Europe and can be used in a great number of places, mostly stores. Diners Club cards are still accepted, sometimes in places that won't accept other cards.

Concerning credit cards, please be aware that there is a "plastic war" being waged between American Express, Visa, and MasterCard. Perhaps you have noted television advertisements announcing that certain establishments won't accept American Express—only Visa (who, by the way, sponsors the ads). *International Travel News* reported that, while in Europe, some readers had to pay a supplemental charge to cash American Express traveler's checks in stores and other commercial establishments. Their readers have also reported that some banks in Scandinavia have been charging flat fees to cash traveler's checks, regardless of the denominations and the issuing company. To combat this, we suggest carrying traveler's checks only in denominations of $100. In general, check first before cashing traveler's checks and, wherever possible, cash the checks in the bank or office of the issuing company.

Picking pockets is an art. The art is practiced in Europe. Gentlemen's breast pockets are the main targets. Foil 'em by sewing on two medium-size buttons, one above and one below the pocket opening. Loop a piece of shoelace or strong string around the buttons when carrying valuables. Avoid carrying anything more valuable than a handkerchief in hip pockets. Ladies' purses should be the shoulder type and carried that way at all times. Don't let the thought of pickpockets alarm you while in Europe. Just think what they could be doing to you back in the United States—on Main Street and in broad daylight.

Don't go to Europe without a rail pass. There's a pass for every type of traveler. Standing in long lines to buy tickets isn't what you came to Europe to do. Ride first-class coaches. Each first-class car is marked by a yellow stripe running high along its side.

The Language Barrier

Don't worry if you can't speak the language—a surprising number of Europeans speak yours. But when you speak with them in English, do so slowly and distinctly and try not to cloud your speech with slang and colloquial expressions. Most Europeans speak at least two languages. If you are a monolingual North American, remember that it is you, not the European, who is limited in the ability to communicate.

We have concluded that you can't learn to speak a foreign language unless you become involved in it. To become involved, you should live where it is spoken. Short of this, the experience can be created to a certain degree by "living there" electronically. With even a few foreign words, your trip—and you—become more interesting. Berlitz, the name synonymous with language instruction, has cassette courses in French, German, Italian, and Spanish. Short of an intensive crash course with cassettes, the alternative is to carry phrase books in the language of the countries you plan to visit. Again, Berlitz is a good source.

Europeans write numbers in a manner different from ours. Printed or typed numbers are identical, but when written by hand, they can look somewhat dissimilar. The number "1," for example, looks very much like a "7" with an inclined top. The European number "7," however, is identified by a short stroke across its center. Europeans reverse the order of the month and day when writing numbers. November 15, 1994, appears as "15/11/94" and not as "11/15/94," as we are accustomed to writing it. Be aware of this, particularly when making train reservations in Europe.

Pictographs are symbols used throughout Europe to identify people, places, and things by a uniform sign language. Study the pictographs in the Appendix of this edition, starting on page 619, before leaving on your Eurail trip. With pictographs, "speaking the language" comes easily.

All praise to the hotel concierge we talked about on page 18. He or she can be most helpful in solving the language problems you may encounter. For example, if you plan to take a taxi to a restaurant the concierge has recommended, ask him or her to write out the instructions for the taxi driver. The same for shopping and the like. With the degree to which English is spoken throughout Western Europe, there is only a slight chance that you may have to use the concierge's notes. They are, however, reassuring.

Above all, do not reject the idea of a Eurail trip because of the so-called language barrier. Most of the operating personnel aboard the trains speak English, as do most of the tourist information people.

The Eurostar train exiting the portal at Folkestone terminal ushers in a new era in international rail travel. Linking London with Paris and Brussels, the train provides direct passenger service from London to Paris in three hours and from London to Brussels in three hours, fifteen minutes. As services expand, all of continental Europe will be linked with England, Scotland, and Wales. (Photo courtesy Britrail Travel International.)

2   HOW TO USE *EUROPE BY EURAIL*

This chapter is devoted to the format and organization of the chapters to follow, which in turn describe each base city and the day excursions that may be taken out of these cities on a day that you select. Thus, we begin to unfold the virtues and advantages of our "Base City–Day Excursion" program.

Before you begin planning for your Eurail adventure, wc would like to explain some of the details of the Eurail system, specifically, the composition of its trains and the functions of its rail stations. Following, you will find a description of the train schedules appearing in the book as ancillary information to the base cities and day excursions, along with an insight into the manner in which the day excursions are organized. The chapter closes with a brief comment on the special features contained in this edition of *Europe by Eurail.*

Pragmatic Information

Have you ever read a travel book that prattled on and on with vagaries such as "Arriving in Brussels you will fall in love with the medieval charm of its main square, the Grand'Place. Quite near, you'll come upon the lovely Gallerie de la Reine or perhaps you might like to go strolling along the nearby Rue des Bouchers"? This style of writing might be great when read from the comfort of an armchair in Peoria—but don't try it out on a bewildered tourist standing on a train platform in one of Brussels's *three* railway stations. That traveler needs detailed, pragmatic information—and needs it in a hurry.

Pragmatism, by definition, is a practical approach to problems. The arriving traveler needs just that and none of the pleasing prattle mentioned above. "Grand'Place? How do you get there? Gallerie de la Reine? What's that in English? How far—and in what direction—is it from the Grand'Place? Rue des Bouchers? (Back in Peoria they told us to stay out of places like that!)"

Europe by Eurail takes the pragmatic approach, giving its readers at least a minimal amount of walking directions, explanation, and translation. Using it, you'll find the Grand'Place in Brussels by exiting from the central railway station in a downhill direction and walking toward the highest spire on the skyline. The Gallerie de la Reine (Gallery of the Queen) is pinpointed at the intersection of Rue de la Colline and the main thoroughfare called Rue du Marché-aux-Herbes—one block off the Grand'Place in the direction of the central station. Rue des Bouchers (Street of the Butchers) becomes somewhat more inviting when it is described as "lined with a variety of moderately priced restaurants."

Europe by Eurail picks up the traveler disembarking from the train on arrival from another base city (or at the airport if it is the first stop in Europe) and leads him to the money exchange, the hotel reservation office, and the tourist information office. Later, when the traveler is settled, *Europe by Eurail* explains the base city's highlights and the day-excursion opportunities awaiting the traveler. Our book doesn't delve deeply into the tourist attractions of the base cities. This we leave to the expertise of the city's tourist information folks. The personnel in the tourist information offices are professionals, especially trained and experienced in presenting the best of their cities. Rely upon their advice and their recommendations.

Hotels and Restaurants

Europe by Eurail does not rate hotels or restaurants, as there are many excellent guidebooks devoted to such endeavors. Besides, trains are *our* "thing." We do drop a hint now and then regarding an unusual dining spot that has taken our fancy. But we are fully aware that what is one man's "steak" can become another man's "hamburger."

In cities that host a multitude of conventions and festivals throughout the year, hotels can be booked to capacity and the city's tourist information office may assume the attitude of the typical hotel clerk: "Sorry, we are fully booked." One case in point is Milan, Italy. From experience, we have found that a personal look at the hotels clustered near the train terminal may produce a room or two. The "Memo on Milan" appearing on page 386 describes such a search.

Translations

Europe by Eurail does not go into detail on language translations. Beyond pictographs, we believe Berlitz is better suited to that. One phrase book published by Berlitz covers commonly used travelers' phrases in fourteen European languages. Berlitz also publishes a *European Menu Reader* that covers food terminology in the same fourteen languages—a helpful aid when you and the kids invade a European McDonald's only to find that no one behind the counter can translate "Big Mac" into their native tongue.

Berlitz also has a series of pocket-sized phrase guides in French, German, Italian, and Spanish featuring commonplace phrases, along with more than 2,000 useful words to use when shopping, eating, seeing a doctor, making friends, and so on. The advantage of a written guide in a single European language is that you don't need to thumb through endless pages searching for the language of the country you are in. Berlitz guides are offered by most bookstores featuring travel publications.

The Passenger Trains of Europe

Passenger trains in Europe range from the sleek TGV (*train à grande vitesse*) and EuroCity "name" express trains running on the main lines to the perky little omnibus rail cars that ply the suburban lines between the cities and their suburbs. In between, you find the national InterCity trains that provide express services within a country's borders, plus a whole stable of various passenger cars (carriages) including plush compartment interiors and businesslike commuter conveyances. Almost without exception, every one is sparkling clean. Despite the demise of the passenger train on other continents, the passenger train is "alive and well" in Europe. But don't take our word for it. Go see for yourself.

Flagships

The TGVs and the EuroCity trains are the flagships of the fleet. With the exception of the EuroNight sleepers and the hotel trains, they are basically "day trains" and are "back in the barn" well before midnight. Presently, none of the TGVs or the regular EuroCity trains have sleeping accommodations, but they make up for it with restaurants, snack bars, and cocktail lounges. They are comfortable, convenient, and every bit the "luxury liners" of the European rail fleet.

Ride a TGV, EuroCity, or InterCity train whenever there is one going in your direction. As a holder of a Eurailpass, you are entitled to ride them absolutely free without payment of surcharge. On many of the trains running throughout Scandinavia, seat reservations are required; but this is no great problem, because all Eurail routes are linked by a computerized reservation system that is available in every major rail terminal. Even without an advance reservation, your chances of climbing aboard a EuroCity or InterCity within continental Europe with a Eurailpass in hand are good. Many EuroCity trains require seat reservations; others do not. It's best to check the train departure board. If there is an R next to that train, then seat reservations are mandatory and you should not board without a reservation. Seat reservations are mandatory for all TGVs but made easy with automatic reservation-ticket dispensers in every rail station served by the TGVs. You will be fined if you do not have a seat reservation on a TGV.

You should announce your intended destination each time you present your Eurailpass to a train conductor. If you happen to be on the wrong train, or in the wrong coach, he will advise you accordingly—information that we're sure you'd like to have.

In addition to the fleet of EuroCity trains in Europe, several countries have their own luxury class fleets. Germany operates its InterCity Express (ICE) service between its major cities. Finland has a flashy new line of "Rapid" trains. Italy has its "Pendolino" line, while Spain has the "Talgo" and AVE. France is on line with its TGV. All of the above require supplemental fares *unless you are traveling with a Eurailpass.* Unfortunately, the Spanish AVE trains require supplemental fares regardless of whether you have a point-to-point ticket or a rail pass.

Seat Reservations

Seat reservations are mandatory on all long-distance trains in Spain. This includes most first- and second-class cars. Details of the Spanish reservation system are discussed in the chapters on the Spanish base cities of Barcelona and Madrid.

Seat reservations are mandatory on the InterCity and Lyntog (lightning) trains of Denmark, as well as Sweden's Rapid and Express trains. But unlike reservations in Spain, you can pay for the seat reservation aboard the train if you did not have time to obtain it in the station. The cost of seat reservations in Europe is approximately $5.00 (U.S.) and is not covered by the Eurailpass. In Switzerland there are no reserved seats unless the train is going into another country.

Seat reservations become more important the farther south you go in Europe. The trains run less frequently and are more crowded. As a rule of thumb, *always* have seat reservations when traveling in Italy and Greece. As we mentioned previously, seat reservations are mandatory in Spain.

Train Splitting

Many international trains in Europe have multiple destinations. Accordingly, passenger coaches are "split" en route. All trains in Europe display side boards announcing their departure point, stops en route, and final destination. Check before boarding to make certain you'll end up where you want to be. Announcing your destination to the conductor as he checks your Eurailpass is one sure way of double-checking. Aboard trains "splitting" coaches, it is wise to remain in your own coach when the train halts at a terminal. The "splitting" process takes place very quickly, and you could easily end up at the wrong destination—sans suitcase and members of your immediate family.

Express Trains

The mainstay of the European rail system is its regular express trains. They convey both first- and second-class coaches and usually make more intermediate stops than the EuroCity, InterCity, and Rapido trains. First-class coaches are identified by a yellow stripe over the train windows or a large number 1 on or near all doors. Finding the proper coach to board while the train is standing in the departure station is easy: Look for the yellow stripe or the number 1 identifying the first-class conveyances, then check the sideboards for the destination you want. If you hold a seat reservation, locating the coach is made simpler by the fact that the reservation slip will show both the car number as well as the number of the seat being reserved for you. Plan to board the train at least several minutes before its scheduled departure. European railroads pride themselves on their punctuality; so they hold to their schedules—whether you are on the train or not.

European trains stop for a short time only at intermediate stations to let passengers on and off. Stops of only one or two minutes are not unusual. Consequently, to position yourself on a platform where the first-class coaches will halt, check the illustrated train-composition boards displayed on the platforms. They will save a lot of scurrying around when the train arrives. Another way of assuring that you are positioned properly on the platform is to ask the uniformed "starter," who will be on the platform a minute or two before the train arrives.

If your itinerary calls for changing trains en route, ask the conductor what track you will be arriving on and what track your connecting train will depart from. Changes between EuroCity, InterCity, and "name" express trains often take place conveniently between tracks served by the same platform. When you change from an express to a local, even though the express may be running late, the local (or subordinate) train will usually wait beyond its regular departure time to accommodate transferring passengers.

Every European railway station has its arrival and departure times posted. These timetables usually list all the intermediate stops, as well as the final destinations. They also list the platform and track the train will arrive on or depart from. Should the station have digital displays, as many of the main train terminals in Europe do today, the information posted on these displays will take precedence over the printed schedules. But the track numbers seldom, if ever, change.

The posted timetables usually show departure times on a yellow sheet and arrival times on a white one. Many European railroads now provide minischedules listing train services between two specific points. Help yourself. They are free of charge.

Base-City Railway Stations

Some base cities have a single central station, others have more than one. Single or multiple, all are described in this book in the same format for each base city. You will find under each station name the subtitles dealing with where to change money, obtain hotel bookings, and secure tourist information, train information, train reservations, and Eurailpass validation—in that order. These informative sections appear in the same order as the normal pattern a traveler follows when arriving: First change some money or cash a traveler's check and get a hotel room, then pick up some information about the city, find out when the day-excursion trains leave and the tracks they depart on, and, finally, make reservations for the train to the next base city.

Eurailpass validation is the last item mentioned, as you only do that once—on arrival in the first base city. Each rail station has an office or ticket window designated to perform this validation. If you have trouble finding that office, go to the train information center and ask directions. When validating your Eurailpass, sign the pass only after the railroad official has asked you to do so. Although it is not a part of the validation procedure, we suggest that you write the starting and ending dates of your pass-validation period on a piece of paper and hand it to the clerk, along with your pass and passport. Be certain the clerk agrees to the dates before he enters the validity period on your pass. Errors can be corrected, but it is a long procedure. The clerk then enters your passport number, stamps your pass, and detaches the validation slip from the pass. Remember, once validated, your pass is neither refundable nor replaceable.

If you cancel your trip or for any other reason want to return your pass (prior to validation), return it to the travel agent or the Eurailpass issuing office where you purchased it within one year of the issue date. All refunds are subject to a minimum 15 percent cancellation fee. Be sure you read the Conditions of Use on your pass.

Guard your Eurailpass with the same attention you give to your cash, your traveler's checks, and your passport. Lost or stolen Eurailpasses are not refundable, however a Lost Rail Pass Protection option is available for an additional $10 per pass. The program reimburses the traveler for 100 percent of any additional rail-ticket expense in the event that the pass is lost or stolen in Europe. Be certain to obtain a police report of loss or theft and keep receipts for any additional rail transportation purchased.

Rail Pass Express, Inc. is an authorized Eurailpass issuing office with a complete stock of Eurailpasses and a wide variety of single-country and regional rail passes. To order yours, call toll-free (800) 722–7151.

Train Schedules

Train schedules are listed at the end of each base-city chapter. With few exceptions, those listed will be EuroCity or InterCity trains, and in most cases, the connections will be shown in daytime schedules. This particular section of the base-city chapters should prove to be extremely helpful when you are initially planning your Eurail trip. Not all base cities can be reached from another in the same day, although most can. Overnight trains are seldom listed: You go to Europe to see it, not sleep through it.

Please remember that these train schedules, as well as those provided for the day excursions, are *for planning purposes only*. Every care has been taken to make the timetables correct at press time, but *Europe by Eurail* and its publisher cannot be held responsible for the consequences of either changes or inadvertent inaccuracies. You are again reminded to check the train schedules posted in the rail station(s) of the base city shortly after your arrival to assure that no changes have occurred. Many of the rail stations are being expanded and modernized in order to accommodate the ever increasing traffic on the European rail system. In doing this, some temporary schedule changes may have to be made, including platform changes. Follow the advice of America's famous frontiersman Davy Crockett: "Just be sure you're right, then go ahead!"

Day Excursions

Each day-excursion section begins with the distance and average train time, because we are well aware that there are some days when you prefer a short trip rather than a great adventure.

The distance is restated in the day-excursion schedule, along with other informative notes such as days of operation and *Thomas Cook European Timetable* references. Trains departing the base city are normally on morning schedules; trains returning from the day excursion usually run in the late afternoon and early evening.

Special Features

Special features in this edition of *Europe by Eurail* include pictographs, beginning on page 619, and a list of European tourist information offices in North America, which can be found on pages 633–35. If the twenty-four-hour time system boggles your mind, consult the Thomas Cook universal clock reproduced on page 625. Fares between base cities are listed on page 626. Regarding the point-to-point fares, if you are trying to determine whether or not to purchase a rail pass, sketch out your intended itinerary and then add the fares between the points you will be traveling. You will probably be amazed at the bottom line. Nine times out of ten, a rail pass will come out dollars ahead. Consult our list of European rail passes beginning on page 627.

Where do you get a passport? Check out page 632 for a list of U.S. Passport Offices. Airline and toll-free hotel numbers are on page 636.

Readers who want to preplan their rail-tour itinerary will find particular interest in chapter 26, in which three rail tours are described in detail.

Ferries and catamarans play an important part in linking the seventeen Eurailpass countries into one system. Chapter 27 is devoted to descriptions of these maritime services and how Eurail travelers may use them.

Central Station in Amsterdam is the city's center of transportation. Canal boats in foreground provide city sightseeing tours. Many are equipped with cassette-tape descriptions in several languages.

3 AMSTERDAM

One of the most unusual cities in Europe, Amsterdam is a "fun city"—fun to see, fun to be in. It is a pleasant, human city where handsome houses stand on quiet canals, shoppers walk uninterrupted on streets without vehicles, and street organs play in the parks (even on rainy afternoons). It is the kind of city that, when you are lost, sends a smiling old gentleman on his bicycle or a bevy of flaxen-haired schoolgirls to your rescue. Amsterdam is a patient city whose people listen as you read Dutch expressions from a guidebook—then respond in perfect English. Amsterdam is a city to fall in love with.

Day Excursions

The *Europe by Eurail* day excursions described in this chapter are to Alkmaar, home of the world-famous cheese market; Enkhuizen, for its Zuider Zee Museum, which depicts what Dutch life was like before the Zuider Zee was sealed off from the North Sea; Haarlem, for the Frans Hals Museum and more aspects of life in the Netherlands; and Hoorn, for browsing in a medieval market. The day excursion to the open-air Zuider Zee Museum at Enkhuizen is the latest addition to the roster. The day excursions have been selected to present a cross section of the Netherlands, from its rural to its sophisticated side.

The Netherlands Railways has many of its own day excursions waiting for you upon your arrival. Because Holland is a very compact country, it is possible to take any one of the day excursions from any railway station within the country and return to your point of departure the same day, a strategy similar to that outlined in *Europe by Eurail.* To find out more about these day excursions, ask at the train information office in the Amsterdam central station for the brochure *Touring Holland by Train.* The publication is updated annually by the railroad's publicity and design department. Eurailpass holders pay only for the added attractions of the excursions, such as entrance fees and meals. The rail-transportation part of each day excursion is already covered by the Eurailpass.

Day-excursion opportunities out of Amsterdam are virtually unlimited. Other Dutch cities, such as The Hague, Rotterdam, and Utrecht, are less than an hour away. In just two hours, you could be in Antwerp, Belgium, shopping for diamonds. Add another thirty minutes and you could have lunch in Brussels before shopping for lace. Continue your shopping splurge—the quaint town of Delft, where the world-renowned Delft blue pottery is made, is only forty minutes' train time from Amsterdam.

Arriving and Departing

By Air: Amsterdam's Schiphol Airport is one of the most modern and efficient air terminals in the world. It was built to be convenient. At latest count, the airport provides flights to 200 destinations in eighty-five countries by more than eighty international airlines. After you have cleared customs, turn right and proceed to the KLM information center at the far right end of the arrival hall. There you can get all the information you may need for getting into downtown Amsterdam. Rail service between the airport and Amsterdam's Central Station takes about twenty-two minutes and costs 8 guilders. Trains run approximately every fifteen minutes. If your destination is in the southern part of the city, you can board a train for the Zuid (South) Station as well. In fact, direct train service from Schiphol Airport to many other points in the Netherlands, such as The Hague, Rotterdam, and Delft, is available. Within Holland call 06–9292 for bus, tram, subway, and rail connections (50 guilders per minute), or for international train information call 06–9296. Eurailpass is accepted on the trains.

KLM Road Transport operates a shuttle-bus service between Schiphol Airport and the major hotels of Amsterdam. The bus stops at the Barbizon Centre, Hotel Pulitzer, Krasnapolsky, Holiday Inn, Sonesta, and Barbizon Palace hotels. The one-way fare is 15 guilders, and tickets may be purchased on the bus. If your hotel is not listed above, ask at the KLM desk for the listed hotel nearest to yours and get off there—first checking that your hotel is only a short distance away. Otherwise, a taxi may better serve your needs. A taxi takes about forty-five minutes and costs 45–60 guilders. Again, the KLM desk will be helpful.

By Rail: The Amsterdam Central Station is the focal point of all rail, tram (trolley), bus, and Metro (subway) traffic within the city. All train service for the listed day excursions departs from, and arrives in, this station. Trams, buses, and the Metro (entrance) are available immediately in front of the station, the hub of Amsterdam's city-transportation network; practically everything in Amsterdam begins and ends here. Canal-boat terminals also may be found immediately outside the station. The closest of these is the Holland International pier. It is just across the bridge on the right. A canal tour costs approximately 11 guilders for adults and 8.50 guilders for children aged four to twelve and senior citizens over age sixty-five. Boats for sightseeing line the city's pier-studded canals.

The schedules appearing at the end of this section list train services—most of which are direct—between Amsterdam and twelve other base cities: Barcelona, Berlin, Berne, Brussels, Copenhagen, Hamburg, Luxembourg, Milan, Munich, Nice, Paris, and Vienna.

Amsterdam Analysis

Though picturesque, by European standards Amsterdam is not an ancient city. In the thirteenth century it was a small fishing village tucked behind a protecting dam on the Zuider Zee. It wasn't until the seventeenth century that it emerged as northern Europe's most prosperous port. Dutch influence declined at the end of that century, but Amsterdam survived in style, having been built on ninety islands linked by more than 1,000 bridges arching 160 canals. Although their interiors have been altered many times, the fronts of seventeenth-century houses along the canals remain unaltered.

A boat trip on Amsterdam's canals and other waterways is, undoubtedly, the best way to see the city for the first time. Tour-boat terminals are scattered throughout Amsterdam. All of them are excellent. During summer evenings, when the buildings along the canals are illuminated and the canal bridges are outlined by tiny lights, the tour boats offer a "Candlelight and Wine" cruise. This is a perfect way to meet Amsterdam.

It doesn't take too long to discover that Amsterdam is multilingual. The Dutch laughingly refer to their language as "more of a throat condition than anything else" and readily join you in your native tongue. English is the primary second language spoken in the Netherlands, but French, Spanish, German, and many others are heard daily.

Amsterdam's old "inner city" is famous for its compactness. Its museums, markets, monuments, shopping streets, and other attractions are all within walking distance—or a short tram ride—from your hotel. Amsterdam boasts the largest historical inner city in Europe, with more than 6,800 National Trust buildings.

The city has more than forty museums, including the famous Rijksmuseum (closed on Mondays), where Rembrandt's renowned *Night Watch* may be viewed along with an extensive collection of his other dazzling works. For a double treat, visit the Van Gogh Museum, just around the corner from the Rijksmuseum. If you're into museums, you can purchase the Museum Card from most of the VVV tourist offices and at the Rijksmuseum, which allows free access to more than 400 of Holland's museums. The card is valid for a full year (40 guilders for adults, 25 for persons over age sixty-five, and 15 guilders for those under the age of nineteen).

Dining in Amsterdam is an exercise in international cuisine. The expression "you can eat there in any language" is no exaggeration. First decide what type of food you want—Hungarian, German, Yugoslavian, Greek, Scandinavian, Japanese, or Indonesian—then select from among the many restaurants offering such dishes. Our favorite is Restaurant Indonesia, at 18 Korte Leidsedwarsstraat, and it can be reached by taking tram 1, 2, or 5 from the Central Station to the Leidseplein area, about a twelve-minute ride. Their specialty is an eighteen-dish rijstafel (ricetable). Go there hungry. We guarantee you won't go home that way.

Touring Amsterdam's canals by pedal boat has become an interesting way of seeing the city at your own pace. The rental craft are available year-round at several city mooring locations. Maps are provided, together with suggested routes and descriptions of the places you will pass. You provide the pedal power.

Amsterdam Central Station

Emerging from a massive modernization program, Amsterdam's Central Station has managed to preserve its old-world charm while at the same time adding extensive passenger-handling facilities. It has never been a sparkling example of chrome and polished marble, as many rail terminals in Europe have become in their renovations. The Central Station's facade is unchanged. Its ability to handle incoming and outgoing passengers alike, however, has been improved drastically.

Although it abounds in digital train-information displays, the station still provides the standard train-departure posters with their yellow background giving train-departure information by separate directions. Rail service throughout the Netherlands is so dense—departures approximately every half-hour—that these sectional timetables to Rotterdam, Utrecht, and other cities are most helpful.

Amsterdam's Central Station is virtually a city within a city, with restaurants, snack bars, specialty shops, fruit stands, and candy shops operating over extended hours—a good place to stock up for a trip.

A word of caution regarding the station. It's the originating point for long-distance express trains, including the EuroCity network. This means that lots of tourists will be boarding. Tourists attract pickpockets. Watch when boarding, particularly for people who are apparently traveling without luggage and are following you closely with only an empty shopping bag in hand. Chances are that they are "shopping" for your wallet and plan to leave the train before it departs.

Money-exchange office "GWK" is on the street side of the station foyer. It is open daily, twenty-four hours per day.

Hotel reservations can be made at the VVV Amsterdam Tourist Office located in the NZH Koffiehuis (coffee house), just outside the station's main exit or in the Central Station. See page 40 for its hours of operation.

Tourist information for all of Holland, including Amsterdam, is available from the VVV Amsterdam Tourist Office located in the train information office on the far right of the main station hall as you exit from the trains or at the office in front of the rail station.

Train information may be obtained in the office of the Netherlands Railways (national trains 06–9292, for international trains, 06–9296), located on the far right of the main station hall as you exit from the trains. This office has the familiar "i" sign. It's open daily 0630–2230. It uses the customer-number system, so take a number as you enter. Seat reservations as well as Eurailpass validation may be made in this office. Complete information regarding the Netherlands Railways day-excursion program is also available. Remember, when having your Eurailpass validated, write out the starting and ending dates on a piece of paper and have the railroad representative agree to the correctness of the dates before the information is entered on your pass.

Tourist Facilities

The VVV Amsterdam Tourist Office and the GVB (Holland's transportation system) are located next to each other in the buildings immediately in front of Amsterdam's Central Station at Stationsplein 10. Look for the distinctive white Dutch facade slightly to the left as you exit from the station. The VVV Amsterdam Tourist Office is located in the NZH Koffiehuis and is an ideal place to stop and enjoy refreshments while you attend to your various tourist-information needs.

This VVV office can provide complete city and national information for all of the Netherlands. Amsterdam services include hotel, pension, and hostel bookings, as well as a wealth of printed information regarding the city and its surroundings. Maps of Amsterdam are available at a vending machine for 3.50 guilders. The NZH also maintains a telephone information service. Just dial 06–34034066 Monday through Saturday, 0900–1700. Two other offices are located at Leidseplein and Stadionplein.

From the transportation office (GVB), you can obtain a complete map of Amsterdam's transportation network, including the subway. A variety of tourist transportation tickets, which are now accepted on all trams, buses, and subway trains, can be purchased there, too. Ask about the Day Tickets and National Strip Card. Another feature of Amsterdam's transportation office is its telephone information service. Dial 06–9292 for assistance.

The tourist and transportation offices are open 0900–1700 daily. The Dutch are noted for their industrious ways, and the folks in charge of Holland's public relations are probably some of the hardest-working people in the country.

Amsterdam abounds in travel agencies, so there is no problem getting to see the city. There's a potpourri of short tours around Amsterdam to select from. There are eight canal cruise companies to choose from when selecting a means of cruising on the city's vast network of canals. There are boarding points scattered throughout Amsterdam, including one at the VVV Amsterdam Tourist Office in front of the central rail station. During your visit to the VVV office, ask for the illustrated color brochure, *Excursions Amsterdam.* The brochure describes the various cruise and bus programs, including the popular nighttime, candlelight tours.

In many respects, Amsterdam is Europe's answer to every other city of the world claiming to be different or, in some manner, unique unto itself. It is distinctly different yet bears a similarity to all the favorite cities you have ever known. As we said at the beginning, it's a city to fall in love with, and most people do.

40

From Amsterdam ...

TRAIN CONNECTIONS TO OTHER BASE CITIES

TO:	DEPART	ARRIVE	TRAIN NUMBER	COOK'S TABLE	NOTES
Barcelona	1452	1020+1	1286	48	(5) (6)
Berlin (Zoo)	0902	1715	2343	22	(7)
	1302	2116	2345	22	(8)
Berne	0800	1712	EC 105	38	
Brussels (Midi)	0853	1138	EC 82	18	(1)
Copenhagen	2009	0725+1	1237	22	(5)
Hamburg	0902	1411	2343/IC 826	22	(2)
Luxembourg	0853	1449	EC 82/EC 97	210	(3)
Milan	1755	0745+1	201	39	
Munich	0800	1615	EC 105	28	(4)
Nice	1647	1039+1	1186	48	(9)
Paris (Nord)	0853	1425	EC 82	18	(1) (10)
Vienna	2056	1058+1	EN 215	35	

Daily departures unless otherwise noted. Make reservations for all departures.

(1) Daily, except Sunday
(2) Transfer in Osnabrück
(3) Transfer in Brussels Nord. See Cook's Table 210
(4) Transfer in Mannheim to ICE 593
(5) Couchettes only
(6) Transfer in Port Bou to Train 63
(7) Arrives 1729 on Saturdays
(8) Arrives 2126 on Saturdays
(9) Daily June 22 through September 5; otherwise, Fridays and Saturdays only
(10) Not August 15; arrives 1835 July 1 through August 31

Cheese market porters convey their product to the Weigh House during the Friday cheese auction in Alkmaar. Photo courtesy of Netherlands Railways.

From Amsterdam . . .

A DAY EXCURSION TO ALKMAAR
DISTANCE BY TRAIN: 24 miles (39 km)
AVERAGE TRAIN TIME: 30 minutes

There is a cheese market in Alkmaar every Friday from mid-April to mid-September. Alkmaar is such a picturesque town, however, that it deserves a visit any time of the year. The Netherlands Railways operates rail service between Amsterdam and Alkmaar every fifteen minutes. Consequently, you can go to Alkmaar as early as you like and then return to Amsterdam at your leisure and when you are ready—unlike the tour-bus visitors.

Alkmaar is famous not only for its cheese; it is steeped in Dutch history as well. It was here at Alkmaar in 1573 that the Spanish were first compelled to retreat their occupying forces; hence, the Dutch expression "victory begins at Alkmaar." A festival is held annually on the eighth day of October to commemorate the breaking of the Spanish siege.

Upon arrival, you may obtain train information at the ticket window in the Alkmaar station. English is spoken. The service is provided 0500–2345 Monday through Saturday. Either the ticket agent or personnel at the travel agency located to the left as you exit from the station will be glad to give you instructions for reaching the square in the center of Alkmaar. We recommend that you go to the VVV office on the town square for complete information regarding Alkmaar.

An easy route to the town square is to follow the street, Geesterweg, running perpendicular to the front of the station and the VVV signs leading you across a bridge toward a large church (Church of St. Laurens). Pass the church on its left side and pick up Lange Straat, still walking in the same direction. Pass the Town Hall, which will be on your right; four blocks farther, at a canal, turn left to the Weigh House, where the cheese market is held. The VVV office is located in the front of the Weigh House. Hours of operation are 0900–1730 Monday through Wednesday, 0900–1800 Thursday and Friday, and 0900–1700 Saturday; closed Sunday.

Ask at the tourist office about seeing Alkmaar by canal, a popular way to see the town. The boats depart from Mient (near Waaggebouw). Adult fare is 6 guilders; children under twelve, 3.50 guilders. During the cheese market on Fridays, boats sail every twenty minutes from 0930. During May, June, July, and August, they depart daily on the hour from 1100. In April, September, and October, they sail Monday through Saturday, every hour on the hour, from 1100, depending on the weather. The canal trip takes about forty-five minutes (telephone 117750).

The cheese auction is *the* thing to see in Alkmaar. The square explodes into

ALKMAAR—*WORLD FAMOUS CHEESE MARKET*

A Day Excursion from Amsterdam

DEPART FROM AMSTERDAM CENTRAL STATION	ARRIVE IN ALKMAAR STATION	NOTES
0822	0853	(1)
0852	0923	(1)
0922	0953	(1)
0952	1023	(1)
1022	1053	(1)
1052	1123	(1)

Other departures every thirty minutes throughout the day

DEPART FROM ALKMAAR STATION	ARRIVE IN AMSTERDAM CENTRAL STATION	NOTES
1633	1719	(1)
1703	1749	(1)
1733	1819	(1)
1803	1849	(1)
1833	1919	(1)
1903	1949	(1)

Other departures every thirty minutes throughout the day

(1) Daily, including holidays

Distance: 24 miles/39 km
Reference: Thomas Cook Table 225

a frenzy of color and activity as cheese porters trot across the square wearing red, blue, green, or yellow hats according to the group they represent. This auction has continued for more than 350 years and attracts thousands of tourists. It is not, however, merely a tourist attraction. It is a genuine auction, at which cheese merchants sample the product, bargain for the best price, and conclude the sale "on hand clap." From there the porters move the cheese to the Weigh House, where the weigh master checks the weight and calls it out in a loud voice; then the porters take the cheese from there to the buyers' warehouses.

Alkmaar has been involved in the production of cheese for centuries. Its cheese makers founded their guild in 1622, only two years after the Pilgrims landed on Plymouth Rock. Unique in the curatorial world, Alkmaar's Cheese Museum attracts visitors from far and wide from April through October. The museum is open Monday through Saturday, 1000–1600. (It opens at 0900 on Fridays due to the cheese auction.)

Another unique museum is dedicated to the history of beer production. Featuring the fine skills of brew masters and covering 5,000 years of beer-making history, the city's National Beer Museum De Boom deals with all aspects down through the ages that have determined the various characteristics of beer, including the current Dutch favorite, pale lager. It is interesting to note that despite the complicated brewing equipment utilized today, the art of brewing has remained a natural process relatively unchanged from earlier times.

Both the Cheese Museum and the Beer Museum are but a few steps from the city square, where the cheese auction takes place. From April through September, the Beer Museum is open 1000–1600 Tuesday through Saturday and 1300–1700 on Sunday. October through March, the hours are 1300–1600 Thursday through Sunday. Literature describing both museums is available in the Alkmaar VVV office.

Alkmaar is a charming town. It is crisscrossed by canals that, in turn, are spanned by humped stone bridges. The shining red roofs of its old houses are guarded by the towering vaults of the aged St. Laurens Church, constructed in 1520. Four blocks south of St. Laurens stands Molen van Piet, a windmill built in 1769.

To spend a perfect day in Alkmaar, ask the cooperation of the VVV personnel in mapping out a walking tour. Also ask about seeing Alkmaar by canal boat. There are an amazing number of things to do and see: among them, a visit to the Municipal Museum and the Dutch Stove Museum; on a Friday or Saturday morning, visit the active fish market that started back in 1591; or take a look at the stately wooden gabled house complete with an embedded cannonball as a memoir of a war now past. Sample the famous Edam cheese at either lunch or dinner. Time moves slower in Alkmaar. Relax and enjoy life.

A canal bridge in an Enkhuizen open-air museum leads to the town "center" in this reconstructed village representative of life on the Zuider Zee between 1880 and 1932, when the Zee was sealed off from tidal waters and turned into a fresh-water lake. Four polders—land areas that were under the surface of the sea—were reclaimed. They are used today as prime agricultural areas. The train to Enkhuizen enters the polder area just after passing Hoorn, another landlocked harbor town in this interesting area.

From Amsterdam . . .

A DAY EXCURSION TO ENKHUIZEN
DISTANCE BY TRAIN: 37 miles (60 km)
AVERAGE TRAIN TIME: 1 hour

This day excursion from Amsterdam was made possible by the opening of the Zuider Zee Open Air Museum in Enkhuizen, east of Hoorn. The museum was opened formally by Queen Beatrix on 6 May 1983 after eighteen years of preparation and construction. The site consists of 135 houses and workshops, gathered from coastal towns throughout the area, that were doomed to destruction as a result of the closing off of the Zuider Zee from the tidal waters of the North Sea.

Getting to Enkhuizen by train has been greatly facilitated by the Netherlands Railways line to Hoorn via Purmerend, with a direct extension through to Enkhuizen. Modern commuter-type stations line the route, and the entire area is expanding and benefiting from this service. The schedule on the next page tells it all. Enkhuizen is the end of the line—you can't miss it. But if you have kids on the excursion, tell them, "Enkhuizen is fifty-two minutes into the mission." Start timing from "lift off" out of the Amsterdam Central Station; the train service is so punctual that your offspring will think you are astronaut material.

Enkhuizen has succeeded in preserving its seventeenth-century character. The old center of the city contains a picturesque fisherman's quarter and a corresponding essential from those days, a farmer's corner. From within the old sea wall, which was constructed to protect the city from storms on the Zuider Zee, you will find a shopping center accompanied by sidewalk cafés and restaurants.

A visit to the outdoor museum in Enkhuizen begins with a boat trip. Bear left approaching the railway station after disembarking from the train and walk along the right side of the boat yard in front of the station to its far end. The route is well marked; just follow the signs. As you round the station, you pass by the local VVV office, so we suggest that you stop in for a map and some up-to-the-minute information about the town and its attractions. The VVV office is open daily, 0800–1700 from mid-April to mid-September. The remainder of the year, it is open Tuesday through Saturday 1000–1700. If you want to phone ahead, the number is 02280–13164.

Board the launch at the pier. It runs every fifteen minutes, and its first stop is the parking lot by the main ticket office. Town planners, insisting that vehicular traffic remain outside the town and museum area, provided this facility. It works well. Once they have purchased admission tickets, rail and auto passengers alike board the launch once again for a fifteen-minute ride to the museum.

ENKHUIZEN—*ZUIDER ZEE MUSEUM*

A Day Excursion from Amsterdam

DEPART FROM AMSTERDAM CENTRAL STATION	ARRIVE IN ENKHUIZEN STATION	NOTES
0819	0921	(1)
0849	0951	(1)
0919	1021	(1)
0949	1051	(1)
1019	1121	(1)
1049	1151	(1)

Other departures at nineteen and forty-nine minutes past the hour throughout the day until 2319

DEPART FROM ENKHUIZEN STATION	ARRIVE IN AMSTERDAM CENTRAL STATION
1609	1714
1639	1744
1709	1814
1739	1844
1809	1914
1839	1944

Other departures at nine and thirty-nine minutes past the hour throughout the day until 2309.

(1) Daily, including holidays

Distance: 37 miles/60 km
Reference: Thomas Cook Table 225

Admission for adults is 14 guilders; for children four to seventeen, 9 guilders and adults sixty-five and over, 11 guilders. Children under four are admitted free.

The Zuider Zee Open Air Museum was founded to collect and show as many items as possible of the Zuider Zee culture before it was closed off in 1932 by the construction of the Afsluitdijk barrier dam. A stroll through the museum reveals much about those times. The trades are well represented by a foundry, a steam laundry, a sail loft, and a smokehouse, to name but a few items. There's a fishing village on the quay and a town center complete with a church and a general store, where postcards and wooden shoes and other souvenirs are for sale. Snacks and various Dutch food specialties are also available, as are tours led by English-speaking guides. Check at the museum office for information. You will pass it just after the foundry. The open-air museum is open from mid-April to mid-October from 1000–1700 daily. The indoor portion, known as the Binnen Museum, is open throughout the year (except December 25 and 26 and January 1). When the outdoor museum is closed, the entrance fee is 5 guilders for adults and 4 guilders for children ages four to seventeen and adults over sixty-five.

A visit to the Weigh-House Museum, housed in a structure dating from 1559, recalls the days when Enkhuizen was the center of the cheese-and-butter trade for the region. Oddly enough, in the seventeenth century, the second floor of this structure housed the Enkhuizen Guild of Surgeons. These facilities, together with a historic hospital, are open for inspection. The Weigh House Museum (or "Waagmuseum") is open Tuesday through Saturday, 1000–1200 and 1400–1700; Sundays, 1400–1700; closed on Mondays.

You may note a touch of Amsterdam in the heart of the old city. The style of the city's recently renovated town hall is much like that of the Palace on Dam Square in Amsterdam. Its grand style is reminiscent of the area's extensive trade and industry that once abounded in the area. Another point of interest is the old town's prison located immediately behind the town hall.

For the small fry, Enkhuizen offers Sprookjeswonderland (Fairyland), situated in a park setting. It contains a children's zoo with a deer park and a farm, complete with a "hugging" barn. Fairyland is open daily from mid-April until mid-October, Monday through Saturday, 1000–1730; Sundays, 1300–1730.

It doesn't end here. The town of Enkhuizen is a living museum in itself. The Zuiderkerk church, with its spiraling tower and copper-clad roof, dominates the skyline of the city, assisted by the wooden bell tower of Enkhuizen's other church, the "Wester." Together with the ramparts and fortress walls, Enkhuizen recalls a rich past. Through its preservation of the past, Enkhuizen is assuring its future.

Sun dial marks the center of the inner courtyard in Frans Hals Museum in Haarlem.

From Amsterdam . . .

A DAY EXCURSION TO HAARLEM
DISTANCE BY TRAIN: 12 miles (19 km)
AVERAGE TRAIN TIME: 15 minutes

Haarlem is close to Amsterdam, and this trip has the shortest travel time of any day excursion described in this edition of *Europe by Eurail.* It is also one of the most interesting.

The train service to and from Amsterdam is so frequent that you may go and come at your leisure. We recommend that you go early and be prepared to stay late. There's an aura of antiquity surrounding Haarlem that will attract and hold you.

The VVV office is situated on the south right-hand corner of the railway station as you exit. (The train bringing you to Haarlem is headed in a westerly direction as it enters the station.) The office is marked with an ample sign reading VVV HAARLEM and cannot be missed. Attendants are competent in assisting with any information you may need, and they will be happy to help you in the planning of your day excursion. The office is open 0900–1730 Monday through Saturday.

Haarlem remained relatively undamaged by both world wars. What you find there in the Grote Markt (Great Market), the old center of the town, has authentic origins dating from the thirteenth century. Haarlem was put to the sword in July 1573, when it fell to its Spanish besiegers and its citizens were butchered. Its devastation, however, was not on the scale that modern weapons could perpetrate.

With the release in 1976 of the motion picture *The Hiding Place,* the attention of the world was drawn to a quaint little watchmaker's shop established in 1837 at 19 Barteljorisstraat in the heart of Haarlem. It was here in the shop and home of a Christian, Opa ten Boom, and his family that Jewish refugees fleeing the wrath of Nazi Germany were hidden for a time during World War II. A hiding place was built in a bedroom where the refugees could go in case the Germans made a surprise inspection. The ten Boom family operated the refuge for more than eighteen months, until they were betrayed on 28 February 1944.

At the time of the betrayal, six persons were concealed in the hiding place. They escaped while the Gestapo was still in the house. The ten Boom family, however, were imprisoned in a concentration camp for their acts of mercy. The ten Boom house is now a museum. It is open for visits from 1100 to 1630 Tuesday through Saturday from April 1 through October 31. It closes one hour earlier the rest of the year. Entrance is free. Check with the VVV for directions and details.

The old center of Haarlem is not so large as to require transportation to its

51

HAARLEM—*AND THE FRANS HALS MUSEUM*

A Day Excursion from Amsterdam

DEPART FROM AMSTERDAM CENTRAL STATION	ARRIVE IN HAARLEM STATION	NOTES
0833	0850	(2)
0903	0920	(1)
0935	0952	(1)
1003	1020	(1)
1033	1050	(1)
1103	1120	(1)
1133	1150	(1)

Other departures every thirty minutes throughout the day until 2203

DEPART FROM HAARLEM STATION	ARRIVE IN AMSTERDAM CENTRAL STATION	NOTES
1512	1529	(1)
1542	1559	(1)
1612	1629	(1)
1642	1659	(1)
1712	1729	(1)
1742	1759	(1)
1812	1829	(1)
1842	1859	(1)

Other departures every thirty minutes throughout the day until 2212

(1) Daily, including holidays
(2) Monday through Friday only

Distance: 12 miles/19 km
Reference: Thomas Cook Table 245

points of interest, but the city bus system is available to assist if necessary. You will want to visit the Great Market and see the town hall and the Church of Saint Bavo, then proceed to the world-famous Frans Hals Museum and from there to the Teylers Museum before returning to the railway station.

The Great Market is actually the central square of Haarlem, in which the noblemen of Holland staged their tournaments during the Middle Ages. Today, it is traditionally the social gathering place of the townspeople. A part of the town hall was once a hunting club. The Church of Saint Bavo houses a pipe organ that was once played by the eleven-year-old Mozart.

On foot, head south from the station, crossing the Nieuwe Gracht (New Canal), and proceed to the city's central square, using the tower of the great church as your point of destination. As you enter the square, the church stands on your left, the town hall on your right. This square has been termed the most beautiful in Holland. A pause here in one of the many restaurants, outdoor cafés, or ice cream shops is recommended.

Time permitting, before leaving the Great Market, you may wish to visit the Meat Hall and the Fish Hall. No longer functioning by their descriptive names, both structures are now employed in the exhibition of modern visual art. The seventeenth-century architect Lieven de Key designed the Meat Hall, which is said to be one of the finest examples of Renaissance architecture in the Netherlands.

From the western end of the church, follow the street running south from the square to the Frans Hals Museum, just before the canal. This street has several names—Warmoes, Schagchel, and Heiligland—appearing in that order as you move to the museum through some of the most heady seventeenth-century atmosphere to be found anywhere in Europe.

The Frans Hals Museum is a moving experience. It's open Monday through Saturday, 1100–1700, and Sunday, 1300–1700. Perhaps nowhere else can you find such a perfect combination of setting and display. The building is a gorgeous sight—its inner courtyard a magnificent example of seventeenth-century architecture. The versatility of the museum's collections is unusual. In one section, the peak achievements of Haarlem's seventeenth-century painters may be viewed; in another wing of the museum, visitors may view an exhibition of modern Dutch art. Admission for adults, 6 guilders; children and senior citizens, 3 guilders.

A left turn at the canal below the museum takes you to the Turf Markt on the Spaarne River, where another left turn takes you winding along the river to Holland's oldest museum, the Teylers Museum, just beyond Damstraat (Dam Street). Here you will be treated to a rich collection of drawings and paintings by Michelangelo, Raphael, Titian, and Rembrandt. The Coin and Medal Room displays Dutch coins and medals from the sixteenth to the twentieth century. The museum also includes a collection of fossils and minerals.

Hoorn statue of the East India Company's founder, Admiral Jan Pieterszoon Coen, marks the center of the main square in Hoorn.

A DAY EXCURSION TO HOORN
DISTANCE BY TRAIN: 26 miles (42 km)
AVERAGE TRAIN TIME: 40 minutes

Ever since its harbor slowly silted in the eighteenth century, the city of Hoorn has taken to slumbering—except on Wednesdays from mid-June to mid-August, when it awakens and brings back to life its medieval trades and craft guilds to stage an Old Dutch Market.

In stalls grouped around the statue of Admiral Jan Pieterszoon Coen (founder of the East India Company) in the square the town calls Rodesteen, Hoorn's seventeenth-century crafts of clog making, net mending, basket weaving, and many others come to life while groups of folk dancers perform with musical ensembles. If you are not particularly fond of mingling with the crowd, this colorful spectacle may be viewed from the comfort of the Old Dutch Tavern on Rodesteen Square.

Although the Zuider Zee has been landlocked since the strait to the North Sea was sealed off in May 1932, Hoorn has managed to maintain its status of a port by establishing four harbor areas with more than 1,100 moorings for commercial and recreational watercraft. The pursuit of water sports, including wind surfing and water skiing, may be observed—or participated in—throughout the season in Hoorn.

Steam-engine buffs will find interest in Hoorn, too. You can travel on a genuine steam train from Hoorn to Medemblik and back in old-fashioned coaches. Your Eurailpass pays for the round-trip steam-train ride. The Netherlands Railways operates a day excursion, "Historical Triangle," during the spring and summer months. Starting either in Hoorn or Enkhuizen, a steam train plies between Hoorn and Medemblik and a boat between Medemblik and Enkhuizen. The VVV office in Amsterdam or the train information office in Amsterdam's Central Station can provide details for this triangle trip. Information for finding Rodesteen Square, as well as the departure point and tickets for the steam train to Medemblik, is also available in the Hoorn railway station.

On Wednesdays, you'll find the Old Dutch Market merely by following the crowd. At other times, cross the main street in front of the railway station, bear right to the first street, then turn left to the next intersection. Here, you turn right for one block, and then you go left. The market is at the end of this street. Green signposts scattered along this route indicate the VVV office is located at Nieuwstraat 23, on a small side street off Rodesteen Square. Summer hours are 0900–1800 Monday through Saturday, and 1900–2100 Thursday evenings.

HOORN—*OLD DUTCH MARKET*

A Day Excursion from Amsterdam

DEPART FROM AMSTERDAM CENTRAL STATION	ARRIVE IN HOORN STATION	NOTES
0819	0900	(1)
0849	0930	(1)
0919	1000	(1)
0949	1030	(1)
1019	1100	(1)
1049	1130	(1)

Other departures at nineteen and forty-nine minutes past the hour throughout the day until 2319

DEPART FROM HOORN STATION	ARRIVE IN AMSTERDAM CENTRAL STATION	NOTES
1635	1714	(1)
1705	1744	(1)
1735	1814	(1)
1805	1844	(1)
1835	1914	(1)
1905	1944	(1)

Other departures at five and thirty-five minutes past the hour throughout the day until 2335

(1) Daily, including holidays

Distance: 26 miles/42 km
Reference: Thomas Cook Table 225

Day excursions by train to Hoorn are popular trips out of Amsterdam in the summer. Local trains bear special markings (on Wednesday) from mid-June through mid-August, when the Old Dutch Market is staged. Take these trains for the festive mood they create among passengers; but regular train service between Amsterdam and Hoorn runs about every half-hour throughout the day, so you have the option of going and returning whenever you feel like it.

The steam train operates daily from July through mid-August; so Hoorn stages this market plus many other attractions on days other than Wednesday. In fact, the steam train continues to operate through September and October from Tuesday through Sunday once the Old Dutch Market has closed for the season. (For more complete details, check the Netherlands Railways day-excursion brochure.)

Wednesdays during the summer are, of course, the times of high activity in Hoorn, but you may go there at any time throughout the year and spend an enjoyable day in this ancient town on the Ijsselmeer, a freshwater lake that was once part of the Zuider Zee. It is one of Holland's loveliest cities. As an important fourteenth-century fishing harbor, it grew in stature until the seventeenth-century East Indies trade made it rich. The warehouses and mansions of the East India merchants that still line its streets make exploring the town on foot a sheer delight. You can obtain a street map with a recommended walking tour from either the VVV office or the ticket office in the railway station. Other information is available there as well.

At Rodesteen Square you may inspect the seventeenth-century Weigh House and the Westfries Museum, which houses a collection of antiques, paintings, and objects associated with the city and its surroundings. The museum is crammed with beautiful paintings of Hoorn's citizen soldiers and other memories of Hoorn's "golden age" during the seventeenth century.

Be certain to stop at the fifteenth-century calligrapher's workshop. Here is where Hoorn's wealthy merchants had their contracts and correspondence penned prior to the invention of the printing press later in the century. Of course, you will need no guide to point out the direction to the city's century-old coffee roaster if it is in operation.

It's time for a word of caution regarding Hoorn and the area surrounding it. Earlier mention of Enkhuizen and Medemblik might lead a visitor to plan a one-day excursion of the whole area to take it all in and then rush off to another province of the Netherlands to do it again—and again. If you do, take a lot of photographs—as the Japanese do—so that when you go back home you can have the film developed, prints made . . . and then find out where you have been.

Take time to smell the flowers. It took Hoorn many centuries to become what it is today. Relax and enjoy it.

Western facade of the Parthenon, symbol of Athens, stands on the Acropolis overlooking the city. Built between 447 and 432 B.C., the structure has withstood the ravages of man and nature since pagan times.

4   ATHENS

Despite being one of the easternmost cities in Europe, Athens has a distinct Western appearance. Modern Athens surrounds the splendor of its ancient Acropolis, which has a nobility that survives time and change. That first glimpse of the Parthenon from the window of the plane or train bringing you to Athens remains a once-in-a-lifetime experience.

Today, the rail system of Greece presents a challenge to Eurailpass travelers. Joining the Eurailpass-sponsoring countries in 1978, Greece had only begun modernizing its rail network the year before. Narrow-gauge lines are the only rail beds in use throughout the Peloponnesus (the southernmost part of the country). To the north, with the exception of a handful of international express trains, the standard-gauge rails carry too few trains too slowly for the too distant terminals along the right of way. Nevertheless, with a little perseverance, traveling by train in Greece can be pleasurable and rewarding.

Day Excursions

Until the standard-gauge railway running north between Athens, Larissa, and Salonika becomes a double-track section, we are limiting our surveyed day-excursion selections to local Athens and the Peloponnesus peninsula of southern Greece. Riding a narrow-gauge train through areas steeped in the history of Western civilization is sufficiently stimulating to make the traveler overlook the lack of air conditioning, posh dining cars, and other amenities. Argos, the oldest continuously inhabited town in Greece, is one such adventure. Corinth, both modern and ancient, is rich in Greek history, from Alexander the Great down through Roman rule. Patras, port city and scene of the most spectacular carnival in Greece, is still another place to see on the Peloponnesus. Piraeus, main port of Athens, closes the quartet of rail excursions. A must here is a ride on Athens's subway system in quest of culinary delights from the surrounding sea.

The revised schedule of the Akropolis Express on the standard-gauge railway between Athens and Larissa provides an opportunity to spend four hours in Larissa during a day excursion out of Athens. We consider the route as not surveyed, because several years have passed since our last trip on that line. Departing Athens at 1000, you will arrive in Larissa at 1504 and depart again at 1908 to arrive back in Athens by 2305. Although the IC 55 does not haul a restaurant car, there is some food available. Also you will find an abundance of cafés and patisseries on the town square. Larissa, the "citadel," is the capital of Thessaly, and, for a time, it was the home of Hippocrates, the Father of Medicine.

Arriving and Departing

By Air. The Athens Hellinikon Airport lies 6 miles southeast of the city center and has two terminals. The East Air Terminal (or New Air Terminal) serves foreign airlines, and the West Terminal (or Olympic Terminal) serves domestic and international flights for Olympic Airways only. The West Terminal is currently undergoing extensive renovations.

Express yellow buses run between the airport and Syntagma (Constitution) Square at a fare of 160 drachmas and a journey time of about thirty minutes. Regular city buses (blue) charge a lower fare, but we cannot recommend using them, particularly when carrying baggage. We also found their schedules to be confusing unless you read Greek. Taxis run the route in about twenty minutes, and fares are not too bad (approximately $9.00 U.S.). There is a currency exchange office immediately outside the customs area in the airport. Baggage carts are available. If you are departing Athens by air, the airport's tax-free shopping area offers a wide selection of Greek wearing apparel, liquors, and delicacies. Unlike many tax-free shopping facilities, the one in Athens's airport has some reasonable values, but you can't bargain with the sales people—leave that for shopping in the city.

By Train. If you are traveling by Eurailpass, it is unlikely that you will be arriving in Athens from Istanbul or Belgrade (in the former Yugoslavia) because the Eurailpass is not accepted in Eastern European countries (except for Hungary). Arrivals from these points, and others in northern Greece, terminate in Athens's Larissa Station, a standard-gauge facility. If you come on a Eurailpass via the Adriatic ferries and the port of Patras, the Peloponnesus Station (narrow gauge) will be your arrival point. The two stations lie parallel to each other, with a connecting, overhead footbridge. Each has a train-information booth with a limited amount of city information available. Both stations have taxi stands and bus service, but we recommend that new arrivals use the taxi. The taxi fare from the station area to the tourist office on Syntagma (Constitution) Square is inexpensive and well worth the extra drachmas.

If you are in the mood for some high adventure and don't mind rail-travel hardships lasting forty-one or more hours in order to travel 1,470 miles between Athens and Munich at roughly 35 miles per hour—then the rail route lying between Germany and Greece, passing through Austria and the former Yugoslavia, might be your piece of cake. Before signing up for such an endurance contest, however, consider that your Eurailpass may be "inoperative" during the time you are transiting the area that was Yugoslavia. Due to the unsettled nature of this region, you may encounter travel delays at the Greek and Austrian borders.

The Railway Stations—Larissa Station & Peloponnesus

ATHENS'S LARISSA STATION serves the standard-gauge rail lines to the north.

Money-exchange office is located at the north end of the train platform. Its only sign reads BANK—which, when you think about it, is entirely adequate. So are its operating hours: 0800–1830 Monday through Friday; 0900–1400 Saturday; 0900–1300 Sunday.

Hotel reservations are not available. Proceed to the tourist information office, in the National Bank of Greece Building on Syntagma Square.

Tourist information is limited. The train-information-booth attendants can help, but full tourist information service is available only in the Syntagma Square office.

Train information can be obtained in a booth to your immediate left when entering the station. The train information booth is open daily, 0600–2330. The telephone number is 823–7741.

Baggage can be stored in a "Left Baggage Office." It is located to the right as you enter the station and is open 0630–2300.

Train reservations are best obtained at the Hellenic Railways office at No. 1–3 Karolou Street or No. 6 Sina Street. Get taxi instructions from the tourist office on Syntagma Square.

Eurailpass validation is available at the Hellenic Railways' main office. They will predate your Eurailpass if you wish. Eurailpasses also can be validated at ticket windows in the stations, but only on your departure day.

ATHENS'S PELOPONNESUS STATION serves the narrow-gauge lines to the south.

Money exchange office is not available. Use the footbridge to cross to the Larissa Station Bank, or use the exchange services in the tourist information office on Syntagma Square.

Hotel bookings reservations are not available. Proceed to the tourist information office on Syntagma Square.

Tourist information is limited. The train-information-booth attendants can help, but full tourist information service is available only in the Syntagma Square office.

Train information can be obtained in a booth to your immediate left when entering the station. The office is open 0730–1900 daily throughout the summer. The hours are split, 0730–1230 and 1630–1900, the rest of the year. The telephone number is 513–1601.

Train reservations are best obtained at the Hellenic Railways' office at No. 1-3 Karolou Street or No. 6 Sina Street. Get taxi or bus instructions from the tourist office on Syntagma Square.

Greek guards parade at the tomb of the country's unknown soldier in front of the Greek Parliament Building facing Syntagma (Constitution) Square. The walls behind the guards celebrate Greek victories since 1821. You also can see the ceremonial guards at the Presidential Palace.

Eurailpass validation is available at ticket windows in the stations, but only on your departure date. The Hellenic Railways' offices will predate your Eurailpass validation.

Tourist Facilities

Foreign visitors arriving in Athens seem to congregate in Syntagma (Constitution) Square. They are attracted there like a needle to a magnet—a very strong magnet. The National Tourist Organization of Greece has wisely placed its main tourist information office in the vicinity of Syntagma Square in the National Bank of Greece Building. Telephone: (01)322–2545. It's easy to locate. Facing the Parliament Building from the bottom of the square in the café area, the tourist information office is just across the street on the left at No. 2 Amerikis Street. Telephone: (01)322–3111; fax: 322–2841.

The tourist office offers complete services for the tourist, including hotel and pension accommodations, money exchange, and tour information about Athens. Most of the tours being offered are bus tours that include some walking. Consequently, you should inquire as to the tour's duration and terrain before signing up, and don't forget to wear comfortable walking shoes. To avoid the daytime heat, select an evening tour when available. Most of the tourist attractions are illuminated.

The Athens city tourist office is an excellent source for information concerning other areas of the country. Be certain to inform the attendant you speak with that you hold a Eurailpass. Otherwise you might find yourself signing up for a bus tour when a rail trip would suffice for the transportation to the site you want to see. The banking office is open 0800–1830 daily throughout the year. The hotel desk, operated by the Hellenic Chamber of Hotels, is in operation Monday through Saturday, 0830–1400. Tourist information attendants are on duty daily, 0800–1300 and 1430–2000.

All about Athens

Although there is more to Athens than the Acropolis, it should be the first place to visit during your stay in the city. All else in and around Athens becomes secondary to this symbol of classic perfection that has stood majestically above Athens for about 2,500 years. Don't rush your visit or you will regret it. Plan to spend an entire day, and if you go there during the summer months, go prepared with some sun screen, sun hats, bottled water, and comfortable shoes. You will be outside during the entire visit, and walking around and through the ruins will absolutely ruin a pair of high heels.

The Parthenon is the focal point of the Acropolis, but there is much more to see. Study the Propylaea, the impressive entrance to the sanctuary, along with the Temple of Athena-Niki and the elegant row of maidens along the facade of the Erechtheion. You can peer down on the Theater of Dionysis from the rim of the Acropolis, but go there later to feel its "presence."

During the tourist season, a light-and-sound show of the Acropolis is presented. It, too, should not be missed. It is given in several languages, so be certain to select the right program. The program in English starts at 2100. You view the show from an opposite hillside and it can cool down considerably. You may want to take a light sweater or pullover. The Athens city tourist office can provide you with all the details for a wonderful evening.

The Romans made their presence known in Athens, too. A group of ruins dating back to the days of Julius Caesar clusters about the Roman Forum at the beginning of Aeolou Street. There are so many other sights to be seen that we recommend a guided tour as the only means of possibly scratching the surface of this wonderful city where Western civilization began.

With an extensive history like Athens, you may expect to find a full retinue of museums. You won't be disappointed. Be aware that you may be required to check any bags, including purses, and that most museums charge a fee for videotaping within the museum. If your stay in the city is limited, we suggest visiting the Benaki Museum, located on the corner of Vassilissis Sofias Avenue and Koumbari Street (telephone 361–16178). In its twenty-eight chambers, you will see exhibits ranging from the Bronze Age to the beginning of the twentieth century. As you pass through the centuries of statuary development, take note of the style by which the sculptors slowly developed the technique of depicting fingers and toes.

The modern city of Athens also holds much interest for visitors. You must visit the Tomb of the Unknown Warrior, with its colorful guards. Go to a café on Syntagma Square for coffee and pastry. Climb the time-worn steps leading through the Plaka Quarter, which hugs the base of the Acropolis.

Select one of Athens's "tavernas" and enjoy its food, music, and dancing. To experience a popular form of Greek entertainment, visit a Bouzouki nightclub. Bouzouki music is similar to American blues in that the music reflects the pain and pathos often present in love and friendships. Before you participate in the traditional plate breaking, check with the management as to the cost per dozen. You could end up spending a lot of drachmas.

Tourists are targets for ploys and pranks throughout the world. Athens is no exception. A waiter may suggest that you consume bottled water with your meal. After all, you may have been warned not to drink the regular water. Bottled water is a good idea, but insist that the waiter open the bottle *at your table*. Otherwise, you might receive an opened bottle of water that was just recently filled from the water tap in the kitchen. Or order a bottle of carbonated water. That's hard to bootleg!

TRAIN/FERRY CONNECTIONS TO OTHER BASE CITIES

Routing: Depart Peloponnese Station by train to Patras. Depart Patras by ferry to Brindisi, Italy. Depart Brindisi, Italy, for selected base city.

DEPART ATHENS	TRAIN NUMBER	ARRIVE PATRAS	DEPART PATRAS	ARRIVE BRINDISI	NOTES
0950	308	1438	1700	0930+1	(1)
1202	IC 12	1518	1900	1000+1	(2)
1459	314	1912	2100	1300+1	(2)

TO:	DEPART BRINDISI	ARRIVE MILAN	TRAIN NUMBER	COOK'S TABLE	NOTES
Milan	1313	2315	IC 578	390	(3)
	2022	900+1	1950	390	(3)*

	DEPART BRINDISI	ARRIVE ROME	TRAIN NUMBER	COOK'S TABLE	NOTES
Rome	0652	1520	962	390	(3)
	2241	0810+1	956	390	(3)**

* Train 922 arrives 0840+1 but does not always have sleepers (train 1950 does).
** Train 950/2 does not have sleepers; 956 does.

(1) Train daily, ferry summer only
(2) Train daily; ferry schedule varies month to month
(3) Daily

The central square in Argos is a good place to start exploring nearby Greek and Roman ruins. The modern town covers much of the ancient city.

From Athens . . .

A DAY EXCURSION TO ARGOS
DISTANCE BY TRAIN: 89 miles (144 km)
AVERAGE TRAIN TIME: 2 hours, 30 minutes

History comes out to meet you on this day excursion. Argos lies in the plain of Argolis on the Peloponnesus peninsula, land of myth and magic. Your mind can run rampant as you journey there. The *Iliad,* the *Odyssey,* and the beautiful Helen hover over all travelers who enter.

Modern history appears first as the train crosses the Isthmus of Corinth. Below the railroad bridge lies the canal connecting the Aegean and Ionian seas. Alexander the Great, Caesar, and Nero all failed in their attempts to construct the waterway through four miles of solid rock. A French engineering firm finally succeeded in 1893. Watch for it about an hour and twenty minutes after leaving Athens. The best view is from the right side of the train. The railroad bridge is only 108 feet long; so if you intend taking pictures, have everything poised and ready to go, for it passes quickly.

Medieval history is next in line as you approach Argos, where the hillsides northwest of the city reveal at their highest point a Venetian fortress, which dominates the White Chapel of the Prophet Elias and Our Lady of the Rocks Convent lying below.

Ancient history unfolds in Argos itself, where a 20,000-seat theater has been hewn from a hillside next to the remnants of a Roman bath. Five miles east of the town lie the Argive Heraeon and the scattered remains of Greece's oldest recognizable temple (800 B.C.). Tiryns, legendary birthplace of Hercules, is also in the area. These last two sights are not on the rail line and are best visited by taxi from Argos. Reasonable fares can be arranged.

Argos does not have a tourist information office. Neither does it have a tourist police office such as one finds in many of the smaller towns throughout Greece. But these absences present no great hardship, for most of its sights are within the city limits. The area must be the birthplace of all Greeks who have ever worked in the United States as waiters. We met two of them by just standing on a corner and looking perplexed. Try it—it's an easy way to pick up an English-speaking guide who will even recommend the best eating places in town, lead you to them, and then recommend items on the menu!

The railway station is about a kilometer from the town square in Argos. To reach it on foot, walk straight out of the station to the main road, where a road sign points to the right in the direction of town. Taxis are available for a nominal fare.

For sightseeing, orient yourself with the church in the town square. From its front door, you can reach the Argos museum by crossing the street, turning

ARGOS—*OLDEST GREEK TOWN*

A Day Excursion from Athens

DEPART FROM ATHENS STATION	TRAIN NUMBER	ARRIVE IN ARGOS STATION	NOTES
0745	422	1030	(1)
0818	1420	1049	(1)(2)
0930	424	1208	(1)

DEPART FROM ARGOS STATION	TRAIN NUMBER	ARRIVE IN ATHENS STATION	NOTES
1500	423	1742	(1)
1731	1423	2004	(1)(2)
1941	425	2225	(1)

(1) Daily, including holidays
(2) Second class only

Distance: 89 miles/144 km
Reference: Thomas Cook Table 980

left, and proceeding to the first cross street, where you then turn right. The museum is half a block farther on the left-hand side of the street. It is open daily, except Tuesdays. Admission is charged. It has an excellent collection of archaeological exhibits. Unfortunately, it does not have any literature published in English, but the curator will provide a verbal explanation of his collection.

The ancient theater and Roman ruins lie on the outskirts of town, in the direction of the hillsides. They are a five-minute taxi ride or a fifteen-minute walk from the museum. On foot, turn left at the next street beyond the museum and walk until you reach the next main intersection. Turn right, and walk straight ahead to the site. If there is the slightest tinge of archaeology in your blood, you'll love this spot. It is relatively unchanged and a perfect place to probe and peer for priceless treasures.

The theater has ninety tiers, which were cut into the hillside on rather a steep angle, making it possible for a perfect, uninterrupted view of the stage area from any seat in the house. Oddly enough, the 20,000 seating capacity of this amphitheater is more than adequate for the present 19,000 population of Argos.

Argos is the oldest continuously inhabited town in Greece. Many archaeologists suspect that it may be the oldest in all of Europe. Legends, many of them the basic stuff from which most of Greek mythology sprang, have their origins in Argos and the area surrounding it. In the legendary time of Danaus, story tellers relate how his fifty daughters slew their husbands on their wedding night and then tried to make amends with the devil by trying to fill a bottomless cask with water carried in sieves from the river Stykes. If this would happen in our times, no doubt Congress would investigate—taking equal time to determine the outcome.

The legend does, however, have a happy ending. One of Danaus's daughters, realizing that it could ruin her honeymoon, thought it over once or twice and then let her spouse escape the murderous nuptial-night activities. For this, she was rewarded by becoming the ancestral matriarch of a long line of mythological heroes.

The modern town of Argos was built up over ancient ruins from previous centuries of conflict. The last ethnic group to participate in that particular form of urban renewal was the Turks, who ravaged the town in 1397. As a result, Argos has scant visible remains of its ancient origins except the theater and the Roman baths. There is great speculation, however, as to what lies under the first layer or two of Argos's real estate. A French organization has been probing about the area since 1952. Artifacts it has found are displayed in the town's museum.

Archaic temple of ancient Corinth, built circa 500 B.C. and destroyed by the Romans in 146 B.C., was rebuilt in Roman times and dedicated to Apollo. Seven of its monolithic Doric columns are still standing.

From Athens . . .

A DAY EXCURSION TO CORINTH
DISTANCE BY TRAIN: 57 miles (91 km)
AVERAGE TRAIN TIME: 1 hour, 35 minutes

This day excursion runs from modern Greece back through the millennia to the Bronze Age. You have the opportunity to see modern Corinth, a typical "new" Greek city, and its port on the Peloponnesus. You may delve as well into the hillside of ancient Corinth, where Saint Paul established a church, Nero fiddled around with a canal, and Julius Caesar implemented an earlier version of the Marshall Plan.

There is a great deal of history to be noted en route to Corinth, for the railroad skirts the Aegean Sea and crosses the Isthmian Canal before arriving in Corinth. Watch for the canal when the train is about one hour and twenty minutes out of Athens. The center of the canal runs 285 feet deep through solid rock. The railroad bridge passes 200 feet above the level of the water for a spectacular view.

Greek and Roman rulers (the infamous Nero included) periodically attempted to breach the Isthmus with a canal, but until a French company using modern methods succeeded in the years 1882–93, all failed. The ancients hauled their small ships across the Isthmus on rollers. Vestiges of the portage road are still visible just after the train crosses the bridge. Watch on the right side of the train for the best view. Have your camera poised and ready—the train traverses the area quickly.

The present "new" city of Corinth, moved to its site in 1858 after an earthquake destroyed "old" Corinth, was leveled in turn by an equally devastating earthquake in 1928. The site has had its share of earth tremors; ancient scribes record devastations in A.D. 522 and 551. Termed an "undistinguished town," new Corinth is interesting in that it represents a community rebuilt on antiseismic principles of low buildings that, paradoxically, give it an air of impermanence.

For fear of pirates, old Corinth was built well back from the sea. This strategic position served the city well. It prospered and became one of the three great city-states of Greece, along with Athens and Sparta. Things went reasonably well until Corinth led the Achaean League against the Romans in 146 B.C. The Romans won the ball game and, à la Carthage (as was the custom in those days), laid waste to Corinth. After the city withstood a hundred years of total desolation, Julius Caesar decided to rebuild Corinth, and it blossomed into one of the great trading cities of the Roman Empire.

During his eighteen-month sojourn in Corinth, Saint Paul became alarmed about the sinful ways of the Corinthians and frequently "read the riot act" to

71

CORINTH—*AND THE ISTHMIAN CANAL*

A Day Excursion from Athens

DEPART FROM ATHENS STATION	TRAIN NUMBER	ARRIVE IN CORINTH STATION	NOTES
0854	IC 20	1024	(1)
0950	308	1152	(1)
1202	1C 12	1330	(1)

DEPART FROM CORINTH STATION	TRAIN NUMBER	ARRIVE IN ATHENS STATION	NOTES
1556	303	1750	(1)
1746	IC 15	1912	(1)
1955	IC 25	2122	(1)
2131	305	2322	(1)

(1) Daily, including holidays

Distance: 57 miles/91 km
Reference: Thomas Cook Table 980

the city fathers. Because of his violent condemnation of moral laxity, he was charged with inciting a riot. Instead of dispensing punishment, the city fathers issued Saint Paul a reprimand—and the suggestion that he leave town as soon as possible, which he did.

Historians estimate that at one time the ancient city of Corinth had a population of more than 460,000; today, its citizens number about 21,000. Although termed a citadel, the old city was attacked repeatedly and conquered down through the ages. During their sweep through Greece, the Turks took over the city in 1458 and again in 1715. In 1458, the Turkish conquest ended when they retreated hastily in ships. The siege of the city in 1715 was described in prose by Lord Byron. There is little Turkish architecture visible in the Corinthian area, due mainly to the short time they were on the premises.

There is excellent bus service between the city and the archaeological site. Departures are daily on the hour from 0615 to 2100. The one-way fare is 160 drachmas. Round-trip cab fare, including a reasonable wait, runs about 1,000 drachmas. The bus terminal is on the south side of the city park. The sign over the terminal reads ΑΡΧΑΙΑ. A taxi will take you there from the railway station for a nominal fare.

To reach the bus station on foot, turn left after leaving the station and then right onto Damaskinou Street and right again onto Ermou Street, just before the Hotel Belle Vue. Turn left at this point and, three blocks later, you'll arrive at the bus terminal on the far left-hand corner of the city park. For further information regarding new or old Corinth, check with the "Tourist Police." Walk through the park past another bus terminal to a pharmacy on the right-hand side. Turn right and find the police station half a block farther down the street on the left-hand side.

Excavations have been in progress on the site of old Corinth for many years. Literature describing the excavations and the contents of the museum is available as you enter the site. Between 1925 and 1929, extensive excavations were made. Among the findings, an inscription was found that recorded the story of Androcles and the lion. According to Roman history, Androcles removed a thorn from a lion's paw. Later, when he was sentenced to death and thrown to the lions, the lion remembered Androcles' kindness and let him off without a scratch.

In ancient Corinth, you must pay for admission to the grounds and an additional fee to enter the museum. It is open Monday through Friday, 0730–2100 (or sunset), and on Sundays, 1000–1300 and 1500–1900. Plan to spend a minimum of four hours at the site. There is a lot of walking. Several canteens serve refreshments outside the main entrance.

Broad steps running from the arcaded shopping center of modern Patras mark the path to the Venetian-Turkish citadel overlooking the city and its harbor. The foundations of a Roman odeum can be seen below the fortress.

From Athens . . .

A DAY EXCURSION TO PATRAS
DISTANCE BY TRAIN: 138 miles (222 km)
AVERAGE TRAIN TIME: 4 hours

Patras is the third largest city in Greece. It is also the country's western gate way. Located at the entrance to the Gulf of Corinth, Patras has been a Greek seaport since the beginning of recorded history. Ships large and small are constantly arriving in, and departing from, its harbor. The ferry services of the Adriatica and Hellenic Mediterranean lines ply between Patras and Brindisi, Italy. If you are a Eurailpass traveler, no doubt you will either enter or leave Greece through the Port of Patras.

Patras is the port where the majority of Greek emigrants sailed for the United States. It is interesting to note that in 1922, refugees fleeing Asia Minor arrived at the pier in Patras penniless. Many of them paid for their passage to America by selling their oriental carpets, which they had carried on their backs from their homelands. Since the early 1960s, Patras has developed into a major Adriatic ferry port.

Eurailpass holders are cautioned to use either the Adriatica or the Hellenic Mediterranean Line if they intend paying for their deck passage with the Eurailpass. Although other ferry companies operate between Greece and Italy, these lines are the only ones honoring the Eurailpass.

Spreading below its Venetian castle, Patras is where Saint Andrew taught Christianity and was crucified. The saint's head rests in a shrine following its return from Saint Peter's, Rome, in 1964. It was here in Patras in 1809 that Lord Byron first set foot on Greek soil.

The railway station in Patras lies on the quay, but it's about 500 yards from the pier where ferries depart for Brindisi. You'll spot the pier to the right as the train slows for its stop in the Patras station. A tourist information booth is located at the entrance to the ferry terminal. For complete information regarding Patras and its surroundings, we suggest that you visit the office of the Greek National Tourist Organization at 110 Iroon Polytechniou Street. Ask at the rail station or the ferry terminal for directions. Otherwise, turn right at the quay and walk well beyond the ferry terminal and look for the signs leading to the office. There also is an information office at the entrance of the port of Patras (at Glyfada).

The quay is an interesting part of Patras. The long mole, with its benches for resting, extends into the harbor and is a favorite place from which to watch the activity in the harbor. From it you can photograph the arrival of the ferryboats running between the ports of Patras and Brindisi.

Patras has two noteworthy celebrations: the stately procession of Saint

PATRAS—*PORT CITY*

A Day Excursion from Athens

DEPART FROM ATHENS STATION	TRAIN NUMBER	ARRIVE IN PATRAS STATION	NOTES
0756	IC 10	1145	(1)
0854	IC 20	1215	(1)
1202	IC 12	1518	(1)
1343	IC 22	1703	(1)

DEPART FROM PATRAS STATION	TRAIN NUMBER	ARRIVE IN ATHENS STATION	NOTES
1325	303	1750	(1)
1557	IC 15	1912	(1)
1803	IC 25	2122	(1)

(1) Daily, including holidays

Distance: 143 miles/230 km
Reference: Thomas Cook Table 980

Andrew on November 30 and a spectacular carnival during the last ten days before Lent. The city also conducts a classic-theater season during the summer. We suggest a walking tour of Patras starting at the Trion Symmahon Square across from the station and on the right. The long arcaded avenue leading off the park in the direction of the city's heights is studded with stores, restaurants, and specialty shops.

Continue walking on this avenue (Ayiou Nikolaou) to the foot of a broad flight of steps, which will bring you to the site of the ancient Patras Acropolis. A wonderful view of the city, its harbor, and the surrounding hills and mountains may be enjoyed from this point. If you return to the base of the steps and proceed to the left on Yeoryiou Street, it will lead you to the Odeum, a characteristic Roman theater. It was discovered in 1889, but enterprising building contractors subsequently removed much of its marble, requiring the theater to be restored extensively in 1960.

Visitors seeking Saint Andrews Church should begin their quest at the Trion Symmahon Square and walk southwest along Andreou Avenue to the church, which stands by the sea at the avenue's end. A park dedicated to Andrew, the patron saint of Scotland, is across from the church.

To reach the city's museum, turn left at the Trion Fountain in Trion Symmahon Square and walk for two blocks, then turn right and walk for two more. The museum has an extensive collection of classic Greek and Roman statues plus a collection of prehistoric pottery. There is an admission charge.

The area surrounding Patras is steeped in Greek history. Patras may be used as a "base city" when visiting Olympia, original site of the Olympic Games. In Olympia, you can visit the site of the Olympic flame, which is carried by runners to any point in the world where the games are to be held. Also of interest is the arch commemorating Nero's "victory" in a chariot race staged in A.D. 67. The emperor's chariot was pulled by ten horses, while all other competitors had to make do with four—needless to say, Nero won.

Another interesting side trip can be made to the Achaia Clauss Winery, five miles outside Patras, to view the wine-making process and sample a bit of the product. If interested in either excursion, you may obtain information at the tourist police office.

Culinary delights abound in Patras. A sea-bass dish, *tsipoures,* is a specialty of the area. This and other Greek dishes are available in the tavernas scattered throughout the upper part of town. An American-style restaurant lies just before the Hellenic Lines office on the quay. Customers may stow their suitcases and backpacks there free of charge while waiting for the ferry.

Picturesque port of Mikrolimano forms a semicircle lined end to end with seafood restaurants. One of two small harbor basins in Piraeus, it has fresh fish from the sea that lures tourists daily throughout the year.

From Athens . . .

A DAY EXCURSION TO PIRAEUS
DISTANCE BY TRAIN: 5 miles (8 km)
AVERAGE TRAIN TIME: 20 minutes

Piraeus, main port of Athens, basks in the warm embrace of the Saronic Gulf just a few miles and minutes outside the heart of Athens. Piraeus today is one of the principal ports of the Mediterranean. It serves both commercial shipping and pleasure craft. Most tourists go to Piraeus not to view its remains of antiquity but, rather, to enjoy the picturesque atmosphere of its port and to indulge in some of the wonderful seafood served in its restaurants.

Throughout the centuries, Piraeus has had its successes and its failures. In 86 B.C., the Roman General Sulla destroyed the city and its docks, and for centuries Piraeus was considered an unimportant village. Its reconstruction began only in 1834, when Athens became the capital of Greece. Resettled by islanders, Piraeus grew rapidly throughout the nineteenth century and played a large part in the revival of Athens.

Between 1854 and 1859, Piraeus was occupied by an Anglo-French fleet to prevent Greek nationalists' forays against Turkey, an Allied power in the Crimean War. In World War II, the port was put out of action in April 1941 by a German air attack. The ammunition ship *Clan Fraser,* carrying 200 tons of TNT, together with two other ships loaded with ammunition exploded and destroyed the port.

You won't need your Eurailpass for this day excursion. You'll be traveling on Athens's privately owned electric line. The line is the "subway" for the city. A major portion of the rails running to Piraeus, however, are above ground.

You begin your journey from Omonia Square in the city. It connects with Syntagma (Constitution) Square via Stadhiou Street, which, by the way, starts right outside the entrance to the tourist information office. The entrances to the underground terminal are clearly marked. Be certain to purchase your tickets before boarding. The station uses a center platform for all trains, so check the directional signs for Piraeus before boarding.

Most of the trains operating on this line are of wood construction, an oddity in this day of stainless steel and aluminum. Although quaint, the equipment is maintained in excellent condition and is most enjoyable to ride. Travel at off-peak hours to avoid the crowds. Service is frequent throughout the day. Train etiquette in Greece dictates that men relinquish their seats to ladies and that the young do the same for elders. When in Greece, do as the Greeks do.

Leave the electric train at the end of the line in Piraeus. The terminal lies right at the harbor. To stroll along the quay, exit the station straight ahead,

PIRAEUS—*SEAFOOD BY THE SEASIDE*

A Day Excursion from Athens

Electric subway trains operated by the Athens Electric Railway run every few minutes between the Omonia Square Station in Athens and the port rail terminal in Piraeus.

The journey takes about twenty minutes. Passengers are cautioned to board Piraeus-bound (south) trains from the subway platform in the Omonia Square Station. Trains to Kifissia (the northern suburbs of Athens) depart from the same platform.

Distance: 5 miles/8 km
Reference: Thomas Cook Table 980

turning left at the side along the sea. Commercial ships and ferries to hundreds of island points occupy the piers along the waterfront of the main harbor. The railway station serving the Athens-Peloponnesus Line is to the right of the subway terminal. Trains for Patras, Corinth, and Argos originate from there, but passengers are not accepted for the short ride between Piraeus and Athens.

In addition to its main harbor, Piraeus has two small-craft harbors, Zea and Mikrolimano. Zea shelters pleasure craft, and Mikrolimano features fishing craft and seafood restaurants, the latter rimming its waterfront like pickets of a fence. Bus No. 20 will take you to either of the smaller ports. Board it from the bus terminal on the left side of the train station. Bus No. 20 stands in the far line, facing away from the sea.

After skirting the main harbor, the bus passes through a built-up area before it again sides with the sea at Zea. If Mikrolimano is your destination, ride four stops beyond Zea and dismount. The Castella Hotel is on the left side at the bus stop. From there, walk down to the harbor. If you're going for lunch, try to arrive before 1230, when the area is invaded by a horde of tour buses packed with hungry tourists. At night the tables in the restaurants overlooking the sea groan under their loads of fresh fish, luscious lobsters, and opulent oysters. Top off your evening by climbing the hill behind Mikrolimano for a magnificent view of the Mediterranean's Saronic Gulf.

Many restaurants employ solicitors to influence your selection of eating places. You can ignore them. We have found that the better places lie to the right of the harbor. "Kanaris 2" is one of the more expensive restaurants, but it is well worth it.

While on the subject of price, a word of caution: Check menu prices carefully before ordering. Many menu prices are given for one kilo (2.2 pounds) of fish—a price that the government requires the restaurants to list. Certainly, your platter won't hold that much, but some places will try to charge you on that basis. *Caveat emptor*—let the buyer beware.

During the summer, Piraeus is considerably cooler than Athens. Should the temperatures soar during your stay in the Greek capital, take a quick trip on the Athens subway to the seaside at Piraeus. In the evening, the tavernas and night clubs there provide a resort-type life style. The city's night spots feature popular singers.

Lacking museums, Piraeus's archaeological discoveries are displayed in the Athens National Museum. Of particular interest is a collection of statuary stored and forgotten by General Sulla in 86 B.C. Perhaps the general lost his claim check.

A young admirer of costumed horses relaxes in Barcelona. The statue of Christopher Columbus is seen in the background.

5   BARCELONA

Barcelona has a very special atmosphere. Actually, it is more European than Spanish. Yet, there isn't another city in Europe to compare it with—even Marseilles, the other great Mediterranean port. Big, beautiful, and rich, Barcelona is there to be seen and appreciated. Basically, Barcelona is an elegant, sophisticated city, characterized by a modern, futuristic outlook adapted perfectly to a profound respect for the traditions of the past.

Barcelona is steeped in history. Founded in ancient times by the Phoenicians, it was named "Barca" by the Carthaginians in honor of the Barcinos, the third-century–B.C. ruling house of Cartagena. Barcelona witnessed Hannibal's army moving northward to strike at Rome. By the time of Augustus Caesar, Barcelona was a growing city under Roman rule. On his return from the discovery of America, Columbus was received in Barcelona by Ferdinand and Isabella. In recognition, the city erected a monument to the explorer. Completed in 1868, you may view it today at the edge of the Barcelona harbor, where the Ramblas meets the sea. To the left of the monument, you stand in awe at the perfect reproduction of Columbus's *Santa Maria*, moored at the quay, and wonder how such a great adventure could have possibly been accomplished in such a small craft.

In more modern times, Barcelona has become Spain's most prosperous port. Although it has developed a thriving industrial complex, complete with burgeoning suburbs, Barcelona wears its centuries-old charm in a manner befitting both a matron and a monarch. International in nature, Barcelona has hosted the World's Fair twice in its history; once in 1888 and again in 1992. Come to Barcelona prepared to enjoy it. It has something for everyone.

Day Excursions

If Barcelona isn't typically Spanish, its day-excursion opportunities are. A visit to Blanes takes you to the Costa Brava (Wild Coast), where the azure of the Mediterranean sky blends harmoniously with the intense colors of the coast and where you will be provided with an opportunity to sample a culinary delight, fish soup. The citadel city of Lerida, stormed by Caesar's legions and conquered by the Moors, carries visitors far back into Spanish history. Stretching south from Barcelona, a strand of fine, golden sand, the Costa Dorada (Gold Coast), leads to one of Spain's most picturesque places, Sitges, with its unusual adaptation of American fast food. Farther south lies Tarragona, Roman in facade but actually a modern metropolis. Blanes, Lerida, Sitges, and Tarragona await your pleasure.

Arriving and Departing

By Air. Barcelona's international airport is fewer than nine miles from the city center. It is serviced by trains running directly from the airport to the Barcelona Sants Station. The trip takes approximately twenty minutes. From the station, you can connect with the regular Spanish railroads, the Barcelona Metro, or transfer to a taxi if you are hotel bound. The airport rail system accepts the Eurailpass. It is *not* possible, however, to have your pass validated at the airport. Furthermore, you will probably spend some time sightseeing in the city and have no need for your Eurailpass during that time. The rule (which applies to arriving in any of the growing number of European airports with train-transfer facilities): Wait and have your Eurailpass validated on the day you *begin* your train travel and not before.

Trains depart Barcelona from the Sants station for the airport every thirty minutes from 0542 to 2212. Trains depart the airport on the same thirty-minute schedule from 0612 until 2242. Tickets for the airport train are available at local train ticket windows in the station. Airport trains depart from Track No. 3. The fare is 285 pesetas weekdays and 325 pesetas weekends and holidays.

Airport busses to Plaça de Cataluna (Cataluna Square) depart every fifteen minutes Monday through Friday 0600–2230; every thirty minutes Saturdays, Sundays, and holidays. The fare is 380 pesetas, and the time en route is fifteen to twenty minutes. The approximate taxi fare from the airport to city center is 1,800–2,200 pesetas.

By Train. Barcelona has a total of eight rail stations—nine, if you take into consideration the one at the city's airport. Fortunately, only one—Barcelona Sants—is involved for arrivals from other base cities or participation in our day-excursion program. The station has also been referred to from time to time as Barcelona "Central." "Sants" was its original name, however, and the Spanish National Railways has designated this as the proper name to officially identify the station.

Veteran rail travelers will recall Barcelona Termino, the city's first rail station, where for many years all trains running to or from France originated or terminated. After being closed for several years for a major renovation in preparation for the 1992 Summer Olympics, the station is operational again under the name Estació de França (the French station). *Most* of the international trains from France and northern European countries now arrive in Estació de França. Check the timetables, however, to be certain.

If arriving in Barcelona from Madrid, the train will halt in Barcelona Sants but then continue onto Paseo de Gracia, an underground station, where it terminates. Unless you are well acquainted with Barcelona and its rail terminals, we suggest that you detrain in Barcelona Sants since it has more facilities to assist travelers than does Paseo de Gracia which, in many respects, has been designed to serve as a Barcelona commuting station.

Barcelona Sants

Still commonly referred to by Barcelona's taxi drivers as "Estació de Sants," this facility is the hub of Barcelona's transportation system, combining rail, metro (subway), air terminal, and bus service in one location.

Barcelona Sants was renovated in preparation for the 1992 Summer Olympics. Many of the station's functions were relocated at that time. It is expected that still further relocation of many services and amenities will be taking place throughout the next few years. Consequently, it is best to follow the strategically placed pictographs in the station for information, restrooms, taxi, telephone, baggage storage, food, and shopping.

The entrance to the Barcelona metro system has not been relocated. It's still to the right of the station's arrival-departure board, leading down from the station's ground level. Neither has the restaurant moved; you can reach the Dos Leones by the stairs leading to the second level just past the snack bar and vending machine area.

Seat reservations are mandatory on all express trains in Spain. Don't board without one. Reservations may be made in Barcelona Sants at the ticket desk in the access area to tracks 9 through 12. If you are making reservations in advance, report to the reservation desk section marked "Venta Anticipada." For same-day departures, report to the section marked "Venta Immediata." That section handles reservations only for the current date. Since reservations may be made up to two months in advance of the departure date, it is sensible to make all of your reservations with one visit to the "Anticipada" section when possible. Trying to get reservations for today and tomorrow—or the future—all at one time can be hectic, to say the least. It has been rumored that the Spanish dance, the adagio, was invented between "Immediata" and "Anticipada." We're checking further on that rumor.

The Spanish railroad's rule that seat reservations are obligatory has been tested personally, and we can assure you that, without them, the conductor will ask you to leave the train at the next station—even if you are carrying a Eurailpass. Avoid the hassle by planning your train trips in advance while in Spain. Waiting until the day of departure to get a seat reservation can be very time consuming.

You may enter the train-platform area just by showing your Eurailpass, but you must have the seat reservation in order to actually depart on a train (other than local commuters). If you must wait until your departure date to reserve a seat, apply for reservations only in the station from which the train initially departs. Allow at least one hour for the reservation process.

Bullfighting, national sport of Spain, thrives in Barcelona. "Most Americans," according to Myra Waldo's *Travel and Motoring Guide to Europe* (Macmillan), "want to see a bull-fight when they come to Spain. And they should—it's all part of the local scene. Not many go a second time."

Barcelona Sants has twelve track platforms running beneath the station's ground level that are accessible by escalators or elevators. Be certain to check the platform and track number on the departure board before descending to the train level.

Money-exchange facilities are prominently located in the center of the station ground level. They are identified by the standard currency exchange pictograph. Hours of operation are daily, 0800–2200. Official bank rates are observed.

Hotel reservations ajoin the Hertz facilities. The service operates 0800–2200 daily. Reservations can be made at this counter with a cash deposit of 100 pesetas.

If you have a credit card, such as American Express, MasterCard, or Visa, you can ask the attendant to advise the hotel to assure the reservation by giving the card number and its expiration date to the hotel's reservation clerk. In any event, as quickly as you have been able to make a hotel reservation, you should proceed immediately to the hotel. Don't stop for dinner or a bullfight. Without your money in their hands, Spanish hotel clerks work on a first-come, first-served basis. So hurry on over as quickly as you can. The last alternative is to have an advance reservation in hand prior to arrival in Barcelona.

Tourist information takes a prominent position in the southeast section of the station between the escalators for tracks 9–10 and 11–12. The facility serves for both rail and city tourist information. Identified by the familiar "i," the office hours are 0900–1900 Monday through Friday; Saturday 0900–1400; closed Sunday. For information regarding places outside of Barcelona, you should visit the Barcelona branch of the Spanish Government Information office. It is located at 658 Gran Via. The tourist information office can provide you with a map and metro (or taxi) information if you need to go there.

For sightseeing information, we suggest you check with your hotel or pension. Several reputable tour companies provide their literature to the hotels, and quite often a city tour can be arranged where the tour bus calls directly to your place of residence for pick-up.

Train information is available at the center of the station between tracks 5–6 with hours from 0630 to 2200. This is where you should inquire regarding seat reservations and how to get them. Although timetables are posted throughout the station, you may want to obtain one of the miniature tables giving information only from Barcelona to nearby day excursion points.

Eurailpass validation is made at selected ticket windows under the Arrivals–Departure Board. Check first with the information desk and they will direct you to the proper window.

The Eurail Aid Office is also located in the Barcelona Sants Station. You can get directions from the attendants at the information desk or telephone ahead to (093) 4903630 if you have a problem.

Barcelona Background

Ramble along the Ramblas, one of Europe's most delightful thoroughfares. Nature was its architect because it began as an ancient path carved out by waters rushing to the sea. Its buildings are insignificant. It is the pulse of its people that makes it interesting. Go there day or night. There's always something to do, something to see. It's the promenade, park, and marketplace of Barcelona. It has a bird market, a flower market, bookstalls, and banks. Sidewalk cafés on the Ramblas are *the* place to be seen—to sit and watch, too.

Barcelona's night life is highly varied. There are discothèques as well as night clubs where you may watch popular shows, or you can select from several supper clubs for dining and dancing. Oddly enough, the area in Barcelona called the Paralelo was the heart of the city's night life at the turn of the century and was nicknamed the "Montmartre" of Barcelona. The Ramblas has long since stripped the area of that exclusive title.

While on the subject of dining, Barcelona conforms to the Spanish tradition of late dinners. In theory, restaurants begin serving the evening meal at 2030. If you should arrive earlier than 2130, however, you will probably have the establishments all to yourself. Fashionable restaurants have their last seatings prior to 2300. Consequently, if you happen to be on the city's streets between 2130 and 2200, don't become alarmed at the sudden, maddening increase in traffic. Barcelona's citizens are not evacuating the city—they're just going out for dinner.

At the city's quay in the harbor, the statue of Columbus serenely surveys the scene, which includes a replica of his flagship, the *Santa Maria*. Aboard, there is hardly room for a good-size flag, let alone a ship's crew. You wonder how he made it, but as an American, you are awfully glad that he did.

Actually Barcelona, as the city is formed today, was created only in 1874 by the joining of twenty-seven separate municipalities. The center of this new metropolitan area is the Plaça de Cataluna, a square rimmed with trees and highlighted by sculptures and fountains—and an abundance of pigeons. The square is actually the intersection where the old and new Barcelona meet.

Running off of the Plaça de Cataluna to the north is the wide thoroughfare known as the Passeig de Gracia, Barcelona's most expensive shopping street. The name should sound familiar because the rail station lying between Sants and Termino stations is located there. If you're on a tight budget, you may want to avoid the use of this station—the shops don't accept Eurailpass, but they do accept every bank card ever known.

From Barcelona ...

TRAIN CONNECTIONS TO OTHER BASE CITIES

TO:	DEPART	ARRIVE	TRAIN NUMBER	COOK'S TABLE	NOTES
Berne	2015	0751+1	EN 272	81	(1)(2)
Madrid	0805(2)	1455	TAL 41	410	(2)
	1200(3)	1905	TAL 377	410	
	1505(2)	2203	TAL 379	410	(2)
	2310(3)	0800+1	875	410	(3)(4)
Milan	1945	1345+1	1142	90	(3)(5)
	2015	0845+1	EN 277	90	(1)(2)
Paris (Austerlitz)	2100	0815+1	474	47	(2)(4)
Rome	1945	1805+1	364	90	(3)(5)(6)

Daily departures unless otherwise noted. Make reservations for all departures. Reservations are mandatory in Spain.

(1) Talgo train, *Pablo Casals,* Gran Classe sleeper, supplement payable, Eurailpass *not* accepted
(2) Departs Barcelona França station
(3) Departs Barcelona Sants station
(4) Sleeper
(5) Couchettes only
(6) Transfer in Cerbère

Beach at Blanes, north of Barcelona, marks the beginning of the Costa Brava resort area on Spain's Mediterranean coast.

From Barcelona . . .

A DAY EXCURSION TO BLANES
DISTANCE BY TRAIN: 38 miles (61 km)
AVERAGE TRAIN TIME: 1 hour, 10 minutes

Blanes is reached easily from Barcelona by train. In a sense, Blanes is the rail-head for Spain's Costa Brava. From Blanes, local buses or coastal passenger boats can take you to many other ports along this rugged and beautiful sea-coast. You really should plan to visit Blanes twice during your stay in Barcelona—once to explore and enjoy Blanes, the second time to see and survey more of the Costa Brava.

Blanes is best described as a typical Spanish coastal village. Tourists are welcome, and Blanes goes out of its way to extend a friendly invitation. But it remains an industrious village engaged primarily in fishing and farming. It is not a "resort" in the usual sense of the word. Perhaps this lack of commercialism is what attracts many visitors.

Trains to Blanes depart from the suburban section of the Barcelona Sants Station. The best way to locate it is to get directions from either the train information desk or the tourist information office in the main section of the station. The service to Blanes is frequent. All the trains to Blanes are one class. Seat reservations are not necessary, but board early. The cars can become quite crowded during peak hours, and seats are on a "first-come, first-served" basis.

The railway station serving Blanes is perched on a hill about a half mile from the center of the village and the sea. Buses that are marked ESTACION-BLANES will take you into town. The bus terminal and a taxi stand are located at Plaça de Cataluna, near the sea.

Another taxi stand is located on the Plaza de España near the Passeig de Dintre. The Oficina de Turismo (tourist information office) is located on Plaça de Cataluna, a few steps from the bus terminal (telephone 9–72–330348). The driver will point it out. Go there first. Blanes has many attractions—and winding streets. The tourist office can supply you with a town map and brochures. From June through September, it's open 0900–2000 Monday through Saturday (also 1000–1400 on Sundays during July and August). In May and October, hours are 0900–1500 and 1600–1900 Monday through Friday and 0900–1400 on Saturdays. During winter, the office is open 0900–1500 Monday through Friday and 0900–1400 on Saturdays.

Blanes curves around the Mediterranean much like Cannes on the French Riviera, but that is the end of the comparison. In Blanes, the tempo is much slower. A stroll along its waterfront is a delightful experience. It is fronted principally by houses of fishermen whose boats lie at anchor in the curve of

BLANES—*BEACHES, BOATS, AND BIKINIS*

A Day Excursion from Barcelona

DEPART FROM BARCELONA SANTS*	ARRIVE IN BLANES STATION	NOTES
0712	0844	(1)
0812	0944	(1)
0942	1114	(1)
1012	1214	(1)
1212	1344	(1)

Additional trains depart daily every 30 minutes until 2212.

DEPART FROM BLANES STATION	ARRIVE IN BARCELONA SANTS	NOTES
1530	1704	(1)
1700	1834	(1)
1800	1934	(1)
1920	2054	(1)
2030	2204	(1)

Additional trains depart daily every 30 minutes until 2130.

* See *Thomas Cook European Timetable,* "Plans of Cities" section, for description of railway stations in Barcelona.

(1) Daily, including holidays. One class only (second class only)

Distance: 38 miles/61 km
Reference: Thomas Cook Table 417

the bay. There is an auction of the day's catch each evening at about 1700 Monday through Friday at the breakwater.

Blanes is not *all* business. It has plenty of fun-in-the-sun places. The town is particularly proud of its beach areas. A sewage-treatment plant ensures the sanitation of the water. Seekers of sun and surf have found the right place. Bathing facilities are excellent.

For other diversions, a delightful botanical garden is located quite near the breakwater where the fish auctions are held. Founded in 1924 by Karl Faust, the garden exhibits more than 4,000 species of regional and international flora. The garden is open 0900–1800 daily from April to mid-October. The hours are reduced during winter.

The Costa Brava (the Rugged Coast) is a breathtaking, ninety-mile stretch of jagged coastline blessed with fantastic beaches and hidden coves. It begins at Blanes. A local cruise-boat company, Crucerus, provides an exceptional opportunity to view the Costa Brava from the Mediterranean, and its boats put in wherever you please if you want to investigate farther on foot.

The Crucerus Line, which identifies its vessels with a blue whale at each bow, operates from June through September; sails north out of Blanes with ports of call at Lloret, Tossa, and San Feliu de Guixols; and continues to near the French border at the resort village of Tamariu (August only). Llorct has undergone a transformation from a simple fishermen's village in the 1950s to a resort with more than one hundred hotels. Tossa was actually the first "resort," attracting visitors even before the Spanish Civil War. San Feliu de Guixols, supposedly founded by Charlemagne, is the largest town on the Costa Brava.

Tamariu, where the blue whales turn and return to Blanes, rivals any coastal area in the world for beauty. You may reach there by departing Blanes at 0900 and arriving in Tamariu at 1300. After lunch, a departure at 1540 will place you back in Blanes by 1945.

Another, shorter combination of port calls would include departing Blanes at 0900, going ashore at Lloret between 0920 and 1000, then proceeding to Tossa. At 1155, you would set sail again, this time for San Feliu de Guixols, where you would arrive in time for a fashionable lunch at 1245. You could linger to explore in San Feliu de Guixols on a leisurely basis, too, because there are three afternoon departures back to Blanes, the latest being at 1545. Late risers coming from Barcelona could still make that luncheon date if they board the Blue Whale departing from Blanes at 1045—that's the sailing that arrives in San Feliu de Guixols at 1245. To obtain a copy of the "Blue Whale" schedule, ask the tourist office for the "Daily Sea Excursions" brochure.

Crave seafood? In Blanes, head for Restaurant Unic Parrilla at No. 7 Puerta Nueva. Try the *sopa casera* (fish soup). It's superb!

Old cathedral cloister in Lerida was formerly a mosque. Restoration is now under way. (Photo courtesy Josep M. Farré.)

From Barcelona ...

A DAY EXCURSION TO LERIDA
DISTANCE BY TRAIN: 114 miles (184 km)
AVERAGE TRAIN TIME: 3 hours

Your transportation to Lerida is an ELT (*electrotren*), a fast diesel rail car that takes you there in comfort through spectacular scenery. Dining facilities are aboard, so you may want to have breakfast while en route. Just the train ride alone is worth the experience. Be certain to make seat reservations well in advance of your day-excursion date, because the train's early morning departure does not allow sufficient time for making the reservation on the same day as you intend to make the day excursion. The ELT departs Sants Station, where same-day reservations are possible but time-consuming.

At "one hour and ten minutes into the mission," your train will stop briefly in Manresa. Surrounded by irrigated lands devoted to the production of fruits and vegetables, Manresa itself is rather lackluster. On a clear day, however, it has a breathtaking backdrop—the ridges of the Montserrat in the Pyrenees Mountains to the north. The ridges, when visible, will be illuminated by the rays of the morning sun. Stay alert for this scenic treat—it's only a fleeting glimpse.

After departing Manresa, the scenery becomes more mountainous. Watch from the left side of the train as it approaches Lerida. The sight is unforgettable. The ancient cathedral, Seo Antiqua, stands as a sentinel atop a hill on the banks of the Segre River. It appears to brood—and well it should. Seo Antiqua has suffered from the passage of time and the hands of men. Constructed in the thirteenth century on the former site of a mosque, it was converted from a church to a garrison fortress in 1707 by Philip V and burned and pillaged in the wars that followed. In 1950 it was reconsecrated, and restoration was begun. A visit is worthwhile. If you are up to it, scaling the tower of Seo Antiqua provides the visitor with yet another sweeping vista of the plain surrounding Lerida.

Upon arrival in Lerida, check in with the Oficina d'Informació Turística (tourist office). A map showing the location of the tourist office in relation to the rail station is displayed in the station's foyer. The tourist office is located at Plaça d'Agelet i Garriga, adjacent to the city hall and historical museum, La Paeria.

You can reach the tourist information office on foot by proceeding directly out from the station and walking along Rambla de Ferran. As you approach the bridge to your left crossing the Segre River, you'll find the office immediately ahead on the right-hand side of the Rambla.

It's about a fifteen-minute walk from the rail station to the tourist informa-

LERIDA—*ANCIENT PROVINCIAL CAPITAL*

A Day Excursion from Barcelona

DEPART FROM BARCELONA SANTS*	TRAIN NUMBER	ARRIVE IN LERIDA STATION	NOTES
0730	623	0924	(1)(2)
0830	TAL 41	1017	(1)(2)
1200	TAL 377	1405	(1)(2)

DEPART FROM LERIDA STATION	TRAIN NUMBER	ARRIVE IN BARCELONA SANTS*	NOTES
1638	530	1915	(1)(2)
1543	TAL 374	1800	(1)(2)
2034	TAL 378	2235	(1)(2)

* *See Thomas Cook European Timetable,* "Plans of Cities" section, for description of railway stations in Barcelona.

(1) Daily, including holidays. Food service available
(2) Reservations mandatory

Distance: 114 miles/ 184 km
Reference: Thomas Cook Table 410

tion office. A taxi can have you there in about five minutes. During the summer, you may prefer taking a taxi because of the heat. From June through September, the tourist information office is open 0900–2000 Monday through Friday, 0900–1400 and 1600–2000 Saturday, and 0900–1400 Sunday. An excellent brochure containing a city map is available. It is more than adequate for planning your visit to Lerida.

Lerida first became important as a military outpost for ancient Rome. If you expect Lerida to be merely an ancient city slumbering in its past, however, you are in for a surprise. The picturesque old quarter of this provincial capital teems with interest. Certain streets are closed to traffic, making it easy for shoppers to pause and ponder a purchase. The streets, though narrow, alternately burst into bright sunlight or welcomed shade. Life in Lerida has taken on new dimensions.

The architecture of Lerida creates a refreshing atmosphere that is seldom found elsewhere. You will begin to sense it almost immediately. Perhaps the use of the *toldos* (awnings) throughout the shopping areas creates the magic. With a Mediterranean-type climate, the awnings are most welcome and certainly make Lerida easy on the eyes. The shopping areas are delightful, and you'll find a good selection there, with prices generally lower than those in Barcelona.

History records that life was not always as leisurely in Lerida as it is now. Caesar's legions stormed it. The Moors conquered it and reigned there from the eighth to the twelfth centuries. Although there is little left of the Roman Legion's remnants, there are considerable mementos from the Moors, including the discernible Mediterranean flavor of the city's markets. The French attacked Lerida frequently; Napoleon attempted to annex it to France but failed. It was under artillery fire as recently as 1936, during the Spanish Civil War. Today, Lerida burgeons with life as peace and prosperity appear to emanate from it. It has taken a well-earned respite—and appears to be enjoying it.

The railway station is efficient and well organized. Cabs stand immediately in front, and the bus stop is in the square just beyond. This area abounds in good restaurants. There are two within a stone's throw of the station's steps: the Casa Luis and Tiell. We liked the back room at the Casa Luis—good food plus air conditioning. Lerida's climate is delightful during the spring and autumn months, but we think you'll prefer air conditioning when dining there during the summer.

While on the subject of gastronomy, we have heard gourmets term the cooking of Lerida as "exquisite." We have our doubts concerning the area's most popular dish, *cazuela,* a typical farmhouse recipe of potatoes, pork, snails, tomatoes, and onions. But there are others.

Scene at Sitges is a facade of the parish church rising from the breakwater of the beach overlooking the Gold coast.

From Barcelona ...

A DAY EXCURSION TO SITGES
DISTANCE BY TRAIN: 25 miles (36 km)
AVERAGE TRAIN TIME: 25 minutes

Sitges, south of Barcelona and known as "the Golden Beach of the Mediterranean," is one of the most cosmopolitan seaside resorts in Europe. Its locale is excellent for both summer and winter relaxation. It's the place to which wealthy Barcelonese flee to escape their city's summer heat. Elegant houses of the wealthy rimming the old town and luxury apartments along its Paseo Maritimo (sea promenade) attest to this.

The town is brilliant with the flowers for which Sitges is famous. The national carnation show—the carnation is Spain's national flower—is held annually in Sitges at the beginning of June. It coincides with the procession of Corpus Christi, when the city streets are paved with spectacular carpets of flowers. Other festivals include Sitges' world renowned carnival, in February; the antique car rally, "Rallye Internationale," in March; and Sant Bartomeu Holiday, at the end of August. With the International Theatre Festival in June and the Film Festival at the beginning of October, Sitges truly is a place to visit at any time of the year.

Train service to Sitges from Barcelona is available approximately every ten minutes on local trains. The local (suburban) trains do not have a seat-reservation system. They operate on a first-come, first-served basis.

Trains for Sitges vary as to their terminals leaving Barcelona. The majority depart from Barcelona Sants, the main Barcelonese rail station, although others may originate from the underground station. Passeig de Garcia, the station nearest Barcelona's city center. A brief check with the train information office, or your hotel information desk, will provide the necessary information for the station located nearest to you.

Sitges has only one train station. As you exit the station, the tourist information office is at the end of the first road to the right at Pg. de Vilafranca. It's identified with a large sign reading PATRONAT MUNICIPAL DE TURISME.

The staff of the Sitges tourist information office is well trained and most eager to assist in the planning of your visit to their city. City maps and brochures are available. A rather exhaustive listing of restaurants, bars, night-clubs, cafeterias, and other helpful information is a part of the city map.

Seafood is the specialty in Sitges, but there are excellent meat and chicken dishes available as well. Name the kind of food you're after, and the tourist office will help you find it.

You can be certain that the "catch of the day" is fresh—the salt air and the Mediterranean are right there to attest to that. Well worth trying are the fish

SITGES—*SPARKLING SEA RESORT*

A Day Excursion from Barcelona

DEPART FROM BARCELONA SANTS STATION*	ARRIVE IN SITGES STATION	NOTES
0704	0726	(1)(2)
0904	0926	(1)(2)
1004	1026	(1)(2)
1157	1222	(1)(2)
1304	1326	(1)(2)

Other local trains are available between the Passeig de Gracia and Sants stations to Sitges.

DEPART FROM SITGES STATION	ARRIVE IN BARCELONA SANTS STATION*	NOTES
1434	1457	(1)(2)
1709	1733	(1)(2)
1857	1931	(1)(2)
2204	2227	(1)(2)
2220	2245	(1)(2)

Other local trains are available from Sitges to the Passeig de Gracia and Sants stations in Barcelona.

* See *Thomas Cook European Timetable,* "Plans of Cities" section, for description of railway stations in Barcelona.

(1) Daily, including holidays
(2) Seat reservations mandatory

Distance: 25 miles/36 km
Reference: Local schedule

parrilladas (grills) offered by the restaurants, or you could try *rice a la cassola,* which contains not only rice but a selection of fish, oysters, lobster, and snails dressed in a special sauce.

Swept up by the culinary circumstances of Sitges, we almost forgot to mention that the tourist office is open daily in the summertime from 0900 to 2100. The remainder of the year, it's open 0930–1330 and 1600–1900 Monday through Friday, 1000–1300 on Saturday, and closed Sunday.

For centuries, Sitges was nothing more than a quiet fishing village on the Mediterranean. Then, in the nineteenth century, it began to develop its commerce with America, wine being its major export. By the turn of the century, Sitges emerged as an elegant summer resort attracting a large number of artists and intellectuals—with the ensuing gathering of the rich, possibly hoping that some of the first groups' talents would rub off on them.

There are three museums in town. Most famous is Cau Ferrat, former home of the painter Santiago Rusiñol (1861–1931) and gathering place for artists. It contains many of his works, plus paintings by El Greco and Casas, and drawings by Picasso. Another museum, Lola Anglada, has an outstanding collection of antique dolls from all over Europe. The Casa Llopis is a fully furnished eighteenth-century home depicting the life of the middle and upper classes at that time. It's crammed with interesting mechanical devices such as music boxes. The museums are open Tuesday through Saturday, 0930–1400 and 1600–1800. They also are open on Sunday mornings.

Should you be inclined to sift some of Sitges' famous golden sand, the tourist office will gladly advise you regarding the beaches, four of which have won the blue European Community Flag for cleanliness. Have fun. As the locals say, "Sitges, this is the life!"

Roman fountain overlooks Tarragona's beach.

A DAY EXCURSION TO TARRAGONA
DISTANCE BY TRAIN: 55 miles (89 km)
AVERAGE TRAIN TIME: 1 hour

Although you may travel between Barcelona and Tarragona on local, one-class suburban trains without seat reservations, we suggest that you go in style on the "Rapido" trains. Book out of Barcelona in the morning, and return by the same type of train service in the evening. The Rapido trains require a supplemental-fare payment, which, of course, is included in your Eurailpass. Just be certain to have seats reserved in advance of departure. The Rapido is a relaxing way to go. You'll find them more conducive to maintaining that "holiday feeling" that Tarragona is bound to induce during your day excursion there.

Check with a train information office in one of Barcelona's rail stations or with your hotel concierge regarding the station in Barcelona where you will be boarding the Rapido. The earliest departure and the latest return Rapido trains use only Barcelona Sants as their terminal.

Tarragona is Spain's "Roman City." It has often been said that the city and its immediate surroundings are among the most fascinating places in the whole of Europe. When Rome ruled its vast empire, Tarragona was considered its finest urban creation. The modern city has a population of approximately 80,000 inhabitants; in Roman times, it had more than 250,000. Although it could never equal Rome, it enjoyed the same privileges. Its citizens held equality with those of Rome.

Though rich in antiquity, Tarragona is nevertheless a modern metropolis with wide avenues and an attractive sea coast. In 1707, British civil engineers surveyed and laid out the system of avenues and promenades that you see today. Its sea front, rising from the azure blue waters up a cliff side drenched in flowers, is supposedly one of the most attractive scenes along the Mediterranean coast.

Tarragona goes back in time to the first millennium B.C. Romans built on the foundations of Iberian ruins. Visigothic, Moorish, and Catalan constructions followed. Through the centuries, the city held the primacy in Spain until finally bowing to the ambitions of Toledo in the eleventh century.

The magnitude of Tarragona can become overwhelming. For example, its walls constructed in 218 B.C. contain blocks of stone so large that modern engineers cannot conceive how they were placed in position before the age of machinery. In some respects, the walls of Tarragona are similar to the great pyramids of Egypt.

Tarragona's tourist information office, Oficina de Turismo, was moved

TARRAGONA—*CITY OF ROMAN SPAIN*

A Day Excursion from Barcelona

DEPART FROM BARCELONA SANTS STATION*	TRAIN NUMBER	ARRIVE IN TARRAGONA STATION	NOTES
0700	IC 161	0800	(1)(2)
0800	697	0858	(1)(2)
0900	693	0958	(1)(2)
0930	IC 163	1030	(1)(2)
1230	TAL 463	1328	(1)(2)
1100	IC 185	1158	(1)(2)

DEPART FROM TARRAGONA STATION	TRAIN NUMBER	ARRIVE IN BARCELONA SANTS STATION*	NOTES
1623	TAL 460	1730	(1)(2)
1829	IC 64	1930	(1)(2)
1927	IC 490	2040	(1)(2)
2027	694	2149	(1)(2)
2223	IC 264	2325	(1)(2)

* See *Thomas Cook European Timetable,* "Plans of Cities" section, for description of railway stations in Barcelona.

(1) Daily, including holidays
(2) Seat reservations mandatory

Distance: 57 miles/92 km
Reference: Thomas Cook Table 415

from the rail-station area several years ago. The Romans didn't plan ahead for rail service. As a consequence, the railway station is a bit remote from the city center. The office is located in the city at No. 46 Rambla Nova, Tarragona's main thoroughfare. It operates 1000–2000 Monday through Saturday. You can contact the tourist office for directions by phoning 232143 from the railway station. You can reach the tourist information office on the city bus line. The city bus stop on the Rambla Nova, where it intersects Fortuny, is less than a two-minute walk from the tourist office. The bus fare is 80 pesetas. Taxi fares vary according to route.

The tourist information office can supply visitors with an illustrated color brochure in English that includes an excellent map to use in conjunction with a walking tour of the city. Allow the tourist-office representative to make suggestions according to your interests, then draw a route on the map. If you should plot an ambitious route that might take more time than you planned for, ask for city-bus information from the tourist-office representative. Plan to use the public buses to the maximum extent possible during your visit. If you must use a taxi, we suggest that you check with the driver concerning the approximate rate before entering his cab. Don't worry about the cabby not speaking English. Ask him to write the fare on a piece of paper.

Although Tarragona's cathedral could be considered modern in comparison to the walls of the city, it should be included in your walking tour. Erected in the twelfth century on the site of the Roman Temple of Jupiter, in its architecture the cathedral depicts its different periods of construction, ranging from Romanesque through Gothic to Baroque. According to theologians, Saint Paul preached at this site. Illustrations of the saint's life may be viewed in the altar area.

The Archaeological Museum is another "must" in your tour. The exhibits are all from Tarragona or its environs. Most of them date from the Roman period. The penetrating stare of Medusa's eyes, cornices from the Temple of Jupiter (where the cathedral now stands), and age-old ceramics are on view. The museum operates on seasonal hours. Consequently, you should check with the tourist information office before going there.

Hungry? While you are in the tourist information office, ask for directions to the Bufet el Tiberi restaurant at 5, Marti d'Ardenya. They feature a buffet of local specialties you're bound to enjoy. Restaurant el Celler and Restaurant el Trull also feature local specialties.

Supporting the thesis that "time flies when you're having fun," time will have flown and you will be returning to Barcelona before you realize it. We wager that Tarragona goes with you.

Broken tower of the Kaiser Wilhelm Church, situated on Berlin's Kurfürstendamm, with its succession of luxury hotels and cafés, stands as a mute reminder of the destruction of war.

6   BERLIN

Although eons apart, the modern city of Berlin and the ancient city of Jericho shared a common occurrence—their walls "came tumblin' down." The *Bible* (Joshua 6) is a bit vague concerning the actual date of the occurrence in Jericho; but for as long as modern man occupies planet Earth, history will chronicle the fall of the Berlin Wall on November 9, 1989, twenty-eight years after it was erected. Berlin is now a whole city; Germany is one country; Berlin is the capital of the new Germany; and communism is on the wane worldwide.

With the demise of the Wall, Berlin has nearly doubled in size. The reunited metropolis is rediscovering its traditional rhythm that made it famous throughout the world. Travelers from around the world are passing the word, "Berlin is worth the trip." Come to Berlin and stand in history.

Day Excursions

Three day excursions have been selected. All of them—Dresden, Leipzig, and Potsdam—are typical German cities in their own right. Since the end of World War II, however, they have been a part of the German Democratic Republic, more often referred to as "East Germany." As a consequence, tourist facilities are more limited and travel is a little slower than that which you may have experienced in the western part of Germany. Your patience will be taxed on occasion; nevertheless, your patience is appreciated by these proud people who are rebuilding their way of life.

Dresden is an important city in the historic German state of Saxony. The city's name is derived from *Drezdzane,* the old Slavic word for forest people, who were early settlers in the area. Dresden is situated on a bend in the Elbe River approximately nineteen miles (thirty kilometers) from the northwest border of the Czech Republic. Although the city's fame comes mainly from its past cultural achievements, Dresden also is economically important. The city's best-known product is Dresden china.

Leipzig is also a part of Saxony and, like Dresden, owes much of its prestige to its cultural accomplishments. The Gewandhaus Orchestra of Leipzig is Europe's oldest orchestra. Both Johann Sebastian Bach and Felix Mendelssohn held positions in the city's conservatory of music. Bach is buried in Leipzig's St. Thomas Church. Perhaps Leipzig is best known for its trade fairs that date back to the Middle Ages and still attract businesspeople from all over the world.

Potsdam owes its appeal to Frederick the Great, who took the concept of *sans souci* (without care or worry) and transformed it into the reality of the delightful Sanssouci Palace. It was also the scene of the Potsdam Conference in 1945, where Harry Truman got to like "Old Joe" (Stalin)—at least for a little while.

Arriving and Departing

By Air: Berlin has three commercial airports, Tegel (TXL), Tempelhof (THF), and Schönefeld (SXL). All three airports are connected with the city center by buses and trains. Tegel, five miles northwest, is your most likely arrival airport. Exiting from Customs, you'll see an information office between two rows of ticket counters. Go there for transportation information. A branch of the Berlin Tourist Office, open 0800–2300 daily, will be to your right. From that position, look over your right shoulder and you will see the money exchange office across the hall.

Schönefeld is served by many European airlines; you should check with the airline taking you into Berlin as to its landing airport. Tempelhof, which served as the Allies' airport during the Berlin Airlift (1948–1949), is in the southwest section of the city. Surrounded by a sea of buildings, it is used only for regional flights.

Tegel Airport is served by bus lines 128 and 109 as well as the Airport-Transport, which takes you from Tegel Airport to the Berlin Zoo rail station in about twenty minutes. If you have baggage, the Airport-Transport system is recommended. The Airport-Transport also serves the Schönefeld Airport as does the S-Bahn line S-9. Both connect with the Berlin Zoo rail station. Standard tickets (*Einzelfahrschein*) for all forms of Berlin transportation may be purchased for 3.20 deutsche marks (DM), or 12 DM for a one-day Berlin-Ticket, at any Berlin Transport Authority office. Look for the sign BVG.

By Train: There are three major railway stations in Berlin: Zoo, Hauptbahnhof (Hbf.), and Lichtenberg. If you are arriving from base cities such as Amsterdam, Berne, Brussels, Hamburg, Luxembourg, or Paris, the Berlin Zoo Station will be the first stop in Berlin before the train terminates in the Berlin Hauptbahnhof. The tourist information office in the Hauptbahnhof is well marked and open daily, 0800–2000. If you disembark at the Zoo Station, Berlin's main tourist information office is located nearby. There's ample time to get off the train since it will stand in the station at least five minutes before proceeding on to the Hauptbahnhof.

If you are arriving from Copenhagen, Oslo, or Stockholm, your train halts first in the Berlin Lichtenberg Station and then terminates at the Hauptbahnhof. From there, you can take an S-Bahn train to Berlin Zoo and the tourist office. When arriving from Munich, if you've selected the rail route through Nuremberg (which we prefer), your train will make its only stop in Berlin at the Hauptbahnhof. If you select the rail route running through Regensburg between Munich and Berlin, your train stops only at the Berlin Lichtenberg Station. Again, you can take the S-Bahn to Berlin Zoo.

The day excursions to Dresden and Leipzig depart from the Berlin Lichtenberg Station. Train service between Berlin Zoo and Berlin Lichtenberg stations is limited. Use the S-Bahn or the city's U-Bahn (subway).

Berlin's Railway Stations

Until the two Germanies were reunited, the Berlin Zoo Station was the primary rail terminal for the Allied section of the divided city. Traveler services in the Berlin Hauptbahnhof and the Berlin Lichtenberg Station are in a transitional period of being reestablished to meet the standards of those available now at Berlin Zoo. Great progress is being made by the German Federal Railroads and the city of Berlin in the rehabilitation of the city's railway facilities. Later editions of *Europe by Eurail* will note the progress as it occurs. In the meantime, we will deal only with the Berlin Zoo Station and its services and facilities.

The Berlin Zoo Station is centrally located in the former "West" sector of Berlin. The majority of the city's hotels, pensions, hostels, restaurants, shopping centers, and entertainment also are in this area. The city's main tourist information office is within easy walking distance. To reach it, exit the Berlin Zoo Station in the direction in which your train came. Cross the first street. Then turn left and walk toward the ruins of the Kaiser Wilhelm Church with its jagged steeple (a stark reminder of war's destructive power) until you see the Europa Center and its globe fountain, which Berliners affectionately refer to as "the wet dumpling." Stay on the left side of the Europa Center. The tourist information office is on the street side of the center, just before the Palace Hotel. It's open Monday through Saturday, 0800–2300.

Descending from the trains into the main hall of the Berlin Zoo Station, there's a train information office (open daily 0800–2100) to the far left alongside a Berlin tourist office branch. Train departure and arrival information is posted on boards above the stairway. A privately operated money exchange office is on the street side of the station. You can reach it by using the exit alongside the tourist information office and then turn to the right. We do not recommend exchanging money there, however, since the tourist office is so close by and offers more favorable rates of exchange.

With the exception of the rail information office in Berlin Zoo, we suggest that you obtain all the services you require, other than train information and Eurailpass validation, from the main tourist office. The branch office in the Berlin Zoo Station is staffed with competent people, but because of its small space—and the swarms of tourists that descend upon it—we prefer the main office and believe you will, too.

By the way, Berlin Zoo is not a baggage cart station, since ramps to the train level are nonexistent and elevators normally are not available for public use. Porters are available by prearrangement, but the best assurance for a no-hassle visit to the new Germany's new capital is to observe the golden rule of rail travelers: Take one medium-size suitcase—nothing else, except perhaps a shoulder bag. *Gut farht!*

Berlin's center, the Kurfürstendamm, a magnificent two-mile stretch of boutiques, shops, cafés, bars, and galleries, is where Berliners gather to watch the world go by. Termed the number one shopping area in Germany, there is always something going on here, whether it is day or night. The Kaiser Wilhelm Church steeple stands as a silent sentinel over the scene.

Berlin's Tourist Facilities

Berlin's tourist information offices are ready to serve you. Should you need informational materials to assist in planning your trip, write to: Berlin Tourist Information, Martin-Luther-Strasse 105, 10820 Berlin, Germany. For direct electronic communication from the United States: Telephone 011–49–30–2123–4, Fax 011–49–21232520, or Telex 183 356. As previously described, the office is in the Europa Center just before the Palace Hotel and is open Monday through Saturday, 0800–2230; Sunday, 0900–2100.

In addition to the standard handouts of a city map and various tour brochures, the Berlin Tourist Office publishes a small booklet entitled *Berlin* that's packed with information and is brilliantly illustrated. Ask for it. The office provides a housing service, but we strongly recommend that you arrange for your accommodations in advance of your arrival. Berlin's many hotels, hostels, and pensions frequently are booked to capacity, thus making Berlin far less accommodating than the little town of Bethlehem back in Year One! All tourist offices charge 5 DM for housing accommodations and provide an excellent map of Berlin and its S-Bahn and U-Bahn free of charge.

There are three other tourist information offices in Berlin. One is located in the main hall of the Berlin Tegel Airport and offers the same services as the main office in the Europa Center. It is open seven days a week from 0800 to 2300. Another office is on the street level of the Berlin Zoo Station, adjacent to the station's train information office. The same services are available during the same hours (closed Sunday). The third office is at the Hauptbahnhof and is open 0800 to 2000 daily.

One of the first items visitors should do on arrival in Berlin is to acquaint themselves with the city's excellent fast-train system, the S-Bahn ("S" is for fast—*snell*) and the U-Bahn (subway). During rush hours, trains run every three to five minutes and approximately every five to ten minutes at other times. The S- and U-Bahn systems are augmented by trams and buses. Fares are reasonable. You can use the entire system for twenty-four hours with a Berlin-Ticket for just 12 DM.

Bus 100, an innovative tourist bus system, makes twelve stops within the unified city, ranging from the Zoological Gardens in the west to Alexanderplatz in the east. You are free to hop off whenever you fancy and hop on another bus when you want. The operator, BVG, will provide you with a free map describing the stops. In effect, you become your own tour guide.

The city even operates an all-night bus system of ten busses and eleven trams to "gather the barflies and the birds of paradise from the disco scene on the Kurfürstendamm."

Once again, Berlin is without boundaries. As it's been explained to us, "Berlin is more than the sum of two halves." We agree.

Berlin Diary

The origins of Berlin date back to the twelfth century. A review of its recent history, however, would be more useful in preparing you for a visit.

For Berlin, World War II ended on the afternoon of May 2, 1945. Of the 245,000 buildings in Berlin before the war, 50,000 had been destroyed or rendered beyond repair. There was no electricity, no gas, no water. Before the war, Berlin had 4.3 million inhabitants; in May 1945, the remaining 2.8 million began the task of clearing away the debris.

In July of that year, Berlin became a four-power city with a joint Allied administration composed of Britain, France, Russia, and the United States. This division into zones turned the former German capital into an island of occupation surrounded completely by a sea of Soviets. East and West were in complete agreement about abolishing Nazism, but they had no common or precise answer as to what would replace it. Moreover, it quickly became evident that the Soviet intention was to gain complete control of the city.

On June 24, 1948, the Soviets sealed off the West's section of the city and, on the basis of "technical disorders," shut off their supply of electricity. They were left with a meager thirty-six-day food supply. A disaster appeared imminent, but two days later the largest airlift in history began. From July 1948 to May 1949, the Western Allies transported, in some 213,000 flights, more than 1.7 million tons of food and other supplies to the beleaguered city. While operating the airlift, seventy members of the Allied Air Forces lost their lives. On May 12, 1949, the siege was lifted. Berliners began demonstrating their political choice by moving en masse to the Western sectors.

By August 1961, faced with mass evacuation of their sector, the Soviets began erecting the Berlin Wall. In 1989, after twenty-eight years of division, the wall that Winston Churchill called the "Iron Curtain" was breached in one night. Before it "fell," more than one hundred people lost their lives while attempting to cross it. The eastern part of Berlin, including its historic center, is once again easily accessible to visitors. Checkpoint Charlie has been dismantled. Its guardhouse is now a museum piece. Except for a small section that will stand as a mute reminder, every vestige of the Berlin Wall has been removed.

Today Berlin is a fascinating city. Don't miss walking on the Kurfürstendamm, its shopping and entertainment street. The Berlin Zoo is one of the finest in Europe, and there's no better place to relax than in the attractive English Gardens, dedicated by Sir Anthony Eden. Berliners now call it the "Garden of Eden." Best of all, stand at the Brandenburg Gate—on either side—and feel democracy in action.

From Berlin ...

TRAIN CONNECTIONS TO OTHER BASE CITIES

TO:	DEPART	ARRIVE	TRAIN NUMBER	COOK'S TABLE	NOTES
Amsterdam	0638	1453	2344	22	(5)
	1038	1853	2342	22	(6)
Brussels (Midi)	0907	1801	EC 46	23	
	2038	0655 + 1	242	23	
Hamburg	1000	1315	IC 538	680*	
	1200	1515	IC 634	680*	
	1400	1715	IC 178	680*	
Copenhagen	0851	1655	1106	51	(1)(7)
	2352	0831 + 1	308	51	(1)
Munich	0906	1706	IC 813	670	(2)
	1106	1903	IC 705	670	(2)
Oslo	1300	0837 + 1	316/IN 682	52	(1)(2)(4)
Paris (Nord)	0707	1905	EC 109	25	(3)
	2049	0908 + 1	242	25	
Stockholm	2238	1553 + 1	318/34	52	(2)(4)

All departures from Berlin Zoo Station unless otherwise noted. Daily departures unless otherwise noted. Make seat reservations for all departures.

* Table 680 subject to major alteration after September 24

(1) Departs from Berlin Lichtenberg
(2) Departs from Berlin Hauptbahnhof
(3) Transfer in Köln to EC 38
(4) Transfer in Malmo
(5) Departs 0613 on Sundays
(6) Departs 1034 on Saturdays and Sundays
(7) June 23 through August 20

The Dresden Zwinger, most famous of the city's many edifices, gets its name from the space between two walls of a fortress. This splendid and festive building is said to be unparalleled in Germany. Built between 1710 and 1728, it is a fine example of late-Baroque buildings. This view, over the balustrades of the Nymph's Bath, imparts an impression of the dynamic quality of the Baroque architectural style.

From Berlin ...

A DAY EXCURSION TO DRESDEN
DISTANCE BY TRAIN: 117 miles (189 km)
AVERAGE TRAIN TIME: 2 hours, 30 minutes

Situated in the wide, gentle valley of the Elbe River, Dresden has always enjoyed the delightful harmony of the river and nature in which to develop from its beginnings as a small Slavonic fishing village. As it grew, its scenic beauty was enhanced in the seventeenth and eighteenth centuries by builders who erected fine examples of baroque and rococo architecture. This, in turn, attracted a great number of artists and writers as Dresden grew into a modern, confident city of a half-million citizens. With its architectural landmarks and its art treasures of Dutch, Flemish, and Italian collections, Dresden gained the well-deserved title, "Florence of the Elbe."

Today's traveler's first impression, however, is not one of that era's splendor. At first, the difference between Dresden's reputation and its actual appearance is somewhat alarming. On February 13, 1945, more than a half-million bombs rained down on Dresden from Anglo-American aircraft. Thirty-five thousand of its citizens died and more than fifteen square miles of the inner city were reduced to rubble. The air raid devastated nearly all of the city's cultural monuments. Dresden was declared dead.

This was not the first destructive blow to ever strike Dresden. In 1491 and again in 1685 much of the city was destroyed by fire. Even as resolute as Dresdeners can be, following the communist takeover of East Germany, they were deterred in rebuilding their city by their communist rulers who ordered many of the remaining majestic ruins torn down to be replaced by a depressing vision of a socialist industrial town. This is what today's traveler sees first. But Dresden is rising like a Phoenix.

Dust from the air raid scarcely settled before restoration began on the Semper Opera House. Forty years to the day, February 13, 1985, Dresden's population celebrated the reopening of this world-famous theater. Many other cultural and historic edifices have either been rebuilt or are under reconstruction. Dresden's *Altmarkt* (old market) is the historic center of the city. Between 1953 and 1956 it was rebuilt in its traditional brick construction. The city's botanical gardens, completely destroyed in 1945, were rebuilt in 1950. Only nine zoo animals survived the air attack, but in 1961 the zoo reopened with a stock of more than 2,000 animals representing nearly 500 species.

With typical Dresden determination, on February 13, 1992, the city announced that the Frauenkirche (Church of Our Lady)—decried by the communists to stand in ruin forever—will be rebuilt. Dresden is returning!

Upon your arrival in Dresden, we recommend that your first stop be in the

DRESDEN—*CHINA, CARILLONS, AND CULTURE*

A Day Excursion from Berlin

DEPART FROM BERLIN HAUPTBAHNHOF	ARRIVE IN DRESDEN HAUPTBAHNHOF	TRAIN NUMBER	NOTES
0824	1012	EC 173	(1)(2)
0924	1119	2373	(1)(3)
1024	1212	EC 175	(1)(2)
1224	1412	EC 177	(1)(2)

DEPART FROM DRESDEN HAUPTBAHNHOF	ARRIVE IN BERLIN HAUPTBAHNHOF	TRAIN NUMBER	NOTES
1536	1726	EC 176	(1)(2)
1736	1926	EC 174	(1)(2)
1936	2126	EC 172	(1)(2)
2136	2326	EC 170	(2)(4)

(1) Daily, including holidays
(2) Restaurant car
(3) Departs Berlin Lichtenberg
(4) Daily, except December 24 and 31

Distance: 117 Miles/189 km
Reference: Thomas Cook Table 680

Dresden Information Center, where you will receive a large "Welcome to Dresden" map with a list of its hotels, museums, and important addresses. A five-minute walk on Prager Strasse across the street from the Hauptbahnhof will take you there. The rest of Dresden—both the Old Town on the left bank of the Elbe and the New Town across the river on its right bank—is still in front of you. If you are an average sightseer, as we are, you can reach the Old Town area on foot from the center in no more than fifteen minutes.

The information center is prepared to assist you in finding those places in the city in which you are most interested. In typical German fashion, the city's *Rathaus* (town hall) has a *Ratskeller* (restaurant) in its cellar where you may enjoy a cold draft and a sample of Saxon food before setting out to see the town.

Among the publications available in the information center is the brochure "Tips for Visitors." It contains a city map, places of interest, sightseeing tours, and just about everything you might ever want to know about Dresden.

One of the many magnificent edifices vying for your attention during your Dresden visit is the Zwinger. It is known as the most important late baroque building in Germany. The name "Zwinger" is a term used in the construction of fortresses and defines the space between the outer and inner ramparts. Heavily damaged in 1945, the reconstruction of the Zwinger was said to have begun "instantaneously" despite communist objections. It was restored to its present condition by 1963.

If you cross the Elbe, be sure to use Dresden's famous Loschwitzer-Blasewitzer Bridge. Opened in 1893, it was the only bridge to remain intact by 1945. The SS had the bridge set for destruction, but two Dresdeners, each unaware of the other's action, cut the wire to the explosives. The grateful populace of Dresden now refer to the bridge as the "Blue Miracle."

Make it a point to visit the newly reopened Dresden Gallery and examine the famous views of the court painter, Bernardo Bellotto. They show the city at the peak of its splendor. The dome of the Frauenkirche (Church of Our Lady) dominates the scenes, and it is gratifying to know that it is being reconstructed even though the project may take several decades to complete.

The church's actual ruins still lie near the Albertinum Museum. The museum was heavily damaged in 1945 but was restored by 1964. It's open daily except Thursdays from 1000–1800.

Largest Rail Terminus in Europe, the Leipzig *Hauptbahnhof,* or central station (above) schedules more than 600 train departures a day from its 26 platforms, thereby serving over 120,000 passengers. Termed one of the most beautiful concert halls in Europe, the *Neues Gewandhaus* (below) seats 2,000 in its main hall.

From Berlin ...

A DAY EXCURSION TO LEIPZIG
DISTANCE BY TRAIN: 113 miles (182 km)
AVERAGE TRAIN TIME: 2 hours, 30 minutes

Like many cities and towns in Europe, Leipzig has an old and a new section. Leipzig's old town is located between three rivers, the Parthe, the Elster, and the Pleisse. No doubt the site selection had much to do with safety, and the proximity to three navigable rivers also indicates an early interest in trade. Leipzig has been known for its great trade fairs since the Middle Ages.

The city's name is derived from *Lipsk,* the original Slav settlement named for the lime trees (*lipa*) growing there. Leipzig has grown and thrived since its recorded beginnings in the eleventh century. Originally a walled city, the walls surrounding the old town were replaced in the eighteenth century by a ring of parks and promenades. Subsequently, Leipzig expanded in all directions by gradually incorporating the suburbs that were growing up around it—a tactic followed by many American cities today. (Some Texans have been compared to Leipzigeans, in that all they want out of life is the opportunity to buy their neighbors' property.)

Originally constructed in 1915, Leipzig's main rail terminal (*Hauptbahnhof*), with its twenty-six platforms, is the largest in Europe. More than 600 trains move through the terminus daily, carrying an estimated 120,000 passengers. There's no need to worry about its size, since the Hauptbahnhof comes well equipped with pictographs. By following them, you'll be in the Leipzig Tourist Information Center (telephone 275318) within five minutes' walking time.

The city's information center is located in the Sachsenplatz just inside the old town. It's open Monday through Friday, 0900–1900, and Saturday and Sunday from 0900–1400. City tours start daily at 1000 and 1330 from the Hotel Intercontinental Leipzig. Built in 1981, the hotel stands in the immediate vicinity of the Hauptbahnhof and towers over its surroundings. You will have no problem locating it.

The main attraction on the old town's market square is the Old Town Hall. It was built in the record time of nine months in 1556 by Hieronymus Lotter. The building is one of the oldest Renaissance town halls still standing on German soil. Although severely damaged by fire during the Allied air raid on December 4, 1943, the building's facade remains almost unchanged from its sixteenth-century beginnings. The city was governed from here until 1905, when a new town hall was erected in a more spacious area. Since 1909 the building has been the Museum of History of the City of Leipzig. Its attractions include the Old Council Chambers, the Mendelssohn Room, and special exhibits.

LEIPZIG—*BACH AND MENDELSSOHN MEMORIES*

A Day Excursion from Berlin

DEPART FROM BERLIN HAUPTBAHNHOF	TRAIN NUMBER	ARRIVE IN LEIPZIG STATION	NOTES
0906	IC 813	1107	(1)(2)
1106	IC 705	1307	(1)(2)

DEPART FROM LEIPZIG STATION	TRAIN NUMBER	ARRIVE IN BERLIN HAUPTBAHNHOF	NOTES
1440	IC 706	1649	(1)(2)
1640	IC 812	1849	(1)(2)
1840	IC 800	2049	(2)(3)
2040	IC 704	2249	(1)(2)

(1) Daily, including holidays
(2) Restaurant car
(3) May 29 through October 30

Distance: 113 miles/182 km
Reference: Thomas Cook Table 670

The new town hall also will attract your attention, particularly because of its 115-meter tower. Built between 1899 and 1905 on the foundations of earlier buildings, it houses both the mayor and the city council.

Within the rim of the old town, the spires of the Church of Saint Nicholas and the Church of Saint Thomas stand as sentinels over the scene. The first mention of Saint Nicholas was made in 1017; Saint Thomas was erected between 1212 and 1222 as the collegiate church of the Augustinian Choir. Its late-Gothic hall was added at the end of the fifteenth century.

The stained-glass windows of Saint Thomas, dating from the end of the nineteenth century, depict three historical personalities closely associated with Leipzig: Johann Sebastian Bach, Martin Luther, and King Gustav Adolf II of Sweden. Saint Thomas became world famous from its association with Johann Sebastian Bach. The great composer served as cantor of the church from 1723 to 1750. Since 1950, the remains of the great composer have lain in the church.

The Church of Saint Nicholas, although containing some of the oldest building remains in Leipzig, recently played an important part in the reunification of Germany. From 1982, the prayers for peace held every Monday under the sheltering roof of the church "transmitted" loud and clear signals to the Leipzig demonstrators—impulses that, during the days of October and November 1989, brought about the "gentle revolutions" that led to the downfall of the communist dictatorship.

Outside Leipzig's old town you can visit the Leipzig Zoo, which was founded in 1878. The city information center will tell you it's a "ten-minute walk," but perhaps a taxi would be better. The zoo is noted for its lions and tigers, including the breeding of some 2,500 purebred Berber lions. An unusual feature of the zoo is its "shop-window" whereby spectators are separated from the animals only by a moat—a *deep* moat, by the way!

Like Munich, at the end of World War II, the city constructed a stadium seating 100,000 spectators from the rubble left by the war. The stadium was the first major building project in Leipzig following the war. Three million cubic meters of rubble were used for the 23-meter-high terraces.

Leipzig's self-anointed title is "The City of Change." It would appear that some name changes within Leipzig have taken place. Karl Marx Square has returned to its original name, Augustusplatz; and Karl Marx University, founded in 1409 as *Universitas Lipsiensis* but renamed in 1952, is now Universitas Leipzig.

With editorial comment of the prior paragraph, one must remember that change is a slow process. The "gentle revolutions" took time and so will the process of putting things back in their proper order.

Sans Souci Park and its palaces, pavilions, and other architectural structures (above) lure visitors around the world to Potsdam. The Rococo-style palace was constructed between 1745 and 1747. The city's *Alten Markt,* or old market (below), was built according to the personal tastes of Frederick the Great.

From Berlin . . .

A DAY EXCURSION TO POTSDAM
DISTANCE BY TRAIN: 22 miles (36 km)
AVERAGE TRAIN TIME: 26 minutes

Originally a small settlement of Slavs, Potsdam first appeared in German chronicles under the name Poztupimi (Under the Oak Trees) in a Deed of Gift dated July 3, 993. There are virtually no oak trees left in present-day Potsdam, but you will find a large number of handsome mansions and palaces from days gone by surrounded by beautiful parks. After a period of almost total insignificance in the Middle Ages, Potsdam eventually entered the sphere of German history in the seventeenth century when Frederick William, the Elector of Brandenburg, decided to make Potsdam his place of residence.

In the eighteenth century, during the reigns of King Frederick William I and his son Frederick II, known as Frederick the Great, Potsdam grew to be a prestigious royal seat and garrison town. Frederick William I established a military orphanage where the boys "learned to work" in nearby factories and also drilled in "square bashing," which came in handy whenever the impoverished peasants could no longer stand their plight and chose to demonstrate in the town square.

Unlike many towns emerging from the Middle Ages, Potsdam was not surrounded by a wall until the eighteenth century. Oddly enough, the wall served not so much as a military protection as it did to prevent soldiers from deserting and dishonest folks from smuggling. Whether the wall contributed to the growth of the town is not known, but Potsdam did flourish under the Fredericks. The old market *(Alten Markt),* the Dutch quarters (Hollandisches Viertel), the Brandenburger Strasse, and the Sans Souci Park and Palace date to the era of their reign.

Frederick II, growing a bit "long-in-tooth," decided he wanted to live "without cares" *(sans souce),* so beginning in 1744 when the palace park was terraced and during the following three decades, "Old Fritz" supervised the building of the palace and several other buildings, including his own tomb as a last resting place beside the palace. The rococo palace was built from sketches by the king himself, together with designs by his architect, Knobelsdorff. With a large number of further additions during the nineteenth century, Sans Souci stands today on a 717-acre complex as one of the largest and most significant parks in Europe.

But "Old Fritz" would not rest. After the Seven Years' War, in which he lost all the battles but won the war, he decided to celebrate his "victory" by building another palace. The two palaces, Sans Souci and the Neues Palais (new palace), await your arrival in Potsdam.

POTSDAM—*WHERE HARRY MET JOE*

A Day Excursion from Berlin

DEPART FROM BERLIN ZOO	TRAIN NUMBER	ARRIVE IN POTSDAM STADT	NOTES
0723	IC 501	0745	(1)(2)
1123	IC 505	1145	(1)(2)

Plus frequent S-Bahn service between Berlin Zoo and Potsdam Stadt

DEPART FROM POTSDAM STADT	TRAIN NUMBER	ARRIVE IN BERLIN ZOO STATION	NOTES
1616	IC 506	1640	(1)(2)
2104	D2245	2126	(1)(2)
2216	EC 102	2240	(1)(2)

Plus frequent S-Bahn service between Potsdam Stadt and Berlin Zoo

(1) Daily, including holidays
(2) Restaurant car

Distance: 22 miles/36 km
Reference: Thomas Cook Table 700

The Potsdam Information Center is located in the old market, a ten-minute walk from the Potsdam Stadt (city) station. Just follow the marked route across the Lange Brücke (Long Bridge) and up the Friedrich-Ebert-Strasse to the center, which is located at Number 5 on the right side of the street. The center is open daily from Monday through Friday from 0900 to 2000. On Saturday and Sunday, the hours are from 0900 to 1800. Telephone 21100, 23385; fax 23012. Ask for the illustrated pamphlet, "Info–Stadtplan Potsdam."

The Potsdam Information Center conducts two bus tours. The first, a city tour that includes as stop at the Cecilienhof Palace, the scene of the Potsdam Conference, runs from 1030 to 1300. The cost is 24 DM. The second tour, which includes a tour of the Sans Souci Palace and its gardens, leaves the center at 1400 and returns at 1700. The cost is 34 DM.

If you like palaces, you've come to the right place. Potsdam abounds with them. Charlottenhof Palace, a part of the Sans Souci complex, comes complete with Roman baths. The baths, by the way, were not intended for the purpose of hygiene but formed a part of a museum-like dream world reflecting the romantic yearnings of the Crown Prince, Frederick William (Fat William). The Marble Palace and the New Garden—called "new" in contrast with the "old" gardens at Sans Souci—were ordered built by "Fat William" when he was crowned in 1786. The Marble Palace is presently closed for restoration.

Potsdam's old town is a great place to browse. Right in the center of it you feel as though you've been transferred to Holland. To attract Dutch craftsmen to Potsdam, more than one hundred middle-class Dutch baroque-style houses were built between 1734 and 1742. The project failed in that it failed to attract Dutchmen in the number expected, but the houses were inhabited, in turn, by Potsdam's craftsmen, artists, and military. Sometimes things just don't work out the way you want them to. Perhaps that is Potsdam's penchant—read on.

The son of Kaiser Wilhelm, Crown Prince William, built a second palace at the New Garden from 1913 to 1915. He named it Cecilienhof after his Crown Princess. Unlike his father, who never returned from his Dutch exile, the ex-Crown Prince *did* move back into Cecilienhof Palace in 1923 and stayed there until 1945. The summer of that year brought a number of interesting guests to Cecilienhof.

From July 17 until August 2, 1945, Cecilienhof played host to the Potsdam Conference, the third and final meeting of the "Big Three"—Churchill, Stalin, and Truman. The first two meetings had taken place in Tehran, Iran, at the end of 1943, and in Yalta at the beginning of 1945. One of the conference aims was the unity of Germany, though what followed was in fact its division. Harry Truman returned from the conference stating that he "liked old Joe." But just like the time when Harry met Sally, things didn't quite work out the way they wanted them to.

Ancient bridge, the Untertorbrücke, spans the swift-moving Aare River at Berne. Old buildings on the left stand in contrast to the city's modern structures on the right bank of the Aare.

7   BERNE

The Aare River embraces Berne in a great natural bend. Like the river, you too will embrace this ancient Swiss city, for once you have trod its cobblestone streets, you can never forget it.

Berne, the federal capital of Switzerland, was built between the twelfth and eighteenth centuries. According to legend, it was named after the first animal caught in the area, a bear, and bears have played a part in its history ever since. The city's bear pits, where the animals are raised and displayed, are a "must" stop on any tour. Another unusual feature of Berne is its shopping arcades— nearly four miles of them. They line the route of the walking tour suggested by the city tourist information office and offer one of the finest selections of wares and food to be found anywhere in the world. The shopping arcades are completely covered, so they are weatherproof as well as traffic-free and totally delightful. On Tuesday and Saturday mornings, there are markets where Swiss farmers sell their meat and produce.

The most striking thing about Berne is its medieval appearance. Some of the buildings in the city's old town date from the thirteenth and fourteenth centuries. The low silhouette of its roof lines appears to be different from most of Europe's other cities with origins in the same era—and indeed it is, for there is a medieval ordinance still in effect today that mandates each roof line be at a different level from adjoining structures. This ancient architectural asset is most visible when you view the city from the Nydeggbrück Bridge crossing the Aare en route to the bear pits. If you miss it, you'll have another opportunity when you view the city from the location of its rose gardens on the high bluff of the Aare's right bank.

Berne is a medieval city, yet it is a new city as well. The old and the new blend together well in Berne. In 1983, the city was listed as a World Landmark of UNESCO. Over the centuries, Berne's citizens have developed a remarkable means of combining modern living with the centuries-old facades of their surroundings. Consequently, the city is genuine and without pretense. Although Berne is not a large city by European standards, it is cosmopolitan, with a wide selection of restaurants, hotels, museums, and concert halls. Modern Berne has grown well beyond the curve of the Aare and into the surrounding foothills. The main commercial, cultural, and political activities of the city, however, still take place in its old sector.

In summer, Berne leads you to believe it is the geranium capital of the world as well as being the federal capital of Switzerland. These flowers bloom everywhere in an eye-dazzling display of color. Berne was voted Europe's most beautiful city of flowers in 1984. You will be bewitched by Berne, beguiled by its bears, and satisfied with its sights. Like Chicago, Berne tugs at your sleeve when you leave.

Day Excursions

Berne is an ideal base for day excursions to almost any point in Switzerland. Geneva is one hour and forty train minutes to the west; you can reach Zurich to the east by rail in only one hour and twelve minutes. Travel north and, in sixty-nine minutes, your train will set you down in Basel on the banks of the Rhine.

You won't find day excursions of the above cities mentioned here because such information is readily available to you in Berne's tourist information office in the central rail station. Between that office and the rail information office directly across the hall, you may obtain everything, including the rail schedules from Berne to your points of interest.

The four-day excursions that we have selected for this edition reveal the natural grandeur of the country. The Golden Pass adventure takes you through Alpine surroundings, in the comfort of a vista-dome rail car, to Lake Geneva and a cruise on the lake before returning to Berne. The outing to Interlaken unfolds a panorama of towering peaks along the shore of the Lake of Thun, where again you have the opportunity of a lake cruise to conclude a memorable day.

Picture-postcard perfect, Lucerne will charm you with its scenery, cuisine, and ambience. Promenade along its ancient walkways, scale nearby Mount Pilatus, or cruise the Lake of Lucerne during your visit. For a peek at a Disney-type setting that has been going strong since the eleventh century, journey to Rheinfelden, where the mighty Rhine River swirls past a medieval setting that stirs the imagination.

Arriving and Departing

By Air. Switzerland's international airports, Zurich and Geneva, connect incoming flights with trains to Berne. Berne is only one hour and thirty minutes away from Zurich's airport and two hours from Geneva's by comfortable passenger trains that depart daily from the airports every hour. In Zurich, the rail station lies immediately beneath the airport's terminal. In Geneva, the rail station and the airport terminal are connected by a plaza.

By Train. Berne has one of the finest, most modern rail terminals in all of Europe. In a sense, it is a small city within a city, with an impressive array of facilities including a spacious underground arcade that connects at its surface entrances with the city's fabled, arcaded shopping walkways. Direct rail transport from Berne to such destinations as Amsterdam, Brussels, Luxembourg, Milan, Munich, Paris, and Venice is available.

Thirty trains a day depart Berne for Zurich at forty-five minutes past the hour; the majority of these trains also stop at the Zurich airport following the city stop. Twenty-seven trains a day depart Berne for Geneva at eighteen minutes past the hour. Upon arrival in Geneva, stay aboard, and nine minutes later you will be at the Geneva airport.

128

Berne's Railway Station

Berne's railway station is a model of efficiency and functionalism. Trains are reached from its ground level via ramps, thus making the use of baggage carts very practical. Surprisingly enough, porter service is still available but there are only one or two porters for the entire station.

With your baggage stacked in one of the station's baggage carts, leave the train platform by descending the ramp, then turn in the direction of track 1 and walk to the end of the passageway, where you will emerge into the station's underground arcade, with its myriad of shops and services. You'll see the escalators directly ahead.

Escalators take you to the other levels of the station. Elevator service is also available. If you have your luggage on a cart, we strongly suggest that you use the elevators. At street level you will find the train and tourist information offices, plus additional facilities such as shops and restaurants. On the subject of food, snack bars and fruit stands prevail on the ground level; more extensive food-service facilities are on the upper levels, ending at the top of the escalators with a full-service restaurant.

Visitors burdened with baggage may want to use the coin lockers on the ground (train) level or the "Handgepack Service" (baggage room) immediately opposite the coin lockers. Taxi service is available from the street level—follow the pictographs—but we urge you to check with the city's tourist information office before attempting to use the public-bus and streetcar services. Their access ramps, fares, ticket machines, and so forth can prove to be rather confusing unless you have been briefed on their operation.

A suburban train station is located on the underground arcade level. To reach it, continue past the escalators that run to the street level and watch for its entrance on the left side of the passageway. This system is operated by a private Swiss railroad. The Swiss Pass is accepted and the Eurailpass is now accepted by some private Swiss railroads such as RBS. Check prior to boarding the train.

The Berne station, like most of the major rail terminals in Switzerland, will accept your baggage and check it through the Zurich or Geneva airports directly to your U.S. port of entry. Trains for both airports depart the Berne station hourly throughout the day. We suggest that you place your baggage on a train an hour or so in advance of your departure for the airport.

Money-exchange facilities, two of them, are located on the ground level of the station. Both may be reached by turning right, just before the elevators, as you come out of the passageway leading from the trains. Both will be on your right as you proceed into the station's arcade. The first office, marked CHANGE SBB, is operated by the Swiss railroads. From April through October it is open 0615–2130 daily, including Sundays and holidays. November through March,

Bear antics in Berne's bear pits attract thousands of visitors to Switzerland's federal capital each year.

The Clock Tower in Berne was the city's western gate until 1250. Dancing figures perform four minutes before the hour.

it closes at 2045. The second facility is a full-service bank, the Schweizerische Volksbank. It is a few more steps away in the arcade, close to the Handgepack Service. Banking hours are 0700–1900 Monday through Friday and 0700–1630 on Saturday, closed Sundays and holidays. There are several banks in the plaza surrounding the station. The rates of exchange are standard throughout the city each day, however, and the rail-station money-exchange facilities are the most convenient. There is also a money exchange machine available twenty-four hours a day near the station at Schwanengasse 4.

Hotel reservations can be made in the city's tourist information office on the station's street level. Turn left coming off the escalator from the ground level, then right at the passageway leading to the street. The office will be a few steps farther on your right. It is identified by a green "i" sign, and during the summer (June–September) it is open 0900–2030 daily. Hours for the remainder of the year are 0900–1830 Monday through Saturday and 1000–1700 on Sunday. There is a charge of 3 francs for the hotel reservation services.

Tourist information is available in the same office where the hotel reservations are made. The Berne City Tourist Information Office is one of the most complete information centers in Europe. Information in many languages, including English, is available for just about every nook and cranny in Switzerland. Most other information offices dispense only city and local area information. Ask here for the booklets *Berne Informations* and *Berne Excursions,* an informative publication listing ten or more day excursions from Berne by rail, lake steamer, and postal buses.

Train information can be obtained from the rail-reservations center immediately across the passageway from the tourist information office. Identified by a blue "i," it is open 0800–1900 Monday–Friday and until 1700 on Saturday, closed Sunday. It dispenses rail information, reservations, and other services, including validation of Eurailpasses. Keep in mind that your Eurailpass is accepted on all of the Swiss federal railways and lake steamers; on the other hand, it is accepted only on a few of the private railroads, the Golden Pass being one of them. To be certain, check your day excursions plans with the train information office. For example, if you plan to ascend the Jungfrau, a Eurailpass will take you to Interlaken, where you must purchase a ticket for the private railroads leading out of Interlaken to Grindelwald or Lauterbrunnen and Wengen en route to the Jungfrau.

Beautiful Berne

There are two excellent means of sightseeing in Berne: on foot or by comfortable motor coach escorted by a multilingual guide. The tourist information office has complete details on both modes. From May through October the bus departs from in front of the railway station at 1000 and 1400 daily; November through March, at 1400 on Saturday; and in April at 1400 Monday through Saturday. The bus tour takes two hours.

If interested in the walking tour, ask at the tourist office for the "Short City Sightseeing Map." It leads you right through the heart of Berne's ancient walled city to its famed bear pits (open daily 0800–1800 April through September and 0830–1600 October through March). From there you return to your point of departure by a different route. According to the instructions appearing on the map, the entire route can be covered in approximately one hour, but without any stops en route. We suggest that you plan for a minimum of two hours and consider yourself lucky if you make it in three. (According to the tourist office, no one has ever returned within the hour.)

Be certain to see the *Zeitglockenturm,* the city's famous clock tower. It first began ticking in the year 1250, and it is still the city's official timepiece today. Try to position yourself in front of the clock no later than five minutes before the hour; the clock's glockenspiel starts promptly at four minutes before the hour as accompaniment to a parade of armed bear figures following a rooster. It's quite a show, and you shouldn't miss it. What makes it tick? Take the forty-five-minute guided tour of the *inside* of the clock tower. Purchase your ticket (5 SFR.) at the tourist office.

You can shop the city's arcades Monday through Friday, 0900–1830 (the shops stay open through 2100 on Thursday), and 0900–1600 Saturday. Or, if museums appeal to you, Berne has plenty to choose from, including the Swiss Alpine Museum, the Swiss PTT Museum, and the Einstein House—even a Museum of Psychiatry.

May we propose a cheese fondue luncheon in Zermatt while viewing the Matterhorn? It can be done very easily as a day excursion during your stay in Berne. Board the 0722 or 0822 express from Berne to Brig. There, you connect with the *Glacier Express* private railroad to Zermatt. The earlier train from Berne will have you in Zermatt at 1047; the later one will still get you there in time for that luncheon at 1145. In fact, you could stay in Zermatt for an early dinner, too. Leaving there on the express at 1910 and changing in Brig, you would still be back in Berne at the respectful hour of 2310—all in the same day!

Eurailpass holders can travel to Brig. From there, a round-trip ticket must be purchased to Zermatt. Swiss Pass holders can ride the entire route at no additional charge. Interested? Check with the Berne tourist office for Zermatt information and the rail office across the hallway for fares.

From Berne . . .

TRAIN CONNECTIONS TO OTHER BASE CITIES

TO:	DEPART	ARRIVE	TRAIN NUMBER	COOK'S TABLE	NOTES
Barcelona	0918	2050	IC 712/70	260/81	(1)
(França)	1918	0910+1	IC 738	260/81	(2)
Brussels (Midi)	1448	2237	EC 90	40	
Hamburg	2148	0831+1	1845	78	
Luxembourg	0648	1200	IC 852/296	280/176	(3)
	1448	1956	EC 90	40	
Lyon (Part-Dieu)	0818	1211	IC 708/5766	260/159	(1)
	1018	1446	IC 716/5768	260/159	(1)
	1418	1818	IC 726/5770	260/159	(1)
Milan	0851	1240	IC 813	82	
	1256	1645	IC 333	82	
	1522	1915	EC 91	82	
Munich	0814	1357	EC 167	75	
	1145	1751	IC 721	75	(5)
Nice	0718	1734	IC 706/370	260/165	(1)
Paris (Lyon)	0700	1124	TGV 422	42	
Rome	0851	1755	IC 813/EC 55	83	(4)

Daily departures unless otherwise noted. Make reservations for all departures.

(1) Transfer in Geneva
(2) Transfer in Geneva to sleeper train EN 274, *Pablo Casals,* Gran Classe sleeper, supplement payable, Eurailpass *not* accepted.
(3) Transfer in Basel
(4) Transfer in Milan
(5) Transfer in Zurich to EC 95

EURAIL TRAVEL NOTE: A timetable bookshop is operated by the Swiss Federal Railways in St. Gallen, Switzerland, where you may purchase the current official timetables of many European countries, as well as a wide range of rail travel literature and rail maps. St. Gallen is one hour by train from Zurich in the direction of Austria and Germany. Call at Room 224 in the St. Gallen rail station or telephone ahead on 071–22–1021, extension 208, for details.

Breathtaking splendor of the Swiss Alps unfolds for passengers aboard the famed "Golden Pass" train in the heart of Switzerland.

From Berne . . .

A DAY EXCURSION THROUGH THE GOLDEN PASS
DISTANCE BY TRAIN: 65 miles (104 km) to Montreux
TOTAL ELAPSED TIME: 10 hours, 25 minutes

Dollar for dollar (or franc for franc), this day excursion is beyond any doubt the best Eurailpass train-travel value existing today.

We suggest that before setting off on this day excursion, check with the Berne tourist information office. Inform them you are going on the Golden Pass trip and pick up the booklet *Berne Excursions.* (The booklet is usually available in the train information office as well.) Trains run through the Golden Pass rather frequently, and you may want to follow a somewhat different schedule. We strongly recommend the one we have selected, however, because it uses the *Panoramic Express*, an air-conditioned, vista-dome train with bar service. Need we say more?

Yes, we will go on to state that this schedule will permit ample time for a leisurely lunch in Montreux before boarding a lake steamer to Chillon, where you may go ashore to visit its famous castle before reversing course aboard another lake steamer back through Montreux. Then you'll continue on to Lausanne, where you will ride a funicular adjacent to the steamer dock to the Lausanne train station and your train back to Berne. Whew! It's a day loaded with extras.

We suggest that you also check the weather report the night before embarking on this day excursion. The clearer the day, the better. You will be viewing some of the Alps' most spectacular scenery, and if it's shrouded in clouds, the weatherman just might spoil your day. To get the weather report, you can dial 162 on any Swiss telephone and talk with a weather forecaster who speaks English, or you can ask your hotel concierge to check for you.

InterCity 811 usually departs from the Berne railway station on track 6, but double-check just to be sure. The destination of this train is Brig, and it makes a stop at Thun before it arrives at Spiez. At Thun, the beautiful Lake of Thun comes into view. As you approach Spiez, you'll see Mount Niesen (7,750 feet) towering over this quiet town on the southwestern shore of the lake.

In Spiez you have eleven minutes to cross a platform to board the next train—time enough to enjoy the breathtaking view. Zweisimmen, the next stop and transfer point, lies almost halfway between Spiez and Montreux. When you depart Spiez, you will enter the Golden Pass.

The transfer at Zweisimmen places you aboard the *Panoramic Express* on a narrow-gauge railroad, with Montreux as its destination. The best instruction here is to "follow the crowd" as you move between the standard- and narrow-gauge trains. The Panoramic Express narrow-gauge train will make two stops

THE GOLDEN PASS—*THE ALPS Á LA TRAIN*

A Day Excursion from Berne

COOK'S TABLE	TRAIN NUMBER	DEPART		ARRIVE			NOTES
280	811	Berne	0822	Spiez	0852	Transfer	(1)
276	2312	Spiez	0903	Zweisimmen	0939	Transfer	(1)
275	*	Zweisimmen	0950	Montreux	1136	Lunch**	(1)
252	Lake steamer	Montreux	1350	Chillon	1410	Visit castle	(2)
252	Lake steamer	Chillon	1510	Montreux	1530	Stay aboard	(2)
252	Lake steamer	Montreux	1550	Lausanne	1705	Transfer***	(2)
270	1930	Montreux	1707	Lausanne	1727	Transfer	(1)
260	IC 739	Lausanne	1734	Berne	1842	Terminate	(1)(3)
260	IC 741	Lausanne	1834	Berne	1942	Alternate	(1)(3)
260	1749	Lausanne	2234	Berne	2344	Last train	(1)(4)

* Panoramic Express Vista Dome from Zweisimmen to Montreux—reservations advisable (required in first class)

** Majestic Hotel, between rail station and city pier, recommended. Have your Berne hotel concierge call to make reservations: telephone 63.51.81.

*** From Lausanne pier, cross city park diagonally to rack railroad. Second stop en route is Lausanne Gare Centrale (central station). Eurailpass accepted.

(1) Daily, including holidays
(2) Seasonal, June–September; check at pier
(3) Dining car
(4) Food service

before reaching Montreux (three from mid-December through March, when it calls at Saanenmoser during the skiing season).

The first regular stop is Gstaad, which, you may recall, is the alpine-resort retreat of many famous movie stars including Elizabeth Taylor and Roger Moore. During his lifetime, Richard Burton frequented the area, and the late David Niven maintained a chalet there on a mountainside for many years. Chateau d'Oex (pronounced "day") is an alpine resort, too, but more at the family level, frequented by the Genevese when they grow tired of viewing beautiful Lake Geneva—possibly because it's flat.

Our "wood pile theory" can be tested—at least two-thirds of it—because you will be passing from a German inhabited area into one of French habitation. Based on research we have made during several decades of European rail travel, the theory is: Germans pile wood with precision, Italians pile it artistically, and the French stack theirs with an air of independence. The two regular stops are Gstaad and Chateau d'Oex. Watch what happens to the wood piles between these two points. Gstaad, as the name may imply, is German; it goes without saying that Chateau d'Oex lies in the French-speaking district of Switzerland.

Approaching Montreux, the train descends 2,000 feet to Lake Geneva in much the same manner as a jet airliner does when entering a landing pattern. It whirls through a series of hairpin curves for almost a half hour before coming to rest beside the main Montreux railway station. Have your camera handy at this time, for you are going to see some sensational scenery during the descent.

An examination of our schedule page will inform you that you have several options while visiting Montreux. You can extend your shopping and sightseeing in the city for one hour and fifty minutes if you want to forgo Chillon and yet board the same steamer for Lausanne and not miss any of your friends who may have elected to see the castle made famous by Lord Byron. If it's stormy on Lake Geneva, you can still keep to the schedule by proceeding to Lausanne by rail.

Chillon-bound passengers should scurry to the castle as quickly as possible after the lake steamer docks to ensure maximum use of the time ashore. The steamer proceeds on to the French port of St. Gingolph and then returns to Chillon. Check at the Chillon dock for its return time. Should you miss the boat, you still have another option. Hail a cab back to Montreux, then entrain for Lausanne to join your friends in the dining car en route back to Berne.

Horse-drawn carriages await visitors arriving in Interlaken's west station. These conveyances are a familiar sight along the city's grand promenade, Hoheweg, which is lined with grand hotels and other attractions that draw visitors from all over the world.

From Berne . . .

A DAY EXCURSION TO INTERLAKEN
DISTANCE BY TRAIN: 37 miles (59 km)
AVERAGE TRAIN TIME: 50 minutes

Interlaken can best be described as the cultural and social focal point of Switzerland's Alpine areas. The English poet Lord Byron is said to have exclaimed, "It's a dream!" at his first sighting of Interlaken and its surroundings. Nestled between the Lake of Thun and the Lake of Brienz, Interlaken (Latin for "between the lakes") began in the twelfth century as a small cluster of buildings surrounding a monastery, traces of which can still be seen today. The town's main thoroughfare, Hoheweg, is lined with great hotels, shops, and even a grand casino that is set back from the main promenade and banked with such beautiful flowers that one might think it is a retirement home.

For Interlaken, the Hoheweg plays the same part as does the Champs-Elysées for Paris or the Via Veneto for Rome—it is *the boulevard,* with the ambiance for which the Swiss are famous. Just as in its larger counterparts, you'll find strollers on foot or aboard horse-drawn carriages taking in the sights along with those relaxing over coffee and pastries at the sidewalk cafés. Towering over this entire scene is the Jungfrau, a massive mountain that tops out at 13,642 feet above sea level, a mere eleven miles south of Interlaken. On a clear day the view is dazzling.

Believe it or not, the Jungfrau can be scaled by train. Beginning in Interlaken at its east rail station, a private cog railroad terminates at the Jungfraujoch station, at 11,333 feet, the highest rail terminal in the world. We do not recommend that you attempt to include this rail excursion in your visit to Interlaken because the round trip takes the better half of a day and should be made only in ideal weather. Furthermore, the Eurailpass is not accepted, and the round-trip fare is just as steep as the ascent, 157 Swiss francs per person first class and 147 francs for second class. Plan your "assault" on the Jungfrau for a separate day after you have checked the weather—and your wallet.

If you *must* scale a mountain while in Interlaken, we suggest you select the funicular running up to Harderkulm, which overlooks Interlaken to the south from 4,333 feet above sea level. On a clear day you can see both lakes surrounding Interlaken, as well as the Jungfrau. This can be done in about an hour for only 22.40 Swiss francs per person. The Harderkulm station is only a short walk from Interlaken's Ost (east) station. Ask for directions at the tourist office.

Interlaken has two railway stations, west and east. Coming from Berne you arrive first in the west station. We suggest that you detrain at that point rather than riding another five minutes to the east station. Remember, however, if

INTERLAKEN—*LAKE OF THUN CRUISE*

A Day Excursion from Berne

DEPART FROM BERNE STATION	TRAIN NUMBER	ARRIVE IN INTERLAKEN WEST STATION*
0828	1706	0916
0928	IC 865	1016
1028	1716	1116
1128	IC 871	1216

DEPART FROM INTERLAKEN WEST STATION**	TRAIN NUMBER	ARRIVE IN BERNE STATION
1544	1733	1632
1644	IC 882	1732
1744	1739	1832
1844	1741	1932
1944	IC 890	2032
2141	2446	2232

* Arrives Interlaken Ost (East) Station five minutes later. All train departures are daily.

** Departs Interlaken Ost (East) Station five minutes prior to departing Interlaken West Station. All train departures are daily.

Distance: 37 miles/59 km
Reference: Thomas Cook Table 280

LAKE OF THUN CRUISE
(Operates mid-April through mid-October)

DEPART PIER INTERLAKEN*	ARRIVE THUN	DEPART THUN	TRAIN NUMBER	ARRIVE BERNE
1447	1648	1712	IC 882	1732
1647	1852	1912	1741	1932

* Steamer pier adjacent to Interlaken West Station. Other lake-steamer departures available. Check schedule.

References: Thomas Cook Tables 280 and 281

you are closer to the east station as your visit draws to a close, you can catch the same train from that point, too—but five minutes ahead of the west-station schedule.

The Hoheweg starts at the west station, and the grand promenade extends to the east station. The tourist information office is on the left side of the Hoheweg, about a five-minute walk from the station. During July and August, office hours are 0800–1200 and 1400–1830 Monday through Friday, 0800–1200 and 1400–1700 on Saturday, and 1700–1900 on Sunday. Hours are shorter the rest of the year, and the office is closed Sunday. With a city map in hand, courtesy of the tourist office, you are all set to tour the town. If walking isn't your forte, you may prefer to see the sights from a surrey. These horse-drawn vehicles are available just outside the west station. Rates vary and must be arranged with the driver.

We've never counted them, but we are told that there are more than one hundred restaurants in Interlaken. We do have a favorite among that number, although it's a bit off the beaten path—the Hotel Rossli, No. 45 on the city map. It is run by a friendly gentleman who worked in New York City restaurants for many years before he moved to the German district of Switzerland. The result is German-Swiss food served with a French flair and an American accent—rather unusual.

Interlaken is the starting place for explorations of the Jungfrau region. We suggest that you devote one day to Interlaken and its immediate area and, while you are there, check with the tourist office regarding the other day-excursion possibilities. In addition to the rail ascent to the Jungfrau, you can reach the Schilthorn and lunch in the restaurant Piz Gloria (at 9,744 feet), where James Bond escaped the murderous intents of the opposition by skiing down the world's longest ski slope in the film *Her Majesty's Secret Service.*

Wearers of pacemakers should be wary of the higher altitudes, but there's no reason to miss out on the fun around Interlaken. The Swiss Open-Air Museum at nearby Ballenberg is an ideal alternative and easy to reach by either train or lake steamer departing from the city's east station. Ask for details at the tourist information office.

If the weather is agreeable, a cruise on the Lake of Thun before returning from Interlaken is a must. The ships depart from a pier that can be reached from either the west station by tunnel or the Bahnhofstrasse, where it intersects with the Hoheweg alongside the station. There are additional sailings throughout the day, but either of the two shown on the schedule opposite will take you to the town of Thun (pronounced "tune") at the upper reaches of the lake in late afternoon.

A Lucerne landmark, the *Wasserturm* (water tower) on the side of the city's recently restored covered bridge, the *Kapellbrücke,* is recognized instantly by visitors. The bridge, longer than two football fields, was constructed in the fourteenth century. The 112 murals under its eaves were added in the seventeenth century and refurbished early in the twentieth. Destroyed by fire in 1993, the bridge was rebuilt and reopened April 14, 1994. Rain or shine, crossing the *Kapellbrücke* is a must for every visitor. The city's swan flock calls this area home and welcomes handouts.

From Berne ...

A DAY EXCURSION TO LUCERNE
DISTANCE BY TRAIN: 59 miles (95 km)
AVERAGE TRAIN TIME: 1 hour, 20 minutes

This day excursion is weatherproof. Rain or shine, Lucerne has much to offer. So much, in fact, that you may want to return again and again until you have seen it all—an impossible but challenging task. We've tried it.

Lucerne is in its glory on a bright, sunny day, when the city and its surroundings sparkle with a brilliance that defies description. At the northwestern end of Lake Lucerne, where the Reuss River resumes its swift quest for the Rhine, Lucerne's lakefront, rimmed by the mighty Alps, is an unforgettable sight. But a rainy day in Lucerne (and that sort of thing does happen occasionally) won't dampen your spirits one bit, for there are many things to see that are under cover. The *Kapellbrücke* covered bridge is one example. A symbol of Lucerne, the bridge was built at the beginning of the fourteenth century together with the *Wasserturm* (water tower) at its side. During the seventeenth century, artists painted a total of 112 pictures under its eaves depicting Swiss history, particularly that of Lucerne and its patron saints. Unfortunately, the bridge was destroyed by fire in 1993. The bridge and the artwork were recreated, and the bridge reopened to the public in April 1994.

The Swiss Museum of Transport and Communications in Lucerne is open from March through October on a daily schedule between 0900 and 1800. From November through February, it is open Monday through Saturday, 1000 to 1600; Sundays and holidays, 1000 to 1700. It is the largest and most modern museum in Europe—also one of the most visited. The museum is reached easily from the center of Lucerne by bus No. 2, which departs from the rail station every six minutes for the ten-minute trip, or by lake steamer from the Lido dock (Eurailpass accepted).

Its special attraction is the Longines Planetarium, and the museum also traces vividly the development of Swiss transportation, including rail, road, aeronautical, and water navigation. Tourism since the nineteenth century is also highlighted. Kids from seven to seventy will be fascinated by the operating scale model of the Gotthard tunnel railroad, and everyone will end up breathless following a visit to the museum's *Swissorama* circular theater. With three restaurants to choose from, you can really plan to spend an entire day.

If you want to check in with the city's tourist information office during your visit, it is located immediately outside and to the left of the railway station. Look for the "i" sign just under the HOTEL WALDSTATTERHOF sign or—better still—look for it directly across from McDonald's golden arches. Yep, fast food has invaded Switzerland!

LUCERNE—*AND MOUNT PILATUS*

A Day Excursion from Berne

DEPART BERNE	ARRIVE LUCERNE	NOTES	DEPART LUCERNE	ARRIVE BERNE	NOTES
0731	0846	(1)(2)	1313	1429	(1)(2)
0848	1012	(1)(2)(3)	1513	1629	(1)
0931	1046	(1)(2)	1713	1829	(1)
1048	1212	(1)(2)(3)	1813	1929	(1)(2)
1131	1246	(1)(2)	1913	2029	(1)
1331	1446	(1)(2)	2013	2129	(1)
			2101	2215	(1)

(1) Daily, including holidays
(2) Food service
(3) Transfer in Olten

Distance: 59 miles/95 km
Reference: Thomas Cook Table 265

DEPART LUCERNE	ARRIVE ALPNACHSTAD	DEPART ALPNACHSTAD*	ARRIVE PILATUS
1005	1153	1050	1120
1130	1300	1310	1340
1405	1545	1430	1500

DEPART PILATUS*	ARRIVE ALPNACHSTAD	DEPART ALPNACHSTAD	ARRIVE LUCERNE
1425	1505		
1505	1545	1555	1715
1545	1625	1635	1825
1625	1705	1755	1854

* Via Pilatus cogwheel railway May to end of October. One class only. Eurailpasses are *not* accepted on Pilatus railway. Pilatus is 7,000 feet (2,132 meters) above sea level.

Distance: 3 miles/5 km, Pilatus cogwheel railway
References: Thomas Cook Tables 294 and 286

Travel in luxury between Lucerne and Lugano aboard the William Tell Express. See page 402 for details and schedule.

Lucerne's tourist information office has a city map as well as illustrated brochures on every attraction within the city. From April through October, the center is open 0830–1800 from Monday through Friday. Saturday, the center operates 0900–1700. From mid-May through October, Sunday hours are 0900–1300. From November through March, it is open 0830–1200 and 1400–1800; Saturday, 0900–1300.

If you don't mind mixing fondue with frivolity, by all means eat at the Stadtkeller restaurant, just two blocks north of the *Kapellbrücke's* right-bank entrance. It may be a bit "touristy," but if you like yodeling, alphorn blowing, cowbell ringing, beer drinking, and flag throwing, this is the place. At lunchtime, you should be there no later than 1130. The Stadtkeller is a tour-bus lunch stop and fills up rapidly. You can watch those poor, tired bus passengers try to determine what country they are seeing today.

Turning to a sobering experience, follow up lunch with a visit to *The Dying Lion of Lucerne.* It is one of the world's most famous monuments. It was hewn from natural rock in commemoration of the heroic, fatal defense by Swiss guards of Louis XVI at the Tuileries in Paris at the beginning of the French Revolution in 1792. Mark Twain described the Lion of Lucerne as "the saddest and most poignant piece of rock in the world."

Next door, you will find Lucerne's Glacier Garden Museum, which contains remnants of Lucerne's prehistoric past that were discovered in 1872. Twenty million years ago, Lucerne was a subtropical palm beach on the ocean; twenty thousand years ago, Lucerne was covered by more than a mile of glacier ice. Don't miss it.

On your way to the Lion Monument and the Glacier Garden Museum, you will pass one of Switzerland's most outstanding and attractive restaurants, the Old Swiss House. Built in 1859, the restaurant contains an antique collection of rare beauty. The oil paintings are all originals. The food's superb, too! We suggest that you call ahead for reservations: 041–516171.

Visiting Mount Pilatus as a side adventure during your Lucerne day excursion is pretty much just following the schedule we've laid out for you on the opposite page. Be certain to go on a clear day, for there is nothing more disappointing than a fog-shrouded peak. The world famous Pilatus electric railway, with its maximum gradient of 48 percent, is the steepest cog railway in the world. Eurailpass is not accepted. It's best to purchase tickets at the tourist information office at Frankenstrasse 1. Ask at the station's train information office for the alternate routes to Mount Pilatus. If you have a lot of time, you can take a lake steamer to Alpnachstad. For a breathtaking view and a beautiful way to end your day in Lucerne, descend Mount Pilatus in a cable car to Kriens and catch the bus to Lucerne. Check with the tourist information office for details and discounts available to rail-pass holders.

Upper gate of Rheinfelden dates to 1256. Additional construction and the installation of a clock were completed during the seventeenth century.

A DAY EXCURSION TO RHEINFELDEN
DISTANCE BY TRAIN: 76 miles (122 km)
AVERAGE TRAIN TIME: 1 hour, 30 minutes

If the Disney folks ever want to start another European operation, there's a site ready and waiting for them. It's Rheinfelden.

A medieval jewel set on the banks of the swift-moving Rhine River just above Basel, Rheinfelden stirs the imagination. Much of its wall and many of its watch towers are still standing, and they were erected back in the eleventh century. An island on the Swiss side of the river's channel forms an important part of a bridge linking Switzerland to Germany. In the thirteenth century, it was the site of the famed "Emperor's Palace" described by Schiller in the tale of William Tell. The castle is gone now, and the island serves mainly as a city park; but the swirls and eddies of the mighty Rhine continue to stimulate one's sense of the centuries of history that have unfolded there.

During World War II, the bridge over the Rhine at Rheinfelden was the center of intrigue and mystery. Many downed but uncaptured American and British aviators seeking the sanctuary of Switzerland attempted to flee Nazi Germany from there. Some made it; some were apprehended. In our visits to Rheinfelden, we have talked with residents who still remember those days and the risks that were taken. One person recalled for us her personal escape across the Rhine's waters in a rowboat.

The Rheinfelden railway station sits on a broad bluff above the old city. To reach the tourist information office from there, proceed downhill on Bahnhofstrasse (Station Street) to the bottom of the hill, where it meets Marktgasse, the pedestrian shopping area. Turn left and walk a short block to the office at 61 Marktgasse, near the Swiss Customs station at the bridge leading to Germany. Look for the sign identifying the office: *Offizielles Verkehrsburo* (Official Tourist Bureau). The office operates on a year-round schedule: 0900–1200 and 1400–1800 Monday through Friday and 0900–1200 on Saturday (telephone 831.55.20; fax 831.55.70). Schedule your Rheinfelden visit for any day except Monday, when most stores and restaurants are closed.

Be certain to pick up a city map during your stop at the tourist office. Armed with the map, you can easily wend your way through the labyrinthlike streets to any point of interest and still find your way back to the train station in time for your return to Berne. Check out the shops lining the Rhine. Here you can find bargains in antiques, clothing, and sporting equipment.

When your stomach (or your watch) tells you it's lunchtime, you have more than twenty excellent eating places to choose from in Rheinfelden. Our favorites are the Hotel Schiff and the Café Rheineck close to the river. The

RHEINFELDEN—*WALLED CITY ON THE RHINE*

A Day Excursion from Berne via Basel

DEPART FROM BERNE STATION	TRAIN NUMBER	ARRIVE IN BASEL STATION	DEPART FROM BASEL STATION	ARRIVE IN RHEIN-FELDEN STATION
0648	IC 852	0759	0849	0901
0748	IC 854	0859	0934	0950
0848	IC 314	0959	1049	1101
0948	IC 864	1059	1134	1150
1048	EC 108	1159	1249	1301

DEPART RHEIN-FELDEN	ARRIVE IN BASEL	DEPART BASEL	TRAIN NUMBER	ARRIVE IN BERNE
1658	1711	1701	IC 839	1812
1758	1811	1801	EC 109	1912
1817	1832	1901	IC 893	2012
1958	2011	2152	2549	2312

Note: Semi-fast trains run hourly from Basel to Rheinfelden at forty-five minutes past each hour from 0745 to 2045. Same train service runs from Rheinfelden to Basel on the hour from 0900 to 2200.

Distance: 76 miles/122 km
References: Thomas Cook Tables 280 and 300

Sherlock's City restaurant to the right of the train station is a convenient spot to rally for a brew prior to departure back to Berne. While on that subject, Rheinfelden is home for two of Switzerland's largest breweries, Cardinal and Feldschlösschen. Tours are available on an irregular basis. Excellent restaurants and beer stubes are located at each brewery.

May we suggest that you have lunch by the Rhine? Clustered about the bridge entrance are several eating places offering menus ranging from light snacks to full-course meals. Another suggestion: Pick up some cheese, bread, and wine at one of the market stalls and have your repast on the island as the Rhine provides the background accompaniment. To get to the island, you will have to pass the Swiss Customs station on the bridge entrance. The genial gentlemen in charge there speak English and will wave you through when you show your luncheon selection and point to the island. One caution—don't continue across the bridge into Germany. If that is your intent, have the Swiss officials stamp your passport.

Saline deposits were discovered under the town in 1844, and Rheinfelden quickly developed into an international spa. Its natural brine, which is one of the strongest in Europe, is piped from a depth of more than 600 feet to several bathing facilities in town, including the largest saltwater swimming pool in Switzerland. The tourist office can provide full details. The structures housing the pumps that bring the brine to the surface from the deep wells bear a striking resemblance to the original oil fields of western Pennsylvania, where oil refining first began in North America.

There is an unusual inside-outside saltwater swimming pool in Rheinfelden that you should see during your visit. You can reach it on foot by walking along the Rhine in an upstream direction. The brine-well structures may be seen nearby.

River steamers ply between Rheinfelden and Basel. The option of returning to Berne via Basel and a boat trip on the Rhine becomes an attractive option between May and September, when the service is in operation. Schedules are posted at the *Schifflande* (boat landing) opposite the island. Information on the steamer service to Basel, as well as cruises on the Rhine, is also available in the Rheinfelden tourist information office. Rhine steamers, unlike the lake steamers, do not accept Eurailpass, but the rates to Basel are nominal.

Hotel de Ville, Brussels' medieval town hall, stands in Gothic splendor over the Grand'Place. Brussels' tourist information office is located immediately inside the main gate of the town hall. (Photo courtesy City of Brussels)

8   BRUSSELS

Brussels has stood for more than 1,000 years as a signpost of ideals and ideas, a crossroad of people and events. Less than 150 miles from Amsterdam and 200 miles from Paris, Brussels is a bonanza for travelers desiring to see Europe by Eurail. Few people realize how short distances actually are in Belgium, of which Brussels is the capital. Its most opposite points are only 195 miles apart.

Brussels is old; it celebrated its millennium in 1979. Brussels is new; it's the headquarters of the European Common Market and the North Atlantic Treaty Organization (NATO). Consequently, it has been quite a task to preserve the quaint atmosphere of a city immersed into all this international activity; but Brussels has succeeded, thanks to the attitudes of its one million people. They have maintained a way of life in their city that cherishes the human dimension—and they welcome you to come and share it with them.

Day Excursions

It is difficult to limit the number of day excursions Brussels has to offer. With its central location and numerous EuroCity trains available, a day excursion to Paris, Amsterdam, Luxembourg, or Cologne is quite feasible. With the opening of the Channel Tunnel with its new high-speed trains, even London becomes a possibility. We have elected, however, to present four day excursions going to various points within Belgium itself. We offer Antwerp, city of diamonds and Rubens; Bruges and its famous Markt; Ghent with its Flower Show; and Namur, gateway to the beautiful Ardennes.

Arriving and Departing

By Air. Direct train service between the Brussels national airport in suburban Zaventem and the city is available. The fare is 85 Belgian francs to or from either the north station or the central station in Brussels. Time en route is seventeen minutes. Trains depart every twenty minutes. *Eurailpasses are not accepted.* Taxis aren't cheap. You'll pay about 800 Belgian francs for the six-mile ride. One saving grace, however, is the tip—it's included in the fare indicated on the meter. You'll save 20 to 50 percent by phoning for a Brussels taxi instead of using the vehicles waiting at the airport.

By Train. Brussels has three train stations along its main line: one in the north (Brussel Nord), one in the south (Gare Brussels du Midi), and a mid-city underground station (Gare Centrale). EuroCity trains and the major express trains do not stop in the central station. Change at either the north or south station and then transfer to a local train if Gare Centrale is your destination.

Background on Brussels

Brussels' cosmopolitan population knows how to enjoy itself. Eating and drinking well in Brussels is no problem. Succumbing too easily to gastronomic temptation is the real difficulty. Bruxellois, it is said, is like French cuisine served in German portions—although some lighter touches of the *nouvelle* cuisine are beginning to inch their way into Brussels' menus. In Belgium, beer is not just beer, it's an art form, and the local cafés and bistros are as much an attraction as are the brews they dispense. In Brussels, some offer more than one-hundred different labels of *Belgian* beer alone. For bistro-type dining with a modest price tag, we suggest that you head for the pedestrian-only Rue des Bouchers, a stone's throw from the Grand'Place. Along with the gastronomy, in the evening the area presents numerous sidewalk displays by local artisans.

Latin and Nordic cultures meet in Brussels, making it a city of contrasts. French is spoken by the Walloon people of French origin, and Flemish is the tongue of its Germanic inhabitants. French, German, and Flemish are official languages in Belgium. Consequently, all signs are bilingual in Brussels. English is spoken in all the train stations, hotels, and (the majority of) public places.

The city abounds in things to see and do, ranging from its elegant Grand'Place to historic Waterloo, but we will leave that part of your visit in the good hands of the Brussels tourist information office.

Tourist Facilities

Brussels maintains a tourist information center in the Town Hall at the Grand'Place. The telephone number is (02) 513.89.40; the fax number is (02) 514.45.38. Hotel reservations and theater tickets, as well as information covering the entire city, are available there. The office is open 0900–1800 Monday through Saturday. Sunday hours are 0900–1800 from April 1 through September 30 and 1000–1400 from October 1 through November 30. City maps are sold at the center together with a wealth of free information regarding sightseeing, shopping, restaurants, tours, transportation, and so on.

To reach the Grand'Place from Gare Centrale (Central Station), simply walk downhill in the direction of the town hall's spire until you reach the square. Take a minute to drink in the splendor of the medieval buildings facing the square. You will realize immediately why it is called the most beautiful square in all of Europe. After leaving the tourist information center, check Le Cerf in the square's northeast corner—probably the finest bar in all Europe and an excellent place to rally with friends for a period of "attitude adjustment." It's a coat-and-tie establishment, but well worth dressing for.

City Transportation

Brussels boasts two metro systems since the introduction of its high-speed lines in 1976. The older metro, the one permitting the individual trams (trolley cars) to scurry beneath the city and then surface like a pack of prairie dogs, is still in operation but it is gradually being phased out. Together, the two systems provide Brussels with a highly efficient underground-transportation network. *Eurailpasses are not accepted.* A Tourist Ticket, available for 120 Belgian francs, provides for travel on any underground, tram, or bus service for one calendar day. Ask the Brussels Tourist Office (T.I.B.) for a map and other fare information.

The Railway Stations—North Station, Central Station & South Station

North Station (Brussel Nord) is the gateway to Holland, Germany, Switzerland, Italy, and eastern France.

Money-exchange office is in a corridor to the left when exiting from the trains into the main station area. It is open daily, including Sunday, 0800–2000.

Hotel reservations can be made at the information booth in the departure hall. The hours of operation for this service are 0900–1700 Monday through Friday throughout the year. The American Express and Cook's Travel Service can make hotel reservations and advance reservations in other cities if you would like to use their services.

Train information office is located in the corridor off the left-hand side of the main station area as you exit from the trains. It operates daily, except Sunday, 0700–2100.

Train reservations can be made at ticket window No. 3 or No. 4 in the main station area.

Eurailpass validation is available at the train reservation windows—No. 3 or No. 4.

There is a railway museum located on the mezzanine of the North Station. Turn right when entering the main station from the train area and walk up the stairs at the end of the concourse. The museum holds an interesting collection of rail-transportation vehicles ranging from the first Belgian steam locomotive to some of the present-day diesel and electric traction units. The Belgian railway system is said to be the oldest on the continent of Europe, and the museum is well worth the time of your visit. Admission is free.

The Central Station (Gare Centrale) links both North and South stations via underground trackage. Please note that many of the express trains do not stop there. You may, however, board any of the local trains as a shuttle to either of the main stations and vice versa. Therefore, it is possible to establish

Covered shopping malls appeared in Brussels long before the other cities of Europe. The Galeries Saint-Hubert attract today's shoppers with century-old splendor.

yourself in one of the downtown hotels or pensions quite near Central Station yet be able to make any train connection with a minimum of inconvenience.

Money-exchange office is located in the center hall of the station. As you stand looking at the train information board above the ticket windows, the office is on your right. It is open daily, 0800–2000.

Hotel reservations cannot be made in Central Station. Sabena operates a passenger reservation center next door in the Sabena Building, right next to the airport train-entrance gate. This facility is open 0800–1800 Monday through Friday and 0900–1700 on Saturday. In addition, hotel accommodations can be obtained by visiting the tourist information center in the town hall facing the Grand'Place. (Refer to the previous section on tourist facilities.)

Train information is displayed in the main station area immediately above the ticket windows. This is hourly information. Regular printed schedules are also displayed.

Train reservations are available *only* at North and South stations.

Eurailpass validation must be completed at either North or South station.

South Station (Gare du Midi) is the gateway to London (via Oostende), Paris, and Spain. The station is divided into three sections: a main hall where tickets are sold, a departure hall, and an arrival hall. You can reach the departure hall by passing through the ticket gates from the main hall, but to return to the main hall from either the departure or arrival hall, you must exit the building and re-enter. Use the exits on the west side for this purpose. Coming down the stairs from the train platforms, west is to the left.

Money-exchange office is on the far right-hand side of the main hall as you enter from the street. It also has windows servicing the departure hall. Daily operating hours are 0700–2145.

Hotel reservations are possible at an "Information" booth located in the center of the departure hall. This booth is open 0900–1700 Monday through Friday. If this booth is closed, use the central tourist information office in the Grand'Place.

Tourist information is available on occasion at an "Information" booth in the center of the departure hall. If it's closed, go to the tourist information center in the Grand'Place.

Train reservations can be made in the Railtour (Relations Internationales) office on the far left-hand side of the main hall.

Eurailpass validation is available in the Railtour office (see above).

There is a taxicab reservation system available to passengers returning from Paris on the afternoon and evening EuroCity trains, the Ile de France and the Étoile du Nord. The regular taxi queues on the station's west side are frequently oversubscribed, and waiting is frequently required. If interested in reserving a taxi for your use immediately upon arrival, speak to the conductor soon after departing the Gare du Nord (North Station) in Paris. The conductor will issue a coupon to you with instructions to turn right, to the east, when you descend from the train platform. The taxi stand for this reservation service will be found at the end of the corridor on the right. The waiting taxi has a slightly higher fare rate than the regular Brussels' cabs and you should tip the conductor for his services. If time is money, however, the extra is well spent.

Brussels Bits and Bites

Want to see Brussels and the rest of the European Community in one day? You can. Ask the tourist information office for details about Mini-Europe in Bruparck. You'll see Europe in miniature—more than 300 models of famous buildings and monuments constructed on a scale of ⅕, complete with animation and sound effects. Watch a TGV glide by, an Airbus take off, or Mt. Vesuvius erupt simply by pushing a button.

If you are looking for a souvenir or a gift for someone, we can suggest *pralines* (hand-dipped chocolates), *speculoos* (brown sugar biscuits), or some fine Brussels lace. All three of these Belgian specialties are available from shops in and around the Grand'Place. The attendants at the city tourist information office will be happy to assist you.

If you've never eaten a Brussels waffle, you haven't lived a full and rewarding life. We are not referring to the "Belgian waffle" that you'll find at concession stands in every state fair from Maine to Mexico, nor do we refer to the highly touted desserts served by restaurants using a waffle as a base piled high with candied fruits and buried in whipped cream. These confections are good, mind you, but nothing in the world can surpass the kind of waffle that Brussels offers.

Don't look for the true Brussels waffle in any of the Brussels restaurants, plain or fancy. And you won't find them served in any café or candy shop in the city either. Brussels waffles are a part of the scene—you can only buy them from several small waffle shops located in the area around the city's opera house, and you should only buy them from a shop that actually makes the waffles right on the premises. Look for the sign GAUFRES in French or WAFELS in Flemish.

There's nothing fancy about a Brussels waffle. The vendor will hand it to you wrapped in a small napkin. Bite into it—and your life will be changed from that moment on. *Bon appetit!*

From Brussels ...

TRAIN CONNECTIONS TO OTHER BASE CITIES

TO:	DEPART*	ARRIVE	TRAIN NUMBER	COOK'S TABLE	NOTES
Amsterdam**	0910	1208	2481	18	(1)
	1410	1708	2486	18	(1)
Berlin (Zoo)	0748	1654	413/IC 504	23	(1)(2)
Berne	0715	1512	EC 91	40	(1)
	1219	2012	EC 97	40	(1)(3)
Copenhagen	1847	0825+1	233	21	(1)
Hamburg	0947	1711	417/IC 524	21	(1)(2)
Luxembourg**	0821	1115	956	210	(1)
	1521	1815	963	210	(1)
Milan	0715	1915	EC 91	43	(1)
	1913	0710+1	299	43	(1)
Munich	0748	1711	413/ICE 513	33	(1)(2)
Nice	2013	1039+1	1186	48	(1)(9)
Oslo	1847	1937+1	D233	21	(1)(6)
Paris	0704	0940	TEE 80	18	(4)
	1154	1425	EC 82	18	(7)(8)
	1711	1942	TEE 84	18	(4)
Rome	1513	0945+1	295	43	(1)(10)

* All departures from Gare du Midi. Daily departures unless otherwise noted. Make reservations for all departures (except to/from Amsterdam).

** Hourly service

(1) Stops at Brussels Nord
(2) Transfer in Cologne (Köln)
(3) Transfer in Basel to train 893
(4) Monday through Friday, except holidays
(5) Daily, except Sunday
(6) Transfer in Copenhagen to IN 384
(7) Reservations required
(8) Arrives 1435, July 1 through August 31
(9) Leaves at 1907, Sunday through Thursday, September 6 through June 21
(10) July 1 through September 4

Hand of the giant Antigoon, thrown in the River Schelde by the Roman soldier Brabo, gave Antwerp its name according to legend.

From Brussels . . .

A DAY EXCURSION TO ANTWERP
DISTANCE BY TRAIN: 35 miles (57 km)
AVERAGE TRAIN TIME: 40 minutes

If your wife has convinced you that diamonds are a girl's best friend and if the kids are hankering to see one of Europe's finest zoos—take them to Antwerp. There's satisfaction there for the entire family.

Be certain the train you take from Brussels is marked "Antwerp Central." EuroCity and other through trains continuing to Amsterdam stop only at stations on the edge of Antwerp. The central station is right in the city center. If you do end up in one of Antwerp's suburban stations, board an inbound local train.

The city's name is spelled three ways: "Antwerp" is the English version; in French it is "Anvers"; and its Flemish title is "Antwerpen." Call it what you will, this fine city with nearly half a million people is a marvelous place to visit. Its contrasts will amaze you. Antwerp is Belgium's second city, the third largest port in the world, reputed to be the world's diamond center, and a Renaissance treasure house.

Train-departure information for your return trip to Brussels can be found on the many train bulletin boards located throughout the station. A train information office is located on the street side of the station, between the two main exits.

The train information office does not dispense tourist information, but they will assist you in finding the city's tourist office. There are three suggested means of getting there. On foot, the walk takes about fifteen minutes—you set the pace. Antwerp's Metro system also can get you there, but first stop at the Metro office in the railway station for fare and routing information. In a hurry? Follow the pictograms to the taxi queue. Antwerp's tourist office is located in its Grote Markt (Main Square) at No. 15. Office hours are Monday through Saturday, 0900–1800 and Sunday, 0900–1700. The telephone number is (03) 232–01–03, fax 231–19–37.

Because Antwerp is one of the world's major seaports, it offers an unusual harbor tour that the entire family can enjoy. During the summer, motor launches depart from the Steenplein on the river. With more than 3,000 acres of docks, seventeen dry docks, and six locks (including the largest in the world), the harbor is a spectacle you should not miss. There are a variety of waterborne tours to select from and a short trip on the river Scheldt takes fifty minutes. The port sightseeing tour that we have recommended runs for two and a half hours. A combination zoo-harbor ticket is available, too. This will take care of the kids, but we doubt that mom will forget the diamonds.

ANTWERP—*THE DIAMOND CITY*

A Day Excursion from Brussels

DEPART FROM BRUSSELS MIDI STATION*	TRAIN NUMBER	ARRIVE IN ANTWERP CENTRAL STATION	NOTES
0710	2479	0749	(1)
0810	2480	0849	(1)
0910	2481	0949	(1)
1010	2482	1049	(1)

Plus other frequent service throughout the day

DEPART FROM ANTWERP CENTRAL STATION	TRAIN NUMBER	ARRIVE IN BRUSSELS MIDI STATION*	NOTES
1649	2464	1730	(1)
1749	2465	1830	(1)
1849	2466	1930	(1)
1949	2467	2030	(1)

Plus other frequent service throughout the day

* Also stops at Brussels Centrale and Nord stations

(1) Daily, including holidays

Distance: 35 miles/57 km
Reference: Thomas Cook Table 205

Antwerp boasts twenty museums, among them the Plantin-Moretus, featuring a sixteenth-century printing press. Most of Antwerp's museums are closed on Mondays, but the zoo, which is just to the right as you exit from the railway station, is open daily until sunset. Because you will probably include a visit to the zoo in your day excursion, plan it for the first or last part of the day, for there are plenty of other sights to be seen around town.

If you are interested in the Zoo-Harbor Tour combo ticket, we suggest that you check with the city tourist information office after arriving in Antwerp and pick a time to participate.

Most seasoned travelers put Rubens's House at the top of their list of sightseeing "musts." Rubens ordered the patrician dwelling to be built for himself, and he lived there with his family from 1615 until his death in 1640. Works of the great Flemish master also are kept in many of the museums and churches in Antwerp. The great Flemish artist is buried in St. James Church, where you may view the painting *Madonna with Child and Saints,* which Rubens directed be placed on the altar shortly before his death. Rubens and Antwerp remain inexplicably linked to each other.

Other sightseeing musts are the Cathedral of Our Lady (largest Gothic church in Belgium), with four Rubens masterpieces inside; the Grote Markt (Antwerp's marketplace); and the Open Market (known locally as the Birds Market). The Birds Market is open on Sunday mornings, when miscellaneous wares are sold. All these city highlights will be on the map you receive at the city tourist office, and all are within reasonable walking distance.

The Flemish term it "De Rubenswandeling"—The Rubens Walk. It's all laid out for you in a colorful brochure, its map detailing eleven points of interest associated with Rubens. For variety, there is a Stadswandeling/Rondwandeling—city round-trip walking tour—prepared in a similar format. Both are available at the city's tourist information office.

According to legend, the site of Antwerp was once inhabited by a giant who extracted tribute from all who navigated the river and cut off a hand of those who refused to pay. He was slain by a Roman soldier, who cut off the giant's hand and threw it into the river. Thus, the city's name: *Ant* (hand) and *werpen* from the verb "to throw." In support of the legend, the city fathers erected a statue of Silvius Brabo, the Roman soldier, in front of the city hall. Those not subscribing to the legend say the name was derived from Aenwerpen (higher land). There's always someone who doesn't believe in the tooth fairy.

The Belfry in Bruges rises 280 feet above the city's Markt. On a clear day, those who climb its stairs can see points as far away as the North Sea.

A DAY EXCURSION TO BRUGES
DISTANCE BY TRAIN: 65 miles (105 km)
AVERAGE TRAIN TIME: 1 hour, 7 minutes

Bruges has magnetic attractions—its ancient buildings, great churches, picturesque canals, art treasures, and antique shops. You will leave Bruges with the feeling that you must return again.

There are many things to enjoy in Bruges that date from the Middle Ages and the Renaissance. Probably the most interesting sight is the Burg, where history has been in the making since the ninth century. Surrounding the Burg you will find museums of all descriptions, spectacular church spires, peaceful canals, and fascinating alleyways. If you are up to it, a climb up the Belfry finds its reward in a panoramic view to points as far away as the North Sea.

The rail route from Brussels to Bruges is the main line to the port of Oostende. Consequently, most of the trains going in that direction stop at all three of the main Brussels stations. Check the departure information in the station you plan to depart from in Brussels on your day excursion to Bruges, however, just to be certain. The day-excursion schedule on the following page has more details.

Arriving in Bruges, again check the schedules posted in the Bruges station for your return train to Brussels. Train-departure notices are posted throughout the main station area. Also, there is a train information office inside the main station on the left side as you exit from the train platform. Tourist information is available here, or you can go to the central tourist office in the Burg square. You can get there by boarding any bus stopping in front of the railway station that is marked CENTRUM at the entrance side of the bus. The bus will take you to the Markt. It stops in the center of the square in front of the Provincial Palace. To return to the station, board the bus marked O STATION at the library on the square close to the Markt, which can be reached by walking through Kuiperstraat off the Markt.

The tourist information office is located at Burg No. 11 (telephone 050/44–86–86, fax 44–86–00), close to the Town Hall and the Belfry, a remarkable building that dominates the Markt with its famous 280-foot high octagonal tower. The hours of Bruges's tourist office vary according to the season: April–September, Monday–Friday, 0930–1830; Saturday, Sunday, and public holidays, 1000–1200 and 1400–1830. October through March, hours are Monday–Saturday, 0930–1700; closed on Sunday and public holidays.

During the thirteenth and fourteenth centuries, Bruges stood at the crossroads of traffic between the Mediterranean and the Baltic. Rich cargos piled high on its docks and in its warehouses held treasures of spices, cloth, and

BRUGES—*OLD LACE AND CHURCH SPIRES*

A Day Excursion from Brussels

DEPART FROM BRUSSELS NORD STATION*	TRAIN NUMBER	ARRIVE IN BRUGES STATION	NOTES
0747	530	0854	(1)
0847	531	0954	(1)
0947	412	1054	(1)
1047	232	1154	(1)

Plus other frequent service throughout the day

DEPART FROM BRUGES STATION	TRAIN NUMBER	ARRIVE IN BRUSSELS NORD STATION*	NOTES
1650	515	1757	(1)
1725	667	1829	(1)
1850	517	1957	(1)

Plus other frequent service throughout the day

* Also stops at Brussels Midi and Gare Centrale

(1) Daily, including holidays

Distance: 65 miles/105 km
Reference: Thomas Cook Table 200

other luxuries. The counts of Flanders commissioned architects, painters, sculptors, and goldsmiths from all over civilized Europe to build and decorate their churches, palaces, and guildhalls.

Bruges was bursting at the seams during this period. Hundreds of ships dropped anchor in its harbor. In its medieval magnificence, Bruges boasted a population double that of London. There was no equal to the grandeur of its court—and no one seemed alarmed that the estuary linking Bruges with the North Sea was growing narrower and shallower as the silt from the River Zwyn slowly oozed seaward.

Inexorably, the waterway began to close. Deep-draft ships could no longer navigate the estuary. The docks were abandoned and Bruges became a victim of its own progress, a landlocked city. Today, Bruges is a museum of the Middle Ages, with gabled roof lines casting shadows on its cobblestone streets. Despite the loss of its commerce with the sea, Bruges has managed to maintain its former opulence.

Remnants of grand days past, the canals of Bruges weave in and around the city graced by a bevy of swans. Oddly enough, the birds' presence is attributable to a murder. In 1488, the good people of Bruges beheaded a tyrant named Langhals ("Long Neck"). Miffed by this deed, the counts of Flanders decreed that the "long necks," the symbolic swans, would be kept at public expense forever. Consequently, the city firemen pedal around every morning with bread to feed the swans.

It is not unusual in Bruges to hear English being spoken with a British accent. No, they are not Belgians but British neighbors. Oostende and Zeebrugge, a short distance away, are Belgium's train-ferry ports, and many British avail themselves of the short distance to visit Bruges and the Belgian seacoast on weekends and holidays.

Although walking is the best way to see Bruges, there are other interesting ways of getting around the city, one being by canal boat. You may board behind the Belfry, but first get directions from the tourist office. The canal-boat trip lasts thirty-five minutes. Or, if pedal power appeals to you, see "Bruges With Bart," a tour by bicycle that includes a local guide. Yet another, and no less pleasant, way of seeing the city is by horse-drawn cab. The cabs wait on the Burg (city square) in front of the tea room directly in front of the Belfry.

In addition to all the sights of historic significance in Bruges, there are many stores selling exquisite, handmade Flemish lace, excellent reproductions of Flemish paintings, and colorful ceramics. In general, prices for the products are slightly lower in these shops than in those of Brussels, and the quality is as high. By all means plan to have lunch in one of the restaurants or outdoor cafés surrounding the Markt.

Gothic city center contrasts Ghent's centuries of prominence in Western civilization with its modern moods of progress. (Photo courtesy of C. G. T.—Dede.)

From Brussels ...

A DAY EXCURSION TO GHENT
DISTANCE BY TRAIN: 40 miles (64 km)
AVERAGE TRAIN TIME: 45 minutes

Ghent is one of the true Flemish water towns. Three rivers—the Schelde, the Lys, the Lieve—plus a canal flow through it. This accounts for its more than one hundred bridges and its Celtic name, Ganda, meaning a place of confluence.

In the fourteenth century, Ghent was the second largest city, after Paris, north of the Alps. In 1827, the cutting of the Terneuzen canal made Ghent the second largest seaport in Belgium. In more modern times, Ghent has become world-famous for its flower show and the International Ghent Fair. Both are held in the Flanders Expo, a new trade fair complex a few kilometers from the center of Ghent.

A visit to Ghent is facilitated by the fact that most trains running from Brussels to Ghent stop in all three of the Brussels metropolitan railway stations. Always check the departure information in your station, however, to be certain.

Arriving in Ghent, you will find the train information office just to the right as you enter the main station area from the train platforms. It is open daily, 0700–2100, but you will probably get all the information you need for your return trip to Brussels from the station's bulletin board.

The city tourist information offices are not represented in the railway station. The tourist information center is in the center of the city, in the crypt of the Ghent Town Hall at Botermarkt. The telephone number is (09) 224.15.55. The office is open, April through October, 0930–1830 daily and November through March, 0930–1630 daily. To reach the tourist information office, take tram No. 1 to the town center. Ask for the city information brochure to help plan your own walking tour of Ghent.

The map provided by the tourist information office outlines three different walking-tour suggestions. Each is color-coded, and a chart of its places of interest is color-coded, too. The prominent points are shown in dimension on the map, thereby facilitating your sightseeing.

The city information brochure is in color and contains descriptions of all the places of interest. With the brochure in hand, you are all set to see Ghent on foot. If you didn't bring your walking shoes with you, the city's tourist office can arrange a taxi tour for you with an English-speaking guide. A bit expensive—but shoes are expensive, too!

Saint Michael's Bridge, in the heart of the city, is a good place to begin your walking tour. The view from here is impressive, with church towers and guild

GHENT—*HISTORIC BEAUTY*

A Day Excursion from Brussels

DEPART FROM BRUSSELS NORD STATION*	TRAIN NUMBER	ARRIVE IN GHENT STATION	NOTES
0747	530	0830	(1)
0847	531	0930	(1)
0947	412	1030	(1)
1047	232	1130	(1)
1147	534	1230	(1)

Plus other frequent service

DEPART FROM GHENT STATION*	TRAIN NUMBER	ARRIVE IN BRUSSELS NORD STATION	NOTES
1548	665	1629	
1648	666	1729	(1)
1748	667	1829	(1)
1848	668	1929	(1)
1948	669	2029	(1)
2048	670	2129	(1)
2315	521	2357	

Plus other frequent service

* Also stops at Brussels Midi and Centrale stations

(1) Daily, including holidays

Distance: 40 miles/64 km
Reference: Thomas Cook Table 200

houses rimming the skyline. In the distance you can see the Castle of the Counts, one of the most imposing feudal fortresses in Europe today. This castle played a prominent role in Ghent's history during feudal times. The tradespeople had united in a number of strong guilds and could offer armed resistance against their feudal lords, the counts, when said gentry came to collect the rent. The town hall and the Belfry, symbols of civic freedom, were also erected during that period. The Castle of the Counts was completely restored in 1887 and is well worth your inspection.

If you can select a Sunday to visit Ghent, you will be able to join the crowds of townspeople and farm folk as they browse and bargain around the flower market on Kouter Square, opposite the Ghent Opera House. The vegetable and fruit markets are held Monday through Friday at the Groentenmarkt. As the commercial activity diminishes, the social activities gain tempo.

In early times Ghent, like many other Flanders towns, was involved in warding off the Norse invaders coming off the beaches of the North Sea to loot and plunder. Later, Ghent was able to turn its activities to more peaceful enterprises. Like Bruges, it became known throughout the civilized world as a trading center. Growing in opulence, Ghent fostered the emerging artists of Flanders and today is considered the cradle of Flemish Art.

Each September and October, Ghent plays host to the Flanders Festival of Music. Some of the world's greatest musicians and the most celebrated Belgian orchestras and choirs perform. Many other special events take place in Ghent each year. International regattas are held every May at the Georges Nachez Aquatic Stadium. During the summer season many of the city's historic places, such as the Castle of the Counts, are illuminated at night. A carnival is staged each year from the third to the fourth Sunday in July.

Hungry? Opposite the town hall you'll find the Hotel Cour St. Georges. Its chefs can come up with substantial Belgian fare. Although Ghent lies inland from the North Sea, it is, in fact, a seaport and offers some exceptional seafood. If you enjoy shellfish, try the Belgian specialty, *moules marinières* (steamed mussels) for a real treat.

Although not recommended, it is possible to visit both Ghent and Bruges in one day excursion. If pressed for time, go to Bruges in the morning, have lunch, then take a local train in the direction of Brussels and get off in Ghent.

Fountain in the park marks location of tourist information office in Namur. A modern shopping mall is nearby.

From Brussels . . .

A DAY EXCURSION TO NAMUR
DISTANCE BY TRAIN: 43 miles (69 km)
AVERAGE TRAIN TIME: 50 minutes

If you would like to revisit the eighteenth century, go to Namur. It is one of the most attractive towns in Belgium. Its tourist information office offers five excellent walking tours to select from. For the footsore and those wanting to range farther afield during their day excursion, you can book an "All-In-One" ticket that includes boat tours, cable-car ascensions, and a traction-train ride around and through the Citadel of Namur, complete with underground explorations.

There is frequent train service between Namur and Brussels. We suggest that on arrival, you go directly to the Namur tourist bureau, a beautiful circular building set in a small park quite near the railway station. Although a train information office and train-departure bulletins are in the station, the tourist bureau can also provide the information you will need for your return trip to Brussels. In other words, you'll have an opportunity to kill two birds with one stone.

The pathway leading to the tourist bureau is marked at strategic positions by signs pointing to the TOURISME ACCUEIL (tourist reception) area. In the Namur station, you leave the train-platform area via an underground ramp. Once on the ramp, walk past SORTIE 1 to SORTIE 2 and take the escalator to the street level. Bear right around the "C & A" store and proceed to the park, where the tourist bureau will be in plain view at Square de l'Europe Unie, telephone (081) 222859. The bureau is open Monday through Friday, 0900–1200 and 1400–1700. In summer, it is also open on Saturday and Sunday, 0900–1900.

For complete information regarding the walking tours, purchase the booklet *The Little Guide to Namur* at the tourist bureau. The bureau will provide a free town map plus all the assistance you need, including information on the "All-In-One" ticket, should you elect that option.

Tour No. 1 takes you around the town's shopping area. On Saturday mornings, don't miss the colorful flower market at the Fountain of Angels and the Leopold Square shopping center. Tour Nos. 2 and 3 lead you from the tourist bureau around the many museums and monuments. Probably you will not find such a concentration of them anywhere else in Europe. Namur has seven museums—good reason for having two tours instead of just one. Tour No. 4 offers a more rustic itinerary for those who prefer parks and greenery to museums and monuments. It leads you to the Marie-Louise Park, the Academy of Music and Arts, and the Namur Casino (which is open year-round if you'd care to wager a franc or two) and includes a walk along the Meuse River to the Park of Flowers.

NAMUR—*GATEWAY TO THE ARDENNES*

A Day Excursion from Brussels

DEPART FROM BRUSSELS MIDI STATION*	TRAIN NUMBER	ARRIVE IN NAMUR STATION	NOTES
0821	956	0920	(1)
0921	957	1020	(1)
1021	958	1120	(1)
1121	959	1220	(1)

DEPART FROM NAMUR STATION	TRAIN NUMBER	ARRIVE IN BRUSSELS MIDI STATION*	NOTES
1622	990	1721	(1)
1722	991	1821	(1)
1822	992	1921	(1)
1922	993	2021	(1)
2022	994	2121	(1)
2122	995	2221	(1)
2222	996	2321	(1)

* Also stops at Gare Centrale and Brussels Nord stations

(1) Daily, including holidays

Distance: 43 miles/69 km
Reference: Thomas Cook Table 210

By the way, all five tours originate and end at the Tourism Pavilion (the tourist bureau), where you pick up your guide booklet. Attendants there will be glad to advise you concerning the time required for each walking tour so that you won't miss your return-train connections to Brussels.

Throughout all the previous tours, the dominating landmark of Namur—the Citadel—looms on its skyline. Tour No. 5 is devoted entirely to this magnificent sight. The Citadel is in the center of the Parc du Champeau. The walk there can be delightful, particularly if you ascend via the cable car that departs from the Place Pied-du-Chateau. The tourist bureau will provide full details. You can also reach the Citadel by bus. Board bus No. 3 or No. 5 in the town square, adjacent to the railway station. A tour of the Citadel is included in the "All-In-One" ticket, too.

The Citadel of Namur sits at the confluence of the Meuse and the Sambre. Two thousand years of history are contained within its walls. Originally a Celtic stronghold with primitive fortifications, it was altered into a strongly defensive castle. Underground fortifications were added in the fifteenth century and again expanded century after century until modern weaponry brought a cessation of such defenses in the eighteenth century. Throughout its history, however, the Citadel, as one of the most important strongholds of Europe, faced twenty sieges!

Namur's tourist office has a wide selection of excursions for you to select from. Here are but a few. The Gardens of Annevoie, famous for their eighteenth-century style of flowers and fountains, are open 0900–1900; a visit can be made in forty-five minutes. A restaurant and tavern are on the grounds. Cruises on the River Meuse are available in a variety of schedules, including a picnic on board or ashore.

Continuing with Namur's excursion offerings, the city is justly proud of its space-telecommunications ground station and offers a tour of the facility that includes guide service plus a documentary film. The visit requires one and a half hours; food and beverage self-service is available. For aquatic buffs, a kayak or boat trip down the river Lesse is available, with departures daily throughout the season at 1000 and 1400. Looking for something a bit less strenuous? Perhaps a water tour of the Caves of Neptune would fill the bill. It's a forty-five-minute tour and includes a twenty-minute boat ride plus a sight and sound show.

Namur is the gateway to the Ardennes, the forests and mountains of Belgium. It has all the amenities of a holiday resort. Should you find yourself with time to spare while in Namur (a very unlikely thing), take a stroll on the Boulevard de la Sambre, an attractive, tree-lined avenue. If, on the other hand, you are looking for exquisite gifts, the Rue de l'Ange has excellent shops.

Hungarian parliament building (top), situated on the Danube, is probably the most familiar landmark in Budapest. Eight bridges span the Danube in Budapest. **Chain bridge** (below), opened in 1849, was destroyed during World War II, then rebuilt and reopened to mark the centenary of its inauguration in 1949.

9 BUDAPEST

Hungary, the seventeenth member country to join the Eurailpass system, is a unique addition in that it is the first Eastern European nation to do so. Of the country's 10.7 million inhabitants, 2.1 million live in its capital city of Budapest. Tree-lined boulevards and spacious public squares bordered by magnificent buildings make Budapest one of the most attractive and beautiful capitals of Europe. Hungary welcomes more than 24 million visitors annually, the majority of whom pass through Budapest, pausing to enjoy its special charm and atmosphere.

The city is a combination of two ancient towns, Buda on the west bank of the Danube and the community of Pest on the east bank. Buda stands on a terraced plateau and contains relics of a Turkish occupation; Pest rises from a plain and is the site of the Houses of Parliament, the Palace of Justice, the Museum of Fine Arts, and the National Museum. Buda and Pest are linked by eight bridges over the Danube, including one of the largest suspension bridges in Europe.

Termed "The pearl of the Danube," the city's origins date back to about 10 B.C. when the Romans established the colony of Aquincum on what is now Buda. The Vandals took it over from the Romans in A.D. 376 and, in turn, management changed hands frequently during invasions by the Tartars and the Turks until armies under Austrian leadership liberated what was left of the towns in 1686. Some Roman ruins withstood the assaults and may be seen even today.

Present-day Hungarians descended from the Magyars, a nomadic, horse-riding people who conquered the land in the ninth century. The Magyars spoke a language unlike any other language of Europe, except Finnish, and even today other Europeans have difficulty understanding it. English, however, is spoken by many Hungarians, so you should not encounter language problems, particularly in hotels and restaurants.

A bit of Hungarian modern history would be good to keep in mind during your visit. During World War II, the Hungarian government sided with the Axis powers. In April 1945 the country fell to Russian troops. Encouraged by the Polish defiance of the Soviet Union, Hungarians staged a revolt in 1956 that was quickly suppressed by Soviet troops and tanks. Hungary was under the Soviet aegis until 1989, when the Soviet troops left the country. The Hungarian People's Republic became the Republic of Hungary with a newly elected democratic government—a coalition of six parties.

The paradox of the growing interface of Hungary with Western democracies is evident. In Budapest, people are lining up in front of McDonald's, and Western tourists are everywhere. Hungarians are wonderful hosts, so enjoy them and keep your thoughts and attention on lighthearted affairs rather than the more weighty ones of state. 'Nuff said?

Day Excursions

Two combination day excursions have been selected for your Hungarian explorations once you have broken the spell that Budapest can cast. The first combination involves Balaton and Siofok, resort towns along the shores of Lake Balaton, a large, long lake lying to the southwest of Budapest. The second set takes you south through Hungary's great plain to the historic cities of Kecskemet and Szeged.

Arriving and Departing

By Air: Budapest's international airport, Ferihegy, consists of two terminals, about four kilometers from each other, and is nine miles (fourteen kilometers) southeast of the city. There is no rail transportation between the airport and the city. Airport minibus and taxi service are available. Time en route to the city's main bus station on Erzsébet (Elizabeth) Square is thirty minutes; the fare is 200 forints from either Terminal No. 1 or Terminal No. 2. The bus stop at the airport is located immediately to the right of the main exit. The airport taxi stand is further to the right, about 200 feet beyond the bus stop. Taxi service is available twenty-four hours a day. All taxis have meters. IBUSZ operates an information office at Terminal No. 1 at the airport. You will find it on your right as you approach the main exit. The office is open daily between 0800 and 2300. Customs control uses the red-green corridor system just like the western European countries. If you have nothing to declare, you should use the green corridor.

By Train: Vienna is the Eurailpass "gateway" to Hungary and its capital, Budapest. If you depart Vienna from the Westbahnhof (West Station), you'll arrive in Budapest at the Keleti (East) Station. When departing Vienna's Südbahnhof (South) Station, your train will terminate in Budapest at the Deli (South) Station except for the Avala Express, which arrives at the Keleti Station. The Wiener Walzer and the Orient Express trains leave Vienna from the Westbahnhof; the Lehar express departs from the Südbahnhof. The rail routes for all express trains is the same, except for the arrival and departure stations, so check with a rail information office in one of the western European countries as to the train best suited to your Hungarian travel plans. By the way, the Orient Express is not the plush, expensive one. It's the regular train that operates year-round between Paris and Budapest.

To put the rail terminal complexes of Budapest and Vienna into a different perspective, obtain a copy of the Thomas Cook Rail Map of Europe. Panel No. 30 on the map depicts the rail facilities of Budapest while panel No. 12 provides the details of the trackage in Vienna. Panel No. 30 outlines the entire territory between the two cities and makes an excellent travel reference for your rail adventure.

The Railway Stations

Keleti (East) Station, originally constructed in 1884, has undergone extensive improvements and restoration during the past few years. The old charm, however, is still evident. Statues of George Stephenson, the inventor of the locomotive, and James Watt, creator of the steam engine, grace its entrance. The modern touch is found in the digital departure boards displayed at the platform entrances.

Stairs at the front of the station take you to the city's Metro, a modern two-line subway system, but arrivals burdened with luggage should opt for the taxi queue immediately outside the station on the right. A word of caution: Be sure that the taxi you hail has a meter—and uses it.

Keleti Station has available all of the usual tourist services, including IBUSZ Travel. However, we recommend that you wait and either visit an IBUSZ office in your hotel or the main service center in mid-city at Ferenciek tére 10 (telephone 118–6866). IBUSZ operates offices in all three Budapest rail stations, but we have found them to be crammed to capacity on every occasion. The main center caters more to Western visitors and offers full facilities, including hotel and rail reservations, currency exchange, and tour programs. However, if you must use the Keleti IBUSZ facility, proceed to the sign FOREIGN RAILWAY TICKETS—SEAT RESERVATIONS on your right when exiting from the trains. Note that window 2 is for currency exchange, window 3 for hotels, and window 6 is where you request tickets and seat reservations. Pay for all services in cash (U.S. dollars, forints not accepted).

Deli (South), a modern concrete edifice located on the Buda side of the Danube, features a huge supermarket on the ground level. Trains arrive overhead on uncovered platforms that lead to a covered concourse, with an enclosed waiting room and ticket office just beyond. The designation of Deli as Budapest's "south" station is a bit confusing in that it actually lies to the west of the city; but you'll get used to it. A visit to the supermarket is a must. The products and produce selections offered may be fewer than those offered by even your local Seven-Eleven store, but it's a great place to pick up the local flavor and mix with the citizens.

The Metro line Z terminates at the Deli Station, with direct connections to the other two rail stations, Keleti and Nyugati. To access, follow the "M" pictographs leading from the train level; same for taxis.

Nyugati (West), gateway to the East European cities, stands at the head of Teréz Street just before Nyugati Square. Although Western visitors will probably have little need to utilize its facilities, the station has an IBUSZ office as well as the usual amenities found at Keleti and Deli.

Budapest station Nyugati (top), one of the city's three major rail stations, provides rail service to eastern Germany, Czechoslovakia, Romania, and Bulgaria. The station was constructed by George Eiffel, the designer of the Eiffel Tower in Paris. Train arrives in **Budapest's Deli Station** (below). The Keleti Station (not shown) has direct rail service between Moscow and Western Europe.

Tourist Facilities

The central office of the IBUSZ Hungarian Travel Company offers a complete selection of services for visitors, including money exchange, hotel reservations, travel reservations (including rail and air), tour bookings, and general tourist information. On your first visit, it's best to get to the central office by taxi. Just show the taxi driver the name and address appearing on page 177, or ask your hotel concierge to write it on a separate piece of paper. Once you have located the office and have one of their maps in hand, you'll be able to make subsequent visits just like a local citizen.

The IBUSZ central office is open Monday through Friday from 0800 to 1630; Saturday between 0800 and 1200; and is closed on Sunday. In addition, IBUSZ has branch offices in many Budapest hotels, including the Astoria, Aquincum, Atrium Hyatt, Budapest, Marriott, Erzsébet, Flamenco, Helia, Hilton, Hungaria, Korona, Novotel, Penta, Stadion, Taverna, Thermal Hotel Margitsziget, and Volga. Inquire at the hotel desk for operating hours and the extent of the services offered.

When the IBUSZ office provides you with a city map and other information, ask them to suggest where to stay, what to eat or drink, where to eat or drink it, where to go for entertainment, and what to buy. In the interest of promoting Hungarian foods, IBUSZ can make suggestions for restaurants and pastry shops to visit. Perhaps they can even tell you where to find recipes for those famous Hungarian dishes.

If you are interested in organized tours, the IBUSZ offers quite a selection of sightseeing and tour activities. The "City Tour" is a three-hour sightseeing adventure by bus to Budapest's famous spots, including Castle Hill for a panoramic view. You may also take a two-hour sightseeing cruise on the Danube.

For a night on the town, you have the option of a Goulash Party with wine and a show, or you can pull out all the stops with the "Budapest By Night" tour, which offers dinner, a floor show, dancing, and wine tasting accompanied by Gypsy music. If you can work it in, the full-day Danube Bend bus tour on the right bank of the Danube to the towns of Esztergom, Visegrad, and Szentendre is well worth it. The area is not accessible by train, and the vistas along the river are captivating.

FROM BUDAPEST

A Day Excursion to Balaton

DEPART FROM BUDAPEST	TRAIN NUMBER	ARRIVE IN BALATON	NOTES
0700(5)	862	0948	(1)(3)
0715(5)	8512	1040	(1)(3)
1015(6)	202	1324	(1)(3)

DEPART FROM BALATON	TRAIN NUMBER	ARRIVE IN BUDAPEST	NOTES
1458	863	1748(5)	(1)(3)
1649	203	1953(6)	(1)
1843	8601	2153(5)	(1)(3)

Distance: 112 miles/180 km
Reference: Thomas Cook Table 891

A Day Excursion to Kecskemet

DEPART FROM BUDAPEST	TRAIN NUMBER	ARRIVE IN KECSKEMET	NOTES
0700(4)	700	0813	(1)(2)(3)
1030(4)	712	1143	(1)(2)(3)

DEPART FROM KECSKEMET	TRAIN NUMBER	ARRIVE IN BUDAPEST	NOTES
1642	713	1805(4)	(1)(3)
1921	7001	2046(4)	(1)(3)

Distance: 66 miles/106 km
Reference: Thomas Cook Table 895

A Day Excursion to Siofok

DEPART FROM BUDAPEST	TRAIN NUMBER	ARRIVE IN SIOFOK	NOTES
0700(5)	862	0841	(1)(3)
0715(5)	8512	0915	(1)(3)
1015(6)	202	1209	(1)(3)

DEPART FROM SIOFOK	TRAIN NUMBER	ARRIVE IN BUDAPEST	NOTES
1608	863	1748(5)	(1)(3)
1804	203	1953(6)	(1)(3)
2012	8601	2153(5)	(1)
2120	8243	2258(6)	(1)(3)

Distance: 72 miles/115 km
Reference: Thomas Cook Table 893

A Day Excursion to Szeged

DEPART FROM BUDAPEST	TRAIN NUMBER	ARRIVE IN SZEGED	NOTES
0700(4)	IC 700	0910	(1)(2)(3)
0705(4)	710	0935	(1)(3)
1030(4)	IC 702	1240	(1)(2)(3)

DEPART FROM SZEGED	TRAIN NUMBER	ARRIVE IN BUDAPEST	NOTES
1530	713	1805(4)	(1)(3)
1650	IC 703	1900(4)	(1)(2)(3)
1810	7001	2046(4)	(1)(3)

Distance: 119 miles (191 km)
Reference: Thomas Cook Table 895

Notes for Balaton, Kecskemet, Siofok, and Szeged
(1) Daily, including holidays   (4) Nyugati (West) Station
(2) Reservations obligatory   (5) Deli (South) Station
(3) Food service available   (6) Keleti (East) Station

From Budapest . . .TRAIN CONNECTIONS TO OTHER BASE CITIES

TO:	DEPART	ARRIVE	TRAIN NUMBER	COOK'S TABLE	NOTES
Munich	1225(3)	2036	EC 62	61	(1)(2)
Paris	1530(3)	0930+1(7)	262	32	(1)(2)
Rome	1530(3)	0930+1	262/235	88	(1)(2)(8)
Vienna	0555(3)	0920(5)	346	890	(1)(2)
	0820(3)	1146(5)	EC 24	890	(1)(2)
	1225(3)	1550(5)	EC 62	890	(1)(2)
	1530(3)	1900(5)	262	890	(1)(2)
	1725(3)	2050(5)	466	890	(1)(2)
	1830(3)	2145(6)	344	890	(1)(2)

(1) Daily, including holidays   (5) Vienna Westbahnhof Station
(2) Food service available   (6) Vienna Südbahnhof Station
(3) Keleti (East) Station   (7) Paris Est (East) Station
(4) Deli (South) Station   (8) Transfer from Vienna Westbahnhof to Südbahnhof

The little mermaid of Copenhagen keeps watch on the city's harbor. The statue has become famous as the symbol of Denmark's capital.

10 COPENHAGEN

Danes are a fun-loving people, and their sparkling humor is unsurpassed. For example, Victor Borge, one of Denmark's leading exponents of such jocularity, explains that his ultra-expensive, concert grand piano is "every bit as good as a Rolls-Royce, except," quips Victor, "it has smaller wheels." This is typical Danish humor, and this fairy-tale land of Denmark abounds in it. No doubt you will find the Danes to be the most happy and humorous of all Europeans. Why are the Danes that way? One of our Danish friends explains it in this manner: "For centuries, we Danes were the most feared of the Vikings, destroying and plundering at will. Now, we've got that all out of our system and have nothing left to do except to be happy!" This happy attitude exists not only in Copenhagen but throughout the country.

Legend has it that the ancient Vikings, fierce as they were, never missed the chance to throw a party whenever the opportunity presented itself. It would appear that their descendants are just as enthusiastic when it comes to having a good time. In summer, there are festivals throughout Denmark where eating, drinking, singing, and dancing are the orders of the day. In winter, the Danes go inside for their celebrations, where eating, drinking, singing, and dancing are the orders of the day. Oddly enough, this never seems to be monotonous to the Danes—or their visitors.

Day Excursions

Five delightful day excursions await whenever you can break away from the charm that is distinctly Copenhagen's. Admittedly, this is a difficult thing to do because the Danish capital has so much to offer, what with its Tivoli Gardens, Circus, and pedestrian-only shopping streets; but leave it you must. The entire country is a fairyland. Go out and enjoy it. Get to know *all* of Denmark. The day excursions will introduce you.

Jutland is the Danish mainland, the tip of the European continent that reaches northward toward the Scandinavian peninsula. Aarhus is Jutland's cultural center and Denmark's second largest city. Fans of William Shakespeare will, no doubt, make Helsingør (Elsinore) their prime day-excursion choice. Castle buffs will head for Hillerod and its gracious Frederiksborg Castle. Odense, birthplace of Hans Christian Andersen, will delight day excursioners of all ages. Roskilde is loaded with Danish folklore and history, including a Viking-ship museum and Denmark's most important medieval building, the Roskilde Cathedral, for centuries the final resting place of Denmark's royalty.

Arriving and Departing

By Air. Copenhagen's Kastrup Airport is six miles (ten kilometers) southeast of the city. There is no train transportation between the two points, but frequent airport-coach, public-bus, and taxi service are available. The coach ride to the downtown SAS terminal (located at the main railway station) costs 28 kroner. For only 12 kroner, public bus No. 32, 32H, or 63E will take you from the airport to the Town Hall Square, near Tivoli Gardens, and to the railway station, where your ticket still entitles you to transfer to any other bus within one hour from the time of purchase. Taxi service has a minimum charge of 7.15 kroner per kilometer plus a 12-kroner "start" charge. The airport has money-exchange facilities, and you may obtain hotel reservations at the service department, which is located in the airport's arrival hall. The airport operates a tax-free shop, but only departing or in-transit passengers are permitted to use it. Remodeled in 1987, the shopping area is one of the largest and most modern in Europe. As at most other airport "tax-free" operations, however, there are very few real bargains, except on liquor or tobacco.

By Train. Copenhagen has four major railway stations, but, unlike the situation in Paris, only the central station, Kobenhavn Hovedbanegaard, is of concern to Eurailpass travelers. Signs in and approaching the station are marked KOBENHAVN H. Through-passengers to the Swedish ferry port of Helsingborg (via Helsingør north of Copenhagen) need only assure that they are in a coach properly marked for the crossing. Frequently (such as is the case at Helsingør), seven or eight coaches arrive at the ferry dock, but only three or four are loaded for the trip—the other coaches having completed their part of the journey. Check before boarding the train and also advise the conductor of your destination. If you do miss the connection and get stranded, the ferry service is very frequent.

For hydrofoil service between Copenhagen and Malmo, check with the train information office. Connections may be made either by public bus from the central station to the hydrofoil pier or by taxi directly from your hotel. If you are burdened with luggage, it goes without saying that the taxi would be the service to use.

For rail service between Oslo or Stockholm and Copenhagen, it's a tossup between using the hydrofoil or taking the ferry crossing between Helsingborg (Sweden) to Helsingør (Denmark). The hydrofoil route is about one hour faster—aside from the time spent getting from the station to the pier. Check Cook's Tables 465 and 466 for details. We prefer the ferry. You don't have to change conveyances, Eurailpass is accepted, and tax-free shopping is on board, not the case with the hydrofoil routing.

Copenhagen's Station—Kobenhavn H.

The abbreviation of Hovedbanegaard (Central Station), an "H," reflects the efficiency of this huge train complex right in the heart of the city. All tracks run below street level, and the architecture of the station blends well with the locale. Kobenhavn H. is suggestive of a great Viking hall with two great wooden archways that span its enclosed area. The axis of these arches runs east and west, with baggage and storage facilities in the center. Thus divided, the two passenger areas are separated physically and also in function: The south bay serves arriving passengers; the north bay is for those departing.

The station is served by twelve tracks joined by six exits as you ascend from train level to the station's arrival area. *For your orientation, upon arrival you will exit in a northerly direction.* The Tivoli Gardens flank the station's east side, and a huge square fronts the station to the north. The arrival hall serves mainly for baggage handling. Lockers are available in numerous sizes and require 3-6 Danish kroner to operate. The lost-and-found office and the politi (police station) are alongside tracks 11 and 12.

Most services are located in the north departure area. Here you will find the SAS coach terminal, a cafeteria, and an excellent restaurant in the northwest corner. Taxi service is available at both the north and the east exit. City bus lines also serve the station, but inquire at the train information office before using one. Train arrival-and-departure information is displayed in bulletin form at both the arrival exits and the east and west entrances. Modern, airport-style digital displays give train-departure information automatically at each departure gate and on the train platforms. Elevator service, as well as stairways, is available between the station and the train platforms. If you are using a baggage cart, be certain to use the elevators to move your baggage between the two levels. The carts cannot negotiate the stairs. We've noted some disastrous results when it's been attempted.

Money exchange is available in two locations—one in the arrival hall and another in the departure hall. Arriving, you will find the office on the left of the exit for tracks 1 and 2. The sign reads DEN DANSKE BANK. The hours of operation are 0700–2200 daily. On the departure side of the station, a similar banking facility will be found opposite the gate for tracks 9 and 10. Operating hours for money exchange are 0900–2200. With the traveler's-checks war being waged, ask if there are supplemental charges before cashing them.

Hotel reservations can be made through the Copenhagen Tourist Association, which operates "Room Service" in the central railway station. It is identified by a sign, KIOSK P., located between the post office and the police station. The Room Service personnel do an excellent job and are authorized to

Danish youngsters go motoring in the Tivoli Gardens, stellar attraction in Copenhagen for "children of all ages."

accept advance payments on behalf of the hotels to ensure reservations. Operating hours are seasonal: May 1 through September 15, 0900–2400 daily; September 16–30, 0900–2200 daily; October and April, 0900–1700 Monday through Saturday; November through March, 0900–1700 Monday through Friday and 0900–1200 on Saturday.

Tourist information can be obtained at 22 Hans Christian Andersen Boulevard (telephone 01–111325); this building faces the impressive town hall. To reach the tourist office on foot, exit the central station and walk around the front of the Tivoli Gardens on Vesterbrogade to where it intersects with Hans Christian Andersen Boulevard. Turn right at this point. The office will be on your right and readily identifiable by the familiar "i" sign. This is a well-equipped tourist information center, and you can get interesting brochures and pamphlets on just about every tourist attraction in Denmark from the multilingual attendants. During May, June, and September, the office is open 0900–1800 Monday through Saturday and 0900–1300 on Sunday; during July and August, 0800–2000 Monday through Saturday and 0800–1300 on Sunday; from October through April, 0900–1700 Monday through Friday and 0900–1200 on Saturday.

Train information is available at three windows located between the entrances to tracks 3/4 and 5/6 on the departure (north) side of the station. This office is for train information only, so your inquiries should be limited accordingly. One or more of the windows is open daily throughout the year between 0700 and 2300. Train information bulletins are displayed at this location. Departures are printed on yellow paper, and arrivals are on white. During the times that international trains are arriving or departing, Danish State Railways personnel wearing "Information" hats will be seen in the station. They speak English and are eager to assist you.

Train reservations can be made through the large reservations office on the north side of the station, just opposite the departure gates for tracks 1/2 and 3/4. Inside the office, any attendant can assist you in your needs for seat and berth reservations. The operating hours for these services are 0800–2100 daily.

Eurailpass validation is available, in the same office where international tickets are purchased, 0630–2400 daily.

An Inter-Rail Center is located in the middle section of the south side of the station between tracks 2 and 4. You can enter the center with a Eurailpass or a ScanRail Pass. You can pick up information on what's going on in the *Copenhagen This Week* brochure, and the center personnel can help with reservations for inexpensive places to stay. For a few kroner, you can even take a shower.

Copenhagen Condensed

Tivoli Gardens is open from May through mid-September. It's not the world's largest amusement park, but in our opinion, it is the world's greatest. It has been in business since 1843. Each year, people come from all over the world to enjoy its very special blend of attractions old and new. Tree-lined walks, resplendent with flowers, and sparkling illuminations form the backdrop to its theaters and open-air amusement areas. Four evenings each week, the park closes with a giant display of fireworks.

During its day of entertainment for young and old alike, international artists appear at the Tivoli Concert Hall, Gilbert & Sullivan scenarios are acted out at the Pantomime Theater, and the Tivoli Boys Guard parades frequently to the delight of all. There's also an impressive assembly of quality rides to thrill you, games to play, and seven great restaurants to select from when you get hunger pangs. Tivoli cannot be described adequately in words; it must be experienced.

Want more? Tour the city's world-famous breweries, Carlsberg and Tuborg. Get details from the tourist office. Yes, they provide samples of their products. The circus is in session May to October just opposite Tivoli Gardens. Carefully restored, Cirkusbygningen is home to the only permanent circus in Scandinavia. Off-season, it serves as a hall for concerts, musicals, and ballet.

Denmark has a hefty 25 percent Value Added Tax (VAT). It may be avoided in two different ways. Have your purchases sent home. This way, you pay only the purchase price of the item plus shipping and insurance. Second plan, take the goods home yourself by paying the VAT; save your purchase slips and get the VAT refunded at the Copenhagen Kastrup Airport tax-free shop. In that case, plan to arrive at the airport an hour ahead of your regular reporting time.

Shopping? Copenhagen can accommodate you. Most shops are open Monday through Thursday, 1000–1730 or 1800; Friday, 1000–1900 or 2000; and Saturday, 1000–1300 or 1400. You'll learn quickly about Stroget (pronounced "stroy-it"). It's not one but actually five different shopping areas, each designated pedestrian-only and lined with shops that might make you want to hide your credit cards. All the well-known Danish specialties are in profusion here. Cafés and restaurants are interspersed throughout Stroget, so you can get anything from a hot dog to a five-course banquet. Please, don't go home before you have tried the Danish waffle–ice cream combination.

Year-round, visit *Den Lille Havfrue* (The Little Mermaid), symbol of today's Copenhagen. We have yet to see a more beautiful, soul-touching statue anywhere in the world—and we've been around it twice. The city is loaded with pretty girls. By the way, fellows, girl watching is absolutely free of charge in Copenhagen—but don't touch.

TRAIN CONNECTIONS TO OTHER BASE CITIES

TO:	DEPART	ARRIVE	TRAIN NUMBER	COOK'S TABLE	NOTES
Amsterdam	2105	0954+1	232/EC 140	22	(4)
	2205	0952+1	1236	22	(1)(5)
Berlin (Lich.)	0720	1507	305	51	
	1241	2107	1107	51	(6)
	2230	0704+1	309	51	
Berne	1905	1212+1	483/EC 101	50/280	(2)
Brussels (Midi)	2105	1055+1	232	21	
Hamburg	0920	1429	EC 187	50	
	1230	1722	EC 185	50	
Munich	0730	1838	EC 189/ICE 589	50	(3)
	1905	0921+1	483	50	
Oslo	0945	1937	IN 384	466	
	1235	2216	IN 392/ICE 94	466	(7)
	2145	0737+1	382	466	(8)
Paris	2005	1126+1	1232	25	(9)
Stockholm	1115	1929	IN 286	465	
	2315	0747+1	292	465	
Vienna (Westbf.)	1520	0830+1	EC 183/EN 491	50/64	(3)

Daily departures unless otherwise noted. Make reservations for all departures.

(1) Couchettes only
(2) Transfer in Basel
(3) Transfer in Hamburg
(4) Transfer in Duisburg, Germany
(5) June 16 through September 10
(6) June 24 through August 21
(7) Transfer in Gothenburg (Göteburg)
(8) May 29 through August 28
(9) June 17 through September 11

The Old Town of Aarhus, open throughout the year, features more than seventy half-timbered houses transplanted from every region of Denmark. The Mansard Warehouse (above) is nearly four hundred years old. Moved to Old Town in 1926, it houses special exhibitions of Denmark's history. The Tannery (below), constructed in 1650, was moved to its present site in 1947. (Photos courtesy Aarhus Turistourean.)

A DAY EXCURSION TO AARHUS
TRAIN AND FERRY DISTANCE: 139 miles (223 km)
AVERAGE TRAVEL TIME: 4 hours, 30 minutes

People have lived in Aarhus ever since the Vikings settled at the mouth of the river, where it meets the bay. There the Norsemen constructed a harbor, built houses, and erected a church. During the 1960s, contractors excavating under a bank in Aarhus came upon the remains of a semicircular rampart that the Vikings of a thousand years ago used to protect their small community. Today, the site is a museum, where you can see the reconstructed ramparts with a typical house of that time, together with tools and other belongings used by the first inhabitants of Aarhus. This museum, and an outdoor collection of more than sixty half-timbered houses known as the "Old Town," are "musts" during your visit. Between the two, you will be able to range through Danish history from the Vikings to the era of Hans Christian Andersen.

Aarhus has many other worthwhile attractions. It's Denmark's second largest city and Jutland's uncontested cultural center. Being one of the country's oldest cities makes it all the more interesting, but one of the special features of this day excursion enhances it to a point where a visit to Aarhus becomes a must. The feature referred to is the delightful ferryboat ride from Zealand to East Jutland.

It isn't imperative that you take the 0658 train out of Copenhagen, but the earlier departure will give you many more options of travel routes and sightseeing opportunities than the later departure at 1015. The early train reaches the Kalundborg ferry pier at 0836, in time for you to transfer to the ferryboat for its 0910 departure. This involves a short walk up an overhead ramp to the ferry dock. The train coaches are not conveyed onto the ferry, so don't wait aboard the train at the pier or you'll end up back in Copenhagen on the same train on the same day without ever seeing Aarhus.

Between Kalundborg and Aarhus, the ferry sails the Kattegat and rounds the island of Samso. The trip takes three hours; but there's plenty of scenery, and the ship has a pleasant cafeteria with an ample supply of smorgasbord and beer aboard. Time goes quickly, and you will probably meet some Aarhus residents, who are always eager to tell you about their city. You can return to Copenhagen via this same route, but we recommend the "great circle" tour, which includes stops at the cities of Fredericia and Odense and a trip aboard the Nyborg-Korsor ferry (see Cook's Table 450). You can stop in both Aarhus and Odense on this trip, but it makes for a long day and is not recommended.

Arriving in Aarhus, disembark and follow the signs to the main rail station,

AARHUS—*JUTLAND'S CULTURAL CENTER*

A Day Excursion from Copenhagen

DEPART FROM COPENHAGEN STATION	ARRIVE IN AARHUS STATION	NOTES
0638	0955	(5)(6)
0658	1220	(2)(4)
1015	1520	(1)(2)
1050	1355	Sunday only
1250	1555	(4)

Via catamaran or ferry crossing Kalundborg–Aarhus
Transfer to catamaran/ferry at Kalundborg.

DEPART FROM AARHUS VIA ODENSE	TRAIN NUMBER	ARRIVE IN COPENHAGEN STATION	NOTES
1526	IC 152	1948	(1)(3)
1626	IC 156	2048	(1)(3)
1726	IC 160	2148	(1)(3)
1826	IC 164	2248	(1)(3)

Via Odense and Nyborg–Korsor ferry
Stay aboard train at Nyborg.

DEPART FROM AARHUS STATION	ARRIVE IN COPENHAGEN STATION	NOTES
1640	1942	(6)

Via catamaran crossing Aarhus–Kalundborg
Transfer to train IC 552 at Kalundborg.

(1) Daily, including holidays
(2) Via ferry crossing Kalundborg–Aarhus
(3) Via ferry crossing Nyborg–Korsor (circuitous route)
(4) Monday through Saturday
(5) Via catamaran crossing Kalundborg-Aarhus
(6) Monday through Friday

Distance: 139 miles/223 km
References: Thomas Cook Tables 450 and 451

where you mount stairs leading to the station's main concourse. Lift (elevator) service is available should you or a member of your party require it. After turning left, walk to the end of the corridor. The train-information office is to the left at the end of the corridor. It is open daily from 0800 to 1900. A small "Supermarket" is also in the station. It's a good place to replenish your personal larder if the ferry trip took its toll. It's open from 0800 to midnight.

City maps and other information may be obtained at the city tourist office located in the town hall. To reach it, exit the station and cross the street. Turn left, proceed to the first traffic light, and cross the street to the SAS building. From this point, you will see the town hall close by on the left. The tourist office has its entrance at the fountain, telephone (86) 121600. From mid-June to mid-August, it is open 0900–2000 daily; mid-August to mid-September, 0900–1900 daily; September 16 through mid-June, 0930–1630 weekdays and 1000–1300 on Saturday. A money-exchange service is available in the tourist office when banks are closed.

The "Old Town" in Aarhus is a part of the city's botanical gardens that has been transformed into a Danish market town typical of the seventeenth century. Its half-timbered houses have been transferred there from every region of the country to re-create an entire landscape complete with narrow streets, shops, public squares—even a millrace. Be certain to visit it. Check with the tourist office for the seasonal hours of operation. To reach it, follow the city map for a ten-minute walk or take the No. 3 bus.

Admission to the Viking Museum is free. It's a scant three blocks from the tourist information office. You may want to visit other attractions, however, by taking the bus. The small investment of 45 kroner buys a tourist ticket that is valid for an unlimited number of bus rides for twenty-four hours. With it, you may participate in a two-and-one-half-hour guided city-bus tour, which departs daily from the tourist office at 1000 from mid-June through August.

South of Aarhus you'll find the Prehistoric Museum at Moesgaard, one of Denmark's top attractions. The museum contains collections from the Stone Age, the Bronze Age, the Iron Age, and the Viking period. To get there, take bus No. 6 from the railway station and use the tourist bus ticket. The museum, open daily from 1000 to 1700 in the summer, is closed on Mondays during winter.

Guardians of the straits, the cannon of Kronborg Castle were the "enforcers" of Helsingør's collection of "sound dues."

From Copenhagen . . .

A DAY EXCURSION TO HELSINGØR
DISTANCE BY TRAIN: 26 miles (44 km)
AVERAGE TRAIN TIME: 45 minutes

It's the lure of Shakespeare's Hamlet that usually brings visitors to Helsingør (Elsinore). The town has many other attractions, however, not the least of which is the world's biggest and best ice cream cone. Read on, MacBeth!

Local train service between Copenhagen and the town of Helsingør (sometimes referred to by its older name, "Elsingore" or "Elsinore") runs every half-hour throughout the day and is interspersed with frequent express train service. We urge you to plan an early arrival in Helsingør.

The Helsingør railway station is the terminus for the train ferries that ply between Denmark and the town of Helsingborg in Sweden. The distance across the sound between the two countries is less than three miles. This is the reason why Helsingør was founded there and also the reason why it flourished from 1426 through 1857 by the collection of the "sound dues" from all merchant ships that passed.

If you are interested in maritime ferry operations, Helsingør is the place to observe it. More than sixteen ferries and passenger boats utilize this port. Arrivals and departures take place almost endlessly throughout the day and into the night. You will probably note upon arrival in the Helsingør station that rail cars are being loaded or unloaded from the tracks immediately on your right. When you emerge from the station, you will see that this operation also includes passenger cars, trucks, and foot passengers.

This active port averages seventeen million passengers a year. In addition, it carries approximately one million passenger cars across the straits, along with 200,000 railway cars, 150,000 trucks, and 15,000 tour buses—packed with tired, confused bus-tour people who think every day must be Tuesday because, to them, every country looks like Belgium.

For details regarding the "sound dues," Hamlet, the Kronborg Castle, walking tours—and the ice cream cones—call the Helsingør tourist office, which is conveniently located just across the street on the left side of the station at Havnepladsen 3, telephone (49) 211333. Look for the TURIST AGENCY sign at the end of tracks 1 and 2 if more explicit directions are needed. Words of caution—obey the traffic signals when crossing to the tourist office, and use the designated walkway. A local, private railroad uses the street as a siding, and it could be hazardous to your health. From June through August, the tourist office is open 0930–1900 Monday through Friday; 1000–1800 Saturday. During the rest of the year, hours are 0930–1700 Monday through Friday and 0900–1300 on Saturday.

HELSINGØR—*HAMLET'S HIDEAWAY*

A Day Excursion from Copenhagen

From Copenhagen to Helsingør:
Trains depart daily every thirty minutes at 25 and 55 minutes past the hour from 0625 through 2325. Check with the train-information office in the Kobenhavn (H) Terminal.

From Helsingør to Copenhagen:
Trains depart daily every thirty minutes at 14 and 44 minutes past the hour from 0614 through 2344. Check with the train-information office in the Helsingør train station.

Ferries Between Helsingør, Denmark, and Helsingborg, Sweden:
Most Copenhagen-Helsingør trains connect with ferries to Sweden. Eurailpass is accepted for passage. Ferries connecting at Helsingør for Copenhagen depart Helsingborg about forty-five minutes earlier, at 1030, and fifty minutes past each hour. If desired, you may combine a day excursion to Helsingør, Denmark, with a round trip to Helsingborg, Sweden.

Distance: 26 miles/44 km
Reference: Thomas Cook Table 463

The tourist office is well equipped with information about the town of Helsingør and many other places of interest throughout Denmark as well. The office is housed in a building erected in 1890. There are many other buildings in town of more ancient vintage. For example, nearby No. 27 Strandgade is the oldest half-timbered house in town. It was built in 1577. Other structures date back to the fifteenth century. The tourist office has published a bulletin titled "Take a Walk in the Old Town Elsinore." (The modern town is spelled "Elsinore" in English, "Helsingør" in Danish.)

Another of the tourist office's publications is *Helsingør-Hamlet's Town.* It describes, in great detail, Kronborg Castle, the churches of Saint Olai and Saint Mary, and the Carmelite monastery. These highlights of Helsingør are all close at hand for your inspection.

1985 marked the 400th anniversary of Kronborg Castle, the city's most famous landmark. It was built by Christian IV between 1574 and 1582. With this formidable fortress came the rapid development of the town under its protective shelter. For several centuries, Helsingør was the second largest city in Denmark. The castle is open May through September from 1030 to 1700. During April and October, hours are 1100–1600; November through March, 1100–1500. (It is closed on Mondays.)

Hamlet's residency in the castle was imaginary, but the play was performed there from 1916 until 1954, when performances were curtailed for financial reasons. It was again performed in 1979, but there are no definite plans for the future. In the castle the King's Chamber, the Queen's Chamber, and the Great Hall must be seen to appreciate the once-great splendor of this fortress. Cannon still stand along the seawall, but they are fired only on festive occasions.

While admiring the Great Hall, you'll probably note that there are no fireplaces or other heating devices in evidence. Apparently, they were overlooked by the royal architect. This created no problem for the royal occupants, however, when they wanted to lay on a royal mid-winter bash; they merely marched the several thousand men of the royal guard into the area and the troops' body heat sent the mercury soaring—along with a few other atmospheric additives, no doubt.

Helsingør is one of Denmark's oldest populated places. Documents dating back to 1231 record its development. In the vaults under Kronborg Castle, there is a statue of Holger Danske, a Viking chieftain, who voyaged to the Holy Land as a crusader about A.D. 800.

While in Helsingør, make certain that a part of your tour includes a stop at the Raadhus (town hall). In its council chamber, you can see a stained-glass window that depicts the history of the town. Outside of the town hall you will see a narrow street (Brostraede) leading to the sea. Follow it. The ice cream shop is located there.

Frederiksborg Castle, viewed across the lake from the town square in Hillerod, has a picture-book quality that attracts visitors from all points of the world. The town square bustles with activity during market days on Thursday, Saturday, and (occasionally) Monday.

From Copenhagen . . .

A DAY EXCURSION TO HILLEROD
DISTANCE BY TRAIN: 19 miles (30 km)
AVERAGE TRAIN TIME: 40 minutes

Hillerod can become the crowning touch to your visit to Denmark. The town has an atmosphere distinctly its own. A picture-book lake rests in the town's center, faced on one side by the old town and its market square and on another by the majestic Frederiksborg Castle. Words fall far short of the actual experience that comes from visiting Hillerod and its Frederiksborg Castle, for there are few places in the world where nature and culture blend together so perfectly.

The castle actually spans three islands. The first of its structures erected by Frederik II in 1560, occupied the largest island. The balance of this imposing castle complex was built by Christian IV between 1600 and 1620. Until 1840, Frederiksborg Castle served as the coronation church for succeeding Danish monarchs.

In 1859, a disastrous fire destroyed the interior of the main building, and irreplaceable treasures were lost forever. The chapel and all of its valuable contents, however, remained relatively undamaged. Among those items was the celebrated chapel organ built by Esaias Compenius in 1610. The chapel organist plays the organ every Thursday between 1330 and 1400. During the summer, hymns are played hourly on the castle carillon. The castle has been restored, at first by royal contributions and public donations and, more recently, by philanthropic support from J. C. Jacobsen, owner of the Carlsberg Brewery and the Carlsberg Foundation.

Train service between Copenhagen and Hillerod is fast and frequent. Trains depart Copenhagen daily at two, twenty-two, and forty-two minutes past the hour throughout the year. Additional trains are run on weekends and holidays. The train information office at either station can provide a local train schedule. The schedule is a good thing to have in your pocket during your day excursion in Hillerod, for we are certain that you will be consulting it for later train departures once the captivating beauty of Hillerod and the Frederiksborg Castle begin to unfold.

We suggest that you go immediately to the city's tourist office at Slotsgade 52 upon arrival in Hillerod. Turn left as you exit the station, then bear right at the first intersection. The street running downhill at that point ends at the market square by the lake. The tourist office is next to the castle on the right-hand side of the street. If you like, you can obtain a brochure in the railway station that contains a city map to help guide your way.

At the Hillerod tourist office, besides asking for brochures describing the town and castle, also ask for those suggesting rambles and bike tours. You can

HILLEROD—*PICTURE-BOOK SCENERY*

A Day Excursion from Copenhagen

DEPART FROM COPENHAGEN STATION	TRAIN NUMBER	ARRIVE IN HILLERROD STATION	NOTES
0814	Local	0853	(1)
0914	Local	0953	(1)
1014	Local	1053	(1)
1114	Local	1153	(1)

Additional hourly service at 34 and 54 minutes past the hour through 0034

DEPART FROM HILLEROD STATION	TRAIN NUMBER	ARRIVE IN COPENHAGEN STATION	NOTES
1508	Local	1617	(1)
1608	Local	1717	(1)
1708	Local	1817	(1)
1808	Local	1917	(1)

Additional hourly service at 08, 28, and 48 minutes past the hour through 0028

(1) Daily, including holidays

Distance: 19 miles/30 km
Reference: DSB Kobenhavn-Hillerod Timetable

rent a bike for the day (40 kroner) at the tourist office and enjoy Hillerod's scenic bike paths. The tourist-office hours are 0900–1800 Monday through Friday and Saturday, 0900–1700, from May through August, and 0900–1600 Monday through Friday and Saturday, 1000–1300, from September through April. The tourist office is closed on Sundays and holidays. Should you want to phone ahead to inquire regarding scheduled events, you may do so by dialing 42–26–28–52.

The shop-'til-you-drop group will enjoy Hillerod's newest shopping center, the "Slotsarkaderne," with more than forty-seven specialty shops. It, too, is conveniently located on Slotsgade. When coming from the railway station, the glass-covered Slotsarkaderne shopping mall is on the left-hand side of Slotsgade.

The Frederiksborg Castle (like Mount Everest) is there and cannot be denied. No doubt it will be the first stopping point on your tour of Hillerod. A tour boat plies between the castle and the marketplace from May through September at 1100 and 1700. It is really a delightful way of seeing both the city and the castle. The castle is now the home of the National Historical Museum of Frederiksborg, an independent section of the Carlsberg Foundation.

The museum is open daily from 1000 to 1600. The admission charge is 30 kroner for adults, 5 kroner for children. The museum houses the famous Compenius organ. There is an interesting open-air exhibit, known as the North Seeland Folk Museum, by a small pond in a corner of the Castle's gardens. It was originally built around 1790 as an exhibition site and now houses the pictures and objects of Hillerod's history.

The castle gardens were laid out in 1720 in the style of French baroque. In another section of the castle garden known as the *Indelukket,* you can inspect a charming little country house built in 1562 for the king to conduct informal entertainment.

There is a museum in the Provinsbanken (bank) at No. 16 Slotsgade on your way to the castle. It should attract coin collectors of all ages. It comprises a very fine collection of Danish and foreign coins as well as other means of payment used in ancient times. Illustrations tell the story of political, historical, and cultural aspects of money and coinage. The museum is open during banking hours. Just outside Hillerod, you may want to visit an exhibit of dolls in costumes. You can reach it on bus No. 736. The display features seventy dolls with handmade costumes that present the history of dress as well as the history of man. You'll see everything from Queen Victoria to the bustle that your great grandmother used to wear.

Market day in Hillerod is an event you won't want to miss. On Thursday and Saturday (occasionally on Monday) from 0900 to 1300, the market is alive with activity. Hillerod is also noted for its shops that display Danish art and handicraft items.

Hans Christian Andersen was born in this house in Odense on April 2, 1805. His fairy tales have made him and the City of Odense famous throughout the world. Odense is today the destination for thousands of tourists from all corners of the globe who come to see his home town. Many of Andersen's stories were set in or near Odense. Each summer, the Hans Christian Andersen Play is performed in the Funen Village open-air theater in Odense. (Photo courtesy Odense Tourist Association.)

From Copenhagen . . .

A DAY EXCURSION TO ODENSE
DISTANCE BY TRAIN AND FERRY: 103 miles (165 km)
AVERAGE TRAVEL TIME: 2 hours, 40 minutes

Hans Christian Andersen, Denmark's famous teller of fairy tales, was born in a tiny yellow house in Odense on 2 April 1805. One hundred years later, the city bought the house and turned it into a museum—probably the best investment that the city fathers ever made. Tourists of all ages still flock to this magic point to see what his early life was like and to wonder what developed the imagination that would captivate the entire world.

Many of Andersen's stories were set in or near Odense. Most of the locations can be seen today. The small, half-timbered house where he was born, now the nucleus of the Hans Christian Andersen Museum, is set in a cluster of other small houses from the same period. A visit there is like stepping back into the nineteenth century.

The house of Hans Christian Andersen is not the only attraction in Odense. There are at present seven museums in the city under the auspices of the municipal authorities. The city is Denmark's third largest. Industrial and vigorous in its life style, Odense has smart shops, spacious parks, and sparkling residential areas. Situated, as it is, in the center of Denmark's second largest island, the Isle of Funen, the city is the focal point for those wishing to explore the island's rolling countryside. Seekers of either urban or rural Denmark will find it here.

The German emperor Otto III officially mentioned Odense for the first time in a letter dated 18 March 988. Although there were people living there at the time and a church had been previously erected, the present-day residents of the city have taken the emperor's date as a benchmark and declared 1988 as the "1,000th Anniversary of Odense."

The train trip to Odense is an interesting one, with the train traversing the two largest islands of Denmark and crossing the sea between them on a modern train ferry (the coaches are actually loaded aboard the vessel). Passengers are free to go topside during the hour-long crossing to view the coastlines or to relax in the ship's lounge or restaurant. This particular part of the trip is a rewarding travel experience. Actual participation (as a passenger) in the loading and unloading of the train ferry is an excitement to be enjoyed by everyone. The efficiency of the loading and unloading operations and the punctuality of departures and arrivals never cease to amaze even the most seasoned traveler.

When you arrive in the Odense railway station, look for the train information booth located conveniently on the far left side of the main station hall. There you can obtain train information and a map of the city from the booth's

ODENSE—*HOME OF HANS CHRISTIAN ANDERSEN*

A Day Excursion from Copenhagen

DEPART FROM COPENHAGEN STATION	TRAIN NUMBER	ARRIVE IN ODENSE STATION	NOTES
0655	IC 121	0935	(1)(2)
0755	IC 125	1035	(1)(2)
0855	IC 129	1135	(1)(2)
0955	IC 133	1235	(1)(2)

Via ferry crossing Korsor–Nyborg
Stay aboard train at ferry dock.

DEPART FROM ODENSE STATION	TRAIN NUMBER	ARRIVE IN COPENHAGEN STATION	NOTES
1408	IC 140	1648	(1)(2)
1508	IC 144	1748	(1)(2)
1608	IC 148	1848	(1)(2)
1708	IC 152	1948	(1)(2)
1808	IC 156	2048	(1)(2)
1908	IC 160	2148	(1)(2)
2008	IC 164	2248	(1)(2)
2108	IC 168	2348	(1)(2)

Via ferry crossing Nyborg–Korsor
Stay aboard train at ferry dock.

(1) Daily, including holidays
(2) Seat reservations mandatory

Distance: 103 miles/165 km
Reference: Thomas Cook Table 450

attendants. The information booth is open Monday through Saturday, 0600–2100; and Sunday, 0700–2200. The Danish Railway Museum is just behind the station. It contains an interesting collection of trains. From May through September it is open 1000–1600 daily; October through April, it is open 1000–1300 on weekdays and on Sunday and holidays, 1000–1600.

The map you receive at the train information booth shows how to proceed to the main tourist information office, which is located in the Radhuset (the town hall), telephone 6612 7520. The map also shows the location of the birthplace of Hans Christian Andersen and the Open Air Museum in Funen Village. The tourist office and the Hans Christian Andersen house are quite close to each other—about a ten-minute walk from the railway station. From June 15 through August 31, the main tourist office operates 0900–1900 Monday through Saturday and 1100–1900 on Sunday. The rest of the year, the office is open 0900–1700 Monday through Friday and 1000–1300 on Saturday.

The Hans Christian Andersen house is open daily during April and May, 1000–1600. During June, July, and August, the daily hours are expanded to a 0900–1800 schedule. September brings a return to the 1000–1600 schedule, and the schedule for the rest of the year is 1000–1600 daily. The house is well worth a visit. The area surrounding Hans Christian Andersen's home, with its little colored houses and cobblestone streets, is very attractive.

If you are visiting the museum area at mealtime, we suggest that you eat in a charming little restaurant across the lane, Under the Linden Tree. It's but one of a score of excellent restaurants in Odense. The tourist information office has a handy pocket guide describing many of these eating establishments in the city. You'll find an interesting selection—including such names as Jensen's Boefhus and Den Grimme Ælling (Ugly Duckling).

A Hans Christian Andersen fairy tale is presented from mid-July through the first week in August at the Open Air Theater in Funen Village. The village is one of the largest open-air museums in Denmark, characterized by a coherent layout of landscape and a real village of seventeenth-century houses assembled from the Island of Funen and the surrounding islands. Here you will find farms with animals, a rectory, a school—even a brickyard and a forge. The theater seats 2,000 people.

Odense has a museum for every interest—from art to transportation. The Brands Klaedefabrik Art Gallery (European Museum of the Year, 1988), Danish Museum of Printing, Danish Press Museum, and the Museum of Photographic Art are all located in Brandts Passage. The Odense Adventure Pass will provide either free or reduced-price admission to Odense's many museums, sights, and the zoo. To reach the zoo, board one of Odense Aafart's covered cruise boats for a relaxing journey.

Viking ships undergo restoration in the maritime museum of Denmark's ancient capital, Roskilde.

From Copenhagen ...

A DAY EXCURSION TO ROSKILDE
DISTANCE BY TRAIN: 19 miles (31 km)
AVERAGE TRAIN TIME: 25 minutes

Since Roskilde is so close to Copenhagen, you might think that it would be so much like Denmark's capital city that a day excursion there would be pointless. On the contrary, Roskilde is as different from Copenhagen as night is from day. Known as the "Town of Viking Ships and Royal Tombs," Roskilde warrants a visit. In fact, it is difficult to see all that you might want to see in Roskilde in just one day.

Roskilde was Denmark's original capital, with a history dating back to the tenth century. Copenhagen began to gain prominence only about midway through the twelfth century, when Bishop Absalon realized that the harbor of Roskilde would allow only limited expansion, while Copenhagen's was of greater potential. The German city of Lübeck, also recognizing the new city's potential, attacked and burned Copenhagen twice (in 1249 and 1369). Consequently, Copenhagen is a relatively new city, while Roskilde is older in both grace and face.

We recommend at least three things to do during your day excursion: (1) visit the cathedral, (2) take a tour, and (3) visit the Viking Ship Museum. To organize your itinerary, check in with the tourist information office. It's a ten-minute walk from the railway station, or a taxi will get you there for about 45 kroner. If walking, exit the station and proceed downhill to a store marked S & E. Turn left at this point to the city square. The tourist office is only about 300 yards off the pedestrian street at Gullandsstraede 15, telephone (42) 352700. Office hours are 0900–1700 Monday through Friday and 0900–1300 on Saturday. During July and August the hours are extended to 1900 Monday through Friday, 0900–1700 on Saturday, and 1000–1400 on Sunday.

Roskilde's twin-spired, brick cathedral dominates the city's skyline. Its construction was begun in 1170 on the same site where King Harald Bluetooth erected a church in A.D. 960. Today it's considered Denmark's most important medieval building. It is an international attraction primarily because it has been the burial place of Danish royalty for centuries. Thirty-eight kings and queens of Denmark are buried there, representing the longest reign of family monarchy in the world.

The cathedral is one of Denmark's first brick buildings, and it is said that it has as many tales to tell as it has bricks in its walls. Originally, a limestone edifice was erected on the foundation of Harald Bluetooth's church, only to be torn down and replaced slowly by the present brick structure, which was completed in the year 1280.

ROSKILDE—*THE VIKING SHIP MUSEUM AND THE CATHEDRAL*

A Day Excursion from Copenhagen

DEPART FROM COPENHAGEN STATION	TRAIN NUMBER	ARRIVE IN ROSKILDE STATION	NOTES
0655	IC 121	0713	(1)(2)
0755	IC 125	0813	(1)(2)
0855	IC 129	0913	(1)(2)
0955	IC 133	1013	(1)(2)
1055	IC 137	1113	(1)(2)
	Plus other frequent service		

DEPART FROM ROSKILDE STATION	TRAIN NUMBER	ARRIVE IN COPENHAGEN STATION	NOTES
1426	IC 132	1448	(1)(2)
1526	IC 136	1548	(1)(2)
1626	IC 140	1648	(1)(2)
1726	IC 144	1748	(1)(2)
1826	IC 148	1848	(1)(2)
	Plus other frequent service		

(1) Daily, including holidays
(2) Seat reservations mandatory

Distance: 19 miles/31 km
Reference: Thomas Cook Table 450

SPECIAL ATTRACTIONS

Roskilde Festival—Greatest rock-and-jazz festival in northern Europe; last weekend in June.

Some less significant, but nevertheless interesting, features of the cathedral are its granite measuring column and a 500-year-old clock. The column was used to measure the height of royal visitors. The tallest, Peter the Great of Russia, checked in at six feet ten inches! The clock features Saint George and the dragon. Installed since about 1500, Saint George mounts his trusty horse each hour and attacks the dragon, which screams in pain before going off to dragon heaven to be refurbished for the next hour's performance.

The cathedral is open to visitors (except when services are being conducted) weekdays, April through September, 0900–1645, and October through March, 1000–1445. Sundays and holiday hours are 1230–1645 May through August and 1230–1445 September through April. Admission is 5 kroner.

If you visit Roskilde on a Wednesday or a Saturday morning, you will find the city's market in full operation. The market is unique in that it isn't limited to the sale of meats, poultry, fish, and produce—the usual bill of fare that you find throughout Europe. The market activities include a flea market operation that could rival the best American garage sale ever held. All of this activity takes place in the town square called "the Staendertorvet" fronting the Town Hall. You are not required to purchase anything at the market—but we bet that you will. Go and see for yourself.

The Viking Ship Museum is an interesting addition to Roskilde's many attractions. Five Viking ships, circa A.D. 1000 to 1050, are being restored piece by piece in this most modern of maritime museums on the banks of the Roskilde fjord. For centuries legend had it that a barrier at the fjord's narrowest point actually had a Viking vessel beneath it. The legend was only partially correct in that a cofferdam operation in 1962 revealed that not one but five such vessels had been sunk there to protect Roskilde's harbor from enemy fleets.

Admission to the museum is 30 kroner. It's open daily, April through October from 0900–1700; November through March, 1000–1600. The site is located downhill from the cathedral. The map provided by the city's tourist information office will guide you on your way.

One word of caution. Recalling that the tourist office was downhill from the rail station and that the Viking Ship Museum was downhill from that office and the cathedral, allow a little more time to reach the train station when you decide to return to Copenhagen. It's uphill from the Viking ships, and time, tides, and Danish trains wait for no one.

Just six miles west of Roskilde is the Prehistoric Village-Historical-Archaeological-Experiment Centre at Lejre, representing one of the most profound studies of prehistoric housing. Ask the tourist office for complete details, including free bus connections from the small station in Lejre to the center.

O'Connell Monument, standing at the foot of O'Connell Street in Dublin, pays tribute to the memory of Daniel O'Connell, "The Liberator," who secured passage of the Catholic Emancipation Act in 1829. The body of this noted lawyer and lord mayor of Dublin lies in the crypt of the O'Connell Memorial Tower in Glasnevin Cemetery.

11 DUBLIN

Ireland, the sixteenth member country to join the Eurailpass system, is a unique addition in that it is the first English-speaking nation to join. About one-third of the Republic of Ireland's population lives in or near Dublin. And because the country is slightly smaller in size than Pennsylvania, with no part of it more than seventy miles from the sea, Ireland's capital city of Dublin is a good starting point for day excursions into the rest of the Republic.

There is no doubt that Ireland is the greenest country of Europe. According to legend, a true Irishman can recognize at least forty shades of green. The breeze that blows across the seas to Ireland is usually humid and proceeds to drop its moisture from the time it touches the Irish shoreline on the Atlantic Ocean until it's well out into the Irish Sea. A raincoat or an umbrella—or both—is essential equipment for your visit. But the sun also shines a bountiful bit of the time, and most of the rain takes place as showers that disappear as quickly as they come.

Dublin is one of Europe's finest capitals. Its O'Connell Street is as broad a boulevard as any other main street in Europe. Dublin is rich in domestic architecture. Stately Georgian mansions and the less pretentious homesteads of its citizenry all share a common attraction in that no two doorways look alike. The delightful doors of Dublin, with their solid shades of enamel and sparkling brass fixtures, are as fine a trademark as any city could hope to possess.

The face of Dublin has changed somewhat from the days when Molly Malone wheeled her wheelbarrow through its streets wide and narrow, but its citizens remain unchanged. They still have time to be genuinely interested in you, thoughtful in the consumption of their beloved Guinness stout, and wondrously literate when discussing any subject you might choose to talk about. In Gaelic, *céad mile fáilte* means "one hundred thousand welcomes!" You'll hear it frequently.

Dublin is a beautiful metropolis set in a country rich in natural beauty, but it is the people who give it the stuff of which memorable holidays are made. Dublin has television, but Dubliners prefer the theater and books to the tube. Dubliners love to read. You'll find them doing so while sitting on park benches, walking in the park, riding on a bus, or sitting in a hotel lobby. If a Dubliner is scurrying to catch a bus but spies a friend, he'll stop to chat. There's always another bus.

Dublin is the home of the Guinness Brewery. Dubliners lovingly refer to it as the city's "water supply." As a visitor to Dublin, it would be a breach of etiquette to leave town before making a visit to the brewery to see where "Uncle Arthur," as Dubliners affectionately refer to their brew, is created.

Day Excursions

The roster of day-excursion selections from Dublin reads like banners in a Saint Patrick's Day parade moving down Fifth Avenue—Cork, Galway, Killarney, and Kilkenny. The only thing missing is McNamera's Band. The city of Cork is the Irish Republic's second largest metropolis. Cork provides a double treat when you tread its fascinating quays *and* kiss the renowned stone at nearby Blarney Castle. Galway, western capital of Ireland, has all the charm of an ancient city plus the vigor of its expanding industries and popular holiday-resort attractions. Galway has a genuinely bilingual culture. The Irish language "survived" in Galway. And what could be more Irish than Killarney, where horse-drawn "jaunting cars" still meet arriving trains? These "cars" are a festive feature of the city, and their drivers are by far the friendliest and most informative guides to be found. The town's main economic base is tourism— which speaks well for its friendliness. The combination of Kilkenny Town and Kilkenny Castle forms a delightful duo of attractions offering everything from cats and choir lofts to castle tours and witches' tales. Superb shopping awaits visitors in the Kilkenny Design Centre opposite the castle. Kilkenny bears a history of invasions by foreigners, but they seldom returned to their own lands.

Arriving and Departing

By Air. Ireland has two gateways for air travelers: Shannon International Airport, on the west side of the Republic, and Dublin Airport, six miles northeast of the city's center. Aer Lingus, Delta, and Translift Airways service both Shannon and Dublin. Other air carriers stop only in Shannon, which has a world-famous, duty-free shopping area featuring items produced in Ireland. Shannon connects with the railway station in Limerick by airport bus service. The forty-five-minute ride costs 3.70 pounds (6.90 round trip). The bus between Dublin Airport and the city's central bus station takes twenty minutes and the fare is 2.50 pounds.

By Train. Connolly station is the terminal in Dublin for trains arriving from Northern Ireland. It is also the terminal for boat trains connecting with the Irish Ferries that sail from the port of Rosslare, south of Dublin, to the French ports of Cherbourg and Le Havre. Coming from London by train requires a transfer to either a Stena Sealink or a B&I Line ferry at Holyhead. The Stena Sealink ferry docks in the port of Dun Laoghaire, a suburb of Dublin, where passengers can transfer to buses for Connolly and Heuston stations. The B&I Line ferry sails to Dublin city.

Irish Trains

The rail system in Ireland is operated by Eireann Iarnrod (Irish Rail). All trains are diesel powered, and much of the equipment compares favorably with the EuroCity trains operated on the Continent. First class is referred to as "super-standard," and second class is known as "standard." Eurailpass holders are entitled to travel in super-standard coaches without payment of any extra fares or supplements (Eurail Youthpass holders must pay a supplement).

Seat reservations are not mandatory, but they are suggested. Advance seat reservations may be obtained from the Irish Rail ticket office at Connolly and Heuston stations and at the Irish Rail Travel Centre at 35 Lower Abbey Street. Reservations are made up to 1700 on the preceding day. Without seat reservations, we suggest arriving in the station about a half hour before your train's scheduled departure time, just in case the travel is heavy on the day you have selected for your day excursion.

First-class coaches are not marked with the conventional yellow stripe as they are in the rest of Europe. The only markings visible on the train exteriors are circular SUPER-STANDARD window markers, many of which also show a figure "1" within the circle. First class is usually divided into smoking and non-smoking sections.

Some trains operate with standard-class coaches only. Although seats may be reserved in standard as well as super-standard coaches, reservations are usually not necessary unless you are traveling on a weekend or a bank holiday. You are required to show your ticket (or Eurailpass) when entering the train platforms in all Irish rail stations, so have it handy.

All food and beverages are served by Irish Rail's own catering service. The service varies according to the type of train. Full-service restaurant cars are hauled only on the main-line routes operating between Dublin–Cork, Dublin–Limerick, Dublin–Tralee, and Dublin–Belfast, and then only on a few express trains. Most catering consists of buffet cars or snack-bar service. Food carts are used on some routes. When traveling on a train hauling a restaurant car, in-seat catering is provided for super-standard passengers. In buffet cars, you can obtain hot food, but trains equipped with snack-bar service offer only sandwiches and other previously prepared food. You may take your own food and beverages aboard. Take some candy treats with you. It's a good way of getting acquainted with other passengers.

The new equipment operated by Irish Rail has been aptly dubbed "The Trains of the Future." The distinctive orange-color units, complete with automatic doors, full carpeting, and air conditioning, embody all of the modern features of the latest rolling stock on the Continent.

The DART (Dublin Area Rapid Transit) is the electric commuter service running around Dublin Bay. Much of the twenty-three-mile route is coastal and gives many different views of the bay. Eurailpass is accepted.

DART is the fastest way of getting around Dublin and its suburbs. It's excellent for short excursions to places such as the charming fishing village of

Georgian town houses ringing St. Stephen's Green in Dublin are some of the finest eighteenth-century houses in the city. Professional offices and apartments lie hidden behind the beautifully preserved doorways and fanlights, lamp posts, and other street furniture. Dublin is the best preserved example of an eighteenth-century European city.

214

Howth at its northern end, or to Dun Laoghaire, the busy harbor for the Stena Sealink ferry to England via Holyhead.

Dublin's Stations—Connolly and Heuston

Connolly and Heuston stations in Dublin are both classified as major train terminals. Heuston Station serves as the departure point for all *Europe by Eurail* day excursions to Cork, Galway, Kilkenny, and Killarney. Connolly Station is the terminal to use when arriving on, or departing for, ferry services to Great Britain and the Continent and for trains to Belfast in Northern Ireland. (A description of Connolly Station can be found in chapter 27.)

The towns of Drogheda and Dundalk are situated on the main rail line between Dublin and Belfast, with the Connolly Station as the terminus in the Republic of Ireland. The northwestern coastal city of Sligo is also reached by train service departing from the Connolly station, as are the towns of Wicklow and Wexford, located south of Dublin in the direction of Rosslare.

The Dublin tourist information office on Upper O'Connell Street is within easy walking distance of Connolly Station. From the station escalator, exit to Amiens Street, turn left briefly onto Talbot Street, turn right at this intersection, and walk straight ahead on Talbot until it intersects with O'Connell. An immediate right turn brings you to the information office displaying the familiar green "i" at 14 Upper O'Connell Street. The telephone number for information is (01) 2844768. If you are having a Big Mac attack, McDonald's is right across the street.

Heuston Station lies to the west of the city center on the south bank of the River Liffey, a short distance from the Guinness brewery—a national monument in its own right. Neither Heuston nor Connolly Station provides facilities for exchanging money or obtaining accommodations and tourist information, but all these services are available at the tourist information office at 14 Upper O'Connell Street. At press time, the tourist information office plans to relocate in June 1995 to the newly refurbished St. Andrews Church on Suffolk Street, near Grafton Street.

City buses depart from the head of track No. 5 in Heuston Station and take passengers to Aston Quay, near the O'Connell Bridge. These buses are marked CITY CENTRE or AN LAR. You can't miss them. There is also a taxi stand on the opposite side of the station immediately beyond track No. 1 and outside the ticket-office entrance.

Heuston Station has eight main tracks. Ticket offices are located on the side of the station serving track Nos. 1 and 2. Train information and Eurailpass validation are available at any of the ticket windows.

Passengers arriving at the port of Dun Laoghaire, in the suburbs of Dublin, after completing passage on the British Sealink ferry service from Holyhead, can be taken by bus to Heuston and then to Connolly Station. The same bus service may be utilized when returning to England by Sealink. Shopping for Waterford crystal? Depart Heuston station via Kilkenny to the town where it's made. Take money!

Tourist Facilities

Visitors coming to Dublin will find it a city well aware that when guests are well treated, they will return. Such is the case with the Dublin tourist information office. As in the better department stores where "the customer comes first," in the Dublin tourist information office, "the visitor comes first." In our opinion, this tourist information office ranks as one of the best in Europe. Located conveniently in the center of Dublin, at 14 Upper O'Connell Street near Connolly Station and the Dublin central bus station, the Dublin tourist information office operates Monday through Saturday, 0900–1700. A money-exchange service is also on the premises and operates on the same days between 0900 and 1630. By the way, the rates of exchange are identical with those at Dublin banks.

The tourist office offers advice and guidance, including brochures and tourist literature, on all aspects of Dublin and Ireland. Guidebooks, timetables, and other items are offered for sale. One publication available in the tourist information office is a brochure entitled *Top Visitor Attractions.* It contains information on public places of interest, operating times, and so forth. It costs 1.95 pounds and will pay for itself many times over.

Other guides available from the tourist information offices include *The Essential Guide to Shopping, Dining & Pubs in Dublin,* the *Heritage Trails* guides, the *Dublin Cultural Connection* (with a 10 percent discount card), and the *Dublin Holiday Guide.* Each costs 1.95 pounds.

The tourist office uses numbered tickets for customer service. Be certain to take a ticket when entering. We congratulate Dublin Tourism, which operates the information offices under the aegis of Bord Failte (Irish Tourist Board), for installing the number system and wish other tourist offices would consider doing likewise. Ask for the fact sheets (20 pence per sheet) describing the free attractions available throughout Ireland. Among its listings, you'll find ancient places, art galleries, craft centers, sporting events, historic buildings, parks, and gardens—many of which are accessible by rail from Dublin.

The Irish Tourist Board has published guide books covering each of the counties in the Republic of Ireland. They are on sale in the tourist offices as well as some book shops and news agencies. Look for them; they are very informative.

Discovering Dublin

Visitors to Dublin frequently follow a pattern similar to those visiting London. They come. They see. They stay—until they realize suddenly that there are other places to see in Ireland and they've run out of time. Our point is, schedule your time in Dublin. Check in with the Dublin tourist information office soon after your arrival. Plan your visit—then follow your plan. Plan, too, to return. Ireland has so much to offer that just one vacation there may not be sufficient.

Let's indulge in a little Irish history for a moment. In 840, a band of Vikings established a settlement in what is now Dublin. In the years that followed, the Danes occupied the town (but not without a hassle from the local lads) until Danish power was finally broken by Irish forces in 1014. For more than a century, the Irish had to be content with fighting among themselves; then, in 1169, the English began to assert their influence militarily and commercially. Inevitably, warfare followed during succeeding centuries, with "England never wholly victorious nor Ireland thoroughly subdued."

Labor unrest marked Ireland's entry into the twentieth century. It was followed by the uprising of 1916 that was ended eventually by the Treaty of 1921 and followed closely by the tragic civil war of 1922–23. All of this left Dublin scarred and battered but basically intact. The economic expansion of the 1960s created an explosion of development in Dublin, with an accompanying growth in its population. It would seem that the nation whose principal export up to now has been people has found the jobs and the economy to keep its people at home.

Now, for a look at the city. Sightseeing on foot in Dublin is easy. During your visit to the Dublin tourist information office, purchase the walking tour guide booklets that are of interest to you: *The Old City Trail, The Georgian Trail, The Cultural Trail,* or the *Rock 'n Stroll Trail* (significant sites in Dublin's music history), which is popular among the younger set. The success of bands like U2 and singers like Sinead O'Connor, who began her career by singing traditional Irish songs, have made Dublin the world's newest rock music capital.

Each of these brochures describes specially selected, signposted walking tours through the center of Dublin and include many points of interest. The tours begin at the tourist information office on O'Connell Street, but are so designed that you can pick up the trails anywhere within the downtown area. The routes cover much of what is of interest historically and culturally to visitors and take about three hours.

One of Dublin's sights to see is O'Connell Street, where, from the Liffey River Bridge, you can look at the pulsating heart of the city. A block away on the river's south bank stands Parliament House (now the Bank of Ireland), which faces the entrance to Trinity College, founded in 1591. The *Book of Kells,* considered its greatest treasure, is housed in the Collonades. Tourist trails lead from that point to St. Stephen's Green at the top of Grafton Street, where its twenty-two acres are surrounded delightfully by splendid Georgian houses.

For an insight into Irish life, visit a Dublin pub. We have found the best time to do so is immediately after dinner. In general, Irishmen treat their pubs as a second home. A Frenchman spends a relatively short time in his café before heading off for lunch, dinner, or whatever. An Englishman goes to his pub for a chat with his friends and the barmaid and perhaps a game of darts before heading homeward. An Irishman, if he has the time (and he generally seems to), is in his pub for the entire evening, and you should plan to join him on the same basis.

The main pub activities are drinking and talking. You are free to sit and watch or join in. To take the latter option, merely turn to your neighbor and mention the weather. With that, the ball's in play. What is revealed then is one of the most fascinating characteristics of the Irish. You'll find that everyone has positive but sensible opinions about a myriad of subjects, including a remarkable knowledge of the outside world. Make certain that what you say about a topic is relevant, for unlike most bar conversationalists, the Irish *listen* when you speak. Extend them the same courtesy, and you will be in for a wonderful evening with some wonderful people.

Many of the pubs in Dublin serve appetizing meals and snacks and provide entertainment in the form of traditional music and song. It's been said by many distraught mothers and wives that it's possible to live in a pub—many of their sons and husbands do. Unless you are a Scot, try not to match the Dubliners' drinking ability or verbal athletics. Listening is a conversational art that you can develop to a fine degree in a Dublin pub.

Dublin is well equipped to offer a wide range of accommodations to visitors. Two exceptions, however, come during the Dublin Horse Show in early August and St. Patrick's Day in March. The principal sporting and social event of the year in Ireland, the horse show attracts thousands of visitors from all parts of the world. Don't plan to be in Dublin during the horse show unless you have *confirmed* reservations. The city is filled to overflowing at that time. If you are planning a visit to Dublin on St. Patrick's Day or during the summer months, it would be wise to check with the Irish Tourist Board in New York (see page 634) or with the Dublin Tourism Telecentre: telephone 2844768 for information; 2841765 for reservations with a credit card; or fax 2841751.

Regarding money, Ireland is a member of the European Monetary System, and only Irish pounds (not the British pound sterling) should be used in Ireland. There are no provisions for changing money aboard the British Sealink ferries to Great Britain. On the other hand, you may exchange currencies on ferries operated by the Irish Ferries Line en route to France.

From Dublin ...

TRAIN CONNECTIONS TO AND FROM PORT OF ROSSLARE FOR FERRY CONNECTIONS TO CHERBOURG AND LE HAVRE, FRANCE

Dublin to Rosslare			Rosslare to Dublin		
DEPART CONNOLLY	**TRAIN NUMBER**	**ARRIVE ROSSLARE**	**DEPART ROSSLARE**	**TRAIN NUMBER**	**ARRIVE CONNOLLY**
(Daily except Sunday)			**(Daily except Sunday)**		
0935	606	1240	0730	633	1030
1335	612	1635	1455	609	1805
1830	620	2135	1800	617	2057
(Sunday)			**(Sunday)**		
1025	670	1325	0915	671	1220
1830	676	2130	1830	677	2130

Note: For more information, telephone (1)8366222
Standard class only on all trains
Distance: 95 miles/168 km
Reference: Thomas Cook Table 637
For ferry schedules to and from France, see page 616 of this edition and *Thomas Cook European Timetable,* Table 1008.

Placid waters of the river Lee flowing through the center of Cork divide the city in two. The best of the old and the new is reflected in the well-patterned architecture in this second city of the Irish Republic.

WARNING
BEFORE KISSING THE
STONE REMOVE ALL
LOOSE VALUABLES

Kissing the Blarney Stone at Blarney Castle near Cork City is said to impart eloquence to all who undertake the task. The village of Blarney is reached by a pleasant twenty-minute bus trip from Cork.

From Dublin . . .

A DAY EXCURSION TO CORK
DISTANCE BY TRAIN: 165 miles (266 km)
AVERAGE TRAIN TIME: 2 hours, 50 minutes

A double treat is in store for those selecting a day excursion to Cork. There's opportunity to capture the excitement of Cork, a city with a heritage that reaches into antiquity, *plus* a chance to kiss the "crown jewels" of Ireland—the Blarney Stone. In fact, there is so much to see and do that you may want to take an additional day to ensure that you've not missed something.

Cork is the second city of the Republic of Ireland. In a manner similar to the way Venice developed, Cork was built over marshlands and water, hence the origin of its name, Corcach (a marshy place). As the city developed, it divided the river Lee into its present-day north and south channels. Today, the city center lies on an island between the two channels, surrounded by endless quays, hump-backed bridges, and ships' masts.

Wandering about the city, you might become confused by coming upon the river when you thought that you had left it behind you a few minutes previously. Each channel of the river Lee runs a winding course under and between the picturesque streets of the city. Patrick Street, one of the major shopping streets in Cork, was once a safe anchorage of ocean going ships.

Cork is so compact that you don't have to search for its scenery. It's there every time you turn a corner. Cork is an enchanting place, and you can be overcome easily by its charm. Caution should be exercised lest you become absorbed by Cork—as so many have been. Norsemen invaded in 860, and Anglo-Normans stormed and captured the city in 1172. Both groups remained in the area and eventually were absorbed by the native population.

The Normans were responsible for bringing to the marshes of Cork the lifestyle of a Continental European city, but the modern center of Cork didn't begin to develop until the mid-eighteenth century, when the city's Butter Exchange captured lucrative markets throughout the world. The best way to see what Cork's citizens did with their marsh and river is to walk its streets, quays, and bridges. Ask for directions from the railway station (or take the short taxi ride) to the city tourist information office on Grand Parade. Once there, pick up the Visitor's Map and Guide.

Cork's tourist information office at Tourist House, Grand Parade, is open in summer Monday through Saturday, 0900–1900. In winter the hours are 0915–1730 Monday through Saturday (closed for lunch 1300–1415). The telephone number is (021) 273251, fax (021) 273504.

The tourist office operates a money exchange, which is open Monday through Saturday, 0915–1330 and 1430–1800. Guided tours of the city depart

CORK—*AND THE BLARNEY STONE*

A Day Excursion from Dublin

DEPART FROM HEUSTON STATION	ARRIVE IN CORK STATION	NOTES
0730	1005	(3)(4)
0820	1050	(3)(5)
1015	1330	(2)(3)
1045	1345	(1)(3)
1320	1620	(1)(3)

DEPART FROM CORK STATION	ARRIVE IN HEUSTON STATION	NOTES
1445	1735	(1)(3)
1730	2005*	(1)(3)
1830	2150	(2)(3)
1900	2200	(3)(4)
1905	2210	(3)(5)

* Arrives 1950 on Sundays

(1) Daily, except Sundays and holidays
(2) Sundays only
(3) Food service available
(4) Monday through Friday only, except holidays
(5) Saturday only

Distance: 165 miles/266 km
Reference: Thomas Cook Table 640

daily at 1100 and 1430. The charge is 3.50 pounds. Telephone (021) 293822 to reserve your place on the tour. Each Tuesday and Thursday during July and August, a free guided tour of the city departs from outside the tourist office promptly at 1930.

We suggest that your first stop after leaving Cork's railway station be the city tourist office. But if your quest is to seek the eloquence of speech one can acquire by kissing the Blarney Stone, perhaps you should go "straight-away" to Blarney Castle. As the tiny village of Blarney is five miles north of Cork, board the bus marked BLARNEY in the city's bus terminal at Parnell Place. It's only a ten-minute walk down Glanmire Road to the river and the bus station.

Purchase a round-trip ticket for 2.50 pounds in the bus terminal before boarding the bus to Blarney. On Sunday the Blarney bus departs Cork on the hour from 0900 to 2300 and returns at thirty-five minutes past the hour. During the week, the Blarney bus runs more frequently, about every fifteen minutes. The ride to Blarney takes about twenty-five minutes. There's a lot of scenery along the route, so you might want to have your camera or camcorder ready. Since it's safe to assume that your bus driver will be Irish, don't hold back on your questions. He's got answers that he probably hasn't used yet!

The bus stops in the center of Blarney, and Blarney Castle is clearly visible to the left. Admission to the Blarney Castle is 3.00 pounds; admission to the Blarney Castle and Blarney House is 4.50 pounds. Blarney Castle, with its eighty-five-foot keep, was built in 1446. The Blarney Castle you see today is actually the third to be erected on the same site. The first such structure was built of wood in the tenth century. It was replaced by a second structure, made of stone, but it too was demolished, except for some foundations. The present castle was built in 1446.

There are many legends regarding the origins of the Blarney Stone. According to one, it was brought to Ireland from the Holy Land during one of the crusades. Apart from the legends, a MacCarthy professing to be a Baron of Blarney and true to Queen Elizabeth never fulfilled any promise or condition he made to her highness. His "fair words in soft speech" caused the queen to term them as "just blarney."

In order to gain the eloquence of the stone, you must scale the castle to its roof top, then be lowered backwards from the battlements in order to kiss the Blarney Stone—a rewarding task for those vigorous enough to accomplish it. Short of kissing the stone, kiss someone returning from the battlements—then pass it on. What the world needs now is more eloquence—so get it any way you can.

Salmon weir, as viewed from the Salmon Weir Bridge beside the cathedral in Galway, is one of the city's most popular sights. Shoals of salmon making their way to the spawning grounds can be seen in the clear water of the Corrib River during salmon season.

From Dublin . . .

A DAY EXCURSION TO GALWAY
DISTANCE BY TRAIN: 129 miles (208 km)
AVERAGE TRAIN TIME: 3 hours

John Fitzgerald Kennedy, thirty-fifth president of the United States, came to Galway in June 1963. He was given the "Freedom of the City" during his visit. A memorial plaque was erected in his honor and may be seen in the park bearing the name of the late president.

Like some of Ireland's other cities, Galway was established initially by foreigners. It was originally a Norman port. Richard II of England granted Galway a charter making it independent—in effect, a city-state. The "Tribes of Galway," an oligarchy of fourteen Norman and Welsh merchant families, ruled the city during this time, and a thriving trade with Spain developed. The Spanish Arch was erected in 1594 to protect Spanish ships unloading in Galway. Tradition tells us that Spanish merchants strolled along the "Spanish Parade" in Galway leading from the arch. The area, known in modern times as the Long Walk, can be reached on foot from the tourist office by walking four blocks south on Merchants Row. Spanish architecture is still evident in the city.

Gaeltacht is the name given to those communities throughout Ireland where Irish is the spoken language in common use. Such communities are generally bilingual, however, English being the second language. Galway City, and the county from which it takes its name, is the center of this common linguistic and cultural heritage. Until the sixteenth century, all of Ireland spoke Gaelic, but the pressures of a central English system began to erode the situation. It wasn't until the end of the nineteenth century that Galway, and the west of Ireland in general, became the focal point of a new reawakening into the Celtic past. Although an ancient city, Galway has now become the fastest growing city in Ireland with a population of 50,000—5,000 of whom are students.

Supposedly, the word "lynching" entered the English language through an act of Galway's chief magistrate, James Lynch-FitzStephen, elected to his post in 1493. According to a popular but dubious legend, his son, Walter, murdered a Spanish visitor and then confessed to the crime. He was condemned by his own father, but no one could be found to carry out the execution. So Judge Lynch, no doubt a firm believer in "spare the rod and spoil the child," hanged his own son and afterwards retired into seclusion. Lynch's castle stands today on Shop Street, and the Lynch Memorial attesting to this stern and unbending justice lies nearby, close to the Church of St. Nicholas, erected in 1320. Legend has it that Columbus worshipped in the church before setting out on his voyage of discovery to America.

GALWAY—*ON THE BAY*

A Day Excursion from Dublin

DEPART FROM HEUSTON STATION	ARRIVE IN GALWAY STATION	NOTES
0755	1105	(1)(3)(4)
0920	1220	(2)(3)(4)
1100	1350	(1)(3)(4)

DEPART FROM GALWAY STATION	ARRIVE IN HEUSTON STATION	NOTES
1510	1810	(1)(3)(4)
1805	2110	(1)(3)(4)
1810	2110	(2)(3)(4)

(1) Daily, except Sundays and holidays
(2) Sundays only
(3) Standard class only
(4) Light refreshments available

Distance: 129 miles/208 km
Reference: Thomas Cook Table 645

Emerging from the railway station, you'll see Eyre Square and the JFK Memorial Park in its center. Fronting the square is the Great Southern Hotel, a hostelry combining the charm of both old and new and an ideal place to halt for a libation or a luncheon. Irish hotel service is really an enjoyable experience.

The Galway tourist information office is located in Victorian Place off Eyre Square. The traditional green "i" signs will lead you to it. If you would like to call ahead to the office before leaving Dublin, you may do so by dialing (091) 63081.

The tourist information office is open all year. During the summer, hours are Monday through Saturday from 0900 to 1900, with the same hours on Sundays during July and August. The services that the office renders include a money-exchange bureau. You will find maps of the city and its surrounding areas plus an informative guidebook, *Tourist Trail of Galway City* (walking tour), a must purchase for visitors planning to wander about this historic city with its narrow winding streets and old houses.

If you are interested in remaining in the Galway area for a day or so, the tourist information office will assist you in finding suitable accommodations for a nominal reservation charge. Remember, when the attendant asks you how much you want to pay, the answer isn't "as little as possible." If you have a budget figure, or one you won't exceed, that's the information they are seeking.

The Aran Islands lie thirty miles offshore. They are among the last outposts of traditional Irish life and culture. Ferry service to the islands operates from Galway City, Spiddal, Doolin, and Rosaveal, and air service is available from Connemara airport. The islands can be visited in a day, but you may want to extend your visit. For ferry or flight schedules and complete information regarding the Aran Islands, check with the Galway tourist office.

An unusual feature of Galway is its downtown salmon weir, where shoals of salmon swim in the clear river en route to spawning grounds. This unique sight may be viewed from the Salmon Weir Bridge crossing the Corrib River by the city's cathedral. It's not unusual to come upon some of the parish priests on the shore of the river hoping—and praying—that they will be able to contribute to the cathedral's larder with the donation of a big, fresh salmon.

Two items of priceless value are on display in the Bank of Ireland at 19 Eyre Square. They are the Silver Sword and the Great Mace, said to be two of the finest examples of Irish silver work remaining within the Republic. The sword, which is the older, dates from the early seventeenth century. Several names of Galway mayors are recorded on it. The Great Mace, made in 1710, is 5 feet long.

Kilkenny Castle's extensive gardens, green parks, and a restored interior attract many visitors to the castle throughout the year. (Photo courtesy Irish Tourist Board.)

Kilkenny Design Workshops, as seen from the castle gate, are housed in former stable buildings. Products displayed and sold here are selected from throughout Ireland.

From Dublin . . .

A DAY EXCURSION TO KILKENNY
DISTANCE BY TRAIN: 81 miles (130 km)
AVERAGE TRAIN TIME: 1 hour, 49 minutes

Kilkenny combines Old World charm with today's progressiveness. Situated on the banks of the river Nore, Kilkenny is an ancient city of stone in which centuries of architectural styles blend together in perfect harmony. Nothing seems out of place in Kilkenny; yet within the city, activities range from the restoration of its thirteenth-century castle to sixteen craft workshops producing the latest designs of Irish products.

Kilkenny has what you could term "instant atmosphere." Kilkenny Castle dominates the scene and sets the theme. It is one of the most impressive castle sites in Europe. Utilizing the Nore River as a protecting moat running below its steep cliffs, it is strongly reminiscent of the great bastions seen along the Rhine. Under the protective shadow of the castle, the compact city has developed without much change over the centuries.

The defenses of Kilkenny Castle were breached only once. Cromwell and his armies laid siege to the castle in March 1650; the castle's garrison surrendered only after four assaults. Under the terms of the surrender, the castle's defenders and the townspeople who had fled their homes for the protection of the castle were permitted to march out "with their colors hoisted."

Make the Kilkenny tourist information office your first stop after arriving on the train from Dublin. To reach it, turn left onto John Street after leaving the station and walk to the bridge crossing the river. Cross the bridge and John Street then becomes Rose Inn Street. Continue walking up Rose Inn Street and you will find the office in the Shee Alms House on the right. To call ahead from Dublin or from the Kilkenny station, the phone number is (056) 51500. The tourist office is open all year. During the summer it is open Monday through Saturday from 0900 to 1800 and Sunday, 1100–1700. You'll receive a free map of the city, along with a wealth of information about the city and its surroundings.

Continuing uphill toward the castle, you will see the design workshops housed in the former castle stables. There is a permanent exhibition-and-shopping area where the latest designs are displayed and sold. The silver, textiles, and pottery products are elegant, expensive—and well worth it. Keep in mind that items mailed from the Design Centre are tax free. Or, if you prefer to take them with you, ask for a "Cashback Voucher." The workshops are open Monday through Saturday, 0900–1800. The Design Centre is open 1000–1800 on Sunday from April through December.

Although Kilkenny Castle is undergoing extensive restoration, the complet-

KILKENNY—*GHOSTS AND GIFTS GALORE*

A Day Excursion from Dublin

DEPART FROM HEUSTON STATION	ARRIVE IN KILKENNY STATION	NOTES
0735	0925	(1)(3)(4)
0950	1140	(2)(3)
1135	1316	(1)(4)

DEPART FROM KILKENNY STATION	ARRIVE IN HEUSTON STATION	NOTES
1602	1750	(1)(4)
1850	2035	(2)(3)
1913	2100	(1)(3)(4)

(1) Daily, except Sundays and holidays
(2) Sundays only
(3) Standard class only
(4) Light refreshments available

Distance: 81 miles/130 km
Reference: Thomas Cook Table 642

ed portions are open to the public. These include the great hall of the castle and the dining room. The basement houses a modern art gallery. Also open to view are the formal gardens and extensive parklands surrounding the castle. Kilkenny Castle was the chief residence of the Butler family from 1391 until 1935—almost 550 years.

In general, the history of Kilkenny Castle has not been very warlike, possibly because its imposing defenses were such as to deter attackers. The great hall of the castle is now employed as an exhibition gallery, and the effect is stunning. The hall, 150 feet long by 27 feet wide, is breathtaking in its dimensions, topped by a hammer-beamed roof thirty feet high at its apex. Admission to the castle, which is floodlit during the summer, costs 1.00 pound per adult, 40 pence per child.

The city of Kilkenny is a double-cathedral city, boasting not one but *two* cathedrals—Saint Canice's and Saint Mary's. Saint Canice's is the most ancient and is reputed to be one of the most beautiful thirteenth-century cathedrals in Ireland. The tower of Saint Mary's, built in 1843, rises 200 feet above the city.

One of Kilkenny's most interesting landmarks is Kytler's Inn, which has the distinction of being the oldest residence in the city and, by tradition, the house of the witch Dame Alice Kytler, born there in 1280. Dame Alice seems to have been a very nice lady except that she acquired and disposed of husbands—four in all—in rapid succession. This aroused the curiosity of the local folks, and in 1324 she was charged by Bishop de Ledrede with witchcraft, heresy, and criminal assaults upon her husbands. Brought to trial and condemned to burn at the stake as a witch, Dame Alice eluded her accusers and this horrible fate by escaping across the Irish Sea to England, where she disappeared from the pages of history. Her maid, Petronilla, was not as fortunate; the bishop had her burned at the stake as a suitable substitute. Locals claim that Petronilla's ghost still haunts the cellar of what is now the Kytler Inn on St. Kieran Street—possibly asking for back wages? In any event, excellent food and beverages await all.

During your visit to the Kilkenny tourist information office, plan to see the CityScope Exhibition featuring Kilkenny as it was in 1640. The twenty-one-minute presentation depicts the walled city at the height of its power and influence. Also include the Doll Houses and Miniatures Exhibition. Another place of interest is the Rothe House, an Elizabethan merchant's house built in 1594, where you will see a collection of period costumes and furniture.

Guided walking tours of Kilkenny are available (from mid-March through October) through the services of Tynan Tours, official guides appointed by the the city of Kilkenny. The tourist office has the details.

Jaunting cars of Killarney provide a traditional way for visitors, such as the Fergusons (above), to see many of Killarney's famous sites. Jaunting cars have access to many roads in the area prohibited to other forms of transportation. Storytelling by the jarveys (drivers), such as Dermot Cronin, shown below with his horse Dolly, enlighten and amuse passengers as they enjoy this unique sightseeing experience.

From Dublin ...

A DAY EXCURSION TO KILLARNEY
DISTANCE BY TRAIN: 185 miles (298 km)
AVERAGE TRAIN TIME: 3 hours, 30 minutes

Killarney ranks as the number-one tourist attraction in the Republic of Ireland. Consequently, when you go, expect to find tourists there in large numbers. This should not deter you from visiting Killarney but alert you to the fact that you should go there with a plan in mind: Spend a minimum amount of time in the town and a maximum amount outside of the town in the beautiful Kerry countryside.

Arriving in Killarney, make your way directly to the town's tourist information office and avoid the solicitations of the horse-drawn jaunting-car drivers that you will meet along the way. The jaunting cars are a real and permanent part of Killarney, but unless you know specifically where you want to go and what you want to see, it's best to consult the tourist office before contracting with one of the drivers.

Jaunting-car rates are usually based on four passengers. If your party is fewer than four, the tourist office may be just the place to find other passengers willing to share the cost. The central jaunting-car stand in Killarney is a stone's throw from the tourist office; so you won't have to return to the railway station.

Making your way past the queue of jaunting cars at the rail station may be easier said than done. The car drivers are convincing people. After all, they've been doing this sort of thing ever since the horse and the wheel became associated. If you stop to consider their offer, you just might be hustled politely but persuasively into the seat of a jaunting car before you can say "Erin go brae." Even if your plans include a jaunting-car ride, please wait until *you* have decided in the tourist office what you want to do.

To reach the tourist information office in Killarney, turn left on Railway Road just after passing the Great Southern Hotel on your left as you leave the railway station. Railway Road crosses Muckross Road a short distance from the station and almost immediately ends as it runs into Main Street. The jaunting-car stand will be on your left at this point. The tourist information office is housed in the Town Hall just ahead on your left. During July and August, the office is open Monday through Saturday, 0900–2000, and Sunday, 1000–1800. In June and September, it's open Monday through Sunday, 0900–1800, and November through May, hours are 0915–1730 Monday through Friday (closed 1300–1400) and 0915–1300 Saturday. The usual services are available, including accommodations and money exchange (not available on Sunday).

KILLARNEY—*LAKES AND JAUNTING CARS*

A Day Excursion from Dublin

DEPART FROM HEUSTON STATION	ARRIVE IN KILLARNEY STATION	NOTES
0850	1216	(2)(3)(4)
0900	1240	(1)(4)

DEPART FROM KILLARNEY STATION	ARRIVE IN HEUSTON STATION	NOTES
1453	1820	(1)(4)
1739	2050	(2)(3)(4)

(1) Daily, except Sundays and holidays
(2) Sundays and holidays only
(3) Standard class only
(4) Food available

Distance:　185 miles/298 km
Reference: Thomas Cook Table 640

The town of Killarney has many attractions. Saint Mary's Cathedral probably ranks highest. Also of special interest are the picturesque lanes leading off Main Street, which beckon with intriguing names such as Barry's Lane, Green Lane, and Old Market Lane. Ask in the tourist office for their town-trail booklet. It will lead you to these lanes and many more places of interest.

There are many eating places in town to choose from. We found the food at the Flesk Restaurant to be tasty and satisfying. It's on Main Street a few doors past the tourist office on the left-hand side. One of the favorite spots of the locals, too, the Flesk is known for its daily fresh fish specials, such as wild salmon, and its live Dingle Bay lobsters. Four-course menus range from 8 to 12 pounds.

Things to see in the countryside surrounding Killarney are so numerous that making decisions on what to do and see can become difficult. Don't let rain dissuade you from going on an excursion. It may rain in Killarney, but seldom for long periods. "No sooner is an excursion determined upon," wrote Lady Chatterly about Killarney in 1839, "than rain and storm appear; and no sooner is the excursion abandoned, than all is sunshine again."

Throughout the world, weather forecasters are envious of Killarney's "half day by half day" forecast. It means that any weather, good or bad, doesn't often last more than half a day; if it is wet in the morning, it will probably be fine in the afternoon—or vice versa.

Lady Chatterly was right, take it as it comes. Change your plans with the changing sky. Opportunism is essential when visiting Killarney and, usually, gives splendid returns—but take an umbrella.

Within easy jaunting-car distance from Killarney, Ross Castle, on the banks of Lough Leane, rates high among the sights to see, as do Muckross Abbey and nearby Muckross House. The latter, a dignified nineteenth-century manor now a museum of local folk life, includes an operating craft center where a blacksmith, a weaver, and a potter ply their trades. Admission is charged for the museum, but guided tours of the abbey and its environs are free for visitors throughout the year.

The classic Killarney countryside excursion is by jaunting car to Kate Kearney's cottage, a coaching inn, where you are fortified with Irish coffee. Then, setting out by pony through the Gap of Dunloe, you are refreshed again at Lord Brandon's Cottage before returning by boat to Lough Leane and to Killarney by jaunting car. You can obtain information on prices from the tourist office.

The Great Southern Hotel, opposite the railway station, is a fashionable hostelry of great beauty. Its Punchbowl Bar is a good place to meet people—or wait out the weather just in case you forgot our advice regarding umbrellas.

Hamburg City Hall, the Rathausmarkt (above) provides a majestic background for café patrons relaxing in the Alster Arcades. The area evokes memories of St. Mark's Square and the Piazetta in Venice. A cruise on Hamburg's canals (below) opens up many unusual perspectives of stately homes, public parks, and the architecture of the city's "Old Town," where there has been no noticeable change in the skyline for many centuries. (Photos courtesy Hamburg Tourist Board.)

12   HAMBURG

The Free and Hanseatic City of Hamburg is an impressive title—for an equally impressive city. Its 1.6 million residents are intensely proud of their city and are most anxious to show it. Hamburg is the largest in a league of "Hansa" cities in German that medieval merchants organized to secure greater safety and privileges in trading. For a long time, nobility was barred from entering this affluent city that sits poised between the Elbe River and Alster Lake.

Hamburg is full of surprises. For example, it has more bridges than the combined total of Amsterdam and Venice. The city's harbor is one of the leading ports in Europe and ranks as one of the top twelve container ports in the world—notwithstanding the fact that it is 68 miles inland from the North Sea! Chartered in 1189, Hamburg occupies a 288-square-mile area, 20 percent of which is covered by water. To the delight of residents and visitors alike, about 10 percent of the city's total area has been landscaped into public parks. Many of these areas date back to the eighteenth century, when landscaping was fostered by the city's wealthy residents as one of the arts.

Day Excursions

Due in large part to its commerce, Hamburg is situated in the center of a vast railroad network. Consequently, the availability of day-excursion opportunities is virtually unlimited. Bremen, another great Hanseatic city of Germany, is in contrast to Hamburg, although jointly the two provide the largest operation of seaports within Germany today. Bremen got its start as a port city in the tenth century when Emperor Otto I approved the construction of its docks.

To the south of Hamburg, in the midst of the Weser Hills, stands the fascinating town of Hameln, where the tale of the legendary Pied Piper is reenacted every Sunday to the delight of young and old alike. Hameln merits a visit even if you can't be there on Sunday. Relatively untouched by World War II, Hameln's Old Town will hold you spellbound with its cobblestone walks, ancient facades, and cozy eating places.

Ride the new German ICE (InterCity Express) to Hannover for a rewarding day of sightseeing amid the city's beautiful parks and gardens. Hannover is known throughout the world for its trade fair and as the "green metropolis" on the southern edge of the North German Plain. Lübeck is Germany's largest Hanseatic port on the Baltic. The Old Town of Lübeck has been included in the UNESCO list of "Cultural and Natural Heritage of the World." It is one of the oldest and most beautiful towns in Germany today. Go early and enjoy!

Arriving and Departing

By Air. The Hamburg-Fuhlsbüttel International Airport is eight miles north of the city center. Although it has four terminals, all international arrivals and departures utilize Terminal 4. The airport does not have a rail connection to the city, but the city operates an airport express bus service between the airport and a nearby S-Bahn station where frequent train service into Hamburg is available. If you are burdened with baggage, we suggest using the Airport-City bus. It departs the airport every twenty minutes, 0530–2300, for Hamburg's Hauptbahnhof (main rail station). The journey takes twenty-five to thirty minutes, and the fare is 8 deutsche marks (DM). The service operates back to the airport from 0540 until 2120. Taxis queue for incoming flights. Follow the pictographs. The average taxi fare to the city center is 35 DM.

The tourist information office is located in the arrivals hall of Terminal 3, Level 1. It is open daily, 0800–2300. The telephone number is 300–51–240. Banking and currency exchange facilities are provided by the Deutsche Bank in the arrivals hall of Terminal 4, 0630–2030 daily. Transatlantic service is provided by U.S. carriers Delta and United; Icelandair and Lufthansa also operate transatlantic services to and from Hamburg.

By Train. The Hamburg Hauptbahnhof appears as though it was constructed to handle the dirigible Hindenburg. The immensity of the structure is impressive. There are fourteen *gleis* (tracks) under the station's roof. Gleis 1 to 4 serve the S-Bahn, the suburban rail service; gleis 5 through 14 are for regular train service. Hamburg is the northern terminus of the InterCity Express (ICE). These sleek new trains glide in and out of the Hauptbahnhof on gleis 13 and 14. If your plans do not include a trip on the ICE to Munich, ride the ICE to Hannover and back. It's a real experience.

Hamburg's Hauptbahnhof

Hamburg's rail station has been updated. There's a host of new facilities—yes, even McDonald's! For a full service restaurant, visit the InterCity Restaurant, accessible by elevator, on the station's second floor front. The Gourmet Station on the main floor features national and international dishes. It's informal. Opposite the Gourmet Station are various boutiques in the "Wandelhalle."

Train information is available daily, 0530–2300, in the Reisezentrum (central ticket office). Eurailpasses can be validated at window 20 or any window marked AUSLAND. Information windows are 21 to 24. If the attendant does not speak English, you will be referred to one who does.

The money exchange is open daily, 0730–2200; the post office, Monday through Friday, 0700–2100, Saturday and Sunday, 0800–2000. International telephones are on the second floor of the post office. Baggage carts are scarce. The baggage room is the best source for a cart or a porter.

238

Tourist Facilities

The Hamburg Tourist Board has four information offices. However, the airport and main rail station offices probably will be all that you need contact. The tourist office at the airport is located in the arrivals hall of Terminal 3 (telephone 300–51–240). It operates daily, 0800–2300. The tourist office at the main station is open daily, 0700–2300 (telephone 300–51–230).

One of the first bits of business is to purchase a Hamburg-CARD. The card is a real bargain. It entitles you to travel free on the city's bus and train systems, its subways, and the port ferries at any time within the card's period of validity. It also provides free admission to eleven museums. Reductions up to 30 percent are available when the card is presented for such activities as the Alster tour, the Port tour, and many others. The Hamburg-CARD is available as a daily card or a multiple-day card. The tourist information office will provide you with a brochure, "City Map and Tips from A to Z," which explains the card's features. Purchase the CARD at tourist information offices, metro (in-city) station vending machines, and at most hotels.

For advance planning, contact the Hamburg Tourist Board administrative office. The mailing address is: Post Office Box 10 22 49, 20015 Hamburg, Germany. The international telephone number is (49) 40–300510, or you can send a fax to (49) 40–30051–253. In addition to general information, the board's information service can provide accommodation bookings; bookings for port tours and Alster cruises; arrangements for guides; and tips on sightseeing, dining, and shopping.

Visitors of Germanic origins will be interested in the Historic Emigration Office of the Hamburg Tourist Board. It is Germany's only historic emigration office, based on the register of German emigrants kept by the municipal authorities from 1850 to 1934. The register has five million names of people who set sail via the Port of Hamburg for a new life overseas. Family tree hunters need the emigrant's name and year of emigration. There is a charge of $30 for the search and a passenger list printout. You may call ahead for information by dialing 40–30051–250 or visit the office between Monday and Saturday, 0900–1800.

During your stay in Hamburg, take a ride on the Hamburger Hummelbahn. By the way, Hamburg-CARD holders get a substantial discount. *Hummel* is German for "bumble bee," and this amazing form of transportation literally "buzzes" all over town. The train does not run on tracks. Its open platforms are ideal for photographing. It's a fun trip. Don't miss it!

Hamburg Highlights

Hamburgians have their port to thank for the development of their city to its present stature. Hamburg is now an expansive metropolis of international busi-

Harbor Birthday, beginning in the first week of May and lasting for three days, is celebrated each year by Hamburgians and visitors alike. Hamburg's harbor was declared "a free port" on that day in the year 1189. Local craft, such as the Harbor Police boat (above), and ships from the seven seas join in the festivities. Book authors George and LaVerne Ferguson (below) were on hand to celebrate the 1992 birthday—and promised to return!

ness and culture. In the first week of May, the Hamburgians begin celebrating their port's "birthday" with pomp and pleasure for three entire days to commemorate the year 1189 when Emperor Frederick Bararossa granted Hamburg exemption from customs duties in the lower Elbe area.

A "free port" means that transit cargo is exempt from all custom duties. All goods may be stored, transported, inspected, sampled, or processed for special storage without formalities or restrictions. For example, coffee, tea, and tobacco are refined in a free port so as to make them immediately consumable when they are forwarded to their final destination, where customs duties are then levied for the first time.

Not all of the harbor area is classified as a "free port." In 1881, Chancellor Otto von Bismark rescinded Hamburg's "free port city" status and restricted it to only have a free port zone. Fortunately, it had little effect. In fact, port trade flourished as never before and Hamburg quickly rose to the rank of the third largest port in the world.

A tour of the harbor by launch is available year-round. (The launches are heated in winter.) In summer, the tour operates every half hour from 0900–1800; for winter tours contact the tourist information office. The launches sail from the St. Pauli pier. From the Hauptbahnhof, take either U2, S1, S2, or S3 to the Landungsbrücken station. Tickets are 14 DM for adults, 7 DM for children. Hamburg-CARD holders board for 11 DM and 6 DM. The tour takes about one hour. Ask for a launch with an English-speaking captain.

From April through October, leisure cruise boats depart from the quay at Jungfernstieg—Hamburg's elegant shopping street—to cruise on Lake Alster. Actually, the Alster is not really a lake. It is a tributary of the Elbe River that has been widened into a lake just before it flows into the Elbe River. This 460-acre lake, an area larger than the entire principality of Monaco, was created when the Alster was dammed in the early thirteenth century.

There is a wide selection of tours available on the Alster ferries, including a one-hour trip along its shoreline, a tour of the city's canal system, a bridge tour where you'll see a sampling of the city's 2,400 bridges, and a twilight tour. A guided tour of the Inner and Outer Alster operates every half hour, 1000–1800; tour duration is about fifty minutes. Adults pay 14 DM and kids 7 DM, unless you hold a Hamburg-CARD, then it's 11 DM or 6 DM. To inquire, visit the Alster-Touristik office on the quay where the boats depart, or call 341141. Brochures also are available in all of the Hamburg Tourist offices.

Hamburg Hints

A first-time visitor to Hamburg may feel much like the proverbial child in a candy store with only enough money to purchase a few items—when all the time the eyes urge the child to buy the entire store. With the visitor, it may be time, more so than money, that limits what one can see and do.

If you are in Hamburg on a Sunday, reserve a good part of the day for a visit to the Fischmarkt (fish market). Dating from about 1703, it is the oldest licensed market in Hamburg where just about everything that is movable is sold or traded. Fish? Well, fish have become incidental to the market's activities; freshly caught fish, however, are still sold any day of the week from fishing boats tied up at the city's pier.

On Sunday mornings, the pubs scattered around the fish market area draw crowds of early-risers and late-night-outers alike. Take in the Sunday morning auction activities held in the Fischauktionshalle (fish auction hall). The auction hall opens promptly at 0500 (0700 in winter), and the auction only lasts until 1000, so hurry. Following the auction, treat yourself to a jazz breakfast right in the Fischauktionshalle.

Shopping is an international pastime and Hamburg is a wonderful place to pursue such interests. No city on the Continent has so many covered shopping arcades. As a jumping-off place, start at the Jungfernstieg where the white ferries depart for water tours of the Alster Lake. Here, you will find covered arcades where shoppers may stroll regardless of the weather. For big department store shopping, head for Monckebergstrasse directly east from the Rathaus, Hamburg's city hall. Or you can get off to a flying start right after arriving by train in Hamburg at the Wandelhalle, the covered mall above the train platforms in the Hauptbahnhof.

Hamburg abounds in museums catering to all interests. As a port city, Hamburg maintains two museum ships, the *Rickmer Rickmers,* a reminder of bygone days when sailing ships ruled the waves, and the *Cap San Diego,* the "White Swan of the South Atlantic." Both museum ships offer discounts to Hamburg-CARD holders and are open daily starting at 1000.

Those interested in erotic art will not want to miss Hamburg's Erotic Art Museum located in the very heart of St. Pauli, between the Reeperbahn and the Hafenstrasse. It's open daily, 1000–2400.

As the night lengthens, St. Pauli, the entertainment district, springs into action with numerous pubs, restaurants, and discos along the (in)famous Reeperbahn, the Hans-Albers-Platz, and the Gross Freiheit. Hamburg has no inhibitions or curfew. See for yourself—there's a four-hour bus tour, "Hamburg at Night," that starts from the Hauptbahnhof at 2000 every evening except Sunday and Monday. The cost is 99 DM and includes admission to selected bars.

From Hamburg ...

TRAIN CONNECTIONS TO OTHER BASE CITIES

TO:	DEPART	ARRIVE	TRAIN NUMBER	COOK'S TABLE	NOTES
Amsterdam	0947	1452	IC 729	22	(1)
	1347	1853	IC 625	22	(2)
	1747	2252	IC 736	22	(3)
Berlin (Zoo)	0651	0950	EC 175	680	
	0851	1150	EC 177	680	
	1051	1350	IC 535	680	
	1251	1550	EC 179	680	
	1651	1950	IC 539	680	
Brussels	0747	1455	EC 29/422	21	(4)
(Midi)	1047	1801	IC 521/EC 46	21	(4)
	1147	1855	IC 823/430	21	(4)
Copenhagen	0719	1208	EC 180	50	
	0919	1420	EC 182	50	
	1519	2020	EC 186	50	
Munich	0907	1438	ICE 585	750	
	1107	1638	ICE 587	750	
	1507	2038	ICE 681	750	
Oslo	0719	2152	EC 180	50	(5)
Paris	0847	1905	ICE 621/EC 38	25	(4)
	1247	2208	ICE 523/EC 32	25	(4)
Stockholm	0919	2329	EC 182	50	(6)
Vienna	2023	0830+1	EN 491	64	

Daily departures from Hamburg Hauptbahnhof unless otherwise noted. Make reservations for all departures.

(1) Transfer in Osnabrück to train 2344
(2) Transfer in Osnabrück to train 2342
(3) Transfer in Osnabrück to train 2340
(4) Transfer in Cologne (Köln)
(5) Transfer in Copenhagen to IN 392 and in Göteborg to ICE 94
(6) Transfer in Copenhagen to IN 282

The Town Musicians of Bremen, from the popular fairy tale by the Brothers Grimm, stands at the west-wing corner of the city's town hall facing the market square in the heart of the old town.

From Hamburg . . .

A DAY EXCURSION TO BREMEN
DISTANCE BY TRAIN: 76 MILES (120 km)
AVERAGE TRAIN TIME: 55 minutes

Admittedly, Bremen is a city of such proportions that it becomes much more than a day excursion. It would take days even to skim the surface of its sights. Bremen is Germany's oldest maritime city. It lies on the Weser River, forty-four miles upstream from the mouth. Bremen is the second largest port in Germany. With so much to see and do in Bremen, we recommend that Eurailpass travelers visiting Bremen for the first time confine their sightseeing to the area in and around the city's market square, then follow up on a second visit with an inspection of the city's extensive harbor facilities. Certainly the charm of the market and its immediate surroundings will beckon the traveler to return again.

Finding your way from the Bremen railway station to the market square is an easy task. A city tourist information kiosk is immediately opposite the railway station (telephone 30–800–5051). The attendants there can give you a considerable amount of information regarding Bremen. Particularly valuable is a brochure entitled "Bremen, the Free Hanseatic City" (1 DM). The brochure contains background information on all aspects of Bremen.

The most direct route to the market square is down Bahnhofstrasse, which begins in front of the station. Proceed to where it intersects with Sogestrasse and crosses a former moat. A landmark at this point is a large windmill, seen in the distance on the right when crossing the bridge. Proceeding two blocks straight ahead on Sogestrasse brings you to the threshold of the old city center. A short walk through a shopping area and you are in the market square, where the cathedral, the *Rathaus* (city hall), and the Liebfrauenkirche are all clustered.

Bremen's oldest resident, the statue of Roland, erected in 1404, is the center of attraction in the market square. Roland is a symbol of justice and freedom. Legend has it that Bremen will not pass away as long as the stone giant is still standing in the marketplace. Legend also has it that the city fathers have a replacement ready just in case worse comes to worst.

No one is quite certain as to Roland's origins. City history first mentions the existence of the knightly statue in the marketplace in 1366, but it was made of wood and went up in flames. So did its wooden replacement. The stone statue has fared better.

The seventeenth-century facade of the Rathaus makes it one of the most photographed public buildings in the world. Rising above the town hall are the twin towers of the eleventh-century Saint Peter's Cathedral, site of an ancient

BREMEN—*AND THE TOWN MUSICIANS*

A Day Excursion from Hamburg

DEPART FROM HAMBURG HAUPTBAHNHOF	TRAIN NUMBER	ARRIVE IN BREMEN STATION	NOTES
0747	EC 29	0843	(1)(2)
0847	IC 621	0943	(1)(2)
0947	IC 729	1043	(1)(2)
1047	IC 521	1143	(1)(2)
1147	IC 823	1243	(1)(2)
1247	IC 523	1343	(1)(2)

DEPART FROM BREMEN STATION	TRAIN NUMBER	ARRIVE IN HAMBURG HAUPTBAHNHOF	NOTES
1616	IC 524	1711	(1)(2)
1716	IC 522	1811	(1)(2)
1816	IC 620	1911	(1)(2)
1916	IC 728	2011	(1)(2)
2016	IC 520	2111	(1)(2)
2216	IC 724	2311	(1)

(1) Daily, including holidays
(2) Restaurant car

Distance: 115 miles/183 km
Reference: Thomas Cook Table 650

sand dune where the earliest Bremeners sought refuge from the surging tides of the Weser.

Seek out the cellar of the town hall. It is said that the people of Bremen are most at their ease in a cellar—and this cellar is one of the best. It's a Rathskeller with more than 600 varieties of German wines to sample. Chances are if you find it, it may be a while before you see the light of day again.

The bronze statue of Bremen's "Four Musicians" (the donkey, dog, cat, and rooster) is stashed away in a cranny between the Rathaus and the Liebfrauenkirche, the Church of Our Blessed Lady. Be certain you find and photograph it, or you kids will never forgive you. The "Four Musicians" is one of several statues erected in Bremen honoring the Brothers Grimm fairy tales. If you delve into the true origins of the odd assortment of these domestic animals, apparently they are symbolic of a peasants' revolt against aristocracy rather than the Grimms' version of frightening off robbers—but don't tell the kids.

The Bottcherstrasse, a narrow street leading off the market square, was redeveloped as a center for arts and crafts, with shops, workshops, art collections, and fine restaurants—even a casino. At the end of the street you will come to the Martini Church on the banks of the Weser. Boat tours of the Bremen harbor depart from the pier immediately in front of the church.

Another area that you can reach on foot by walking upstream along the banks of the Weser is the Schnoor. The oldest surviving residential area within the city of Bremen, it boasts quaint little houses, inns, and workshops dating back to the sixteenth, seventeenth, and eighteenth centuries.

The tourist information kiosk hours are 0930–1830 Monday through Friday (until 2030 on Thursday), 0930–1400 Saturday, and 0930–1530 Sunday. City sightseeing tours depart daily from the bus station in front of the main railway station at 1030. Tickets must be obtained beforehand at the tourist information office. Trips around the harbor depart the Martini Church jetty daily at frequent intervals from March through October. The trip lasts one and a quarter hours.

Anywhere in Bremen, the marketplace, the Bottcherstrasse, and the Schnoor included, you may come upon a chimney sweep garbed in his traditional swallow-tailed coat and high, black hat. Reach out and touch him, for it is said that it brings good luck. Everyone does, and it's quite an exciting time when one passes through a crowd. Legends old and new abound in Bremen. Enjoy your visit.

Pied Piper of Hameln leads procession of town's children through the city's square in a reenactment of the famous legend. The pageant may be seen each summer on Sundays at noon. (Photo courtesy of Hameln Tourist Information.)

A DAY EXCURSION TO HAMELN
DISTANCE BY TRAIN: 240 miles (395 km)
AVERAGE TRAIN TIME: 2 hours, 45 minutes

If a time machine is ever invented, its first journey might well be to Hameln to confirm—or dispel—the legend of the Pied Piper.

Fact or fable, the town's archives reflect that on June 26, 1284, an itinerant Rattenfanger (rat catcher) attired in a multicolored costume trilled his flute, and 130 children followed him out of town to an unknown fate. Only three children survived—one boy had returned for his coat and was left behind, a little blind lad lost his way, and a mute youngster returned but was unable to tell the story.

This most famous kidnapping supposedly happened in retribution for the town's elders' not paying the Pied Piper for his previous performance, when he trilled the town's burgeoning rat population to the Weser River, where they drowned. Moral of the story: You have to "pay the Piper."

The story of Hameln's Pied Piper is the most well known of all German folklore. It appeared in Grimm's *German Legends* and has been translated into at least thirty languages. There are probably as many theories as to what actually happened as there are children who disappeared—maybe more. The most probable explanation relates to the colonization of an area in the Czech Republic to which many citizens of Hameln migrated after being recruited by wealthy noblemen during the same time in history. Peasants were referred to frequently as the children of towns, so it is quite possible that the tales became tangled. In any event, the present citizens appear to be happy that it worked out the way the Brothers Grimm recorded it.

Every Sunday from mid-May through mid-September, a live performance of the event is staged in the town square. The colorful Piper, plus fifty or so of the town's children (attired in charming "rat" costumes) and another twenty adults representing the town mayor and citizens of Hameln, begin their performance promptly at noon.

You will have about twenty minutes to change trains in Hannover. Aboard the train to Hameln, you'll realize you are approaching it when you see the silhouette of the famous Piper on the railroad control tower. On arrival, proceed immediately to the tourist information office, a short walk from the Hameln railway station. Walk through the square in front of the station, turning right onto Bahnhofstrasse. At the first traffic light, turn left onto Deisterstrasse. When you note a tree-lined shopping plaza on the right of the main street, look for the tourist information office near the next main intersection on the right.

If you plan to arrive in Hameln on the 1135 train for the performance at

HAMELN—*WHERE THE PIED PIPER PLAYED*

A Day Excursion from Hamburg

DEPART FROM HAMBURG HAUPTBAHNHOF	ARRIVE IN HANNOVER		DEPART FROM HANNOVER	ARRIVE IN HAMELN		NOTES
0705	0821	ICE 583	0848	0935	3814	(1)
0907	1021	ICE 585	1048	1135	3818	(1)
1107	1221	ICE 587	1248	1335	3822	(1)

DEPART FROM HAMELN	ARRIVE IN HANNOVER		DEPART FROM HANNOVER	ARRIVE IN HAMBURG HAUPTBAHNHOF		NOTES
1422	1509	3819	1537	1651	ICE 588	(1)
1622	1709	3823	1737	1851	ICE 586	(1)
1822	1909	3827	1937	2051	ICE 584	(1)
2023	2109	3835	2137	2253	ICE 582	(1)

(1) Daily, including holidays

Distance: 240 miles/395 km
References: Thomas Cook Tables 703 and 750

noon on Sunday, we suggest that you go directly to the town square and check in later with the tourist information office.

Hameln's tourist information office is open, from May through September, 0900–1300 and 1400–1800 Monday through Friday; 0930–1230 and 1500–1700 on Saturday; and 0930 to 1230 on Sunday. During the balance of the year, the office is open weekdays only, 0900–1300 and 1400–1700.

Adjacent to the tourist office on the right is a beautiful park, the Burgergarten, where you might spend some time while waiting for the office to open. The park is readily identified by its pleasant green gate with the silhouette of the Pied Piper. The tourist information office conducts guided tours every day from May through September at 1500 Monday through Saturday; on Sunday they start at 1000. These guided walking tours take about one hour and cost 3.5 DM per person.

If you're making your own walking tour, turn right when leaving the tourist information office and take the pedestrians' underground route. Follow the signs reading ALTSTADT (Old City). When you leave the underground passageway, you will be on Osterstrasse. The "Gaststatte Rattenfangerhaus (Pied Piper House), which is a charming café, will be to your immediate left. Either pause for refreshments here or proceed on Osterstrasse to the town hall, situated at the end of the street by the marketplace. En route, you will find several other attractive restaurants and cafés.

The Sunday performance of the Pied Piper legend is performed from a platform in front of Hameln's Hochzeitshaus (festive hall). We suggest arriving in the area at least twenty minutes prior to noon and positioning yourself in one of two places before the audience gets too large and your view partially blocked. It's mostly a "standing room only" performance because only a few chairs are provided.

The first place suggested is the edge of the raised area. If you plan to photograph the presentation, equip your camera with a wide-angle lens or one that can zoom to catch the close-up action. Otherwise, stake out a place on an elevated door step of one of the stores across the market square facing the festive hall. A telephoto lens is necessary from this vantage point, but you'll be shooting over the heads of the audience.

The Pied Piper isn't Hameln's only attraction—sightseeing in the Alstadt alone could fill your entire day. During the summer, it is possible to take a steamboat trip on the Weser River or stroll through the extensive woods surrounding Hameln. The old and the new have been blended successfully in Hameln. Happily passed over by World War II, the city is a living example of yesterday and today.

Hannover King Ernst August sits astride his stallion in front of the Hannover central train station. "Underneath the tail" (of the stallion) is a popular rendezvous point in Hannover.

A DAY EXCURSION TO HANNOVER
DISTANCE BY TRAIN: 111 miles (178 km)
AVERAGE TRAIN TIME: 1 hour, 30 minutes

Hannover is known throughout the world for its trade fair and as the "green metropolis" on the southern edge of the North German Plain. One of the many highlights in this city of parks and gardens is the famous Royal Gardens of Herrenhausen. In its 300-year-old landscaping, you will find the only example in Germany of early baroque gardens that have survived in their original form.

The history of Hannover is interesting in that it produced the lineage of Britain's present royal family. George I of England was born in Hannover, as was his son and successor, George II. Thoroughly German in tastes and habits, both monarchs made frequent trips back to Hannover, where they also ruled under the title of "Elector." George III, who presided over the loss of Britain's American colonies, was the grandson of George II and the first English King George to be born on British soil.

The Hannover rail station, constructed initially between 1876 and 1879, has had numerous improvements, although it has retained its original nineteenth-century facade. Fourteen tracks now serve passenger traffic from an elevated platform. A concourse at ground level connects all the tracks with the main station area. Running under the main station area and extending under the station's plaza and into the city is a shopping mall.

If you can avoid the temptation of shopping, you can easily reach the city's tourist information office by exiting the station and turning to the right. The tourist office is on the right in the Hauptpost (main post office) building. Watch for the "Red Thread," a painted red line that runs directly to the information office. Hours of operation are 0830–1800 Monday through Friday, and 0930–1400 Saturday (telephone 511–301422; fax 511–301414). The office operates an official money-exchange facility.

The "Red Thread" is actually an unusual walking tour of the city. Follow the red line that runs through the city's sightseeing points, but do it with a Red Thread booklet that you can pick up at the tourist office for 3 DM. The booklet fits easily in your hand—or it's small enough to slip into your pocket if you want to avoid looking like a tourist. It contains a map outlining the walking tour of approximately two hours' duration and describes thirty-six points of interest you will pass while following the Red Thread. Take a camera with a wide-angle lens. Each point of interest has been numbered and the number placed so that if you stand on the number while photographing the scene, you'll have the best shot possible.

Highlights of the Red Thread walking tour include the Passerelle,

HANNOVER—*FOLLOW THE RED THREAD*

A Day Excursion from Hamburg

DEPART FROM HAMBURG HAUPTBAHNHOF	TRAIN NUMBER	ARRIVE IN HANNOVER	NOTES
0705	ICE 583	0821	(1)
0802	ICE 793	0915	(1)
0907	ICE 585	1021	(1)
1002	ICE 785	1115	(1)
1107	ICE 587	1221	(1)

DEPART FROM HANNOVER	TRAIN NUMBER	ARRIVE IN HAMBURG HAUPTBAHNHOF	NOTES
1607	ICE 576	1721	(1)
1737	ICE 586	1851	(1)
1843	ICE 784	1956	(1)
1937	ICE 584	2051	(1)
2043	ICE 792	2158	(1)
2243	ICE 782	2358	(1)

(1) Daily, including holidays

Distance: 111 miles/178 km
Reference: Thomas Cook Table 750

Hannover's walking mall where you'll have more opportunities to shop, and the city's 1852 opera house. The old city wall and the new city hall are also passed en route. Hannover's oldest half-timbered building, dating from 1566, is also seen on the tour, which ends "under the stallion's tail"—unless you have succumbed on the tour route to the charm of the local frauleins or bierstubes.

Bus tours of Hannover are conducted daily (except Sundays and holidays) from May through September and twice weekly on Wednesday and Saturday the remainder of the year. The tour, which is described in English, takes two and one half hours; a tour ticket costs 20 DM for adults and 10 DM for children and college students. The Hannover city tourist office also can suggest a variety of sightseeing opportunities, including a cruise on Hannover's downtown lake, Maschee.

Hannover's zoo is less than five minutes from the central station by U-Bahn Line 6. The stop is called "Krüpcke." As one of its features, the zoo has the world's largest antelope collection. All of the zoo's animals are exhibited in modern, fenceless enclosures.

The Great Herrenhausen Garden and Garden Theater is one of Europe's greatest tourist attractions (3 DM entrance fee for people 14 years and older). It should not be overlooked during a visit to Hannover. Herrenhausen Avenue, facing the gardens, is lined with 1,219 lime trees set in four rows; they link Hannover's inner city with the gardens of the former summer residence of the Royal House of Hannover in Herrenhausen. Many sections of the garden have remained unaltered through the centuries.

The garden is open throughout the year from 0800 to 1630 in winter and until 2000 in summer. Throughout the summer, the ornamental fountains of the garden operate from 1100 to 1200 and again from 1400 to 1600 Monday through Friday. On Saturday and Sunday, the hours are 1100–1200 and 1400–1700. Either U-Bahn No. 4 or No. 5 will take you to the Herrenhausen Garden, or you will be able to see a portion of the gardens during a stop on the city bus tour.

Hannover has six major museums spanning 6,000 years of history. Entry to all is free, except the Busch Museum in the Georgengarten, a natural park developed in the eighteenth century. In sharp contrast to the baroque world of the Herrenhausen Garden, the Georgengarten is a mature example of English landscape gardening.

Many of Hannover's residents believe that a day in their city should have forty-eight hours. The refurbished city center alone—an ambler's paradise (reserved entirely for pedestrians) with shops, cascading fountains, and cafés—can captivate you for longer than the hours in a normal day. With the frequent train service between Hamburg and Hannover, you can easily extend your stay into evening.

City gate of Lübeck (above) marks the entrance to Germany's Hanseatic city for the Baltic Sea. Totally destroyed by fire in 1157, the present city dates from 1159. **Lübeck's city square** and town hall (below) were heavily damaged during World War II but are now fully restored. Between 1806 and 1815, Napoleon I garrisoned his troops in this area.

From Hamburg . . .

A DAY EXCURSION TO LÜBECK
DISTANCE BY TRAIN: 39 miles (63 km)
AVERAGE TRAIN TIME: 38 minutes

The Hanseatic City of Lübeck extends its hospitality in a phrase, "Welcome, to yesterday, today, and tomorrow." The city's origins go back to around 1000 A.D. when "Liübice" was established as a royal seat, artisan settlement, and a trading center on the banks of the Trave River near the Baltic Sea. Today, parts of the old town of Lübeck have become a UNESCO World Heritage Site, and tomorrow is well in the hands of its energetic citizens who number more than 210,000.

Destroyed by fire in 1157, the present city dates from 1159 when it was rebuilt. In 1358, it was chosen as the administrative headquarters for the Hanseatic League. Between 1806 and 1813, Napoleon I held Lübeck as a part of his empire. Until the turn of the twentieth century, when it began to build its own industries, Lübeck was known only as a Baltic port. Its industrial strengths and strategic maritime location, however, brought destruction to Lübeck during World War II. During the night of March 29, 1942, most of Lübeck's industrial complex and some one-fifth of its Old Town were destroyed by Allied aerial bombardment.

In 1949, the reconstruction of Lübeck, including the historic Old Town, began. The results have been that Lübeck's Old Town is now included in the UNESCO list, the "Cultural and Natural Heritage of the World." As Germany's largest Baltic port, this proud city has once again become a center of economic, cultural, and commercial interests.

Lübeck is noted for two culinary specialties that you should sample during your visit, marzipan and *rotspon*. Marzipan, as a sweet specialty, is produced in a countless variety of forms. We suggest you try a piece of marzipan cake. The origins of marzipan are hidden in history. The Lübeck version is that during the famine of 1407, bakers produced a bread made from the stocks of almonds since wheat flour was unavailable. Others believe that marzipan originated in Venice, and the recipe came to Lübeck through trade links.

In the early days, when salt was used to preserve fish, ships sailing out of Lübeck began carrying salt mined in the Lübeck area to fishing ports along the French coast of Biscay. Rather than return empty, the ships brought back casks of French wine to mature in Lübeck prior to bottling. A combination of sea climate and storage in Lübeck's wine cellars brought about an amazing improvement in the quality of the wine. This was first discovered in 1806 during Napoleon's occupation, when French officers found that the Bordeaux wine from Lübeck's wine cellars tasted considerably better than at home. We

LÜBECK—*RENAISSANCE AND ROTSPON*

A Day Excursion from Hamburg

DEPART FROM HAMBURG HAUPTBAHNHOF	TRAIN NUMBER	ARRIVE IN LÜBECK	NOTES
0704	E 3006	0748	(1)
0719	EC 180	0756	(1)
0804	E 3014	0847	(1)
0904	E 3018	0948	(1)
0919	EC 182	0955	(1)
1104	E 3028	1148	(1)
1304	E 3040	1348	(1)

DEPART FROM LÜBECK	TRAIN NUMBER	ARRIVE IN HAMBURG HAUPTBAHNHOF	NOTES
1605	E 3053	1650	(1)
1809	E 3067	1854	(1)
1948	EC 183	2027	(1)
2009	E 3079	2055	(1)
2139	EC 181	2215	(1)

(1) Daily, including holidays

Distance: 38 miles/63 km
Reference: Thomas Cook Table 665

suggest you try a glass of *Lübecker rotspon* and judge for yourself.

Visiting Lübeck by rail is easy, since there is a city tourist information office located right in the train station. It is situated opposite track No. 1 and is open Monday through Saturday, 0900–1300 and 1400–1800. The telephone number is (0451) 72300. Purchase the illustrated brochure of Lübeck from the information office. It's well worth the investment.

Lübeck's architecture ranges from Gothic to neoclassical and you can find typical examples of these as well as Renaissance, baroque, and rococo in almost every part of the town's old section. Frequently, the various styles can be seen side by side. For example, starting with the College of Music at the head of Grosse Petersgrube you can see all five styles mixed together in harmonic unity within one small block of the town.

With Lübeck's illustrated brochure in hand you can become your own tour guide, or you might want to opt for one of the town's regular guided walks that start from the tourist office in the marketplace. The guided walks take about two hours to complete. The tourist office in the train station has full details and can give you directions for finding the marketplace.

After you leave the train station, your point of reference will be the Holstentor, an imposing structure perched prominently at the head of the harbor just before the bridge leading over the Trave River into Old Town. Built between 1464 and 1478, more as a prestige symbol for the town than to protect its harbor, the unique design of its twin towers has become the symbol of Lübeck. The museum of city history housed in the Holstentor is very interesting and it features a model of Lübeck in 1650.

After crossing the river, follow Holsten Strasse, which leads directly to Lübeck's Rathaus (town hall) in the marketplace. It is one of the oldest town halls built in Germany between the thirteenth and sixteenth centuries and certainly one of the most beautiful. By the way, the Ratskeller Restaurant in the basement of the Rathaus is a delightful place to pause for lunch or to sample a glass of *rotspon*. We can also recommend the Schiffergesellschaft Restaurant at No. 2 Breite Strasse, site of a meeting house built in 1535 for shipmasters and brimming with treasures from the world of shipping. Credit cards are not accepted. Bring money—lots of it—but the ambience and food are worth it. (Closed on Mondays.)

For an aerial view of Lübeck, cross Holsten Strasse from the marketplace to Petrikirche (St. Peter's Church). Destroyed in the war, the church no longer has its own parish since its restoration, but it serves as a popular center for meetings, concerts, and exhibitions. Here you can ride the elevator to a viewing platform 162 feet (50 meters) above the city.

Shops in Lübeck are open Monday to Friday, 0900–1800 and Saturday, 0900–1300. The Deutsche Verkehrsbank operates in the rail station daily.

Helsinki railway station, located in the Railway Square in the city center, dates from 1914. Buildings surrounding the square are linked to a pedestrian tunnel containing many specialty shops, food stores, and restaurants.

13   HELSINKI

Helsinki is a city born of the sea, and it is from the sea that it draws its soul and nature. It is the beautiful daughter of the Baltic—a jewel with the blue sea as its setting. Helsinki is a modern city. Here the visitor does not come face to face with the past as he does in many long-standing European capitals. Great fires destroyed the original Helsinki many times, but it was always rebuilt. The only original remains of the trade-and-seafaring town that Swedish King Gustav Vasa founded in 1550 at the mouth of the Vantaa River are the foundations of a church.

Helsinki did not become Finland's capital until 1812. Now it has become very cosmopolitan, the heart of cultural and artistic experiences for the Finns. The city's colorful market square on the harbor is characterized by the glittering sea and an abundance of flowers and fruit, white sea gulls and busy saleswomen. Helsinki has an ambience that is all its own, supported by a friendly population and the physical comforts to enable you to enjoy fully its many features.

Surrounded as it is by the sea, there is a lot of island hopping you can do while visiting Helsinki. A ride on a ferryboat will take you to Korkeasaari, Helsinki's zoo; by ferry you can also reach Suomenlinna, a fortress island started by the Swedes, captured by the Russians, and shelled by the British before being given to Finland, which used it as a part of its sea defenses until 1973.

Should you tire of all this activity, you can plan to relax in one of Helsinki's excellent saunas.

Day Excursions
When you have finally broken the fine Finnish spell Helsinki casts over its visitors, you will want to venture forth into the Finnish countryside. We have selected four such adventures for your pleasure. They are Hanko, Lahti, Tampere, and Turku. Hanko, Finland's southernmost city, is a very popular summer resort with miles of wide beaches, good fishing, sailing, and all types of amusements. Lahti, site of the 1978 World Ski Championships, is about sixty-five miles north of Helsinki and provides an opportunity to ride trains plying between Helsinki and Saint Petersburg. Also north of Helsinki lies Tampere, Finland's second largest city. Both industrial and recreational, Tampere has much to offer visitors year-round. Turku, Finland's gateway to the west, was its former capital and an important cultural center before Helsinki was founded. Wherever you go, the friendly Finns will make you feel right at home. Enjoy Finland as the Finns do.

Arriving and Departing

By Air. Helsinki's Vantaa International Airport is eleven miles north of the city's center, about a twenty-five-minute ride by bus. Finnair buses run between the airport and the Finnair City Terminal next to the main rail station on a frequency of two to four times an hour. The single fare is 22 markkaa. The city operates bus line No. 615 between the airport and the station square on the same frequency, and the fare is 15 markkaa. Taxi service between the airport and the main railway station takes about twenty minutes and costs about 100 markkaa on the meter.

Passengers should check in at the airport a minimum of forty-five minutes before departure time for overseas flights. Also, you should contact Finnair several hours before flight time to check weather conditions at the airport.

Just in case you were too busy sightseeing while in Finland and forgot the shopping, there are tax-free shops in the departure lounge of the Vantaa Airport just loaded with gifts of Finnish origins.

By Train. Helsinki is served by a single train terminal, the Great Central Terminal, which was designed by Eliel Saarinen, the prominent Finnish-American architect. The terminal lies right in the heart of Helsinki and is close to everything. The train platforms have a total of fourteen tracks. The tracks are not covered, so an umbrella or a raincoat will come in handy if you are arriving in, or departing from, Helsinki during inclement weather.

By Ship. The Silja Line ferries arriving from Sweden dock at Helsinki's South Harbor. The Viking Line ferries dock at Katajanokka Harbor. Each ferry company maintains spacious passenger facilities complete with food services, lounges, currency exchanges, and connections to public transportation. Shipping activities in the harbor present many photographic opportunities.

The Helsinki Card

The Helsinki Card is a veritable key to the city. The card opens the doors of museums and other places of interest in and around Helsinki. It grants you free travel on buses, trams, trains, and the Metro in the metropolitan area. The card provides a free guided sightseeing tour by bus and free entry to about fifty museums. Showing the card in department stores brings you a free gift; it will spoil you in many of the city's restaurants, theaters, the opera, and concerts. A ninety-six page brochure describing the scores of opportunities the Helsinki Card provides may be obtained from the Helsinki City Tourist Office or in the Hotel Booking Centre at the railway station, as well as at some travel agencies, hotels, and department stores. The cards are issued for periods covering twenty-four hours for 105 markkaa, forty-eight hours for 135 markkaa and seventy-two hours for 165 markkaa. Kids ages seven to sixteen pay reduced rates. It's a value you can't refuse.

Tourist Facilities

During the summer, Helsinki operates an unusual form of sightseeing—a tram (streetcar) named "3T." It circles the city and takes in most of its important sightseeing points. Board the tram from the rear, where you pay your fare to a cashier and receive a pamphlet containing a map and descriptions of the sights you'll see on your tour. Electronic billboards at the front and midsection of the tram will display a number indicating the point on the map you are approaching as well as the name of the tourist attraction. Have your camera ready throughout the tour. The round trip takes about forty-five minutes. The adult fare is 9.00 markkaa; kids up to age twelve ride for only 4.50 markkaa.

Another way to become acquainted with the city is to take a guided bus tour. A city tour departs from the railway square from June through August at 1100 and 1300 daily. The fare is 60 markkaa, the duration one and a half hours. The same tour is conducted on a more limited schedule throughout the year. Check with the Helsinki tourist information office or the information office in the rail station for details.

Other tours originate at the Silja Line or Viking Line terminals in the harbor area. These tours run two and a half hours, and some schedules include lunch. Again, the tourist information office has the details, or you can contact the tour operator, Ageba, by calling 669–193.

Helsinki's market square, besides presenting unusual flowers, fish, vegetables, fruits, and souvenirs, also can provide visitors with coffee and delicious sugared buns at the square's tent café. The usual hours of operation for facilities in the market square are 0700–1400 Monday through Saturday. Most shops in Helsinki are open 0900–1800 (or 2000) weekdays and 0900–1400 on Saturdays.

The underground shopping area beneath the railroad station is open until 2200 every day, including Sunday. It's a great place when returning late from a day excursion to pick up a loaf of crusty bread, tasty cheese, and a beer—but on the other hand, there's always room service.

In addition to the tourist information facilities provided by the city tourist office, a mobile information center housed in a microbus and marked with a large green information "i" is found occasionally on the market square near the enchanting statue of Helsinki's mermaid, *Havis Amanda*. On May Day, she is crowned with a "student cap."

Helsinki's Railway Station—The Central Terminal

This imposing structure lies in the heart of Helsinki, and as we mentioned before, it is close to everything. The main hall of the station offers innumerable facilities to passengers. Food services, banking facilities, and a hotel booking office can be found there. In addition, a large cafeteria on the main

Streetcar named "3T," a unique boon to Helsinki's visitors, follows a figure-8 route throughout the city on a forty-five minute sightseeing trip. Tram 3T passes many principal points of interest such as *Havis Amanda* (the little mermaid) in the market square, the Olympic Stadium, and the railway station. Also included is a view of the city's south harbor and its Olympic Harbor passenger terminal where ferries depart for Sweden, Estonia, Poland, and Russia.

level serves fast-food specialties for the hurried traveler. On the floor above, a modern *ravintola* (restaurant) serves from 0900–0100 daily.

A limited number of porters meet the main trains. A baggage-storage area is available on the far right of the main hall entering from the trains. Similar to Munich's Hauptbahnhof, Helsinki's Central Terminal connects with a vast underground system lined with shops and restaurants. This subterranean arcade connects with a number of other buildings in the vicinity of the train terminal, making it possible to move about in a wide area without having to brave the elements on cold or rainy days. Baggage lockers are scattered throughout the station. A standard charge is required for all lockers, regardless of size.

Money exchange is located at the Kansallis-Osake-Pankki (KOP) Bank across the street from the rail station in the arcaded area at No. 10 Kaivokato. Hours of operation are 0915–1615 Monday through Friday, with extended hours during the summer.

In the event you are continuing your Eurail journey back aboard the Silja Line, a money-exchange service is offered aboard by the ship's purser. The rates are governed by the Swedish banks but have basically the same exchange rates as the on-shore facilities in Helsinki.

Hotel reservations are available at the hotel booking center located outside the main railway station on Railway Square. The office will be directly in front of you as you leave the station through the main exit. A charge of 10 markkaa is made for either a single- or double-room reservation. The office does not take deposits. The charge is 15 markkaa for three persons and 18 markkaa for four persons. This is the only hotel-reservations office in Helsinki. Hours are 0900–1900 weekdays, 0900–1800 on Saturday, and 1000–1800 on Sunday. Winter hours (from September 16 to May 15) are Monday through Friday, 0900–1700.

Tourist information. The central tourist information office operated by the city is located in the market-square area of the harbor at Pohjoisesplanadi 19. To reach this office, board tram No. 3T immediately in front of the train station. The fare for adults is 9.00 markkaa; for children, 4.50 markkaa. Following a ride of approximately ten minutes, the tram will pass the Silja Line Terminal. Disembark at the next stop, which is the market square on the harbor.

The tourist information office is readily identified by a green "i" sign. Hours of operation are 0830–1800 on weekdays and 0830–1300 on Saturday and Sunday (in summer). Telephone 90–1693757. It is not possible to make hotel reservations in this office. The office just outside the central railway station must be used.

Train information can be obtained on the left side of the train station's main hall. Train-seat reservations can be made at window Nos. 1–8. Eurailpass validation also can be accomplished at these windows. Seat reservations may be made between 0700 and 2100 daily. The charge for seat reservations on the "Rapido" trains is 9.00 markkaa. Reservations on these trains are obligatory.

Highlights of Helsinki

The Helsinki Tourist Office publishes interesting information sheets describing tours to such places as the island fortress of Suomenlinna (the "Gibraltar of Finland"), museum information, details concerning visits to the submarine *Vesikko,* the coastal artillery museum, and the Korkeasaari Zoo on an island off the coast of Helsinki. Ferry connections and fares to Helsinki's many islands and schedules for summer theaters and the Finnish National Opera also are provided.

Summer restaurants and cafés are also listed in this informative publication, together with their opening and closing times. Menus vary from borscht to burbot and roe to reindeer. But don't tell the kids about the reindeer—they might associate it with Rudolph! Helsinki has it all—from the avant garde to the classical.

Sail to Saint Petersburg. Founded in 1703 by Peter I (the Great), Russia's second largest city (formerly Leningrad) may be visited on a special cruise out of Helsinki thanks to a program offered by the Baltic Express Line. There is train service between Helsinki and Saint Petersburg.

The Baltic Express Line's sailing schedule is a visa-free cruise to Saint Petersburg that entails a four-day cruise aboard the, M/S *Konstantin Simonou.* The Eurailpass is not accepted on this cruise. It does, however, get you to Helsinki, where you can join the cruise for an overnight sailing to Saint Petersburg, departing Helsinki at 1730.

Interested? If so, contact the Bergen Line, Inc. (general agents) by writing to them at 505 Fifth Avenue, New York, NY 10017—or better still, call them at (800) 323–7436 or (212) 986–2711 (fax: 212–983–1275) at least one month prior to your U.S. departure.

From Helsinki ...
FERRY CONNECTIONS TO BASE CITY STOCKHOLM

TO:	DEPART	ARRIVE	VIA	COOK'S TABLE	NOTES
Stockholm	1800(2)	0830+1(3)	Ferry	1250	(1)
Stockholm	1000(4)	1900(3)	Ferry	1250	(6)
via Turku*	2000(4)	0700+1(3)	Ferry	1250	(5)

* For train connections from Helsinki to Turku, see *Thomas Cook European Timetable,* Table 490.

Eurailpass holders are entitled to discounted passage on Silja Line ships between Stockholm and Turku or Helsinki.

(1) Daily, including holidays (except January 15, 17, 19)
(2) South Harbor, Silja Terminal, Helsinki
(3) Silja Terminal, Stockholm
(4) Silja Terminal, Turku
(5) Daily, except May 29 and 30, September 4 through 8, and December 24, 25, and 31, 1995
(6) Daily, except January 1, 3, 10, 17, and 24; April 17 through 21; September 12 and 13; and December 24 and 25, 1995

Emigration monument on Hanko's waterfront, a granite pillar topped by swans in flight, to commemorate more than 500,000 Finns and Russians departing their homeland for a new life in North America, Australia, or Canada between 1880 and 1930.

A DAY EXCURSION TO HANKO
DISTANCE BY TRAIN: 85 miles (137 km)
AVERAGE TRAIN TIME: 2 hours, 15 minutes

Hanko is Finland's southernmost town. It is best known as a summer resort; but as the climate in this part of Finland often is very mild, you can visit Hanko in any season. In September, for example, the seawater is still warm enough for swimming. If you do not want to swim, you can lie on the beach, take a walk in the surrounding area, go for a bicycle tour, hire a horse, or just relax. Hanko in autumn is an unusually peaceful place. No matter when you go there, you will find clean water, lots of fresh air, and quite a few things to do.

The peninsula where Hanko lies, known long ago among seafarers, was used for centuries as a harbor where sailing vessels could seek refuge from storms or winter ice packs. With time on their hands, many navigators, merchants, and soldiers kept themselves busy by carving their names or family coats of arms in the rocks along the shoreline of the harbor. More than 600 of these carvings have been found. Due to these inscriptions, the area gained the title "Guest Book of the Archipelago," and you may inspect this handiwork while participating in any of several sightseeing cruises available in the harbor area.

Hanko did not begin as a town until the 1870s. With the introduction of iron ships, winter navigation became possible, and Hanko's peninsula was found to be well suited as a year-round harbor. Both a railway and harbor were constructed, and Hanko was well on its way to becoming an important part of the Finnish economy.

By the end of the nineteenth century, Hanko was a fashionable summer resort, especially among the Russians coming from the Saint Petersburg area. The Russian influence is visible in the architecture of many wooden villas in Hanko, most of which are in the Spa Park. The peninsula on which Hanko lies was ceded to the Soviet Union in 1940 but was regained in 1941.

Hanko is inseparably linked to the sea. There are about ninety islands just within its town limits! The town has four small boat harbors, including the largest harbor for visiting boats in all of Finland, two commercial harbors, four industrial harbors, and the only rail-ferry loading facility within Finland. None of this activity is detrimental to tourism; in fact, it attracts it. More than 300,000 tourists visit Hanko annually. They come not only for the long sandy beaches and aquatic sports but for the more than 1,000 events that take place every year.

The day excursion to Hanko requires a change of trains at Karjaa, which you reach in just over an hour from Helsinki. In Karjaa, you will transfer to a

HANKO—*SOUTHERNMOST CITY*

A Day Excursion from Helsinki

DEPART FROM HELSINKI STATION	TRAIN NUMBER	ARRIVE IN HANKO STATION	NOTES
0650	121	0842	(1)(2)(3)
0902	123	1052	(1)(2)(3)
1202	125	1357	(1)(2)(3)

DEPART FROM HANKO STATION	TRAIN NUMBER	ARRIVE IN HELSINKI STATION	NOTES
1410	128	1602	(1)(2)(3)
1610	130	1802	(1)(2)(3)
2120	136	2310	(1)(2)(3)

(1) Daily, including holidays
(2) Light refreshments available from Helsinki to Karjaa
(3) Transfer in Karjaa (train numbers refer to Helsinki-Karjaa trains)
    (Trains between Karjaa and Hanko are second class only.)

Distance: 85 miles/137 km
References: Thomas Cook Table 490 and 491

local train that makes an interesting trip through southern Finland's woods and lakes before reaching Hanko. Board the front car and you can ride right behind the engineer. The Hanko station is the last stop on the line, so there's no chance of missing it.

The Hanko City Tourist Office is located at Boulevarden 10 and can be reached in about a ten-minute walk from the railway station. Depart the station and proceed along the overpass crossing the railroad, which will be on your left as you arrive. Turn left immediately after the overpass and proceed down Berggatan Street to where it intersects with Boulevarden.

The city tourist office is at the intersection and is open Monday through Friday, 0900–1700, year-round; it is closed Saturday and Sunday. If you want to telephone ahead with inquiries regarding hotel reservations or tourist information, the number is 11–280–3410; the fax number is 11–280–3412.

Between the years 1880 and 1930, thousands of emigrants set off from Hanko for the United States, Canada, and Australia. In 1967, a statue commemorating this period was erected near the beach, a short distance from the tourist office. Depicting wild birds in free flight, this "independence monument" is well worth the time to visit. Also worthwhile is a visit to the Fortress Museum in the Eastern Harbor and the City Hall Art Gallery, which features exhibitions from local, Finnish, and foreign artists.

To experience Hanko's spa history, visit the famous Hanko Casino, or "Summer Restaurant Casino." To get there, head down Boulevarden toward the sea. Turn left onto Appelgrenintie. Or, turn right instead and head for the luncheon buffet at the Hotel Regatta at Merikatu 1 (telephone 11–248–6491).

Hanko has several other interesting restaurants, some of which are open year round in the Eastern Harbor area. You can find seafood served Italian style or homemade Finnish foods. If you feel a little on the wild side, try the Gamerestaurant Sisapiha. Located at 1, Satamakatu, this restaurant specializes in wild boar, willow grouse, pheasant, and reindeer (telephone 11–24–87824).

Other tours of Hanko and its surroundings can be arranged through the city tourist office. Brochures, maps, and special information leaflets are available, and guides can be hired. Sea cruises operate every day from June to the end of August. The sea tours start at the Eastern Harbor at 1300 daily and last about two hours. Tickets are sold on board. Fishing trips also may be arranged, but before angling off, check with the tourist office and obtain a general fishing permit from the town's post office. Hanko is packed with exciting as well as relaxing things to do. Have a good visit!

View from the top. In earlier editions of *Europe By Eurail*, we used a photograph taken from the bottom of the Lahti trio of ski jumps, the most impressive one being the ninety-meter (295-foot) Olympic-class giant. Here, we have photographed the jumps and the other sports facilities clustered around their run-out area *from the top*. Quite a different point of view!

272

A DAY EXCURSION TO LAHTI
DISTANCE BY TRAIN: 81 miles (130 km)
AVERAGE TRAIN TIME: 1 hour, 30 minutes

Lahti is the seventh largest city in Finland, with nearly 100,000 inhabitants. It is particularly noted for its timber and wooden furniture, brewers' products, and clothing. It is equally famous as a winter sports center. Sporting events have always played a prominent role in Lahti's life-style. The Salpausselka Games, as well as the Finlandia and other skiing events, have made Lahti famous worldwide.

Perhaps the most spectacular sight in Lahti is its 115-meter ski jump, located in the Lahti Sports Center. The jump is about a fifteen-minute walk from the tourist information office. It merits everyone's inspection. An observation platform on top of the jump can be reached by elevator and is accessible to visitors during summer months, Monday through Friday, 1000–1800; Saturday and Sunday, 1000–1600. In addition to the 115-meter ski jump, there are smaller ski jumps and practice areas nearby. The ski-jump area actually is a year-round attraction for tourists. In addition to the observation platform, there is an open-air, heated swimming pool at the foot of the ski-jump complex.

The Sports Center is not the sole attraction in Lahti. The city also has the most powerful broadcasting station in Finland. A unique Radio and TV Museum stands beneath the tall radio masts. The museum is open Monday through Friday, 1000–1700; Saturday and Sunday, 1100–1700. The museum contains more than a thousand items of great interest in the field of radio technology. The tourist information office has complete details.

In Lahti, general fitness is a feature of everyday life. There are illuminated trails for walking, jogging, and skiing—about forty kilometers of them—as well as unilluminated trails. Summer weekly events include outdoor theater, concerts, a lively marketplace, and hiking.

The city is unique in that it is one of the few metropolitan areas where you can live in a one-family house in the center of the city on the shore of a lake. (We would like to suggest that the city planners of America go to Lahti to pick up a few pointers.) Much of Lahti's housing is spread over a wide area, along the city's green hillsides and lake shores. Many visitors are surprised to find Lahti so sophisticated and versatile. The infrastructure of quality department stores, good hotels, and good restaurants coupled with civic convention centers capable of handling large numbers of people are the elements of Lahti's success. Lahti is modern yet traditional.

Arriving from Helsinki, you will find the Lahti railway terminal on the left-hand side of the train. Use the underground exit and proceed in the direction of

LAHTI—*SKI, SKATE, SAIL, OR CYCLE*

A Day Excursion from Helsinki

DEPART FROM HELSINKI STATION	TRAIN NUMBER	ARRIVE IN LAHTI STATION	NOTES
0802	81	0927	(1)(2)
1030	11	1159	(1)(2)
1122	75	1247	(1)(2)
1332	1	1500	(1)(2)

DEPART FROM LAHTI STATION	TRAIN NUMBER	ARRIVE IN HELSINKI STATION	NOTES
1456	2	1626	(1)(2)
1735	12	1901	(1)(2)
1830	76	1956	(1)(2)
2040	4	2202	(1)(2)
2130	82	2256	(1)(2)

(1) Daily, including holidays
(2) Buffet car

Distance: 81 miles/130 km
Reference: Thomas Cook Table 499

track No. 4 to the station. The terminal has a snack bar on the right as you enter from the trains. Ticket windows and train information are also on the right. Some tourist information is available in the rail station, as well as in the Sports Center and the city's Market Square, throughout the summer; however, we suggest you check in with the city's main tourist information office at No. 3, Torikatu, telephone (918) 8184565 or 8184568. To dial from outside Finland, use country code 358 and drop the 9 from the area code.

To reach the main office from the rail station, proceed directly out of the station along Rautatienkatu Street until you reach Aleksanterinkatu Street. Here, you turn left and walk to Torikatu Street. Following a right turn, you will find the office at the intersection of Torikatu and Vapaudenkatu streets. Take heart, it's easier than it sounds. During the winter, the office is open Monday through Friday, 0800–1600; during the summer months (June, July, and August) Monday through Friday, 0800–1700, and Saturday, 1000–1400.

The friendly staff of the Lahti City Tourist and Marketing Bureau arc happy to help in all matters concerning sightseeing in their beautiful city. They can arrange for city sightseeing tours and cruises on nearby lakes and even make hotel and restaurant reservations for visitors. The office has an excellent selection of travel brochures and leaflets on Lahti, its surrounding areas, and other points of interest throughout Finland. Shopping for excellent Finnish glassware can be a full-time occupation for a visitor. Numerous department stores, as well as specialty shops, located throughout the city feature fine Finnish glassware and other high-quality items. The city is well known for its ready-to-wear garments for both men and women. The Finnish furniture industry is centered around Lahti. Lahti bread and beer are known all over Finland for their quality.

In summer, Lahti's cultural life includes performances in the Kariranta open-air theater and the open-air concerts at the Mukkula Tourist Center. Lahti provides an interesting as well as relaxing day-excursion site; it's a year-round attraction you shouldn't miss.

Sights to see while in town include the Historical Museum, the Museum of Military Medicine, the Ski Museum, and the Museum of Art. The City Tourist and Marketing Bureau conducts a two-hour city tour every Wednesday starting at 1700 from mid-June through mid-August.

Lahti has been described as Finland's most American city. Founded in 1905, Lahti is, historically speaking, a young city, but it has grown more rapidly than towns of similar age or older. One reason for its vigorous development is its geographic position in the center of southern Finland, at the junction of major traffic routes. Another, we might add, is its friendly, courteous people.

Nasinneula Observation Tower, tallest such tower in Finland, adjoins aquarium and planetarium in Tampere's Särkänniemi recreation area. Tampere is Finland's third largest city.

From Helsinki . . .

A DAY EXCURSION TO TAMPERE
DISTANCE BY TRAIN: 116 miles (187 km)
AVERAGE TRAIN TIME: 1 hour, 55 minutes

Tampere is the youngest of the "triangle towns" of Finland, the others being Helsinki and Turku. The reference to a triangle comes from the fact that all three cities are approximately 93 miles (150 km) apart from each other. The town of Tampere was granted its charter in 1779 by Gustavus III, who was king of both Sweden and Finland at that time. From a modest start, Tampere developed into an industrial and resort center early in the nineteenth century. Today, Tampere is the third largest city in Finland and the biggest inland city in all of Scandinavia with its 175,000 inhabitants.

Tampere is a city of lakes and parks. Its two major lakes are connected by rapids flowing over three waterfalls. Tampere is considered to be a "small" city. The city center is located on a narrow isthmus that is divided by the rapids. The "smallness" actually means that all shops, stores, restaurants, and other places are within easy reach of each other, which makes Tampere an easy city to explore on foot.

Among the noteworthy places to see and visit during your day excursion in Tampere is the city's *Särkänniemi,* an amusement area containing a dolphinarium, an amusement park, and a children's zoo which are open daily in summer. An aquarium, a planetarium, an observation tower, and the Sara Hildén Modern Art Museum also are located in the complex. These attractions are open daily throughout the year.

In the Särkänniemi aquarium, you will find some 2,000 fish of more than 200 species from all over the world. There is a seal tank, too. The seals are fed daily at 1100 and again at 1600.

In the planetarium, a veritable sea of 6,000 twinkling bodies will open up before you. Here you will see both past and future movements in space projected on the planetarium's dome ceiling in a thirty-minute space adventure.

The Särkänniemi also offers a separate amusement park area complete with a roller coaster ride, big and small bumper cars, and many other attractions. The little ones in the family will love getting to know all the fluffy animals in the children's zoo. Art lovers will enjoy the Sara Hildén Art Museum, with its outstanding collection of contemporary art. The paddle-wheel steamboat *Finlandia Queen* starts its two-hour cruises from the Särkänniemi quay from June through August running weekly from Tuesday through Sunday. Need we say more—except that the Särkänniemi is the place to be?

Another place of interest in Tampere is the revolving auditorium of the Pyynikki Summer Theater. It is world renowned and was the first of its kind

TAMPERE—*CITY OF THEATERS*

A Day Excursion from Helsinki

DEPART FROM HELSINKI STATION	TRAIN NUMBER	ARRIVE IN TAMPERE STATION	NOTES
0658	69	0855	(1)(2)
0958	67	1155	(1)(3)
1258	55	1455	(1)(3)

DEPART FROM TAMPERE STATION	TRAIN NUMBER	ARRIVE IN HELSINKI STATION	NOTES
1500	68	1658	(1)(3)
1804	56	2000	(1)(3)
1956	160	2152	(1)(2)
2058	70	2300	(1)(2)

(1) Daily, including holidays
(2) Buffet car
(3) Restaurant car

Distance: 116 miles/187 km
Reference: Thomas Cook Table 495

when it opened in 1959. Nearby Pyynikki Park and Pispala Ridge, with their old timbered houses, also are worth visiting.

In Tampere, you can find a good cross section of Finnish architectural history. It ranges from charming wooden houses and art nouveau houses in the center of the city to the most modern designed office buildings and red brick factory buildings at the city's rapids. Tampere's oldest building is the Messukyla stone church, which dates back to the fifteenth century. The city's cathedral with its architecture and frescoes is a good example of Tampere's art nouveau period. A newer place of worship is the Kaleva Church, a strikingly modern construction completed in 1966. Another fine example of modern Finnish architecture is the city's main library. The Moomin-Valley Museum in the same building also is worth a visit. If you are interested in architectural design, Tampere can come up with a good serving of it.

In the center of Tampere, there is the Verkaranta Arts and Crafts Center with Finnish articles of high quality on exhibition. Close by, you can browse about in Tampere's colorful old market hall and the outside markets that surround it. If you happen to be in town during the summer (June–August), there's a concert at 1900 at the Old Library Park in the city center on Tuesdays. Folk dance groups perform at 1830 on Wednesdays.

Every visitor to Tampere receives a key to the city. The "key" constitutes an indispensable information brochure, *Key to Tampere*. It's a twenty-page, pocket-sized brochure that is updated annually to include the latest information on the city's places and events. The brochure includes a map of the city with numerical identifiers for points of interest and their hours of operation and, where applicable, admission charges.

You may pick up your key to the city in the tourist information office located at No. 2 Verkatehtaankatu. It's an easy ten-minute walk from the rail station down Hämeenkatu Street, which lies directly in front of the rail station. After four blocks, just before the river, turn left to Hatanpään valtatie. The city tourist information office, a red brick building beside a small park, will then be in front of you.

From June through August, the office is open Monday through Friday, 0830 to 2000; Saturday, 0830 to 1800; and Sunday from 1130 to 1800. During winter, the operating hours are 0830 through 1700 Monday through Friday, closed Saturday and Sunday. The telephone number is 31–2126652 or 2126775; fax 2196463. Sightseeing tours leave the tourist office at 1400 daily, June through August. The tour takes about one and a half hours.

Suomen Joutsen, the "Swan of Finland" (above), highlights Turku's harbor area. Built in France in 1902, the ship served as a school for seamen until 1988. It is now open to visitors every summer. **Cloister Hill** (below), an out-of-the-way 1779 settlement of Turku, escaped the city's disastrous fire of 1827. Some thirty workshops now form a handicrafts museum showing occupations of that era. (Photos courtesy Matti Kivekäs.)

From Helsinki . . .

A DAY EXCURSION TO TURKU
DISTANCE BY TRAIN: 124 miles (200 km)
AVERAGE TRAIN TIME: 2 hours, 15 minutes

Turku is a city of contrasts, where past and present meet and blend. Finland's oldest established town, Turku celebrated its 760th anniversary in 1989. Turku was never founded; it seems it was always there. It developed naturally at the crossing of the northern trade routes at the mouth of the Aura River. The present population of approximately 160,000 is hard working, industrious, and friendly.

Your Eurailpass enables you to choose from two forms of traveling to Turku. You can go by train on a day excursion from Helsinki, or you can take the Silja ferry from Stockholm (see chapter 27 for complete details on ferry crossings). Whether you go by train or ferry, Turku deserves an extended examination because it has many interesting sights to offer.

Turku has three rail stations. Arriving from Helsinki, your train will make a brief stop at the Kupittaa suburban station before arriving in the city's main station. Do not detrain at Kupittaa. If you arrive in Turku on a day excursion from Helsinki and your train is scheduled to terminate at the ferry port (the third stop), we suggest that rather than getting off at the main station (second stop), stay aboard the train and ride to the end of the line. There you can inspect the Silja Line's ferry terminal at the mouth of the Aura River and then, time permitting, visit the nearby Great Castle of Turku, the museum ship *Sigyn,* and the sailing ship *Suomen Joutsen* (the "Swan of Finland"). Return to the town either on foot or by taxi. The taxi fare is approximately 30 markkaa; the walk from the port to the station should take about twenty to thirty minutes, and there's a lot to see en route. Bus service also is available. Bus No. 1 plies between the town's marketplace and the port. The bus fare is 8.00 markkaa.

Turku's tourist information office can be reached by proceeding from the rail station down Humalistonkatu, which will turn into Humlegardsgaten. Turn left at Eriksgatan and proceed for two blocks, then turn right onto Auragatan. The tourist information office will be at your right near the city hall.

From June through September 15, the tourist information office in Turku is open 0800–1930 Monday through Friday, Saturday and Sunday, 1000–1700; from September 16 through May, 0830–1800 Monday through Friday, Saturday and Sunday, 1000–1700. The telephone number is 21–233–6366; fax 21–233–6488. At the harbor, check with the Silja Line desk for city information and directions to the city.

Tours depart the Aurakatu tourist office Monday through Saturday from

281

TURKU—*FINLAND'S FIRST CAPITAL*

A Day Excursion from Helsinki

DEPART FROM HELSINKI STATION	TRAIN NUMBER	ARRIVE IN TURKU STATION	NOTES
0650	121	0912(2)	(1)(3)
0902	123	1116	(1)(3)
1202	125	1416	(1)(3)
1402	127	1616	(1)(3)
1606	EP 129	1816	(1)(5)
1706	131	1916(2)	(1)(3)
1838	133	2051(2)	(1)(3)

DEPART FROM TURKU STATION	TRAIN NUMBER	ARRIVE IN HELSINKI STATION	NOTES
0830(4)	124	1102	(1)(3)
1043	126	1302	(1)(3)
1343	128	1602	(1)(3)
1543	130	1802	(1)(3)
1700	132	1918	(1)(3)
1935	134	2200	(1)(3)
2042(4)	136	2310	(1)(3)

(1) Daily, including holidays
(2) Arrives at Turku Harbor 10 to 15 minutes later
(3) Light refreshments available
(4) Departs from Turku Harbor, departs 13 minutes later from Turku Station
(5) Restaurant car

Distance: 124 miles/200 km
Reference: Thomas Cook Table 490

mid-June through August. Check with either of the city's tourist information offices for full details regarding sightseeing opportunities in and around Turku.

The Great Castle of Turku, which is only a brief walk from the Silja Line terminal, was begun in the 1280s. It is the largest castle in Finland. It once served as a prison but now provides a magnificent banquet hall for state and civic functions. Also of interest to visitors is the historical museum that is housed in the Great Castle. Its collection provides insight regarding 400 years of Finnish history. Hours of operation are 1000–1800 daily from April 16 through September 15; 1000–1500 from September 16 through April 15 (on Mondays 1400–1900 in winter).

The Turku Cathedral, another thirteenth-century structure, is open throughout the year. Check with the tourist office regarding the times you may visit the cathedral. Turku Cathedral, the major medieval ecclesiastical building in Finland, is regarded as the national shrine. You will see many interesting neoclassical buildings surrounding the cathedral. Turku boasts two major universities—one Finnish and one Swedish—with a combined student body exceeding 15,000.

During the early hours of the day, the bustling marketplace is full of life. There you will see brisk bargaining amid a brilliant display of flowers, fruit, vegetables, and fresh fish. Fire destroyed a major part of Turku in 1827, but Cloister Hill, a neighborhood of carpenters and stonemasons, escaped damage. Today the area houses the Cloister Hill Handicraft Museum with workshops that reflect the eighteenth and nineteenth centuries.

The word "turku" means "market place." The city, born out of the needs of commerce, is still one of the largest commercial centers in Finland. The Hansa Shopping Center, the country's largest, is adjacent to the city's marketplace and features more than one hundred shops and boutiques—plus a supermarket. Also there is a hotel, theaters for movies and live performances, a gym, eighteen restaurants, and four banks. Whew!

Tower of Belem guards entrance to Lisbon's harbor on the Tagus River. Once in midstream, it's now at the water's edge on the north bank due to changes in the river's course from medieval times.

14   LISBON

Lisbon doesn't just "happen"—you have to plan for it. It's the westernmost capital of Europe and, except for Athens, the southernmost. Geographically speaking, Lisbon is in the boondocks. You must decide on going, then put some extra effort and planning into the going. It's worth it.

Lisbon's main railway station, Santa Apolonia, is the western terminus of all European rail traffic. With this in mind, we suggest that you plan either to begin your Eurail travels in Lisbon or end them there. The "open jaw" air-excursion plan is ideal. It means you arrive in one European city and depart from another. For example, you could fly to Lisbon, Eurail throughout Europe, and return home by way of Amsterdam—or Athens. Talk it over with your travel agent. There are countless ways in which your Eurail plans can include the lovely, lively city of Lisbon.

Day Excursions

We have selected four day excursions out of Lisbon for your continuing pleasure in Portugal once you have roamed about in its capital city for awhile. Each day excursion has been selected to give you a distinctly different portrayal of the Portuguese landscape, its local customs—even its regional cuisine.

Lisbon's riviera comprises the twin towns of Cascais and Estoril. The area is Mediterranean by nature but geographically Atlantic. The coast line is highly cosmopolitan but spotted here and there with charming little enclaves of fishing villages and local industries. For contrast, we have selected Coimbra, which reveals Portugal's academic nature. This fine old university town was at one time the capital of Portugal. You'll not find a more imposing city anywhere.

Travelers typically picture Portugal in its seafaring role. For that image, we suggest Setubal, with its fishing port, fine beaches, hillside castles, and exceptional seafood. En route to Setubal, you will have the opportunity to cross the broad channel of Portugal's Tagus River and view the Tagus Bridge spanning the estuary. The bridge bears a striking resemblance to the Golden Gate Bridge in San Francisco.

Castle buffs will also have a field day in Sintra, where the rail line sets them down amid three ancient castles and close to Cape Roca, the most western point of Europe. If you go there, "where the land ends and the sea begins," the local tourist office can issue you a certificate proving you made the trip. We've even gone so far as to recommend which castle you should see first.

Arriving and Departing

By Air. The Portela de Sacavem International Airport serving Lisbon lies only five miles to the north of the city. Frequently air travelers are treated to an aerial view of Lisbon while their airplane circles for a landing. The approach and landing is similar to that at Hong Kong—you believe the pilot may have elected to land downtown.

Lisbon's airport has all of the usual passenger services and shops available. They are well marked by pictographs. There is no train service from the airport to the city, but public bus service between the airport and the city is available. A special Green Line bus transports passengers from the airport into Lisbon, with a final destination of Santa Apolonia railway station, for 270 escudos, but the buses can be very crowded and you will probably end up taking a cab from the Santa Apolonia Station to your hotel.

We suggest you take a taxi. The cab fares are very reasonable. From the airport to the city center a taxi ride with your luggage costs about 1,000 escudos, depending on how much luggage you have and your destination. Taxis are metered; a tip is appreciated.

The airport has a tax-free shop that is available only to departing international passengers. Following the usual pattern, with the exception of alcohol and tobacco, most other items can be found in the city at lower prices.

By Train. Lisbon has four railway stations; but only one, Santa Apolonia, serves as an arrival point for international trains. Porters usually meet the trains and can herd you through the crowds and into a taxi much faster than you could do it alone.

A taxi-reservation system is available but doesn't seem to work too well. If you don't use a porter and find that the taxi line is too chaotic, walk directly out of the station to the Museu Militar (Military Museum), straight ahead and about one-hundred yards distant. There, you can hail an inbound taxi with ease. Don't feel bad about pulling this ploy. It's all part of the game where taxis are concerned in Lisbon.

Bus No. 9 runs from Santa Apolonia Station to the Rossio Station in downtown Lisbon. The fare may be minimal, but the buses frequently are crowded to capacity, making it rather difficult for you and your suitcase to board the same bus at the same time. Because taxi fares are very reasonable and meters are used, we suggest you take advantage of them and leave your forays on Lisbon's public transportation system to a time when your luggage is safely stacked in your hotel room.

Libson's Rail Stations

Santa Apolonia is the only railway station in Lisbon with international train service.

Money exchange is located in the main hall of the station on the left side as you exit from the trains and beyond ticket window No. 10. The official exchange rate is paid. The service is open daily from 0830 to 2030.

Hotel reservations can be made at a combined train and tourist information office maintained in the station. To reach it, turn to the right as you exit from the trains and walk past ticket window No. 1. Turn right again, and the office bearing the familiar "i" over its door will be in view directly in front of you.

The office hours apparently vary—the posted ones are 0900 to 2000—but the train officials advise that they are actually from 0930 to 1730. The variance, no doubt, is caused by the office staff being on duty primarily during the hours when international trains are arriving. In any case, the office is available to assist in finding hotel rooms for visitors and to provide them with information about Lisbon and Portugal.

Tourist information is available in the station through the services of a combined train and tourist information office (see above). The official tourist information office for the city of Lisbon is located in the city center near the Rossio Station. To get there, take a taxi or bus No. 9, 46, or 39 to the Praca dos Restauradores. The building has three main doors. Enter the one on the left, marked TURISMO. Brochures and maps describing Lisbon, as well as the major tourist attractions throughout Portugal, are available. Office hours are 0900–1730 daily. Some of Portugal's most beautiful señoritas staff this office. Let them help you discover the city that according to legend was founded by the Greek hero, Ulysses—a city of contrasts in which the old and the new rub shoulders at every step.

Train information can be obtained at the office described under the "Hotel Reservations" section. Train information bulletin boards are posted in the station. Those headed CHEGADAS are for arrivals; PARTIDAS indicates departures.

Train reservations can be made at the combined tourist and train information office described previously. Remember that seat reservations on trains going to Spain are obligatory.

Eurailpass validation. If you are beginning your Eurail travel in Lisbon, present your Eurailpass at ticket window No. 11 in the hallway of the Santa Apolonia Station. This window and the others providing international service operate 1000–1800 daily. The Eurail Aid Office is located one floor above in the Servico de Fiscalizacao de Receitas office. Take the elevator around the corner from window No. 10 one floor up.

The following is a description of the other rail and rail/ferry stations in Lisbon. Since the Santa Apolonia Station is the only station handling international travel, Eurailpass validation is available there only.

* * *

Rossio Station is located in the heart of Lisbon. It's on the immediate left of the Teatro Nacional (National Theater) in Rossio Plaza. Entering from the

Terreiro do Paco (above) is the departure point for ferry service to Barreiro Station on the south bank of the Tagus River. En route by ferry (below), a splendid view is given of the "25 of April" Harbor Bridge, seen in the background. It has provisions for a railway and will someday replace the scenic ferry service.

plaza, go up *all* the escalators to reach the train platform level. Train schedules are posted in an alcove beyond track No. 10. This station serves commuter lines to the west of Lisbon. Trains for the day excursion to Sintra depart from here on track No. 5.

Taxis are available at the rear of the train level. If you arrive at the station by taxi, you will be at the track level and won't have to use the escalators. Taxis arrive at the station on a separate ramp that cannot be used by private vehicles or pedestrians.

Campolide Station is the first station stop for trains departing from Rossio Station. It's immediately beyond the tunnel that starts at the end of the Rossio Station train platforms. It's a commuter stop that you should not use when returning from your day excursion to Sintra.

Cais do Sodré Station is the terminus of the suburban lines running to Estoril and Cascais. Departures on its five tracks are shown on a television screen suspended between track Nos. 2 and 3. You may reach this station from Rossio Station on bus No. 45 or No. 35 from the Santa Apolonia Station; however, taxis are recommended. They stop in front of the station.

Terreiro do Paco Station has no trains, only ferryboats that cross the Tagus River to the Barreiro Station, where trains depart for southern Portugal. The ferry runs every half hour. Be certain to board the ferry line to Barreiro, where further rail connections can be made. The other ferry line serves Cacilhas, a commuter station with no rail connections. Eurailpasses are accepted for the ferry crossings.

On a summer's evening, you might want to catch a breeze and see the city from the ferry on a round trip to Barreiro and back.

Likable Lisbon

The city rates high in the climate category. Summers can be hot but are seldom oppressive. If it does get too hot, however, feel free to use the Terreiro do Paco-Barreiro ferry service to cool off. The long autumn is delightful. Winter, at its worst, is best described as "nippy" with plenty of sunshine. Lisbon was all but destroyed by a great earthquake in 1755. It owes its wide avenues and plazas to the foresight of city fathers who rebuilt the city on a grand scale.

Lisbon has three distinct districts—the shopping areas clustered around Rossio, the more ancient areas such as the Moorish quarter in the west and Alfama to the east, and the "new Lisbon" with modern high-rise structures stretching out to the airport and the north. A day can easily be spent in any one of them.

Of particular interest to western visitors is the Alfama district, which suffered the least damage during the earthquake and has thereby been able to preserve much of its old facade and narrow, winding streets. The tourist office has an excellent illustrated brochure describing Alfama, including a map with a suggested walking tour.

At least one evening of your stay in Lisbon should be devoted to dining out in a typical Portuguese restaurant and listening to "Fado," the plaintiff, nostalgic, tragic music of the countryside. Lisbon abounds in such establishments. Our recommendation goes to the Forcado Restaurant, Rua da Rosa No. 221, in the Bairro Alto section of town. Ask your hotel to call ahead for reservations on 36–85–79.

Fado packs more pathos into one song than does a thirteen-week series of your favorite soap opera. Typically, the man and the woman are forced to part. The man, as an example, is coerced into going on a long sea voyage, but his ship sinks in a hurricane and everyone aboard perishes—except our hero, who makes it into a lifeboat, only to be attacked and eaten alive by a giant white shark. The messenger bearing the news of his demise is struck by lightning before he can deliver the message; the woman, seeing the message being swept down the rain covered street, dashes after it—only to be run over and trampled to death by a team of horses. It's all good clean fun and you shouldn't miss it!

Either your hotel or the tourist office can arrange for a sightseeing tour of Lisbon. Highlights of any tour will include the Jeronimos Monastery of Belem and the Tower of Belem. Along with these monuments of earlier years you will be sure to see and enjoy Lisbon's more modern side by visiting such edifices as the Discoveries Monument, inaugurated in 1960. The most modern symbol of Lisbon is its bridge spanning the Tagus River, which is equal to the Golden Gate in its structural beauty.

From Lisbon . . .

TRAIN CONNECTIONS TO OTHER BASE CITIES

TO:	DEPART	ARRIVE	TRAIN NUMBER	COOK'S TABLE	NOTES
Madrid	1155	1956 (3)	31	80	(1)(2)
(sleeper)	2155	0837+1 (4)	335	80	(1)(2)
Paris*					
(couchettes)	1703	1500+1	311	46	(1)(2)(5)

* No day trains. Distance is 1,173 miles/1,887 km

(1) Daily, including holidays
(2) Seat reservations mandatory
(3) Madrid Atocha station
(4) Madrid Chamartin
(5) Transfer in Hendaye (French border) to TGV 8530 (departs Hendaye 0934)

Fishing fleet at anchor in Cascais harbor portrays dual role of village as a port and year-round resort. Estoril, Portugal's posh resort, is only four train minutes away.

From Lisbon . . .

A DAY EXCURSION TO CASCAIS AND ESTORIL
DISTANCE BY TRAIN: 16 miles (26 km)
AVERAGE TRAIN TIME: 30 minutes

Portugal boasts miles and miles of sun-drenched, sandy beaches. Probably the most famous stretch lies just to the west of Lisbon along the Costa do Estoril. Here, the two towns of Cascais and Estoril offer a wide variety of scenes to suit the tastes of everyone.

Famed as a resort for royalty and a playground for deposed monarchs and international sportsmen, Estoril has recently widened its welcome to include the rank-and-file traveler. A bevy of moderately priced hotels now dot the seascape, which once was all but dominated by the Casino, a super complex of gaming rooms, bars, restaurant, and movie theater—all fronted by formal gardens.

Estoril's twin town, Cascais, played the country-cousin role for years with its fish market and colorful harbor. Now Cascais has its own string of hotels, yet it manages to maintain a slightly lower key atmosphere than its chic neighbor.

The point of departure in Lisbon for the Costa do Estoril is the Cais do Sodré, a small, suburban-type railway station near the waterfront. We suggest a taxi as the best means of getting there. Departure information on television screens will guide you to the next train. Service is frequent, with trains running every fifteen minutes during peak passenger periods and every thirty minutes otherwise.

There is a snack bar just to the right of track No. 1 if you want to tote your own picnic lunch and have forgotten to pick one up in town. All the trains are one class. Cascais is the end of the rail line; Estoril is two stops before Cascais. If Estoril is your destination, stay alert and get off at the proper station. But with Cascais at the end of the line, there's no way you can miss the beautiful Costa do Estoril with its fabulous beaches and swimming pools, golf, tennis, sailing, shooting ranges, and much, much more.

Estoril is recommended as the first stop on your visit to this coastal area because the tourist office, which is quite near the Estoril railway station, can provide you with all sorts of information for the entire Costa do Estoril area, including Cascais. To reach this office, use the underpass from the ocean side (the trains run on the left) to the city side. Cross the wide boulevard immediately in front of you and walk straight ahead to the Hotel das Arcadas. You can see its sign from the station. The tourist information office (telephone 268–01–13 or 268–70–44) functions daily throughout the year from 0900 to 2000.

CASCAIS AND ESTORIL—*LISBON'S RIVIERA*

A Day Excursion From Lisbon

Trains depart from Lisbon's Cais do Sodré Station every twenty minutes. (See *Thomas Cook European Timetable,* the "Plans of Cities" section, for a description of train stations in Lisbon.)

Trains run to Estoril in twenty-nine minutes. Cascais is three minutes beyond Estoril. All trains are one class only.

Train departure information is shown on television in Cais do Sodré between track Nos. 2 and 3. Printed schedules are posted in the station foyer opposite public telephone booths.

Distance: 16 miles/26 km

If you plan to enjoy the beach while you are in Estoril, all you need to do is retrace your steps from the tourist information office to the ocean side of the underpass, where excellent beach facilities, including lockers, cabanas, and restaurants, can be found. The tourist office has complete details, brochures, and prices. The beach at Cascais is somewhat smaller but more intimate. A quick four-minute train ride will get you there.

The area abounds with attractions, and the climate is ideal. Spring never seems to know when to arrive, so the flowers bloom twice a year. Posts have been placed along the rocky areas of the beach to indicate surf-fishing spots. Tennis courts are in profusion as are swimming pools, for those not satisfied with sun and surf.

On Sundays during the summer, Lisbon flocks to the Monumental de Cascais, the bull ring, for excitement. Bullfights in Portugal are different from those in Spain in that the bull is not killed but taken by the horns (literally) and forced to a standstill. The proceedings end more on a comic note rather than the tragic end of a Spanish bullfight.

A championship eighteen-hole golf course, Estoril Palacio, with temporary memberships, is available—as is a miniature golf course for those who just want to "putter" around. Both are available year-round and are in immaculate condition. The comfortable club house has a large terrace overlooking the golf course, a restaurant, and a swimming pool in case mom and the kids want to pass the time of day while dad's out on the links.

On Wednesday mornings, Cascais is the site of a regional open market that is well worth a trip from Lisbon to see. Gypsies in their traditional garb and golden earrings hawk everything imaginable. Farmers' wives, suspicious of supermarket packaging, can be seen scrutinizing their chickens while they are still alive, healthy, and squawking loudly. Flower vendors appear to be almost submerged beneath a tidal wave of splendid color created by the flowers and plants they are offering for sale.

Tradition has it that you should bring your own market basket to the market—no plastic, please. To reach the market quickly after arriving in Cascais, bear to the right around the plaza in the front of the rail station and continue to the right onto Avenue 25 de April. Two short blocks farther you'll spy the market—probably hear it, too.

Some Eurail travelers establish themselves in a local resort hotel in or near Cascais or Estoril, then commute to Lisbon for sightseeing or for continuing on with other day excursions. The fast and frequent train service from Cascais and Estoril and the abundance in both towns of hotels to fit any budget, large or small, makes this idea very feasible. No day is long enough on the Costa do Estoril, so perhaps this is the answer. It sure sounds like a good alternative.

Old university peers down upon the city of Coimbra from its vantage point 300 feet above the Mondego River. Poets have done much to immortalize the charm of Coimbra, first capital of Portugal.

A DAY EXCURSION TO COIMBRA
DISTANCE BY TRAIN: 135 miles (218 km)
AVERAGE TRAIN TIME: 2 hours, 3 minutes

Coimbra is one of Portugal's most charming cities. It has a unique blend of the old and the new. Site of the oldest university in Portugal, it has ancient buildings that seem to blend perfectly with the modern spirit of its students. Until 1911, Coimbra was the only university in Portugal. Founded in 1290 in Lisbon, it was transferred to its present site in 1307 to compensate for the removal of the capital from Coimbra to Lisbon.

Six kings were born in Coimbra, and from the middle of the eleventh century, the city was the headquarters of the Portuguese forces dedicated to driving the Moors back to north Africa. As a fortress, and now as a university, Coimbra occupies an imposing position from its hillside, 300 feet above the Mondego River.

There is a pleasant air of antiquity surrounding Coimbra. Its origins are lost in the mists of time. The Romans named the city Aeminium. Scene of the largest Roman archaeological site in Portugal, it was sacked by the Vandals and overrun by the Saracens. Only during the Christian reconquest, which reached its climax in 1064, did the city begin to grow and develop with the special character it has today.

Coimbra's cathedral is said to be the finest Romanesque building in Portugal. The first stone of the structure was laid in 1162. Inside the cathedral, visitors may see its Gothic tombs and art collection. A later addition to its attractions, Portugal dos Pequeninos (Portugal of the Little Ones), in which you will find scaled-down facsimiles of Portuguese architecture, gives grownups something to marvel at—and kids something to play in. Time is a fleeting thing in Coimbra. Get there early to enjoy every moment.

Trains from Lisbon stop at the Coimbra B. Station, which is a short distance north of the city center. You may take a shuttle train into its main station or hail a cab. We suggest the latter because the taxi can take you directly to the Municipal Tourist Board located on Largo da Portagem, at the approach to the great bridge spanning the Mondego River. If you do ride the shuttle train, on arrival walk four blocks away from the station, upstream along the river, until you come to the bridge approach. The tourist information office is just off Largo da Portagem on Avenida Navarro, which continues to run along the river.

The tourist information center has numerous brochures and maps to assist visitors. Just be aware that when the attendant suggests a visit to the university area, the short distance between where you are and where you are going

COIMBRA—*UNIVERSITY TOWN*

A Day Excursion from Lisbon

DEPART FROM SANTA APOLONIA* STATION	TRAIN NUMBER	ARRIVE IN COIMBRA B.** STATION	NOTES
0722	IC 511	0946	(1)(2)(3)
0805	IC 531	1013	(1)(2)(3)
0810	IR 811	1045	(1)(3)(5)
0900	IR 823	1132	(1)(3)(5)
1100	IC 521	1308	(1)(2)(3)
1135	IR 825	1400	(3)(4)

DEPART FROM COIMBRA B.** STATION	TRAIN NUMBER	ARRIVE IN SANTA APOLONIA* STATION	NOTES
1549	Alfa 122	1750	(1)(2)(3)
1703	IC 512	1912	(1)(2)(3)
1819	Alfa 124	2020	(1)(2)(3)
1914	IR 810	2135	(1)(3)(5)
2129	IR 532	2335	(1)(2)(3)

* See *Thomas Cook European Timetable,* "Plans of Cities" section for description of railway stations in Lisbon.
** Take shuttle train to main station.

(1) Daily, including holidays
(2) Seat reservations required
(3) Food service available
(4) Fridays and Saturdays only
(5) Seat reservations recommended

Distance: 135 miles/218 km
Reference: Thomas Cook Table 445

involves an elevation of about 300 feet—the university sits on a hilltop over-looking the river. Unless you are a born mountain climber, we suggest that you go by taxi to the top and then walk downhill. Like "Jack and Jill," we climbed up the hill and haven't been able to carry a bucket of water since.

The tourist information center is open 0900–1800 Monday through Friday, 0900–1230 on Saturday and Sunday. They reopen after lunch from 1400–1730. Speaking of lunch, the center can provide you with a map of the city showing the locations of its hotels and eating establishments. *Leitao* (roast suckling pig) is a specialty of the area. Having washed this down with an ample supply of *vinho verde* (green wine), another regional feature, you should be in a mood to cross the river and visit the "Portugal of the Little Ones"—but don't tackle the hill unless you go there in a taxi.

This unusual children's garden, planned more for educational purposes than for entertainment, attracts "children of all ages" because of its exacting con-struction and organization. Children can come in close contact with its build-ings and monuments, thereby learning by looking, asking, and touching. The garden has five sections. The first is a children's house (actually a day school) where local children attend kindergarten.

The areas that follow represent the architectural styles of continental Portugal, Coimbra, the monuments of Portugal, insular Portugal, and, finally, the overseas territories. The city map will guide you to this wonderland. Check with the tourist center as to hours of operation, for they vary according to the season.

Back in the center of the city you will find the monastery of the Holy Cross, Santa Cruz. Its initial construction began in the twelfth century. Later addi-tions included a charming Renaissance sacristy and a magnificently carved facade. In the choir loft of the monastery, you can examine the pictorial record of the voyages made by Portugal's famed navigator, Vasco da Gama, who was the first European to reach India by the sea route.

While across the river, you may want to visit the remains of the Santa Clara convent. It was destroyed by floods, but you may visit the ruins. Ask the tourist office for details.

A visit to Coimbra is like stepping back into the pages of history. It is truly one of the loveliest and most picturesque cities of Portugal. It's an enjoyable experience, one we're certain that you will not forget.

Third port of Portugal, Setubal has seen development of many industries, but fishing remains its main resource. The area is world famous for Portuguese oysters and sardines.

From Lisbon ...

A DAY EXCURSION TO SETUBAL
DISTANCE BY TRAIN: 18 miles (29 km)
AVERAGE TRAIN TIME: 35 minutes

This is a colorful, interesting day excursion from beginning to end. You start at the Lisbon Terreiro do Paco Station, which is actually a marine terminal for ferryboats crossing the Tagus River. After a pleasant twenty-five-minute boat ride, you disembark at the Barreiro Station, where you board a southbound train for Setubal.

The ferry crossing is a memorable experience. It provides an outstanding view of Lisbon, a panoramic scene of the entire city from the sea. Built on seven hills, like Rome, Lisbon appears to cascade down to the water's edge as your ferry moves away from its shore.

Gazing seaward, your eyes sight the Tagus Bridge, a modern miracle of engineering. It has the highest bridge towers and the longest span of its kind in Europe and looks every bit like the Golden Gate Bridge in San Francisco. For an abbreviated day excursion, we suggest you ride the ferry to Barreiro and back. The boats run about every half-hour throughout the day and into the evening. The first-class section is aft, and a snack bar sells a reasonable variety of food and beverages. On a warm summer evening, it's great! Your ticket is your Eurailpass.

Docking at Barreiro seems to stir up the local folks, for they charge off the boat like a horde of lemmings bent on self-destruction. Don't join the melee— the ferry arrives in ample time, and Eurailpassers will find plenty of empty seats waiting for them in the train's first-class coaches.

Taking a ferry a half-hour ahead of schedule will give you some time to browse around Barreiro's station. Avoid the snack bar in the station. The one on the ferry is much nicer—cleaner, too.

The railroad right of way you'll be traveling on between Barreiro and Setubal was completed in 1860. Aside from the fact that this project was one of the first of its kind in Europe, it gives one the impression that Setubal has been an aggressive, alert community for many decades.

The city's port facilities are highly developed and capable of handling even the largest ocean-going vessels. The bay of Setubal is a glistening example of the success resulting from the proper combination of commerce and recreation. During your visit, you should plan to move to a high point of vantage to see this for yourself. We would like to suggest that you plan lunch from such a vantage point. Later, we'll tell you about the menu and view from Saint Philip's Castle.

Setting out in Setubal, take a taxi downtown to the Regiao de Turismo de

SETUBAL—*SEASIDE AND CASTLES*

A Day Excursion from Lisbon

DEPART FROM LISBON TERREIRO DO PACO FERRY TERMINAL	ABOARD	ARRIVE IN BARREIRO* STATION	NOTES
0825	Ferry	0855	(1)
0950	Ferry	1020	(1)

DEPART FROM BARREIRO* STATION	ABOARD	ARRIVE IN SETUBAL STATION	NOTES
0925	Train	1018	(1)(2)
1035	Train	1123	(1)(2)

DEPART FROM SETUBAL STATION	ABOARD	ARRIVE IN BARREIRO* STATION	NOTES
1650	Train	1738	(1)(2)
1806	Train	1900	(1)(2)
1912	Train	1955	(1)(2)
2132	Train	2218	

DEPART FROM BARREIRO* STATION	ABOARD	ARRIVE IN LISBON TERREIRO DO PACO FERRY STATION	NOTES
1750	Ferry	1820	(1)
1910	Ferry	1940	(1)
2000	Ferry	2030	(1)
2240	Ferry	2310	(1)

* See *Thomas Cook European Timetable,* "Plans of Cities" section, for description of railway stations in Lisbon.
(1) Daily, including holidays
(2) Second class only

Distance: 18 miles/29 km (from Barreiro)
Reference: Thomas Cook Table 448

Setubal-Costa Azul (regional tourist office). It operates Monday through Saturday in the summer, 0900–1900, and Sunday, 0900–1230. It's closed throughout the winter. If you want to call ahead for information, the travel office numbers are 524284, 527033, 529789, or 529507. If there's no answer, try 534222, which is the town hall tourist information office located in Praça do Bocage, where there will be someone on duty at all times to assist you.

There are two tourist information offices in Setubal. As capital of the district, Setubal houses the *Regiào de Turismo de Setubal* (regional tourist commission) located in Travessa Frei Gaspar, No. 10. The city tourist information office, although it operates in conjunction with the region, is located in a separate office across from the park, *Praça do Quebedo*. If your taxi driver doesn't understand English, point to either of the above italicized names; he will be able to get you to either.

The city happens to be the third largest in Portugal, but its rural atmosphere seems to deny it. Uncrowded and unhurried, Setubal is not a resort in the strict sense of the word, but it has a lot to offer visitors. The tourist commission office can assist in planning your day there. Everything is more or less laid back. If you are seeking relaxation, you'll find it in Setubal. Everyone is nice, and nobody seems to be in a hurry.

The Palmela Castle is about five or six miles from Setubal. The castle has been converted into a *pousada* (resting place), or inn, and offers a fantastic view of the surrounding countryside. The trip to the castle, an impregnable fortress in medieval times, is well worth the time. The most convenient way of getting there is by taxi (the most economical way, too, if you have a few fellow passengers to share the fare).

Setubal has a remarkable assemblage of monuments and fine old buildings. The Church of Jesus is said to be one of the most beautiful small churches ever built. Next door, the Town Museum displays a priceless collection of old masters. There is also a Maritime Museum and the Bocage Monument, which honors the city's great poet.

Luncheon in Saint Philip's Castle overlooking Setubal is an unforgettable experience. This castle also has been converted into a *pousada* and commands an impressive view over both land and sea. A local taxi will take you there, and the inn will telephone for another when you are ready to return. Lunch is inexpensive, and you couldn't buy a better view for twice the price. The menu features local specialties such as *sopa do mar* (fish soup) and a variety of tasty fish and shellfish.

Spend some time strolling through Setubal's colorful harbor area before returning to Lisbon.

Pena Palace, rebuilt in the nineteenth century, occupies the highest point overlooking Sintra. Royal families summered here.

A DAY EXCURSION TO SINTRA
DISTANCE BY TRAIN: 17 miles (28 km)
AVERAGE TRAIN TIME: 45 minutes

Former home of Portuguese kings. Ancient castles. Palaces. Three separate villages towering above the countryside with fantastic views. Close by Cape Roca, the westernmost point of continental Europe "where the land ends and the sea begins." A luxury hotel that is really an eighteenth-century palace. The place Lord Byron termed, "a glorious Eden." All of this, and more, is Sintra—which you can reach from Lisbon in less than one hour by train.

Sintra is a comfortable day excursion. Trains departing Rossio Station throughout the day and into the late evening hours make a visit there uncomplicated. Actually, Sintra is the end of the line for trains departing Rossio on track No. 5, so all you need do is get aboard, relax, and go.

The Rossio Station is located in the heart of Lisbon. It can be reached by the Lisbon subway or by bus, but if you are not within walking distance from your hotel, we recommend going there by taxi. By subway, bus, or on foot, you will enter the Rossio Station from street level and reach the train platforms by a series of escalators.

By taxi, you arrive via a hillside roadway at the train-platform level. If you want to check train schedules before departing for Sintra, you will find them posted in an alcove just to the right of track No. 10. Station stops on the Sintra line are not displayed in the coaches of the train, but that's no problem in that you are riding to the last stop anyway. All passenger coaches on the Sintra line are single-class commuter types. Seating is on a first-come, first-served basis, so we suggest being in the Rossio Station well before the scheduled departure of the train you intend taking.

Departing the Rossio Station, trains immediately enter a tunnel. When they emerge, a short stop is made at the Campolide Station at the other end of the tunnel. We make mention of this because you may mistake this station for Rossio when returning from Sintra and get off the train at that point. Stay aboard. The Campolide Station is a commuter-type facility and very limited in taxis and bus services.

As the train moves westward out of Lisbon, a backward glance will again reward you with a view of the city and its seven hills. Ahead, as the train travels on to Sintra, you will begin to note rising hills and rock outcroppings. It was in this area that prehistoric man erected tomblike monuments called *dolmens.* There are still a few remaining.

SINTRA—*MOUNTAIN PEAKS AND PALACES*

A Day Excursion From Lisbon

Frequent suburban trains run between Lisbon's Rossio Station and Sintra. The journey takes forty-five minutes. (See *Thomas Cook European Timetable,* "Plans of Cities" section, for a description of train stations in Lisbon.)

All trains are one class only. Trains for Sintra depart from track No. 5 approximately every sixteen minutes. Ride the train to the end of the line.

Schedules for all trains departing and arriving Rossio Station are posted in an alcove to the right of track No. 10.

Distance: 17 miles/28 km
Reference: Local schedule only. (Not listed in *Thomas Cook European Timetable.*)

Arriving in the Sintra rail terminal, you will note that there is no tourist information available other than a posted notice concerning the location of the tourist information office in the city. The Sintra tourist office is located in the city center, about one kilometer from the train station. You can reach it by taxi or by boarding the bus marked S. PEDRO, which leaves from near the station (at Correnteza). On foot, it is an interesting fifteen-minute walk.

The bus stops near the fire station, a short distance from the National Palace of Sintra and the tourist information office. The tourist office can supply you with maps and guidebooks to help you select where to go and what to see. The tourist office is open daily from 0900 to 1900 and from 0900 to 2000 June through September. It is closed January 1, May 1, Easter Sunday, and Christmas Day. Call ahead for information on 923 11 57.

There is no public transportation to most of the places of tourist interest. You must take a taxi or a horse-drawn carriage. The taxis are not equipped with meters. The Sintra tourist office can inform you about taxi fares. The fare, by the way, includes up to four passengers plus a fixed amount of time for you to complete your sightseeing, so you don't have to worry about the meter ticking away. You should also ask about the half-day tour, which includes Pena Palace, the Convent of Capuchos (the Cork Convent), Cape Roca, and the Gardens of Monserrate.

Of all the sights in the area, we suggest that you see the National Palace of Sintra (Palacio Real) first, followed by a visit to the Pena Palace (Palacio da Pena) and Pena Park. There is a nominal admission to the palace grounds. If you are taking a tour of the palace, a tip for the guard is appropriate. (There are no guides.)

Pena Palace is more than one hundred years old, and its commanding position atop the highest peak in the area makes it well worth the visit. The tourist office will provide information for other sights in the area surrounding Sintra. The Pena Palace is closed on Monday; the National Palace of Sintra is closed on Wednesday.

Other points of interest are the Moorish Castle, the Convent of Capuchos, the Gardens of Monserrate, and the Queluz Palace. The latter captures much of the style of Versailles, although it is considerably smaller. A luxury restaurant is housed in the old kitchen area of the Queluz Palace. It is closed on Tuesday.

If you are interested in seeing the Atlantic from Cape Roca, the local tourist office can provide you with a certificate verifying that you did, in fact, visit there. You can purchase the "usual" certificate or a special one. Either certificate attests to the fact, in Portuguese (translation on the back), that you stood on the most western part of the European continent—a point that is closer to New York than Dublin, Ireland.

Luxembourg City, a complex of old and new patterns superimposed one upon the other, was once one of the world's most powerful fortresses. (Photo courtesy of Luxembourg City.)

15   LUXEMBOURG

The Grand Duchy of Luxembourg is one of Europe's small countries. Germany borders it to the east, France to the south, and Belgium adjoins it on the north and west. Luxembourg now vies with Switzerland in the field of international banking. A substantial number of corporations doing business in the European community maintain accounts there. Despite its financial strengths, the Grand Duchy is confined to 999 square miles, making it smaller than the state of Rhode Island.

The Grand Duchy once dominated an area nearly 300 times its present size. In more recent times, as well as in the past, Luxembourg's fate and fortunes have been linked with those of Belgium. The forces of the French king Louis XIV conquered the city of Luxembourg in the mid-seventeenth century. Subsequent fortifications built by the French and succeeding conquerors earned the city the title "Gibraltar of the North."

Luxembourg was overrun by the Germans during World War I, but its independence was restored by the Treaty of Versailles. It was occupied again by German forces during World War II. During the Battle of the Bulge in December 1944, the tides of war surged around Luxembourg. Liberated earlier by U.S. Forces, the city was recaptured by the Germans, who executed many members of the Belgian and Luxembourgese underground before Luxembourg was again taken by the Allied Forces.

Luxembourg's monetary unit is the Luxembourg franc, which has the same value as the Belgian franc. Belgian money is circulated freely throughout the Grand Duchy, but Luxembourg francs are not accepted in Belgium. If you cash a traveler's check in Luxembourg and plan to leave immediately, insist that you receive Belgian francs or the currency of the country where you are going.

Day Excursions

Four day excursions have been selected for the Grand Duchy and its surrounding countries. Each is distinctly different in its points of interest. The day excursion to Clervaux takes you through the rugged north country of the Grand Duchy, where the Ardennes campaign was contested bitterly in 1944. The day excursion to Koblenz is saturated with scenic views along the Moselle and Rhine rivers and the charm of Koblenz, one of the oldest cities in Germany. Metz measures up to a most interesting day excursion into France. The German city of Trier, founded by Augustus Caesar, provides an exciting opportunity to explore many Roman ruins and to titillate your taste buds with the most delectable Moselle wines.

Arriving and Departing

By Air. Luxembourg, because of its central European location, the excellent air services of Icelandair, and the city's convenient rail connections, attracts an increasing number of visitors annually. Findel, the city's international airport, is only four miles outside the city limits. Regularly scheduled flights to Luxembourg from New York are provided by Icelandair.

Findel has long been one of Europe's most modern airports and has expanded its runways and parking ramps to accommodate more arrivals and departures. All usual airport services are available, including tax-free shopping for departing passengers. Bus service from the airport terminates at the Luxembourg rail station and downtown air terminal. Municipal buses (Bus No. 9) depart every half-hour throughout the day and evening. The one-way bus fare is 35 Luxembourg francs plus 35 francs for each suitcase. A Luxair bus straight to the rail station costs 120 francs with no charge for luggage. On the other hand, taxis to town are expensive, ranging from 400 to 600 francs. All taxis are equipped with meters. No tips are expected.

By Train. The City of Luxembourg is served by a single railway station located conveniently in the city center. Connections can be made directly to Belgium, France, Germany, and the Netherlands from the station. The city tourist information office, the downtown air terminal, and the city bus terminals are all clustered conveniently about the railway station, which, like the airport, has been modernized to handle an increasing number of passengers.

There is a wide selection of food services to choose from in and around the station area. Inside, there's a regular cafeteria, a menu restaurant, and a gourmet dining facility. The first two are located on the ground floor just off of the station's foyer; the full-service dining room is on the second floor. Standing in front of the station, you can view an abundance of eating establishments offering everything from fast food to leisurely dining. We dare you to pass the bakery shop on the corner to the left of the cinema without going in and buying something. Your nose will lead you to it.

Luxembourg Central Station

Constructed originally in 1912, the Luxembourg rail station underwent a complete interior renovation in 1979. Other improvements, such as digital display boards for train arrivals and departures, have been added since then. The facade of the station is unchanged, but the services you find inside are modern.

The rail terminal in Luxembourg is actually located in what historians call the "new city." From 1855 to 1866, when the first rails were laid, the gorge of the Alzette River remained too wide to be bridged. Consequently, the rail station was established on the far side of the gorge opposite the city as it existed then, and the new section of the city began to develop around it.

The station has three platforms (*quais*) serving five tracks. Track 1 is served by platform 1, which is directly connected to the station with level access to the platform. Trains arriving on the other tracks, however, require passengers to utilize an underground tunnel to reach the main station hall.

To eliminate the inconvenience of hauling baggage up and down the stairways to and from the platforms, a system of elevators was installed that serves the outer tracks. To utilize the elevator service from the station to the outer train platforms, take the hallway running off to the right of the main hall until you arrive at the entrance to the elevator service tunnel. It is just beyond the last ticket window and right before you reach the baggage room.

The entrances to the elevators serving the train platforms are marked clearly, although it seems a bit confusing when you first use them. You descend from the train platform to a tunnel. There, you walk a short distance to another elevator, which you ascend to the station level; you then take another short tunnel into the main hallway.

The station is one of the few remaining rail terminals in Europe with porter service, and it's limited. The porters work for tips. As a rule of thumb, they expect about 30 francs per piece of luggage, regardless of size.

Money exchange office is located on the right side of the main station hall as you enter from the train-platform area. The standard money-exchange pictograph identifies the facility. Hours of operation are 0900–2100 daily. An additional exchange facility is located in the nearby air terminus, which also houses the Luxembourg tourist information office. Operated by a local bank, this exchange is open 0830–1200 and 1330–1600 Monday through Friday. It is closed Saturday and Sunday.

Hotel reservations should be made through the tourist information office. They assist in securing hotel accommodations and do so without charge. There are numerous hotels on the side streets near the station in addition to some charming smaller hotels within reasonable taxi or city-bus distances. The four-star President Hotel is across the street from the rail station.

Should you prefer the American-style chain hotels, the Sheraton is located near the Findel Airport.

Tourist information is obtained in the air-terminus office, which stands to the right of the railway station as you leave the main exit. It is easily identified by its AIR TERMINUS sign and the usual "i." Upon entering the air terminus, you will find the tourist information office on your left. In addition to making hotel reservations, they can also provide information on youth hostels, camping grounds, and holiday flats and chalets available to tourists. The office is open 0900–1930 daily in summer.

Equip yourself with a map of Luxembourg and the colorful brochure *Discover Luxembourg*. In addition to the walking tours described in this last

Luxembourg railway terminal bustles with train departures and arrivals to and from the neighboring countries of Belgium, France, and Germany. Passenger facilities and services have been added, including a lift service for baggage carts and the handicapped.

publication, the information office can provide a schedule and description of conducted bus tours in and around the city. Tour No. 1, the basic sightseeing trip, departs from Platform 5 at the downtown bus terminal every Tuesday through Saturday (April 1–October 31) at 1000 and lasts about one and a half hours. A sightseeing tour of the city and its suburbs is offered every Tuesday, Thursday, Saturday, and Sunday (June 1–September 30) beginning at 1430.

The other tours take you through the Ardennes and the Moselle Valley; but much of the area seen on these tours can be enjoyed during the day excursions to Clervaux, Metz, and Trier, so don't duplicate your efforts.

Train information office is to your immediate left when exiting from the train platform area. It's readily identified by the universal "i" alongside an illuminated sign reading, RESERVATIONS, RAIL TOUR-LUXEMBOURG. The hours of operation are 0700–2000 daily, including Sunday and holidays. A minitimetable describing the best train connections between Luxembourg and other major European cities is available in this office. Included in the timetable are the departing and returning hours of selected trains to Brussels, Paris, Rotterdam, Basel, Cologne, Frankfurt, Munich, Vienna, Copenhagen, Milan, and Rome.

Train reservations for EuroCity, InterCity, and regular express trains can be made in the train information office. Sleeper reservations may also be made here. Remember, the Eurailpass covers only your first-class rail transportation. Sleeper accommodations are separate and vary in cost according to the type you select from those available on the trains you intend to travel on and the distance of your overnight journey.

Eurailpass validation can be accomplished in the train information office daily between 0700 and 2000. Due to the popularity of Icelandair as a transatlantic air carrier, this office probably validates as many, or possibly more, Eurailpasses than even the major stations in Europe's capitals. If you are an arriving passenger on Icelandair and plan to leave Luxembourg on the next available train, we suggest that you taxi to the rail station in order to avoid the crowd.

Eurail Aid Office: A Eurailpass traveler who loses his or her Eurailpass or encounters other related problems will be directed by the train information office to report to the Eurail Aid Office, Room 407 on the fourth floor of the CFL (Luxembourg Railroad Building). Entrance to this building is to the immediate right of the downtown air terminus. You should present identification at the reception desk in the lobby. This office, which is open weekdays 0830–1200 and 1400–1730, is closed Saturday, Sunday, and holidays. During that time, the train information office in the station is prepared to render assistance.

Luxembourg Limelight

"The soldier, above all other people," said Douglas MacArthur, "prays for peace, for he must suffer and bear the deepest wounds and scars of war." Such is the drama of 5,100 grave sites in The American Military Cemetery near the village of Hamm, three miles outside the city of Luxembourg. Among the crosses standing row on row, you will see one marked "George S. Patton, Jr., General, Third Army, California, December 21, 1945." Solemn in its simplicity, beautiful in the manner whereby it attests to the American spirit, this cemetery must be seen. It is a moving, memorable moment. The guided bus tours operated from Luxembourg City will take you there as a part of their tour program, or you can taxi there for about the same price as the airport-to-rail-station fare. A return taxi may be summoned by telephone.

Luxembourg's low value added tax (VAT) of 13 percent makes it a bargain base city in comparison to some other European cities. Even residents of Luxembourg's neighboring countries make purchases of tobacco, alcohol, and fuel in the Grand Duchy because the taxes are lower.

Although hotel rates and restaurant prices are lower than those of most other European cities, the quality is not. Some Luxembourgers actually believe "the way to a man's heart is through his stomach," and they've made believers out of us. Try the smoked pork with broad beans or the delicate Ardennes ham cut paper-thin. For a real treat, try trout from the Moselle accompanied by a fine Luxembourg wine—all at popular prices. Luxembourg abounds in international cuisine. One of our favorites is the L'Hotel-Restaurant Italia at 15–17 rue d'Anvers (telephone 486626), which offers excellent Italian specialties. Phone ahead for reservations—it's popular with the local folks, too.

From Luxembourg . . .

TRAIN CONNECTIONS TO OTHER BASE CITIES

TO:	DEPART	ARRIVE	TRAIN NUMBER	COOK'S TABLE	NOTES
Amsterdam	0827	1402	984	210/18	(1)*
	1127	1800	987	210/18	(2)*
Berne	1001	1512	EC 91	40	
	1459	2012	EC 97	40/280	(3)
Brussels (Midi)	0827	1121	984	210	*
	1206	1435	296	210	
	1659	1921	EC 96	210	
Milan	1001	1915	EC 91	43	
Munich	1033	1810	IR 2431	720/650	(6)
Paris (Est)	0711	1101	351	173	(4)
	0744	1122	353	173	(5)
	1307	1708	EC 54	173	

Daily departures unless otherwise noted. Make reservations for all departures.

* Similar service hourly

(1) Transfer in Brussels Nord to train 2483
(2) Transfer in Brussels Nord to train 2486
(3) Transfer in Basel to IC 893
(4) Sundays only
(5) Daily, except Sundays
(6) Transfer in Koblenz to IC 613 (runs daily except Saturday)

Sherman tank from General Patton's Third Army bristles in courtyard of Clervaux Castle. Armored vehicles from both American and German forces have been placed throughout the Ardennes, where bitter World War II Battle of the Bulge was fought.

From Luxembourg . . .

A DAY EXCURSION TO CLERVAUX
DISTANCE BY TRAIN: 38 miles (61 km)
AVERAGE TRAIN TIME: 54 minutes

Clervaux is a medieval town nestled in the valley of the Clerf River deep in the Ardennes of northern Luxembourg, through which runs the scenic rail route from Luxembourg through Liege in Belgium to Amsterdam in the Netherlands. There is a world of history in Clervaux, ranging from the twelfth to the twentieth century. It's all there waiting for you.

The scenic beauty of the train ride begins the moment you leave the Luxembourg station and the train crosses a viaduct high above the Alzette River. Take a seat on the left side of the carriage to enjoy best a spectacular view of the city of Luxembourg from the viaduct.

Have your camera ready and start shooting a moment after the train clears a short tunnel just beyond the rail station. The morning departure is best for photographing the ramparts of Luxembourg because the sun will be shining directly upon them at a rather low level at that time. You will pass the same scene on the later departures; however, the sun will be at a higher angle and the shadows will be less dramatic.

Clervaux is the fourth express-train stop en route after stops at Mersch, Ettelbruck, and Kautenbach. Beyond Ettelbruck, you enter the hilly and heavily wooded Ardennes, where the Battle of the Bulge was fought during World War II in December 1944. Some of the buildings along the right of way still bear the scars of this engagement. Don't be alarmed if you should spot a German or an American tank at a road intersection en route. The locals have intentionally placed it there.

The Clervaux railway station is a fifteen-minute walk from the town's main square. It's a delightful stroll along the river and easy to do with the aid of several maps of Clervaux posted along the way with "you are here" arrows to assist you.

Start at the station by walking along the main street in the direction the train came from. When you reach the town square, turn right and follow the paths and steps leading up to Clervaux Castle. The Clervaux tourist information office is located at the entrance to the castle in a towerlike structure on the right-hand side as you face the castle. The office is open from Easter through June, 1400 to 1700; July and August, 1000–1200 and 1400–1800; September and October, 1300–1700.

Clervaux is packed with points of interest. Three of the most prominent ones are the DeLannoi Castle, the Benedictine Abbey of St. Maurice and St.

CLERVAUX—*MEDIEVAL CHARM*

A Day Excursion from Luxembourg

DEPART FROM LUXEMBOURG STATION	TRAIN NUMBER	ARRIVE IN CLERVAUX STATION	NOTES
0810	110	0900	(1)
1010	112	1100	(1)
1210	114	1300	(1)
1410	116	1500	(1)

DEPART FROM CLERVAUX STATION	TRAIN NUMBER	ARRIVE IN LUXEMBOURG STATION	NOTES
1451	117	1539	(1)
1751	119	1839	(1)
1936	121	2024	(1)
2051	123	2139	(1)

(1) Daily, including holidays

Distance: 38 miles/61 km
Reference: Thomas Cook Table 219

Maur, and the parish church. All three tower over the town and its surrounding countryside.

The DeLannoi family are some of Franklin Delano Roosevelt's maternal ancestors. The DeLannoi Castle has so much to offer that we recommend you concentrate on it first and see the rest of Clervaux's sites in the time remaining at the end of your visit. The castle was heavily damaged during the Ardennes offensive in 1944, but it is being restored. It now houses the "Battle of the Bulge" museum, an exhibition of ancient Luxembourg castle models, and the world famous "Family of Man" photo exhibition of Edward Steichen, an American citizen born in Luxembourg.

No one is quite certain about the castle's origins. There are several hypotheses; some historians believe that it was built on top of an ancient Roman citadel, while others speak of Celtic origins. In any event, it has been established that the oldest part of the castle dates back to the twelfth century.

There's an immediate impact upon entering the castle's outer courtyard. One of General Patton's tanks is parked there, along with its chief antagonist, a German Army 88-mm cannon. Kids (up to age 60) will enjoy climbing aboard the tank to inspect its armor and speculate as to the role it played during the liberation of Clervaux and the Battle of the Bulge.

Bear in mind that by 19 December 1944, the castle you see now was reduced to a burned-out hulk. The authentic restoration that has been accomplished by the townspeople of Clervaux and the Duchy of Luxembourg is laudatory.

The "Family of Man" exhibit and the castle model exhibit are immediately inside the first gate leading off the courtyard. The "Bulge" museum is located farther along toward the center of the castle off an inner courtyard.

In preparation for the "Family of Man," ask the Luxembourg tourist office for a copy of the information sheet it has prepared describing the exhibition and the career of its creator. Steichen considered the Clervaux castle an ideal location for his exhibition. The collection was given to the Grand Duchy of Luxembourg by the U.S. Government in 1975, three years after Steichen's death. The castle is open to visitors 1000–1700 daily July through September 15. On Sunday, bank holidays, and during the off-season, hours are 1300–1700. There is an admission charge.

You may want to enjoy lunch in the castle. The Café du Vieux Chateau, dating from 1671, is a part of the castle's outer courtyard. During the summer, the café provides tables and chairs in the courtyard for its patrons. You will find the café just inside the tower gate and on the left. It was constructed originally as a dwelling for the guardian of the castle. Today, it would be a good place to launch hang gliders.

Moselle and Rhine rivers meet at Deutsches Eck (German corner) in Koblenz. Massive mooring pillars in foreground and distant skyline of city's Alte Burg (old castle) section stretch along the Moselle.

From Luxembourg . . .

A DAY EXCURSION TO KOBLENZ
DISTANCE BY TRAIN: 101 miles (163 km)
AVERAGE TRAIN TIME: 1 hour, 14 minutes

Just as there is a subtle difference between Rhine and Moselle wines, so is there a difference between the scenic beauty of the two great rivers from which the wines take their namesakes. At the rivers' confluence in Koblenz, however, you will be able to enjoy both. Koblenz claims that it can offer 2,000 years of history to its visitors—and all within the span of a few hours. The historical background of this city in the very center of Germany's Rhineland makes this no idle boast.

The area around Koblenz was settled originally by the Celts. Julius Caesar, dividing and conquering as he went, arrived with his legions and established domain along the Rhine's western banks. Roman tranquillity thrived here until the fifth century, when Rome's power weakened and the Franks took over. Koblenz has noted the waxing and waning of many empires since then.

Napoleon's "memorable campaign against the Russians" was inscribed on the St. Castor's fountain in the city during 1812. In 1814, the tables were turned when the Russians captured the town and added a postscript, "seen and approved" beneath the original inscription. At the Deutsches Eck, a monument erected at the confluence of the Rhine and the Moselle in 1897, the statue of the German emperor Wilhelm I was toppled into the Rhine by the U.S. Army's Corps of Engineers in 1945. The base of the monument was made as a memorial to German unity in 1953 by President Theodor Heuss. Since September 1993, Wilhelm I is back—in minimodel form on top of the monument.

Koblenz suffered extensive damage during World War II but was reconstructed in its historic pattern, even to the typically narrow streets—to the annoyance of motorists but to the joy of its visitors.

The Koblenz railway station is just far enough away from the meeting of the Moselle and Rhine rivers and the city's major tourist attractions to cause a "walk or ride" decision soon after arrival. The city tourist information office can assist in this decision-making process.

If your decision is to walk—and it's all downhill to the river—we suggest you proceed to that office by using the pedestrian crossing in front of the train station. If you need to convert monetary holdings from francs to marks, you may do so before leaving the station at the Exchange-Geldwechsel-Cambio alongside ticket window No. 6, to your left as you exit from the track area. If you decide to ride, the tourist office will help you hail a cab or provide you with the city's bus schedule together with information on fares and boarding.

KOBLENZ—*HEART OF THE RHINELAND*

A Day Excursion from Luxembourg

DEPART FROM LUXEMBOURG STATION	TRAIN NUMBER	ARRIVE IN KOBLENZ STATION	NOTES
0930	3037/E 3960	1141	(1)(2)
1033	IR 2431	1237	(1)
1433	IR 2433	1637	(1)

DEPART FROM KOBLENZ STATION	TRAIN NUMBER	ARRIVE IN LUXEMBOURG STATION	NOTES
1617	E 3971/3054	1826	(1)(2)
1719	IR 2430	1923	(1)

Note: Returning from Koblenz at 1519 via Trier (see below) provides two hours to become acquainted with Germany's oldest town.

DEPART FROM KOBLENZ STATION	TRAIN NUMBER	ARRIVE IN TRIER STATION	NOTES
1519	IR 2336	1639	(1)(2)

DEPART FROM TRIER STATION	TRAIN NUMBER	ARRIVE IN LUXEMBOURG STATION	NOTES
1841	IR 2430	1923	(1)

(1) Daily, including holidays
(2) Transfer at Trier

Distance: 101 miles/163 km
Reference: Thomas Cook Table 720

During summer (June 15–October 14), the city's tourist information office is open 0830–2015 Monday through Saturday. On Sunday, it operates 1400–1900. If you are planning to stay in Koblenz, the tourist office will be glad to make hotel reservations for you at a nominal charge for the service.

Regarding that "walk or ride" decision: Regardless of your choice, ask for a city map and a copy of the Koblenz *Tour of the City* brochure. It lists thirteen outstanding points of interest along the shorelines of the two rivers. There is no charge for these documents.

If you have elected to see Koblenz under your own foot power and guided by the city map, a ten-minute walk down the Markenbildchenweg brings you to the Rhine, and a left turn at that point sends you in the direction of the Deutsches Eck, where the Rhine meets the Moselle. The riverside gardens along the Rhine join up with those on the Moselle to provide a delightful five-mile promenade along their banks.

If you plan to whiz around the city on wheels, Bus No. 1, marked RHINE (DEUTSCHES ECK), will deposit you on the promenade at a point opposite the Rheinkran, an antique building that once housed the harbor crane. The bus route takes you through the narrow streets of the old city along the Moselle and past the Deutsches Eck before reaching its final stop on the Rhine. Returning to the train station, the bus follows a more direct (and less interesting) route through the town's shopping areas. If your "walk or ride" decision is still up for grabs, we suggest you compromise by taking the bus outbound and returning on foot. From the river to the station, the bus is bannered HAUPT-BAHNHOF. The bus ride takes about fifteen minutes. Allow at least that same amount of time if you're walking.

Make the Koblenz Weindorf (Wine Village) a must stop during your visit. It consists of four taverns clustered around a village square that, in turn, is enclosed within a real vineyard along the Rhine. The taverns are actual copies of half-timbered houses found in the notable German wine areas. Six hundred or more guests can be accommodated in the taverns and more than 1,000 outside when the weather is good—as it usually is.

The wine village was built on the occasion of the 1925 German Wine Exhibition. Since then, it has achieved fame for its products and romantic atmosphere. The village offers an excellent menu and wine list daily from 1100 to midnight. From November through March, an advance booking is required.

We hate to be spoilsports, but the last train returning to Luxembourg departs at 2219. The good news is that there are early morning trains departing at 0537, 0633, and 0826.

Metz Cathedral, shown here at its central nave, is one of the most luminous in the world. It houses the largest surface stained-glass windows in France. The cathedral was formed from the junction of two churches facing different directions.

From Luxembourg . . .

A DAY EXCURSION TO METZ
DISTANCE BY TRAIN: 39 miles (63 km)
AVERAGE TRAIN TIME: 53 minutes

Throughout its 3,000-year history, Metz has been a great Roman city, the center of the Carolingian Empire, an independent republic, a part of Germany, and a bastion of France. Poised at the confluence of the Moselle and Seille rivers, Metz claims the oldest church in France, the fourth-century Pierre-aux-Nonnains. The city's Cathedral of Saint Etienne (thirteenth to sixteenth century) houses two of the largest surface stained-glass windows in the world.

Metz further claims the largest railway station in eastern France, and truly it is. Due to its size, visitors arriving by rail may find the facilities somewhat confusing. Arriving from Luxembourg in the north, Eurailpass travelers are advised to take the southern stairway rather than the northern one when transiting from the arrival platform to the main station hall via the underground passageway. When you emerge into the rail station's main foyer, you will see the tourist information office on the left.

A map of Metz and a copy of *Transports Par Minibus* describing the two minibus lines operated by the city for visitors will prove to be invaluable, particularly to first-time visitors. If the tourist office in the station is closed, these aids may be obtained from the main tourist office, Office de Tourisme, Place d'Armes. Another recommendation: Turn right leaving the station tourist office and walk the length of the station hall to the departure gate (served by the northern underground passageway). Reasons: You will pass the station's cafeteria midway in the corridor and may want to eat there later; the station's north end houses the train information office and faces the city square on Avenue Foch, one of Metz's main thoroughfares. Money can be changed in the Post Office, the huge red building in front of the station, Monday through Friday, 0800–1900, and Saturday, 0800–1200.

As a part of the German empire, Metz was returned to France only at the end of the first World War, during which it was badly damaged. The city again suffered much damage during World War II, when it was occupied by the Germans from 1940 to 1944.

The center of attraction in Metz is its gothic cathedral of Saint Etienne. The cathedral has been described as the "apotheosis of light" due to the luminescent quality of its stained-glass windows. One of the cathedral's two towers stands 300 feet over the city. To climb it is sheer exercise, but the view is well worth it.

There are many pictographs scattered throughout the Metz rail-station areas to assist visitors wending their way through its labyrinth. You will find them

METZ—*MOSELLE STRONGHOLD*

A Day Excursion from Luxembourg

DEPART FROM LUXEMBOURG STATION	TRAIN NUMBER	ARRIVE IN METZ STATION	NOTES
1001	EC 91	1043	(1)
1307	EC 54	1355	(1)
1459	EC 97	1540	(1)

DEPART FROM METZ STATION	TRAIN NUMBER	ARRIVE IN LUXEMBOURG STATION	NOTES
1604	EC 96	1649	(1)
1913	EC 90	1956	(1)

(1) Daily, including holidays

Distance: 39 miles/63 km
Reference: Thomas Cook Table 173

very helpful. We are not suggesting that you drag a string behind you so that you'll be able to retrace your steps. The Metz rail station is a labyrinth, however, and it's not too difficult to lose your bearings as you wander about it.

The city of Metz operates a minibus service consisting of two lines, A and B. You can use this service to reach the city's main tourist information office. Board either line at the bus terminal directly in front of the rail station. Get off at the Hotel de Ville (town hall) stop in front of the cathedral. The tourist office will be on the right in the Place d'Armes.

In addition to the cathedral, Metz has many interesting sights, such as the fourteenth-century St. Louis market square with its Italian influence. Its majestic buildings are constructed of yellow limestone, which seems to give them an aspect of light. The city's theater, Place de la Comedie, is another typical example of this "brightness."

The two lines of the minibus service together cover the major points of the city's sights and shopping areas. The two lines frequently cross each other as they make their way through the city, but each, in turn, terminates at the main railway station.

The minibus stops throughout the city area are marked with devices very similar in appearance to barber poles, to which are attached maps showing the course of the bus making that particular stop. Each pole is marked with the name of the stop, and inside the bus is a circular chart showing all of the stops that the bus makes. By noting first the name on the pole stop and then relating it to the map inside the bus, you can easily identify your position within the city.

Both minibus lines operate from 0730–1930 daily except Sunday and holidays. A bus leaves the main railway station approximately every six minutes. Bus tickets are available in the bus.

From mid-June to mid-September, the Metz tourist office operates a walking tour that covers the highlights of the city with an English narration.

If you are sightseeing on your own in Metz, you should include the city's Gallo-Roman collections together with an impressive display of seventeenth-century paintings by Dutch masters and artists of the French School.

Top off your visit with a stroll along the city's Esplanade on the banks of the Moselle River.

Porta Nigra, the strange gateway building of Trier, is one of many Roman remains in the German city known centuries ago as the "Second Rome." Floodlights bathe the monument at night.

A DAY EXCURSION TO TRIER
DISTANCE BY TRAIN: 32 miles (51 km)
AVERAGE TRAIN TIME: 41 minutes

"Before Rome, there was Trier." Although this is legend, it is also a historical fact. Evidence of human settlements as early as the third century B.C. have been discovered in and around the city of Trier. Further legend attributes the founding of Trier in 2000 B.C. to the Assyrians. But history more soberly attributes its roots to the Emperor Augustus, who founded (or refounded) Trier in 16 B.C., thereby beginning Trier's part in Roman history.

In A.D. 117, Trier became the capital of Rome's province of Belgica Prima and the seat of the emperor's court. History records that no less than six Roman emperors held court here. The town's population swelled to more than 80,000 citizens, and its cultural growth kept pace with its expanding population. Many magnificent edifices and archaeological finds attest to this growth today.

Trier grew to be known as the second Rome. By the end of the third century A.D., it had become the capital of the western part of the Roman Empire. Its many monuments from that time attest to its greatness. In ancient Roman records, Trier was the first place north of the Alps to bear the name of "town."

Trier's pride is the Roman gateway building, the Porta Nigra (Black Gate), standing on the town's northern edge. Known as the "northern gate of the Roman Empire," it takes its name from the dark patina that formed over its limestone facade. It was transformed into a church during the eleventh century, but Napoleon restored the building to its original appearance in 1804. Other Roman ruins still remaining are the Barbara Baths (A.D. 150), the Imperial Baths (A.D. 300), an amphitheater (A.D. 100) and a bridge crossing the Moselle River.

Trier fell to the Franks in the fifth century, but the city's life did not end at that time as many did in such conquests. During the thousand years that followed, churches, monasteries, convents, and mansions were built literally on top of, and around, its ancient structures. A cross, erected in 958 to signify Trier's right to conduct a market, marks the Hauptmarkt (central market) of today's city. The fourteenth-century Romanesque cathedral has among its treasures the "Holy Coat," said to have belonged to Christ.

On the other side of the coin, in 1818 a man was born in Trier who had ideas that grew up in opposition to civilization as it existed up to that time. The man was Karl Marx.

The Trier railway station has all the usual services, including a money-exchange office, if you need to convert from Belgian or Luxembourg francs to

TRIER—*GERMANY'S OLDEST TOWN*

A Day Excursion from Luxembourg

DEPART FROM LUXEMBOURG STATION	TRAIN NUMBER	ARRIVE IN TRIER (Hbf.) STATION	NOTES
0830	3035	0910	(1)
0930	3037	1010	(1)
1033	IR 2431	1115	(1)
1230	3043	1310	(1)

DEPART FROM TRIER (Hbf.) STATION	TRAIN NUMBER	ARRIVE IN LUXEMBOURG STATION	NOTES
1644	3052	1732	(1)
1742	3054	1826	(1)
1839	IR 2430	1923	(1)
2144	3062	2224	(1)

(1) Daily, including holidays

Distance: 32 miles/51 km
Reference: Thomas Cook Table 720

German marks. The tourist information office (telephone [651] 978080) is about a ten-minute walk from the rail station. It is located immediately in back of the Porta Nigra monument.

A taxi stand is located at the right-hand front of the station, but unless you encounter inclement weather, we suggest you proceed on foot directly down Bahnhofstrasse, which runs from the station into Theodor-Heuss-Allee leading to the Porta Nigra. Avoid the din of traffic by using the park pathways on the left of the main thoroughfare for a relaxing stroll.

The tourist office in Trier is open 0900–1830 Monday through Saturday and 0900–1530 on Sunday. If the office is closed, we suggest that you use the coin-operated machine that dispenses a hotel list and city map. Operating instructions are in English.

Trier's tourist information office runs guided tours of the city from Monday through Friday at 1400. For those who want to inspect this ancient city at their own pace, the tourist office has an information brochure and city map for sale. A booklet describing Trier in greater detail is also available.

For those who wish they had packed a picnic lunch before leaving Luxembourg, there's a second chance to do so at a market area located one block in front of the railway station. A wide selection of food and beverages is available. The market is on the left side of Bahnhofstrasse, the street immediately in front of the rail station.

Trier is an appealing city. It probably can attribute much of this appeal to the fact that it has been an imperial residence since the days of the Caesars. Strolling through Trier, you will see examples of Renaissance, baroque, and rococo architecture standing side by side. More recently, during the nineteenth century, several impressive citizens' houses of outstanding architectural beauty were built in the city.

Not all of Trier's attributes are readily visible, for beneath the city in the storage cellars of its wineries there are vats and casks capable of holding more than three million gallons of the Moselle, Saar, and Ruwer wines produced annually in the area surrounding the city.

A small street to the side of the great cathedral in Trier is named Sieh Um Dich (Look Around You)—an expression that depicts the city's greatness, for you can see two thousand years of history in just about as many steps. In fact, one of the tours conducted by the city bears the title, "Trier—2,000 steps—2,000 years."

King of France, Louis XIV garbed in ancient Roman armor astride a spirited stallion marks the center of the huge Place Bellecour, largest square in Lyon. The city's central tourist information office is also in the square.

16 LYON

Lyon, for the most part, is essentially a very modern city. It bustles with industry, trade fairs, and business. Its origins, however, go back to Roman times. Founded in A.D. 43, its old town stands on a hillside of volcanic soil containing some of the richest archaeological sites in France and still contains an unspoiled area of fourteenth- and fifteenth-century houses.

The city of Lyon claims to be the world capital of gastronomy, and it has some impressive credentials to back this claim. The gastronomical tradition comes from its geographic position in the center of such great culinary areas as Bourgogne, Savoy, Beaujolais, and many others. With tongue in cheek, Lyon citizens say that the whole world cannot come from Lyon—there has to be at least a little from elsewhere. With *our* tongue in cheek, we note that Lyon now has four McDonald's fast-food establishments within its city limits. Touché!

Although proud of its history and devoted to preserving its antiquity, Lyon forges ahead toward the twenty-first century with a constant, modernizing, building-and-expansion program that rivals even that of Paris—sometimes even outstripping it. Part-Dieu, a complete and separate metropolis on the left bank of the Rhône, rises like a modern phoenix above the rest of Lyon, most of which was built during the eighteenth century. Lyon's contrasts are great. By virtue of these contrasts, Lyon is becoming one of the great cities of France and of Europe.

Day Excursions

Contrasts continue in the selection of day excursions from Lyon, the third largest city in France. A scant twenty-five miles short of Geneva, the town of Annecy and its crystal-clear lake wait to charm you. Annecy's old quarter, lying back from the lake, has one of Europe's finest marketplaces.

Dijon vies with Lyon for gastronomic honors. During your visit to Dijon, you will want to shop for its world-renowned product, mustard. But that's not all it has to offer. The history of Burgundy breathes in Dijon, its capital, and you will want to catch its scent.

Grenoble is situated in the midst of a breathtaking panorama of mountains. A ride on its *téléphérique* will provide an even more remarkable view of the city and the countryside surrounding it. Via TGV from the Part-Dieu station in Lyon, Grenoble is only a scant 70 minutes away!

Vienne, only twenty miles to the south, is almost a suburb of Lyon, but the town is altogether different in a variety of ways. Some of the best preserved Roman buildings and amphitheaters in all of Europe await your inspection there. One of the world's finest restaurants, La Pyramide, waits for your visit.

Arriving and Departing

By Air. The Satolas Airport, which serves Lyon, lies fifteen miles (twenty-three kilometers) to the east of Lyon. International air service between Lyon and New York is provided by Air France. Frequent air service to Paris, Frankfurt, Brussels, and Amsterdam provides additional connections for passengers with North American destinations.

The best transportation between the airport and Lyon's Perrache Station is the airport bus service operating between the two points. Daily runs are scheduled every twenty minutes throughout the day. The trip takes thirty-five to forty-five minutes; the fare is 40 francs. Limousine service is also available direct to most of the city's hotels. Allow on the average for forty-five minutes en route.

Passengers arriving or departing Lyon by air can obtain some air service information from the Lyon City Information Office on the second floor of the Perrache station annex. The Air France office closest to the station is located at 17 rue Victor Hugo. Telephone 78–427900.

By Train. The TGV service from Paris calls at Part-Dieu before going on to terminate at Perrache, and all service to Switzerland departs from the Part-Dieu station. Otherwise, Perrache continues to handle all major train traffic. During this transition, please consult the notes on page 339 to be certain that you are using the proper terminal.

The facilities being provided by Gare de Perrache have been enlarged and expanded by the addition of an ultramodern annex appended to the front of the present station building. This annex houses a bus terminal, the terminal for the city's metro system, and a bevy of offices, shops, snack bars, and restaurants. The terminal for the airport bus and local taxi services is also located in the annex. Access to the annex is gained by escalators immediately in front of the station's main doors. Pedestrian traffic, moving from the station through the annex and into the city, utilizes another escalator system to exit into Lyon's park, Place Carnot. The park, with its statues, fountains, and waterfalls, is one of the city's showplaces and an excellent place to spend a few quiet moments.

Gare de Perrache, together with its annex, is a large and sprawling complex. Access to its train platforms is possible through underground tunnels as well as escalators that descend from the ticket office and the waiting-room areas. There's an abundance of pictographs throughout the station to assist you in reaching where you want to go. Don't hesitate to ask for directions, however, if you need them. The French are accustomed to such questions in German, Italian, and Dutch, too.

Lyon's Central Station—Gare de Perrache

The city of Lyon has a number of railway stations, but we are concerned only with two, the century-old Gare de Perrache and the one just added in the last decade, Part-Dieu. Please consult page 339 for departures to other base cities as well as for the individual day-excursion schedules. We revise and update our text and schedule material annually. Some changes can take place, however, after we have gone to press. *Always* consult the schedules posted in the stations first.

Currently, the day excursion to Annecy departs from Part-Dieu; and the mid-morning departure to Dijon, along with the first train to Grenoble, uses Part-Dieu, too. Otherwise, you will be utilizing the venerable Gare de Perrache for all of your rail services. Transportation between the two rail terminals is facilitated by Lyon's new, ultramodern metro (subway) system that serves both rail stations.

Until Part-Dieu begins full operation, we are limiting our detailed description of passenger facilities to Gare de Perrache. At a time when the rail traffic at Lyon's newest station warrants it, descriptions of its service will follow in subsequent editions. Stay tuned.

All of the tracks in Gare de Perrache, with the exception of track A, require using underground passageways to pass between the trains and the station proper. The platforms are numbered, and the tracks are identified by the letters of the alphabet. There are two underground passageways—*Sortie Nord* and *Sortie Sud* (north and south exits). Use of either will take you to platform No. 1 and, in turn, to exits leading to the street side of the station. If you have any baggage, be prepared to carry it. Baggage carts for passenger use are not available, probably due to the platform stairways. The previously mentioned escalators serve only the tracks reserved for express-train service.

There are times in the Perrache station when two trains are scheduled to depart on the same track—one in each direction, of course. Check for the departure position (north or south) of the day-excursion trains; otherwise, you might be standing at the wrong end of the track as your train departs. Train-departure signs are displayed in the underground passageways at the bottom of the platform stairways. The north passageway, however, will not list a south-bound departure, nor the south a northbound one, unless it is a train running through Lyon Perrache and not originating there. All train departures are displayed over the ticket windows in the main station hall.

The station restaurant, located on the north end alongside track A, next to the north-passageway staircase, has a feature not normally found in European railway stations—a take-out window à la Wendy's. Look for the sign PROVISIONS A EMPORTER.

Fourvière Basilica stands on a hilltop overlooking the bustling city of Lyon. Nearby Renaissance dwellings are among the finest in Europe. (Photo courtesy of Gilles Defaix and Lyon Tourist Office.)

Money-exchange services are available in the Perrache station. From the train information area, follow the pictographs and proceed either by escalator or elevator to the station's TGV departure lounge on the second level. The Thomas Cook office at that location is open daily from 0800 to 2000. If you have arrived in Lyon from another country and have an accumulation of foreign notes crammed in your wallet, this office can exchange them for French francs at official rates.

To reach the bank, use the escalator on the side of the station annex facing Place Carnot, the city park immediately in front of the station. When you reach ground level, walk down the steps alongside the waterfall to the fountain at the bottom. At this point, turn to the right between the fountain and the waterfall, and then proceed across the square. When you approach the first street, you will see the bank across the intersection to your left. This is the only bank in the vicinity of Place Carnot.

Hotel reservations for within the city of Lyon may be made at any of the tourist information offices operated by the city for a nominal fee. For advance hotel reservations in other parts of France, the offices will charge 30 francs for the service.

Tourist information can be obtained at any of five information offices. The most convenient one is located within the Perrache station annex on the first floor above ground level. You can reach it by using the escalator located in the front of the station and following the conventional "i" signs to the office.

The office hours in the Perrache station annex are 0900–1300 and 1400–1800 Monday through Friday and 0900–1700 Saturday. The city's central tourist information office, Pavillon du Tourisme, is located in Place Bellecour, two subway stops from Gare de Perrache. This office is open 0900–1900 weekdays, 0900–1800 Saturday in summer; in winter the office closes one hour earlier. (Telephone 78.42.25.75; fax 78.42.04.32.) The city also maintains a tourist information office on Fourvière Hill near the Roman theaters on the hillside where the city was founded in 43 B.C. This office is open daily, including Sunday, from 1000 to 1300 and again at 1330 until 1800.

A three-hour sightseeing bus tour of Lyon is operated each year from March 30 to October 31 by Lyon Vision, a private company endorsed by the Lyon Tourist Authority. The buses are equipped with headsets providing explanations of the tour sights in five languages including English. The fare for adults is 110 francs; children under age sixteen, 55 francs. Buses depart daily at 0930 and 1430. Ask for a folder at the tourist office.

Train information office is located within the main building of the Perrache station. Use the main entrance, turn right once you have entered the hall, and proceed through an archway to the train information office. It is open

0800–1920 Monday through Saturday and 0900–1200 and 1400–1830 Sunday and holidays.

The French National Railroads produces *Fiche Horaire* (mini-timetables) that can be very helpful. A selection is normally kept immediately outside the train information office door and inside the office on the left-hand wall. These timetables may eliminate standing in line to make inquiries.

Train reservations may be made in the train information office at any one of the operating windows. We did not find the train information staff too adept at English. Consequently, we recommend your reservation requests be written before making inquiries. Train names, train departure and arrival times, and destinations all blend together easily in international travel language.

Eurailpass validation is handled at any window in the train information office, but we suggest you write the starting and ending dates on a piece of paper and obtain concurrence from the attendant before the entry is made on your Eurailpass.

Lyon Locale

As mentioned previously, the City of Lyon has an ultramodern metro (subway) system. One of its main terminals is in Gare de Perrache; there's another in the rail terminal at Part-Dieu. Trains run every three to ten minutes from 0500 to 2400 daily. A single-ride ticket costs 7 francs; a book of six tickets, 36 francs. One-day tourist tickets also are available for 20 francs.

Le Vieux Lyon (Old Lyon) is a charming area to visit. For your convenience, use the *funiculaires* (funicular) to gain the summit. Take bus No. 44 from the station annex and ask the driver to let you off at the St. Jean bus stop. The funicular station is located at rue St. Jean and avenue Max, immediately to the left of place St. Jean.

Or, join the Lyon Tourist Office's guided tour, "A Stroll Through Old Lyon," which is conducted on foot over a two-hour period. Old Lyon is said to be the most extensive Renaissance area in France. Old Lyon covers about one mile along the right bank of the Saone River at the foot of Fourvière Hill. Departures are daily throughout the tourist season at a charge of 50 francs. An evening tour also is available. Check with the tourist office for the daily schedule. Telephone (33) 78.42.25.75.

While visiting the Fourvière Hill area, check out Lyon's answer to Paris's Eiffel Tower located behind the basilica. The Lyonese claim their tower is five feet higher than the Parisians', and it is—above sea level, that is.

338

From Lyon . . .

TRAIN CONNECTIONS TO OTHER BASE CITIES

TO:	DEPART*	ARRIVE	TRAIN NUMBER	COOK'S TABLE	NOTES
Milan	0659	1340	410/IR 2011	45/350	(1)
	1231	1940	417/IR 2023	45/350	(1)(2)
	1714	2305	218	45	
Nice	0933	1426	TGV 843	151	
	1245	1738	TGV 845	151	
Paris	0900	1102	TGV 716	150	(3)
	1100	1316	TGV 616	150	
	1500	1704	TGV 624	150	
	1700	1910	TGV 628	150	
Rome	0659	1820	410/IC 611	45/360	(1)

* All departures from Lyon Part-Dieu station unless otherwise noted.

Daily departures unless otherwise noted. Make reservations for all departures.

(1) Transfer in Torino Porta Nuova
(2) From Lyon Perrache Station
(3) Daily, except Sunday

Old quarter of Annecy, lying back from the lake along the Thiou River, forms a picturesque part of the city. A network of narrow streets in the quarter is reserved for pedestrians on market days.

A DAY EXCURSION TO ANNECY
DISTANCE BY TRAIN: 99 miles (160 km)
AVERAGE TRAIN TIME: 2 hours, 25 minutes

A crystal-clear lake, a spectacular view of the Alps, foothills that touch the town, an old quarter where quaint canals cross arcaded lanes, an engaging market selling everything from apples to zinnias—these are Annecy.

Annecy is a health spa as well as a popular holiday center. It has innumerable hotels, casinos, and, best of all, the lake. The basin in which the lake lies is so protected against pollution that the latter is almost transparent in its purity. The Thiou River, flowing out of the lake and through the old quarter of Annecy, runs through canals and meanders around islands en route to the Rhône and the Mediterranean.

Annecy (pronounced "Ahn-see") still remains largely undiscovered by North Americans, although it has long been a retreat of the French themselves.

Tour-boat operators offer a wide variety of tours around the "sea" of Annecy. Rapid tours, lasting just over an hour, have frequent departures. The more vigorous traveler can opt to cycle around it. Either mode will provide a spectacular view of alpine meadows, rivers, waterfalls, and the bountiful natural riches surrounding the lake.

The city of Annecy has an excellent tourist information office, but there's no evidence of its existence in the railway station. The quickest way to reach the information office is via bus No. 1 from in front of the station to Place de la Liberation, where you'll find the office in the Bonlieu Center at 1 rue Jean Jaurès. The telephone number is 50-45-00-33; fax 50–51–87–20.

On foot, use the underground pedestrian passageway to the left of the station as you exit. Continue to walk a block ahead to rue Vaugelas. Here, you turn left and walk four blocks to where rue Vaugelas ends at place de la Liberation (a large open area). While in the area, be sure to visit the town hall, Hôtel de Ville, a short walk along quai Chappuis. The picture on the opposite page was taken there. Exercise caution when crossing the street. The locals stage a "Grand Prix" on occasion.

The route on foot is actually far less complicated than it appears. En route, you will pass many interesting places, and you have an opportunity to soak up some of the local culture. So, unless you are pressed for time or the old feet have played out on you, we recommend that you do it under your own power at least once.

The tourist information office is open 0900–1830 daily, 0900–1200 and 1345–1830 on Sundays. If for any reason you find it closed, you will be

ANNECY—*ALPINE LAKE*

A Day Excursion from Lyon

DEPART FROM LYON PART-DIEU STATION	TRAIN NUMBER	ARRIVE IN ANNECY STATION	NOTES
0659	410	0903	(1)
0909	5407	1111	(1)

DEPART FROM ANNECY STATION	TRAIN NUMBER	ARRIVE IN LYON PART-DIEU STATION	NOTES
1557	5420	1811	(1)
1711	5422	1920	(1)
1904	5424/418	2101	(1)(2)

(1) Daily, including holidays
(2) Transfer in Aix les Bains

Distance:　　99 miles/160 km
Reference: Thomas Cook Table 167

instructed to go to the bureau of information in the city hall, which is open until 1900 daily, except Sunday and holidays.

The tourist information office has several brochures describing the city and its lake, including an illustrated booklet, *Through the Old Town*. The office also contains bulletin boards with numerous announcements of cultural events in Annecy. The office conducts a tour every day from July through September at 1000 and 1430.

From the bridge crossing the Thiou River, you will catch your first glimpse of the Palais de l'Isle sitting astride the river. As its name suggests, this curious palace was an island stronghold. It remains one of the most arresting old-time monuments of Annecy. Its oldest sections date from the twelfth century. At one time it housed the municipal offices of Annecy, the high judges' private apartments, and it has also served as a dungeon.

Beyond the Palais de l'Isle lies the enchanting marketplace of Annecy's old quarter. A network of narrow streets filled with every type of shop imaginable is augmented on market days by hundreds of stands erected in the streets, where only pedestrians are allowed to pass.

Along with the chic boutiques and appliance shops, the marketplace vends every imaginable food product, pastry, flower, and condiment. Lavender, picked in the Alps, and locally manufactured culinary wares are also available. Follow our suggestion and hold your shopping in abeyance until you have visited Annecy's old-quarter marketplace.

The picturesque medieval appeal of Annecy stems from both the French and Italian civilizations as a result of having changed sides several times during the two thousand years of its existence. The area became a part of the French empire in 1792, although it reverted to the Italian Kingdom of Sardinia in 1815. It was not until 1860 that all of Savoy, where Annecy is situated, was again reunited with France as a reward to the French for helping Italy in her war with Austria.

Annecy slipped quietly into the twentieth century with the introduction of TGV train service directly from Paris. The distance from the Lyon station in Paris to Annecy is covered in just three and a half hours—a trip that formerly consumed at least eight hours. Currently, there are four trains daily, making the possibility of a day excursion to Annecy from Paris a reality.

Word reaches us that Annecy has slipped even further into modern times when the town's Imperial Palace Hotel opened a casino. It's operated by a German group on French soil, and with Switzerland just across the lake, we suggest that you approach it with caution.

Departing Paris on TGV 931 at 0709, you would arrive in Annecy at 1050; boarding TGV 936 in Annecy at 1920, you would be back in Paris by 2254. It's a full day but a fun-packed one, too.

The White Bear of Pompon, sculpted by Dijon's favorite son, François Pompon, stands in Parc Darcy. Known for the simplicity of his work, sculptor Pompon's keen sense of observation caught each animal in characteristic pose.

From Lyon . . .

A DAY EXCURSION TO DIJON
DISTANCE BY TRAIN: 119 miles (190 km)
AVERAGE TRAIN TIME: 1 hour, 30 minutes

Say "Dijon" to any American who likes to eat well, and he will respond, "mustard." Mention Dijon to any Frenchman, and his eyes will roll and his hands will fly as he describes the gastronomic wonders of the Burgundian city's pastry shops, restaurants, cassis (black-currant liquor), *and* mustard—but not necessarily in that order. Dijon, the ancient capital city of Burgundy, has something for everyone. It sets a fine table, lives its history, and preserves its art.

Dijon is the gateway to France's most famous wine region. It became important historically in 1015 when Robert I, Duke of Burgundy, made it the capital of his duchy. The city's most brilliant era, however, was from the fourteenth through the eighteenth centuries, when it gained most of its art and beautiful monuments.

Dijon cannot be visited in a hurry. Actually, an entire day can easily be spent visiting its Palace of Burgundy Dukes and the Museum of Fine Arts, which is housed in the palace. The museum, founded in 1783, is the most important in France after the Louvre in Paris. Don't miss the huge banquet room of the palace. Identified as the Guards Room, the tombs of the dukes are located here. They provide some descriptive background as to how the populace rated the four "Valois" Dukes of Burgundy: Philip the Bold, Jean the Fearless, Philip the Good, and Charles the Rash.

Modern art has made an entry in the palace in the form of a department housing an exhibition of impressionist works from the Granville collection. There's also a gallery devoted completely to the works of local artists from the Burgundy area.

The city is particularly proud of its artistic sons, among them François Pompon (1855–1933). Sculptor Pompon began his career as a Burgundy marble cutter. He attended Dijon's school of fine arts before further studies and apprenticeships in Paris. He sculpted 300-plus works, almost all depicting animals. His fresh, clear style has astonishing simplicity. One of his finest works, *The White Bear,* stands in Dijon's Parc Darcy.

Engrossing as Dijon's works of art can be, don't forget to break for lunch—another Dijon work of art that can't be hurried. Whatever entree you select, we are certain that you will want to enhance it with a dab or so of Dijon mustard. A word of caution, make that dab a small one and determine first if it suits your palate. Dijon's favorite condiment has some varieties that exceed the fire power of any Mexican pepper.

DIJON—*CUTTING THE MUSTARD*

A Day Excursion from Lyon

DEPART FROM LYON STATION	TRAIN NUMBER	ARRIVE IN DIJON STATION	NOTES
0816(2)	5072	1032	(1)
0934(3)	5014	1115	(1)
1249(3)	6636	1432	(1)

DEPART FROM DIJON STATION	TRAIN NUMBER	ARRIVE IN LYON STATION	NOTES
1544	5053	1744(4)	(1)
1657	6132	1840(3)	(1)
1917	5073	2133(2)	(1)
2043	6106	2226(4)	(5)

(1) Daily, including holidays
(2) Perrache Station
(3) Part-Dieu Station
(4) Part-Dieu Station (arrives in Perrache Station twelve minutes later)
(5) Daily, except Saturday

Distance: 122 miles/197 km
Reference: Thomas Cook Table 149

Dijon's railway station is unique in that its main hall is circular. Although unique, this unusual architectural design is quite efficient. Train departures out of Dijon are displayed over the ticket-window areas on a circular-bulletin-board display. Further, departure information is divided according to the destination: for example, Paris, Lyon, and Marseilles.

Train information is available in the area marked INFORMATION VOYAGEURS on the right as you enter the main hall of the station. The office is open 0830–1900 Monday through Friday and 0830–1830 Saturday. A map showing the location of the city's tourist information office in relation to the rail station is displayed prominently in the station's foyer.

The Dijon tourist information office is located on Place Darcy. It is easily reached by exiting through the main doors of the station and bearing to the right onto avenue Maréchal Foch. Average walking time is five minutes. Use the Hotel Climat de France as a landmark in crossing the square in front of the station and positioning yourself on avenue Foch. Proceed along avenue Foch a block from the station. As you approach Place Darcy, you will find the tourist information office on the left-hand side of the street.

The operating hours of Dijon's city tourist information office are 0900–2000 daily from April 11 through November 15 (open until 2100 June 1–September 15); 0900–1200 and 1400–1900 daily the remainder of the year. The telephone number is 80–43–42–12.

The tourist office displays a room-availability list immediately outside the office entrance. This depicts the number of vacancies existing in the various hotels of Dijon and its surrounding areas. Within the tourist office, you will find hotel-reservations facilities and money-exchange services. The office charges a nominal fee for each call within Dijon to secure hotel reservations.

The tourist office has an excellent selection of English brochures describing Dijon. Due to the varied number of tours the office conducts, we recommend that you discuss the current schedules with them before selecting one. If you desire to make your own inspection of Dijon, ask for the excellent brochure describing a walking tour of historic Dijon that takes you past the major points of interest within the city.

The Saint Benigne cathedral probably holds the record for being destroyed and rebuilt more times than any other place of worship in France—four times since its origins back in the sixth century! The present church was built between 1281 and 1325.

Also constructed in the thirteenth century, the church of Notre Dame in Dijon fared better over the centuries. Both edifices are typical Burgundian Gothic.

High-riding téléphérique conveys visitors from the heart of Grenoble's old quarter to a summit overlooking a panorama of the city. Museums and restaurants are at the peak.

From Lyon . . .

A DAY EXCURSION TO GRENOBLE
DISTANCE BY TRAIN: 80 miles (129 km)
AVERAGE TRAIN TIME: 1 hour, 23 minutes (1+10 via TGV)

Grenoble will remind many North Americans of Denver, Colorado. Lodged on a wide plain, butted against the swift waters of the Isere River, and back-dropped by the French Alps, it is a breathtaking scene of man and nature in concert. Grenoble is a big city. It attracts visitors at all times of the year and bids them a warm, friendly welcome. Your day excursion has the potential of becoming an extended visit.

Grenoble is the capital of the French Alps. It lies at the feet of three majestic mountain ranges at the crossroads of a number of large valleys. Its majestic Isere River was first bridged by Roman legion engineers in 43 B.C.; Napolcon employed the concealment of the area to move his armies into the Italian campaign; and modern mountaineering was born on its towering peaks.

Grenoble unfolds the past as well as the present in its monuments and art. The Musée de Grenoble houses one of the finest collections of old and modern masters in France. The classics of Rubens and Watteau, along with those of Utrillo and Picasso, adorn its galleries. The Cathedral of Grenoble dates to the twelfth century. Its early Renaissance Palace of Justice was built in the sixteenth century.

The University of Grenoble was founded in 1339—making it one of the oldest in Europe—and is considered by many academics as one of the best in France. Grenoble's student population exceeds 40,000, more than 6,000 of whom are foreigners from 150 different countries. With university students nearby snow-covered slopes, it was inevitable that winter sports should develop in Grenoble. The 1968 Winter Olympics were hosted by Grenoble, and many other sports gatherings, including the Davis Cup finals, have taken place in the city's magnificent Sports' Hall.

Excitement in Grenoble is to be found aboard its unique téléphérique de la Bastille as it scales the first heights of the city beyond the Isere River. The upper terminal is located at the top of the city's Guy Pape Park, where a spectacular view of the city and its surrounding countryside is provided. Dominating the heights, the Bastille, a nineteenth-century fortress, houses a military museum as well as a restaurant featuring traditional, regional dishes.

From the top of the Guy Pape Park, on a suitable day, you may opt to descend on foot through the park to the Jardin des Dauphins (Dauphins' garden) on the banks of the Isere or tarry with a visit to the museum of vintage cars near the upper terminal before descending via the téléphérique.

The Grenoble railway station has three platforms. Unless your train arrives

GRENOBLE—*AND THE BASTILLE CABLEWAY*

A Day Excursion from Lyon

DEPART FROM LYON STATION	TRAIN NUMBER	ARRIVE IN GRENOBLE STATION	NOTES
0705(2)	—	0824	(4)
0818(2)	—	0941	(6)
1000(3)	5448	1145	(1)
1212(2)	—	1335	(1)
1411(2)	5451	1530	(1)
1630(2)	—	1758	(6)
1720(2)	6304	1837	(1)

DEPART FROM GRENOBLE STATION	TRAIN NUMBER	ARRIVE IN LYON STATION	NOTES
1600	5454	1726(2)	(1)
1658	5456	1816(2)	(1)
1723	—	1906(3)	(1)
1755	5458	1911(2)	(5)
1916	—	2044(2)	(5)
2106	—	2257(3)	(1)

(1) Daily, including holidays
(2) Part-Dieu Station
(3) Perrache Station
(4) Monday–Friday only
(5) Daily, except Saturday
(6) Monday through Saturday

Distance: 80 miles/129 km
Reference: Thomas Cook Table 154

on track No. 1, access to the main station hall is by subterranean passageway. Consequently, the use of baggage carts is limited by the stairways leading to the passageway. Porter service is limited, too, so go to Grenoble as unfettered as possible.

A modernization program of the station's facilities may remedy this situation. Such modernization is already evident: Train-departure information is given by a digital display on the station wall beneath a large clock.

Grenoble's central tourist information office is located some distance from the railway station. It's in the midst of a labyrinth of winding streets, making it rather difficult to reach from the station. With the increasing number of visitors arriving in Grenoble aboard the TGV high-speed services, however, the situation will no doubt be corrected.

The tourist office is located at 14, rue de la République and can be reached by either of the tramways in the direction of Grand Place or Universités. Your stop is Maison du Tourisme. The center of town is a series of one-way streets. MAISON DU TOURISME signs are displayed at many intersections to assist pedestrians and motorists alike. The downtown tourist office is open 0900–1900 Monday through Saturday. It is also open on Sundays and holidays from 1000–1200. The telephone number is 76–42–41–41; the fax number is 76–51–28–69.

To ride the téléphérique de la Bastille, wend your way to the banks of the Isere River and then to the Jardin de Ville (city garden). From practically any point on the river front, you'll be able to see the "bubbles" of the cableway flying up and down the hillside in groups of three. A photographic hint: Ride the rear "bubble" up and the front one down for better views of Grenoble and its environs. A city map will assist you in getting around in Grenoble.

TGV service has made a Grenoble day excursion from Paris practical. Departing Paris at 0650 places you in Grenoble at 0945, or late risers can leave at 1004 for arrival at 1310. There are six TGVs Monday through Friday. The last departs Grenoble at 1923 and arrives at Gare de Lyon in Paris at 2231. Three TGVs run on Saturday and Sunday.

Roman Temple of Augustus and Livia stands in perfect preservation in the center of Vienne. The city boasts numerous Roman remains plus classic buildings of the Renaissance and a world-famous restaurant.

From Lyon . . .

A DAY EXCURSION TO VIENNE
DISTANCE BY TRAIN: 20 miles (32 km)
AVERAGE TRAIN TIME: 24 minutes

Turn a corner in Vienne and you turn a page of history. Roman in origin, this charming city lies on the Rhône River to the south of Lyon but so close (twenty miles) that it could be mistaken easily for a Lyon suburb. Such is not the case. Vienne is distinctly different.

Among the remains of this once-great city of the Roman Empire, and dating from the first century B.C. to the end of the third century A.D., stand a temple, an amphitheater, and a pyramid that was once the center of a Roman circus. Roman Vienne spread to both sides of the Rhône River, where ruins of a warehouse and baths have been uncovered.

The building that houses Vienne's tourist information office is a large, modern structure standing on the left bank of the Rhône. It is not more than a ten-minute walk from the railway station, a distance spanned by three city blocks. A statue to the fallen during 1914 and 1940 stands in the square fronting the railway station. Take a moment to pause and reflect here. Note, too, that many of the names have family extensions in North America. Depart from that point down Cours Brillier to the tourist information pavilion, which is located at No. 3 on the left-hand side of the street.

From mid-June to mid-September, the tourist information office is open 0900–1300 and 1400–1900 Monday through Saturday, 1000–1300 and 1400–1900 on Sunday. The telephone number is 74–85–12–62. There are several brochures with English translations inserted. The available maps are descriptive, and they make orienting yourself an easy task.

Attendants at the tourist office will assist by marking a suggested walking tour on your map. The majority of the city's sights, concentrated in the old north quarter, allow visitors to move quickly from one attraction to another.

After visiting a few of the structures, drop in on the Museum of Fine Arts, where the relics rest after their excavation from the various sites. Collections of bronze, ceramics, and jewels are on display.

Perhaps the most impressive Roman ruin of Vienne is the Temple of Augustus and Livia, which is perfectly preserved. One almost expects toga-clad senators to step through its portals and into a local pastry shop. The temple is surrounded by more modern structures in the center of the city. No doubt the close proximity of other buildings has helped shield and preserve the temple through the ages during which it has occupied its position.

The great amphitheater of Vienne was cleverly built into the slope of the hillside on which the town now stands. In its original state, it could hold

VIENNE—*OF ROMAN ORIGIN*

A Day Excursion from Lyon

DEPART FROM LYON STATION	TRAIN NUMBER	ARRIVE IN VIENNE STATION	NOTES
0756(2)		0823	(7)
1221(2)		1243	(1)
1308(2)		1355	(7)

DEPART FROM VIENNE STATION	TRAIN NUMBER	ARRIVE IN LYON STATION	NOTES
1402		1431(3)	(1)
		1442(2)	(1)
1807		1837(2)	(6)
1924	—	1950(3)	(1)
2008		2137(2)	(5)
2243	5528	2302(2)	(1)

(1) Daily, including holidays
(2) Perrache Station
(3) Part-Dieu Station
(4) Departs from Part-Dieu Station on Saturday and Sunday and holidays
(5) Sunday only
(6) Monday through Friday
(7) Daily except Sundays and holidays

Distance: 20 miles/32 km
References: Thomas Cook Table 151

15,000 spectators. It was covered entirely by soil in the first century, but excavations between 1922 and 1938, when activities were curtailed by World War II, have brought to life some very beautiful remnants of statuary, coins, and jewels from the era.

The amphitheater, modernized with stage lighting, is now the scene of many fine theatrical presentations in Vienne for thousands of spectators throughout the summer season. Similar lighting of the Temple of Augustus and Livia makes an evening visit to the city a memorable one.

The pyramid was erected in the center of a Roman circus to guide the racing chariots. History does not relate why the pyramid was never finished. For centuries it was believed to be the tomb of Pontius Pilate, who, according to a twelfth-century legend, had died in Vienne while living there in exile. Little else remains of the circus site, but your imagination stirs when you stand there.

The city's famous restaurant, La Pyramide (named for its location on Boulevard Fernand-Point at the former Roman circus), has been endorsed by many gourmets as the world's finest. Reservations are recommended at La Pyramide, which is closed every Wednesday and Thursday at noon in season and annually from November through mid-December. Call ahead on 74–53–01–96 or fax 74–85–69–73. It's expensive, but you only live once!

When departing from the main part of town, you can reach Vienne's pyramid and the restaurant La Pyramide by taking the main road running to the south, Cours de Verdun (RN 7), to Boulevard Fernand-Point, on your right. When proceeding from the tourist information office at Cours Brillier, head south on Quai Riondet and turn left onto Boulevard Fernand-Point.

Vienne has its share of medieval buildings, too. Most of them are still being lived in and look very much as they probably did back in the fifteenth and sixteenth centuries. The mixture of ancient and medieval architecture makes a visit to Vienne a most interesting experience.

Roman poets term Vienne *Vienna Pulchra*—beautiful Vienne. It remains that way today, steeped in a magnificent lesson in history. Vienne, however, is not a town buried in history. It is very much alive, vibrant, and industrious. Still a center of a lively wool trade, the town manufactures chemicals and flourishes from other industries, too. The people of Vienne are justly proud of their industrial endeavors set in the midst of a richly wooded countryside.

Chamartin Station is a Madrid showplace. Services and facilities provided by this modern train terminal mirror those at airports and emphasize efficiency and passenger comforts.

17 MADRID

Madrid is in metamorphosis. Although its history as a human settlement dates back to the Paleolithic period, Madrid as a city with little more than 400 years of history to its name is still a youngster when compared to other Spanish cities.

Tourism accounts for much of the change that is descending upon this city of broad boulevards, restful parks, and sparkling fountains. Tourists come in droves, like invaders—over the mountains and out of the skies. Although it may tax the friendly nature of the Spaniards on some occasions, the citizens of Madrid are still some of the most hospitable people in Europe.

The Spanish National Railways, RENFE, have completed a comprehensive program of modernizing their rolling stock, rights of way, and terminals. Madrid's shining Chamartin Station is the epitome of the program. Its facilities and conveniences surpass those of even the most modern European air terminals.

Spain's growing armada of sleek Talgo trains, with their complete articulation, low center of gravity, and interior spaciousness, glides in and out of Chamartin Station today on scheduled runs that put airlines to shame. The Talgo even changes its track gauge *automatically* while crossing the border into neighboring France.

RENFE's high-speed AVE (Alta Velocidad Expanola) trains were inaugurated in April 1992 for the opening of EXPO '92 in Seville. Like the French TGV, AVE trains cruise at 186 miles per hour. These 329-passenger trains even have headsets with music channels, TV monitors, and movies. Rail pass holders must pay a supplement of 15 to 40 percent, depending on class, to ride the AVEs. Seat reservations are required. Instead of a five- or six-hour trip to Andalucia, you can now take day excursions to Cordoba (two hours, twenty minutes) and Seville (two hours, thirty minutes) from Madrid. AVE trains depart from Madrid's refurbished and modernized Atocha Station.

Day Excursions

By contrast to modern Madrid, five day excursions will take you back in history to ancient Spain: (1) Toledo—where Visigothic and Moorish conquerors ruled; (2) Burgos—birthplace of the glorious El Cid; (3) Avila— walled city of the eleventh century; (4) El Escorial—with its "eighth wonder" monastery; and (5) Aranjuez—site of the Bourbons' splendid palace of the eighteenth century. All excursions are reasonable in time and distance. Each is distinctive, and each will help in unfolding the past, as well as the present, glory of the Spanish nation.

There's just one difference in Spanish day excursions that you need to be aware of. You just can't decide on the spur of the moment to "jump on a train and go." You *must* have seat reservations before boarding the train. Plan your day excursions at least a day in advance of the intended departure date. Also, make the seat reservations for a round trip. It's rather unlikely, but it could happen on a weekend or national holiday that you arrive at the day-excursion point without a return reservation only to learn that the returning trains are fully booked.

Arriving and Departing

By Air. Madrid's international airport, Aeropuerto de Barajas, is ten miles east of the city. There is no train service between the airport and the city center. There is a duty-free shopping area in the Barajas airport, and it is loaded with Spanish products. You should attempt to complete your shopping prior to departing from the airport; however, the shops are always ready to sell you that last-minute gift you forgot to buy for Aunt Mabel. Expect to pay a little more than you would for the same item in town.

A bus service operates between the airport and the Plaza de Colón Terminal in Madrid, where connections with the nearby RENFE Apeadero and Madrid Metro systems can be made. The buses are air-conditioned. The one-way fare is 320 pesetas. Buses depart each terminal about every fifteen minutes throughout the day, and the trip takes about forty minutes.

A taxi stand is located immediately adjacent to the bus stop in the Colón Terminal. The taxi fare between the city and the airport, 1,800–2,200 pesetas, varies according to the distance traveled. Transit time for both taxi and limousine services is usually about thirty minutes.

By Train. Madrid has two main railway stations—Chamartin and Atocha. They are connected by underground trackage, and you may travel from one to the other on "Apeadero cercanias" trains or any through train scheduled to stop at both. The Atocha Station has a special underground terminal, Atocha Apeadero, for such traffic.

In Chamartin, the Apeadero cercanias trains depart from track No. 1. Always check with the train information hostesses at the booth in the center of the station before boarding, for a train may be departing from another track ahead of one on track No. 1.

Eurail, Euro, and Spain rail passes are accepted on the Apeadero cercanias, but not on the Madrid Metro. There are two intermediate underground stops between Chamartin and Atocha: Nuevos Ministerios in the government building area and Recoletos at the main post office.

Chamartin is the terminal for most long-distance trains and international trains. Therefore, a complete description of Chamartin will be given, while only a brief sketch of Atocha will be presented. Day excursions depart from both stations, so be certain to check the schedules in this edition, then double check with the schedules posted in the rail stations, too. Many hotels in Madrid post current schedules of the closest rail station in their lobbies.

Madrid's Main Station—Chamartin

You get the feeling that you are arriving in an international airport, rather than a railway station, when you ride the escalator up from the train level into Madrid's sparkling Chamartin Station. The spacious main hall provides easy access to the twenty-one tracks below, and the station concourse has all the amenities a rail traveler could want, including a competent staff of porters to assist you with your baggage.

Train departures and arrivals are displayed on digital bulletin boards throughout the station. There are two snack bars, one between track Nos. 3 and 4 and another between track Nos. 17 and 18. Here, and in the cafeteria and restaurant that you reach by an escalator opposite track Nos. 4 and 5, you will see train departures displayed on television screens located in prominent positions. There's no danger of enjoying a cup of coffee—or a full-course meal— and missing your train's departure.

By the way, the snack bars sell a box lunch called a *Bolsa de Viaje.* You might like to take one with you on your day excursion. You will have a delicious menu selection of sandwiches, snacks, and beverages to choose from. Ask at the cashier desk when entering. It will save a rush later if your train is about to depart.

The Chamartin Station is located in the suburbs of Madrid; but the RENFE Apeadero system, Metro line No. 8 (pink), the bus service, or taxis will get you to your final destination within the city with minimal inconvenience. All public transportation is available either right in, or adjacent to, the station and marked plainly with pictographs.

For information, go to the train information center, the tourist information office, or to the hotel reservations service in the station. All of these places are manned by competent people who are genuinely eager to assist you. (We prefer the train information center—for reasons that we'll explain later.)

Money exchange facilities are located opposite track Nos. 17 and 18. The sign reads BANCO DE FOMENTO, and pictographs will lead you there. It is open 0830–2300 daily. The facility is operated by one of the major banks in Madrid, and the rates of exchange are identical with the bank's offices in the city.

Hotel reservations can be made under the INFORMACION HOTELERA sign opposite track Nos. 6 and 7. The office is open 0730–2300 daily. A nominal charge is made for each reservation. Madrid is a large city, so be certain that you ask for lodging near one of the rail terminals or close to public transportation.

City of fountains, Madrid is colorful both day and night. Beautiful Plaza de la Cibeles, fronting the Spanish Palace of Communications, is enhanced by these dancing waters.

Tourist information is available opposite track Nos. 10 and 11. This office is operated by the Madrid province and can provide information about Madrid or, in fact, any other Spanish city or location. Brochures describing all of the day-excursion points are usually available in English. The office operates 0830–1400 and 1700–2200 daily. When the office is closed, the hotel office opposite track Nos. 6 and 7 will assist you.

Train information is available at a *mostrador* (center) in the middle of the station, between the entrances to track Nos. 9 and 10, which is staffed by a bevy of cute, well-informed señoritas. If you can keep your mind on the questions, they can come up with answers. The center is actually a large, oval-shaped counter area placed prominently in a strategic position and "decorated" attractively. When you see it, we know you'll agree. By the way, lest we forget, it's open daily from 0700 to 2300.

Train reservations are obligatory in Spain for all express and international trains. Start at the train information center by informing one of the attractive attendants stationed there of the date, destination, and train (by number and departure time) on which you wish to reserve seats. She will then assist you in preparing a small memo that, you, in turn, will hand to a less attractive male clerk in one of the ticket windows numbered from 1 to 8 behind the train information center. Present your Eurailpass together with your seat reservation request to the clerk, and there will be no charge for the seat reservation.

We believe that it is proper Spanish etiquette to return to the train information center to thank the pretty señorita for the part she played in helping you obtain the seat reservation.

The reservation form is a computer card. Under the column "Asiento" you will either find a seat number or the entry "S.R." This means "Seat Reserved," but no specific number is assigned. You are assured that there will be a seat available in the *coche* (coach) you'll be traveling in, but you should ask the conductor where to sit when you board the train. This type of seat reservation is given frequently when you request a seat on the same day you travel. Seat reservations are available up to departure time. *Be certain to have them.*

We have intentionally tested the Spanish railroad's mandatory seat-reservation requirement and can personally report to our readers that they mean what they say. If you do not have a reservation—even though you have a rail ticket or a rail pass—you will be asked politely, but firmly, to leave the train at the next station.

Eurailpass validation must be accomplished at the station where you board a train for the first time in order to have the dates of validity entered on the pass. In Spain, this is extremely easy to remember, since you cannot board a train there *unless* you have a seat reservation (except for local trains, of course). Your Eurailpass can be validated in the Chamartin Station at ticket windows 1 through 8—the same windows where you make your seat reservations.

Madrid's "Expo" Station—Atocha

Although the Atocha terminal's train traffic was reduced with the opening of the Chamartin Station, all of its services continue to operate: currency exchange, tourist information, hotel reservations, and train information.

It is also possible to make seat reservations at the Atocha rail station even if the train now departs from Chamartin. (You may now obtain seat reservations in any Madrid station for trains departing from any other station.) The station's pleasant interior is well marked with pictographs, making it easy to locate all of its services and functions. All operating hours are identical with those of Chamartin. The day excursions to Aranjuez and Toledo depart from this station.

Madrid Memorandum

Should you plan to attend a bullfight in Madrid, remember what Ernest Hemingway wrote: ". . . It is a tragedy; the death of the bull, which is played, more or less well by the bull and the man involved and in which there is danger for the man but certain death for the bull."

If Papa's words are too strong to take, Madrid can offer many other attractions. The Prado Museum is incomparable. Housing more than 7,000 works of art, the museum is particularly noted for its fine collections of the Spanish masters—Goya, Velazquez, El Greco, Murillo, and Zurbaran. It is closed on Monday. Madrid's park Buen Retiro offers a place for mid-city meditation amid its several exhibition halls, flower gardens, and lake. Night entertainment varies from the expensive clubs featuring international reviews to the crowded bistros where you can rub elbows with the populace.

As in all European cities, people watching can become a full-time pastime. The Spanish are among the most polite and precise people of Europe—in fact, of the world. You will note this in the manner in which they act in public, the manner in which you are escorted and seated in a restaurant, and the way the concierge hands you the hotel key.

One thing you will learn soon after arriving in Madrid is that the city isn't being evacuated nightly at about 2100—the traffic jams you witness are merely the city's well-to-do diners en route to dinner. Madrilenos (residents of Madrid) like to eat late in the evening, and some of the better restaurants don't open until 2100. When photographing the fountain on page 360, in fact, we spent two hours at a traffic circle waiting for traffic to subside.

Visit several of Madrid's *chiringuitos,* a combination German-style beer garden and discotheque. Numerous *chiringuitos* and cafés line the Paseo de la Castellana, which becomes Paseo del Prado as it nears the Prado Museum. You may even want to join the Madrilenos in a *cerveza* (beer) and *tapas* (numerous small appetizers).

From Madrid . . .

TRAIN CONNECTIONS TO OTHER BASE CITIES

TO:	DEPART*	ARRIVE	TRAIN NUMBER	COOK'S TABLE	NOTES
Barcelona	1100	1800	TAL 374	410	
(Sants)	1600	2235	TAL 378	410	
	2310	0800+1	874	410	
Lisbon	1405(4)	2145	TAL 30	433(6)	
	2230	0845+1	332	433	
Paris	1000	2300	203	45	(2)(3)(5)
	1930	0830+1	EC 406	46	(1)

See *Thomas Cook European Timetable,* "Plans of Cities" section, for description of railway stations in Madrid.

 * All departures from Madrid's Chamartin Station, unless otherwise noted.
Seat or sleeper reservations are mandatory in Spain.

(1) Arrives at Paris Gare d'Austerlitz
(2) Transfer in Hendaye to TGV 8596
(3) Daily, except Sundays and holidays
(4) Departs from Madrid Puerto de Atocha
(5) Arrives in Paris Gare Montparnasse
(6) Daily, except Saturday

Royal Palace of Aranjuez is framed by iron latticework surrounding its grounds. Dating from the eighteenth century, this classic building is an interesting place to visit.

From Madrid . . .

A DAY EXCURSION TO ARANJUEZ
  DISTANCE BY TRAIN: 30 miles (49 km)
  AVERAGE TRAIN TIME: 50 minutes

In the eighteenth and nineteenth centuries, Aranjuez was the favorite hangout for Spanish royalty. It's now a popular place for Madrid's citizenry to gather on weekends. Consequently, we would like to suggest that you take this day excursion sometime during the week to avoid the crowds that you will probably encounter on the weekend.

The town of Aranjuez and its surroundings have often been described as the "Oasis of Castille," due in part because Aranjuez nestles on the banks of the Tagus River, which nurses dense groves of poplars and rich vegetation. The jade green waters of the river apparently favor the growth of trees. This fact manifests itself in the city's Circus of the Twelve Streets, a square from which twelve beautifully shaded avenues radiate.

As your train approaches Aranjuez, you begin to get the feeling that perhaps you are crossing a border and entering a different country. The impression comes from the fertile, wooded valley formed by the Tagus and the Jarama rivers. With an eye for aqua, the Romans founded the area and there erected a temple to the god Jupiter. *Ara Jovis,* Latin for "the place of Jupiter," became, when translated into Spanish, the city's modern name.

Aranjuez closely resembles Versailles in its parks and palaces. In fact, the lavish and elegant interior decorations of the Palacio Real (Royal Palace) and the Casa del Labrador (Cottage of the Farmer) probably outstrip the French showplace in sheer luxury. You have to see it to believe it.

Trains for Aranjuez depart from the Atocha Station in Madrid. If you have not made seat reservations, plan to arrive at the station fifteen to twenty minutes before train time to obtain them from any of the ticket windows, designated "Largo Recorrido," directly opposite the timetable bulletins in the station's north hall.

If you're going to Aranjuez on a Sunday or a holiday, we strongly recommend that you make seat reservations at least one day before or plan to take the early train, which is second class only and does not require reservations.

Upon arrival in the Aranjuez train station, proceed immediately to the tourist information office (Oficina de Información de Turismo) by taxi. City buses go there by a round-about route. Taxis go there directly, and the fare is reasonable.

The tourist information office is located at No. 1 Plaza del Puente de Bancas across from the Jardín (garden) del Parterre and near the Palacio Real. The telephone number for the tourist office is 891.04.27.

ARANJUEZ—*SPANISH ROYAL RETREAT*

A Day Excursion from Madrid

DEPART FROM MADRID CHAMARTIN*	DEPART FROM MADRID ATOCHA*	TRAIN NUMBER	ARRIVE IN ARANJUEZ STATION	NOTES
0800	0815	TAL 20	0840	(1)
0900	0915	TAL 220	0945	(1)
1315	1330	Local	1408	(1)(2)

DEPART FROM ARANJUEZ STATION	TRAIN NUMBER	ARRIVE IN MADRID ATOCHA*	ARRIVE IN MADRID CHAMARTIN*	NOTES
1926	Local	2004	2017	(1)(2)
1928	TAL 25	1959	2013	(1)
2025	TAL 225	2059	2113	(1)

* See *Thomas Cook European Timetable,* "Plans of Cities" section, for description of railway stations in Madrid.

(1) Daily, including holidays
(2) Second class only

Distance: 30 miles/49 km
Reference: Thomas Cook Table 420

There are a variety of tickets available in the palace for Aranjuez attractions. The combination ticket for everything includes a guided tour of the Royal Palace. You may purchase a ticket for the palace tour alone if your time is limited. During spring and summer, the palace is open 1000–1830 Tuesday through Sunday. It closes one hour earlier in autumn and winter.

Sightseeing highlights in Aranjuez include the Royal Palace, where you will see the Porcelain Salon, the Throne Room, and the "monumental" grand staircase that was installed by Philip V. The Museum of Royal Robes, which displays the court dress of sovereigns up to the nineteenth century, is closed periodically for the cleaning and restoration of its displays. Should you be fortunate enough to visit the Royal Palace at a time when the museum is open, you will be able to admire the curious mixture of French elegance and Spanish sobriety reflected by the garments. In a total of eighteen rooms, you will find exhibits of the different royal and courtly costumes from the time of the Catholic kings up to the period of the last Spanish monarchy.

No doubt, the most interesting place to visit in the Royal Palace is the Farmer's Cottage, or House of the Peasant Farmer—if only for its name. A workhouse for peasants (poor ones, at that) once stood on the site where a Versailles-type Trianon now dominates the scene. Never has a so-called "cottage" displayed such extravagant furnishings. The richness of the furniture, paintings, marble, and porcelain is truly breathtaking.

You reach the Farmer's Cottage by strolling through the Prince's Garden, a spacious bit of landscape that was created by the Spanish king Charles IV (1748–1819). Indirectly, King Charles contributed to the history of North America by ceding the Louisiana Territory to France through his disastrous involvement in the French Revolution. You can muse about this while strolling—and wonder what might have happened to New Orleans if Charles had not been so involved in gardening.

Other places to visit are the Casa de Marinos (Sailors' House), which houses the royal vessels of six Spanish sovereigns; the Parterre Garden, which extends along the eastern front of the palace and across from the tourist office; and the Jardin de la Isla (Island Garden), which you reach by crossing a canal adjacent to the palace. Most of the sights are closed on Mondays.

The tours operate from 1000–1300 daily all year. Afternoon hours are 1530–1830 (May–September 15), 1500–1800 (February–April and September 16–October 15), and 1430–1730 (October 16–January 31).

Medieval fortifications, the walls of Avila date to the eleventh century. Visitors may walk the paths atop the walls.

From Madrid . . .

A DAY EXCURSION TO AVILA
DISTANCE BY TRAIN: 70 miles (112 km)
AVERAGE TRAIN TIME: 1 hour, 30 minutes

Avila is the great walled city of medieval Spain. It is forever associated with Saint Teresa of Jesus, one of the greatest mystics of the Catholic Church. It is the highest provincial capital in Spain, with a cathedral that looks more like a fortress than a place of worship. Only recently has the city spread to the outside of its eleventh-century walls. Seeing it is fascinating and makes the comfortable train trip worthwhile.

The entire city gives the impression that it is a rocky castle perched on a hillside. Viewed from a distance, Avila seems like a giant stage set for a medieval drama.

Avila lives under the influence of Saint Teresa. You will see evidence of this at practically every turn you make within its walls, positioned just as they were in the sixteenth century when she walked its streets. Termed the City of Saint Teresa, Avila also is known as the City of the Knights, because they were responsible for the construction of its walls in the eleventh century. You will notice the knightly presence in the proud coats of arms blazoned on the doors of its stately mansions.

Trains to Avila depart from the Chamartin Station in Madrid. Seat reservations are obligatory. We suggest you obtain them at least one day in advance of your trip. It is possible to request seats right up to departure time in the Chamartin Station, however, by asking at any of the ticket windows from No. 1 to No. 8. Write out your request and show your Eurailpass. Train service to Avila is also available from Madrid's northern station, Principe Pio.

Avila's railway station is about a mile from the center of the city. Although tram service is available, we suggest that you take advantage of the reasonable taxi fares to go directly to the tourist information office (Oficina de Turismo) at No. 4 in the Plaza de la Catedral (Cathedral Plaza). There is a taxi stand on the far right of the station as you exit.

During summer the tourist office is open 0900–1500 Monday through Friday. After siesta, it is open 1600–2000. Saturday hours are 1000–1400; Sunday and holidays, 1100–1400. The telephone number is (920) 21.13.87; fax (920) 25.37.17.

Across the street from the tourist office is the Gran Hotel Palacio Valderrabanos. Don't let the name scare you. This former nobleman's residence is an excellent place to have lunch. Its door dates from the fifteenth century.

A visit to Avila wouldn't be complete without a walk on its walls, which

AVILA—*WALLED CITY*

A Day Excursion from Madrid

DEPART FROM MADRID* CHAMARTIN STATION	TRAIN NUMBER	ARRIVE IN AVILA STATION	NOTES
0800	IC 131	0925	(1)
0900	TAL 61	1021	(1)
1000	203	1126	(1)

DEPART FROM AVILA STATION	TRAIN NUMBER	ARRIVE IN MADRID* CHAMARTIN STATION	NOTES
1325	202	1458	(1)
1615	TAL 78	1742	(1)
1834	Local	2013	(1)
1952	TAL 60	2120	(1)

* See *Thomas Cook European Timetable,* "Plans of Cities" section, for description of railway stations in Madrid. Seat Reservations mandatory on trains, except Locals

(1) Daily, including holidays

Distance: 70 miles/112 km
Reference: Thomas Cook Table 431

you may begin from the National Parador near the tourist office. Get a briefing from the tourist information office before setting out.

The walls are more than one and a half miles around and completely enclose the city. Construction began in 1085. The average height is thirty-three feet, and there are ninety towers and nine gateways. It took nine years to build the walls surrounding Avila. The enormity of the project is overwhelming when you realize that the walls average about ten feet in thickness. During July and August, the walls are illuminated nightly from 2200 to midnight.

The cathedral forms a part of the great wall and, as mentioned previously, has the distinct look of a fortress rather than a church. Its austere exterior is in contrast to its interior, which has many beautiful details. In the cathedral's museum you may see a portrait painted by El Greco and a colossal silver monstrance, made in 1571 by Juan de Arfe, which weighs nearly 200 pounds. There is a nominal admission charge to the museum.

Saint Teresa's Convent, erected in 1636, marks the site where she was born in 1515. Her first convent, San José, stands in Avila, as does Nuestra Señora de Gracia, where she was educated. The religious and historic places in Avila are generally open both in the morning and again in the afternoon, but some of the hours are seasonal. Inquire at the tourist information office concerning those places that you might wish to visit.

A very pleasant walking tour of Avila can be arranged with the help of the tourist office. After seeing and walking on the great wall, you should include a visit to the main square, named after Saint Teresa, as well as one to the Plaza de la Victoria, also known as the Constitution Square.

With all of the physical activity involved in sightseeing, the inner man no doubt will begin to crave reconstitution in the form of a substantial meal. You have come to the right place. The cuisine of the area, although medieval in style, is fit for a king's palate. The trout taken from the Tormes River is renowned for its distinctive flavor; the roast suckling pig, lamb, or veal dishes are equally excellent and served with a hearty accompaniment of vegetables.

When you return to the railway station, check with the train information office regarding the track number of your train to Madrid. It often varies, and it could be embarrassing to find yourself standing on one platform while your train to Madrid arrives at another. A moment of inquiry might save a minute or so of frantic scrambling later. If you prefer, telephone RENFE at Avila railway station: 22.01.88.

El Cid, legend of Spain's eleventh century, guards the city of Burgos. His final resting place is in the city's cathedral, where he lies in state with his wife, Ximena.

From Madrid . . .

A DAY EXCURSION TO BURGOS
DISTANCE BY TRAIN: 211 miles (340 km)
AVERAGE TRAIN TIME: 3 hours

El Cid, immortalized by the epic poem *Cantar de Mio Cid,* was born in Burgos. A stunning equestrian statue stands in the city square attesting the exploits of *El Cid Campeador* (The Lord Champion), and he lies in state beside his wife, Ximena, in the city's thirteenth-century cathedral.

The cathedral is one of the most majestic in Spain. Its twin spires rise to greet you long before your Talgo train comes to a halt in the Burgos Station. The first stone of the cathedral was laid in 1221, and the construction was completed thirty years later. There is so much history and detail both inside and outside the cathedral that your entire time in Burgos could be spent in a study of it. By all means, take the Talgo and enjoy a full day in El Cid's city.

The city of Burgos, situated in the valley of the Arlanzon River, lies halfway between Madrid and the French border. The entire city is filled with beautiful little squares and streets. Divided by the course of the Arlanzon, Burgos's apparent modern-day tranquillity hides the hectic history of the city. In its early years, Burgos was devastated repeatedly until the ninth century, when it was renewed to become the capital of Castile.

It was from Burgos that the Castilians began their campaigns against the Muslims by which they eventually won back Madrid in 1083 and Toledo in 1085. During this time, the coffers of the city swelled with the tributes it extracted from the defeated Moorish princes.

Don't let the distance to Burgos deter you from making the trip. The Talgo "glides" there at an average speed of 76 miles per hour through the scenic Old Castile region. It was in this area during the eighth century that the first resistance to the Moors' invasion was mounted. From this Burgos gained the name "the Shield of Castile." In more recent history, Burgos was the headquarters of General Franco during the Spanish Civil War. The Generalissimo issued the cease-fire of the Spanish civil war in Burgos on 1 April 1939.

Seat reservations are obligatory on the Talgo trains. Any of the ticket windows from No. 1 to No. 8 in the Chamartin Station can provide seat-reservation service. The Talgos ply between Madrid and Irun on the French border and are booked heavily. For this reason, we recommend that you obtain your reservations as early as possible even though they can be requested right up to departure time. Ensure a pleasant day excursion by booking early.

Arriving in Burgos, you can taxi to the tourist information office (Oficina de Turismo). It is located at No. 7, Plaza Alonso Martinez, a shaded walkway that runs from the Arch of Santa Maria to El Cid's statue. It's a fifteen-minute

BURGOS—*HOME OF EL CID*

A Day Excursion from Madrid

DEPART FROM MADRID CHAMARTIN STATION*	TRAIN NUMBER	ARRIVE IN BURGOS STATION	NOTES
0920	343	1230	(1)(2)
1000	203	1332	(1)

DEPART FROM BURGOS STATION	TRAIN NUMBER	ARRIVE IN MADRID CHAMARTIN STATION*	NOTES
1903	Tal 200	2209	(1)

* See *Thomas Cook European Timetable,* "Plans of Cities" section, for description of railway stations in Madrid. Seat reservations mandatory on express trains.

(1) Daily, except Saturday
(2) Second class only

Distance: 211 miles/340 km
Reference: Thomas Cook Table 431

walk. On foot, exit the station and go straight ahead until you cross the Arlanzon River. Turn right and proceed along General Franco Avenue to the arch where the walkway Paseo del Espolón begins.

The tourist office is open 0900–1400 and 1630–1830 Monday through Friday and 1000–1330 Saturday. The office is closed on Sunday and holidays. Maps of the city and its surrounding area are available, together with brochures (in English) that provide you with excellent background on the cathedral and other points of interest. Cathedral tours are available; admission to the cathedral is 220 pesetas.

El Cid, a legendary hero with a "have sword, will travel" attitude, fought for the Moors and against them. Born Rodrigo Diaz, a native of Vivar some six miles from Burgos, his exploits drew much attention during the later decades of the eleventh century. Referring to both Spaniards and Moors alike, he said, "They are all the same, as long as they pay my price."

El Cid first supported the Castilians, but his victories against the Moors drew the envy of Alfonso VI, who had assumed the Castilian crown from his brother, Sancho II, under somewhat dubious circumstances. Even though he was married to the king's cousin at the time, El Cid was banned from the kingdom and became a soldier of fortune.

He finally met defeat by the Moors and died in 1099. His widow, a legend herself, continued to hold out against the Moors and returned to Burgos in 1102 with El Cid's body. Buried first in a monastery outside of Burgos, he was finally interred at her side in the Burgos Cathedral in 1942. Legend had finally transferred the ruthless warrior into a chivalrous knight of great valor.

Sometime during your day excursion, stop off to see El Cid's statue in the city square just beyond the tourist information office. Also be certain to stop and examine the Santa Maria Arch en route to the cathedral. Its gateway has defended against invasion of Burgos since the fourteenth century.

The Casa del Cordon, a fifteenth-century house so named from the huge cord of rope carved in stone fronting its entrance, forms the backdrop for El Cid's statue. It was here that Christopher Columbus was received in formal audience by the Spanish monarchs on his return from his second voyage to the Americas.

Anytime you have lunch in mind, we suggest the Ojeda Restaurant located at the beginning of Calle Vitoria, No. 5. It's great for a light snack or a full meal. Its outside tables are delightful in summer.

Eighth wonder of the world according to many, the palace monastery built by Philip II in Escorial dominates the skyline with its massive, austere structure. The king watched the construction from a hillside seat about five miles away.

From Madrid . . .

A DAY EXCURSION TO EL ESCORIAL
DISTANCE BY TRAIN: 32 miles (52 km)
AVERAGE TRAIN TIME: 60 minutes

El Escorial is an immense building that was erected as a palace-monastery by Philip II of Spain to celebrate a victory over France at St. Quentin in 1557. Supervised personally by the king, the project was a stupendous one that would even boggle the minds of today's shopping-mall developers.

Just as Versailles will be forever associated with Louis XIV, Escorial will serve to perpetuate the memory of Philip II. John Hay, the nineteenth-century American historian, said of Philip: "He was so true a king, so vain, so superstitious, so cruel, it is probable so great a king like him never lived." Part monastery, part palace, part cathedral—El Escorial reflects its builder's times and temperament.

Philip II will go down in history as the Spanish king who mounted the Armada against England. He had tried to bring England into the Spanish Empire once before by marrying Mary Tudor, who earned the nickname "Bloody Mary" for her overzealous persecution of English Protestants.

Covering eight acres, the building has 9 towers, 16 courtyards, 86 staircases, 1,200 doors, and 2,673 windows. The building, resembling a giant rectangle, runs for several city blocks along its longest axis. A force of 1,500 workmen labored twenty-one years between 1563 and 1584 to complete it. Wear your best pair of walking shoes—you'll need them.

The scale of El Escorial is so grand that it appears cold and drab from a distance and must be studied at close range. The railway station is a half-mile from the town. Buses that meet the trains run to the town square. Taxis, which stand to the left of the station exit, will take you to the town square or the tourist information office (Oficina de Información de Turismo) for about 350 pesetas.

The information office is located at No. 10 on a picturesque street named Floridablanca that runs the length of the monastery's northern wall. It's downhill from the town square and located easily. Year-round hours of operation are 1000–1400 and 1500–1700; it is closed on Saturday afternoon and Sunday. The telephone number is (91) 8.90.15.54.

There is an admission charge of 350 pesetas to the Monastery of San Lorenzo de El Escorial. It is open from 1000–1800 in summer, until 1700 in winter, and closed on Monday. No tickets are sold within one hour of any closing time. An extra charge is made for taking cameras into the monastery.

El Escorial was a small village at the base of the Guadarrama Mountains when Philip II selected it as the site for the building of his palace-monastery-

EL ESCORIAL—*WORLD'S EIGHTH WONDER*

A Day Excursion from Madrid

DEPART FROM MADRID ATOCHA	DEPART FROM MADRID CHARMARTIN	ARRIVE IN EL ESCORIAL	NOTES
0702	0716	0812	(1)(2)
0832	0847	0937	(1)(2)
1032	1046	1137	(1)(2)
1232	1246	1337	(1)(2)

DEPART FROM EL ESCORIAL	ARRIVE IN MADRID CHARMARTIN	ARRIVE IN MADRID ATOCHA	NOTES
1617	1708	1722	(1)(2)
1817	1908	1922	(1)(2)
2017	2108	2122	(1)
2217	2308	2322	(1)

* See *Thomas Cook European Timetable,* "Plans of Cities" section, for description of railway stations in Madrid.

(1) Daily, including holidays
(2) Seat reservations required

Distance: 32 miles/52 km
Reference: RENFE schedule, not listed in *Thomas Cook European Timetable*

cathedral. The village has since grown into a town, but the main occupations of its townspeople remain the maintenance and promotion of the monument, El Escorial.

The treasures of El Escorial include paintings by Bosch, Rembrandt, Tintoretto, and Titian. Spain's martial adventures are displayed in the Hall of Battles, which features paintings by such Italian artists as Grenello, Tavorone, and Castello. On its walls hang tapestries of Spanish country life woven over sketches drawn by Goya.

Looking through the leaded-glass windows of El Escorial, you may look upon the formal gardens and the hedge mazes on the palace grounds towards the stony hills beyond, which for all the world look like the mountains of Arizona or New Mexico. To see it scattered with snow in the winter transports you back to the Middle Ages.

It is a favorite spot for short holidays by Madrid's citizenry. August 10 marks the feast of Saint Lawrence, patron saint of the town and the monastery. Visits during the week are recommended because the close proximity of El Escorial to Madrid attracts many people on the weekends, especially during summer.

When hunger strikes, strike back with a snack or luncheon at one of the town's many restaurants. The tourist office can provide a list of the local eating establishments. We like the Alaska Restaurant on the Plaza de San Lorenzo, one block downhill from the town square. Summertime meals there are served outside under a grove of delightful shade trees. If you have packed your own lunch, there are numerous plazas and promenades for you to enjoy.

In his later years, the king took on a deep devotion, which clouded his brain before his death in 1598. In the midst of the grandeur he had created, Philip II lived in a Spartan chamber in monastic poverty. This apartment is on the second floor and well worth the climb for the contrast.

The pixilated king had a seat carved out of rock some five miles distant from El Escorial where he would go and watch its construction. If interested, have the tourist office provide more details. The seats are hard, but the view's terrific.

Two related attractions in the area, although on a smaller scale than the monastery, are of interest to visitors. Casita del Principe (the Prince's Cottage) is on the route to the station. Casita de Arriba, a hunting lodge, is two miles farther on. Both are open 1000–1800 (1700 in winter) and closed on Monday. Both were constructed by Charles III (1759–1788). His friendship with France and hostility towards Great Britain led to the alliance in support of the American Revolution.

Toledo's landscape, outside its walls (above), contains both a Roman arch and a Moorish fortress. Toledo's charms, such as its narrow streets (below), attract thousands of visitors who come each year to enjoy the grandeur of Spanish history as well.

From Madrid . . .

A DAY EXCURSION TO TOLEDO
DISTANCE BY TRAIN: 57 miles (91 km)
AVERAGE TRAIN TIME: 1 hour, 30 minutes

Some fifty-seven rail miles south-southwest of Madrid, the Imperial City of Toledo rises towards the heavens, seemingly immersed in a sea of intense light. The city sprawls over an enormous crag that appears to be challenging space, while the fast-flowing River Tagus cradles the city as if it were anchored in its turbulent waters. In the words of the Spanish writer Cossio, Toledo is "the city which presents the most complete and characteristic ensemble of all that is genuinely Spanish land and civilization." Viewing Toledo, others have said that not only can the presence of Castile be felt, but above all, the spirit of Castile can be seen in its red earth and violet sky.

Domenico Teotocopulo arrived in Toledo in 1577. The arrival of a Cretan in a city so fundamentally Spanish should have gone unnoticed and unrecorded. It would have, too, except that Señor Teotocopulo, better known as El Greco, happened to be a painter of some renown. From that time onward, El Greco painted and bequeathed his best to Toledo. In turn, the city has become a museum of his works.

El Greco's *View of Toledo* bursts into the third dimension of space as you approach the city on Paseo de la Rosa, which leads from the railway station past the San Servando Castle and across the Tajo River. The Castilian sky often becomes a luminous mantle surrounding the golden silhouette of the city. As described previously, Toledo is as spectacular as it is rich in history. According to an old Spanish expression, "A traveler but with a single day in Spain ought, without hesitation, to spend it seeing Toledo."

Although Toledo is probably the city that most perfectly epitomizes the fundamentals of Spanish history, its origins are shrouded in legend. Livy, one of Rome's earliest historians, described it as a "small, fortified town." Under the Romans, Toledo became an invaluable stronghold of great strategic importance, minting its own coinage and boasting a grand circus and aqueduct. From Roman-civilization origins, Toledo became the coveted prize of the different civilizations that succeeded one another down through the centuries in Spain.

History relates that many folks have visited Toledo in other years and liked it. The Romans named it Toletum. The Visigoths made it a monarchical seat until they abandoned the town to the Moors, who apparently named it Tolaitola. In 1085, Toledo fell to the Christians and became Spain's imperial city. El Cid was its first governor.

Trains departing Madrid for Toledo leave from the Atocha Station. They are all one class, and seat reservations are not mandatory. In fact, the only way

TOLEDO—*CITY OF HISTORY*

A Day Excursion from Madrid

DEPART FROM MADRID ATOCHA STATION*	ARRIVE IN TOLEDO STATION	NOTES
0720	0838	(1)(2)(3)
0909	1027	(1)(2)
1050	1208	(1)(2)(3)
1220	1338	(1)(2)(3)

DEPART FROM TOLEDO STATION	ARRIVE IN MADRID ATOCHA STATION*	NOTES
1420	1538	(1)(2)(3)
1630	1748	(1)(2)(3)
1750	1908	(1)(2)
1925	2043	(1)(2)(3)
2130	2248	(1)(2)(3)

* See *Thomas Cook European Timetable,* "Plans of Cities" section, for description of railway stations in Madrid.

(1) Daily, including holidays
(2) Seat reservations required
(3) One class only

Distance: 57 miles/91 km
Reference: Thomas Cook Table 432

to reserve a seat on this train is to occupy it. Do so early, well in advance of train-departure time, or you could find yourself standing all the way to Toledo.

The distance from the Toledo railway station to the center of the city is considerable; in other words, it's a short ride but a long walk. There is a public bus service from the rail station into town. The bus leaves every fifteen minutes. The bus stops first at the tourist information office (Oficina de Información de Turismo) at Puerta de la Bisagra before terminating in the main square of the city, Plaza de Zocodover (Marketplace). There also is a tourist information kiosk in the main square, which is open 1000–1800 Monday through Saturday and 1000–1500 on Sundays.

The other option is a taxi. In any event, do check in with the tourist information office. It is the only place in town where you can get the official word, maps, and helpful brochures.

The tourist information office is at the end of a park, immediately across the street from the main gateway to the old city, Puerta Nueva de Bisagra. Its hours of operation are 0900–1400 and 1600–1800 on weekdays, 0900–1500 and 1600–1900 on Saturdays, and 0900–1500 on Sundays. The telephone number is (925) 22.08.43.

Toledo has something to see practically every time you take a step. The main sights for a one-day visit would be: (1) the Alcazar, the city's thirteenth-century fortress with origins back in the third century, when it served as a Pretorian palace during the Roman period; (2) the cathedral, outstanding for its design and works of art, its first stone having been laid by King Ferdinand III in 1226; and (3) the El Greco House and the Museum of Santa Cruz, which houses twenty-two paintings by El Greco.

There are many more interesting places to see in Toledo. Merely walking the narrow cobblestone alleys is an experience. By the way, wear your most sensible pair of walking shoes. Cobblestones wear out more slowly than feet do.

Although there are numerous eating establishments scattered the length and breadth of Toledo, most visitors seem to congregate in the main square, Plaza de Zocodover (Marketplace). Here, you will find the Café Bar Toledo and the Telesforo to be convenient spots to sample some local sandwiches and *tapas* (appetizers). Or, if you've experienced a "Big Mac attack," you may satisfy your hamburger pangs at McDonald's.

There are any number of restaurants to select from, as well as a bevy of sidewalk cafés, just off the main square in Barrio Rey. Local partridge stewed in red wine and *tortilla a la magra,* an omelet, are traditional dishes. With visitors from all over the globe, it's extremely easy to get involved here in people watching—people meeting, too. An aperitif on the plaza is a lovely way to end a perfect day.

Cavernous is the main hall of Milano Centrale, principal railway station of Milan.

18 MILAN

Like the American news commentator Paul Harvey, who's not interested in the past but only interested in what will happen tomorrow, Milan lives more to gain its future than to review its memorable past. Yet despite the "tomorrow" thrust of Milan—visible in the growing number of high-rise structures and the accelerating pace of its population—Milan is ancient and has much to show for it.

For instance, the Duomo (cathedral) is the second largest church in Italy, a beautiful example of Gothic stonework begun in 1386. *The Last Supper,* Leonardo da Vinci's famous painting, may be seen in the refectory of the Santa Maria delle Grazie convent. It was painted between 1495 and 1498.

Like a typical Milanese, Leonardo was concerned with the future, and his drawings of machines in flight, together with some of his futuristic inventions, are exhibited in the Leonardo da Vinci National Museum of Science and Technology.

To gain its future, Milan has created one of the most extensive fairgrounds in Europe; each year, thousands of businesses display or investigate products there. Milan does not live up to the stereotype of the Italian town. Lunches tend to be shorter, conversations seem more direct and to the point, and the Milanese appear to be in a bit of a hurry.

Unlike many Italian cities, transportation is abundant and unusually dependable. Several decades ago, the five o'clock train never left Milano Centrale on time; today, the five o'clock train leaves at five o'clock. Hotel services rival the finest in Europe; shops are sophisticated, efficient. In a word, Milan "works."

There is one crucial thing about Milan. It is virtually impossible to get a hotel room in the city during those periods when the major fairs are in progress—September, October, and early March. Forget about August. That's when the Milanese go on vacation and the majority of the hotels are closed.

Day Excursions

A total of four day excursions have been selected for Milan. The first two take you south of Milan into the Italian peninsula to Italy's gastronomic capital, Bologna, and the birthplace of Christopher Columbus, Genoa. Another day excursion will take you to where Switzerland meets Italy, Lake Lugano, the Swiss city with an Italian flair. The remaining day excursion will take you east to "the Queen of the Adriatic," Venice, and the romance of its gondoliers and grand canals. You'll enjoy each of them.

Arriving and Departing

By Air. Milan has two airports serving international travelers. Milan's main international airport, Malpensa, is thirty miles northwest of the city, and fifty to sixty minutes is required to reach the downtown air terminal. Closer in, Milan's Linate Airport is located slightly more than six miles to the east of Milan; transit time is twenty to forty minutes. Check with your airline regarding which airport will be used for your flight.

No rail service is available from either airport. Regular bus, limousine, and taxi services, however, are available at both air terminals. The limousine charge per passenger between the Linate Airport and downtown destinations is between 2,500 and 4,000 Italian lire; for Malpensa, more distant, the fare is 7,000 lire.

We recommend the limousine service, particularly if you are burdened with baggage. The municipal buses are crowded, and the taxi services are quite expensive.

By Train. Milan has no fewer than seven railway stations, but luckily, readers have to be concerned with only one, the Milan Central Station (Milano Centrale). All EuroCity trains and the trains for the listed day excursions arrive and depart from this station. The schedule appearing on page 391 lists rail services between Milan and ten other base cities: Amsterdam, Barcelona, Berne, Brussels, Luxembourg, Munich, Nice, Paris, Rome, and Vienna. EuroCity and InterCity trains use Milan's central station daily. In rail service, Milan ranks second only to Paris.

Memo on Milan

As we indicated previously, there are times when the city reaches the visitor saturation point and NO VACANCY signs go up all over town. Should you arrive in Milan without hotel reservations and this is the situation you encounter, you have two alternatives to consider.

If there is no housing in Milan, you can leave town. A EuroCity train can have you in Como within thirty-two minutes, where hotel rooms probably will be more plentiful. In fact, you may be taken with the idea of residing in this lovely lake location throughout your stay in the area. There is express-train service back to Milan every morning.

An alternative is a fast but systematic search of the concentrated hotel area adjacent to the railway station. There is a covey of luxury and first-class hotels to the left of it. Dominating the scene is the seventeen-story Michelangelo, with the Bristol, the Anderson, the Andreola, and the Splendido close by.

For lower cost but comfortable lodgings, walk two blocks on Via Roberto Lepetit, beginning at the Michelangelo, to Piazza San Camillo. Within this distance, you pass the Florida, the Colombia, and the Boston hotels. No luck? Turn right at the Plaza onto Via Napo Torriani. Between this point and Piazza

Duca d'Aosta three short blocks ahead (where you can again see the station), you pass on your right the hotels Berna, Atlantic, and San Carlo; on your left, the Milano, Garda, Flora, Bernina, and Augustus.

If you have not found a room by this time, head back to Milano Centrale and one of the EuroCities. By this time, you'll be sure to fall in love with Lake Como.

While on the subject of hotels, it should be noted that there are limited services available in Milan to assist you in your quest for accommodations. The tourist information office in the railway station is not equipped to provide this service. This office will, however, give you directions for reaching the main tourist office located on Piazza del Duomo, in the center of the city.

The main tourist office charges a nominal fee for their services, but they are not authorized to accept deposits to guarantee that your reservation will be honored on your arrival at the hotel or pension. If you have made a room reservation through either of these offices, we suggest that you proceed immediately to your hotel to confirm your reservation in person. Italian hoteliers operate on a "first come, first housed" basis, and even though you have a reservation, someone else may end up with the room.

Milan's Railway Station—Milano Centrale

Milan's central station is enormous, probably the largest in Western Europe—at least it appears to be. Such immensity can be confusing or even frightening, particularly on your first encounter, when you have no idea of where anything is located. We've got it all worked out for you.

Money exchange office can be reached by going through the archway leading off *binari* (track) No. 15. Once through the archway and into the main hall of the station, you will see the office marked CAMBIO CHANGE on the far side and to the left. The exchange office operates daily from 0800–2000; Sundays and holidays, 0900–1430.

By all means, avoid the so-called "money changers" who frequent this area. Like the gypsies in the Paris Metro, their main purpose is to relieve you of your money. The gypsies do it by picking your pocket; the "money changers" are much more gentle in their approach—they just short-change you. You will find the best rates inside the exchange office at the counter.

Tourist information is on the left-hand side of the money-exchange office. Maps of Milan and tour information are available. As mentioned previously, this office is not equipped to assist in locating hotel or pension accommodations. Hours of operation are 0800–2000 daily, Sunday and holidays, 0900–1230 and 1430–1800. Telephone 669–0532. A hallway on the left side of the tourist office will lead you to a public telephone office where you can make operator-assisted phone calls.

The Duomo, second largest church in Italy, graces the main square of Milan.

To reach the central tourist information office, take bus No. 65 in front of the station to Piazza del Duomo, site of Milan's cathedral. Attendants in the railway station information office will direct you. The central tourist office's hours are 0845–1800 daily throughout the year.

Train information can be obtained from an office marked with a black "i" located at the extreme right end of the station as you come from the trains. Illuminated flags indicate what language is spoken at the windows. The British flag means English is spoken. Hours of operation are posted as 0700–2300.

Train reservations for EuroCity, InterCity, and express-train services are made in an office separate from the one dispensing train information. To reach it, go through the main station hall and descend to the station foyer on the lower (street) level. Turn to the left and look for a huge door marked BIGLIETTERIA EST. Go through the door, turn to the left, and you will see ticket windows directly ahead. This office operates 0800–2200 Monday through Friday and 0800–1300 on Saturday and Sunday.

Eurailpass validation requires that you descend to the street level via the escalator in the middle of the station, make a right turn, and look for a sign, BIGLIETTER OVEST. Then proceed to windows 20 or 22 marked INTERNATIONAL TICKETS.

Food services range from trackside vendors to a full-service restaurant. The restaurant, with a large and efficient self-service cafeteria next to it, is located on the far left side of the main hall as you exit from the trains. A snack bar is also there.

In this snack bar, as in the various smaller ones scattered throughout the main hall and track area, you need to purchase tickets for the particular food or beverage you desire from a cashier, then give the tickets to a counter attendant. The system works, but now you know how the Italian immigrant felt when he ordered his first American hamburger and was asked if he wanted it with mustard, catsup, lettuce, tomato, pickles—and "was that to go?" (Hang in there!)

If this is your first rail trip into Italy, this will probably be your first acquaintance with the trackside vendors. Similar to the pushcarts that graced many of the streets in old New York, they offer a convenient variety of refreshments—and the price is right.

Baggage-checking facilities may be reached by taking the exit at the end of tracks 6 and 7. Across the main hall and to the right, you'll see a sign, DEPOSITO BAGAGLI. Rates vary according to what you store. The facility is closed every morning between 0230 and 0400.

The main baggage room, located on the street level of the station, can be reached either from the plaza facing the Michelangelo Hotel or from the bottom of the main escalator, between the street level and the train concourse. Hours of operation are 0700–2230 daily. Through experience, we have learned that you should check items to be forwarded at least one day in advance, and then only to other major points in Italy. We would not advise forwarding anything to France or Switzerland.

There is a checkroom in the restaurant-and-cafeteria entrance that is convenient and safe to use for temporarily storing suitcases and wearing apparel while you are eating or searching the hotel area for a place to stay. If you check your baggage here, it is most important that you find out when the attendant plans to leave. Otherwise, you could return to collect your duds only to learn they have been moved to a safe area until the operation starts again in the morning. The hours of operation are posted as "0700–2400," but it appears to be an individual enterprise rather than one under the supervision of management.

Station miscellany. Milan's railway station has many services within its vast area that the casual traveler may never note. There is a large and rather comfortable first-class lounge leading off the street side of the main hall. Its entrance is just to the left of the tourist information office.

Milano Centrale is a multilevel station, but elevator service from the train level to the street level is available. The entrance on the train level is inside the first-class lounge. If you have a Eurailpass, you have full access to the passenger lounge and elevator service.

All major entrances to the station provide escalator service. Taxi service is available at both side entrances and the front, and bus service is in the Piazza Duca d'Aosta in front of the station. Pictographs of the station's facilities are located conveniently at the end of many tracks.

Double-check your departing train number and platform location. For example, when departing Milan for Munich aboard EuroCity 10 Leonardo Da Vinci, you will note that signs in the station indicate the train's destination as MONACO. In Italian, this means "Monk," and Munich (in German) is the "City of Monks"—and you are on the right train and not bound for Monaco, which, in French, means Monte Carlo. InterCity 346/7 Ligure is the proper train to board if you are in fact going to Monaco and Monte Carlo via Genoa.

Emerging from the train platforms, if you detect the aroma of an American-style hamburger, it's coming from Wendy's. To get there, turn right in the station hall and take the escalator at the far end to the street level. Skirt the tram terminal to the left then look for the WENDY'S sign on the first group of buildings in front of you.

From Milan . . .

TRAIN CONNECTIONS TO OTHER BASE CITIES

TO:	DEPART	ARRIVE	TRAIN NUMBER	COOK'S TABLE	NOTES
Amsterdam	2125	1133+1	200	39	
Barcelona	1815	0935+1	2197	90	(4)(5)(6)
(Franca)	2000	0910+1	EN 276	90	(1)
Berne	0825	1212	IC 332	82	
	1025	1438	EC 90	82	
	1225	1612	IC 334	82	
	1525	1938	IC 336	82	
	1725	2138	EC 40	82	
Brussels (Midi)	1025	2237	EC 90	43	
	2135	1930+1	298	43	
Luxembourg	1025	1956	EC 90	43	
Munich	0700	1430	EC 86	76	
	1530	2240	EC 83	76	
Nice	0640	1120	IC 347	90	
	1415	1946	2191	90	
	1815	2339	2197	90	(4)
Paris (Lyon)	0905	1628	IC 330	44	(2)
(sleeper)	2100	0722+1	EN 216	44	
Rome	0905	1400	IC 557	370	
	1000	1455	IC 537	370	
	1300	1755	EC 55	370	
Vienna (Sudbhf.)	2010	0850+1	2113	88	(3)

Daily departures unless otherwise noted. Make reservations for all departures.

(1) Pablo Casals, special fares apply
(2) Transfer in Laus to TGV/EC 24
(3) Arrive 0857 Sunday through Wednesday
(4) July and August only
(5) Change in Port Bou
(6) Couchettes only

Neptune's Fountain is a landmark of Bologna's Piazza Maggiore and Piazza del Nettuno. Marketplaces leading off this lively square display a mouth-watering assortment of epicurean specialties.

From Milan . . .

A DAY EXCURSION TO BOLOGNA
DISTANCE BY TRAIN: 136 miles (219 km)
AVERAGE TRAIN TIME: 1 hour, 45 minutes

Bologna specializes in two areas—thinking and eating. When you think about that fact, you'll probably conclude, as we did, that it isn't too bad a life style to follow. There are worse!

Bologna's university (oldest in Europe) was founded in 1088. By the thirteenth century, its student body numbered 10,000. One of its more recent students, Guglielmo Marconi (1874–1937), studied wireless telegraphy there. The university was noted for employing women professors. One such educator, Novella d'Andrea, was said to be so beautiful in face and body that she had to give her lectures from behind a screen to avoid distracting her pupils.

On the eating side of the ledger, there's no doubt that Bologna deserves its rank of gastronomic capital of Italy. Endless strings of sausages and thousands of cheese varieties adorn the windows of its delicatessen shops. Restaurants lined along the city's arcaded streets are filled with people consuming delicacies to the accompaniment of fine wines.

The city has much to offer architecturally, too. An ensemble of rare Italian beauty is concentrated in its two enjoining squares, the Piazza Maggiore and the Piazza del Nettuno. Combined with the Piazza di Porta Ravegnana, the heart of Bologna even today reflects its Renaissance greatness.

One of Bologna's architectural features is the great number of arcades lining the city's principal streets. This permits "weatherproof" shopping, a feature that is enjoyed by visitor and citizen alike.

Neptune's Fountain (Fontana del Nettuno) is the focal point of its piazza. Completed in 1566, it aptly depicts the vigorous nature of Bologna. Saint Petronius Basilica, facing the Piazza Maggiore, was begun in 1390 but remains unfinished even today.

The Piazza Ravegnana contains not just one leaning tower but two. The taller, built by the Asinelli family in 1109, stands 330 feet tall with a tilt exceeding seven and a half feet. The other, the Garisenda Tower, is only 165 feet high, but it leans out ten feet over its foundation. If you're in good physical condition and feel like climbing 486 steps, there's a fine view at the top of the Asinelli Tower.

In order to appreciate fully Bologna's beauty, we recommend that you first call at the city's tourist information office for maps and brochures.

There are two tourist information offices within the city. (A third one is located at the airport.) When you arrive by train, we suggest that you call on the office in the railway station. The Piazza Medaglie d'Oro lies directly in

BOLOGNA—*ITALY'S GASTRONOMIC CAPITAL*

A Day Excursion from Milan

DEPART FROM MILAN CENTRAL STATION	TRAIN NUMBER	ARRIVE IN BOLOGNA STATION	NOTES
0750	P 505	0928	(1)(3)
0800	IC 533	0944	(1)
0900	IC 535	1044	(1)
1000	IC 537	1144	(1)
1005	IR 2127	1220	(2)

Plus other frequent service throughout the day

DEPART FROM BOLOGNA STATION	TRAIN NUMBER	ARRIVE IN MILAN CENTRAL STATION	NOTES
1616	IC 538	1800	(1)
1716	IC 540	1900	(1)
1816	IC 542	2000	(1)
1916	IC 544	2100	(1)
2016	IC 546	2200	(1)
2120	IC 578	2315	(1)

Plus other frequent service throughout the day

(1) Daily, including holidays
(2) Daily, except Sunday
(3) Reservations required (Pendolino)

Distance: 136 miles/219 km
Reference: Thomas Cook Table 370

front of the station. As you emerge from the main entrance of the station, incline to the right and enter the hall of the railway station exit. You'll find the tourist information office on the left side. It operates Monday through Saturday, 0900–1900. The telephone number is 246541; the fax number is 251947. This office is closed on Sunday.

For Sunday arrivals, or when you find yourself in need of additional information regarding Bologna, call upon the tourist information office in the heart of the city at No. 6 on the west side of Piazza Maggiore. This office is open on Sunday from 0900 to 1300.

To reach it, turn left when exiting the rail station and walk two blocks to Via Dell'Independenza, one of Bologna's main avenues. Turn right onto the avenue, and a delightful ten-minute walk will bring you to Neptune's Fountain. Then, continue your walk in the same direction a short distance into Piazza Maggiore. During the week, this office is open throughout the day from 0900 to 1900. The telephone number is 239660 (fax: 231454).

Bologna is the capital of Emilia-Romagna, a northwest-to-southeast slice of the Italian peninsula just below its juncture with the European Continent. An economically strong region, with the nation's highest employment rate, Emilia-Romagna holds the uncontested title of the "richest gastronomic region in Italy."

Restaurants, as mentioned previously, are plentiful, and the food they prepare is good. Many of them are in the luxury class, but you can also dine very well in the less expensive restaurants. Many maintain an "open kitchen," which you're welcome to inspect and where you may chat with the cooks.

Enjoy your culinary adventures while in Bologna, for the bad news is that you will probably not be able to find those delights back home. For example, the famous prosciutto of Parma is absolutely unlike any American prosciutto—and, like most Italian meat products, it cannot be sold in the United States.

Bologna is an ideal base for exploring the Emilia-Romagna area. Among the towns to visit are: Faenza, for its ceramics; Ferrara, for its fortress; Ravenna, for its early Christian art; Rimini, for its Adriatic beach; and, of course, Parma, for its ham and Parmesan cheese. All are about one hour or less by rail from Bologna. All of these cities may be visited out of Milan, too. Consult the schedules in Milan's Central Station.

Genova Brignole is one of two main train stations in Genoa. The city sightseeing tour begins at the other station, Porta Principe.

From Milan . . .

A DAY EXCURSION TO GENOA
DISTANCE BY TRAIN: 93 miles (150 km)
AVERAGE TRAIN TIME: 1 hour, 25 minutes

Ride the InterCity Ligure out of Milan to Genoa in the morning. Enjoy a leisurely walk along Genoa's avenues. Lunch in full view of the city's great harbor—largest in all of Italy. Board InterCity 684 late in the afternoon and be back in Milan for dinner that same day. Or fall in love with Genoa by lunchtime and return to Milan on InterCity Ligure on its return run to Milan just before midnight. The relatively short time en route between these cities makes a "set your own pace" schedule ideal.

The Ligure sets the pace for the day, averaging 62 miles per hour between Milan and Genoa on its nonstop mountainous dash to and from the Mediterranean. Note that the Ligure runs at an early hour—0640—and arrives in Genoa's Porta Principe Station ninety minutes later at 0810. If this limits some of the late sleepers in your group, either of the railway schedules shown on the next page may be more convenient.

Be mindful that Genoa has two major railway stations, Porta Principe and Brignole. If you come from Milan, Porta Principe is the first stop after the train emerges from a tunnel. Digital schedule boards in both stations advise what time the next connecting train departs for the other station. To be certain, board your returning train to Milan from Porta Principe because many through trains do not call at Brignole. You can, however, ride any shuttle train from Brignole north to the next stop, which is Porta Principe.

The Porta Principe station has two escalators between street level and the elevated train platform. The tourist information office is on the right-hand side of the station foyer after the second escalator coming from the trains. Hours of operation are 0800–2000 Monday through Saturday, and the telephone number is 262.633.

A boat tour of the city's harbor is an excellent way for visitors to acquaint themselves with Genoa. To reach the quay, turn right leaving the station, then make another right turn as you pass the bank on the corner. Walk downhill to the pedestrian crossing. Cross, and continue to walk downhill until the harbor is sighted to the left. After turning left and passing through Piazza Principe, you'll arrive at the Maritime Building. The tour boats are berthed on its right side. The tour runs every two to three hours starting at 0830 when a minimum of fifteen persons is present.

Most visitors link Genoa with Christopher Columbus (1451–1505). This association begins as you leave the Porta Principe Station fronted by Piazza Acquaverde, where a statue stands in honor of Columbus. You will find a

GENOA—*GREAT PORT OF ITALY*

A Day Excursion from Milan

DEPART FROM MILAN CENTRAL STATION	TRAIN NUMBER	ARRIVE IN GENOVA P.P. STATION	NOTES
0640	IC 347	0810	(1)
0815	IR 2183	1005	(1)
0910	IC 640	1047	(1)

DEPART FROM GENOVA P.P. STATION	TRAIN NUMBER	ARRIVE IN MILAN CENTRAL STATION	NOTES
1513	IC 682	1650	(1)
1554	IR 2163	1745	(1)
1713	IC 684	1850	(1)(2)
1848	IR 2167	2040	(1)
1913	IC 688	2050	(1)
1954	IC 2171	2145	(1)
2225	IC 349	2355	(1)(2)

Note: Genoa has two main railway stations—Porta Principe (P.P.) and Brignole. Porta Principe is the first station when arriving from Milan.

(1) Daily, including holidays
(2) Food service available

Distance: 93 miles/150 km
Reference: Thomas Cook Table 355

quarter-scale model of his flagship, the *Santa Maria,* exhibited in the foyer of the Genoa Brignole Station should you go there.

A part of the city bus tour takes you to the Church of San Stefano, where Columbus was baptized, and into the Piazza della Vittoria—a vast expanse of lawns where the three ships of his fleet, the *Niña, Pinta,* and *Santa Maria,* are depicted in grass and flowers.

Another tourist information office is located at Via Roma 11 (on the second floor) just in front of the Government Palace (Prefettura). Hours of operation are 0800–1330 and 1400–1700 Monday through Friday and 0800–1330 on Saturdays. The telephone number is (010) 541.541, fax (010) 581.408.

Plan a walking tour of Genoa. Depart Genova Porta Principe Station and follow Via Balbi to Via Cairoli, which connects with "the street of Kings"— Via Garibaldi. At the end of Via Garibaldi, turn right (south) and proceed to the city's center, Piazza de Ferrari. From this point, you can continue along Via XX Settembre to the park in front of the Brignole Station or return on foot to the Porta Principe Station by turning south and walking along the harbor. Both tourist information offices have maps to assist you in the walking tour. Be certain to include Genoa's great new aquarium.

The city of Genoa lies beside a fine natural harbor at the foot of a pass in the Italian Apennines. It rivals Marseilles as the leading European port on the Mediterranean. Genoa's harbor facilities, which were damaged heavily during World War II, have been expanded and modernized. Shipbuilding is the leading industry of Genoa.

Ever since its birth, Genoa's calling has been the sea. Genoese ships transported Crusaders to the Middle East and returned laden with booty. Genoese merchants, profiting from the newly created demand in Europe for goods from the Middle East, expanded their operations throughout the Christian world. Genoese forts and trading posts soon spread throughout the Mediterranean and the Aegean seas, creating a rivalry between Genoese and Venetians.

Genoa is proud of its Lanterna, the lighthouse that has become the international symbol of the city. Built on the site of an ancient tower in the first half of the sixteenth century, it has guided mariners to its safe harbor for more than four centuries.

In the time of Christopher Columbus, another son of Genoa, Andrea Doria (1468–1560), did much to promote the development of the city's maritime power. Serving as captain-general of Genoa's navy until defeated by Spanish forces in 1522, he served the French briefly before restoring the republic of Genoa as an ally of the Holy Roman Emperor, Charles V. Doria's birthplace can be seen during the tour of the city.

Serenade on the square evokes a quizzical look from young visitors to Lugano. The area between Piazza Cioccaro, at the bottom of the cable car, to Piazza Riforma, near the lake, abounds with shops and food stores of every description. Many believe it to be the best shopping area in Lugano.

From Milan . . .

A DAY EXCURSION TO LAKE LUGANO, SWITZERLAND
DISTANCE BY TRAIN: 48 miles (77 km)
AVERAGE TRAIN TIME: 1 hour, 15 minutes

Lake Lugano is known as the Swiss Riviera. Sheltered from the north by the Lepontine Alps, it is favored with a climate that is exceptionally mild. Claiming to serve the sunniest of all central European resorts, the local weatherman has the meteorological data to prove it. Considered a year-round resort, the city of Lugano sponsors a multitude of events to attract visitors. Although Lugano is a very short distance from Milan, you will be crossing the Swiss border on this day excursion. *Don't forget your passport.*

In past years, Italian money was accepted readily by Lugano merchants, but there is a growing reluctance to accept it now, so we suggest that you change some currency into Swiss francs for use during your visit. There is a currency-exchange desk in the railway station (open daily, 0515–2230), and the town abounds in banks and *cambio* (exchange) offices that offer official rates.

There is no tourist information office in the station, probably because the center of the city is so close. There is a hotel-reservations-and-information office to your immediate right as you leave the station. Train information may be obtained in the office bearing the "i" sign to the left of the main exit.

To reach the city center, ride the *funicolare* (cable railway) to Piazza Cioccaro and proceed on foot downhill to the hub of Lugano, Piazza Riforma. Mark this route well in your mind because you will use it again when returning to the railway station.

Lake Lugano is a short walk away from Piazza Riforma as you continue in a downhill direction. At the lakefront, turn left past the park; there you will find the tourist office at 5 Riva Gioc. Albertolli. The most informative of their brochures is *Lugano, Southern Switzerland,* which is printed in several languages and is free of charge.

Maps of the area are available at costs ranging from 1.80 to 8.00 (Swiss) francs. The biggest problem is deciding what to do with so many possibilities being offered in and around Lugano.

If Lake Lugano beckons, there is a choice of nine round trips by boat, each offering an opportunity for a special vista. If the mountains seem attractive, ascent is made possible by both cableways and funiculars in many different directions. Two funiculars, one at each end of Lugano, will carry you swiftly up 3,000 feet to breathtaking views of either Monte Bre or Monte San Salvatore.

The list doesn't stop there. Motor-coach opportunities to visit either Sonvico or Tesserete—typical Swiss mountain villages—may be selected, and

LAKE LUGANO—*THE SWISS RIVIERA*

A Day Excursion from Milan

DEPART FROM MILAN CENTRAL STATION	TRAIN NUMBER	ARRIVE IN LUGANO STATION	NOTES
0725	IC 250	0851	(1)(2)
0825	IC 386	0954	(1)(2)
0920	EC 8	1054	(1)(2)
1025	IC 388	1154	(1)(2)
1125(3)	EC 4	1254	(1)(2)

DEPART FROM LUGANO STATION	TRAIN NUMBER	ARRIVE IN MILAN CENTRAL STATION	NOTES
1632	EC 57	1735	(1)(2)(4)
1706(3)	EC 5	1835	(1)(2)
1806	IC 387	1935	(1)(2)
2006	IC 381	2135	(1)(2)
2206	IC 389	2335	(1)(2)

(1) Daily, including holidays
(2) Food service available
(3) Supplement payable in Italy
(4) Reservations required

Distance: 48 miles/77 km
Reference: Thomas Cook Table 290

The William Tell Express

The William Tell Express is a luxury day trip between Lucerne in the German-speaking part of Switzerland to Lugano, the major resort town in Switzerland's Italian-speaking Ticino. The journey begins in Lucerne aboard the 800-passenger *Undterwalden,* a paddle-wheel steamer built in 1902 and meticulously restored in 1985. Crossing first from Lucerne to Fluelen on the eastern end of Lake Lucerne, passengers then board a first-class Swiss express train to Lugano via the 100-year-old Gotthard Railway. Eurailpass is accepted; reservations are mandatory; and the reservation fee of $45 includes a three-course meal aboard ship and a souvenir. For reservations and additional information, call (614) 793–7650.

The William Tell Express operates between May 23 and September 26: Depart Lucerne 1125; arrive Fluelen 1452 and depart 1514; arrive Lugano 1724.

even a journey to the world-renowned resort of St. Moritz is possible. In fact, anything's possible—just ask at the Lugano tourist information office.

For a relaxing day on the lake, select the cruise to the Swiss Miniature Village, a unique exhibition of towns, hamlets, castles, mountains and railways—all on a scale of 1:25. It's an all-day outing, but it has wooed millions of other visitors—why not you?

The city tourist information office in Lugano can help you plan your day. If you would like to remain in the local area, they will gladly mark out a walking tour of the city and its interesting areas for you. If a festival or special exhibition is going on at the time of your visit, by all means avail yourself of the opportunity.

Much of this civic activity takes place in the main square, Piazza Riforma. Take a coffee break at one of its sidewalk cafés. You might be treated to a street troubadour—or a sidewalk opera. After you have paid for your coffee, everything that follows is free.

For lunching at ease in Lugano, you may want to make it a stand-up affair by selecting from a vendor's cart at lakeside or perhaps aboard a lake steamer. For an enjoyable sit-down meal, we offer this recommended list of quality restaurants: Bianchi (famous and expensive), Galleria, Gambrinus, Orologio, and Da Armando. All of these are in the center of Lugano.

Shopping in Lugano is a pleasant experience. The place to do this is concentrated in the market area stretching from the bottom of the funicolare to the city square fronting the lake. Mouth-watering food vies for your attention along with a wide selection of Swiss products and crafts. We have yet to see a visitor enter the market area around lunchtime and not emerge a few minutes later with a sandwich in hand rivaling anything that Dagwood could concoct.

Shopping in this market area may, for the most part, be done in the shelter of overhead arcades, so one does not have to be concerned with the weather. If you have been looking for specialty items of the Ticino area of Switzerland, you will find them here. Although firmly Swiss, the market in Lugano has that piquant touch of Italy.

During our repeated visits to Lugano, we've discovered a retreat on its lake that can no longer stay a secret. It's Gandria, a small cliff-side village that clings precariously to the mountains descending from the east into the lake. Gandria has no streets, but there is a bus stop on the mountainside above. The best access is by lake steamer. If you want to share in our secret, inquire at any steamer pier regarding schedules. You will want to take the Lugano-Porlezza line and plan to have an early dinner in Gandria. It's superb!

St. Mark's Square (Piazza San Marco) shown above, is the social center of Venice and perhaps the most famous square in the world. Equally famous, **the gondoliers of Venice** (below) provide sightseeing tours while singing and telling stories—and hoping for a generous tip at the end of the voyage

From Milan . . .

A DAY EXCURSION TO VENICE
DISTANCE BY TRAIN: 166 miles (267 km)
AVERAGE TRAIN TIME: 2 hours, 45 minutes

Upon arrival in Venice, the American humorist Robert Benchley telegraphed his publisher, "Streets are flooded, please advise." Things have changed little since. Venice is situated on 120 islands surrounded by 177 canals in a lagoon between the Po and Piave rivers at the northern extremity of the Adriatic Sea. The islands on which the city is built are connected by 400 or so bridges. Not only by its site, but also by its architecture and history, Venice is known as "the Queen of the Adriatic."

As your train eases across the railroad and highway causeway connecting the city with the Italian mainland, you can't help but wonder how and why Venice came to be. History records that the city was founded in A.D. 452 when the inhabitants of several northern Italian cities sought refuge there from the Teutonic tribes invading Italy during the fifth century. The Huns were repulsed, as were the Saracens in A.D. 836 and the Hungarians in A.D. 900, as the Venetians improved their fortifications and erected bulwarks of masonry to protect their growing city from the sea and from their enemies.

During the Crusades, Venice began developing trade with the Orient, and the city quickly became the center for this commerce with the East. During the thirteenth and fourteenth centuries, Venice went to war with its chief commercial rival, Genoa, and won. Through other wars of conquest, Venice became the leading martime power of the Christian world by the end of the fifteenth century. Its greatness was then challenged by the Turks and other Italian states, and its power eroded as quickly as it had developed. In 1797, Napoleon Bonaparte conquered Venice and turned its government over to Austria. Through subsequent political maneuvers and revolts, Venice became part of the newly established kingdom of Italy in 1866.

As your train draws to a halt in Venice's Santa Lucia Station, you should proceed to the head of the train and then enter the main hall of the station. Inside, you will find a train information office on the immediate left side of the hall. No tourist information is available at this office. Beyond that, you'll see a sign directing you to a buffet with self-service in the front and complete restaurant service further on. The station digital train information board is prominently displayed above the buffet sign. On the right-hand side in the station hall, you will find telephones, ticket windows, newspaper stands, and specialty shops. We suggest that you shop at the newsstand for a guidebook and a map of Venice. We were fully satisfied with the one we purchased, *A Day in Venice*, by Bonechi. It is updated annually. Coupled with a large-scale map of the city,

VENICE—*GRAND CANAL AND GONDOLAS*

A Day Excursion from Milan

DEPART FROM MILAN CENTRAL STATION	TRAIN NUMBER	ARRIVE IN VENICE SANTA LUCIA STATION	NOTES
0705	IC 641	0952	(1)(2)
0810	IR 2093	1125	(1)
0905	IC 647	1140	(1)(2)(3)
1105	IC 649	1359	(1)(2)

DEPART FROM VENICE SANTA LUCIA STATION	TRAIN NUMBER	ARRIVE IN MILAN CENTRAL STATION	NOTES
1605	IC 656	1855	(1)(2)
1625	IR 2108	1945	(1)(2)
1725	IR 2110	2045	(1)(2)
1825	2112	2145	(1)
1925	2114	2245	(1)
2005	IC 664	2255	(1)(2)

(1) Daily, including holidays
(2) Light refreshments
(3) Arrives Venice Mestre Station

Distance: 166 miles/267 km
Reference: Thomas Cook Table 352

you will be ready to proceed on a particularly interesting day excursion.

Just prior to exiting the station, you'll see a tourist information booth on wheels. Be sure to obtain full details regarding the canal transportation system. Water taxis are extremely expensive; the public water buses are far more affordable. Also, ask for a map of Venice, even though it's on a much smaller scale than the one you purchased. The canal navigation services (*Linee di Navigazione Lagunaire*) are described in full detail on the reverse side of the map. For this day excursion, we propose that you purchase a one-way water-bus ticket from the rail station to San Marco on Line 1 and return to the station on foot.

Ticket in hand, board Line 1-Accelerata at Station 2 in front of the rail station. The dock and vessels are marked PIAZZALE ROMA-FERROVIA-LIDO, and the boat should be moving to your left as you come from the station. Boats proceeding to the right terminate at Station 1, Piazzale Roma, where you're required to disembark and purchase another ticket to get back on course! Line 1 moves along the Grand Canal until emerging into open water from the canal at Piazza San Marco (St. Mark's), the center and most frequented part of Venice. The Grand Canal is the principal traffic artery of Venice. It is lined with churches, museums, palaces—even a fish market—so keep your guidebook open so you can recognize these landmarks as you glide by. It's just like watching a Venetian travelogue—only you are there!

Go ashore at St. Mark's and revel in the staggering sights before you. St. Mark's Bell Tower dominates the scene, but it won't be long before you'll find yourself standing in front of the Cathedral. If time permits, take the elevator to the top of the Bell Tower for a spectacular view of vibrant Venice. By the way, don't forget to feed the pigeons.

With so much to see, be mindful of the time or you will miss the train back to Milan. You can't hail a taxi at the last minute since there are none, so allow at least forty-five minutes to return from St. Mark's to the Santa Lucia Station by water bus. Or start ambling through Venice by following the signs, ALLA FERROVIA (to the rail station). They are posted everywhere and easy to follow. Allow two hours to reach the station, although a pace slightly faster than an amble should get you there about thirty minutes sooner.

En route, you will cross the Rialto Bridge—the best place to view the Grand Canal and a good place to shop, too. There are twenty-four shops right on the bridge and a variety of vendors selling their wares along both sides of the canal. Further on, you will cross the Ponte Degli Scalzi (Station Bridge) and arrive at the rail station where you started.

We're sure you will return to Venice, but heed the plight of the tourists laden with suitcases on the water buses—come back with minimum luggage or stow it in the lockers at the Venice Mestre Station.

Heart of Munich, the Marienplatz (St. Mary's Square) is dominated by the Rathaus (town hall) on the right. The twin towers of the Frauenkirche (Church of Our Lady) loom in the background.

19   MUNICH

Colorful road signs on just about every highway entering Bavaria declare it to be "Freistaat Bayern," the Free State of Bavaria. Insurrection? Not really. It is the manifestation of the free and roisterous spirit of its citizens, who love their homeland and feel that there is no place quite like it anywhere else in the world. We agree; you will, too.

Munich, the capital and heart of Bavaria, is situated in the center of a vast plain washed by the Isar River. The immaculate and astonishing beauty of its countryside is visible in any direction. Rimmed by the Alps to the south and dark green pine forests in all other quadrants, Munich becomes the gateway to day excursions galore. With a population of well over a million, Munich is Germany's third largest city, but it still retains its unmatched roisterous elegance.

Munich's mood is always festive, but twice a year the tempo soars even higher as the city observes Fasching and Oktoberfest. Fasching celebrations are held during January and February. The festivities could be compared to Mardi Gras, only Muncheners get a head start on everyone by cranking up just after New Year's Eve and never letting up until the sun sets on Ash Wednesday!

During this period of Fasching revelry, thousands of masked balls and parties are staged. Many are in fancy dress, and sometimes masks are worn because individuals don't wish to reveal their identities to their partners—who are seldom the ones they came in with. If they are, it's a *complete* surprise when the inevitable unmasking takes place.

The coming of Lent really doesn't dampen Munich's spirits one drop, for it marks the beginning of the strong beer season. Munich's monks, limited to one meal a day throughout Lent (but with no limit on their drinking), started this ancient custom that still prevails today. They asked the brew masters if, during Lent, they could increase the regular alcoholic content of their product; the brew masters agreed—and everyone apparently has lived happily ever after. By the way, there are six major breweries in Munich.

Oktoberfest, instituted by a Bavarian King in 1810, actually takes place during the latter part of September and ends the first weekend in October. About 660,000 gallons of beer are produced by the city's breweries and dispensed directly from huge, chilled barrels in enormous tents serving as beer halls. Bands play throughout the day and long into the night while drinkers wash down sausages, roast chicken, and oxen with five to six million liter-size drafts of the world's finest brews.

Munich also has the finest delicatessen in the world. Its name is Dallmayr's. Extravagant beyond description, it demands to be seen. If for no other reason, go to Munich to savor the sights and scents of Dallmayr's!

Day Excursions

South to the Alps and Garmisch. Into the Alps to Berchtesgaden. Through the Alps to Austria and its beautiful cities of Innsbruck and Salzburg. North to Nuremberg, Ulm, or Rothenburg and the Romantic Road. For a special adventure, up the peak of Germany's highest mountain, the Zugspitze. Take your choice—and your leisure. Enjoy *both* Munich *and* the day-excursion opportunities that it has to offer.

Arriving and Departing

By Air. Munich opened its Franz Josef Strauss Airport in 1992. The new airport features a system of passenger modules connected by a system of walkways, referred to as PTS (Passenger Transport System), that run the entire length of the terminal on level 03. The PTS also connects with the central area, where there is a twenty-four-hour information area staffed by multilingual personnel.

Rail transportation between the airport and the city is provided by Munich's rapid transit train system's (S-Bahn) No. 8 line, with stops at the Marienplatz (city center) and the Hauptbahnhof (main rail station). From the central area, descend to level 02. Between 0455 and 0015 a train departs every twenty minutes. The forty-one-minute ride costs twelve deutsche marks (DM) for a one-way ticket.

There are taxi stands in front of modules A, B, C, D, and E. Due to traffic congestion, the time it takes to travel between the airport and the city by road can exceed one hour and can cost 100–120 DM. Check at the taxi information desk in the central area of the airport. For advance taxi arrangements and information, telephone 773043 in Munich or fax 773590.

By Train. Munich has several suburban stations, but most international trains stop only at the Hauptbahnhof. Schedules given at the end of this section list InterCity and express-train services between Munich and eleven other base cities: Amsterdam, Berlin, Berne, Brussels, Budapest, Copenhagen, Hamburg, Milan, Paris, Rome, and Vienna.

Munich's Hauptbahnhof is actually a city within a city. In addition to the regular rail-station services described on page 411, all you need do is descend one level on any one of the station's many escalators to discover a veritable city of shops, ranging from bakeries, beer stubes, fruit stands, and supermarkets, as well as the subway entrances to many of Munich's department stores. This shopping colossus extends from the Hauptbahnhof all the way to Karlsplatz-Stachus—more than one quarter of a mile. Most shops in the immediate Hauptbahnhof area are open late during the week as well as on weekends and holidays.

Munich's Railway Station—The Hauptbahnhof

Like *every* public building and thoroughfare in town, Munich's railway station gets scrubbed clean every night. On the end of tracks 28 through 35 (where there is ample sunlight throughout the day), flowers are grown. As mentioned previously, the station is a veritable city within a city. In addition to its shopping arcades, it even has its own hotel.

The Hauptbahnhof's transport services include the city's U-Bahn (subway) system. A station is located directly under the plaza in front of the railway station. The Munich Hauptbahnhof is the center of train, tram, bus, suburban train, and subway services for the entire city of Munich.

Eurailpasses are not accepted on the U-Bahn nor on the city bus and tram lines. Eurailpasses are accepted on the Munich S-Bahn (suburban) service, however, because the system is operated by the Deutsche Bundesbahn (DB) or German Federal Railroads. A description of the S-Bahn (*schnell,* or "fast") system appears on page 416.

Money exchange office is marked GELDWECHSEL-EXCHANGE-CAMBIO and is located in the far left corner of the main station hall next to the main entrance. Its hours are 0600 to 2300 daily. This facility is operated by the Deutsche Verkehrs-Kredit-Bank and offers a service not usually found in other exchanges. It *will* accept foreign coins (except coins from Eastern Europe). Most exchanges will only accept notes. If you have collected a variety of coins moving from country to country, here's your chance to unload if you're willing to accept 30 percent less than the total value.

Hotel reservations can be made in the tourist information office located at the end of track (*gleis*) 11. You may see a sign reading FREMDEN-VERKEHRSAMT, but don't let that frighten you—you're at the right place! A nominal charge is made for reservations. The attendants are very helpful in finding local reservations.

The office is open 0800–2200 on weekdays and 1100–1900 on Sunday. For reservations in other cities, the "ABR" travel service in the front of the station can provide such services, or you may patronize the American Express office. (Its location is given under "Tourist Facilities.")

The InterCity Hotel is located conveniently in the train station. As you are exiting from the train-platform area (by passing through the first set of doors on your way to the main concourse of the station), turn to the right just before the main concourse hall and walk to the street entrance. The hotel will be on the left just before the doors leading to the street. It's soundproof, comfortable, and convenient, but get reservations early—it's also popular. Telephone (89) 545560; fax (89) 54556610.

Tourist information may be obtained in the same office where local hotel reservations are made (at the end of track 11). City bus tours can be arranged there, or perhaps you would prefer such arrangements be made by your hotel. Maps—such as the one mentioned earlier—are available in this office, and you can often obtain a brochure describing day-excursion sites by asking at the counter. Most of the brochures and maps are sold, but the city map is provided free of charge.

Another tourist information service, EurAide, is available in the Munich Hauptbahnhof. This office is located alongside gleis 11, four doors down from the Railway Police (Bahnpolizei) station. EurAide caters to the needs of English-speaking travelers and operates under a contract with the German Federal Railroad. The office specializes in answering Eurail-related questions. They also can make room reservations, and they have information on tours of Munich and using the city's public transportation systems.

Train-information office is located at the end of gleis 20. A sign over the door says INFORMATION. (*Only train information is available in this office.*) It is open 0630–2300 daily. If you want to work out your own day excursion, this office can provide you with the information pertaining to the train service to and from the day-excursion point.

We suggest that, before you enter the train information office, you prepare a listing or an itinerary of the rail trips you intend to make. Too many people enter the office without a thought of where they want to go or when they want to get there. This office can tell you what train to take and the time that it leaves the Munich Hauptbahnhof. They are not a travel agency, however, and you shouldn't ask for suggestions of things to do.

Train reservations for EuroCity, InterCity, and express-train services are made in the "ABR" office. Its full name is "Amtliches Bayerisches Reiseburo"—one good reason for the abbreviation. It is located in the extreme front end of the station on the right-hand side, directly opposite the money-exchange office. Hours of operation are 0900–1800 Monday through Friday and 0900–1200 on Saturday. It can be very crowded, particularly on weekends and during the summer tourist season.

If you need the services offered by this office, we strongly recommend calling there at least one day in advance of your intended rail trip.

Eurailpass validation is accomplished in an office on the right-hand side of the station hall. You can enter the ticket office by going through a door marked SONDERSCHALTER (special ticket office). During the summer, it's air-conditioned. If for any reason you want to purchase train tickets, use windows 12 to 14, where English is spoken.

Food services are available in several parts of the station. The most famous is the stand-up wiener-and-beer stube immediately to the right of the entrance into the main station concourse. Behind it, there are three full-service restaurants with posted prices and menus.

Memo on Munich

The population of Germany is divided into two distinct groups—those who live in Munich and those who would like to live in Munich. This expression by the Germans themselves—many of whom live hundreds of miles away—supports the thesis that Munich is indeed a very special place to live as well as to visit.

Munich's heart pulsates at the Marienplatz, the city's central square. From the tower of the new town hall in the center of the Marienplatz, a glockenspiel chimes every morning at 1100 (again in summer at 1200 and 1700) and is followed by a performance of mechanical figures including knights on horseback and a crowing rooster. You will have to see it to believe it.

Dallmayr's delicatessen is nearby. Facing the glockenspiel, walk around the right side of the town hall to the smaller square in the rear. Dallmayr's store will then be in plain view immediately across the street to your right at 14 Dienerstrasse. You really don't have to buy a thing—the sights and the aromas are wonderful, and they are free.

Here are some statistics to support the previous statement regarding Munich's spare-time value: approximately one hundred historic buildings, four castles and two hundred churches, fifty-three art collections and museums, and sixty-nine performing theaters—all within the city limits and most of them within reasonable walking distance from the Marienplatz. An excellent illustrated folder containing a city map showing the exact location of each of the above points of interest is published by the Munich tourist information office.

There are fourteen additional places of interest, including the 1972 Olympic Park, identified in the folder by color-coded circles. For ardent admirers of the brew master's art, the map also pinpoints twelve of Munich's most famous beer gardens. The Hofbrauhaus (the state-owned beer hall) is a short walk from the Marienplatz via Dallmayr's delicatessen. (It would be un-American not to stop!)

The Hofbrauhaus dates back to the year 1589. It is no longer operated as a brewery but beer is drayed in to be consumed daily from one-liter (one-and-three-quarter-pint) mugs while bands play lively tunes, often accompanied by the singing of the drinkers. There's a full-service restaurant on the second floor, where decorum is a bit more in evidence.

The Platzl (a bustling beer hall and restaurant), directly across the street from the Hofbrauhaus, is another place to go for oom-pa-pa music, yodeling, and delicious Bavarian food.

For those visiting Munich for the first time, a guided tour by bus is recommended highly. Check either with the city tourist information office in the railway station or with your hotel.

Olympic Tower dominates the skyline of Munich's Olympia Park, scene of the 1972 games.

Tourist and Transportation Facilities

In Munich, Cook's Travel Service is represented by "ABR" (see "Train Reservations"). The American Express office is at 6 Promenadeplatz. Facing the glockenspiel in the Marienplatz, walk to the left side of the town hall and then straight ahead to the tram tracks. At this point, turn left and walk one block to the Promenadeplatz. The Amex office is situated about halfway down the street on the left side.

Munich's S-Bahn system, one of the finest urban-transportation systems found anywhere in the world, is operated by the German Federal Railways. *Eurailpasses are accepted for travel throughout the entire S-Bahn system.* The Eurailpass *is not accepted* on the U-Bahn (underground or subway system) nor the Strassenbahnen (street railway system), more commonly referred to as the trams. These two systems plus the buses and trams, however, are excellent ways of moving about in Munich. There are special fares and day tickets, too, so check with the city's tourist information office for details and fare information.

All of Munich's public transportation operates on the honor system. You must have a ticket for any conveyance you board, but you may not be asked to show it—then, again, you may be asked by a plain-clothes representative flashing an official-looking badge for your ticket. If you are apprehended without a valid ticket, you will be fined 60 DM on the spot. If you can't pay the fine, you must go to the Munich Public Transport Office to work out some sort of payment agreement.

The S-Bahn has eight main operating lines, S-1 through S-8. All of these lines converge on the Marienplatz. Each originates at a point in the suburbs or countryside some distance from Munich, moves above ground to the city's perimeter, then plunges underground through its heart and finally terminates, back on the surface, at a distant point on the opposite side of the city.

Use this system for suburban transportation in and around Munich all that you can, for your Eurailpass covers it. You can obtain maps and fare information at the tourist information office. A chart of the S-Bahn and the U-Bahn systems appears on the following page.

Luncheon in Munchen

Munich abounds with excellent eating places ranging from the Hofbrauhaus to countless beer gardens and gourmet restaurants. In case you tire of city dining, we suggest that you take a southbound S-1 train on the S-Bahn from the main transfer station of the S-Bahn under the Marienplatz and get off in the Village of Aying—about a forty-minute ride. Walk four blocks toward the church steeple to the Aying Hotel, where you'll find the best Bavarian food, beer, and atmosphere.

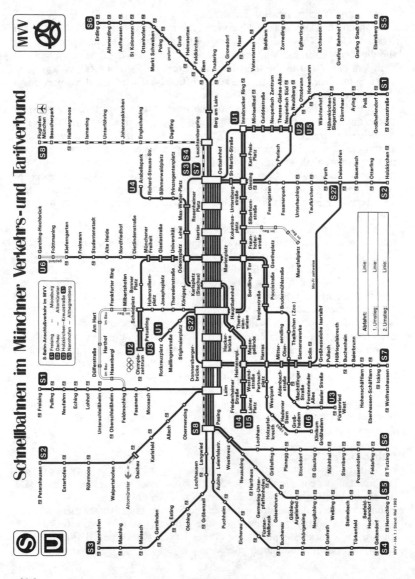

Schnellbahnen im Münchner Verkehrs- und Tarifverbund

MVV

MVV · HA 1 / Stand: Mai 1992

416

From Munich . . .

TRAIN CONNECTIONS TO OTHER BASE CITIES

TO:	DEPART	ARRIVE	TRAIN NUMBER	COOK'S TABLE	NOTES
Amsterdam	0850	1751	IC 614	28	(1)
	1050	1951	IC 612	28	(2)
	2211	0857+1	214	28	
Berlin (Hbf.)	0856	1649	IC 706	670	
	1056	1849	IC 812	670	
	1456	2249	IC 704	670	
Berne	0810	1345	EC 92	75	(3)
	1402	1945	EC 166	75	
Brussels (Midi)	0650	1556	IC 616	33	(4)
	0850	1801	IC 614	33	(5)
	0950	1855	EC 18	33	(6)
Budapest (Keleti)	0825	1643	EC 63	61	
	2319	0808+1	D269	61	
Copenhagen	0720	1808	ICE 682	50	(7)(9)
	0920	2020	ICE 680	50	(8)
	1928	0925+1	D482	50	
Hamburg	0721	1251	ICE 682	750	
	0921	1451	ICE 680	750	
	1321	1851	ICE 586	750	
Milan	0700	1355	EC 81	76	
	1530	2250	EC 87	76	
	2330	0830+1	289	76	
Paris (Est)	0750	1620	EC 66	32	
	1350	2220	EC 64	32	
	2106	0704+1	260	32	
Rome	0930	2030	EC 85	76	
	2030	0815+1	D287	76	
Vienna (Westbhf.)	0825	1305	EC 63	67	
	1625	2105	EC 65	67	
	2319	0632+1	D269	67	

Daily departures unless otherwise noted. Make reservations for all departures.

(1) Transfer in Cologne (Köln) to EC 148
(2) Transfer in Cologne (Köln) to EC 150
(3) Transfer in Zurich to IC 924
(4) Transfer in Cologne (Köln) to EC 38
(5) Transfer in Cologne (Köln) to EC 46
(6) Transfer in Cologne (Köln) to D430
(7) Transfer in Hamburg to EC 184
(8) Transfer in Hamburg to EC 186
(9) Monday through Saturday only

Electric powered boats operate on the Königssee (King's Lake) near Berchtesgaden in the Bavarian Alps region.

Multiple echoes of a boatman's horn resound over the Königssee to the delight and amazement of passengers aboard.

From Munich ...

A DAY EXCURSION TO BERCHTESGADEN
DISTANCE BY TRAIN: 112 miles (180 km)
AVERAGE TRAIN TIME: 3 hours

Don't let the train time to Berchtesgaden deter you from making this day excursion. The train follows a route that passes through some of the most beautiful countryside in the world, and the tours waiting for your arrival in Berchtesgaden are simply out of this world.

After Adolf Hitler seized power in 1934, he ordered the expansion of the facilities in Obersalzberg, an appendage to Berchtesgaden, with the intent of making it the equivalent of a summer White House. Der Führer's dream was destroyed, however, when the greater part of Obersalzberg was demolished by an air attack on 25 April 1945.

If possible, take the early train out of Munich so as to arrive in ample time to select a tour and still have time for a relaxing lunch in one of Berchtesgaden's charming inns. Current schedules are always posted in the main hall of the Berchtesgaden railway station.

The U.S. Armed Forces maintain a recreational facility at Hotel General Walker on the Obersalzberg, about 3 miles above Berchtesgaden. Tours are conducted for U.S. military personnel only. For civilians, Berchtesgaden Mini-Bus Tours specializes in English-speaking historical tours of Berchtesgaden's sights, including the Obersalzberg and Eagle's Nest. They are located in the Berchtesgaden Tourist Office (Kurdirektion) opposite the railway station. To reach the tourist-information office, cross the street in front of the station at the traffic light, incline to the left, following the KÖNIGSSEE sign. The office is located in a large cream-colored building on the right-hand side.

The village of Berchtesgaden has many attractions. Among them is the Folk Museum housed in the Adelsheim Castle (Schloss Adelsheim) where you will find displays of wood carvings and the famous Berchtesgaden wood-ship boxes.

If you are opting for an overview of this beautiful mountain retreat, ask for directions to the Obersalzberg cable car lift. The lower lift station is only about a ten-minute walk from the rail station. Then, in another ten minutes, a ride that rivals anything you've ever experienced in Disney World will lift you to a view from atop the Obersalzberg Mountain.

In addition to sightseeing in Berchtesgaden and its immediate surroundings, there are many interesting guided tours that can be taken outside of the village. The most popular ones for North Americans are visits to Obersalzberg, the Salt Mines, the Königssee, and the Eagle's Nest.

Tour schedules are seasonal, with the exception of two programs—trips to the Salt Mines and to Obersalzberg. These are conducted year-round. Tours on

BERCHTESGADEN—*ALPS, LAKES, AND SALT MINES*

A Day Excursion from Munich

DEPART FROM MUNICH HBF. STATION	TRAIN NUMBER	ARRIVE IN BERCHTESGADEN STATION	NOTES
0650	E 3501	0928	(1)
0751	IR 2095	1028	(1)
0951	IR 2191	1228	(1)
1050	E 3513	1328	(1)

DEPART FROM BERCHTESGADEN STATION	TRAIN NUMBER	ARRIVE IN MUNICH HBF. STATION	NOTES
1533	IR 2098	1807	(1)
1633	EC 3540	1910	(1)
1721	IR 2096	2007	(1)
1933	IR 2094	2200	(1)

(1) Daily, including holidays; transfer in Freilassing (train numbers refer to Munich–Freilassing trains)

Distance: 112 miles/180 km
References: Thomas Cook Tables 790 and 791

the Königssee (King's Lake) and to the Eagle's Nest are, of course, limited to the warmer times of the year.

The Obersalzberg tour features a visit to the former location of the Berghof, Adolf Hitler's official home and the site of many pre–World War II conferences. Included on the tour is a trip through its air-raid shelters and bunkers, which provided protection to the conferees in the event that the Allied air forces wanted to disrupt the proceedings.

The Salt Mines are located a few miles outside the town of Berchtesgaden. The tour is a thrilling experience. In miner's protective clothing, you ride a mine train, slide down chutes, and cross over subterranean lakes. The kids love it, but a word of caution—it's not for older folks or the faint of heart.

The Königssee is considered the pearl of Berchtesgaden and provides some of the most romantic scenery to be found in Upper Bavaria. In order to preserve the quietness of the lake and the clearness of its waters, electric boats have been the only crafts permitted to navigate there since 1909. A fleet exceeding twenty such boats is available for sightseeing trips around the lake.

A tour aboard an electric boat runs daily on the Königssee whenever the lake is ice-free. This emerald lake is five miles long and is one of the most enchanting settings in Bavaria. Midpoint in the cruise, the captain shuts down the motor and, in the silence of the lake, lets go with a blast on a trumpet that resounds and resounds again off the alpine palisades surrounding the lake for as many as seven times.

The Eagle's Nest tour begins in May and is conducted daily until winter snows block its access. A bus conveys you to a height of 5,274 feet, where an elevator lifts you the final 400 feet to a never-to-be-forgotten experience.

Despite the publicity gained by the Eagle's Nest's connection with Adolf Hitler, Der Führer only visited there about five times. The "nest" itself is known locally as the Kehlsteinhaus. The road running to the elevator that takes you to the summit is beyond doubt a uniquely daring feat of road building. It's a white-knuckle ride all the way. The tour itself is far less strenuous than that of the Salt Mines, but the weather is all important.

Despite its ancient facade, Berchtesgaden is actually very modern in its tourist and recreational facilities. Should its charm overcome you—as it does many—you might consider an overnight stay. The Berchtesgadener Land tourist information office opposite the rail station, can assist you in finding accommodations. Their telephone number is 8652/967–150; fax 8652/63300.

If you are in town at lunchtime, try the Gasthof Neuhaus, opposite the fountain in the town square. Its selection of *Schmankerl* (Bavarian specialties) is a treat, and their ice cream specialties will make you forget all about Baskin-Robbins—at least for a while.

Zugspitze zenith presents a panoramic view from the highest point in the German Alps. The peak is scaled by both Austrian and German cableways. Eurailpass holders benefit by a discount from the private Bavarian Zugspitze Railway for travel on either the cog railway from Garmisch-Partenkirchen or the Eibsee cableway. Customs formalities are observed when passing at the peak between Germany and Austria. Snow conditions from November to May provide ideal skiing opportunities at the Zugspitzplatt amphitheater.

From Munich . . .

A DAY EXCURSION TO GARMISCH-PARTENKIRCHEN
DISTANCE BY TRAIN: 63 miles (101 km)
AVERAGE TRAIN TIME: 1 hour, 30 minutes

Bavaria's eccentric King Ludwig II spent lavishly, admired Wagner, and went mad—though not necessarily in that order. Two of his famous castles, Neuschwanstein and Linderhof, can be visited on tours from Garmisch-Partenkirchen, as well as the village of Oberammergau (home of the Passion Play) and the Zugspitze, Germany's highest mountain.

Tourism started in the area with the building of a railroad between Munich and Garmisch-Partenkirchen in 1889. Prior to that time, the area waned or prospered according to who was in town. The Romans occupied the area as far back as the first century B.C. For centuries, they operated and protected their ancient military road between the Brenner Pass and the present German city of Augsburg.

At the beginning of the eighteenth century, the area was suppressed, first by the Spanish and then, in turn, by the Austrians and the French. It wasn't until 1802 that the area was finally made a part of Bavaria. Because of its interest in winter sports, in 1966 the twin-city of Garmisch-Partenkirchen became the sister city of Aspen, Colorado, ski capital of the United States.

Tourist information is readily available in the city's tourist information office at the Richard Strauss Platz. Reach it by turning left outside the station and walking downhill about 300 yards to Bahnhof Strasse. Turn left and walk about 150 yards to Richard Strauss Platz and the Kongressaal (Congress Hall). You're there!

Office hours are 0800–1800 Monday through Saturday, and 1000–1200 on Sunday. The telephone number is (08821) 1806; fax (08821) 180–55. The office has tips on walking tours as well as bus information and maps.

The U.S. Armed Forces maintain a recreation center in Garmisch and also conduct tours in the area. Tour participation, however, is limited to U.S. military personnel, their dependents, and retirees. Payment for these tours must be in U.S. dollars. If you qualify, to reach the recreation center, follow the ZUGSPITZBAHN signs to the cog railway station, where the U.S. facilities will be in plain view and just ahead. Follow the signs.

ABR, a German tour agency, offers a wide selection of tours in the Garmisch-Partenkirchen area, including King Ludwig's Neuschwanstein Castle and his Linderhof Castle. The ABR agency is immediately adjacent to the Garmisch-Partenkirchen rail station. Proceed to track No. 1 by turning to the left at the bottom of the stairs leading from the arriving train platform. ABR is visible from the rail station lobby. Most tours are conducted daily.

GARMISCH-PARTENKIRCHEN—*BAVARIA AT ITS BEST*

A Day Excursion from Munich

DEPART FROM MUNICH HBF. STATION	ARRIVE IN GARMISCH STATION	NOTES
0800	0916	(1)
0900	1023	(1)
1000	1116	(1)
1100	1223	(1)
1200	1316	(1)

Zugspitze trains depart Garmisch thirty-five minutes past the hour
from 0835 to 1435.

DEPART FROM GARMISCH STATION	ARRIVE IN MUNICH HBF. STATION	NOTES
1534	1652	(1)
1627	1753	(1)
1734	1853	(1)
1831	1954	(1)
1934	2052	(1)
2027	2152	(1)

Zugspitze trains arrive at Garmisch twenty minutes past the hour from 1020 to 1820.
Depart Garmisch hourly 0835 to 1435 (80-minute journey; last train back at 1600).

(1) Daily, including holidays

Distance: 63 miles/101 km
References: Thomas Cook Table 785, Munich-Garmisch
                   Thomas Cook Table 788, Zugspitze Railway

Garmisch-Partenkirchen (actually two villages that united in 1935) hosted the 1936 Winter Olympics and the World Alpine-Ski Championship in 1978. Just visiting the Olympic facilities can consume an entire day. A downtown shopping spree can do the same, but with more injury to pocketbooks. In wintertime, the Winter Olympics ski jump provides spills and chills, and the Olympic Ice Stadium is open year-round.

To give you some idea of the extensive development of the area, there are twelve cable-car runs plus a cog-wheel railroad that operate throughout the year in or near Garmisch-Partenkirchen. In winter, forty-two ski lifts add their services to assist the crowds of winter-sport enthusiasts who flock to the area. The alpine ski runs extend sixty-eight miles in length, and there are ninety-three miles of tracks for the growing sport of cross-country skiing.

Two of the most popular alpine cable-car runs in summer are the Eibsee-Zugspitze system (9,678 feet) and the Wank Bahn, which takes you to the promontory of the Wank Alp (5,874 feet). There are others as well. One that is particularly convenient starts at the Olympic Ski Stadium on the fringe of Garmisch-Partenkirchen and scales the Eckbauer Alp to a height of 4,127 feet. From any of these points on a clear day, the view is extraordinary.

The Zugspitze is the highest mountain in Germany—9,718 feet to be exact. A cog railway was completed in 1931 to the Zugspitzplatt, along with a cable car that scaled the last 2,000 feet to the top. Another cable car running from Eibsee, a station stop on the cog railway at the 3,500-foot level, was placed in operation during 1963. This system lifts passengers directly to the peak in a spectacular ten-minute ride.

These two systems make a circuitous routing possible—up one way and down another—and here's how it's done. The round-trip fare from Garmisch is 67 deutsche marks (DM) (only 50 DM for Eurailpass holders). The ticket entitles you to ride on any part of the total system. When you arrive in the Garmisch-Partenkirchen station, walk about a hundred yards to your right to the cog-railway station. The cog railway stops in Eibsee about thirty minutes after departing Garmisch. Transfer at this point to the Eibsee cable car.

The cable-car trip from Eibsee to the top of the Zugspitze takes about ten breathtaking minutes. If you are in a hurry to return to Garmisch, you could retrace your trip by returning to Eibsee on the cable car, but we recommend that you proceed to the Sonn Alpine Glacier Restaurant via the "Gipfelbahn" cable car. At the Sonn Alpine, you join up with the cog railway, which terminates there in a huge vaulted hall blasted out of solid rock. Trains depart on the hour, and the trip back to Garmisch takes one hour and ten minutes.

Innsbruck hugs the valley of the Inn River, from which the Alps explode upward to the Tyrolean sky.

A DAY EXCURSION TO INNSBRUCK, AUSTRIA
DISTANCE BY TRAIN: 107 miles (172 km)
AVERAGE TRAIN TIME: 2 hours, 10 minutes

Translated, Innsbruck means "bridge over the Inn River." Situated at the junction of the Inn Valley and the Sill Gap, on the road and railroad route running into Italy through the Brenner Pass, the city is the cultural and tourist capital of the Austrian Tyrol.

Innsbruck is surrounded theatrically by its mountains. There is an exhilarating mountain view from nearly every street corner and every window in town. Looking northward from its main street, Maria-Theresien Strasse, you will confront the towering Alps, which seem to encroach upon the city. The scene is breathtaking. (American kids say it's "awesome!")

This day excursion from Munich to Innsbruck offers an opportunity to explore the Tyrolean Alps in the comfort of a cable car—plus a visit to one of the most picturesque "old towns" in Austria. To top it off, a circuitous return on the Mittenwald railroad is possible; it takes you on a fantastically scenic rail route straight through the heart of the Austrian and Bavarian Alps en route back to Munich via Garmisch-Partenkirchen.

You are in for an eye-filling day. Even the regular rail line running out of Munich is loaded with Alpine scenery. Take a seat on the right side of your coach outbound from Munich for the best views. Keep your eyes on the edges of the pine forest. We can almost guarantee that you'll see a family of deer that way. The fawns venture farther into the clearing but scamper back faster into the woods as the train passes.

When you arrive in Innsbruck, you will note that train information is posted throughout the main station, and a train information office can be found immediately to the right of the exit from the trains.

Most of the shops and restaurants in Innsbruck accept German currency. If you want to change money into Austrian schillings, however, you may do so at a change booth located at your far left just as you exit from the trains. The exchange office hours are 0730–2000 daily. The local tourist-office branch office, also located in the station, is an official exchange, too.

Innsbruck hosted the Winter Olympics in 1964 and again in 1976. From those times, when visitors arrived in hordes, Innsbruck has learned to "go with the flow." That is, its railway station's facilities are changed from time to time to take care of large influxes of visitors, so you may find some of the facilities in locations other than as described, or augmented by additional booths—according to the flow.

INNSBRUCK—*JEWEL OF THE ALPS*

A Day Excursion from Munich

DEPART FROM MUNICH HBF. STATION	TRAIN NUMBER	ARRIVE IN INNSBRUCK STATION	NOTES
0700	EC 81	0836	(1)
0800	E 3607	1039	(1)(2)
0930	EC 85	1118	(1)
1130	EC 15	1320	(1)

DEPART FROM INNSBRUCK STATION	TRAIN NUMBER	ARRIVE IN MUNICH HBF. STATION	NOTES
1641	EC 84	1830	(1)
1705	E 3630	1954	(1)(2)
1837	D 488	2030	(1)
2103	EC 80	2240	(1)

(1) Daily, including holidays
(2) Scenic route via Mittenwald/Garmisch; see Thomas Cook Table 785

Distance: 107 miles/172 km
References: Thomas Cook Tables 785 and 795

SPECIAL ATTRACTION

Innsbruck's unique location in the heart of the Alps makes it a mountain-rambling paradise. If you can't exactly picture yourself climbing Alpine peaks, you can still opt for comfortable walks in the refreshing Alpine foothills. Experienced mountain guides and the special Innsbruck mountain-rambling bus are available at no charge.

Hikes are organized daily. For Innsbruck information, call (0512) 5356 or contact the Innsbruck Tourist Office at (0512) 59850. Meet your guide in front of the Convention Center at 0830. Participation requires a Club Innsbruck membership card, which is issued by your hotel. Members get reduced prices on shopping, cable cars, golf courses, tennis courts, and many other facilities.

Tourist information is available at the "Hotel Information Office," which you can find by leaving the main station hall by the exit on the left-hand side and proceeding past the "Checked Baggage" area. Available for purchase is a large guide map, which you will find well worth the price if you plan a walking tour of the city. Bus tours of the city are available throughout the year. Biking tours are a great way to see Innsbruck, too.

If you decide to become your own tour guide, check the map, then head west for a few blocks to Innsbruck's Arc de Triumph. From this point, turn north and wend your way slowly through the Altstadt (Old Town), which lines both sides of the street all the way to the Goldener Dachl (Golden Roof) at the end of Herzog-Friedrich Strasse. It may come as a mild disappointment, but the so called Golden Roof is actually made of heavy, gilded copper.

We suggest you eat lunch in the Goldener Adler (Golden Eagle), the oldest inn in the city. It was founded in 1390! It is around the corner on the left and can best be described as a delicious experience. If you go there for dinner, enjoy the Tyrolean music in the cellar restaurant. It will complete a perfect evening.

Mountain scaling via cable car? Eurailpass holders get a twenty-percent reduction on the following private lines: Seegrube, Hafelekar, Patscherkofel, and Mutterer Alm. The Seegrube (6,287 feet) and the Hafelekar (7,700 feet) await your conquest, and scaling them by cable car makes mountaineering a sport for all ages.

Ready for that fantastic train trip back to Munich? Board the Express 5430, which usually departs from track 12-B in the Innsbruck Station and returns to Munich via Mittenwald and Garmisch daily at 1705. (Check in the station for the proper departure platform, for it has been known to change during construction and repairing projects.)

You start by crossing the Inn River, then the train begins climbing the steep valley walls that skirt the Inn. Approaching the Alpine station of Hochzirl, you will have a sheer, 1,500-foot vertical view of the river and the green valley through which it runs. Select train seats on the left-hand side for the best opportunity of seeing these sights as they unfold.

Later, the train will stop in Seefeld, a delightful Alpine community, before continuing on to Mittenwald and Garmisch, where the Express 5430 cars are switched to another Munich train. Here, you can stay aboard your coach while it is being connected to the rear of the other train, or you can move across the train platform to a coach immediately behind the engine of the Munich-bound train. This maneuver may save some time when you arrive in Munich because the Express 5430 cars are coupled to the rear of the train—and it's a long walk in from the farthest part of the Munich Hauptbahnhof platforms.

Nuremberg landmark, the Kingsgate, towers over a medieval marketplace restored behind the old city walls.

From Munich . . .

A DAY EXCURSION TO NUREMBERG
DISTANCE BY TRAIN: 125 miles (201 km)
AVERAGE TRAIN TIME: 1 hour, 50 minutes

Nuremberg originated the day excursion! On 7 December 1835, the *first* German train chugged its way from Nuremberg to Furth, a neighboring city, with honored guests *and* two barrels of beer.

On this day excursion the InterCity trains average seventy-four miles per hour between Munich and Nuremberg—considerably faster than back in 1835—and Nuremberg's brew is every bit the match for Munich's, for Nuremberg is a part of Bavaria, too. Get ready for an enjoyable day excursion.

When you arrive in Nuremberg, you will find the tourist office in the railway station on the right-hand side of the main arcade just before the main exit. Operating hours of the office are 0900–1900 Monday through Saturday only. Another tourist information office is in the city hall. Summer operating hours are 0900–1300 and 1400–1800 Monday through Saturday and 1000–1300 and 1400–1600 on Sunday (telephone 911/23360). This office is closed on Sunday from September to May (except during Christmas Market).

Conducted tours of the city depart daily at 1430. Individual tours of the city may be arranged at any time; one of the Tourist Board's experienced city guides will serve as escort.

The train information office is in the arcade on the left of the main exit. Train schedules, posted in several prominent locations in the station, will confirm the departure time and track location of your return train to Munich.

One of the main gates of the old walled city of Nuremberg, the Kingsgate, is directly across from the railway station. Picking up Königstrasse (King Street) at this point, you can follow it to the heart of the old walled area known as the Hauptmarkt (Central Market). Plan to be there at noon, a mechanical clock will entertain you at the stroke of twelve with its seven electors paying homage to the emperor.

Connoisseurs of the brewers' art won't want to miss a visit to Nuremberg's Museum Brewery and Medieval Cellars. The museum is really the Altstadthof brewery, who's motto, "Beer like our Forefathers," is observed today by the use of only the finest materials and brewing methods, which date from the nineteenth century. The cellars, going down eighty-five feet through solid rock, form a labyrinth of tunnels dug in the fourteenth century for the storage of beer. A guided tour is available.

Walking though this medieval city, it is difficult to realize that Nuremberg was all but destroyed in World War II, but rose phoenixlike from its ashes to rebuild its ancient monuments and facades. As in Munich, you don't discuss

NUREMBERG—*BEER, GINGERBREAD, AND TOYS*

A Day Excursion from Munich

DEPART FROM MUNICH HBF. STATION	TRAIN NUMBER	ARRIVE IN NUREMBERG STATION	NOTES
0756	ICE 788	0934	(1)
0856	IC 706	1034	(1)
0956	ICE 786	1134	(1)
1056	IC 812	1234	(1)

DEPART FROM NUREMBERG STATION	TRAIN NUMBER	ARRIVE IN MUNICH HBF. STATION	NOTES
1524	IC 813	1706	(1)
1624	ICE 787	1803	(1)
1724	IC 705	1903	(1)
1824	ICE 789	2003	(1)
1924	ICE 707	2103	(1)
2024	ICE 885	2203	(1)

(1) Daily, including holidays

Distance: 125 miles/201 km
Reference: Thomas Cook Table 750

the destruction—or the reconstruction—with its inhabitants. Like all wars, World War II has come and gone, and Nuremberg is today as it was centuries ago before man was endowed with such terrible powers of destruction.

The headline of the schedule on the opposite page states that Nuremberg offers not only beer, but gingerbread and toys as well. The aroma of Nuremberg's special gingerbread, *Lebkuchen,* fills the Hauptmarkt every Christmas. At other times, the same aroma may be savored—and tasted—in the many pastry shops throughout the city.

The traditional recipes of the original gingerbread are kept secret by the bakeries that produce it. Two such companies invite visitors to sample their products. Arrangements may be made by either of the tourist offices.

Toy shops are in profusion, and the Toy Museum on Karl Street, two blocks from the Hauptmarkt via Augustinerstrasse, has a splendid display of dolls, puppets, and tin soldiers. The museum also houses an interesting model-railway layout, featuring—of all things—the train station in Omaha, Nebraska. Real toy fans will want to be in Nuremberg around the first of February for the International Toy Fair. From the Hauptbahnhof, take the U-Bahn (underground) to Spielwarenmesse.

Nuremberg's most famous citizen was Albrecht Dürer, a man who towered above his time. The stately home in which he lived, from 1509 until his death in 1529, is located two blocks north of the Toy Museum, past the Wine Market, on Albrecht Dürer Strasse. The house holds a collection of the famed artist's works, and the area surrounding it is probably the most interesting section within the walled city. Unfortunately, Dürer's most famous work, *The Four Apostles,* now rests in Munich, but a number of his paintings are exhibited.

If you have any doubt about that first day excursion by train originating in Nuremberg, check in at the Verkehrsmuseum (Transport Museum), three blocks to the right of the train station as you face it. The museum is open daily 0930–1700. There you will find the Adler (Eagle), the first German locomotive, complete with the two beer barrels mounted on its tender.

If you are a model-railroad fan, you will be pleased to note that, in addition to the Toy Museum, two of Germany's largest manufacturers of HO- and N-gauge equipment, Arnold and Fleischmann, are located in Nuremberg. E.P. Lehmann, the manufacturer of G-scale equipment for the increasingly popular outdoor garden railways, is located at Sagnerstrasse 1–5. They have operating layouts, and visitors are welcome. The operating hours are seasonal, so check with one of the city's tourist information offices if you would like to visit.

Picturesque framework building in Rothenburg's well-known *Plonlein* (little place) is one of Germany's most charming sights.

From Munich ...

A DAY EXCURSION ON THE ROMANTIC ROAD
DISTANCE BY TRAIN AND BUS: 345 miles (554 km)
AVERAGE TRAIN TIME: 12 hours, 36 minutes

Too long and too far? Not in the least. The Romantic Road, packed with superb scenery and delightful medieval villages, is worth every minute.

The Romantic Road bus service is available from April through the end of October. For advance seat reservations, write to Deutsche Touring GmbH, Am Romerhof 17, 60486 Frankfurt/Main, Germany (telephone 69/790–3256; fax 69/790–3219). Information is available from Rail Pass Express, Inc., 2737 Sawbury Boulevard, Columbus, OH 43235, USA (telephone 614–793–7650 from 1100–1600 eastern standard time; fax 614–764–0711). In Munich, you may telephone or visit the Europabus office described below.

The Deutsche Bundesbahn (German Railroad) bus that takes you from Munich to Würzburg makes two stops en route: one in Dinkelsbuhl for lunch and one in Rothenburg for sightseeing. After these pleasant interludes, plus a return trip to Munich on one of Germany's lightning-fast InterCity trains, you will wonder where the day has gone.

The Romantic Road bus is unique in that it carries an English-speaking hostess. This trip has become so popular that seat reservations are recommended. Reservations can be made at the Europabus office in the Munich railway station opposite track Nos. 33 and 34. The office is open 0800–1900 Monday through Friday and 0830–1900 on Saturday. The telephone number is 591824. Seat reservations are free of charge, and the Eurailpass is accepted.

The Romantic Road bus has no special markings. Ask for its departure position (which is usually No. 23) when you make reservations. Your reservation assures you of a seat on the bus, but not a specified seat. Be at the bus station at about 0830, therefore, to ensure getting a window seat.

This is a fun trip. The bus stereo plays *The Blue Danube* as you cross the river entering the village of Donauworth, and the lunch stop is an ideal time to meet and chat with your fellow passengers. The bus hostess will suggest a restaurant for lunch. Although you are free to select your own, or skip lunch for sightseeing, we recommend that you accept her suggestion.

Rothenburg is one of the most frequently visited places in Germany. Every year thousands of visitors from all parts of the world come to this ancient walled city. You will see why Rothenburg is picturesque and photogenic. Be sure to take a camera. Probably more photographs have been taken of its Kobolzeller Gate and Siebers Tower than of any other scene in Germany.

The town is a museum piece of medieval character. Most of its 12,500 citizens living within or just outside the city's walls work to serve the tourist in

THE ROMANTIC ROAD—*DELIGHTFULLY MEDIEVAL*

A Day Excursion from Munich

	DEPARTS	ARRIVES	NOTES
	Munich Hbf.	**Dinkelsbuhl**	
Bus	0900	1155	(3)*
	Dinkelsbuhl	**Rothenburg**	
	1205	1245	(3)**
	1225	1300	(3)**
Bus	1445	1530	(3)**
	Rothenburg	**Würzburg**	
Bus	1700	1825	(3)

Return to Munich

via train	**Würzburg**	**Munich Hbf.**	
ICE 681	1823	2038	(1)(2)
ICE 885	1923	2203	(1)(2)
ICE 683	2023	2238	(2)(4)
IR 2187	2041	2316	(1)(2)
ICE 883	2123	0003	(2)(4)

*   Stops for lunch
** Stops for sightseeing

(1) Daily, including holidays
(2) Food service available
(3) Daily, April 1–October 31
(4) Daily, except Saturday

Distance: 172 miles/276 km by bus plus 173 miles/278 km by train
References: Thomas Cook Tables 748 (Bus) and 750 (Train)

some manner. This town has survived, even in the twentieth century, as the "Jewel of the Middle Ages." Enjoy your visit in Rothenburg but keep your eye on the town clock, for the Romantic Road bus continues on its journey to Würzburg and its final destination, Frankfurt, promptly at 1700. If, for some reason, you do miss the 1700 bus departure, the German railroad also operates another bus line between Rothenburg and Steinach, where you can connect with train service back to Munich.

Arriving in Würzburg at 1825, you have the early opportunity of returning to Munich at 1923 aboard ICE 885; or, you might want to have dinner and linger as late as 2041, when the IR 2187 speeds back to Munich. The later departure would allow you to stay in Würzburg for several hours. But remember that the IR 2187 is the last regular train for Munich in the evening. There are several restaurants immediately across from the park fronting the east side of the Würzburg rail station where you could enjoy dinner. The IR 2187 serves limited food selections only.

Rothenburg is loaded with living legends. One concerns the salvation of the town from certain destruction by its wine-drinking mayor. In 1631, during the Thirty Years' War, the town was captured by imperial troops under the command of General Tilly. While the general toyed with the idea of destroying the town and executing its councilors, he was handed a tankard holding more than three quarts of heavy franconian wine to aid his meditation.

The general promised mercy to Rothenburg if one of its councilors could drain the "bumper" in one mighty draft. Mayor Nusch did and thus saved the town. Although he slept for three days and nights following the mighty quaff, apparently he suffered no other effects, for he lived another thirty-seven years and died at the age of eighty—with a smile on his face.

The historic deed is re-enacted daily by a glockenspiel installed in the gable of the Councilors' Tavern at 1100, 1200, 1300, 1400, 1500, 2100, and 2200. Be there!

Historical facts are not quite as clear on another Rothenburg legend. It centers around a Shepherds' Dance that is performed by members of the Shepherds' Guild on Sunday afternoons through the spring and summer months. Based on the thesis that the shepherds found a "treasure" (might have been franconian wine), they dance very happily.

Ulm Cathedral's steeple, highest in the world (528 feet), towers above an express train crossing the Danube River. The town's mayor, Ludwig Kraft, laid the foundation stone of the cathedral on 30 June 1377.

A DAY EXCURSION TO ULM
DISTANCE BY TRAIN: 92 miles (148 km)
AVERAGE TRAIN TIME: 1 hour, 13 minutes

The Gothic spire of the Ulm Cathedral, silhouetted against a blue Bavarian sky, is a scene you are not likely to forget. Poised on the banks of the swift-moving Danube, Ulm is a picturesque representation of a typical Swabian city. Birthplace of Albert Einstein, Ulm has withstood the onslaughts of many conflicts, including Napoleonic campaigns, with great dignity. It is considered a miracle that its cathedral escaped damage throughout World War II, although serious damage was inflicted in the town by Allied bombing. All of Ulm's original facades have now been repaired or replaced.

The spire of the cathedral, with its skyward thrust of 528 feet, is the tallest in the world. Although the foundation stone of the cathedral was laid in 1377, the two towers and the spire were not completed until 1890. When the central nave was completed in 1471, it could hold 20,000 people—twice as many as the town's population at that time. Truly, this was an ambitious undertaking right from the start.

The clear vertical lines and the lightness of the cathedral's architecture are beautiful. The interior is open 0900–1700 daily, except when services are being conducted. There is a small admission charge to visit the nave and ascend the spire.

Speaking of the spire, a breathtaking panorama of Ulm, the Danube, and the surrounding area rewards those who climb its 768 steps. We first climbed (and counted) them in 1974, burdened with three 35-mm cameras and a tripod. We have resisted the temptation to climb again during more recent visits, but we are told by people who have made the ascent that the Alps can be seen on a clear day. We'll take their word for it, but perhaps you will want to see for yourself. A word of caution—the climb is rigorous and should not be attempted unless you have good physical stamina.

You will get a brief view of the Danube and the cathedral when crossing the railroad bridge entering Ulm. Watch on the right-hand side of the train immediately after passing the Neu Ulm (New Ulm) suburban station. The railroad bridge has a pedestrian crossing, so you may want to return to that vantage point again for a more prolonged observation. The bridge can be reached after leaving the station by walking to the right to an intersection where the trolleys swing farther right down an underpass. Continue straight ahead, not turning with the trolleys, on the promenade to the river's edge and the approach to the bridge.

If you are interested in shooting a picture similar to the one on page 438, it

ULM—*WORLD'S TALLEST CATHEDRAL*

A Day Excursion from Munich

DEPART FROM MUNICH HBF. STATION	TRAIN NUMBER	ARRIVE IN ULM STATION	NOTES
0746	ICE 598	0854	(1)(2)(3)
0750	EC 66	0902	(1)(2)(3)
0846	ICE 896	0954	(1)(2)(3)
0946	ICE 596	1054	(1)(2)(3)
1046	ICE 794	1154	(1)(2)(3)
1146	ICE 594	1254	(1)(2)(3)

DEPART FROM ULM STATION	TRAIN NUMBER	ARRIVE IN MUNICH HBF. STATION	NOTES
1505	ICE 593	1615	(1)(2)(3)
1605	ICE 895	1715	(1)(2)(3)
1705	ICE 595	1815	(1)(2)(3)
1805	ICE 897	1915	(1)(2)(3)
1905	ICE 597	2015	(1)(2)(3)
2105	ICE 599	2215	(1)(2)(3)

(1) Daily, including holidays
(2) Food service available
(3) Reservations mandatory

Distance: 92 miles/148 km
Reference: Thomas Cook Table 760

is possible to take it from the vehicle bridge, upstream on the Danube from the railroad bridge. You can reach it from the promenade running along the left bank of the Danube. A 200-mm lens is ideal for the shot because you are more than a half-mile away from the cathedral.

Another route to the Danube is through the *Fischerviertel* (Fisherman's Quarters), which lies to the south of the cathedral. En route, you will pass the picturesque *Schiefes Haus* (Sloping House), which has settled over a canal. If you walk downstream on the Danube's left bank, the river promenade will bring you to the *Metzgerturm* (Butcher's Tower), another Ulm landmark.

The tourist information office is in the staathaus at Münsterplatz. You will have no difficulty finding it. There is a display of tourist information in the railway station that you can check with on arrival. You will find it to your left when entering the station from the train platforms.

The tourist office operates 0900–1800 Monday through Friday and 0900–1230 on Saturday. The office can make hotel reservations, too. Telephone 0731–161–2830 or fax 161–1641 for advance information.

During your day excursion in Ulm, you should visit the Ulm Museum, where you will find displays of art and culture ranging from the Middle Ages to modern times. Notable features are the collections of modern graphics and important examples of late Gothic. There are also exhibits concerning some of Ulm's famous citizens, such as the physicist Albert Einstein and Albrecht Berblinger, the "tailor of Ulm," who in 1811 made man's first serious attempt to fly.

Although the cathedral dominates the scene, a stroll through Ulm will reveal its other aspects—that of a modern city of more than 110,000 inhabitants where you can go shopping in exclusive establishments, boutiques, and department stores. And for refreshment in between times, you will find traditional old taverns, pleasant restaurants, comfortable inns, and good hotels where you may enjoy Swabian specialty dishes accompanied by drafts of good Ulm beer.

If attracted to the Danube—which by the way, isn't blue but brown—an inquiry at the tourist information office will make you acquainted with the various things that you may do on or beside the river. You may, for example, hire a boat or go for a cruise. There are pleasant walks along the Danube's banks, and there is the Friedrichsau Park, where one of the main attractions is its aquarium with a tropical house.

Unique in the field of museums is Ulm's German Bread Museum, which presents an impressive display of that major ingredient of our daily diet. Not only does the museum effectively tell the story of breadmaking, it makes you aware of how serious hunger can be.

The track area of the Nice railway station reflects a mixed motif of Riviera plantings and modern, digital train information. Nice is a focal point for rail traffic to and from Austria, Italy, Spain, and Switzerland, as well as other locations within France. Access to many of the train platforms requires the use of underground tunnels, which makes it difficult for those with baggage carts as well as the handicapped.

20 NICE ... AND THE FRENCH RIVIERA

There are "rivieras" scattered throughout the world, but there is still only one Riviera. It is the dazzling, beautiful coast stretching along the Mediterranean Sea on either side of Nice. There is no match for it. It is still the first, ahead of all pretenders, like an incredibly beautiful woman whom you meet once in a lifetime.

There are those who say the Riviera has been ruined. This is a matter of opinion. In the days before World War I, the Riviera was a haven for rich Russian dukes and English lords seeking escape from the rigors of a more northerly winter. When such aristocracy, particularly the Russian version, began to fade from the scene, summer became the popular season, bringing with it hordes of Americans and others seeking the sun and all sorts of fun, including the nocturnal varieties. So summer rates went up and winter rates went down. This caused many of the surviving aristocrats to complain of the ruination of the area, for who in their class would want to pay less than $300 a day?

People claiming that a place is "ruined" usually mean that it has changed. This is certainly true of the Riviera. The towns and fishing villages that earlier visitors knew have now grown together into an almost continuous resort town stretching from Saint-Raphael to the Italian border. Nice, the largest community in the area, lies about halfway between these two points and becomes the base city for numerous day excursions in either direction. Actually, due to the relatively short distances between points, one could select either Cannes or Monte Carlo as a base city because the French National Railroads' excellent system closely links all three cities. Saint-Raphael should be considered, too, since it's the least expensive.

Those seeking surf and sand should consider staying in Cannes because most of the Riviera is not noted for its beaches. The Alps climb so swiftly behind the azure blue waters of the Mediterranean that most beaches, such as those in Nice, tend to be rocky and filled with pebbles. In other words, the Riviera is not a Miami Beach where the old of France go to die—and a lot of folks are most grateful for the difference.

The Riviera is noted for its spectacular scenery. Every proper ingredient of sea, shore, cliffs, and mountains is present. Grapes and flowers are the predominate crops of its highly cultivated farmlands. It is one of the great flower-growing areas of Europe and probably the most famous center in the world for perfume production. The Riviera is also becoming a center for modern art. The works of many twentieth-century artists can be found there in its museums and exhibition halls. The last time we counted, there were eighteen museums in and around Nice. Picasso spent the last years of his life in a villa overlooking the Mediterranean.

With all of these attractions, plus excellent hotels in every price range and restaurants serving every delicacy imaginable, it would be foolhardy not to explore the Riviera just because one had heard it had been ruined by the abundance of everything it provides.

In selecting Nice as the base city for the day excursions in the area of the Riviera, consideration was given to the features and attractions that the city has to offer. They are many.

In the maze of its narrow streets, you will discover, in variations of light, shade, and fragrances, the fish market, the Palais Lascaris, the public squares of the city—each one different in function but all with an air of grace and function—and, in a sudden burst of sunlight, the beaches.

At Cours Saleya, the flower market, you'll discover what makes Nice so fragrant, so colorful. While there, you will also discover what makes the cuisine of the area so appetizing: A fruit-and-vegetable market flourishes right in the midst of the floral beauty. Mondays are a bit different in the Cours Saleya, for that's when the market is reserved for antique dealers. But, here again, is another opportunity to delve into the priceless things that make Nice so nice.

Turn from the sea in Nice and your eyes confront Mont Alban and its fortress overhanging the harbor. If you choose to go to the Alpine area behind the city, there's a charming narrow-gauge railroad, Chemin de Fer de Provence (Railroad of Provence), that will transport you through rocky gorges and sheer cliffs and Lingostiere, on the invasion route used by Napoleon, to an exceptional panorama of the Alps and the Mediterranean Sea.

For another train ride, this one right within the city, you may board the Nice "little train" at its station on the Promenade des Anglais for a scenic ride through the shady, narrow streets of the Old Town to the Castle Hill of Nice. Once again, your vision will be feted to a vista of the *Baie des Anges* (Bay of Angels) and the Port of Nice.

Day Excursions

With Nice as their pivot point, four wonderful day excursions have been selected. Cannes was picked for its beaches and all the things to be found on them—such as bikinis or something even less. Marseilles, melting pot of the Mediterranean, made the list because of its flare for bouillabaisse and its Bogart background. Monaco (Monte Carlo) made it on the opposite end of the spectrum for its coastline and casino. Saint-Raphael—last, but only alphabetically—is the resort on the Riviera with "something for everyone, and at popular prices."

Arriving and Departing

By Air. Nice and its nearby Mediterranean resorts are served by the Nice Côte d'Azur Airport, four miles west of the city. The airport has a convenient

Rendezvous (meeting place) just beyond the arrival gates and a Bureau des Change (money exchange) and information desk farther into the international terminal, Terminal 1. Terminal 2 is for flights within France. If you are not certain of your transportation mode to your final destination, we suggest that you make inquiry at the airport's information desk or at one of the airline counters inside.

Bus and limousine service is available between the airport and the railway station. The bus fare is 20 francs and it departs every 30 minutes. It makes three stops between the airport and the station; the limousine goes direct. Allow about a half-hour for the bus trip and twenty minutes for the limousine.

Connections for both bus and limousine can be made in the front-left section of the airport building as you exit. Taxi service is also available in the same area of the airport. The taxi fare between the airport and the railway station is approximately 125 francs depending on the route. The trip takes about fifteen minutes. Taxi service between the airport in Nice and the resorts of Cannes and Monte Carlo is also available.

Several resort hotels offer free or reduced-rate transportation to their locations along the Riviera. Again, an inquiry at the airport's information desk will keep you advised regarding what mode to use.

By Train. Nice is a major train terminal on the Mediterranean. Express trains connect directly from there with either Milan or Paris. Direct connections between Nice and Rome are available on the Italian Railways Rapido system, and Berne is connected to Nice by express-train service requiring only a single transfer in Milan. Schedules detailing these services are given on page 449.

When arriving in Nice by train and transferring directly to the airport, the taxi service is suggested for those in a hurry. Otherwise, get the proper bus or limousine information from the transportation office just outside the station on the left. Buses depart every fifteen minutes; limousines operate on a request basis.

Nice Central Station—Gare SNCF Centrale

The exterior of the central station in Nice is deceptive. There is a lot more activity, and there are many more facilities than those you see, thanks to considerable modernization to the station's interior during the last decade. It remains smaller than most major train terminals in Europe, but it seems to function equally as well, with the one exception of ticket services, where long lines are the rule. Here again, the Eurailpass will prove to be an invaluable convenience.

If your luggage has been lost or stolen, if you missed your train, or if you need help with a handicapped or elderly passenger, don't panic. The railway

A top spot on the Riviera is the beach at Cannes Beach along the boulevard La Croisette. Beach umbrellas and other amenities, such as room service, are provided by the nearby hotels.

station provides a helpful service—the SOS Voyageurs SNCF (Travelers' SOS Service). Telephone 93.16.02.61 Monday to Friday, 0900–1200 and 1500–1800, for assistance.

Money-exchange office is outside the main station and on the right as you exit from the trains. The office is operated by Thomas Cook. From June through September, the office is open 0700–2300 daily; the remainder of the year, it operates 0800–2000 daily. The office also has the *Thomas Cook European Timetable* for sale.

The American Express (telephone 93.16.53.53) has its office at 11 Promenade des Anglais, the second bus stop en route from the railway station to the airport. During May through September, it operates Monday through Friday, 0900–1800, and Saturday, 0900–1200. It offers full services to card holders, including personal-check cashing. American Express offices are also located in Cannes, Monte Carlo, and Marseilles.

Hotel reservations are handled by the office bearing the title, OFFICE DU TOURISME ET DES CONGRES on avenue Thiers, outside the station and beyond the train administration office on the left. During the summer (July through September), the office is open daily from 0800–2000. During off-season, its operating hours are Monday through Saturday, 0800–1900, and 0800–1200 on Sunday. A nominal charge is made for giving assistance in hotel and pension reservations.

Room vacancies in Nice and throughout the Riviera are extremely hard to come by during the months of June, July, and August, as well as during the winter holiday period. If possible, reserve your accommodations well in advance by writing ahead (see page 448).

Tourist information is available in the same office where hotel reservations are handled, the Office du Tourisme on avenue Thiers. This office can provide details regarding the companies that conduct guided tours of Nice and its surroundings. A city map and a wealth of information regarding the Côte d'Azur (the Riviera) are available for the asking.

Train-information office is inside the main station on the extreme left side when exiting from the trains. It is open 0800–1830 Monday through Saturday and 0800–1130 and 1400–1730 on Sundays and holidays (tel. 93.87.50.50).

Train reservations may be made in the train information office mentioned above. The office is marked RESERVATION INFORMATION—RENSEIGNEMENTS. To make seat reservations by telephone, call 93.88.89.93.

Eurailpass validation is accomplished in the train information office. Remember, when you are having your pass validated, write out the starting date and the ending date and get the railroad clerk handling your pass to agree to the correctness of the dates before the validation information is entered on your Eurailpass.

Tourist Facilities

The Office du Tourisme (Tourist Bureau) has three offices in the city of Nice plus one in the international terminal at the airport. The one in the railway station can probably best serve all of your needs. If you need to call ahead, the number is 93.87.07.07.

If you are interested in receiving advance information describing Nice and its surroundings, you may write to: Office du Tourisme et des Congres, B.P. 79, 06302 Nice Cedex 4, France (telephone [33] 93.92.82.75; fax [33] 93.92.82.98). Enclose a large self-addressed envelope together with six International Postal Reply Coupons, which you can purchase at your post office. You will receive a city map, a list of restaurants, a list of museums, a listing of current festivities, and an illustrated folder describing Nice and its environs.

Nice offers so many attractions that, on arrival, you should check with the English-speaking telephone service by dialing 93.85.65.83. The city also operates an information booth, Nice Ferber, at the airport; telephone 93.83.32.64.

Hotel rates in Nice and the rest of the Riviera vary according to the season of the year, so be specific when requesting reservations. The most expensive time of the year comes between late March and the end of October. If you are looking for bargain rates, late October through January are the months when the rates are at their lowest.

Notes on Nice

Nice, rated as one of the most accomplished and up-to-date hostesses in the world, boasts more than 300 hotels and 200 restaurants to prove it. Most of these facilities are located in the modern section of Nice, west of the Paillon River, which divides the town in two.

To the east, the old town and port offer many attractions to those who have a feeling for the past. At 300 feet above the old town, in a public park where once a fortress stood, the views are unforgettable. Streets and houses in the old town date from the seventeenth and eighteenth centuries.

As we described in the introduction to Nice, the Marché aux Fleurs (Flower Market), one of the most beautiful and truly native sights in the old town of Nice, is held daily except Monday in the Cours Saleya, a block south of the Prefecture Palace near the opera.

There are twelve casinos within forty miles of Nice and three international ski resorts only two hours away. The world-famous Nice Carnival takes place every February. Other festive events, however, are to be found in Nice throughout the year. The King Carnival takes place just before Lent and rivals New Orleans' Mardi Gras.

From Nice . . .

TRAIN CONNECTIONS TO OTHER BASE CITIES

TO:	DEPART	ARRIVE	TRAIN NUMBER	COOK'S TABLE	NOTES
Brussels (Midi)	1840	0903+1	6708	48	
Lyon (Part-Dieu)	1002	1503	TGV 844	164	
	1518	2011	TGV 848	164	
Milan	0715	1345	1142	90	(1)
	0910	1545	343	90	
	1910	2355	349	90	
Paris (Lyon)	1002	1709	TGV 844	164	
	1518	2216	TGV 848	164	
Rome	0808	1805	365	90	
	2029	0655+1	367	90	

Daily departures unless otherwise noted. Make reservations for all departures.

(1) July 13 through August 29

Riviera landmark for more than fifty years, the Carlton Hotel on La Croisette at Cannes has housed an uncounted number of emperors, kings, millionaires, movie stars, and just plain folks who calculate that because they may never do it again, they'd better do it up grand just once! The hotel served as an officers' rest-and-rehabilitation center during World War II after the liberation of France.

From Nice . . .

A DAY EXCURSION TO CANNES
DISTANCE BY TRAIN: 19 miles (31 km)
AVERAGE TRAIN TIME: 25 minutes

Cannes has been described as a magnet that attracts the famous, the rich, and the dreamers. It also has a reputation of being impossibly expensive. No doubt this is true of La Croisette—the waterfront boulevard of Cannes lined with sandy beaches, extravagant restaurants, and elegant hotels. But this reputation does not apply to all of Cannes by any means. Cannes is a large resort with an official list of more than 5,000 hotel rooms within its city limits and that many again in its suburbs. A hundred yards or so back from the waterfront, hotels charge a fraction of the rates extracted from the famous, the rich—and the dreamers—who must live at the water's edge.

The Cannes railway station is modern and efficient. All services are grouped conveniently in or near its main hall. As you exit from the track area, you can reach the train information and reservations office via the escalator to your right. In the summer, the office is open Monday through Saturday, 0900–1230 and 1400–1830. In the winter, it is open 0900–1900 Monday through Friday. Coin-operated baggage lockers are available on the main level at either end of the station.

The Cannes tourist information office, Syndicat d'Iniative, may be reached by turning left in the main station hall, then taking the stairs located immediately outside. Elevator service is also available. Look for the sign that reads, SERVICES DU TOURISME DE LA VILLE DE CANNES, SYNDICAT D'INITIATIVE ACCUEIL DE FRANCE, SYNDICAT DES HOTELIERS.

The sign is impressive—and so is the service. The office is open daily, 0900–1900, dispensing tourist information for Cannes and its surroundings, as well as providing hotel reservation services for the area.

The city also operates a tourist information office at the Palais des Festivals on boulevard de la Croisette directly across from the Majestic Hotel. This office is open Monday through Saturday, 0900–1830. During July and August, the office is open both Saturday and Sunday, 0900–2000. A full-service American Express banking office is located at 3 boulevard de la Croisette. It operates 0900–1800 Monday through Friday.

Walking through Cannes is enjoyable and easy. Certainly no one would want to miss a stroll along the Promenade de la Croisette, one of the most beautiful and highly celebrated seaside walks on the Riviera. It borders the Bay of Cannes for about two miles until you reach its extreme eastern end at the Palm Beach Casino—with its gaming rooms and gala evenings—on place Franklin D. Roosevelt.

CANNES—*TOP OF THE RIVIERA*

A Day Excursion from Nice

DEPART FROM NICE STATION	TRAIN NUMBER	ARRIVE IN CANNES STATION	NOTES
0702	—	0743	(1)
0808	—	0847	(1)
0905	372	0931	(1)
1038	164	1104	(1)
1130	—	1209	(1)

Plus other frequent service throughout the day

DEPART FROM CANNES STATION	TRAIN NUMBER	ARRIVE IN NICE STATION	NOTES
1516	5003	1540	(1)
1708	370	1734	(1)
1800	6464	1830	(1)
1938	6173	2010	(1)
2358	6132	0025	(1)

Plus other frequent service throughout the day

(1) Daily, including holidays

Distance: 19 miles/31 km
Reference: Thomas Cook Table 164

Along your way, you will see some of the world's finest yachts berthed close by magnificent rose gardens in the Port Pierre–Canto and the famous Palais des Festivals et des Congrés, home of the International Film Festival. We also suggest walking along boulevard Du Midi to the old part of town called "Le Suquet," which overlooks the harbor and offers a marvelous view of the bay.

Except for the brief period in the late fall when the Mistral winds make things a bit uncomfortable, the climate of Cannes is wonderfully mild and temperate. Because of a few canes and reeds growing in the bay, the Romans named the spot "Castrum de Canois," and for centuries Cannes remained a small village inhabited only by fishermen.

History relates that in 1834, the Lord Chancellor of England, Lord Brougham, "whilst" en route to Nice, was prevented in reaching there due to a cholera quarantine and paused briefly in Cannes. Taken by the place, his lordship decided on the spur of the moment to build a house in Cannes and did so, straight away—the transaction in real estate taking a matter of only eight days. For the next thirty-four years, until the time of his death, Lord Brougham left the winter fogs of London for the sunshine of Cannes.

His lordship's example was quickly followed by other English aristocracy, and Cannes' population began to swell accordingly. Alluding to the eight days required to get Cannes underway, locals point out that God took only seven days to create the universe—so Cannes, necessarily, is a cut above all else in the universe.

The center of Cannes is ideal for strolling and shopping. Locals claim that you get more than what you pay for because the area has a theatrical atmosphere about it, and the show is free. Not so on the Croisette, the waterfront. Here the most elegant of shops extol the virtues of high fashion at equally high prices. Window shopping, however, is free to all who come and survey.

Excursion-boat services from the main port take you to the islands of Sainte-Marguerite and Saint-Honorat. Sainte-Marguerite's prison incarcerated the Man in the Iron Mask, and the island named after Saint Honorat has the remains of the monastery the saint started in the fourth century. Boats run daily throughout the year.

Another very delightful boat ride provides an unequaled panorama of the Mediterranean and the Alps each afternoon from June through September. This excursion departs at 1430, cruises the Bay of Cannes and the Esterel Coast, and returns at 1730. If you don't happen to be one of the millionaires with a yacht tied up in Port Pierre-Canto, now's your chance to enjoy the same exhilarating view that they enjoy—at a more reasonable price.

Marseilles' main station has plateau steps for its pedestrian approach.

From Nice ...

A DAY EXCURSION TO MARSEILLES
DISTANCE BY TRAIN: 140 miles (225 km)
AVERAGE TRAIN TIME: 2 hours, 15 minutes

Marseilles, the great port of France, is second only to Paris in population and one of the oldest surviving towns in the world. Although French in character, Marseilles is also Mediterranean but with an international flare. There is much to compare in the character of Marseilles to the contents of its epicurean delicacy, bouillabaisse, and the three ingredients so essential in its making.

Greeks, fleeing out of Asia Minor from the Persians, founded Massalia (Marseilles) in 600 B.C. Their enterprising nature disturbed the Ligurians, who came from Italy, as well as the Iberians coming from Spain, and a lot of head smashing took place until the Greeks appealed to Rome for help.

Romans came by the legions and promptly named the area a Roman province. Hannibal and his elephants created some disturbance in the province, but nothing like that brought about by 360,000 Teutonic warriors in 102 B.C. seemingly bent on destroying the civilized world and all that was in it.

Rome, again to the rescue, dispatched Caius Marius to the province; he in turn dispatched 100,000 of the Teutons near Aix-en-Provence, just north of Marseilles. This saved the day for the province and also decided the future of modern-day France. This also explains why the most popular name for men in the region yet today is Marius.

The French national anthem, *The Marseillaise,* was composed in Strasbourg by a young French military officer, Rouget de Lisle, who entitled it *Chant de Guerre de l'Armee du Rhin,* the war song of the army of the Rhine. The battle song was published and reached Marseilles just at the time when the city was giving a send-off banquet to 500 volunteers bound for Paris and the revolution. Someone sang the new song that had come from the Alsace and immediately the banquet room picked it up in chorus.

The song was an immediate success, and the volunteers sang it in unison at every stopping place en route to Paris, each time arousing the enthusiasm of their listeners. By the time they reached Paris they had become somewhat of an accomplished choir and electrified the Parisians as they marched through the streets of Paris singing the stirring words at the top of their warm, southern voices.

All the foregoing was given to set the mood for your arrival in Marseilles. Although the city is not famous as a tourist center, it is a very enjoyable place to visit. Its unusual character and mixture of peoples cannot be found anywhere else in the world.

The tourist information office is in the center of town near the harbor, about

MARSEILLES—*CITY OF INTRIGUE*

A Day Excursion from Nice

DEPART FROM NICE STATION	TRAIN NUMBER	ARRIVE IN MARSEILLES STATION	NOTES
0637	6636	0905	(1)
0825	6676	1115	(1)
0905	372	1132	(1)
1038	164	1253	(1)
1124	347	1343	(1)

DEPART FROM MARSEILLES STATION	TRAIN NUMBER	ARRIVE IN NICE STATION	NOTES
1520	6130	1755	(1)
1639	349	1905	(1)
1725	6172	2010	(1)
1842	6452	2128	(1)
2035	5001	2302	(1)

(1) Daily, including holidays

Distance:　　140 miles/225 km
Reference: Thomas Cook Table 164

a fifteen-minute walk from the rail station. The telephone number is 91.54.91.11 (fax 91.33.05.03) in case you want to call ahead. To get there, obtain directions from the train information office, which you will find on the lower level in the station. The office is open 0900–2000 daily and can also provide some tourist information, particularly in regard to walking tours of the city. A money-exchange office is located on the track level of the station and operates during July and August from 1600–2100 Monday through Friday and 0800–1700 Saturday and Sunday; the remainder of the year, hours are 0800–1800 daily.

Maison du Tourisme Marseilles (the city tourist office) is housed at No. 4 La Canebiere, just adjacent to the municipal docks. You may taxi there just by showing the driver the address. But, if it's a nice day, here's how to reach it on foot.

Leave the railway station by descending the steps shown in the picture on page 454 to street level. Directly in front is the boulevard d'Athens, a promenade from the original settlers, no doubt. Follow this street to the third traffic signal, including the one at the foot of the train-station steps. Turn to the right onto the boulevard La Canebiere, and just beyond the second traffic light now in front of you, look for the tourist office in the last building on the left-hand side of the street just before the small boat harbor. The office is open July through September, 0830–2000 daily; October through June, it's open 0900–1915 Monday through Saturday and 1000–1700 Sundays and holidays.

In the tourist information office, we suggest that you examine the brochures and other literature on hand and select from a wide variety of leisure pursuits that are offered. Not far from the tourist office, you will find the Vieux-Port and its fish market, which defies description. If you are going to tell the folks back home that you toured Marseilles, then you must visit this fish market. This is one of the few places in the world where you can obtain those three essential ingredients for bouillabaisse: red gurnet, conger eel, and a Mediterranean fish known locally as *rascasse.* Nearby restaurants serve it to perfection.

Here in the Vieux-Port, from a pier known only as the Quai des Belges (Wharf of Belgium), you may take a ferry boat for a fifteen-minute crossing to the island of Chateau d'If, made famous in *The Count of Monte Cristo* by Alexandre Dumas. The castle is an interesting place to visit, and your guide will dramatically conclude your tour by showing you the opening through which the count was said to have made his escape. The visit to the island takes about one and a half to two hours, including the tour of the dungeons where the Man in the Iron Mask and many political prisoners were imprisoned.

Monte Carlo casino overlooks the Mediterranean Sea in Monaco.

From Nice ...

A DAY EXCURSION TO MONTE CARLO
DISTANCE BY TRAIN: 9 miles (14 km)
AVERAGE TRAIN TIME: 20 minutes

The Principality of Monaco lies 4,092 miles east of Philadelphia—two cities inexorably linked by the memories of their princess, Grace Patricia Kelly, who died as the result of a tragic accident on 14 September 1982.

Monaco consists of 0.7 square miles (453 acres) of rocky coastline along the Riviera. It has been ruled by members of the Grimaldi family for the past ten centuries. Its famous gambling casino is located in Monte Carlo, one of four sections that make up the principality. The other three are Monaco-Ville itself (the capital and site of the palace), La Condamine (a commercial and residential area), and Fontvieille (a residential and light-industries section).

Monaco operates a highly efficient bus system consisting of five major lines: No. 1 (Red), No. 2 (Blue), No. 4 (Gold), No. 5 (Brown) and No. 6 (Green), which serves the Fontvieille-Larvotto (beach) area. These are augmented by Line No. 3 serving the beach area during the summer. The bus terminal is a short distance downhill from the railway station. Board bus No. 4 and ask the driver to let you off at the Office National du Tourisme (the National Tourist Office). From June 15 to the end of September, there's a small tourist information kiosk in the station lobby. Check there if you need to get your bearings before leaving the station area.

The National Tourist Office (telephone 92.16.61.16) can provide several items to help make your stay in Monaco more enjoyable. Most important is a map of the principality that shows each important landmark plus the bus system. Eating is ranked high among the many pleasurable pastimes in Monaco, so you should also ask for the *Restaurant Rates* brochure; it will help you select a dining place. The address of this office is 2, boulevard des Moulins. It is open 0900–1900 Monday through Saturday and 1000–1200 on Sunday.

French francs are the legal tender in Monaco, so there is no need to change your currency. Traveler's checks can be cashed at "Credit Lyonnais," a bank opposite the train station, 0900–1200 and 1400–1600 Monday through Friday. The American Express office is just to the west of the casino at 2, avenue de Monte Carlo.

If cracking casinos is your cup of tea, Monte Carlo's public gambling rooms open at 1000 daily. You must be twenty-one to enter. Youngsters are not barred, however, at the National Museum and Collection of Dolls and Automats of Yesteryear, located at 17, avenue Princesse Grace. It is open daily from April to September, 1000–1830; from October to March, it's open daily,

MONTE CARLO—*ROULETTE AND RELAXATION*

A Day Excursion from Nice

DEPART FROM NICE STATION	TRAIN NUMBER	ARRIVE IN MONACO STATION	NOTES
0808	364	0829	(1)
0910	343	0933	(1)
0928	6196	0946	(1)
1002	—	1026	(1)
1910	349	1926	(1)

DEPART FROM MONACO STATION	TRAIN NUMBER	ARRIVE IN NICE STATION	NOTES
1550	—	1612	(1)
1640	—	1703	(1)
1805	1180	1824	(1)
1929	340	1946	(1)
2154	6976	2207	(1)
2322	1144	2339	(1)

(1) Daily, including holidays

Distance: 9 miles/14 km
Reference: Thomas Cook Table 164

1000–1215 and 1430–1830. Admission for adults is 26 francs; for children six to fourteen and students, 15 francs.

Pomp and ceremony still prevail in Monte Carlo. The changing of the guard takes place daily in front of the Place du Palais exactly at 1155. There is no admission charge for this spectacle, but the charge for visiting the Prince's Palace State Apartments is 30 francs; children eight to fourteen pay 15 francs. Tours are conducted daily from June through September, 0930–1830, and during October, 1000–1700. One of Europe's greatest aquariums, the Musee Oceanographique, lies near the palace on the seaside. It is open 0900–1900 daily throughout the year (until 2000 June, July, and August). Admission for adults is 60 francs; for children, 30 francs.

While at the Place du Palais, you should visit the Museum of Napoleonic Souvenirs and Collections of the Palace Historic Archives. It is open between 0930 and 1830 daily from June to September, with reduced hours during the balance of the year. Adult admission is 20 francs; children eight to fourteen pay 10 francs.

Other attractions include the Wax Museum of the Princes of Monaco, the Museum of Old Monaco, and the Museum of Prehistoric Anthropology, the last featuring the Exotic Gardens and the Observatory Cave. The National Tourist Office publishes an annual list of all places of interest in Monte Carlo. The list, which provides visitors with the opening times and admission fees, is provided without charge. When you call for this list, be sure to ask for a copy of the principality's transportation brochure, *Monaco: Getting There and Getting About.* The city's "semi-pedestrianized" zone and its twelve public lifts are described in the brochure together with a map of the bus and minibus systems.

The principality now makes available at no cost to its visitors a twenty-two-page brochure describing the Principality of Monaco and explaining how it operates as an independent sovereign state. This informative publication describes, in four parts, the principality's history, its governmental institutions, its place in the international community, and its economy. We suggest that you write for this particular booklet in advance of your visit to Monte Carlo. Address your request to the Monaco Bureau address appearing on page 634 of this edition.

The grandeur of the Monaco yacht harbor is free of charge and unrivaled. No other small boat port in the world can match its beauty—or its clientele. If you are a millionaire with a yacht and don't have it moored at Monaco, you are just simply not with the program and stand a good chance of being thrown out of the club.

The harbor may be viewed from many vantage points. The view from the casino's restaurant Le Privé is impressive—expensive, too. Probably the best site (at popular prices) is a canopy-covered table at the Portofino Restaurant, which clings to the cliff just above the quai President Kennedy.

Grand Casino in Saint-Raphael offers the Monte Carlo experience on a budget.

From Nice . . .

A DAY EXCURSION TO SAINT-RAPHAEL
DISTANCE BY TRAIN: 37 miles (59 km)
AVERAGE TRAIN TIME: 50 minutes

Saint-Raphael is the Riviera resort that has something for everyone—and at popular prices. Its primary asset is its delightful weather, which is mild in the winter and moderate throughout the entire summer. Sportsmen are attracted by its eighteen-hole golf course, tennis clubs, riding academy, and well-protected bay. Its sixteen miles of coastline fringe magnificent pine forests. Nearby mountainous peaks beckon hikers, while sandy beaches and a casino fill the needs of those seeking sun and fun.

The tourist information office, Office de Tourisme, is located across the street and to the left of the main entrance to the railway station. It is identified by a white "i" sign together with TOURISME in brown letters. It is open 0830–1200 and 1400–1900 Monday through Saturday; Sunday, 0830–1200. Attendants are always eager to assist in planning your day excursion in Saint-Raphael. They can provide you with brochures describing the town and its attractions, plus a map of the area and helpful tips on local restaurants.

The fishing-boat dock in Saint-Raphael is not far from the railroad station. The tourist office can point the way. Here you will find some unusually fine local restaurants where, in the summer, you can dine at tables set under trees close to the boats. It is a relaxing atmosphere, and you will begin to feel like one of the local folks long before dessert is served.

Before leaving the railway station, check the departure schedules for trains going back to Nice. There is a train information office in the station on your right as you exit the train platform. It is open 0830–1145 and 1400–1800 daily. If you require banking services, there are several banks in the immediate area of the station. The tourist office will direct you.

Saint-Raphael has an interesting history. Its modern origins stem from the era of the Roman Empire, when it was a fashionable suburb of the Roman port of Frejus. Napoleon passed through Saint-Raphael in both victory and defeat. In 1799, the emperor and his generals disembarked there upon returning from Egypt; a pyramid standing in the town still commemorates the event. In 1814, he sailed again from Saint-Raphael, this time for Elba and exile. On April 28, as Napoleon, overcome with emotion, was saying good-bye to the soil of France, the English frigate he was to sail in fired a salute of twenty-one guns.

The site where the present town of Saint-Raphael now stands has played an exciting part in the history of the Mediterranean. Because of its natural harbor, which is deep enough to accommodate even the deepest-draught warships, the

SAINT-RAPHAEL—*"IN" PLACE ON THE RIVIERA*

A Day Excursion from Nice

DEPART FROM NICE STATION	TRAIN NUMBER	ARRIVE IN SAINT-RAPHAEL STATION	NOTES
0702	Local	0820	(1)
0905	372	0953	(1)
0945	—	1114	(1)
1038	164	1128	(1)
1124	346	1210	(1)

DEPART FROM SAINT-RAPHAEL STATION	TRAIN NUMBER	ARRIVE IN NICE STATION	NOTES
1658	6130	1755	(1)
1733	6464	1830	(1)
1820	—	1936	(1)
1931	TGV 847	2022	(1)
2035	6453	2128	(1)
2210	5001	2302	(1)

(1) Daily, including holidays

Distance: 37 miles/59 km
Reference: Thomas Cook Table 164

Romans developed it first as a holiday center. The town's casino is built over the original foundations of the Roman baths and a fish-holding tank.

Villas of the rich Romans who had come to Saint-Raphael to "take the sea air" were destroyed by Saracen pirates. By the time the pirates were driven from the area in the tenth century, the land lay deserted. It was not until sometime later that the territory began to recover under the protective surveillance of the Knights Templars.

Development was hindered by poor drainage and the diseases that accompanied this impairment. Even by the time of the eighteenth century, when fishermen and peasants began to rehabilitate the area known today in Saint-Raphael as the "old quarter," they were so weakened by marsh fever that they became known in the region as "pale faces." The introduction of drainage and improved sanitation turned the area into a pleasant land again.

Much of Saint-Raphael's modern development has been due in great part to the establishment of the cut-flower industry started there in 1880 by Alphonse Karr. Although its biggest revenues today are developed by the tourist industry, Saint-Raphael is still a large and prosperous center for cut flowers.

An excellent excursion-boat service operates from Saint-Raphael. The tourist information office will have to provide you with schedules and fares, as they are too varied to mention here. There are short cruises on the Mediterranean as well as full day excursions to many ports of call on the Riviera.

Saint-Tropez, summer home of Brigitte Bardot and one of the better "topless" beaches of France, can be reached from Saint-Raphael by bus. The trip takes one hour and twenty-five minutes in each direction, but connections can be made that allow almost seven hours of visiting and sightseeing in this quaint resort town. For complete details regarding the bus service between Saint-Raphael and Saint-Tropez, consult the rail information office in Nice or Saint-Raphael, or ask for assistance from the tourist office in Saint-Raphael. There is no rail service between Saint-Raphael and Saint-Tropez.

Saint-Raphael is an unpretentious resort. Prices, in general, are more modest here than elsewhere. Should your travel plans call for an extended stay on the Riviera with a limited budget, perhaps you—and your Eurailpass—had better stay in Saint-Raphael. There is a plenitude of inexpensive hotels and pensions concentrated there. There's nothing "cheap," however, about Saint-Raphael—it's class!

Oslo's Sentral Station, serves the city rail service throughout Norway with direct rail connections also to Sweden and Denmark.

21 OSLO

If you are a sun bather, if you love to bask in the sun, go to Oslo; but do it sometime between May and October, for that is when more sunbeams fall on Oslo than on any other capital city in Europe north of the Alps. About 12 percent of Norway's four million people live in Oslo, and soaking up the sun is *the* thing to do in town during the summer. Sauna baths, of course, become the rage for the balance of the year.

With so much good weather on hand, it is only natural that the majority of Oslo's sightseeing services concentrate their schedules into the summer months. In the period beginning with April and ending with October, a myriad of sightseeing opportunities are available to visitors. Fjord cruises of from fifty minutes to several hours are available. Likewise, there are land-and-water combinations to select from that include (among other attractions) a visit to the Kon-Tiki raft museum, a cruise on the Oslofjord, and a view from the top of the famous Holmenkollen ski jump.

The usual type of city bus tours are also available, along with a wide selection of things to be seen. There's an old adage that when the weather is nice, you will never find anyone home in Oslo. That is true. Chances are, you will find that many of the passengers on your tour bus or boat are townspeople enjoying the view along with you.

Day Excursions

When you consider that Norway is larger than the British Isles, you can readily appreciate why we deviated from our usual "Base City–Day Excursion" format for Oslo (but only in one instance). The deviation, for want of a better description, we will term an "out-and-back" excursion. It is between Oslo and Bergen, and it offers an almost limitless variety of travel modes and places to see.

Within the usual "Base City–Day Excursion" concept, we have selected a variety of daytime trips within this lovely Scandinavian country that will permit you to see the beautiful fjords, lakes, and mountains without daily packing and unpacking.

A day excursion to the towns of Larvik and Skien has been planned to take you into Norway's seacoast towns for a look at some breathtaking scenery as well as a close look at the country's ports. Hamar lies to the north of Oslo. Its day excursion affords inspection of the countryside surrounding the town and its extensive railroad museum.

The northernmost day excursion takes you to Lillehammer, site of the 1994 Winter Olympics and one of Norway's best known summer-and-winter resorts. As mentioned, the "out-and-back" excursion features Bergen and a visit to the fjord at Flam.

Arriving and Departing

By Air. Oslo is served by two airports, Fornebu and Gardermoen. Although the Norwegian Parliament decided in 1993 that Gardermoen will be the official main airport in Norway, Fornebu (only five miles southeast of the city) is expected to continue as the main airport for many years. Gardermoen, twenty-nine miles northeast of Oslo, is mainly used for charter flights.

Rail connections to Oslo are not available from either airport, but frequent airport coach and taxi service is. From Fornebu, the time en route is fifteen to twenty minutes; the fare is 30 kroner. The airport coach running between Oslo and Gardermoen takes forty to sixty minutes; the fare, 60 kroner. Public bus No. 31 provides transportation from the Fornebu Airport to the city's National Theater, a point about two blocks from the city hall, for only 5 kroner. Taxi fares from close-in Fornebu Airport are approximately 100 kroner, but this will vary according to the route and the destination. From the Gardermoen Airport, taxi fares should be negotiated with the taxi driver. All taxis are equipped with meters.

The airport coaches operating at each airport are probably the best value transportation since they offer facilities for storing suitcases and packages while en route. The coach driver *may* drop you at your hotel if it's en route into Oslo. The public bus is economical but lacks luggage racks.

By Train. Oslo has several suburban rail stations, but all international trains stop only at the Oslo Sentralstasjon (Oslo Central Station). You will see the station name frequently abbreviated as "Oslo S," and it appears as "Oslo Sentral" in the European timetable published by Thomas Cook.

Oslo Sentral is almost a city within a city. A decade or so ago, the facility was known as the East Station. It has now been transformed into one of Europe's most modern rail facilities. Situated on the eastern fringe of Oslo, it serves as a suitable "doorway" to the Norwegian capital city. Within the station, rail travelers can take advantage of a mini-market area amid a variety of kiosks (small shops) selling everything from apples to zircons.

A portion of the original East Station has been preserved as a market area. You'll find it by walking past the entrance of gate No. 19 at the south end of the new station. Nostalgia exists there. The market area stands on what was once the area devoted to steel rails, nail-spiked wooden platforms, and tiles bearing the patina of wear from countless passengers' feet as they hurried to and from the steam-hauled trains.

You will see the names of Oslo's suburban stations on occasion—National Theatre, Jernbanetorget, and Stortinget—but you should not be concerned with them unless you are commuting to the Oslo suburbs.

Oslo's Central Station—Oslo Sentral

Oslo's rail station is a model of efficiency. Access from the train platforms to the station's main hall is by ramps. Travelers may obtain baggage carts for use on the ramps. The carts are available for a 10 kroner coin from a dispensing rack. The coin is refunded if you return it to a rack when you are finished. Although the carts may be used on the ramps, they cannot be used on the station's escalators. You can, however, use the large passenger elevators located at either end of the main hall when moving from one level to another. The elevators are marked HEIS, which comes close to the word "hoist" in English.

Pictographs are found in profusion throughout Oslo Sentral. Follow them and you will find every service you might need. Baggage storage lockers are located on a balcony to the right of the station's main exit. Access to the locker area is restricted and open only between 0700 and 2300 daily. Ticket offices are on the left-hand side of the station. Domestic tickets are available from 0600 to 2300 Monday through Saturday and 0630 to 2330 Sunday. The international ticket office is located next to the domestic ticket windows and is open daily between 0630 and 2300.

Money exchange facilities are located on the mezzanine level of the station, directly across from the ticket windows. Follow the currency exchange pictographs. From June through September, the money exchange office is open daily from 0700 to 2200. During the balance of the year, the hours are 0800–2030 Monday through Friday and 0800–1400 on Saturday. When the money exchange is closed, you can change money in the station ticket office.

Normal business hours for most banks in Oslo from June through August are Monday–Friday, 0815–1500 (Thursday, 0815–1700). During the rest of the year, banking hours are Monday–Friday, 0815–1530 (Thursday 0815–1700). All banks are closed Saturday and Sunday.

Banks at Fornebu Airport operate Monday–Friday, 0630–2110; Saturday, 0730–1900; and Sunday, 0700–2100. The banks at the Gardermoen Airport are slightly different: Monday to Friday, 0600–2100; Saturday, 0600–2000; and Sunday, 0600–1830.

Hotel reservations can be made in the "Hotel Accommodations Office" next door to the money-exchange office. This service is operated by Oslo Promotion. It will make room reservations for you in hotels, pensions, and private homes. The fee for this service is 20 kroner per bed. Oslo Promotion has an exceptional track record. Few, if any, are ever turned away even though the entire town is "fully booked." Oslo is one of the few European cities where you can arrive without an advance reservation and still be reasonably certain of lodgings that night. The office is open daily from 0800 to 2300. Ask for the Oslo Package brochure. This package combines your hotel (choose from twenty-nine selected hotels) and the Oslo Card (page 471). Prices start from

Sogne Fjord brings a tranquil touch to travelers aboard the spectacular Flam railway, an unusual feat of railroad engineering.

295 kroner per person, per night, double occupancy.

Tourist information and hotel bookings for Oslo are available from an office (tel. 22–171124) located in a separate building directly in front of the main entrance to the rail station. The building is identified with the traditional green "i" with a sign, TRAFIKANTEN, posted immediately above the entrance. The hours of operation are from 0800 to 2300 daily May 1 through September 30; the remainder of the year it's open Monday through Wednesday, 0800–2300, and Thursday through Sunday, 0800–1500 and 1630–2300. During your visit, be certain to ask for *The Official Guide for Oslo* since it will aid you in seeing the various attractions in and around Oslo.

Train information is located in Oslo Sentral's main concourse area on the left-hand side just prior to the moving walkways. The office is open from Monday through Saturday between 0700 and 2300 and Sunday, 0700 to 2330. If possible, get the information you need from the regular arrival and departure digital bulletin boards installed throughout the station. Departures carry the heading AVGAENDE TOG, and arrivals are labeled ANKOMMENDE TOG. The usual system of printing departures on yellow paper and arrivals on white is not followed by the Norwegian railroads.

Train reservations and Eurailpass validation are handled at window No. 4 in the ticket office of the main lobby. The ticket windows are marked BIL-LETTER, and any of the other windows (there are six) can assist you if No. 4 happens to be closed. This office also can make sleeping-car arrangements.

Tourist facilities are described at the tourist information office at Vestbaneplassen opposite Oslo's city hall and the accommodations center in Oslo Sentral. Both sell the "Oslo Card," which provides unlimited use of city transportation, free museum admissions, sightseeing-trip reductions, and other savings.

The Oslo Card can be valid for twenty-four, forty-eight, or seventy-two hours and may be purchased at the following Norwegian kroner rates: twenty-four hours, 110; forty-eight hours, 190; seventy-two hours, 240. Children's cards are 55, 80, and 110 kroner.

Visitors desiring personal-guide services can apply at the tourist information office or call 22–427020 for reservations and tariffs. Students, taxi drivers, and couriers are not permitted to arrange paid guided tours in Oslo and the museums.

A variety of tours in and around the city are available. For details, call at the tourist information office or consult your hotel. You may book the standard sightseeing bus tours, which normally take three hours to complete, or you may want to opt for one of the more specialized tours combining bus and boat transportation. You will find them listed in *What's on in Oslo,* and *The Official Guide for Oslo.*

Oslo Options

Information describing Bygdoy and many other attractions in Oslo is available at the tourist information office at the Oslo Sentral Station or from the Norway Information Centre located directly across from Oslo City Hall at Vestbaneplassen 1. The center offers an overview of Norway, such as general information on all aspects of Norwegian life and tips on where to go and what to see. The attitude of the personnel at the center is, "If we can't tell you what you need to know, we can tell you who does and where to go to get it."

You'll find an interesting exhibition of Norwegian design and culture at the Norway Information Centre. A gallery and gift shop, a newspaper kiosk, and a restaurant serving "Norway's best food in a contemporary setting at an attractive price" are awaiting your visit.

The center is open weekdays from 0900 to 2000 (June 1–August 30) and Saturday and Sunday from 0900 to 1600 (May 1–September 30). Hours are reduced the remainder of the year; closed Saturday and Sunday from October 1 through April 30. You also can ask for information by calling (22) 83–00–50, or you can arrange for guide service by calling (22) 83–83–80. It's that easy.

We suggest that you pay a visit to Oslo's famous Vigeland Park while you are in town. Among the 193 granite and bronze statues by sculptor Gustave Vigeland, you will be able to examine *The Monolith,* the world's largest granite sculpture.

All members of the family will enjoy a visit to Akershus, a medieval castle built about the twelfth century and reconstructed as a fortress during the seventeenth century. Standing at the front of Oslo's City Hall, you can see the fort off to your left. Arkershus's military atmosphere is aided by the presence of two military museums. The Norwegian Resistance Museum chronicles Norway's struggle against the Nazis, and the Norwegian Armed Forces Museum traces the country's military history from the Vikings to World War II.

A word of caution. The fort maintains a garrison of armed sentries who patrol the grounds in dress uniform and plumed headdress. These troops also have a cannon that they fire every day (except Sunday) promptly at 1200. Don't tell anyone else in your group about this—at least not until 1205. Then, regain the confidence you may have lost by taking everyone to McDonald's for lunch. Oslo now has four such establishments. Such is the price for progress.

During your stay in Scandinavia's oldest capital—Oslo was established in 1050 by Harald Hardrade—you should plan to visit the world-famous Kon-Tiki raft, the polar vessel *Fram,* and the collection of viking ships on exhibition at Bygdoy, across the harbor from the city hall. Each vessel bears a proud history in nautical accomplishments.

From Oslo ...

TRAIN CONNECTIONS TO OTHER BASE CITIES

TO:	DEPART	ARRIVE	TRAIN NUMBER	COOK'S TABLE	NOTES
Berlin Hbf.	1015	0701+1	IN385	52	(2)
Copenhagen	1015	2015	IN385	466	
	2137	0705+1	IN381	466	
Hamburg	2137	1225+1	IN381	50	(3)
Helsinki	0820	0830+1	IN57	470/1250	(1)
Stockholm	0820	1441	IN57	470	
	1620	2241	IN59	470	

Daily departures unless otherwise noted. Make reservations for all departures.

(1) Arrives in Stockholm at 1441. Transfer to Silja Line terminal for sailing at 1800.
(2) Transfer in Malmö to train 319
(3) Transfer in Copenhagen to EC189

Bergen's Hanseatic warehouses (above) add a touch of Norwegian seafaring atmosphere to the city's architecture. Shops offer everything from ships' hardware to nautical attire. (Photo courtesy Will Haraldsen, Bergen Tourist Board.) Train to Flam and the fjord has five individual braking systems to assure a safe descent. (Staff photo)

From Oslo ...

AN "OUT-AND-BACK" EXCURSION TO BERGEN
AND THE FJORD AT FLAM
DISTANCE BY TRAIN: 293 miles (471 km)
AVERAGE TRAIN TIME: 6 hours, 40 minutes

Bergen is Norway's second largest city. It is beautifully framed by seven mountains. Two cable cars terminate at mountaintop restaurants overlooking the city. Bergen has a fish market that also has live fish, a sixteenth-century town hall, and a twelfth-century cathedral. It's the home of Edvard Grieg (1843–1907), the most distinguished Norwegian composer of the nineteenth century. The city has a 300-year-old wooden village ("Old Bergen"), a symphony orchestra founded in 1765, and the oldest performing theater in Norway. Inseparable from the sea, Bergen also has the largest aquarium in northern Europe.

Founded about 1070 by King Olaf III, Bergen grew quickly as a commercial center, and during the twelfth and thirteenth centuries, it was the capital of Norway. Built mainly of wood, the buildings were highly susceptible to fire, and the city suffered severe fires in 1702, 1855, and 1916. Bergen was badly damaged during World War II, when it was occupied by the Germans.

Bergen seems forever poised on the edge of an adventure. It's a fascinating mixture of both old and new, and the Bergenese actually seem to enjoy sharing their lovely city with you.

It has been said that a cat has nine lives. If so, this excursion has more route options than a cat has lives. The variations are such that the schedule page can only list the various means of travel options available and a few of our suggestions.

The daily train service between Oslo and Bergen has three daylight trains and one overnight train in each direction. The overnight trains haul sleeping cars between Oslo and Flam as well as Oslo and Bergen. Steamers ply between Bergen and Flam from June 1 through August 31. As a result, many interesting travel options are made available both in time and mode. Before examining some of the options, let's look at the destinations and some of the reasons for going.

Bergen is a nice place to visit because the Bergen tourist office makes you feel right at home, makes hotel reservations, changes money, and cashes traveler's checks. It is located by the harbor at Bryggen 7, telephone (55) 321480. There is a map in the station that will point the way. The tourist office is open 0830–2100 (in summer) Monday through Saturday, and it's open 1000–1900 on Sunday. Flam is the terminus of a spectacular railway—the Flamsbanen. It climbs 2,845 feet from Flam in only 12.4 miles, and between May 15 and September 30, it stops for you to take pictures.

BERGEN—AND THE FJORD AT FLAM

An "Out-and-Back" Excursion from Oslo

The numerous variations for visiting both Bergen and Flam (via Myrdal by rail and steamer from Bergen) are made possible by the following train and steamer services operated by the Norwegian State Railways. All services shown operate daily except as noted. All schedules are subject to change without notice. Schedules and reservations are available in the Bergen and Oslo Sentral stations.

TRAIN NUMBER	DEPARTS	ARRIVES	ARRIVES	NOTES
	Oslo Sentral	Myrdal	Bergen	
ET 61	0742	1228	1424	(1)(2)
ET 601	1048	1621	1833	(1)(2)
ET 63	1609	2053	2242	(1)(2)
605*	2300	0450	0721	(1)(2)(3)
	Bergen	Myrdal	Oslo Sentral	
ET 62	0733	0921	1409	(1)(2)
ET 602	1020	1220	1757	(1)(2)
ET 64	1545	1732	2221	(1)(2)
606**	2300	0105	0700	(1)(2)(3)
	Myrdal	Flam		
Flam Railway	1232	1330		
Flam Railway	1736	1836		
	Flam	Myrdal		
Flam Railway	1125	1224		
Flam Railway	1510	1605		

* 605 also conveys sleeping cars Oslo to Flam, arriving Flam 0545, except Saturday.
** 606 also conveys sleeping cars Flam to Oslo, departing Flam 0010, except Saturday.

Steamer service mid-May–mid-September: Departs Flam 1435, arrives Bergen 2035; departs Bergen 0800, arrives Flam 1320. Reservations mandatory Friday and Sunday to or from Bergen.

(1) Reservations obligatory
(2) Food service available
(3) First- and second-class sleeping cars

Distance: 293 miles/471 km
References: Thomas Cook Tables 481 and 481a

Here are some of the route options available on the Bergen-Flam "Out-and-Back" Excursion from Oslo:

Option 1: 0742 Oslo–1424 Bergen, remain overnight (RON). 1020 Bergen–1220 Myrdal. 1232 Myrdal–1330 Flam. 1510 Flam–1605 Myrdal. 1734 Myrdal–2221 Oslo. **Option 2:** Same as No. 1 to Flam, arriving 1330. 0010 Flam–0700 Oslo (sleeper). **Option 3:** 2300 Oslo–0720 Bergen (sleeper). 1545 Bergen–1732 Myrdal. 1736 Myrdal–1836 Flam. 0010 Flam–0700 Oslo (sleeper). **Option 4:** Same as No. 3 to Flam arriving 1836 (RON). 1125 Flam–1224 Myrdal. 1228 Myrdal–1757 Oslo. **Option 5:** 0742 Oslo–1424 Bergen (RON). 0800 Bergen–1350 Flam (steamer). 0010 Flam–0700 Oslo (sleeper) . . . and so it goes! Don't forget that the steamer service on the fjord between Bergen and Flam runs only from mid-May through mid-September. Options 1 and 4 do not involve the steamer services and, therefore, may be used throughout the year.

NOTES ON THE OSLO-BERGEN RAILWAY. The highest point is Taugevatn, 4,266 feet (1,301 meters), which is reached in about five hours travel time from Oslo, three hours from Bergen. The longest tunnel is Ulriken, approximately five miles (7,660 meters) in length. The total number of tunnels is about 200—they are still counting them. From the Ustaoset station westward, the railway travels above the timberline for more than sixty miles. Have your camera ready on the north (right-hand) side of the train when approaching Myrdal from Oslo. The Myrdal-Flam line and the Aurlandsfjord will come into view. Departing Myrdal for Oslo, ready your camera immediately on the left side of the train for the same spectacular view.

NOTES ON THE FLAM RAILWAY. Although it is only 12.4 miles long, the line descends 2,838 feet from Myrdal to Flam on the Aurlandsfjord, an arm of Norway's longest fjord, Sognefjord, in less than one hour. The Flam line is a fantastic feat of rail engineering with the steepest incline of all Norwegian lines, 55 percent! The line passes through twenty tunnels with a total length of 3.7 miles. The train stops several times during its trip to permit passengers to take photographs. Due to the extreme gradients, the engine and the cars of the Flam line have five separate braking systems, any one of which is able to stop the train.

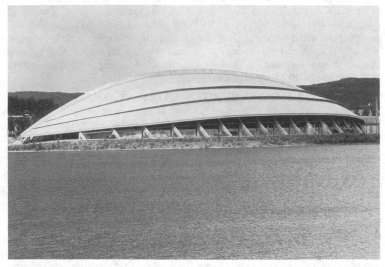

"Viking Ship," Hamar's Olympia Hall, is one of the largest sports halls in the world. It is the architectural symbol of the 1994 Winter Olympics.

From Oslo . . .

A DAY EXCURSION FROM HAMAR
DISTANCE BY TRAIN: 78 miles (126 km)
AVERAGE TRAIN TIME: 1 hour, 45 minutes

On 17 September 1976, en route to Hamar for our first time, we wrote in our notebook: "This train passes through some of God's most beautiful countryside along one of His most beautiful lakes." Nothing has changed since that visit, so please go and enjoy the trip and the city of Hamar as we have and will do again and again.

The countryside is the rich farmland of Hedemarken, and the lake is Norway's largest, Lake Mjosa. The lake is seventy-five miles long, and every foot of it is beautiful. Hamar is situated on the eastern slope of Lake Mjosa at its widest point. The train from Oslo traverses the western shore of the lake to its narrowest point, where it crosses and then continues along the eastern shore to Hamar.

Watch for the bridge that the train crosses about an hour and ten minutes out of Oslo. Station yourself on the right side of the coach for a spectacular view down the lake from the vantage point of the bridge as the train crosses.

It seems that you have hardly settled in your seat when the train glides to a stop in Hamar. Time will pass even more quickly here, for there is much to see and do in this most pleasant city. Two of its feature attractions are the Hedmark Museum and the Norwegian State Railway Museum. These are not stuffy old buildings crowded with relics. Both are spacious, outdoor areas with fascinating displays of what rural and railroad life were like in Norway's earlier times.

For complete information, check in with the tourist office, which is located to the left just outside the railway station at Parkgt.2. The tourist facility is open, mid-June to mid-August, 0800–2000 Monday through Friday, 1000–1800 on Saturday, and 1200–1800 on Sunday. During the rest of the year, the hours are 0745–1520 Monday through Friday only. The telephone number is (625) 21217.

Check with the tourist office regarding transportation to the museums. Both can be reached by public bus. If you perfer a taxi, you will find a taxi stand on your right when leaving the station. Fares by taxi to either museum are approximately 40–50 kroner one way for a maximum of four persons.

Within the Hedmark Museum boundaries are the remains of a medieval cathedral built in 1152. The ruins of the cathedral reveal that, in its day, it was one of the most magnificent churches in Scandinavia. History reveals that the town of Hamar suffered along with the demise of the stately church. Years of civil strife and the Reformation practically wiped out what was once a thriving city.

HAMAR—*HEART OF NORWAY'S LAKE COUNTRY*

A Day Excursion from Oslo (Sentral Station)

DEPART FROM OSLO SENTRAL STATION	TRAIN NUMBER	ARRIVE IN HAMAR STATION	NOTES
0805	ET 41	0940	(1)(2)(4)
0905	351	1048	(1)(3)(4)
1105	ICE 33	1240	(1)(2)(3)(4)

DEPART FROM HAMAR STATION	TRAIN NUMBER	ARRIVE IN OSLO SENTRAL STATION	NOTES
1509	352	1655	(1)(2)(4)
1715	ICE 36	1855	(1)(2)(3)(4)
2058	ET 44	2228	(1)(2)(3)(4)

(1) Daily, including holidays
(2) Seat reservations mandatory
(3) One class only
(4) Food service available

Distance: 78 miles/126 km
Reference: Thomas Cook Table 483

Special Attraction. See Lake Mjosa on an ancient paddle steamer. The *Skibladner* is the oldest paddle steamer in the world still operating. It was built in 1856. Ask the tourist office for excursion timetables and fares.

It was not until 1849 that Hamar once again enjoyed the status and charter of a town. Marking this return to status, the present Hamar Cathedral, replacing its medieval predecessor, was built in 1886.

The museum area also includes Norway's only holography museum and forty buildings from the County of Hedmark. Most of them date back to the eighteenth and nineteenth centuries. One unusual building, the house of a Norwegian emigrant, was built in North Dakota in 1871 and moved to the museum in 1973.

The Odden Restaurant on the museum grounds is open for business from mid-May to mid-September each year. From mid-June through mid-August, the museum is open from 1000 to 1800 daily. During the balance of the year, it is open 1000–1600 Monday through Friday.

The Railway Museum rivals anything the Disney folks have come up with to date. If you are a railroad buff, you'll go bananas over it. Included in its collection of rolling stock are the old royal train, several "stage coach" types, and even an old fourth-class (or shall we say, no-class) wagon—without seats.

Norway's first railway station is among the many buildings found on the seven-and-a-half acre tract covered by the museum. It is open daily May through September, 1000–1600. From October through April, it's closed on Sundays and holidays but in operation on weekdays with the same schedule.

When the Norwegian government closed the Urskog-Holand railway back in 1960, two steam locomotives and a selection of rolling stock from the narrow-gauge line were given to the railway museum together with many structures from this private railway that began operation in 1896. In addition to the two locomotives from the Urskog-Holand line, the museum now has eleven standard-gauge and four narrow-gauge engines—all in operating condition.

Hamar's railway museum is the oldest in Scandinavia, and it is also the oldest technical museum in Norway. No doubt it will still be in full operation during the Norwegian Railway Bicentennial in 2054.

Hamar is also a sporting town, and its Olympic halls can attest to that. Visit Hamar's Olympia Hall, the "Viking Ship," and the Hamar Olympic Amphi Hall, or, the "Northern Lights Hall." The Viking Ship is one of the largest sports halls in the world and the architectural symbol of the 1994 Winter Olympics. The Northern Lights Hall is the world's largest wooden building. Check with the tourist office for opening times.

Skien terminal marks the end of an exciting rail trip through Norway's fjord-and-lake country.

From Oslo . . .

A DAY EXCURSION TO LARVIK AND SKIEN
DISTANCE BY TRAIN: 120 miles (193 km)
AVERAGE TRAIN TIME: 2 hours, 50 minutes

If there's a fjord in your future, you'll probably find it on this day excursion. The greater part of that huge seaway known as the Oslofjord unfolds its grandeur as the train wends its way to Larvik and Skien. The sight of huge tankers and ocean liners miles from the ocean, plying between tree-covered mountains, is a breathtaking sight. You are certain to enjoy this outing.

As the train leaves Larvik en route to Skien, you also leave the fjords but begin to travel in an area of beautiful lakes connected by streams running through a wooded countryside. This, too, is fascinating and well worth the trip.

Because a train departs the Oslo Sentral station on the Oslo-Drammen-Larvik-Skien line every two hours throughout the day, you might consider leaving the train at any point that catches your interest and returning to board the train that follows to continue your journey. It's a nice option to take.

There is no need to seek out the local tourist information office in any of the places you elect to stop, for the train gives you an excellent preview of what each town has to offer as you approach. Basically, the route through Larvik takes you to typical Norwegian seafaring towns, and each seems to offer a different type of land and seascape. In a sense, you'll be window shopping, so be prepared to leave the train on impulse.

A summary of the cities the train passes follows. Be sure to take along a copy of the Norwegian State Railways schedule for this line in order to plan the follow-on portion of your trip as you go.

Drammen (40 km from Oslo): Important center of Norway's timber and paper industries. There are many attractive buildings in town dating back to the seventeenth century. Have your camera handy—the city covers the headwaters of the Drammensfjorden, where it joins the river, and the docks teem with seafaring activities.

Tonsberg (103 km from Oslo): The oldest town in Norway and the seat for centuries of its Viking kings. The *Oseberg* Viking ship now resting in the Oslo Viking Museum was found in a nearby burial mound. The ruins of a Viking castle overlook the town.

Sandefjord (127 km from Oslo): Home of the Norwegian whaling fleet. Regardless of your opinions about this industry, it is interesting to see the fleet being prepared for its annual autumn departure for the Antarctic. There's a whaling museum in town, and there's a spectacular whaling monument in the center of the town square. The coastline around Sandefjord is spotted with many islands and inlets, making it very photogenic.

LARVIK AND SKIEN—*FJORD COUNTRY*

A Day Excursion from Oslo (Sentral Station)

DEPART FROM OSLO SENTRAL STATION	TRAIN NUMBER	ARRIVE IN LARVIK STATION	NOTES
0909	IC 803	1124	(1)(2)(4)
1109	IC 805	1324	(1)(2)(4)

DEPART FROM OSLO SENTRAL STATION	TRAIN NUMBER	ARRIVE IN SKIEN STATION	NOTES
0909	IC 803	1205	(1)(2)(4)
1109	IC 805	1406	(1)(2)(4)

DEPART FROM SKIEN STATION	TRAIN NUMBER	ARRIVE IN OSLO SENTRAL STATION	NOTES
1542	IC 818	1851	(1)(2)(4)
1735	IC 820	2051	(1)(2)(4)
1957	ICE 86	2251	(1)(2)(3)(4)

DEPART FROM LARVIK STATION	TRAIN NUMBER	ARRIVE IN OSLO SENTRAL STATION	NOTES
1628	IC 818	1851	(1)(2)(4)
1826	IC 820	2051	(1)(2)(4)
2042	ICE 86	2251	(1)(2)(3)(4)

TO OSLO VIA NORDAGUTU (CIRCUITOUS ROUTE):

Train number IC 807 departs Larvik 1524, train 582 departs Skien 1641, arrives Nordagutu 1711. Train 587 departs Nordagutu 1850 (daily except Saturdays), arrives Skien 1920. ICE 86 (reservations required) departs Skien 1957, arrives Oslo 2251.

(1) Daily, including holidays
(2) One class only
(3) Reservations obligatory
(4) Light refreshments

Distance: 120 miles/193 km (to Skien)
Reference: Thomas Cook Table 488

Larvik (146 km from Oslo): The city has its own fjord, which connects to the Lagen River. The beautiful lake country we mentioned begins immediately beyond its city limits. An interesting museum is housed in Herregarden, a seventeenth-century manor house built for the counts of Larvik. The building is one of Norway's best preserved wooden structures. A world-famous mineral water, Farris, originates here. The spring from which the water is taken is said to be the only natural mineral-water source known to exist in Norway.

The Larvik District has published an interesting booklet describing the tourist attractions of the area. If you are interested in obtaining a copy prior to your visit to the area, you may write to: The Tourist Office, Box 200, 3251 Larvik, Norway. Otherwise, when in Larvik call at the tourist office, which you will find at Storgt. 48, across from the rail station.

Skien (193 km from Oslo): Situated where the Skien River and Lake Hjelle meet, this city has been an active trading center since the twelfth century. Sawmills were an important part of its industry. The first began here in the sixteenth century. Skien is the birthplace of Henrik Ibsen (1828–1906), famous Norwegian playwright. Ibsen's well-constructed plays dealing realistically with psychological and social problems won him recognition as the father of modern drama.

Brekke Park, which looks out over the river and town of Skien, warrants a visit. There you will find the Museum of Telemark and Grenland. (Skien is the administrative center for the District of Telemark.) In the park there are a number of old houses from different parts of the district, including a reconstruction of Ibsen's home in Oslo with his study, drawing room, and bedroom.

Rather than return to Oslo by retracing your route back through Larvik and the other coastal towns, you might want to return to Oslo via the main rail line running from Stavanger on the North Sea. To accomplish this, board train 584 that departs from Skien at 1810 to Nordagutu, where you'll arrive at 1840. Look around Nordagutu, then board Express ET74 at 2059 bound for Oslo. You will arrive in the Oslo Sentral Station promptly at 2242.

Garmo Stave Church, one of the stellar attractions of Lillehammer's open-air museum, *Maihaugen,* was moved to the museum in 1920 from its eleventh-century site in the Ottadal Valley. The museum is among the largest of its kind in northern Europe and features scores of old churches, farm houses, and displays of costumes, tapestries, silver, and glass. Jacob Weidemann's great wall painting, *May,* is displayed there.

From Oslo . . .

A DAY EXCURSION TO LILLEHAMMER
DISTANCE BY TRAIN: 114 miles (184 km)
AVERAGE TRAIN TIME: 2 hours, 35 minutes

This day excursion is one of the most northerly of any appearing in *Europe by Eurail*. In Lillehammer you will have a sense of really entering the northern reaches of Europe.

Despite its northern latitude, Lillehammer is a famous summer resort. Thanks to its latitude, it is an important winter-sports center as well. Snow conditions for skiing are good from December until April, and the long summer evenings are perfect for enjoying the town's beautiful parks and recreation areas.

If you have succumbed to the charm of Hamar, then you have already been introduced to the beauty of its Lake Mjosa. The train ride to Lillehammer will permit you to see the balance of the lake because Lillehammer lies thirty-five miles to the north of Hamar. Here, Lake Mjosa narrows to the Lagen River and, in doing so, provides a scenic blend of green forestlands and the special green color of the river. If you have ever wondered what most of the world was like before pollution, here is your answer.

In addition to its excellent sports facilities, Lillehammer has some extremely interesting things to do and places to visit. Check with the tourist information office for complete details. The office is only about a five-minute walk from the rail station, at No. 1 Lilletorget. Just follow the signs. The telephone number is 61.25.92.99; fax 61.25.65.85.

The summer hours are 0900–2100 Monday through Friday, 0900–1900 on Saturday, and 1100–1900 on Sunday. The remainder of the year, the office is open 0900–1700 Monday through Friday and 1000–1400 on Saturday; it is closed on Sunday and holidays.

Among the city's attractions, the Museum of Historical Vehicles opens its gates at 1000 daily. Just north of Lillehammer you may visit Lilleputhammer, a scale model town of sixty-two miniature houses, where kids can romp at Hunderfossen Family Park. Ask for details.

The city's stellar attraction is a one-hundred-acre open-air museum known as Maihaugen. It is within easy walking distance of the tourist information office. The office can provide you with a city map as well as several brochures describing the Maihaugen Museum. The museum area is divided into three sections. Each depicts a different mode of Norwegian life. Its origins spring from the private collection of a dentist, Dr. Anders Sandvig.

As a young dentist just out of school, Dr. Sandvig came to Lillehammer in 1885. He soon learned that many of his patients preferred to pay him in kind.

LILLEHAMMER—*NORWAY'S VACATION CENTER*

A Day Excursion from Oslo (Sentral Station)

DEPART FROM OLSO SENTRAL STATION	TRAIN NUMBER	ARRIVE IN LILLEHAMMER STATION	NOTES
0805	ET 41	1020	(1)(2)(4)
0905	Fast 351	1135	(1)(3)(4)
1105	ICE 33	1331	(1)(2)(3)(4)

DEPART FROM LILLEHAMMER STATION	TRAIN NUMBER	ARRIVE IN OSLO SENTRAL STATION	NOTES
1413	402	1655	(1)(2)(3)(4)
1630	ICE 34	1855	(1)(2)(3)(4)
1829	ICE 36	2055	(1)(2)(3)(4)
2003	302	2156	(1)(3)(4)

(1) Daily, including holidays
(2) Seat reservations mandatory
(3) One class only
(4) Food service available

Distance: 114 miles/184 km
Reference: Thomas Cook Table 483

Sometimes it was a farm implement or a piece of furniture. Dr. Sandvig's practice grew, and so did his collection. Eventually, he laid out the museum area and began filling it with old buildings, which he acquired and transported to Lillehammer. Apparently, the museum business was more rewarding than dentistry, for Dr. Sandvig retired from the profession to run the museum personally, which he did until 1946 when he died at the age of eighty-four.

The museum was founded in 1887. There are more than one hundred old buildings in the museum. In the handicrafts section are sixty workshops demonstrating skills of the local craftsmen. The museum is open from 1000 to 1600 daily. From June through August, the peak season, it remains open until 1900. One of the most interesting objects of Norway's past on exhibit in the museum is the Garmo Stave Church, which was built in the Ottadal Valley area in the eleventh century and reassembled at the museum in 1920. Another interesting exhibit is "Slowly We Conquered Our Country," Norwegian history from the Ice Age until tomorrow.

In the dock area of the city from mid-June to mid-August, you can see the *Skibladner,* a paddle-wheel steamer launched in 1856 and still in service today. Its nickname is "White Swan." True to tradition, salmon and strawberries are served on board. It is really difficult to accept the fact that the vessel is now more than 130 years old. It is in as good a condition now as the day it was launched. Some things do get better with age!

If you would like to cruise on this venerable vessel, consult the *Thomas Cook European Timetable.* The *Skibladner* plies between Lillehammer and Hamar, and between the Cook's Timetable and the Lillehammer tourist information office, you could work out an interesting excursion itinerary.

After visiting Lillehammer, if you would like to return to Oslo via a different route, board the bus to Gjovik in front of the railway station at 1725. You arrive in Gjovik at 1830. Board the train for Oslo that departs at 1950. This train returns to Oslo by a different route and arrives in the Oslo Sentral station at 2200. The train service is one-class only, but it's always clean and neat and presents no problem.

The bus fare from Lillehammer to Gjovik is 37 kroner. If you are interested in a brief stopover in Gjovik, a bus leaves Lillehammer at 1550 and arrives in Gjovik at 1655. You will then have time to do some fast sightseeing in this charming little town on the west shore of Lake Mjosa before departing on the 1950 train to Oslo.

Lillehammer was selected as the site for the 1994 Olympic Winter Games. Contact the tourist office for guided tours of the Olympic Park. The ski jumps tower, with a view of the entire town, is open 1000–2000 in the summer. Don't miss it!

Paris landmark, the Eiffel Tower, rises majestically 985 feet above the city. Built between 1887 and 1889, the tower underwent a $40-million face lifting in preparation for its one-hundredth birthday celebration, held in conjunction with the 1989 Paris World's Fair. Lightened by the removal of more than 1,000 tons of unnecessary structural members and concrete, the tower's "new look" includes all new visitor facilities on its three levels and a spectacular night lighting system that seemingly transforms the tower into one of golden lace.

490

22 PARIS

"Every traveler has two cities," wrote Edna St. Vincent Millay, "his own and Paris." Besides being one of the most beautiful and captivating cities in Europe, Paris is the center of one of the most interesting regions of France. Local people call the area around Paris the Ile de France (Island of France), for it is here that the nation began in the forested lands stretching out in all directions around Paris. The city is not only the political capital of France, it's the country's industrial and commercial center as well. To understand and appreciate it, follow the suggestion of British poet and novelist, Lawrence Durrell, watch it "quite quietly over a glass of wine in a Paris bistro."

Day Excursions

Three of the six Paris day excursions have been selected to introduce the traveler to Ile de France: Chartres, Fontainebleau, and Versailles. These places are every bit as important to what Paris is today as the Louvre, the Place de la Concorde, or the Eiffel Tower. The three remaining day excursions venture farther afield in express trains to visit Rennes, Cologne, and Rouen.

Arriving and Departing

By Air. The Charles de Gaulle Airport, seventeen miles north of the city center, is the most probable point of arrival in Paris when coming on a transatlantic flight from North America. If you have baggage, we suggest you make your way into Paris by Air France coach or taxi. Coaches run every twenty minutes between 0540 and 2300, about forty minutes en route, and the fare is 48 francs. Taxis take about the same time en route with an average fare of 180 francs. Tourist information is available from 0700–2300 (telephone 48.62.27.29). Currency exchange is open 0615–2300. The SNCF (French Rail) airport office is open 0730–2015. A new rail system here allows you to immediately board a train to Lyon, Avignon, or Nice without having to transfer to Paris.

The Orly Airport, ten miles south of Paris, also is an international airport. Again, we suggest using an Air France coach or a taxi into the city. Coaches run at twelve-minute intervals from 0530 to 2310, thirty to thirty-five minutes en route. The fare is 32 francs. Same time en route for taxis, average fare 130 francs. Tourist information is available 0600–2330 (telephone 49.75.00.90). Currency exchange is open 0630–2300. The SNCF (French Rail) office is open 0800–2000 Monday–Saturday and 1000–1300 and 1500–1830 Sundays and holidays.

By Train. Paris has six major railway stations, but arriving there by train from one of the other base cities listed in this edition of *Europe by Eurail* will place you either in Gare du Nord (North), Gare de l'Est (East), Gare de Lyon, or Gare d'Austerlitz. Details of these stations follow.

Transfers between rail stations in Paris may be made by bus, Métro, or taxi. If you have baggage, a taxi is your best bet. There are, however, interstation buses that provide baggage storage. Rule out the Métro unless you are without baggage. Suggestion: Consult the conductor on your train at least thirty minutes prior to arrival. If you are transferring between stations to continue your journey, the railroad is obliged to assist you.

Tourist Facilities

The central tourist information office in Paris, Office de Tourisme de Paris, is at 127, avenue des Champs Elysées. Its hours of operation are daily, 0900–2000. Telephone 49.52.53.54; fax 49.52.53.00. You may also consult the Galeries Lafayette travel agency at 40, boulevard Haussman, open Monday to Saturday from 0930 to 1900 (until 2100 on Thursdays). Telephone 42.85.21.20.

Branch offices in the following railway stations are open Monday through Saturday, 0800–2100, during the summer (hours vary from November through April): Gare du Nord, telephone 45.26.94.82; Gare de l'Est, telephone 46.07.17.73; Gare de Lyon, telephone 43.43.33.24; and Gare d'Austerlitz, telephone 45.84.91.70. From May to September a branch tourist office at the Eiffel Tower is open 1100–1800. Telephone 45.51.22.15.

The mainstay of transportation within Paris is its subway system, the Métro. It has thirteen main lines, several with rubber-tired coaches that sort of sneak up on you in the station. The system covers all of the city and much of its suburbs. You can reach all the railway stations in Paris via the Métro.

We recommend that you not use the Métro until you obtain a map from one of the tourist offices and receive a brief explanation of its operation. Many of the Métro stations have an illuminated map in their entrances, where, by pushing the button of your desired destination, the entire route will light up showing what line to take, in what direction, and, when necessary, where to make transfers.

The French refer to transfers as *correspondances*. Although the lines are numbered, the reference you should remember is the *direction,* which refers to the last station on the end of the line in the direction in which you are traveling. For example, Line No. 1 has two *directions:* Grande Arche de la Défense in the west, Château de Vincennes in the east. If you were visiting the Louvre and wanted to see the Place de la Concorde next, look for the direction Grande Arche de la Défense because your destination lies to the west.

At transfer points, watch for the transfer station, then disembark and look for the direction sign for the line you want to transfer to. Proceed to that platform and there determine from the line map how many stops to your destination.

Visitors may purchase a *Paris Visite* (tourist pass) valid for three or five consecutive days, which provides for first-class travel on public transportation in Paris plus discounts on some services and attractions. Prices vary according to the number of zones selected. The pass for all zones for three days is 200 francs and 275 francs for five days.

Question: Are these tourist passes of any value? Answer: If you are staying in Paris for the prescribed number of days and plan to make more than three one-way trips on the Métro or bus systems per day, the pass will definitely save you money, and the convenience gained is invaluable. These passes may be purchased in all of the main train stations in Paris, at Charles de Gaulle Airport, and at Orly Airport.

Offices of both Thomas Cook and American Express are conveniently located in Paris. Cook's is located at 8, place de l'Opéra, which has a Métro stop on both the No. 3 and No. 8 lines. It is open Monday through Saturday, 0900–1900, and Sundays, 1000–1900. American Express has four offices in Paris. The most convenient one is at 38, avenue de Wagram. The American Express offices are open 0900–1730 Monday through Friday. The one at 83 rue des Courcelles is open on Saturday, 1000–1200 and 1400–1700.

Acquaint yourself with the Paris RER, the high-speed, limited-stop rail service that runs *under*—that's right—*under* the regular Paris Métro. If you need to get somewhere in a hurry, the RER's the way to go. For example, we have ridden from Gare de Lyon to the Arc de Triomphe (the Etoile) in less than ten minutes.

The RER (Regional Express) consists of three lines. *Line A* goes west to east from St. Germain-en Laye, La Défense, the Étoile, Auber, Châtelet, Gare de Lyon, and the Marne Valley. *Line B* goes north to south from Roissy-Charles de Gaulle Airport to Gare du Nord, Châtelet, Pont St. Michel, Luxembourg, and the Chevreuse Valley. Finally, *Line C* runs from Versailles and follows the Seine through Paris to the Orly airport.

The Eurailpass is accepted on parts of the RER, but not all, so inquire at the tourist information office or any one of the major Métro stations for specific information. You may also call at the train information office alongside platform 1 in the Gare du Nord for details of the RER.

For train information in Paris, dial 45.82.50.50 and request an English-speaking operator. This service is available daily throughout the year, 0800–2000. For bus information dial 43.46.14.14; and to call a taxi, telephone 47.39.47.39, 45.85.85.85, 49.36.10.10, or 42.70.41.41. To reserve a taxi for the airport, call before 2100 the night before.

EuroDisney opened its gates in 1992. Situated twenty miles to the east of Paris, the resort has attracted millions. With the exception of its French accent, the scene shown below could be Orlando, Florida, or Anaheim, California. The Disney corporation has again excelled by bringing a quality American theme park to Europe.

The Railway Stations

Gare du Nord (North Station) is the gateway to the channel ports of Calais and Boulogne plus Belgium, Germany, and The Netherlands.

Address: 18, rue de Dunkerque, 75015 Paris. Tel. 43.95.10.00.

Money-exchange office (Thomas Cook) is located in the station concourse area at the end of tracks 14 and 15. Hours of operation: 0615–2230 daily except holidays.

Hotel reservations may be obtained in the Paris Convention and Visitors bureau opposite track 19. The charge for reservations varies. Open May to October, 0800–2100, Monday through Saturday. It closes at 2000 from November to April.

Tourist information is in the same office, Paris Convention and Visitors Bureau. This is a branch of the central tourist office located on the Champs Elysées.

Train information is displayed in digital format throughout the station. A rail information office is located at the side of track 1. It is open 0600–2300 daily, including holidays.

Train reservations, including TGV and sleeping cars, may be made in the train information office. A pictograph located between tracks 3 and 4 shows all of the principal services available in the station.

Gare de l'Est (East Station) is the gateway to eastern France, Germany, Luxembourg, and Switzerland. It is located a short distance from Gare du Nord and can be reached on foot or by the Métro.

Address: Place du 11 Novembre 1918, 75010 Paris. Tel. 40.18.20.00.

Money-exchange office (Thomas Cook) is in the main reception hall area opposite tracks 25 and 26. It is open 0645–2200 daily.

Hotel reservations are available in the branch office of the Paris Convention and Visitors Bureau in the station's main reception hall area. May through October, it's open 0800–2100 Monday through Saturday; November through April it closes at 2000.

Tourist information is available in the same office as hotel reservations.

Train information is displayed in digital format throughout the station. A rail information office is located on the left-hand side of the station coming from the trains, opposite tracks 7 and 8. It is open 0700–2100 on weekdays and 0800–2000 on Sunday.

Train reservations may be made in the train information office.

Gare de Lyon (Lyon Station) is the gateway to the Riviera, southeastern France, and western Switzerland. It is located on the right bank of the Seine, some distance south of the north and east terminals.

Address: 20, boulevard Diderot, 75012 Paris. Tel. 40.19.60.00.

Money-exchange facilities are located on the left side of Sortie 1 as you enter the station and proceed toward track A. Hours: 0630–2300 daily.

Hotel reservations can be made in the Paris Convention and Visitors Bureau located in the main ticket hall. Also, tourist information is available here. May through October it's open 0800–2100 Monday through Saturday; November through April, it closes at 2000.

Train information is displayed in digital format throughout the station. The office for train information, marked INFORMATION AND RESERVATIONS, is in the center of the station, to the left of the *Billets Grandes Lignes* area. The office is open 0800–2200 daily except on Sunday and holidays, when it operates from 0800 to 1900.

Train reservations may be made at the office marked INFORMATION AND RESERVATIONS mentioned above.

Restaurant le Train Bleu is located on the mezzanine of Gare de Lyon. Without doubt, it is the most elegant restaurant of any train station in the world. Opened in 1901, it was originally called the Buffet de la Gare de Lyon. Quickly, however, it became the fashionable place for well-heeled passengers to partake of a late supper prior to boarding the Train Bleu, the stylish sleeper that traveled between Paris and the French Riviera, and so it was renamed. The food is good, and the decor is France at the turn of the century at its opulent best: crystal chandeliers, shimmering brass, and mahogany.

Gare d'Austerlitz (Austerlitz Station) is the gateway to central and southern France as well as eastern Spain. It is located on the left bank of the Seine, a short distance from Gare de Lyon, which may be reached on foot or by the Métro.

Address: 55, quai D'Austerlitz, 75013 Paris. Tel. 45.84.14.18.

Money exchange facilities are located within the main hall of the station, close to the ticket windows. Hours of operation: 0630–2300 daily.

Hotel reservations can be made in the Paris Convention and Visitors Bureau office located in the main hall of the station. It's open 0800–1500 daily.

Tourist information. Same office as hotel reservations.

Train information is displayed in digital format throughout the station. A rail information office is located in the foyer of the station just before entering the main hall. It is open 0730–1945 Monday through Saturday.

Train reservations may be made in the train information office.

Other major railway stations in Paris include **Gare Saint-Lazare** (north and west of France) and **Gare Montparnasse** (west of France). In these railway stations, the reservation offices are open every day from 0800 to 2000 and the information offices are open from 0800 to 2030. Telephones: Central reservations office 45.82.50.50; central information office 45.65.60.60. In addition to the six major railway stations of Paris, there are six smaller or suburban-type stations.

Gare des Invalides, another station that begins underground with its trackage until well past the Eiffel Tower, is exclusive for trains running to the Palace of Versailles. **Gare Bercy** and **Gare Charolais** are two auxiliary stations serving the Gare de Lyon complex on the right bank of the Seine. On the Rive Gauche (Left Bank) side, **Gare Tolbiac** serves the Austerlitz station network, and **Gare Vaugirard** performs the same function for the extensive train trackage terminating in the Montparnasse station compound.

A system of buses connects the major Paris stations, Gare St. Lazare, Gare du Nord, Gare de l'Est, Gare de Lyon, Gare Montparnasse, and Gare d'Austerlitz. Operated privately, the system charges a fare slightly higher than that of the Métro, and it is much more convenient for passengers with suitcases than the regular city buses.

Paris Potpourri

Musts during your stay in Paris include a visit to the Louvre, where the *Mona Lisa* and *Venus de Milo* may be viewed, and a cable-car ride up to Montmartre for a view of the "City of Light" or by elevator up the Eiffel Tower to the highest point in Paris. Walk the Champs Elysées to the Arc de Triomphe, and look deep into its "flame of remembrance" for the faces of France and its allies who fought and died in the two world wars. Lunch at a sidewalk café and ride the Seine on a *bateau* (boat); get a gargoyle's point of view from high atop Notre Dame. Dine at Maxim's (if your waistline and wallet can afford it), or better still, treat yourself to a gastronomic delight for gourmets and just plain guys—the soufflé—at Le Soufflé restaurant, located directly behind the Paris Intercontinental Hotel at 36, rue du Mont Thabor. Call ahead for reservations, 42.60.27.19.

Paris has triumphed once again in the arts—this time in a museum that served the city as a train station for nearly forty years. Gare du Quai d'Orsay was inaugurated on Bastille Day, 1900. Designed by architect Victor Laloux, it included a 400-room hotel in part to serve the nearby 1900 World's Fair. By 1939, the Gare d'Orsay was obsolete, its platforms too short to accommodate the longer, electrified trains of the day. In 1971, the city of Paris reluctantly scheduled the structure for demolition, creating an uproar from its citizens equal in furor to the march on the Bastille.

The history of the Gare d'Orsay, although short in time, had made impact. Charles de Gaulle made his announcement to return to power from the hotel in 1958; Orson Wells used the station in the filming of *The Trial* (1952). Under pressure, the government reversed itself and saved both the station and the hotel, which became the Musée (museum) d'Orsay.

Boasting a glorious collection of nineteenth- and twentieth-century French painting and sculpture, the Musée d'Orsay has become one of the brightest attractions in the world of art since it opened in December 1986. The main doors of the Musée d'Orsay are at 1, rue de Bellechasse, at the entry at the Quai d'Orsay station of the RER; the Solferino stop on the Paris Métro is also nearby. In summer the museum is open every day (except Monday), 1000–1800 (closes at 2145 on Thursday and opens one hour earlier on Sunday). Winter hours are 1000–1800. The entry fee is 35 francs. It is usually most crowded on Thursday night and the weekend.

An interesting mix of something old and something new can be found at the Musée du Louvre. Its glass-pyramid entrance designed by I. M. Pei has sparked much controversy, similar to that brought about by Gustave Eiffel and his iron tower. Referred to by the writer Guy de Maupassant as the "disgraceful skeleton," the Eiffel Tower did, of course, become the city's most recognizable landmark. While you ponder Pei's pyramid, visit inside the museum. It's open daily (except Tuesday), 0900–1800 (closes at 2145 on Monday and Wednesday). The entrance fee is 35 francs.

To avoid queueing up and having to purchase a separate ticket for each museum and monument, consider purchasing the Carte Musées et Monuments, which covers entrance fees to about sixty-five museums and monuments in Paris and Ile de France. A one-day pass is 60 francs; three days, 120 francs; and five days, 170 francs. In France, you can purchase the pass at any of the museums, at over 100 Métro stations, or at the tourist information office.

The Champs-Elysées is the most famous thoroughfare in Paris, but you should also see Paris from her most beautiful avenue, the River Seine. Aboard a *bateau* (boat), sights such as The Louvre, Notre Dame, and the Eiffel Tower take on a different perspective—particularly at night when the floodlights of the *bateaux* illuminate the passing scenes. Add a meal served in the tradition of French gastronomy and you will have the best that Paris can offer! Bateaux Parisiens, situated at Port de la Bourdonnais at the foot of the Eiffel Tower, can do it *all* for you. Call ahead on 44.11.33.44 for schedules, rates, and reservations. *Bon voyage!*

From Paris . . .

TRAIN CONNECTIONS TO OTHER BASE CITIES

TO:	DEPART	ARRIVE	TRAIN NUMBER	COOK'S TABLE	NOTES
Amsterdam	0737	1402	281	18	(1)
	1020	1634	283	18	(1)
	1636	2247	287	18	(1)
Barcelona (França)	2115	0825+1	477	47	(2)
Berlin (Zoo)	2101	0858+1	243	25	(1)
Berne	1553	2022	TGV 429	42	(4)
Brussels (Midi)	0737	1049	281	18	(1)
	1129	1404	TEE 83	18	(1)
	1343	1645	EC 39	18	(1)
Dublin					
via Le Havre	1513	1805+1	3147	115/1008/647	(5)(6)
via Cherbourg	1500	1805+1	3311	120/1008/647	(5)(11)
Hamburg	0731	1711	EC 33	25	(1)(7)
	2130	0711+1	235	25	(1)(8)
Lisbon	1555	1305+1	TGV 8543	46	(12)(13)
Luxembourg	1046	1435	357	173	(1)(6)
	1716	2048	EC 53	173	
Lyon (Part-Dieu)	1000	1200	TGV 613	150	(4)(14)
	1400	1602	TGV 625	150	(4)(14)
	2000	2200	TGV 643	150	(4)(14)
Madrid (Chamartin)	2000	0832+1	TAL 409	46	(2)
Milan	0714	1445	TGV 21	44	(4)(9)
	1221	1945	TGV 23	44	(4)(10)
Munich	0747	1611	EC 65	32	(3)
	1345	2211	EC 67	32	(3)
	2230	0850+1	261	32	(3)
Nice	0730	1426	TGV 843	164	(4)
	1041	1738	TGV 845	164	(4)
	1324	2022	TGV 847	164	(4)
Rome (Termini)	1847	0945+1	EN 213	44	(4)
Vienna (Westbhf.)	0747	2105	EC 65	32	(3)
	1943	0925+1	263	32	(3)

Daily departures unless otherwise noted. Make reservations for all departures.

(1) Departs Paris Gare du Nord
(2) Departs Paris Gare d'Austerlitz
(3) Departs Paris Gare de l'Est
(4) Departs Paris Gare de Lyon
(5) Departs Paris Gare St. Lazare
(6) Daily, except Sundays
(7) Transfer in Cologne (Köln) to IC 524
(8) May 29 through September 23
(9) Transfer in Lausanne to IC 323
(10) Transfer in Lausanne to IC 335
(11) Daily, except Saturdays
(12) Departs Paris Montparnasse
(13) Transfer in Irun (Spanish border) to train 312
(14) Arrives Perrache station 10 minutes later

German gun emplacement overlooking Omaha Beach on the coast of Normandy (above) was a prime target for Allied naval guns on D-Day, June 6, 1944. The main hall of the **Caen Memorial** (below) houses an assortment of war memorabilia, but the main theme of the memorial is how war is brought about and the need for vigilance to prevent it from ever happening again.

A DAY EXCURSION TO CAEN & THE NORMANDY BEACHES
DISTANCE BY TRAIN: 148 miles (239 km)
AVERAGE TRAIN TIME: 2 hours, 20 minutes

Five decades have passed since one of the greatest battles in history took place in Normandy. At dawn on June 6, 1944, American, British, and Canadian forces, along with elements of the Free French, assailed the Normandy beaches along a broad spectrum of the coastline at five preselected landing points, Utah, Omaha, Gold, Juno, and Sword. Preceded by the drop of three airborne divisions during the predawn hours, between 0630 and 0730, 120,000 men and about 20,000 vehicles were landed from the sea. The assault upon Adolf Hitler's "Fortress Europe" had begun.

By the night of August 21, seventy-six days later, the Battle of Normandy was over. The German 7th Army had been encircled and forced to surrender. It had cost the Germans 640,000 men—killed, wounded, or taken prisoner. Allied losses were tallied at 367,000 dead or wounded. American losses were set at 127,000 casualties—31,000 of that number died in battle.

The town of Caen was the pivot of the battle and paid heavily for its part in the conflict. By the second day of the invasion, the whole of the town center had been flattened by Allied bombing. The German garrison fought fiercely. It wasn't until July 9 that the British and Canadian troops were able to take the town. The Germans, however, retreated to the right bank of the Orne River, where they continued to direct mortar fire into the ruined town. Caen was not completely liberated until August 9. The Battle of Caen lasted more than two months. Seventy-five percent of the town was destroyed.

For years following the war, Caen was one vast building site in which life was gradually beginning to return to normal. Reconstructed and restored, the town decrees that now is the time for all men of good will to be reconciled. To that purpose, the Caen Memorial has been established on the site of one of the bloodiest battles in history to take you on a compelling journey from the dark years of world wars to a vision of peace.

The memorial is unlike any other museum devoted to the theme of warfare. It employs audiovisual presentations to explain the sequence of events that led up to the outbreak of hostilities in 1939, suffering of the people involved, the preparation for the invasion, and the strategies behind it. Peace can never be taken for granted; consequently, the memorial ends its presentation with a powerful and moving film emphasizing the need for vigilance if we are to have peace in our world in our own time and in our children's.

CAEN—& *THE NORMANDY BEACHES*

A Day or Extended Excursion from Paris

DEPART FROM PARIS ST. LAZARE STATION	TRAIN NUMBER	ARRIVE IN CAEN STATION	NOTES
0655	3301	0915	(1)
0806	3933	1042	(2)
0902	3905	1125	(2)
1032	3337	1301	(3)

DEPART FROM CAEN STATION	TRAIN NUMBER	ARRIVE IN PARIS ST. LAZARE STATION	NOTES
1416	3348	1637	(6)
1529	3316	1745	(1)
1724	3960	1956	(1)
1831	136	2040	(2)
2101	3924	2324	(7)

(1) Schedule varies. Check in station.
(2) Daily
(3) Daily, except Saturday
(4) Daily to June 25 and from Sept. 6
(5) Daily July 4–Sept. 4
(6) Daily, except Sundays and holidays
(7) Sunday only

Distance: 148 miles/239 km
References: Thomas Cook Table 120

Authors' Suggestion:

Allow one day for the Caen Memorial and sightseeing in Caen—a typical day excursion. If you want to tour the landing beaches and the various museums mentioned, you may want to consider purchasing a EurailDrive Pass (any six days travel—four rail and two car—within a two-month period). Call Rail Pass Express at (800) 722–7151 to order. You must know your start date for the two-month period since the pass must be validated for that date at the time of purchase.

The Hertz office in Caen is directly across from the rail station. Reserve your first car rental on your EurailDrive Pass at least seven days prior to your departure for Europe by calling Hertz at (800) 654–3001. The EurailDrive Pass is a true bargain. We didn't have one in May 1992 and paid $174.06 to the Hertz office in Caen for a one-day rental of a Category C car!

If you prefer not to drive, check with the Bus Verts office at the side of the Caen Railway station for Bus Verts' programs for visiting the D-Day landing areas.

This day excursion is a pilgrimage that every American should make. Arriving in Caen, you can proceed directly to the memorial on city bus No. 23. It departs from the bus station outside the rail station on the right. The fare is 5 francs, the trip takes twenty minutes, and the bus stops in front of the memorial. Taxi fare from the station to the memorial is about 40 francs.

The memorial is open daily, 0900–1900 (until 2100 during June, July, and August). Tours are unaccompanied and last at least two hours. Check at the information desk for the starting times of the English language programs. A cafeteria is located on the second floor for refreshments.

Bus No. 23 stops opposite the Caen tourist information office (Office du Tourisme) en route to the station from the memorial—or you can call at the office before going to the memorial. Ask the driver to let you off at boulevard des Allies. Cross the boulevard and proceed one block to where it intersects rue St. Jean. From this point, the tourist office sign may be seen across the street to the right. The tourist office can advise on accommodations in Caen and the Normandy towns close to the beaches.

Conducted tours of the invasion beaches start in Caen and proceed west through the Anglo-Canadian sectors of Sword, Juno, and Gold before arriving in the American sectors of Omaha and Utah. With a Hertz rental car, we suggest that you proceed west from Caen on Route 13 past Bayeux, LaCambe, and Carentan until reaching Ste.-Mere-Englise, the first town in France to be liberated on D-Day, June 6, 1944. Visit the Airborne Museum with its CG4-A glider and a C-47 airplane and gaze in wonder at the 82nd Airborne paratrooper's predicament when his parachute caught on the church steeple opposite the museum.

Proceed from there to the Utah Beach Landing Museum at Ste.-Marie-Du-Mont. An audiovisual presentation explains how Utah beach was used to land about one million men on its shores. Your next stop should be Pointe-Du-Hoc, which was captured by the 2nd Ranger Battalion in a spectacular assault on June 6, 1944, scaling 100-foot cliffs to destroy a German battery of coastal guns. The Rangers made it, but they paid a high price for their valor—seventy-seven dead with an overall casualty rate of about 60 percent.

Leaving Pointe-Du-Hoc, head east to Colleville-St.-Laurent, where on a summit overlooking the Omaha landing beach you enter the American cemetery. Pay your respects to the 10,000 Americans resting there. To paraphrase Sir Winston Churchill, "This part of a foreign field shall forever be American."

En route back to Caen, stop in Bayeux at the Memorial Museum that you passed earlier while en route to Ste.-Mere-Eglise—time permitting. Otherwise, plan to return there the following day and plan to visit the Anglo-Canadian sectors as well. Take advantage of your EurailDrive Pass.

Chartres Cathedral—nonmatching spires and unmatched beauty. (Photo courtesy office de Tourisme de Chartres.)

From Paris . . .

A DAY EXCURSION TO CHARTRES
DISTANCE BY TRAIN: 55 miles (88 km)
AVERAGE TRAIN TIME: 50 minutes

Mention Chartres and anyone who has been there recalls the Cathedral of Notre Dame but not much more. This is a pity, for Chartres has many attractions that apparently are overshadowed by the cathedral to the extent that the average visitor arrives in Chartres, tours the cathedral, and then leaves. Don't be one of them, or you won't know what you are missing.

To mention a few of Chartres' "other" attractions, we start with the town itself. Beguiling, gabled houses galore line its streets. Make it a point to stroll through the old quarter of town along streets with the appealing names of rue du Soleil d'Or (Street of the Golden Sun) or rue des Ecuyers (Street of the Horsemen).

Food is another one of Chartres' attractions, so plan to dine there during your visit. There are many excellent restaurants: the one in the ancient inn of the Grand Monarque, for example, or another, the Vieille Maison (Old House). Chartres is a charming hostess. Allow her the time to entertain you.

The rail route to Chartres originates in the Montparnasse station, which serves the suburbs of Paris as well as the western part of France. There are four Métro stations (Routes 4, 6, 12, and 14) in or adjacent to the Montparnasse railway station. Consequently, it is easy to reach from other parts of the rail network. Route 4 connects directly with Gare du Nord (North Station) and the Gare de l'Est (East Station) in Paris.

Trains departing Paris for Chartres from the Montparnasse station also stop in Versailles. This station is some distance from the Palace of Versailles, however, and should not be used for that day excursion. (Consult page 522 of this edition for schedule information.) Trains running from Gare des Invalides take you directly to the palace area.

On arrival in the Chartres station, check the train departures for Paris on the posters displayed in the main hall near the ticket windows. During the summer months, the cathedral is illuminated at night. If you want to see this, check for a train departing Chartres at a time later than those shown in the schedule on the opposite page.

The cathedral is in plain view from the railway station and will draw you like a magnet. Here is how to reach it and the Chartres tourist information office, which is located in the same area. Exit the station, cross the street in the direction of the cathedral, and continue straight ahead until you come to a large square. Bear left at the square and follow the CATHEDRAL signs that you will begin to see from that point onward.

CHARTRES—*CATHEDRAL COUNTRY*

A Day Excursion from Paris

DEPART FROM PARIS MONTPARNASSE STATION	TRAIN NUMBER	ARRIVE IN CHARTRES STATION	NOTES
0700	—	0756	(4)
0856	3859	0954	(3)
0958	3759	1031	(3)
1114	—	1227	(1)

DEPART FROM CHARTRES STATION	TRAIN NUMBER	ARRIVE IN PARIS MONTPARNASSE STATION	NOTES
1404	—	1507	(1)
1525	—	1636	(2)
1645	—	1759	(1)
1937	13624	2022	(1)

(1) Daily, including holidays
(2) Monday–Friday only
(3) Daily, July 2–September 3
(4) Daily, except Saturdays

Distance: 55 miles/88 km
Reference: Thomas Cook Table 125

The tourist information office is in a building at the far end of the cathedral square. Its sign reads, OFFICE DE TOURISME. Hours vary according to the season, but it is usually open 0930–1830 Monday through Saturday. On Sunday, it is open 1000–1230 and 1430–1730. The office is open on Sunday during the winter 1030–1300. The telephone number is 37.21.50.00.

The Cathedral of Notre Dame in Chartres is said to be the most beautiful Gothic cathedral in Europe. Its stained-glass windows, the superb lines of its pillars and vaulting, and its interior are overwhelmingly beautiful. Fire destroyed the original eleventh-century building. The present cathedral was rebuilt between 1194 and 1220.

It is interesting to note that the cathedral has two nonmatching spires. The plain one of simple architecture was built first; the elaborate spire in late Gothic followed later. On Sunday afternoons at 1645 during July and August, you can enjoy the organ recitals at the cathedral. Admission to these performances is free.

The district surrounding the cathedral is noted for its medieval houses. Time permitting, you should walk down to the river for a look at the old houses and bridges close to the restored Romanesque Church of Saint André.

The tourist information office has a special walking-tour program for the Old Town incorporating the rental of a prerecorded "walkman" cassette in English. The length of the recording is sixty minutes.

The Cathedral of Chartres may be the most famous of the city's attractions. As we mentioned previously, however, there is quite a bit more to this ancient town. In addition to the Church of Saint André, there are others that warrant your inspection. The church of Saint Pierre is a Gothic masterpiece. Its stained-glass windows dating back to the fourteenth century, when added to those of the cathedral, make Chartres the metropolis of stained glass.

The Episcopal Palace, now the Museum of Fine Arts, has a lovely seventeenth-century facade in addition to its interesting contents. The exhibit includes a unique collection of harpsichords, painted wood carvings and art from Oceania, and a great deal of French, Flemish, and Italian paintings.

To assist visitors in seeing *all* of the city's attractions, Chartres has introduced *Le petit train de Chartres* (The little train of Chartres). Daily, from April through October, the "train" departs on the hour from in front of the cathedral on a thirty-five-minute tour of "Old Chartres." The first departure is at 1000; the last departure, at 1800. Adults ride for 30 francs; kids can go for only 15 francs. All aboard!

Horseshoe staircase in White Horse Court, Fontainebleau, was the backdrop for Napoleon's farewell and departure to exile on Elba.

From Paris . . .

A DAY EXCURSION TO FONTAINEBLEAU
DISTANCE BY TRAIN: 37 miles (60 km)
AVERAGE TRAIN TIME: 45 minutes

The Palace of Fontainebleau is most famous today as the residence of Napoleon Bonaparte, but the site attracted the presence of the kings of France and other royalty as far back in history as the twelfth century. For many, Fontainebleau signifies the spirit of France more so than does Versailles.

In 1169, Louis VII had the chapel of his manor at Fontainbleau consecrated by Thomas à Becket, the famous English archbishop of Canterbury. The palace that stands today probably owes more to the imagination of Francis I of France than any other of its monarchs. In 1528, he had the remains of prior centuries torn down and rebuilt; he then filled the new structure with sumptuous jewels, weapons, statues, and pictures—among them the *Mona Lisa*—as a suitable reclining place for his mistress, the Duchess d'Etampes. In 1539, with the place set in order, he received his great rival, Emperor Charles V, in the new diggings.

The fortunes of Fontainebleau slumped under the reign of Louis XIV. He was giving more attention to his new project at Versailles and his dalliances with Madame de Maintenon; but his successors, Louis XV and Louis XVI, were faithful to the palace as an autumn residence. Slowly, Versailles became the "in place" with French courtiers, and only the old retainers showed up to probe the forest surrounding the château for wild game. Fortunately, Fontainebleau survived the French Revolution much better than did Versailles and other royal residences closer to Paris. (Suburban living had its advantages even then.)

Fontainebleau has probably bedded more queens, court favorites, and royal mistresses than all other palaces in France. (Versailles had its headliners, like Pompadour and Du Barry, but Fontainebleau was more discreet.) Under the new management of Francis I, the Duchess of Etampes was granted a chamber that later became known as the "King's Staircase" when Louis XV needed freer access to her apartments. Madame de Maintenon moved to Fontainebleau under the auspices of Louis XIV in 1686 and into a room that bears her name even today.

Since the beginning of the seventeenth century, every queen of France has slept in the queen's bed chamber within the palace. Marie Antoinette ordered the bed that now graces the chamber, but because of unfortunate developments, she never had the opportunity to lay her head on its pillows.

When Napoleon Bonaparte became Emperor of France in 1804, he had Fontainebleau refurbished and refurnished to receive Pope Pius VII, who had

FONTAINEBLEAU—*PALACE OF KINGS*

A Day Excursion from Paris

DEPART FROM PARIS GARE DE LYON STATION*	ARRIVE IN FONTAINEBLEAU STATION	NOTES
0831	0909	(1)
1043	1128	(1)
1136	1213	(1)
1248	1328	(1)

Plus frequent commuter service
Trains call at Melun twelve minutes before reaching Fontainebleau.

DEPART FROM FONTAINEBLEAU STATION	ARRIVE IN PARIS GARE DE LYON STATION*	NOTES
1337	1416	(1)
1554	1654	(1)
1721	1806	(1)
1926	2017	(1)

Plus frequent commuter service
Trains call at Melun twelve minutes after leaving Fontainebleau.

* See *Thomas Cook European Timetable,* "Plans of Cities" section, for description of railway stations in Paris.

(1) Daily, including holidays

Distance: 37 miles/60 km
Reference: Thomas Cook Table 155

come to crown him as Emperor of France. From 1812 to 1814, the pope was also in residence in Fontainebleau—only this time he was not an invited guest but Napoleon's prisoner.

Not all of Napoleon's residence at Fontainebleau was surrounded with the fringe benefits befitting an emperor of his stature; he had some bad days, too. He signed his abdication in a room known now as the "Abdication Chamber" (formerly a bathroom) on 6 April 1814. Nineteen days later, he bade farewell to his officers and bodyguard in the Court of the White Horse from the horseshoe-shaped grand staircase that is now the main entrance to the palace.

Fontainebleau, unlike Versailles, possesses the secret of intimacy, no doubt due to the fact that each successive generation of kings or emperors added a wing of his own to the structure. The palace is full of nooks and crannies. There are back staircases and tapestries that pull aside to reveal secret hallways. Living in Fontainebleau, its occupants were surrounded by romance and intrigue. In a sense, it probably was the earliest version of the present "no-tell motel," but it had far more class!

The Germans used Fontainebleau as a military headquarters during World War II. Following the war, it served as a seat of the North Atlantic Treaty Organization (NATO) until 1965, when it became a public museum.

Before history consumes all the space available for this day excursion, we feel it only fair that the reader should be instructed on how to reach the palace from the railway station in Fontainebleau. Take the No. 1 bus marked "Château" from the station to the palace. The ride takes ten minutes.

The palace and its grounds are closed on Tuesday. Otherwise, the grounds are open every day from 0800 until dusk. Tours through the royal apartments are conducted 0930–1230 and 1400–1700 from April 1 through September 30. From October 1 through March 31, tours are conducted 1000–1230 and 1400–1700. There is no admission charge to the palace grounds, but tour charges are 23 francs. For information, telephone 60.71.50.70.

If you take the tour, and you should, your tour guide will lead you first through the Red Room, scene of Napoleon's abdication, then, in turn, through the Council Room, the Throne Room, and the Queen's Bedroom. From there, you pass through the Royal Apartments, then down the King's Staircase to the Oval Court, where the tour ends. It's intriguing.

The gardens and parks surrounding the palace are lovely throughout the year. You are invited to bring your own picnic lunch and spread it out on the royal grass as long as you don't litter the imperial landscape.

Wooden houses, constructed in the seventeenth century, still exist in Rennes. They can be recognized by the absence of overhangs and the quality of their construction. Facades are flat and are characterized by the extensive use of Saint Andrew's crosses and diagonal beams. They surround the "new town" of Rennes, where some of the finest untouched examples of eighteenth-century architecture add a classic touch to the city.

512

From Paris . . .

A DAY EXCURSION TO RENNES
DISTANCE BY TRAIN: 232 miles (374 km)
AVERAGE TRAIN TIME: 2 hours, 4 minutes

There's an expression that has been making the rounds of the travel trade for some time now, "Half the fun is in the going." Rennes fully qualifies as such a day excursion, since you can go there on the TGV Atlantique, the pride of the French rail fleet and holder of the world's rail speed record. Once outside of Paris and onto its special right-of-way, the TGV (*train à grande vitesse* or train of great speed) accelerates to 186 mph and you will be experiencing the finest rail travel in the world.

It's not a "seat belt" ride. It is smooth and totally enjoyable. Outbound in the morning, you can enjoy breakfast as the French countryside flashes by; inbound returning to Paris, you are in for a "Happy Hour" you'll never forget!

The only word of caution we have for riding the TGV is to be certain that you have a seat reservation. You can obtain seat reservations in Gare Montparnasse, the TGV Atlantique's home station in Paris, or at the time you purchase your Eurailpass in the U.S.

Rennes is unique in that it doesn't remind you so much of France as it does the area around Cornwall in Britain. As the cultural capital of the French province of Brittany, it has some strong ties to its Celtic origins in its architecture and gastronomy. Rennes stands at the confluence of the Ille and the Vilaine rivers. This junction of waterways came to the attention of Julius Caesar, and in 56 B.C., his legions conquered its original Celtic settlers, the Riedones. After this flurry of activity, however, things settled down for the balance of the Middle Ages.

At the beginning of the eighteenth century, Rennes still looked as it had for several hundred years—with narrow alleys and houses constructed of lath and plaster and no running water for sanitation or fire fighting. History records that in the evening of 22 December 1720, a drunken carpenter set fire to a pile of shavings, which, in turn, set fire to his house and then spread rapidly throughout much of the town, destroying a thousand or more other buildings before it burned itself out.

The part of the town destroyed by that fire was rebuilt in stone along well-ordered lines. Gabriel, architect to the French King Louis XV, then designed a new Town Hall. Thus, Rennes developed its "New Town" that stands yet today and awaits your inspection following your arrival in its ultra-modern train station designed specifically for the high-speed TGV Atlantique.

RENNES—*CAPITAL OF BRITTANY*

A Day Excursion from Paris

DEPART FROM MONTPARNASSE STATION	TRAIN NUMBER	ARRIVE IN RENNES STATION	NOTES
0725	TGV 8705	0929	(3)(4)
0820	TGV 8709	1035	(1)(4)
0920	TGV 8713	1124	(1)(4)
1120	TGV 8719	1324	(1)(4)
1420	TGV 8737	1630	(1)(4)
1520	TGV 8641	1724	(1)(4)

DEPART FROM RENNES STATION	TRAIN NUMBER	ARRIVE IN PARIS MONTPARNASSE STATION	NOTES
1304	TGV 8630	1520	(1)(4)
1514	TGV 8738	1720	(1)(4)
1603	TGV 8746	1820	(1)(4)
1714	TGV 8754	1920	(2)(4)
1818	TGV 8664	2040	(1)(4)
2008	TGV 8782	2220	(2)(4)

(1) Daily
(2) Daily, except Saturday
(3) Daily, except Sunday. Runs to July 1 and from August 29.
(4) Reservations mandatory

Distance: 232 miles/374 km
Reference: Thomas Cook Table 125

Arriving in Rennes, check in with the city's tourist information office in the rail station. It's located on the station's mezzanine level, and you will see it immediately after stepping off the escalator coming from the TGV arrival platform. On a scale of one to ten, this office gets a ten for its location, appearance, and knowledgeable staff. Operating hours are 0800–1900 Monday through Friday; Saturday and Sunday the office is open 1000–1300 and 1500–1800. Telephone 99.53.23.23; fax 99.53.82.22.

With a population of 200,000, Rennes describes itself as a youthful, well-established, and dynamic city that is striving to uphold the best interests of its citizens and the surrounding area as it moves toward the year 2000. Well equipped with prestigious theater and museum facilities and augmented with a city orchestra and the National Centre for Dramatic Art, the city plays a major role in the cultural activities of the region.

In the first week of July, during the *Tombees de la Nuit* (Summer Festival), Old Rennes is illuminated with spotlights while ballets, songs, plays, or visual arts presentations are performed. Daytime attractions include the contemporary architecture of the Law Courts, *Le Triangle,* and the cultural center. Saturday mornings are always special with the open-air market.

Evenings in Rennes are pleasant. The city is home to numerous eating places offering a wide range of local or exotic cuisine—each establishment exhibiting a character all its own. Located close to the Atlantic Ocean as well as the English Channel, Rennes offers a selection of seafood second to none. For fine seafood served in an authentic fifteenth-century house, dine at l'Auberge St. Sauveur, located at 6, rue St. Sauveur (telephone 99.79.32.56). Being a university city, Rennes is not without its places where students gather. The bars in the Rue Saint-Michel and Rue Saint-Malo attract the younger set, and there are plenty of concerts, plays, or films to keep the elders fully occupied, too.

Guided tours depart daily at 1500 and 1800 from July 1 to August 31 from the tourist information office at Pont de Nemours in the center of the city. From the rail station, take Avenue Janvier to the River Vilaine, where a left turn puts the office in view two blocks farther on. Summer hours run from 0900 to 1900 Monday through Saturday.

The TGV Atlantique service to Rennes opens up another day excursion opportunity, Mont-Saint-Michel, one of the great wonders of France. Operated by Les Courriers Breton, a special luxury bus runs between the rail station in Rennes to Mont-Saint-Michel, taking only one hour and ten minutes. The bus runs daily during the summer and Friday through Sunday only during the balance of the year. For details, check with the House of Brittany in Paris, the Tourist Information Office in Rennes, or Les Courriers Breton in Saint Malo 99.56.79.09.

Joan of Arc, patron saint of France, was burned alive by her English captors on 30 May 1431, on the site now marked by an aluminum cross in Rouen's main square. Nearby the memorial stand a covered market and a modern church dedicated to the memory of Saint Joan. The contemporary church displays the Renaissance stained-glass windows taken from an older church just prior to its destruction by bombing in 1944.

From Paris . . .

A DAY EXCURSION TO ROUEN
DISTANCE BY TRAIN: 87 miles (140 km)
AVERAGE TRAIN TIME: 1 hour, 15 minutes

Rouen was established by the Romans, who selected the site as the first point from the sea where a bridge could be built across the Seine. Rouen became the capital of Normandy at the beginning of the Christian era, and, despite many thrashings in many wars, it still contains a number of lovely churches, towers, and other reminders of its colorful past, such as half-timbered houses and town clocks. Rouen is steeped in history. During the Hundred Years' War, the city was held by the English from 1419 to 1449. Joan of Arc was burned at the stake in Rouen by the English in 1431.

Your train from Paris will arrive in Gare Rive Droite, the rail station in Rouen on the right bank of the Seine. Several hotels, restaurants, and bars are clustered about the station's plaza. The city abounds with eating and drinking establishments—even McDonald's—so finding refreshments in Rouen during your visit will be no problem.

Since there is so much to see and do in Rouen, we recommend that you proceed to the city's tourist information office with minimum delay. Their genial staff will assist you in organizing a sightseeing program. The office is five minutes away from the station by taxi; ten minutes or so on the No. 12 bus, which stops at the Palais de Justice (Palace of Justice), just two blocks away from the office. Walking—and it's downhill all the way—takes about twenty minutes. Follow Rue Jeanne d'Arc from in front of the station, turning left at Rue du Gros Horloge (Big Clock). After walking under the clock, bear right at the Cathedral plaza for a few yards to the tourist office.

The tourist office has prepared an English-language pamphlet describing a tour itinerary of approximately two hours. It starts at the tourist office and takes the visitor to the principal points of interest within the boundaries of the historical town center. The railway station appears on the map, so you need not worry about finding your way back to the station.

First stop on the tour is the city's cathedral, which stands as one of the most beautiful examples of French Gothic architecture. Construction began in the twelfth century. It was leveled by a devastating fire in 1200, however, and it was not until the fifteenth century that it began to take on its present appearance. The cast-iron spire atop the cathedral's central tower is a nineteenth-century addition. Heavily damaged during the Second World War, restoration work on the cathedral still continues.

In order to rebuild the cathedral, Rouen had to revive the medieval skills of its original creators. The cathedral's attractiveness is said to lie in the infinite

ROUEN—*JOAN OF ARC MEMORIAL*

A Day Excursion from Paris

DEPART FROM PARIS ST. LAZARE STATION	TRAIN NUMBER	ARRIVE IN ROUEN RIVE DROITE STATION	NOTES
0815	3163	0949	(2)
0915	3139	1026	(1)
1042	309	1202	(1)
1234	3141	1345	(2)

DEPART FROM ROUEN RIVE DROITE STATION	TRAIN NUMBER	ARRIVE IN PARIS ST. LAZARE STATION	NOTES
1647	308	1816	(1)
1727	13176	1858	(4)
1830	13178	2000	(3)
1948	13188	2120	(4)
2115	3156	2237	(4)
2212	3158	2327	(3)

(1) Daily
(2) Daily, except Sunday
(3) Sundays and holidays only
(4) Monday–Friday

Distance: 87 miles/140 km
Reference: Thomas Cook Table 115

variety of its architecture, and tales abound relating to these variations. The flamboyant Butter Tower, totally different from the rest of the cathedral's structures, was said to have gained its name from the fact that it was built with money paid by the faithful members of the parish for the privilege of consuming butter during Lent.

Following the tour itinerary suggested by the tourist office, the midway point of the tour will be the Palace of Justice. Three short blocks beyond, you will enter Rouen's old market area, with its narrow streets and half-timbered houses. There are more than 700 structures in Rouen illustrating the typical architecture of the city from the Middle Ages to the end of the eighteenth century. The houses were termed "half-timbered" because their external and internal walls were constructed of timber frames and the spaces between the structural members were filled with brick plaster or wattle—woven reeds covered and plastered with clay. You'll note that the upper stories of many half-timbered houses in Rouen project out over the ground level. By doing so, the lower part of the house was protected against inclement weather.

Born a peasant in 1412, Joan of Arc believed she heard celestial voices. In 1429, during the Hundred Years' War when the English were about to capture Orleans, Joan convinced Charles VII (then Dauphine of France) of her divine mission and led the French to a decisive victory. But Charles chickened out in chasing the English back across the Channel, so Joan took charge but was captured by the English at Compiegne in 1430. Subsequently, she underwent fourteen months of interrogation by her captors until burned at the stake in the Old Market Square at Rouen on 30 May 1431. The Maid of Orleans, national heroine and patron saint of France, by her valor decisively turned the Hundred Years' War in France's favor.

The place in the old market where Joan of Arc met her fate is marked by a huge cross of concrete and metal. Towering over it is a modern church, completed in 1979, its roof representing the flames of the stake. It blends masterfully into the scene against a background of black-and-white-timbered houses. The impact of history can be felt here.

Last stop on the city tour is that huge clock you may have passed under en route to the tourist office. It was positioned at ground level until 1527, when the people of Rouen asked that it be raised so they could see it better. The city council obliged by housing it in the elegant Renaissance structure you see today. The clock is unique in that it has only one hand. The globe at the top, which is no longer functioning, used to indicate the phases of the moon. Although the clock was converted to electricity in 1928, the original mechanism is still in place.

Triton and nymph statues line a broad fountain pool at the Palace of Versailles. The Hall of Mirrors is in the background.

A DAY EXCURSION TO VERSAILLES
DISTANCE BY TRAIN: 11 miles (18 km)
AVERAGE TRAIN TIME: 30 minutes

The only way to understand the powerful influence that was exerted by France during the centuries of rule by her monarchy is to visit Versailles. Here, only at Versailles, can you come to appreciate the spiritual, artistic, and political renown of France and its lineage of kings.

In 1623, Louis XIII (1601–1643) ordered a hunting lodge built on a hill named Versailles in place of a windmill that had occupied the site until then. His orders were followed immediately because there was no arguing with kings in those days. The lodge was erected. Liking the spot so well, he then ordered the lodge replaced by a grand mansion, which was completed in 1634.

His son, Louis XIV (1638–1715), the Sun King, liked the spot, too, hated the crowds in Paris with equal vigor, and envied his finance minister his fine home at Vaux le Vicomte to the extent that he came up with an order that put his dad's to shame—"Build a palace at Versailles to surpass all palaces!" Orders being orders, before long 36,000 men aided by 6,000 horses were at work building palace walls, digging lakes with canals to connect them, and transplanting a forest when the king and his gardener decided that God had planted it in the wrong place to begin with. Work continued on Versailles over a period of fifty years.

The Sun King made certain that nothing from the outside world would be imported for Versailles if it could be created or found in France. The result was an extraordinary showcase of French culture.

Urged on, first by Madame de Pompadour and then by Madame Du Barry, Louis XV (1710–1774) also ordered additions to the palace, including the Petit Trianon, which Louis XVI (1754–1793) gave to his wife, Marie Antoinette, when he came to the throne.

Despite the splendor of this edifice, Marie and her courtiers were drawn to the fantasies of a hamlet erected for her by her loving husband. There, among other rural objects, stood a dairy barn complete with cows, among which Marie and her companions would cavort—much to the consternation of the bovines, who had never observed such carefree antics before among the peasants of the land.

Versailles is an extraordinary complex of marvels where the kings of France stood in insulation against the distant horrors of the Revolution. Its restoration to the original is a marvel in itself—a testament to the inheritors of its tradition.

VERSAILLES—*CELEBRATED SITE OF FRANCE*

A Day Excursion from Paris

DEPART FROM PARIS INVALIDES STATION*	ARRIVE IN VERSAILLES STATION*	NOTES
0829	0842	(2)
0845	0915	(1)
0945	1015	(1)
1114	1127	(1)

DEPART FROM VERSAILLES STATION	ARRIVE IN PARIS INVALIDES STATION*	NOTES
1453	1507	(1)
1541	1609	(1)
1641	1709	(1)
1746	1759	(1)

* See *Thomas Cook European Timetable,* "Plans of Cities" section, for description of railway stations in Paris.

(1) Daily, including holidays
(2) Daily, except Sundays

Distance: 11 miles/18 km
References: SNCF Indicature Officiel: Ville à Ville; Thomas Cook Table 125a

Note: An alternate mode of transportation is via the RER (express metro), Line C, from Paris Austerlitz Station to Versailles Rive Gauche. Trains run every fifteen to thirty minutes from 0530–0030. Journey time via RER is thirty-seven minutes.

Depart Paris for Versailles from any station on the RER Line C in Paris. The RER Line C runs between Orly Airport and Versailles. Suggested stations are Austerlitz, Orsay, Pont St. Michel, or Invalides, the railway station close to the Hotel des Invalides, which was founded by Louis XIV to serve as a military hospital and home for veterans. Gare Invalides can be reached via Métro line 8 or 13. Get off at the "Invalides" Métro stop.

Trains for Versailles also run from the Montparnasse station, but those should not be used. The station in Versailles to which this line connects is a considerable distance from the palace. Trains running from Gare Invalides, however, take you to within easy walking distance. The trains on RER Line C running from Gare d'Austerlitz in Paris terminate in Versailles. Therefore, stay on the train until it reaches the end of the line. The main function of this station appears to be assisting visitors coming to Versailles to see the palace, and it docs an excellent job. Bilingual signs and voice announcements will assist on your arrival.

Turn right as you exit the rail station and walk about one-hundred yards to the next main intersection, the one at the traffic light. Turn left at this point and proceed to the palace, which is readily visible from the intersection.

The palace is open from May 2 to September 30 from Tuesday to Sunday, 0900–1800; it closes one hour earlier the remainder of the year. Guided tours inside the buildings and around the grounds may be taken, or you may purchase a small guidebook and conduct your own tour. Admission to the palace is 40 francs. The one-hour guided tour is an additional 23 francs.

Even with the crowds of visitors coming to Versailles on a weekend or a national holiday, it is difficult to realize how life on such a grandiose scale could take place. Let your imagination run by visualizing throngs of court favorites, courtiers, teams of prancing horses pulling royal carriages over the cobblestones of the courtyard, chambermaids scurrying about, valets rushing with the linens of the gentry, and butchers carving the roasts for the banquets under the surveillance of the king's hounds—all of this seventeenth-century tumult, cacophony, and frenzy taking place on a scale many times greater than any Cecil B. DeMille production. Perhaps then you can envision the magnitude, the grandeur, the pandemonium that was Versailles!

It is impossible to see Versailles completely in one visit—three perhaps, but nothing less than that. Consequently, set priorities (and this may sound silly) by going there the first time and just wandering around. Go back the second time and take the tour. Return the third time to see the things you missed or wanted to see again from the times before.

During your visits, remember the windmill that once stood on the hill of Versailles. Before that, there was nothing there but God's trees—the ones Louis XIV moved.

Vatican Rotunda marks the center of the Holy City within the city of Rome. A million visitors pass under this dome each year.

23 ROME

Italians refer lovingly to Rome as the "Eternal City." In the days of the Caesars, all roads led to Rome. Today, the same may be said of railroads. Rome is connected to other famous cities—Naples, Florence, and many others—by the Italian State Railways system.

No one knows exactly when people first started living along the Tiber River where Rome developed. Archaeologists continue to find evidence of still earlier civilizations than that of the Romans buried under those remains that they have already identified. Etruscans ruled the area long before the Romans. Remains of that earlier Mediterranean civilization continue to be discovered in and around Rome.

Rome has already had two periods of greatness in the civilized world, each of which has had a significant impact upon that civilization. Two thousand years ago, Rome ruled a good part of Europe and the Middle East. Rome contributed roads, architecture, art, law, literature, and political experience to the entire area.

Conquered by barbarians during the fifth century A.D., the city managed to remain the home of the popes, and through them and their armies, political power was regained. During the Renaissance, Rome again became a great center of art and learning. Since 1870, when Italian troops captured the city from Pope Pius IX, Rome has been the capital of Italy.

Readers considering "open jaw" (arrive in one European city, depart from another) air transportation to and from Europe should give serious consideration to Rome as either their entry or exit point. For example, in the spring, enter Europe through Rome and wend your way northward as the weather improves. Leave from Amsterdam. In autumn, reverse the procedure. Follow those lingering fall days southward from Amsterdam to Rome. By planning a Eurail vacation itinerary in this manner, you can assure yourself of having more moderate weather.

As a matter of fact, the average daily temperatures of Amsterdam and Rome vary by ten to twelve degrees Fahrenheit—Rome's, of course, being the higher. So, when in Rome, do as the Romans do. Move north as the mercury soars in the summer, south again when it begins to sink.

Day Excursions

When the charm of Rome begins to wane, four interesting day excursions await your visit: Anzio, scene of an Allied beachhead during World War II; Florence, one of the most prominent art centers of the world; Naples, with its world-renowned Isle of Capri; and Pisa, where the tower really tilts.

Arriving and Departing

By Air. Leonardo da Vinci Airport is twenty-two miles southwest of Rome. A new train service (Direct Link) is now available from the airport directly to Stazione Termini (Central Rail Station) in Rome. The trip takes about thirty minutes and costs 12,000 lire. There are fifteen air-conditioned trains that run daily in both directions. There is also train service, called Metropolitan Link, from the airport to Stazione Tiburtina, with stops at Ponte Galeria, Muratella, Magliana, Trastevere, Ostiense, and Tuscolana. Departures are every twenty minutes 0600–2200. The journey takes approximately forty minutes and costs 7,000 lire. You should also be aware that pickpockets love to ride the airport trains After all, where else could one find such a concentration of pocketbooks and wallets?

Here again, a word of caution: When you arrive at the railway station in Rome, beware of the many willing "helpers" eager to carry your luggage and find you a cab. If you need a taxi, carry your own bag and get in the regular taxi line. Taxis into the city from the airport? We'd caution against it unless your airline representative can arrange it and determine the fare beforehand. On the average, expect to pay at least $40, maybe more.

By Train. As mentioned previously, the central railway station in Rome is the Roma Termini. Trains for all the listed day excursions arrive at, and depart from, this station. The schedule on page 531 lists InterCity and express-train services between Rome and eleven other base cities: Amsterdam, Berne, Brussels, Budapest, Luxembourg, Lyon, Milan, Munich, Nice, Paris, and Vienna.

Rome's Rail Station—Roma Termini

Rome has several suburban stations, but the InterCity and express trains stop only in the main station—Roma Termini. The station has had some facelifting and expansion in the past several years. It is now like a city within a city. In its main concourse, the section separating the train platforms from the main hall, you will find a map of the station showing all the services available in the station and their location. It is positioned in front of the Sesante office on the Via Marsala (Marsala Street) side next to Spizzico Pizza. A bar and restaurant are located conveniently on the concourse, and on the lower level of the station you will find services you normally associate only with the most modern airports—barbershops, hairdressers, showers, and lounges.

Money-exchange facilities are located throughout the railway station. In the main concourse, there is an office just to the left of *binari* 12, between gateways 2 and 4. Hours are usually daily, 0830–1930, and 0830–1430 on holidays. In the main hall, another currency exchange is operated by the Bank of Rome. Turn left when entering the hall from the concourse and walk past all the ticket windows to the bank. The bank's hours are Monday–Friday, 0825–1335 and 1440–1600; holidays, 0825–1155; closed Saturday and Sunday. You also can change money in the Sesante office that you passed on the way to the bank. Here, the hours are 0900–1300 and 1400–1715 Monday through Saturday. On Saturdays money may also be changed at Via Marsala, No. 36.

Hotel reservations Hotel reservations can be made in the Sesante office on the Via Marsala side of the main concourse next to Spizzico Pizza. A yellow sign reads, in large letters, SESANTE, then, in small letters at the bottom, CIT. Office hours are 0900–1300 and 1400–1730 Monday through Saturday.

Tourist information regarding Rome and its province is available from the official city tourist information office, Ente Provinciale Per Turismo-Rome, located at 5 Via Parigi, telephone (06) 688991. Office hours are 0815–1915 daily; the office is closed on Sundays and holidays. To visit this office, exit the main entrance of Roma Termini, skirt the left side of the city square in front of the station, and proceed past Museo Nazionale Romano (the National Roman Museum) to Via Parigi. Turn right at that point, then look for the office on the left-hand side of the street.

If you require more extensive information about Italy and its other cities, we suggest you visit the National Tourist Office, ENIT, at 2 Via Marghera, one block east of the railway station (telephone 4971282). For tours in Rome and vicinity, the Sesante office in the main hall of the railway station will be happy to oblige.

Train information may be obtained from eight free-standing computer touch-tone screens from which you can gather schedule information for your destinations. The computers are located in front of the public telephone service area, Posto Telefonico Publico, in the main center of the station, where the ticket windows are located. Just following the i (information signs).

Train reservations can be made at ticket windows 35 through 42. The cost of the reservation varies depending on destination. To assure that you receive the proper reservation, we suggest that you first determine the day and date of your travel, the number and departure time of your train, and its arrival time at your destination. This information can be taken from any of the train schedules posted throughout the station.

Print this information on a plain piece of paper, starting with the date, the train number, and the departure time. Draw a short arrow, then add the arrival time of the train and, finally, the name of the destination. Indicate the number of reservations required, then present the information to the attendant together with the Eurailpasses you will use for the trip. Submission of this information may draw a small grin from the attendant making the reservations, but it will save time in completing the transaction.

Eurailpass validation may be made at ticket window No. 1 in the office

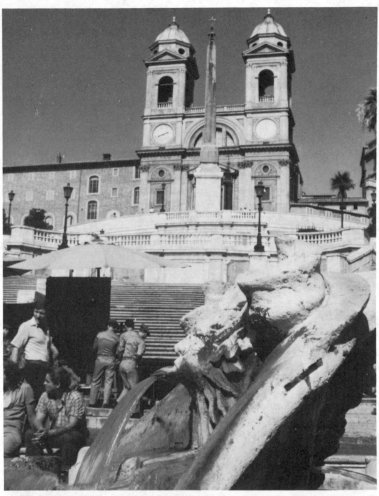

Spanish Steps in Rome were actually built with funds provided by a French Ambassador. The Barcaccia Fountain flows at their base. In May, the steps are covered with blooming azaleas.

528

marked INFORMAZIONI CAMBIO EXCHANGE FERROVIARIE CHANGE WECHSEL located in the center of the train station near the main entrance facing the bus station.

If you plan an early morning departure on the first day you use your Eurailpass, either allow an extra hour at the station that morning or inquire at one of the validating windows mid-evening the night before about the possibility of predating the validation.

Tourist Facilities

Rome abounds with tourist facilities. Every citizen seems to know the exact location of everything and seems to be eager to direct you. But Rome has more than three million citizens, and each has a different opinion regarding the best way to get there—even if it's only around the corner.

Consequently, depend on the hotel staff or the city policemen, not the man on the street, for reasonably correct information. Above all, watch out for the "cab and coin" man. He'd be more than glad to take you where you want to go but probably at three times the regular rate. The legitimate taxicab service in Rome is moderate in price and equipped with meters. Ask your hotel personnel to hail one for you or telephone. Telephone numbers to call in Rome for radio-dispatched cabs are: 3570, 4994, or 63898.

To make a telephone call in Italy, a telephone card is needed. You can buy them at any tobacco or newsstand for 2,000, 5,000 or 10,000 lire. Within the city, it costs 200 lire for the first 9 minutes. It's also possible to use 200 or 500 lire coins for calls. Except for the rail station, don't waste your time looking for a pay phone in a public area. For the most part, you'll find them only in bars and restaurants.

Cook's Travel Service has two locations in Rome. One is at 21/a Piazza Barberini. It's open 0830–1800 Monday through Saturday (telephone 4828082 or 4828083). The second office is at Via della Conciliazone and it is open 0830–1700 Monday through Saturday and 0900–1700 on Sunday (telephone 68300435). American Express has a convenient location in Rome near the Spanish Steps at 38 Piazza de Spagna. The number there is 67641. Either agency can assist in making train or hotel reservations in Rome or any other of the base cities. Both conduct excellent tours, in English, of Rome and its surroundings.

Rome is a great walking city. First, get a map from your hotel or the tourist office, then find your way to the Spanish Steps and walk down Via Condotti—with detours down some of the side streets—to the Tiber. Sightseeing musts include the Pantheon, the Coliseum, and, close by, the Forum. Set aside at least a few hours for a visit to the Sistine Chapel and St. Peter's.

Reflections on Rome

According to legend, Rome was founded by Romulus and Remus, who, in their infancy, were nursed by a wolf. Apparently there is some truth to the tale, because some Roman males still behave in a wolflike manner, particularly in the presence of a pretty foreign woman.

Going around Rome is like moving through history. Columns that looked down on the mighty Caesars, walls that saw Saint Peter and Saint Paul passing, statues sculpted by Michelangelo—these are Rome, where present-day life flourishes in the midst of monuments from past civilizations. Sights such as the Forum, the Coliseum, St. Peter's, and so many others must be seen during an initial visit and revisited on each return to Rome. (Throw a coin in the Trevi Fountain as a down payment on your return trip.)

Once more, a word of caution: When walking in Rome, keep pocketbooks, camera bags, etc. away from the curb side of the street and on a short leash. Motor-scooter thieves find them easy targets.

So vast is the city that it is essential to take some of the organized tours in order to see all of it. We recommend the tours conducted by the Sesante CIT travel service. The CIT (Compagnia Italiano Turismo) is the general passenger agent for the Italian State Railways, and its tours can be booked through most hotels and pensions.

To dine differently, try Da Meo Patacca at 30 Piazza Mercanti (telephone: 58161198)—excellent food and entertainment. For that once-in-a-lifetime splurge, dine in the rooftop restaurant of the Hassler Hotel, Rome's finest hostelry; it overlooks the Spanish Steps. The view of the city from there on a summer's evening is unmatched. Telephone 679–2651 for reservations. Ignore the cost. You only live once!

From Rome . . .

TRAIN CONNECTIONS TO OTHER BASE CITIES

TO:	DEPART	ARRIVE	TRAIN NUMBER	COOK'S TABLE	NOTES
Amsterdam	1605	1133+1	IC 544/200	39	(3)
Berne	0920	1938	EC 552/IC 336	370/280	(1)
Brussels (Midi)	1635	1048+1	1294	43	(4)
Budapest (Keleti)	1920	1328+1	234/263	88/61	(5)
Luxembourg	1635	0804+1	1294	43	(4)
Lyon (Part-Dieu)	1000	2111	IC 622	360/45	(2)
Milan	0805	1300	EC 52	370	
	0905	1400	IC 534	370	
	1105	1600	IC 536	370	
	1205	1700	EC 54	370	
	1605	2100	IC 544	370	
Munich	0725	1830	EC 84	76	
	2035	0830+1	286	76	
Nice	1225	2200	362	90	
	2330	1010+1	366	90	
Paris (Lyon)	1910	1007+1	EN 212	44	
Vienna (Süd)	0745	2046	EC 30	88	
	1920	0857+1	234	88	

Daily departures unless otherwise noted. Make reservations for all departures. Depart from Rome Termini unless otherwise noted.

(1) Transfer in Milan to IC 336
(2) Transfer in Torino Porta Nuova to train 418
(3) Transfer in Milan to train 200
(4) May 30 through September 3
(5) Transfer in Vienna (from Vienna Süd to Vienna West) to train 263, arrive in Budapest 1328+1

Peaceful harbor on Anzio's waterfront has been restored from the ruins left at the Allied beachhead in 1944. Numerous seafood restaurants rim the quay, where local fishermen unload their catch daily.

A DAY EXCURSION TO ANZIO
DISTANCE BY TRAIN: 35 miles (57 km)
AVERAGE TRAIN TIME: 1 hour

"Nothing more beautiful, nothing more agreeable, nothing more peaceful," wrote Cicero about Anzio. The Roman emperor Nero was born in Anzio. The villa where he spent his childhood and studied music still stands. Anzio's sandy beach attracted many important leaders over the centuries, which made it a VIP sanctuary, so to speak. Roman emperors such as Tiberius, Hadrian, Antoninus, and Commodus found escape from Rome and their affairs of state in Anzio.

American and British forces stormed ashore at Anzio and nearby Nettuno on 22 January 1944 to establish a beachhead, which they held until the taking of Rome on 4 June 1944. The devastated town that endured both the crossfire of the Germans and the bombardment of the Allied fleet offshore during that time has been restored completely, but row upon row of white crosses mark the graves in nearby military cemeteries, where lie 7,862 American and more than 6,000 British troops killed between Sicily and Rome. Those missing in action, 3,194 of them, "sleep in unknown graves." A visit to these cemeteries is a sobering event.

If you, like the Roman emperors, want to escape the rigors of Rome or, on the other hand, wish to pay tribute to fallen comrades, Anzio extends a warm and pleasant welcome to all.

Because of the city's proximity to Rome and frequent train connections, Eurailpass travelers might consider accommodations in the area during their visit. Anzio, together with the neighboring sea resorts stretching southward to it from Lida dei Pini, can offer a wide selection of housing amenities and accommodations. If you are interested in exploring the possibilities of such a suggestion, telephone Anzio's tourist information office on either (06) 9845–147 or 9848-135 for details and rates. For a longer stay, villas and apartments are available for rent at moderate rates.

Commuter trains depart the Roma Termini frequently for Anzio. For complete information regarding train service, check the *Partenze* (departure) information board in the main hall of Roma Termini.

Anzio is listed in the Roma-Nettuno section. It is one stop before Nettuno and the end of the line. Nettuno is where the American beachhead was established in World War II. We suggest that you inform the train conductor regarding your destination. He will be glad to alert you.

Upon arrival in Anzio, you will find directions for reaching Nettuno and the American Military Cemetery posted inside the train station; but we suggest

ANZIO—*HISTORIC BEACHHEAD*

A Day Excursion from Rome

DEPART FROM ROME TERMINI STATION	TRAIN NUMBER	ARRIVE IN ANZIO STATION	NOTES
0755	Local	0900	(1)
0955	Local	1100	(1)
1135	Local	1240	(1)
1255	Local	1400	(1)

DEPART FROM ANZIO STATION	TRAIN NUMBER	ARRIVE IN ROME TERMINI STATION	NOTES
1516	Local	1635	(1)
1608	Local	1725	(1)
1814	Local	1915	(1)
1918	Local	2020	(1)
2020	Local	2130	(1)(2)
2159	Local	2240	(1)

(1) Daily, including holidays; one class only
(2) To Rome Ostiense Station

Distance: 35 miles/57 km
Reference: Thomas Cook Table 393

that, before proceeding, you check with the Anzio tourist office and obtain the details for the bus service running between Anzio and Nettuno.

When leaving the Anzio railway station, walk downhill along the palm-lined avenue to Garibaldi Square. Then, continuing on Via Pollastrini, walk downhill to the Anzio port, where you will find the city's tourist information office to the right and on the waterfront.

Summer hours for the tourist office (June–September) are 0900–1230 and 1700–2000 Monday through Saturday. Off-season hours are 0800–1400. If the office is closed, directions will be posted on how to reach another office in Anzio where information is available.

Places to visit in Anzio are, of course, the beach area and the harbor, where the Allied forces landed. The debris of the invasion is gone, and the beach is now lined with cabanas. The beach area is interesting, particularly if you are going there to swim, for the sand is excellent and the surf, usually moderate.

The harbor holds many interesting places to investigate, too. Watercraft of all types are moored there, and the waterfront is lined with seafood restaurants to which fishermen sell their catch right from the dock.

Deciding where to have lunch can be difficult—they all look inviting. On the street side of the harbor you will find a number of smart shops with eye-catching selections of nautical clothing.

Aside from the beach and the port area, places of particular interest are Nero's Grottoes, those ancient warehouses of the port located at the northern end of the Riviera Mallozzi. Beyond Anzio's western harbor wall lie the remains and mosaics of Nero's villa, which runs from the beach up to the level of Via Fanciulla d'Anzio. It's an impressive sight.

At the foot of the Innocenzio wharf in Anzio you can examine the remains of an eighteenth-century fort, and from the wharf itself, there is a view of the gulf with the Astura Tower and Circeo visible in the distance. The monument commemorating the Allied landings in 1944 is situated nearby on the western shore.

Nettuno, a seaside town of Saracen origins, is less that three miles distant. The American Military Cemetery is located there. The two British cemeteries are in Anzio. En route to Nettuno, you'll pass the Villa Colonna on the right and the Villa Borghese, with its magnificent gardens, on the left.

Anzio's involvement with the sea is reflected in its festivals. One such festival, the "Festa del Mare" (Feast of the Sea), is held in June in honor of Saint Antony of Padua, patron saint of the town.

Facade of Il Duomo, cathedral in Florence, was erected during 1871–83 by Emilio de Fabris.

A DAY EXCURSION TO FLORENCE
DISTANCE BY TRAIN: 197 miles (317 km)
AVERAGE TRAIN TIME: 3 hours

We suggest this day excursion to Florence for the traveler on a time-compressed itinerary. It is impossible to see all the beauty of Florence in one day. A week—or a lifetime—could easily be devoted to such a pursuit. No other city in the world pays more homage to the genius of man and his ability to create and, in turn, appreciate beauty than does Florence.

Although a part of Italian history since 200 B.C., it wasn't until the turn of the eleventh century that Florence began to develop power and influence. Coincident with this growth came the development of the city's powerful guilds.

Florence was established on those banks of the Arno River spanned by the bridge of the Roman road *Via Flaminia* and where the Ponte Vecchio (old bridge) still stands today. With the single exception of Ponte Vecchio, all of the city's bridges were destroyed in 1944 during World War II. In 1966, a major flood damaged numerous art treasures in Florence, but many have been restored in succeeding years by the use of sophisticated techniques.

The tourist information office in the station concourse at the end of track 16 (in front of the pharmacy) can be helpful to those coming for the day. The first item everyone needs is a city map. They are available here. Hotel reservations can also be arranged. If the map supply has been depleted, you can either get a suitable one from the CIT (the Gray Line office) outside the station or purchase the illustrated book *Florence, Pisa and Siena* at the newsstand inside the main hall of the station. An excellent map of Florence is contained in this informative book. The tourist office is at 1R, Via Cavour. The telephone number is (55) 290832. Take a taxi there or board bus 1, 6, or 17. This office is open 0800–1915 Monday through Saturday and 0800–1330 on Sunday.

A train-reservations office and a money exchange are located inside the main station hall. The train reservations office is open every day from 0700 to 2000. The money exchange is open 0820–1920 Monday through Saturday.

You can see most of the city's highlights by walking and, when needed, by taxi. Start by walking or taking a taxi to Il Duomo (the cathedral) in the center of Florence. Here you can examine the three huge bronze doors of the Battistero (baptistery), enjoy the view from the top of the cathedral's cupola, and enter the Museo dell'Opera del Duomo (cathedral museum), where you will find the priceless Altar of Saint John the Baptist displayed.

Except on Monday when it is closed, the Galleria dell'Accademia (Academy Gallery) is next. Walk three blocks on Via Ricasoli, off Piazza

FLORENCE—*CITY OF BEAUTY*

A Day Excursion from Rome

DEPART FROM ROME TERMINI STATION	TRAIN NUMBER	ARRIVE IN FLORENCE STATION	NOTES
0725	EC 84	0918	(1)
0805	EC 52	1958	(1)
0905	IC 534	1058	(1)
1000	IC 622	1151	(1)
1105	IC 536	1258	(1)
1205	EC 54	1358	(1)

DEPART FROM FLORENCE STATION	TRAIN NUMBER	ARRIVE IN ROME TERMINI STATION	NOTES
1602	EC 55	1755	(1)
1702	IC 541	1855	(1)
1802	IC 543	1955	(1)
1902	EC 545	2055	(1)
2002	EC 53	2155	(1)
2102	IC 719	2255	(1)

(1) Daily, including holidays

Distance: 197 miles/317 km
Reference: Thomas Cook Table 370

Duomo's north side, to Piazza St. Marco. *David* by Michelangelo is displayed there. This alone may be worth your entire trip to Europe. The gallery is open weekdays (other than Monday) from 0900 to 1900; on Sunday from 0900 to 1400. Admission is 10,000 lire.

Taxi from here to Piazza della Signoria, which lies on the opposite side of the cathedral near the Arno River. (A brisk walk and some expert map reading will get you there in about twenty minutes.) This is the former center of Florence. The concentration of art treasures here is immense. The building with the tower is Palazzo della Signoria (Palace of the Lords), also known as Palazzo Vecchio (the Old Palace). Among its wealth of treasures is the little chapel of Eleonora of Toledo, with its magnificent frescoes by Bronzino (1503–1572). It is open weekdays (closed on Saturday), 0900–1900, and there is an admission fee. On Sunday, the museum is open 0800–1300.

On the south side of the square, you will see the Loggia dei Lanzi, which picked up a few other names, such as "Loggia dei Priori" and "Loggia della Signoria," since it was built in 1376. Statuary such as *Hercules and the Centaur* (1599) and *Rape of the Sabine Women* (1583), both by Giambologna, surround Cellini's *Perseus* (1545).

The Galleria degli Uffizi (Office Gallery) is, in fact, a converted office containing the priceless works of art acquired by the Medici family. Located on the right flank of Palazzo della Signoria, it has forty-five exhibit rooms. Its vast collection includes the ancient sculpture *Medici Venus* from 300 B.C., Leonardo da Vinci's *Adoration of the Magi,* and Michelangelo's *Holy Family,* plus an entire roomful of Rembrandts. It is open 0900–1900 on weekdays, except Monday, and 0900–1400 on Sunday. Admission is 10,000 lire.

This concludes your "quick" tour of the world famous "City of Art, Florence," and it's time to taxi back to the rail station for the train back to Rome—unless, of course, you have succumbed to Florence's charms. It's a difficult decision to make. If you are still ambulatory, the walk back to the station will take about twenty minutes.

Aside from its buildings, art galleries, museums, and parks, Florence has had an interesting and rather hectic development as a municipality and seat of government. It was ruled by the Medici family until 1737, when the family died out and its leadership was assumed by Grand Duke Ferdinand III (1769–1824). Driven out by the French in 1799, the duke made several abortive attempts to resume power. He wasn't successful, however, until 1814.

Ferdinand's successor, Leopold II (1797–1870), held on until he was expelled in 1849. Florence was the capital of Italy under King Victor Emmanuel from 1865 to 1871, when the seat of government became Rome.

Patriot Giuseppe Garibaldi's statue stands in Naples's central square, Piazza Garibaldi, facing the central railway station.

A DAY EXCURSION TO NAPLES
DISTANCE BY TRAIN: 134 miles (216 km)
AVERAGE TRAIN TIME: 2 hours

In the true sense of the expression, Naples is a world apart. There is no other place in Italy quite like it. In fact, there's no place that we have visited in the rest of the world quite like Naples. When you go there, you don't really see Naples—you feel it, hear it, taste it. After you've been to Naples, you come away either loving it—or hating it. You alone must be the judge.

Naples itself is a coalescing of gaiety and sadness. Its inhabitants, the Neapolitans, are expressive, noisy, and vivacious. They are imaginative, superstitious, and (about a third of them) unemployed, either by choice or by circumstance—it's difficult to determine which. But as a consequence, crime is rampant, so watch your wallets, pocketbooks, cameras, and such. To be more concise, don't take anything to Naples that you can't afford to leave there.

Don't go to Naples in fear of your life; just be cautious. The Neapolitans don't want to harm you; they are only interested in your valuables. They want you to enjoy yourself and come back again—with more valuables. Deal only with official agencies. If you plan to take a city tour or sign up for a trip to Vesuvius and Pompeii, do it in an office, not on the street. Ignore the uniformed gentlemen that approach you on the street or in the rail station wearing badges proclaiming they are "official guides." There are several small shops on the square facing the station where you can buy such a badge, too.

Now for the fun part. Spaghetti was invented in Naples, as well as Neapolitan-style ice cream. Pizza first saw the light of day in Naples. If you can, enjoy a pizza in one of the pizzerias located in the old quarter of Naples. If you do, you'll probably not patronize your local pizza parlor for at least thirty days following your return home. The Neapolitan version of a Cajun fish-fry, *frittura di pesci,* is also well worth sampling. So much for tasting Naples.

You can't avoid hearing Naples. The musical style of *Bel Canto* is exclusively that of the Neapolitans. *Santa Lucia, Funiculi-Funicula,* and *O Sole Mio!* are but part of the repertory you will hear being played by hurdy-gurdies, all of it mixed in with the constant background noise of the crowded streets. Dray animals such as mules wear bells so that their presence can be acknowledged in the crowd.

If you haven't developed a feel for Naples after exposure to some or all of the above, you should take an early train back to Rome.

The railway-station complex in Naples can become downright confusing. You will find the Napoli Centrale and Napoli Piazza Garibaldi terminals side

NAPLES—*CITY BY THE BAY*

A Day Excursion from Rome

DEPART FROM ROME TERMINI STATION	TRAIN NUMBER	ARRIVE IN NAPLES STATION	NOTES
0710	IC 741	0907(2)	(6)
0720	D 2385	0953(5)	(6)
0810	IC 691	1000(2)	(3)(6)
0915	E 973	1126(5)	(3)(6)
1010	IC 743	1200(5)	(1)(3)

DEPART FROM NAPLES STATION	TRAIN NUMBER	ARRIVE IN ROME TERMINI STATION	NOTES
1457(5)	IC 546	1650	(3)(6)
1557(5)	IC 554	1750	(3)(6)
1657(5)	IC 694	1850	(3)(6)
1853(2)	IC 756	2050	(6)
1957(5)	IC 700	2150	(3)(6)

(1) Daily, except Sundays and holidays
(2) Piazza Garibaldi Station
(3) Food service available
(4) Centrale Station
(5) Mergellina Station
(6) Daily, including holidays

Distance: 134 miles/216 km
Reference: Thomas Cook Table 405

by side in the city center and flanked by the two narrow-gauge railway stations serving the Circumvesuviana Line from Naples to Pompeii and Sorrento. To minimize the confusion, we are recommending the exclusive use of Naples's Mergellina Station, which is located in its suburbs. Each train shown on the accompanying schedule to Naples makes its first stop at the Mergellina Station.

If you bypass or overshoot the Mergellina Station and end up in the city center, take the subway from platform No. 4 under Piazza Garibaldi for a four-stop ride to Mergellina. Your Eurailpass is accepted on the subway system. Complete tourist facilities are found at the Mergellina Station. Money-exchange services, train information, and food services are all housed within the terminal. A train-information-and-reservations office is located in the Napoli Centrale station. It's open daily, 0700–2115.

The *official* city tourist information office is located at the bottom of the stairs descending from the train platforms and to your immediate right. The telephone number is (081) 405311. Detailed information, including maps and tour information on Naples and its surrounding areas, can be obtained there. The office is open 0900–1900 Monday through Saturday. Naples's main youth hostel is located immediately behind the Mergellina Station. Trolley lines 1 and 2, which serve most of the metropolitan area, run close by; but the trolleys are operated by the city, so Eurailpasses are not honored.

Naples, a city with a population well over one million, is just large enough so that unguided sightseeing can become difficult. Several reputable tour operators provide excellent service. The CIMA city tour is one we can recommend. It departs the CIMA office at 114 Piazza Garibaldi at 1425 daily. This office is located two and a half blocks from the main railway station on the left side of the square.

CIMA conducts tours to Vesuvius and Capri with departure times late enough in the day to ensure connections with trains out of Rome. The tour to Capri departs daily at 1000. We suggest that to ensure connections, you make arrangements with CIMA a day in advance.

Local trains leave the Napoli Circumvesuviana railway station for Pompeii and Sorrento. To reach this station, walk in the direction of the Garibaldi statue in the center of Piazza Garibaldi. Just before reaching the statue, turn left on Corso Garibaldi and proceed to the station, which is close by. The train time from Naples to Pompeii averages about twenty-five minutes. To Sorrento, the average time is sixty minutes. Pompeii is fifteen miles from Naples; Sorrento is twenty-eight. A complete schedule of the Napoli-Sorrento rail service appears in Table 406 of the *Thomas Cook European Timetable.* Eurailpass is not accepted on this line.

Leaning Tower declination is most noticeable when compared to the cathedral standing close by in the Square of Miracles in Pisa.

From Rome . . .

A DAY EXCURSION TO PISA
DISTANCE BY TRAIN: 208 miles (335 km)
AVERAGE TRAIN TIME: 3 hours

Many consider Pisa to be the most beautiful city in Italy. We do not contest that opinion. The town possesses one of the loveliest architectural groupings in Europe. Known either as the Square of the Miracles or the Piazza del Duomo (Cathedral Square), it contains, in addition to the famous Leaning Tower and the cathedral, the Baptistery and the Campo Santo (the burial ground), each in its own stead a masterpiece of sculpture and architecture.

If you have never been to Pisa and actually stood and looked at the Leaning Tower—you are in for the surprise of your life when you do. Any photograph, painting, or motion picture you may have seen of the tower prior to your personal encounter is immediately stripped from your mind. It's no optical illusion—it *really* leans.

After arriving in Pisa, ride bus No. 1 from the station plaza to Piazza dei Miracoli (Square of the Miracles). Dismount from the bus on the southern end of the square—the direction in which the tower is leaning. You will have no doubt whatsoever that: (1) the tower leans; (2) it's leaning in your direction; and (3) you had better get out of its way before it leans too far and topples on you. No other work of art provokes the instinct of self-preservation like this one. You can spend hours gazing at it, but there is never a moment when you are not consciously aware of the trajectory it will take if it topples.

Bonanno Pisano began the construction of the tower in 1174, but the project was not completed until 1350. The primary reason for the delay in its completion was that the tower began to tilt when it reached its fourth level. With an annual increase of about one millimeter per year, the tower was closed to public access in 1990.

The astronomer and physicist Galileo (1564–1642) lived in Pisa and used the buildings of the Piazza del Duomo to conduct studies concerning the laws of gravity, the acceleration of falling bodies, and the movement of the pendulum. He used the Leaning Tower to work out his theories on gravity and acceleration and the cathedral for the accurate measurement of time. Galileo was said to have quarreled with his scholars over his theory of the rotation of the universe. During the Inquisition, when compelled to renounce his theory that the world turned, not the universe—because the Pope thought otherwise—in despair he whispered, "Nevertheless it *does* turn."

When at last you can turn your attention away from the tower, you will realize that Piazza dei Miracoli holds some other fantastic forms of real estate that warrant your inspection. Among them is the cathedral, on which construc-

PISA—*NEW SLANT ON AN OLD SCENE*

A Day Excursion from Rome

DEPART FROM ROME STATION	TRAIN NUMBER	ARRIVE IN PISA STATION	NOTES
0630	IR 2440	1025	(1)
0740	IC 606	1053	(1)(2)
1000	IC 622	1253	(1)
1100	E 1146	1445	(1)

DEPART FROM PISA STATION	TRAIN NUMBER	ARRIVE IN ROME STATION	NOTES
1435	Exp 365	1805	(1)
1534	E 1149	1920	(1)
1704	IC 613	2005(5)	(1)
1904	IC 615	2220	(1)(2)
1945	IR 2455	2340	(1)(2)

(1) Daily, including holidays
(2) Food service available

Distance: 208 miles/335 km
Reference: Thomas Cook Table 360

tion was initiated in 1063. The first work of art to catch your eye is the splendid bronze doors of its entrance. Inside the cathedral and opposite the pulpit, Lorenzi (according to legend) hung a bronze lamp on a chain so long that Galileo figured that it must be the first pendulum and proceeded to work out the theory of isochronism—one of the better "isms" existing today.

Just beyond the cathedral, the baptistery that was started in 1152 by Diotisalvi is topped by a mind-boggling cupola consisting of a cone projecting through a dome. The dome is 115 feet in diameter and has a remarkable echo. History relates that Pisa was in close contact with the Mideast because of its sea traffic during the Middle Ages and got the idea from Arabian architects.

Last of the edifices within the confines of the Piazza dei Miracoli is the building known as the Composanto (cemetery). It began when fifty-three shiploads of earth were transported from Calvary in the Holy Lands to the site and then surrounded by the building, which, after being completed in 1283 by Giovanni Pisano, was frescoed by local Tuscan artists. The structure suffered damage during World War II bombings, but repairs have all but removed those scars.

During its days of prominence, Pisa was in close touch with the Orient. As a result, you'll note an eastern flavor in its architecture. In the ninth century, the city was a naval power of considerable proportion. Pisa and its ally, Genoa, drove the Saracens out of Sardinia and Corsica in the eleventh century. Pisa's powers, however, then went on the wane. No longer allied with Genoa, the city was taken by Florence in 1406, proving that, as is so often the case in history, your allies are never there when you *really* need them.

Back to the Leaning Tower for an update. By using sonar soundings of the ground, the foundation of an ancient village was discovered under the north side of the tower. This explains why the north side of the tower has remained relatively stable, while the south side has sunk almost three-quarters of a meter. Various plans have been proposed to stabilize the tower. One plan is to use sonic waves to break up the ancient foundation under the north side so that it will sink at the same rate as the south. Another proposal requires a ring of steel to be inserted into the base of the landmark. Perhaps the Italian Public Works Ministry should expedite its plans. In 1987, a study revealed that the tower was 16.8 feet off plumb.

For a spectacular meal, visit the Ristorante Antonietta, a delightful Tuscan-Italian restaurant at 179 Via Santa Maria, immediately south of the square. It serves excellent food, and the location can't be beat. According to our best high-school geometry, if the tower topples, it will fall some thirty feet short of the first table at Antonietta's.

For more information about Pisa, stop by the tourist office in the station plaza, telephone (050) 42291, or the one in Piazza Duomo, telephone (050) 560464.

Stockholm station offers travelers services of all descriptions. The restaurant at the far end houses an English pub and a gambling casino as well as two eating establishments.

In size, Sweden is larger than California but smaller than Texas. The country is composed of a combination of forests, lakes, and islands. It is one of the most prosperous countries in Europe and supports a large and efficient industrial complex. Its citizens enjoy a superb quality of life and one of the highest standards of living in the world—and pay for it with one of the world's highest personal-income-tax rates.

It is difficult to realize that less than a century ago, Sweden was one of the most backward countries in Europe. Sweden today is the result of a blending of just the right amounts of socialism and capitalism, which has resulted in a virtually classless society. You may be able to sense this when you are in contact with the Swedes, even the trains' operating personnel. Everyone works, but no one takes a servant's role. Everyone is equal, and each job is equally important.

Cities are identified with the feminine gender. This makes Stockholm *very* feminine, for she is a city with a will of her own and a whimsy of changing her mind. Stockholm declares her intentions of retaining the old, then in the same breath states her love of progress and things modern.

For example, look at Stockholm's Gamla Stan (Old Town). It has narrow cobblestone streets that wind their crooked ways over paths unchanged since the Middle Ages past houses bearing the same facades they had when erected. But behind these old facades you find the most modern of business establishments and apartments whose decors rival those of similar dwellings anywhere in the world. With the delicate touch of a female, Stockholm has made this dualism work in every quarter.

Another example is Sergels Torg, Stockholm's space-age city center. It exists comfortably surrounded by other structures centuries older. Call it what you will, but most people call Stockholm beautiful.

Day Excursions

To introduce you properly to this "new" country, we have selected a group of day excursions that will give you an excellent cross section of life in Sweden. Eskilstuna is often referred to as "Sweden's Sheffield," although it bears little resemblance to its English counterpart. Next, a trip southward through Ostergotland, where the city of Norrkoping will unfold its industrial life styles.

Uppsala brings another contrast, that of a university town. Admittedly, planning day excursions in Sweden is made difficult by the distances involved between the centers of population, but all of these are within reasonable travel times and well worth the time to visit.

Arriving and Departing

By Air. The name of the international airport that serves Stockholm is Arlanda. It lies twenty-four miles (forty km) northwest of the city. Transportation to the city is provided by airport coach. Time en route is about forty-five to sixty minutes—depending on traffic—and the coach terminates in Stockholm at the World Trade Centre next to the Central Station.

This is a convenient location, as it is close to several major hotels and the Stockholm subway (the Tunnelbanan) and across the street from the main taxi stand in front of the railway station. The airport-coach fare for a single trip is 50 kronor for adults, reduced rates for children. If departing Stockholm by air, call 686–3773 (until 2000) or 797–9821 (twenty-four hours a day) for the departure time of the coach to take to be in time for your flight.

Limousine service is also available between Stockholm and Arlanda Airport. The limousine fare for a single trip is 356 kronor for one person plus 90 kronor for each additonal person. Taxis are available twenty-four hours daily. The taxi stand is located just outside the arrivals hall of the airport. The taxi fare is about 400 kronor.

By Train. Stockholm has several suburban stations, but international trains stop only at the main station in the center of the city, Stockholm Central. All of the day excursions out of Stockholm depart from Stockholm Central.

There's a bevy of suburban rail stations in Stockholm. Although you will not be using them for the day excursions, we mention them here so if your train should temporarily halt at one of them, you will know to stay aboard until reaching Central Station. The suburban stations are Stockholm Sodra/Flemmingsberg (south) and Stockholm Ostra (east).

The city's Central Station is modern, well organized, and easy to move about in. International trains usually arrive on track 17 or 18, but this does not mean that you are in for a long walk, because the tracks are clustered around the station complex.

Porters have been replaced by the "do-it-yourself" luggage carts. Insert a 5-kronor coin in the lock. It's refunded when you return the cart to a rack.

Train platforms, by the way, are referred to in Sweden as "spoors." A service you will find only on trains operated by the Scandinavian countries is drinking water supplied in cartons that may be obtained at no charge in the restaurant car.

Stockholm's Central Station

The population of Stockholm is about 1.5 million, and it appears as though half of that population passes through Central Station daily. At least that is the impression you get if you arrive in Stockholm during the morning or evening rush hour. Otherwise, the passenger traffic in this station seems to be as normal as that in any other train terminus in Europe. A probable reason for all the congestion at the rush hours is the Stockholm subway (Tunnelbanan). Its main terminal is connected directly to the railway station.

The station does an excellent job of moving its passengers to and from the trains. It also provides a full complement of services for the traveler. An arcade of shops, on the lower station level in the proximity of the exits from tracks 17 and 18, provides all types of foodstuffs, beverages, tobacco, newspapers, and so forth.

The *Servus*—Sweden's answer to the American supermarket—is a good place to restock your larder. It is located in the same area within the station. There are also shops in the main station-concourse area where you may purchase food and soft drinks.

The station's food-service facilities range from a cafeteria to a restaurant with its own gambling casino. The cafeteria is located on the main level of the station to the far right as you stand looking into the station from the train exit. It can be identified by its sign, CAFE OAASEN. Cafeteria service is continuous from 0600 until 2200, it is a good place to have breakfast, lunch, or dinner.

The Centralens Restaurang (restaurant) Orientexpressen has the previously mentioned casino. You'll see its sign on the right side of the station as you exit from the track area. In addition to the casino, the complex includes a pub and a restaurant with good food at reasonable prices. The "all you can eat" breakfast in the restaurant section is a real bargain. The restaurant has an expansive but relatively inexpensive luncheon-and-dinner menu featuring many Swedish specialties.

Across the street from Central Station, along the street Vasagatan, you can find a number of excellent food facilities ranging from fast to fancy.

Money exchange is located in the main station concourse and to the right of the main exit as you proceed from the track area. The office displays the regular pictograph sign plus one reading VAXELKONTOR and another, VAXEL EXCHANGE. It is open for business on a daily basis between 0800 and 2100.

Banks in the center of the city are open Monday through Friday from 0900 to 1700. They close at 1500 on the day before a holiday, which the Swedes refer to as a *halvdag* (half day). Many stores close earlier, too. Exchange rates are standard and posted in the newspapers.

Hotel reservations can be made through the Stockholm Information Service, which operates a hotel-accommodations locating service in the train station. It is located immediately to the right of the lower-level exit from international-train-arrival tracks 17 and 18. The office is a few steps down a corridor from the exit doors, and as they say in England, "You can't miss it." A large sign that says HOTELLCENTRAL TURISTINFORMANTION will prevent you from doing otherwise.

Stockholm's city hall, with its magnificent chambers, is one of the city's most renowned sights.

The office is open daily, 0800–2100, June through August; 0800–1900 daily in September; 0800–1700 Monday through Friday and 0800–1300 Saturday and Sunday the rest of the year (closed Saturday and Sunday in December and January). Small charges are made for obtaining hotel rooms and space in youth hostels. Advance payment for rooms is accepted by this office. The advance payment will assure that the hotel or pension will hold your room until your arrival. If your accommodations are located some distance from the train station, this can be a welcomed service.

Tourist information for Stockholm and its surrounding areas is available in the same office, "Hotellcentral Turistinformantion," or in the main tourist center, located at Sweden House, Kungsträdgården, telephone (08) 789–20–00.

The main tourist center is open 0900–1800 Monday through Friday and 0900–1500 on Saturday and Sunday. Inquiries about the "Sweden At Home" plan of meeting Swedes with similar interests should be made at the latter information office. Both offices sell an excellent publication, *Stockholm Guide.*

Train information is displayed on bulletins following the usual format. Departures are printed on yellow paper; arrivals appear on white. Train information is readily available throughout the station, including key positions just inside the main entrance and again in the corridors leading to the track areas.

Local train information, usually for commuter trains, is displayed by a bank of large-screen, closed-circuit television sets. The train information office is located in the main concourse to the left of the main exit. Hours of operation are 0700–2300 Monday through Saturday and 0730–2300 on Sunday. Only train information is available in this office.

Train reservations are made in a large ticket office located in the main hall to the right as you proceed from the track area. A sign, FARDBILJETTER PLATSBILJETTER, identifies it. Take a queue number for seat reservations and sleeping-car accommodations. The office is open 0540 (0700 Sunday)–2300 daily.

Eurailpass validation should be completed before making your first train trip. Operating personnel aboard the trains can validate the pass, but they are required to charge for the service. Validation is free in any regular railway station. In Stockholm's Central Station, use window 19 in the main ticket office.

Stockholm Sights

The city has excellent transportation facilities for sightseeing in Stockholm. An extensive network of bus and subway systems makes it easy to reach practically any point in the city from any other point.

Your key to the use of these city transportation facilities is The Stockholm Card, which provides free admission to forty-five of the city's museums as well as free sightseeing and transportation throughout the Stockholm area. Its prices are: 135 kronor for twenty-four hours; 270 for forty-eight hours; and 405 for seventy-two hours. One adult and two children (under age eighteen) can use the same card. Children between ages six and seventeen pay half price.

The card is on sale at the tourist center in Sweden House and at the central station. It is sold undated and is stamped with the date and hour the first time you use it. With the card, you will be given a folder explaining its use.

With this card in your pocket, you can expand your day-excursion itinerary to include places of interest in and near Stockholm. For example, you can make a day excursion to Norrtalje, with its quaint port, and have lunch aboard a vintage steamer permanently moored there. You can also ride one of the Stockholm Transit Authority (SL) buses to Furusund, a narrow passage for ships entering and leaving the city's harbor. You can have lunch in a quaint Inn at Furusund or stay aboard and ride on two ferries to Blido in the outer archipelago.

Yet another alternative use for the card would be to take a bus ride to historic Vaxholm for a great Swedish lunch at the waterfront hotel overlooking the old fortress and then to explore the shops there at leisure. Stockholm has a full fifty-five museums to explore, so it is difficult to single out but a few recommendations. There is one, however, that we are sure you won't want to miss: the *Vasa* Museum.

In 1628, Sweden proudly launched what was then the world's largest warship and pride of the nation, the *Vasa*. She carried the name of the royal family, along with sixty-four cannon, and was presumed to be unconquerable. But the nation's joy was short-lived. The *Vasa* capsized in the harbor during her maiden voyage. She was raised in 1961, painstakingly restored, and now rests in a museum especially constructed for her preservation. The warship is enthroned in the middle of a great hall, displaying the *Vasa* in all her grandeur. The cobblestone ground floor suggests a quay, and the restored warship can be viewed from various perspectives from four levels.

Vasa is unique since it is the oldest fully preserved warship in the world. Films of the raising and the restoration of the *Vasa* are shown hourly in the museum, and guided tours following the film are conducted during the summer.

From Stockholm . . .

TRAIN CONNECTIONS TO OTHER BASE CITIES

TO:	DEPART	ARRIVE	TRAIN NUMBER	COOK'S TABLE	NOTES
Berlin Hbf.	1406	0701+1	IC 37/319	52	(3)
Budapest (Keleti)	1006	1628+1	29/1011	52	(4)
Copenhagen	0612	1450	IN 21	465	(5)
	1030	1851	IN 287	465	
Hamburg	0612	2027	IN 21	50	(1)
	1806	0904+1	IN 391	50	(5)
Helsinki	1800(2)	0830+1	Ferry	1250	
Oslo	0736	1405	IN 51	470	
	1535	2206	IN 53	470	(6)
	2300	0740+1	398	470	(6)

Daily departures unless otherwise noted. Make reservations for all departures.
See *Thomas Cook European Timetable,* Table 1250, for train-ferry connections
from Stockholm to Helsinki via Turku.

(1) Transfer in Copenhagen to EC 183
(2) Depart from Silja Line terminal. No sailings on December 24.
(3) Transfer in Malmö to train 319
(4) Transfer in Malmö to train 1011
(5) Summer only
(6) Daily, except Saturdays (daily in summer)

Rademacher Forges, built in 1658, are unique. Today's craftsmen demonstrate their various skills by using traditional methods from centuries past to form their gold, copper, and iron into colorful trinkets for sale. Craftsmen include a coppersmith, a knifesmith, a goldsmith, and an engraver.

A DAY EXCURSION TO ESKILSTUNA
DISTANCE BY TRAIN: 73 miles (117 km)
AVERAGE TRAIN TIME: 1 hour, 40 minutes

Eskilstuna is unique in that it has preserved its industrial birthplace in the midst of a great industrial expansion. In a quiet section in the center of Sweden's "steel town," the well-preserved Rademacher Forges stand today just as they have for the last 300 years. Be certain to include a visit to this area during your day excursion.

The Rademacher Forges are the scene of many entertainment programs for visitors to Eskilstuna. In spring and late summer, the "Eskilstuna Guards" present concerts there. Folk dancing and theater performances may be seen in this locale throughout July. Descendants of the "smiths" are still at work forming gold, copper, and iron into colorful trinkets for sale.

The forges were erected in 1658 under the supervision of Reinhold Rademacher. Originally twenty in number, six have been preserved as a tribute to the heritage of modern Eskilstuna. The entire area surrounding the forges was restored in 1959 to commemorate the city's tricentennial. The Faktorimuseet is a museum of technology and industrial and cultural history situated in the old Musket Factory.

To expedite your arrival and orientation in the Eskilstuna station, look for a RESTAURANG sign in red with white letters and a VANTSAL sign in blue with white letters. Enter the station at this point. Inside the station, look for an UPPLYSNING sign on the left just beyond the ticket windows. Ask here for a map of the city and instructions for reaching the tourist office opposite the town hall, called the Fristadstorget.

Exit by the front of the station and follow Drottninggatan Street to Rademachergatan. Turn left off Rademachergatan and walk one block to Bruksgatan. The Rademacher Forges are to the right, and the tourist office is in the Rademacher Forges at Hamngatan 19. The office is open 0930–1800 Monday through Friday in June through August; from September through May, 1000–1200 and 1300–1500 (telephone [016] 514500; fax [016] 514575).

Eskilstuna is situated in the most populous part of Sweden. Named after the eleventh-century English missionary Saint Eskil, Eskilstuna is the center of the Swedish steel industry. Its parks and squares, combined with its sparkling charm, do seem, however, to make it unlike any steel town visited previously.

A statue of Saint Eskil stands in the churchyard of the Fors Kyrka. Both the statue and the church are worthy of a visit. The church and statue are marked as No. 6 on the Eskilstuna map. It can be one of your stops when you are en route back to the railway station, which is No. 24 on the map.

ESKILSTUNA—*SWEDEN'S STEEL CENTER*

A Day Excursion from Stockholm

DEPART FROM STOCKHOLM STATION	ARRIVE IN ESKILSTUNA STATION	NOTES
0810 (bus)	1025	(1)
1010 (bus)	1215	(1)
1210 (bus)	1415	(1)

DEPART FROM ESKILSTUNA STATION	ARRIVE IN STOCKHOLM STATION	NOTES
1530 (bus)	1750	(1)
1730 (bus)	1940	(2)
1830 (bus)	2040	(3)
1930 (bus)	2140	(1)

(1) Daily
(2) Saturdays, Sundays, and holidays only
(3) Monday through Friday

Distance: 73 miles/117 km
Reference: Thomas Cook Table 471

Eskilstuna's town charter dates from 1659. In 1971, five surrounding rural communities, together with the town of Torshalla, merged with Eskilstuna. Torshalla is more than 650 years old. Its name was derived from the Nordic god, Thor, who was worshipped by offertory gatherings of the barbarians occupying Torshalla.

Some fifty prehistoric monuments are to be found in the immediate area surrounding Eskilstuna, the best known being the Sigurd Rock carving—Scandinavia's first "strip cartoon." The tourist information office can help in finding transportation to the carvings.

The Park Zoo (Parken Zoo) in Eskilstuna ranks as one of Scandinavia's most visited tourist attractions. In addition to the zoological gardens, there are an amusement park known as the Tivoli, a heated swimming pool with water slides, and Phantom Land, a popular play area for children. For the younger set, the zoological gardens offers its famous Flamingo Valley and a petting zoo in its animal park. The zoo is noted for its collection of animals that are unique and rare to Sweden, including a dwarf panda, a snow leopard, and a family of white tigers. In the wild, the white tiger is thought to be extinct. To our knowledge, Eskilstuna's Park Zoo and the Mirage Hotel in Las Vegas, Nevada, are the only places in the world where one can still see these animals in any number. Park Zoo and the other attractions surrounding it open daily at 1000 from May through the first Sunday in September. It's fun for the whole family.

The city is well endowed with works of art. Its art museum has more than a hundred items on display. It is particularly proud of its collection of Swedish art from the fifteenth century to the present. The museum is open daily, except Monday, from 1200 to 1600. Exhibitions of contemporary art succeed each other at intervals of between three and four weeks throughout the year.

Eskilstuna's Djurgard open-air museum of cultural history is centered around Sormlandsgarden, a typical nineteenth-century farm commune, and Herrgarden, a manor house from the same period. The farm is complete with a hay barn, stables, a storage shed, and a curious apparatus used for shoeing oxen. The manor house includes a number of rooms furnished in different periods of history.

Eight miles outside Eskilstuna by public bus lines is Sundbyholm Castle. Built by an illegitimate son of a Swedish king, it has been restored fully, and a restaurant has been added.

Karl Johans Park in Norrkoping features this beautiful fountain among its world-famous cactus displays.

A DAY EXCURSION TO NORRKOPING
DISTANCE BY TRAIN: 101 miles (163 km)
AVERAGE TRAIN TIME: 2 hours

Ripley's *Believe It or Not* featured Norrkoping many years ago. People would *not* believe that 25,000 cactus plants were growing in Sweden. It's true. They are growing there even today. The place is Norrkoping, and the cactus plantation is one of many things to see in this delightful Swedish city during your day excursion there.

The city is one of Sweden's most important industrial cities. A walk in the old industrial section is recommended. You'll find industrial buildings dating from the nineteenth century. There are many archaeological relics to see within Norrkoping, including Bronze Age rock carvings. The town hall has a carillon that is prized by its citizens. It helps the ambience of the town that has been referred to often by visitors as the Paris of the North. Norrkoping is a town full of experiences just waiting for you.

Norrkoping's tourist information office is located conveniently near the railway station. You will find it on the corner of Tradgardsgatan and Drottninggatan, 200 meters from the station. In summer, a branch of the agency also operates from a booth in the park opposite the station.

The tourist office is open 0900–1900 Monday through Saturday in summer. From September through May, the office is open 1000–1700. The telephone number is (46) 11-151500.

While at the tourist information office, inquire about the Kolmarden-Norrkoping Card. It's a special ticket that gives you a multitude of visitor admissions and discounts. To mention just a few: sightseeing by boat; entrance to the Lofstad Castle; a complimentary ride on the old Number 1 tram; and free admission to the animal and nature park, Kolmarden.

The railway station becomes the "pivot point" for many of Norrkoping's major sights. The ruins of the Johannisborg Fort lie on the left of the station; the 3,000-year-old Bronze Age carvings are in the Himmelstalund Park on its right; and the city's world-famous Karl Johans Park is directly in front of the station.

As indicated, there is plenty to do and see in Norrkoping. Let the tourist information office help in planning your day. Be sure to ride on old Number 1, a tram restored from around 1902, when such conveyances were the mainstay of the town's transportation. A guide is frequently aboard.

Other sights near the railway station are the Gamla Torget (Old Square), the Radhus (town hall), and the Hedvigs Kyrka (German Church). All are clustered in the city's center.

561

NORRKOPING—*THE NORTHERN CACTUS CENTER*

A Day Excursion from Stockholm

DEPART FROM STOCKHOLM STATION	TRAIN NUMBER	ARRIVE IN NORRKOPING STATION	NOTES
0806	IC 25	1005	(1)(2)(3)
1006	IN 29	1205	(1)(2)(3)
1206	IC 33	1405	(1)(2)(3)

DEPART FROM NORRKOPING STATION	TRAIN NUMBER	ARRIVE IN STOCKHOLM STATION	NOTES
1555	IC 10	1753	(1)(2)(3)
1755	IN 42	1953	(1)(2)(3)
1955	IC 46	2153	(1)(2)(3)

(1) Daily, including holidays
(2) Seat reservations mandatory
(3) Food service available

Distance: 101 miles/163 km
Reference: Thomas Cook Table 465

Beyond doubt Karl Johans Park, in front of the railway station, is the best kept park of its kind in the world. Its appearance can only be described as manicured, so detailed is the attention it receives. From its fountain to its floral arrangements, it reflects a quiet blending of nature's most beautiful assets into an atmosphere of contentment and relaxation. Its tranquillity is broken pleasantly at intervals by the chattering of countless parakeets housed in an aviary near the fountain.

The famous cactus plantation that was featured in Bob Ripley's *Believe It or Not* is in Karl Johans Park at the opposite end from the railway station. Approximately 25,000 cactus plants are rearranged annually according to a new theme by the city's able gardeners. The motifs vary from year to year, reflecting important events within the community. A primary reason for the high quality of the cactus and floral displays is the presence of Sweden's National School of Gardening and the Flower School.

If roses are your favorites, go to the Himmelstalundsparken (Himmelstalund Park) and visit its rosery. You can combine this visit with an inspection of the Bronze Age rock carvings, also a part of this park, that are to the right of the railway station.

All that remain of the Johannisborg Fort now are the gate tower and its ramparts, but these are enough to convey a mental image of how this magnificent construction (started in 1613) must have looked.

The time to hear the carillon in Norrkoping is at 0955, 1155, 1455, or 1655. A position in front of the Radhuset (council house) at one of these times will permit you to listen and enjoy the tune it plays. Following the carillon performance, it might be a good time to stroll along the banks of the nearby Motala Ström River in the old city center and relax a bit. You can follow the river down to the old Dyer's House to see how wool was made and dyed in the old days. There's also a café where you can relax and have a snack.

Twenty-five kilometers north of Norrkoping is the largest animal and nature park in Europe—the Kolmarden Zoo. There are no bars or cages, and the animals thrive in large outdoor pens. Check with the tourist office for transportation details.

Unusual statue of Swedish folklore stands in front of Uppsala's railway station to greet visitors.

A DAY EXCURSION TO UPPSALA
DISTANCE BY TRAIN: 40 miles (66 km)
AVERAGE TRAIN TIME: 43 minutes

No other town in Sweden has such a long recorded history as Uppsala. This is where Sweden began. As far back as the sixth century, it was the political and religious center of the expanding Swedish kingdom. According to the ancient legends, pagans from all reaches of the kingdom came to Uppsala every ninth year to feast and offer up sacrifices until the eleventh century, when Christianity began to take over. Legend has it that one of the kings of the period, King Aun, got all wrapped up in the nine-year cycle by sacrificing one of his sons each cycle. His tenth and last son put an end to old dad—and to the cycle, too! Sort of the start of Swedish scams, don't you think?

Modern Uppsala won't remind you of Oxford or Heidelberg—or Bryn Mawr, for that matter. Uppsala is a university town but with an academic environment distinctly its own. The city and the area surrounding it enshrine a great deal of Swedish history encompassing religion (pagan and Christian alike), academe, and politics. This composite results in a city of multifaceted interests, architecture, and customs.

Gamla Uppsala (Old Uppsala) lies three miles north of the present city center. Here, the graves of the sixth-century Ynglinga Dynasty kings are found. The pagan religion of the Vikings persisted here well into the eleventh century. A twelfth-century church, heralding the advent of Christianity, then replaced the pagan temple. The area now is an open-air museum, accessible to visitors daily during June, July, and August.

Uppsala Castle stands on a hill overlooking the city. Begun in the 1540s by King Gustav Vasa as a symbol of his power over the church, it was completed during the reign of Queen Christina. Partially destroyed by fire in 1702, much of the castle has been restored. The church didn't plan to go down without a fight. The bishop had cannon mounted on the church pointing at the castle. They still point that way today.

The great hall of the castle is frequently the scene of historic events. Both the coronation banquet for Gustavus Adolphus and Queen Christina's abdication took place within the castle's walls. Each April 30, undergraduates and alumni of the university assemble there to celebrate the arrival of spring. Nearby, the Gunilla Bell is rung daily at 0900 and again at 2100. The castle is open 1100–1600 daily from mid-May to mid-September. A more restricted schedule is followed during other periods of the year.

Three-quarters of Uppsala were destroyed by fire in 1702. It was in the subsequent period of reconstruction that the character of the city changed. The

UPPSALA—*UNIVERSITY CITY*

A Day Excursion from Stockholm

DEPART FROM STOCKHOLM STATION	TRAIN NUMBER	ARRIVE IN UPPSALA STATION	NOTES
0713	IC 880	0800	(1)(2)(3)
0813	IC 958	0900	(1)(2)(3)
1013	IC 960	1100	(1)(2)(3)(5)

DEPART FROM UPPSALA STATION	TRAIN NUMBER	ARRIVE IN STOCKHOLM STATION	NOTES
1457	IC 961	1544	(1)(2)(3)(4)
1657	IC 963	1744	(2)(3)(4)
2040	IC 965	2130	(1)(2)(3)
2140	IC 885	2227	(1)(2)(3)

(1) Daily, including holidays
(2) Seat reservations mandatory
(3) Food service available
(4) Daily, except Saturdays
(5) Daily, except Sundays

Distance: 40 miles/66 km
References: Thomas Cook Tables 476 and 478

university and its scholars began to dominate, and the reputation of the university spread throughout the civilized world. The present university building was opened in 1887.

The university library houses a collection of more than two million bound volumes and 30,000 manuscripts. The library is open to the public. Weekday access is permitted only during university holidays and vacation periods, but anyone may enter on any Saturday throughout the year between 0900 and 1700.

In Uppsala, Saint Erik, Saint Olof, and Saint Lars's church is usually referred to as the cathedral. Two of its patron saints, Erik and Olof, were Christian kings in Scandinavia during the eleventh and twelfth centuries, when the Christians finally had the pagans on the run. Lars died a martyr's death in Rome in A.D. 258. Building of the cathedral started in the late thirteenth century, and it took a century and a half to complete. It has been ravaged by fires, and its towers collapsed, but with Swedish determination it was restored. English-language tours of the Uppsala Cathedral are conducted during the summer months.

With so many places of interest in Uppsala, a visit to the city's tourist information office should be the first item on your agenda. The office is about a five-minute walk from the railway station. To go there, exit the station and walk diagonally through the small park in front to the main street, Kungsgatan. Turn right, then turn left on Vaksalagatan (the next crossing). Walk until you reach the square (Stora Torget) where all the city buses meet. Follow the street Drottninggatan from the square and cross the small river Fyrisan. Turn right immediately after the bridge, and the tourist office is at No. 8 on the left-hand side of Fyristorg. It is identified by the traditional "i" sign. The telephone number is (018) 117500.

The tourist office can provide you with a city map and a brochure that describes the city's places of interest in great detail. The brochure also gives a summary of Uppsala's history from pagan days to the present. The tourist information office's hours are 1000–1800 Monday through Saturday and 1000–1700 on Sunday from June through August; September through May, the office is open 1000–1800 Monday through Friday and 1000–1400 on Saturday.

Vienna's Westbahnhof (West Station) is one of two major rail terminals in the city. **Paddle-wheel boat** plies the Danube en route to Vienna.

25 VIENNA

Anyone seeking the "real Europe" will find it in Vienna. For centuries the city has been a living source for Western art and culture. The pace of living is slower, which you will notice almost at once, for leisure is the city's tempo. In fact, the cost of living is lower there than in many of the other capitals of western Europe. Vienna developed the waltz, and the city has moved in leisurely three-quarter time ever since.

Vienna's social life centers around its coffee houses. Visiting them during your stay is a must. The Viennese "invented" coffee. According to legend, in 1683 the Turks were defeated in their attempted siege of the city and decided to go home. They left some bags of coffee beans behind. The local folks swarmed out of the city and carried the bags back behind its protective walls and began experimenting. A gentleman by the name of Kolschitzky evolved a clear brew—unlike the Turks who, to this day, serve it with the grounds—and Vienna was so elated that it erected a bronze statue to his memory.

Vienna is many things, but primarily it is music. You may visit the Strauss home where the *Blue Danube Waltz* was written, thrill to the voices of the Vienna Boys' Choir, or marvel at the white Lipizzan stallions as they dance to music in the Spanish Riding School.

Two thousand years ago, the Romans had a fortified military camp, *Vindobona,* on the Danube where modern Vienna is located today. In the course of history, Vienna—or "Wien," as it is identified by Europeans—has always found its fate linked to its geographic position at the eastern end of the Alps, at the edge of the great plains of eastern Europe, and on a great river that provided a natural thoroughfare long before the Romans began building their roads.

Merchants met there at the crossing of the ancient trade routes. Crusaders passed through on their way to the Holy Land, and in 1683, the Turks not only left some coffee—they also abandoned their quest of three centuries to conquer the heart of Europe at the gates of Vienna.

Day Excursions

Because of its location on the Danube River and the eastern reaches of the Alps, Vienna can offer some unusual day-excursion opportunities. Among them are tours on the Danube and through the Austrian Alps. The Danube tour is made possible through the facilities of the Austrian Railroads and its associated steamship lines. Express trains can whisk you from Vienna to Salzburg in time for lunch—followed by dinner—and still return you in time to slumber in Vienna. Local trains can take you to Baden, one of the most famous sulfur-bath spas in Austria.

Arriving and Departing

By Air. Schwechat Airport, approximately eleven miles (eighteen kilometers) southeast of Vienna, introduced its airport train service in 1977, but it still warrants considerable improvement. We recommend the airport bus service, which connects with the West and South railway stations as well as with the city air terminal. The fare is 60 schillings; time en route is twenty minutes. The bus-departure point is immediately outside and to the left of the airport's arriving-passenger exit.

The airport train service connects with the Wien-Nord (Vienna-North) and the Wien-Mitte (Vienna-Middle) rail stations. The fare from Wien-Nord is 36 schillings; time en route, thirty-seven minutes. The fare from Wien-Mitte is 28 schillings; time en route is thirty-three minutes. For schedule details, consult the *Thomas Cook European Timetable.* At the airport, the entrance to the railway station will be on your left after the baggage-claim area.

The Vienna Tourist Board maintains an information office at the airport. It is located to the left of Customs in the arrivals hall. Daily hours: June to September, 0830 to 2300; October to May, 0830 to 2200. Visitor information and hotel-room reservations are available.

Taxis are available twenty-four hours daily. A taxi reservation/information desk is located in the arrivals hall of the airport.

By Train. The Westbahnhof (West Station) and the Südbahnhof (South Station) are Vienna's major railway terminals. Both will be described fully. Wien-Nord and Wien-Mitte, mentioned earlier, are commuter-type stations; no further mention of them will be made.

Vienna's Railway Stations—Westbahnhof Station & Südbahnhof Station

The city has two major railway stations. The Westbahnhof (West Station) is the gateway to Germany, Switzerland, and the rest of northern and central Europe. The Südbahnhof (South Station) is the gateway to southern and eastern Europe. For our purposes, we consider the Westbahnhof as Vienna's primary station because all arrivals from other base cities featured in *Europe by Eurail* terminate there.

Westbahnhof Station has two levels. Arriving by train, you will be on top of the elevated level. The taxi stand is on the left as you leave the train platform. You may descend by stairs, elevator, or escalator to the main station concourse, which is at street level.

Money-exchange office is identified by a sign, EXCHANGE-WECHSELSTUBE. It is located to the right of the escalators on the top level in the main station concourse. The office is open 0700–2200 daily.

Hotel reservations can be made in the glass kiosk identified by the sign,

REISEBURO AM BAHNHOF, located to the left of the escalators on the main station concourse. It is open 0615–2300 daily. A nominal charge is made for reservations. Vienna is an international meeting place. It can, therefore, be fully booked at times.

Tourist information is available in the same glass kiosk, same hours, 0615–2300. Otherwise, we suggest that you proceed to the city's main tourist information office, located at 38 Kärntnerstrasse. To reach it from the Westbahnhof, take the Underground, U3 line, to Bellaria. Then, either change to U2, or take tram 2 along the Ring to the Opera House. The tourist office is alongside the Opera House on the righthand side.

The city tourist information office sign reads OFFIZIELLE TOURIST INFORMATION and is further identified with a green "i" sign. It is open 0900–1900 daily. The telephone number is 5138892. The tourist office also makes hotel reservations.

Tram tickets, by the way, are sold in tobacco shops (there's one in the Westbahnhof) for 20 schillings per ticket. You can buy a twenty-four hour Vienna Network Pass for 50 schillings or a three-day pass for 130 schillings. There's also an eight-day strip ticket for 255 schillings. The tickets are valid for use on the subway, trams, and buses. Vienna has an excellent public transportation system with reasonable fares.

Train information may be obtained from the information office marked, REISEBURO AM BAHNHOF, located in the kiosk to the left of the escalators at ground level. This office is open daily, 0700–2045. From 0600–2200 daily, train information also is available by telephone by dialing 1717.

Eurailpass validation can be provided by the train information office if you are beginning your Eurail tour in Vienna.

Train-reservations service is provided by the train information office marked REISEBURO AM BAHNHOF in the Westbahnhof or in the Reiseburo Oesterreichisches Verkehrsbuero (travel agency) located in the Opernringhof, the building opposite the State Opera House on Ringstrasse. The hours are 0830–1730 Monday through Friday and 0900–1200 on Saturday.

The American Express International office at 21-23 Kaerntnerstrasse also can make train reservations, as well as advance hotel reservations in other cities, for its card members. The telephone number is 51.54.00, and the office is open 0900–1730 Monday through Friday and 0900–1200 on Saturday.

Südbahnhof Station (South Station) is a three-level terminal with the train platforms located on the middle and top levels. It has all of the services that are available to passengers using the Westbahnhof, but because it is not the terminal in Vienna for arrivals from other base cities described in this book, a more limited description follows.

Strauss statue in The Stadtpark commemorates musical contributions made by composer Johann Strauss.

Money-exchange office is located in the lower level of the station immediately to the right of the main staircase. The office is open 0630–2200 daily.

Tourist information, including hotel reservations, is available in the station's information service office just beyond the money exchange. (Look for the "i" sign.) The office is open 0630–2200 daily. This office also can assist with train reservations, Eurailpass validation, and other tourist information.

To get to the main tourist information office (at 38 Kärntnerstrasse next to the Opera House) from the Südbahnhof, take the "D" trolley to the Opera House.

Tourist Facilities

Vienna's U-Bahn (subway), Stadtbahn (metropolitan or old underground), and Schnellbahn systems connect with many important points in and around Vienna. Ask the tourist information office about the guide on public transport in Vienna.

As mentioned previously, Vienna's transit system offers visitors a three-day pass (the Three-Day Vienna Ticket) for unlimited travel on all municipal subways, commuter railroads (within the city limits), trams, and bus lines, including private bus lines operating under transit-system fares. The cost is 130 schillings for unlimited travel over more than 300 miles of routes. For visitors staying three days or more, it's a real bargain.

The visitor's pass is also sold at the city's tourist information counter at the airport, the State Opera underground mall, Westbahnhof and Südbahnhof stations (in the offices of the Austrian Travel Agency), and all city offices for transit-system advance sales throughout the city.

The pass is printed in three languages (German, French, and English) and comes with a folder that gives a survey of the transit system. Considering that the three-day pass costs less than five one-way regular fares purchased on board or seven rides purchased in advance, the pass is a super bargain. Another advantage: Many trams have no conductors, and tickets must be purchased from automatic vending machines—many of which give instructions only in German.

Vienna's tourist office offers a wide variety of ways to see Vienna. There are fifty walking tours, each with a different theme. The themes span the spectrum from "Pure Hapsburg, The Hofburg and Its Emperors" to "Chow-houses, Boozers, Brothels, and Other Houses of Ill Repute." For a real moving experience, tour Vienna by bicycle. Call Vienna-Bike at 319.12.58 to book your bike and your tour. For a ride through the good old days, take Vienna's two-hour 1929 Tram Tour. For information and reservations, telephone 587.31.86.

Vista of Vienna

A word of warning about Vienna. It is very easy to commit suicide there with a knife and a fork. Most local folks ignore this peril. If you care to join them, by all means try the sugar tarts and don't dare miss the *Apfelstrudel* (apple cake). Along with coffee, the Viennese invented the croissant roll in the shape of a Turkish crescent. Eating one demonstrates how one feels about such people who would dare lay siege to such a nice city.

The coffee houses of Vienna are oases of good living at a leisurely pace. The city's pastry shops are temples of a cult dedicated to the most sophisticated blends and aromas possible. Beware! Ye who enter leave all thoughts of calories and waistlines behind you.

Our favorite coffeehouse happens to be the original one in Vienna, the Sacher Café, a part of Hotel Sacher immediately behind the Opera House. It has a semiformal but friendly atmosphere. Please wait to be seated and observe the manner in which your order is taken and served by the courteous staff, all under the ever-watchful eye of the headwaiter. Expensive? Well, yes it is; but it always costs more when going first class.

The Viennese like to eat well, and they take great pride and pleasure in giving visitors every opportunity to do likewise. When a Viennese isn't doing something else—he's eating. Vienna has a dazzling array of eating places, from stand-up snack bars and simple little pubs known as *Beisel* to ethnic specialties and gourmet restaurants noted for their nouvelle cuisine treatment of traditional Austrian dishes.

Good food deserves good libation. Austrian beer is tasty and strong. Austria is also responsible for some great vintages. These are bottled and aged; but young, fresh wine is rushed to the taverns, where locals and visitors alike consume it as though it might loose its freshness between sips.

Regarding ticket reservations at the federal theaters (State Opera, "Volksoper," etc.), reservations can be made from outside Vienna, but they must be made *at least* three weeks in advance of the performance. For reservations write to: Österreichischer Bundestheaterverband, Goethegasse 1, A-1010 Vienna, Austria.

Since Hungary became a Eurailpass country, many Eurailpassers transit Vienna on through trains such as the Wiener Walzer without stopping. We suggest that you take advantage of the frequent rail service and stop for a few hours in Vienna en route to Budapest. Baggage can be stored in the "Gepackaufbewahrung" (temporary baggage storage facility) in the Westbahnhof main concourse level. After descending on the escalator from track level, turn right and go to the far end of the concourse just before the station restaurant. The facility will be to your immediate right.

Vienna is many things—Gothic spires, Baroque exuberance, the blue Danube, dancing white stallions, coffeehouses, pastries—and the list is endless. Above all, Vienna is a memory to waltz through your dreams forever.

From Vienna ...

TRAIN CONNECTIONS TO OTHER BASE CITIES

TO:	DEPART	ARRIVE	TRAIN NUMBER	COOK'S TABLE	NOTES
Amsterdam	1844	0857+1	EN224	35	
Brussels (Midi)	0800	2055	EC 28/434	66/20	(1)
	1844	0804+1	EN224	34	
Budapest (Keleti)	0830	1153	EN467	61	
	1005	1328	263	61	
	1320	1643	EC 63	61	
	1820	2143	EC 25	61	
Hamburg	0800	2211	EC 28	64	
	2000	0751+1	EN 490	64	
Milan	1945(2)	0850+1	235	88	(3)
Munich	0900	1336	EC 64	67	
	1600	2036	EC 62	67	
Paris	0900	2218	EC 64	32	
	1940	0930+1	262	32	
Rome	0718(2)	2020	EC 31	88	
	1945(2)	0930+1	235	88	

All departures from Vienna Westbahnhof. Daily departures unless otherwise noted. Make reservations for all departures.

(1) Transfer in Cologne (Köln) to train 434
(2) Departs from Vienna (Wien) Süd
(3) Departs at 2015 Friday through Sunday (train 1235)

Mountain climbing can be done the easy way—from a comfortable train.

From Vienna . . .

A DAY EXCURSION THROUGH THE AUSTRIAN ALPS
DISTANCE BY TRAIN: 541 miles (871 km)
AVERAGE TRAIN TIME: 14 hours, 40 minutes

Unlike oceans and endless plains, mountains seem to be the beginning and the end of all natural scenery. The Austrian Alps—unplanned, undiluted, and uncomputerized—probably provide more beauty than all of the man-made masterpieces in the world laid end to end. The fact that you can watch the splendor of their Alpine panorama unfold from the comfort of a train compartment of an Austrian train makes this a most unusual and thrilling day excursion.

There are two prerequisites for this trip. Take an adequate, large-scale map of Austria along, and try to select a day when good visibility is forecast. For the latter, your hotel should be able to provide a weather forecast, and an ideal map is the one published by Kummerly and Frey entitled "Autriche-Austria." Its scale, 1:500,000, shows both highway and railroad details. Its blue-and-white cover is easily recognizable in the city's newspaper kiosks or the station newsstands, and it's well worth its price.

This day excursion requires changing trains in Salzburg with the option of changing trains en route to Salzburg at Villach. The time between trains in Villach and Salzburg varies according to the schedule you select. Consequently, you might want to consider having lunch in Villach followed by dinner in Salzburg, thereby adding a culinary note to your excursion through the Austrian Alps. Dining aboard also is possible, since all of the trains listed on the schedule haul dining cars.

Please note that the train leaving Vienna in the morning departs from the Südbahnhof (South Station) and the one returning in the evening arrives in the Westbahnhof (West Station).

The Alps in Austria are divided from north to south into three chains: the northern limestone Alps, the central high Alps, and the limestone Alps of the south. These chains are separated from each other by the great furrows that form the river valleys of the Inn, the Salzach, and the Enns in the north and the Drava and Mur in the south. The route we have selected for this day excursion takes you through all three alpine chains.

Even if the weather is good when you leave Vienna, the climate of the Alps varies considerably with differences in altitude. Consequently, you can expect some changes in the temperature and visibility while en route. It isn't unusual to enter a tunnel with the landscape bathed in sunlight only to emerge at the other end in a dark and foreboding storm.

Vienna is 580 feet above sea level. Leaving the city, the train moves along the edge of the Vienna woods. Before arriving in Bruck, you will get an occa-

AUSTRIAN ALPS TOUR—*VIA VILLACH AND SALZBURG*

A Day Excursion from Vienna

DEPART FROM VENNA SÜDBAHNHOF STATION	TRAIN NUMBER	ARRIVE IN VILLACH STATION	NOTES
0722	IC 431	1210	(1)
0922	IC 593	1410	(1)
1122	IC 595	1610	(1)

DEPART FROM VILLACH STATION	TRAIN NUMBER	ARRIVE IN SALZBURG STATION	
1218	EC 10	1453	(1)(5)
1419	IC 593	1653	(1)
1619	IC 595	1853	(1)

DEPART FROM SALZBURG STATION	TRAIN NUMBER	ARRRIVE IN VIENNA WESTBAHNHOF STATION	NOTES
1705	IC 569	2025	(1)(2)
1800	IC 65	2105	(1)(3)
1925	EC 161	2230	(1)(4)
2000	EC 17	2305	(1)

"Max Reinhardt"

(1) Daily, including holidays
(2) IC 569 train is the Bodensee
(3) IC 65 train is the Mozart
(4) EC 161 train is the Maria Theresa
(5) EC 10 train is the Mimara

Distance: 541 miles/871 km
References: Thomas Cook Tables 820 and 800

sional glimpse of the Raxalpe Peak (6,630 feet). This steep-sided limestone massif, due to its proximity to Vienna, has become very popular with city-based mountain climbers. Here, the train follows the first mountain railway (*Semmeringbahn*) built in Europe (1848–54), which runs between Gloggnitz and Mürzzuschlag.

From Mürzzuschlag to Bruck, the train parallels the Mürz River through the last really mountainous pass leading out of the Alps and on to the broad plains fed by the Danube. Bruck lies at the confluence of the Mur and the Mürz rivers in the pleasant setting of the Styrian Alps. After passing Unzmarkt, the peaks of the Zinken (7,255 feet) and the Greimberg (8,115 feet) Alps are visible. You then arrive in Klagenfurt, 1,472 feet above sea level. Summers here are extremely hot, for the town lies in a basin shielding it from the moderating effects of the Mediterranean.

Between Klagenfurt and Velden, the train passes along Lake Woerth before arriving in Villach. The ten-mile lake is rather different from other Alpine lakes in that it receives little in the way of river floodwaters. As a consequence, it is very warm in summer and attracts many water-sports enthusiasts.

Villach is unusual because it has two large swimming pools within its city limits. Normally, there would be nothing unusual about this fact, except that the pools are filled with radioactive water!

As they used to say in vaudeville, "Folks, you ain't seen nothin' yet!" Leaving Villach and approaching the Tauern Tunnel (which is five miles long), you will be able to view Mount Hochalm (11,020 feet). As you leave the tunnel, Edelweiss-Spitze (8,453 feet) stands guard on the left, while Mount Gamskarspitze (9,296 feet) looms on the right.

After pausing briefly at Badgastein—the highest en route station on this day excursion at 2,838 feet above sea level—the train gradually descends into Schwarzach and parallels the Salzach River, which flows past Bischofshofen and the city of Salzburg. The elevation of Salzburg is 1,400 feet. In Salzburg, change trains for Vienna.

Sunsets, although spectacular in this part of the world, come quickly along the escarpment of the Alps, so there is little chance to see the Danube on this day excursion. Take the Danube-cruise day excursion for that purpose. Again, don't forget that you will be arriving in Vienna's Westbahnhof and not the Südbahnhof.

Austrians say if you plan a seven-country trip in Europe beginning in Austria, you'll end up skipping the other six countries. Perhaps they are right. The snow-covered Alps unveiled during this day excursion could well influence you to do just that.

Baroque monument, the Trinity Column, sculpted in 1718 by Stanetti, stands opposite the town hall in Baden's square.

A DAY EXCURSION TO BADEN
DISTANCE BY TRAIN: 17 miles (27 km)
AVERAGE TRAIN TIME: 20 minutes

Baden is situated on the eastern edge of the Vienna Woods and surrounded by extensive vineyards and woodlands. Because it also lies on the edge of Europe's great eastern Pannonian plain, it enjoys a moderate climate, much sunshine, and favorable temperatures. In fact, Baden is in the warmest part of Austria and recognized as a health resort throughout the world. Famous as a spa, Baden sits on ancient thermal water springs—fifteen in fact—with a regular temperature of 36 degrees Celsius (97 degrees Fahrenheit).

The Romans were always keen on baths and took more than a passing fancy to Baden. They called it "Aquae" and spent legions of hours soaking there in the medicinal, hot sulfur springs of the area. "Padun," a name from which Baden is derived, appeared in history books for the first time in 869. In the nineteenth century, Baden became the center of social life in Vienna's growing sphere of influence. Today, it has become a world-renowned spa and vacation spot, full of charm, flowers, and more swimming pools than one can possibly enter in a single day excursion.

Swimming in Baden is a year-round pastime, either outdoors in the thermal and mineral pools or indoors at a new thermal pool. For those who feel that water is only approached safely in a glass or basin, Baden offers other forms of relaxation ranging from quiet paths leading in and around the eastern edges of the Vienna woods to a lively game of Black Jack in its casino opposite Kurpark, where roses and the flowers of Austria's womanhood can be viewed on any summer's day.

Another interesting pastime is visiting the informal wine taverns scattered throughout the town. Since the Middle Ages, every citizen of Baden has had the right in his own house to sell the wine he has produced himself, as well as meat and sausage specialties. These "taverns" are identified by a pole decorated with fir twigs, or you can seek them out by following the tavern signs displayed in prominent places throughout the town.

The signs list all of the wine taverns that are doing business at the time. With even more wine taverns in Baden than swimming pools, visitors bent on engaging in a time-consuming research of taverns might do well to come to Baden as early as possible and leave only when they have discovered the best vintage—or spend the night in Baden, depending upon how much research was conducted.

Train service from Vienna's Südbahnhof to Baden is frequent. Proceed to level 3 in the station for trains departing on tracks 11 through 19 for Baden in

BADEN—*BATHS, CURES, AND CASINO*

A Day Excursion from Vienna

DEPART FROM VIENNA SÜDBAHNHOF STATION	TRAIN NUMBER	ARRIVE IN BADEN STATION	NOTES
0752	E1557	0814	(1)
0852	E1550	0914	(1)
0952	E1651	1014	(1)
1252	E1657	1314	(1)

Plus frequent commuter trains. Check schedules for track Nos. 11 and 19 on top (third) level of the Südbahnhof (South Station). Most trains departing for Graz stop at Baden.

DEPART FROM BADEN STATION	TRAIN NUMBER	ARRIVE IN VIENNA SÜDBAHNHOF STATION	NOTES
1444	E1750	1505	(1)
1644	E1752	1705	(1)
1744	E1754	1805	(1)
1844	E1756	1905	(1)
2044	E1758	2105	(1)

Plus frequent commuter trains. Check schedules in Baden railway station.

(1) Daily, including holidays

Distance: 17 miles/27 km

the direction of Graz. After arriving in Baden, use the station underpass to get to the town side of the tracks. By walking directly through the park in front of the station and bearing right onto Bahnstrasse (Station Street) at the end of the park, you can reach, two blocks farther along, a *Fussgangerzone* (pedestrian area) where, unhindered by vehicles, you can turn right and walk to the town square.

There should be no doubt in your mind that you have reached the square. It is "garnished" with perhaps one of the most unusual monuments ever to be seen. It's the *Pestsaule*. Aptly described in one guidebook as "frothy," it has been there since 1718 with its mind-boggling charm. Just beyond, you will see the more sedate Rathaus (city hall), built along more classic lines in 1815. Adjoining the city hall is a tobacco shop, followed by the Informationsstelle (tourist information office). Details of Baden and its surroundings are dispensed by this office 0900–1200 and 1400–1800 Monday through Saturday and 0900–1200 on Sunday from May to the end of October. The remainder of the year, the hours are 0800–1200 and 1300–1700 Monday through Friday; closed on Saturday and Sunday. The polite and helpful manner of the office attendants reflects the friendly nature of all Baden's citizens.

Today, Baden attracts its share of Europe's upper class, much as it did in centuries past; however, you don't need a crown or a title to receive first-class treatment there. After your day excursion in Baden, you may actually feel like royalty—it's all part of the atmosphere.

Baden is ideal for shopping. Its entire center is a pedestrian zone of streets radiating out from the main square. You won't find a department store in town. The town's retailers prefer to operate small specialty shops. When you tire of bargain hunting, retreat to the city rose garden in Doblhoff Park to watch chess played on a larger-than-life chess board.

In addition to the spa, casino, and parks, Baden has a wide selection of sights to offer its visitors. The town is musically inclined and attests to this pursuit with a beautiful monument to Strauss and Lanner in Kurpark, the city park. From the end of June to mid-September, delightful operettas are performed in the "sommer arena" in the Kurpark. Mozart took up residence in Baden, and the house in which Beethoven resided, at 10 Rathausgasse, is open Tuesday through Friday, 1600–1800, and Saturday, Sunday, and holidays, 0900–1100 and 1600–1800. The tourist office can provide you with the details of this interesting house and its historic background.

Following a lazy paced spring, Baden comes alive at the beginning of June when the roses burst into full bloom. Trotting season begins at the racetrack, and the city cuts the ribbon on the summer season with a festive concert.

Danube cruise ship heads for en route stop under watchful eye of an Austrian school boy waiting to board.

From Vienna . . .

A DAY EXCURSION DOWN THE DANUBE
DISTANCE BY TRAIN AND BOAT: 102 miles (192 km)
TOTAL TIME: 7 hours, 40 minutes

The Danube is Europe's grand river, second in length only to the Volga and stretching almost 1,800 miles across the continent. Eight countries share its waters. As plains, hills, and mountains succeed one another along its course, the Danube can be sluggish, swift, or even wild.

The Danube rises in Germany's Black Forest—the length of a football field away from the watershed of the Rhine. By the time its waters reach the German city of Ulm (page 439), the Danube becomes navigable by river craft. Between Ulm and Vienna, the Danube takes on an Alpine character. The Danube is unusual among the rivers of the world in that it flows from west to east. At its delta, it empties into the Black Sea.

The *Blue Danube Waltz* is a musical expression of the attractiveness and charm of Austria along the banks of the Danube. The vast countryside— fringed by the Austrian Alps on the south—offers a vista of natural beauty enjoyed by visitors from every part of the world. Although the waters of the river do not always display, especially in times of flood, the color of which the song sings, the beauty of the Austrian countryside through which the Danube flows makes it easy to forget that the waters are actually milky white throughout most of the spring and summer.

We recommend taking the 0844 train to Melk, the point from which the cruise on the Danube begins. The later train departing at 1226 will bring you to Melk in time for unhurried connections with the steamer, but Melk itself is steeped in history and warrants your visit. The earlier train will permit you to wander about Melk's ancient streets, still guarded by the watch towers of its town wall, and to visit Melk's Benedictine Abbey, the epitome of Baroque architecture in Austria.

Melk marks the beginning of the Wachau region of the Danube Valley, where ancient castles stand watch over the steep vineyards and orchards that stretch from the castles' walls downward to the banks of the river below. It is the most picturesque section of the Danube. You are going to have an enjoyable cruise.

Ships of the First Danube Steamship Company (DDSG) ply regularly between Melk and Vienna from mid-May through the end of September. *The Eurailpass is accepted and becomes your boarding ticket.* The trip from Melk to Vienna is downstream in the Danube's swift current. It takes five and one-half hours to complete the steamship portion of the day excursion; the train time to Melk from Vienna is one hour and thirteen minutes.

MELK—*ALTERNATIVE CRUISE UP THE DANUBE*

A Day Excursion from Vienna

DEPART FROM REICHSBRUCKE PIER, VIENNA	ABOARD FIRST DANUBE STEAMSHIP	ARRIVE AT MELK PIER	NOTES
0800	(2)	1610	(2)(3)

DEPART FROM MELK RAIL STATION	TRAIN NUMBER	ARRIVE IN VIENNA WEST-BAHNHOF STATION	NOTES
1838	E1825	1940	(1)

MELK—*AND A CRUISE* DOWN *THE DANUBE*

DEPART FROM VIENNA WEST-BAHNHOF RAIL STATION	TRAIN NUMBER	ARRIVE IN MELK RAIL STATION	NOTES
0844	E1824	0947	(1)
1226	E1524	1341	(1)

DEPART FROM MELK PIER	ABOARD FIRST DANUBE STEAMSHIP	ARRIVE IN REICHSBRUCKE PIER, VIENNA	NOTES
1455	(2)	2015	(2)(3)

(1) Daily, including holidays
(2) Runs mid-May through mid-September. Check schedules in Vienna before departing.
(3) Food service available

Distance: 53 miles/85 km
References: Thomas Cook Tables 800 and 845 (steamship)

Melk maintains a tourist information center in its Rathaus (town hall). As you emerge from the bahnhof (rail station), the abbey dominates the foreground. You can't miss it—it's 1,187 feet long. The town hall sits at the base of the abbey, a mere three blocks distant from the rail station.

Information regarding the town of Melk and its surroundings is available in the tourist center. It's open daily from 0900 to 1200 and again from 1500 to 1800; the telephone number is 230732. The steamship line, DDSG, may be contacted on 2088.

The abbey fared poorly in its earlier years. It was gutted by fire during the Turkish invasion of Austria in 1683, but throughout this and other turmoil, the abbey has managed to preserve its artistic treasures. The Stiftskirche (Abbey Church) is the place to visit first if your time is limited.

The Wachau is noted for the quality of the wine it produces. To sample it, have lunch in one of Melk's charming "Heurigen" taverns before proceeding to the DDSG pier, known locally as the "Schiff Station." You can walk or taxi to the pier.

Going aboard the DDSG steamer, you will not need a boarding pass—the Eurailpass serves that purpose—but we recommend that you check with the information desk on the pier for boarding instructions. Once aboard, you will be requested to register your Eurailpass number in a log book. That concludes the formalities, and you're off on your Danube cruise.

Carry a map of the Danube and refer to it often, for it's one fine scene after another. The market town of Spitz, on the Danube's left bank, is readily recognizable because it nestles at the base of the *Tausendeimer* mountain. The name of the mountain (a thousand vessels) doesn't refer to the river traffic—it refers to the fact that the vineyards on its sides in a good year can produce a thousand vessels of wine.

When the steamship calls at Durnstein, with its red roofs, you should recall that it was here that King Richard I, the Lionhearted of England, was captured and held prisoner returning from the Third Crusade. (Like world wars, the Crusades had numbers, too.)

The next port of call will be Krems, which marks the eastern area of the Wachau. Since olden times, Krems has been the hub of the Wachau wine trade. Here, the Danube becomes dotted with islands as the steamer draws nearer to Vienna.

The steamship company operates four different types of ships on this route. Their flagship is the 2,100-passenger *Theodor Korner.* The others of the fleet have an average passenger capacity of about 1,000, but all offer excellent restaurant facilities. By the way, how's the romance department? Perhaps another bottle of wine might help.

Salzburg fortress offers a view overlooking the Kapitelplatz (Capital Place) and the Salzach River beyond.

A DAY EXCURSION TO SALZBURG
DISTANCE BY TRAIN: 196 miles (315 km)
AVERAGE TRAIN TIME: 3 hours, 23 minutes

If Vienna gives you the impression that it is musically inclined, wait until you see and hear Salzburg. This city of 140,000 has frequently been described as a music festival that never seems to end. No wonder—Salzburg is the birthplace of Mozart. His home is now a museum, and his music has become the very soul of Salzburg.

Music isn't the only thing that makes Salzburg an interesting city to visit. It has a huge fortress-castle called Hohensalzburg. Begun in 1077, it is in a complete state of preservation. In summer there is a terrace restaurant on its south side where you may view the mountains surrounding Salzburg as you dine. A feature of Hohensalzburg is its barrel organ—the only one in Austria. It has been named the Salzburg *Stier* (bull). You'll know why when it booms out over the city. It is not exactly what you would term "music," but it is interesting.

It is claimed that one-half of Salzburg's population is always busy entertaining the other half. When you consider that the festival season in the city extends from January through December, one does not wonder what the Salzburgers may be up to at any given moment—they're either busy entertaining or being entertained.

The trip to Salzburg aboard the Mozart Express is an event in itself. Between Vienna and Linz the train skirts the fertile Danube Valley. When the train leaves the river at Linz, you are treated to a rolling tableau of Austrian farmland followed by a magnificent view of the Alps as you skirt their northern escarpment. It seems as though you have barely settled in your seat before the Mozart Express rolls into Salzburg.

On arrival, check in with the Salzburg tourist information office. It is on the train platform of the station alongside *Bahnsteig* (track) No. 10 (telephone 871–712, 873–638). Open 0845–1930 daily, this office has everything you need to make your day in Salzburg an enjoyable one. A map of the city is yours for the asking.

If you elect to conduct your own tour, begin in the old section of the city. To get there, board bus No. 1, 5, 6, or 51 at the *Autobusbahnhof* (bus station) in front of the railway station and ride to the Staatsbrucke, the fifth stop. This places you on the perimeter of the "old town," where most of the sightseeing is located. Orient yourself with the Kapitelplatz (Capital Place), and you are right in the center of everything. We suggest using the Neptune fountain in the center of the square as a rendezvous point.

SALZBURG—*FORTRESS CITY*

A Day Excursion from Vienna

DEPART FROM VIENNA WESTBAHNHOF STATION	TRAIN NUMBER	ARRIVE IN SALZBURG STATION	NOTES
0735	EC 160	1035	(1)(2)
0740	IC 562	1055	(1)(2)
0840	IC 542	1152	(1)(2)
0900	EC 64	1158	(1)(2)
0935	EC 162	1235	(1)(2)

DEPART FROM SALZBURG STATION	TRAIN NUMBER	ARRIVE IN VIENNA WESTBAHNHOF STATION	NOTES
1525	EC 163	1830	(1)(2)
1605	IC 547	1925	(1)(2)
1705	IC 569	2025	(1)(2)
1800	EC 65	2105	(1)(2)
1905	IC 661	2225	(1)(2)
1925	EC 161	2230	(1)(2)
2105	IC 663	0025+1	(1)(2)

(1) Daily, including holidays
(2) Food service available

Distance: 196 miles/315 km
Reference: Thomas Cook Table 800

Directly behind the Neptune fountain, you will find the cable-car station. These conveyances can whisk you to the top of Salzburg and the Hohensalzburg Fortress in a little less than three minutes. There is a foot path leading to the top; it takes a lot of huffing and puffing, however.

While at the top of Salzburg exploring the fortress, be certain to inspect the barrel organ. It booms out a tune at 0700, 1100, and again at 1800 from March through October. This "organ recital" immediately follows the playing of a thirty-five-bell glockenspiel from a tower on the hillside below the fortress. It's no wonder that Salzburg is very much "alive with the sound of music."

The music-festival season starts in January and ends in December. In other words, it never ends. Afternoons in Salzburg may be spent in one of its comfortable coffee houses watching theatergoers and opera buffs flocking to a performance—everyone in formal attire. In Salzburg, elegance is the way of life.

Salzburg has a charming narrow street called Getreidegasse, which is lined with gilt and wrought-iron trade signs. These trade signs are pictorial devices dating back to the time when few people could read. Don't miss walking through it. It is one of the best spots in town to find authentic Austrian souvenirs for the folks back home.

House No. 9 on the Getreidegasse is probably the most visited house in Salzburg. It is the birthplace of Mozart and is now a museum covering three floors. During the winter months, only the first floor is open to the public. The Mozart House at Marketplatz 8 is the home where the Mozart family resided between 1773 and 1787. It was damaged severely during World War II, and all that remains of the original house is the entrance. In the museum, you may view objects relating to Mozart's life from the years 1773 to 1780.

If you have studied Mozart or watched the movie *Amadeus,* you are aware that Mozart died a pauper in Vienna at age thirty-five and that his body was dumped into an unmarked grave there. Mozart's life story supports the expression applicable to too many of the world's greatest artists: "To be appreciated, one must die first."

Music can be heard almost every night year-round in Salzburg. The Salzburg Festival draws thousands of visitors throughout late July and August; they come to the city again during the last week in January for the Mozart Festival. At times like these, the idea of a Salzburg day excursion sounds like a very good proposal.

Because of its location, Salzburg makes an excellent day excursion between the two base cities of Vienna and Munich. You can go on to Munich after your day-long visit in Salzburg. Several express trains run to Munich during the evening. Check the schedules for a convenient one.

French fleet flagship, the TGV Atlantique is the latest edition of the TGV (*train à grande vitesse,* or "high speed train"), which operates at speeds up to 186 miles per hour. These TGV trains carry ten cars; when run in pairs, their capacity reaches almost 1,000 passengers. Access doors between cars have been eliminated, making it easier to move throughout the train. The TGV Atlantique is silver and blue instead of the well-known orange color of the TGV Paris-Lyon line and comprises ninety-five sets of the world's fastest trains.

26   RAIL-TOUR ITINERARIES

In response to readers' requests for rail-tour itineraries combining several base cities and a selection of day excursions into a rail-tour package, three such rail-tour packages are presented herein. The itineraries are similar to those used in our escorted programs and are considered "route-tested."

All of the base cities and day excursions in the following rail-tour packages are cross-referenced to their descriptions appearing elsewhere in this edition. For example, "Lucerne (142–45)" indicates on which pages Lucerne is described in detail. Each itinerary can be completed with a fifteen-day Eurailpass, but a twenty-one-day or even a one-month Eurailpass may be required if a more leisurely pace is desired. You also may want to consider a Flexipass.

Gateway cities are an important pretour consideration. Discuss them with your travel agent before buying air tickets. When suggested gateways are cities other than the rail-tour base cities, we have included rail schedules to assist in your planning. But as stated previously in this edition of *Europe by Eurail,* the schedules of these rail-tour itineraries *are for planning purposes only. Europe by Eurail* and its publishers cannot be held responsible for the consequences of either changes or inadvertent inaccuracies.

The following rail-tour schedules have been compiled on the basis of what we consider to be the best trains running at the best times; but in almost every case, there are several other trains departing at other times that may be more convenient for your purposes. For this reason, take a current copy of the *Thomas Cook European Timetable* with you.

Hotels suggested for the itineraries have been selected for their convenient locations near the railways stations and/or close to public transportation. Listings in the Addendum to this chapter beginning on page 606, however, are not inclusive of the total accommodations available in any of the base cities.

Hotel price ranges are quoted in local currencies *for planning purposes only* and are subject to change without prior notice. To convert the rates to U.S. dollars, consult the Foreign Exchange listing in the financial section of your hometown newspaper.

You should confirm hotel rates either through your travel agent or directly with the hotel. Most of the hotels listed have U.S. representatives through whom your travel agent can make reservations at no extra cost to you.

Hotel ratings are based on government standards. All hotels listed in the Addendum have our recommendation. Many of the properties have been used previously in our escorted rail-tour programs.

Sleek white ICE (InterCity Express) trains are the mainstays of the German Rail System. ICEs travel at speeds up to 125 miles per hour.

EUROPE À LA CARTE

A rail tour using the Europe by Eurail *base cities of Munich, Berne, and Paris in an adventure through the heart of Europe.*

Base Cities

Munich: Germany's fun capital (408–417). Plan ample time for shopping and sightseeing before beginning your exciting Eurail adventure. Allow for jet-lag, too.

Berne: Medieval elegance in the heart of Switzerland (126–133). An all-weather shopping center. Save the sunny days for Berne's eye-filling day excursions.

Paris: Everyone's "second" city and the only one of its kind (490–99). Mix Paris's pleasures with its unusual array of action-packed day excursions.

Gateways

(1) "Open Jaw": Munich inbound, Paris outbound. Discuss with your travel agent for professional advice.

(2) Frankfurt: ICE 897 to Munich departs 1543 and arrives 1915 or ICE 899 departs 1743 and arrives 2115. Return to Frankfurt on ICE 992 departing 0646 and arriving 1014 or ICE 896, 0846–1214.

(3) Amsterdam: EC 105 to Munich, 0800-1322 (Mannheim), change to ICE 593 departing 1328 and arriving Munich 1617. Return to Amsterdam on ICE 894 to Mannheim, 1246–1532, change to EC 104 Mannheim to Amsterdam, 1537–2051.

(4) Paris: EC 65 Mozart to Munich, 0747–1610. Return to Paris on EC 66 Maurice Ravel, 0750–1620.

Base-City Hotels

Munich: The InterCity Hotel, located in the station, is first choice. Quiet, good restaurant, but usually booked up months in advance. Drei Lowen, one block from the station, is convenient. Balance of those hotels listed in Addendum are clustered nearby. Hilton and Sheraton properties in suburbs have easy tram connections to city center.

Berne: Schweizerhof, on the station plaza, is tops in location, restaurant—and price. Hotel Baeren and Hotel Bristol, are more economical and three minutes' walk to station. Other hotels listed also within short walk of station and maintain highest Swiss standards.

Paris: For economy and excellent location, choose Rèsidence Elysées Maubourg, one block from Maubourg Métro stop. Hotel Lyon-Palace-Paris, one short block away from Gare de Lyon's rail, Métro, and RER connections, has excellent neighborhood-restaurant section. Whole list is A–OK.

Europe à la Carte 15-Day Rail Itinerary

Day 1 Munich–Salzburg (588–91): Visit Mozart's birthplace and listen to Salzburg's sound of music.

Day 2 Munich–Garmisch–Partenkirchen (422–25): Host city to Winter Olympics and gateway to ascent of the mighty Zugspitze.

Day 3 Munich–Berchtesgaden (418–21): Explore salt mines, then soar to Hitler's ill-famed Eagle's Nest.

Day 4 Munich-Innsbruck (426–29): World famous for winter Olympics with year-round exhilarating scenery.

Day 5 Munich–Nuremberg (430–33): Germany's leading toy producers spice activities with fresh gingerbread.

Day 6 Munich–Berne: Base-city transfer via Zurich.

Day 7 Berne–Interlaken (138–41): A day in Alpine splendor, return to Berne by Lake of Thun steamer.

Day 8 Berne–Lucerne (142–45): A rain-or-shine outing with Mount Pilatus and Swiss cheese fondue.

Day 9 Berne–Milan (384–91): A change of pace, a change of place to Italy's bustling northern capital.

Day 10 Berne–Paris: Base-city transfer via Geneva.

Day 11 Paris–Rouen (516–519): Visit historic site of France's Joan of Arc.

Day 12 Paris–Rennes (512–15): Half-timbered houses and a ride on the TGV Atlantique.

Day 13 Paris–Fontainebleau (508–11): Visit the scene where Napoleon ruled and later was vanquished.

Day 14 Lyon–Annecy (340–43): Breathtaking scenery, sparkling water, and a charming medieval marketplace.

Day 15 Paris–Lyon (332–39): City of contrast visited after exciting journey aboard TGV, one of the world's fastest trains.

Tour Tips

Make seat reservations immediately on arrival in Munich (see page 414). At minimum, reserve all base-city legs. Reservations are obligatory on TGV and many EuroCity trains.

Scaling the Zugspitze? Check details and discount information on page 425. Don't overlook the Romantic Road (434–437) and the Golden Pass (134–137) day excursions.

TOURING EUROPE BY EURAIL . . . *EUROPE À LA CARTE* BASE-CITY TRANSFER SCHEDULE

FROM	TO	COOK'S TABLE	DEPART	TRAIN NUMBER	ARRIVE	NOTES
Munich	Berne	75	0811	EC 92	1345	(1)(3)(F)
Berne	Paris	42	0700	TGV EC 422	1124(2)	(1)(F)(R)

EUROPE À LA CARTE DAY-EXCURSION SUGGESTIONS*

BASE CITY	EXCURSION	COOK'S	DEPART	ARRIVE	EBE REF**	RETURN	ARRIVE	NOTES
Munich	Berchtesgaden	790	0751	1027	418–21	1633	1910	(1)(4)
	Garmisch-P.	785	0900	1023	422–25	1831	1954	(1)
	Innsbruck	785/795	0800	1040	426–29	2103	2240	(1)(F)
	Nuremberg	750	0756	0934	430–33	1824	2003	(1)(F)
	Salzburg	790	0825	0955	588–91	1905	2036	(1)(F)
Berne	Interlaken	280	0931	0916	138–41	1944	2032	(1)(F)
	Lucerne	265	0848	1046	142–45	1913	2029	(1)(F)
	Milan	82	0851	1240	384–91	1725	2138	(1)(F)
Paris	Annecy	167	0709(2)	1050	340–43	1920	2254	(1)(F)(R)
	Rennes	125	0820(5)	1035	512–15	1817	2040	(1)(R)
	Fontainebleau	155	0831(2)	0909	508–11	1721	1806	(1)
	Lyon	150	1000(2)	1200	328–35	1749	2004	(1)(F)(R)
	Rouen	115	0915(6)	1026	516–19	1647	1816	(1)

* See appropriate base-city chapters for additional day-excursion suggestions.
** Refers to page numbers in *Europe by Eurail* describing day excursion

(1) Daily, including holidays
(2) Gare de Lyon, Paris
(3) Change to IC 924 in Zurich
(4) Transfer in Freilassing
(5) Gare du Montparnasse, Paris
(6) Gare St. Lazare, Paris

(F) Food service available
(R) Reservations obligatory

Spectacular scenery speeds silently by your train window as you pass through some of Europe's most picturesque and beautiful countryside in a never-ending panorama of landscapes.

EUROPEAN ESCAPADE

A more than passing acquaintance with some of Europe's most fascinating sights and cities. From gateway Luxembourg, you travel to Berne, Amsterdam, and Paris, with shopping in Brussels.

Base Cities

Luxembourg: Fortress city, steeped in European and American history (308–15). Virtually a tax-free city; save some of your dollars for Luxembourg shops.

Berne: Medieval settings in the heart of the Swiss Alps (126–33). Berne's arcaded walkways make shopping and sightseeing easy no matter what the weather may be.

Amsterdam: Canals, cheese shops, diamond cutters, and Rembrandt's finest masterpieces await you (34–41).

Paris: City of Light (490–99). Mix Paris's pleasures with an array of action-packed day excursions.

Gateways

Discuss all gateway possibilities with your travel agent, because the tour's circular itinerary provides a wide selection, including all of the base cities plus Brussels. Depart Brussels for Luxembourg at 1219 for two-hours-thirty-minute EuroCity trip; same service returns you to Brussels at end of tour.

Base City Hotels

Luxembourg: Pick a price. Most of the hotels listed in the Addendum are near the station. Book well in advance, particularly in summer tour season.

Berne: Schweizerhof for luxury, but the other listed hotels offer only a shade less at varying prices. All are within walking distance of the station.

Amsterdam: Victoria Hotel, a scant block from the station, is most convenient and highly recommended. Krasnapolsky Hotel is just another stone's throw away but posh, with prices to match.

Paris: Best bargain and good location is Résidence Elysées Maubourg on the Left Bank. Same for independent Lyon-Palace-Paris Hotel, close to Gare de Lyon.

European Escapade 15-Day Rail Itinerary

Day 1 Luxembourg–Clervaux (316–319): An opportunity to visit site of World War II Battle of the Bulge.

Day 2 Luxembourg–Koblenz (320–23): A rail excursion along the Mosel to the Rhine in German wine country.

TOURING EUROPE BY EURAIL . . . EUROPEAN ESCAPADE BASE-CITY TRANSFER SCHEDULE

FROM	TO	COOK'S TABLE	DEPART	NUMBER	ARRIVE	NOTES
Luxembourg	**Berne**	40	1000	EC 91	1512	(1)(F)
Berne	**Amsterdam**	38	1148	EC 104	2051	(1)(F)
Amsterdam	**Paris**	18	0853	EC 82	1425	(1)(F)(R)(3)
Paris	**Luxembourg**	173	1046	EC 357	1435	(2)(4)(F)

EUROPEAN ESCAPADE DAY-EXCURSION SUGGESTIONS*

BASE CITY	EXCURSION	COOK'S	DEPART	ARRIVE	EBE REF**	RETURN	ARRIVE	NOTES
Luxembourg	Clervaux	219	1010	1100	316–19	1751	1839	(1)
	Koblenz	720	1033	1237	320–23	1719	1923	(1)(F)
Berne	Interlaken	280	0928	1016	138–41	1944	2032	(1)(F)
	Lucerne	265	0931	1046	142–45	1913	2029	(1)(F)
	Milan	82	0851	1240	384–91	1725	2138	(1)(F)
Amsterdam	Alkmaar	225	0922	0953	42–45	1803	1849	(1)
	Enkhuizen	225	0919	1021	46–49	1639	1744	(1)
	Hoorn	225	0849	0930	54–57	2005	2044	(1)
Paris	Annecy	167	0709	1050	340–43	1920	2254	(F)(R)(5)
	Rennes	125	0820	1035	512–15	1818	2040	(1)(F)(R)
	Chartres	125	0700(2)	0756	504–07	1841	1950	(5)
	Fontainebleau	155	0831	0909	508–11	1721	1806	(1)
	Lyon	150	1000	1200	332–39	1749	2004	(1)(F)(R)

* See appropriate base-city chapters for additional day excursions.
** Refers to page numbers in *Europe by Eurail* describing location

(1) Daily, including holidays (F) Food service available
(2) Daily, except Sunday (R) Reservations obligatory
(3) Arrives 10 minutes later in July and August
(4) Departs 1055 on Saturdays
(5) Daily, except some Saturdays (check local schedules)

Day 3 Luxembourg–Berne: Base-city transfer via France.

Day 4 Berne–Interlaken (138–41): View of mighty Jungfrau and cruise on Lake of Thun highlight exciting rail tour.

Day 5 Berne–Lucerne (142–145): Sparkling highlights of Switzerland's lake city plus Mount Pilatus ascent.

Day 6 Berne–Milan (384–391): Cross into Italy for a delightful day of sightseeing in fascinating Milan.

Day 7 Berne–Amsterdam: Base-city transfer via Rhine.

Day 8 Amsterdam–Enkhuizen (46–49): Visit the Zuider Zee museum depicting the Dutch battle with the sea.

Day 9 Amsterdam–Hoorn (54–57): Steam-engine ride from Hoorn to Medemblik; the old Dutch Market on Wednesdays.

Day 10 Amsterdam–Alkmaar (42–45): World-famous cheese market and site of Dutch revolt against Spanish rule.

Day 11 Amsterdam–Paris: Base-city transfer via Brussels.

Day 12 Paris–Chartres (504–507): Palaces and castles abound along with Gothic Cathedral of Notre Dame.

Day 13 Paris–Rennes (512–15): Experience TGV Atlantique at 186 miles per hour.

Day 14 Paris–Fontainebleau (508–11): Visit palace where Napoleon relaxed with Josephine—and others.

Day 15 Paris–Lyon (332–39): "Newest" city of France, with Roman history, visited aboard one of the world's fastest trains, a TGV.

Tour Tips

Book all seat reservations when you arrive in Luxembourg (see page 313). Rhine cruise? Depart Luxembourg (Day 2) at 0930, arriving Koblenz at 1141 (transfer in Trier). Transfer to EC 105 at 1152 for Mainz, arriving there at 1242. You'll get a great view of the Rhine from the train. Lunch in the Mainz station restaurant and depart at 1327 in the direction of Koblenz, but get off in Bingen at 1357. Board the KD Line steamer from the Bingen pier at 1415 (Eurailpass accepted). Then relax on the Rhine until reaching Koblenz at 1755. You may also board a steamer in Mainz at 1425, arriving Koblenz at 1615 (daily, except Mondays). Both services operate April through October. Have dinner at the Weindorf (323). Catch the 2017 back to Luxembourg.

En route to Amsterdam from Berne (Day 7), after departing Mainz, watch on the right-hand side of the train for spectacular Rhine scenery to Koblenz.

For great dining aboard, book a restaurant seat on EuroCity *Rubens* departing Brussels (Day 11) for Paris at 1710, from Monday through Friday.

Sylvan scenes and seascapes blend through the itinerary of the tour "Scandinavian Splendor." *Top:* A Swedish express train flashes along placid waters of the countryside against a backdrop of forests. (Photo courtesy of Swedish National Tourist Office.) *Bottom:* The Silja Line's *Finlandia* plies between Helsinki and Stockholm in the Baltic Sea. (Photo courtesy of Silja Line.)

SCANDINAVIAN SPLENDOR

Tour Scandinavian capitals of Copenhagen, Helsinki, Oslo, and Stockholm and board the Silja Line's newest and finest cruise ship for adventure on the Baltic.

Base Cities

Copenhagen: Jovial, entertaining, the fun capital of Scandinavia (182–89). Save it for the grand finale.

Helsinki: Daughter of the Baltic (260–67). A glittering gem set in a picture-book harbor. Make the best of your "shore leave" by enjoying every moment.

Oslo: Friendly, pleasant, and compact (466–73). Take the Bergen-Flam excursion option if time permits.

Stockholm: Striking harbor skyline, a city of islands and waterways (548–55). Sightseeing must include a visit to Old Town, where it all began centuries ago.

Gateways

All the base cities have direct U.S. air service, even Helsinki. The circular nature of the tour's itinerary makes it possible to select any one of the above base cities as both the inbound and outbound gateway. Our choice would be Copenhagen, which is yours?

Base-City Hotels

Copenhagen: Palace Hotel gets the tourists' nod—convenient location, mid-range rates, and so on. The Plaza, facing the station, is great but difficult to book in high season. All hotels listed in the Addendum are acceptable.

Helsinki: No listing, because we recommend using the Silja Line's accommodations for this tour's out-and-back day excursion, but we can recommend the Presidenti if you elect to extend your stay in Helsinki.

Oslo: The Grand Hotel features Old World elegance with modern conveniences—with the exception of price. The Hotel Nobel, with a wider rate range, is near the Grand Hotel.

Stockholm: Take your pick. All three hotels listed in the Addendum face Central Station. Price is probably the deciding factor. All have acceptable restaurants and are clean and well managed.

Scandinavian Splendor 15-Day Rail Itinerary

If Copenhagen is selected as the in-out gateway, we suggest that you spend jet-lag adjustment time there before validating your Eurailpass and leaving for Oslo.

TOURING EUROPE BY EURAIL...SCANDINAVIAN SPLENDOR BASE-CITY TRANSFER SCHEDULE

FROM	TO	COOK'S TABLE	DEPART	NUMBER	ARRIVE	NOTES
Copenhagen (by sleeper)	Oslo	466	0945	IN 384	1937	(1)(F)(R)
		466	2145	382	0737	(1)(R)
Oslo	Stockholm	470	0820	IN 57	1441	(1)(F)(R)
Stockholm	Helsinki	1250	1800	Silja ferry	0830+1	(1)(F)(R)
Helsinki	Stockholm	1250	1800	Silja ferry	0830+1	(1)(F)(R)
Stockholm	Copenhagen	465	1030	IN 287	1851	(1)(F)(R)
(by sleeper)		465	2212	IN 293	0705+1	(1)(R)

SCANDINAVIAN SPLENDOR DAY-EXCURSION SUGGESTIONS*

BASE CITY	EXCURSION	COOK'S	DEPART	ARRIVE	EBE REF**	RETURN	ARRIVE	NOTES
Copenhagen	Aarhus	450/451	0658(4)	1220	190–93	1726	2148	(4)(F)
	Helsingør	463	0925	1020	194–97	1614	1709	(1)
	Odense	450	0855	1133	202–05	1808	2048	(1)(F)
	Roskilde	450	0855	0913	206–09	1726	1748	(1)(F)
Oslo	Hamar	483	0805	0940	478–81	2058	2228	(1)(F)(R)
	Larvik	488	0909	1124	482–85	1628	1851	(1)
	Lillehammer	483	0805	1020	486–89	2003	2156	(1)(F)
Stockholm	Eskilstuna	471	0810 (bus)	1025	556–59	1530	1750	(3)
	Norrkoping	465	0806	1005	560–63	1755	1953	(1)(F)(R)
	Uppsala	476	0813	0900	564–67	1757	1844	(1)(F)(R)

* See appropriate base-city chapters for additional day-excursion suggestions.

** Refers to page numbers in *Europe by Eurail* describing day excursions

(1) Daily, including holidays   (F) Food service available

(2) Daily, except Sunday   (R) Reservations obligatory

(3) Monday through Friday

(4) Via ferry crossing Kalundborg–Aarhus (Monday through Saturday)

Day 1 Copenhagen–Oslo: Scenic base city transfer.

Day 2 Oslo–Larvik (482–85): Put a fjord in your future with an excursion to Larvik and on to Skien.

Day 3 Oslo–Hamar (478–81): Drink in the beauty of Lake Mjosa before exploring the rail museum in Hamar.

Day 4 Oslo–Lillehammer (486–89): Lillehammer can provide an insight into Norway's culture.

Day 5 Oslo–Stockholm: Colorful base-city transfer.

Day 6 Stockholm–Uppsala (564–67): Spend an interesting day in a city that dates from pagan times.

Day 7 Stockholm–Eskilstuna (556–59): See Sweden's "steel city" and visit 300-year-old Rademacher Forges.

Day 8 Stockholm–Norrkoping (560–63): Surprises such as cacti growing in Sweden await your arrival here.

Day 9 Stockholm–Silja Line cruise to Helsinki (260–67): Cruise the Baltic in luxury to Finland.

Day 10 Helsinki–Stockholm (612–13): Set sail again for Sweden after an exciting day ashore in Helsinki.

Day 11 Stockholm–Copenhagen (182–89): Arrive in Denmark's capital after overland rail through Sweden.

Day 12 Copenhagen–Aarhus (190–93): Ferry and rail transportation join to make an exciting day excursion.

Day 13 Copenhagen–Helsingør (Elsinore) (194–97): A rail visit to north Zealand to inspect Hamlet's castle.

Day 14 Copenhagen–Odense (202–05): A rail visit to the birthplace of Hans Christian Andersen.

Day 15 Copenhagen–Roskilde (206–09): Five Viking ships await your inspection in Roskilde's museum.

Tour Tips

Make the Silja Line cruise to Helsinki and back a highlight of your tour. Book a round-trip cabin and spend a carefree day ashore in Helsinki sans luggage. In Helsinki, ride tram 3T for a quick view of this remarkable city. The Silja Line can also arrange extended shore leave in Helsinki if desired.

ADDENDUM: BASE CITY HOTELS AND INFORMATION

All hotel rates, given in *local currencies* applicable at press time, are subject to change. Rates include breakfast on the Continental Plan, taxes, and service charges. The hotels listed are close to the railway stations. The hotel's street location is next to the hotel name. "Tel:" is the telephone number; "Fax:" is the Fax number.

Amsterdam Hotels (rates in Dutch guilders)

Victoria Scandic	Damrak 1-6	Tel: (20)6234255	Fax:(20) 6252997
4-Star	325–445		Zip: 1012 LG
Krasnapolsky	Dam 9	Tel: (20)5549111	Fax: (20)6228607
4-Star	350–425		Zip: 1012 JS
Damrak	Damrak 49	Tel: (20)6262498	Fax: (20)6250997
4-Star	135–305		Zip: 1012 LL
Classic Hotel	Gravenstr. 14–16	Tel: (20) 6233716	Fax: (20) 638156
3-Star	150–225		Zip: 1012NM

To telephone or fax the Amsterdam hotels listed above from the United States, dial 011–31, then the number listed above. Mailing address should include the zip code and country name; for example, 1012 JS Amsterdam, The Netherlands.

Shopping hours: Monday–Friday, 0830/0900–1730/1800. Some shops close for one morning or afternoon each week as posted. Open until 2100 one evening each week. Saturday, 0830/0900–1600/1700.

Banking hours: Monday–Friday, 0900–1600.

Airport rail link: Schiphol Airport 12 miles southwest of city to Amsterdam Central Station. Train time to airport is about 17–22 minutes. Refer to *Thomas Cook European Timetable,* Table 222. Fare is 5.60 guilders.

Airport bus: KLM bus from Schiphol arrivals hall to Central Station area, 30–45 minutes. Fare is 15 guilders; by taxi (meter), fare is approximately 60 guilders.

Berne Hotels (rates in Swiss francs)

Gauer Schweizerhof	Bahnhofplatz 11	Tel: (31)3114501	Fax: (31)3122179
5-Star	320–390		Zip: CH-3001
Bern	Zeughausg. 9	Tel: (31)211021	Fax: (31) 211147
4-Star	125–240		Zip: CH-3011
Bristol	Schauplatzg. 10	Tel: (31)220101	Fax: (31)229479
4-Star	140–200		Zip: CH-3011
City-Hotel	Bubenbergpl. 7	Tel: (31)3115377	Fax: (31)3110636
3-Star	110–190		Zip: CH-3011
Metropole	Zeughausg. 26–28	Tel: (31)3115021	Fax: (31)3111153
3-Star	130–200		Zip: CH-3001

To telephone or fax the Berne hotels from the United States, dial 011–41, then the number listed. Mailing address should include zip code and country: for example, CH-3001, Berne, Switzerland.

Shopping hours: Monday–Friday, 0800–1830; Saturday until 1600.

Banking hours: Monday–Friday, 0830–1630.

Airport rail link: Zurich Flughaven, 7 miles northeast of Zurich. Rail service to Berne departs 42 minutes past the hour. Time en route (through Zurich Hauptbahnhof), 1 hour, 33 minutes. Trains depart Berne for Zurich airport at 45 minutes past the hour. Baggage may be checked through to final U.S. airport.

Copenhagen Hotels (rates in Danish kroner)

Webers Hotel	Vesterbrogade 11	Tel: (31)311432	Fax: (31)311441
4-Star	895–1,450		Zip: DK-1620
Mayfair	Helgolandsgade 3	Tel: (31)314801	Fax: (31)239686
4-Star	725–1,095		Zip: DK-1653
Palace Hotel	Raadhuspladsen 57	Tel: (33)144050	Fax: (33)145279
4-Star	975–1,150		Zip: DK-1550
Plaza	Bernstorffsgade 4	Tel: (33)149262	Fax: (33)939362
4-Star	1,250–1,850		Zip: DK-1577

To telephone or fax hotels in Copenhagen from the United States, dial 011-45 then the number as listed. Mailing address should include zip code and country name: for example, DK-1620 Copenhagen, Denmark.

Shopping hours: Monday–Thursday, 0900/1000–1730/1800; Friday, 0900/1000–1900/2000; Saturday, 0900/1000–1200/1300/1400.

Banking hours: Monday-Friday, 0930-1600; Thursday until 1800.

Airport bus link: Kastrup Airport, 6 miles southeast of city. Central rail station (opposite Tivoli Gardens) 20–30 minutes. Fare is 15–28 Danish kroner. Departs every 15 minutes.

Luxembourg Hotels* (rates in Belgian francs)

Central Molitor	28 Ave. de la Liberte	Tel: 489911	Fax: 483382
*	3,200–4,200		Zip: 1930
Nobilis Hotel	47 Ave. de la Gare	Tel: 494971	Fax: 403101
*	2,500–3,750		Zip: 1021
President	32 Pl. de la Gare	Tel: 486161	Fax: 486180
*	5,000–6,400		Zip: 1024

* Government of Luxembourg does not rate hotels.

To telephone or fax Luxembourg hotels from the United States, dial 011–352, then the numbers as listed. Mailing address should include zip code: for example, 1930 Luxembourg Ville, Luxembourg.

Shopping hours: Monday–Saturday, 0800–1200, 1400–1800. Most stores closed Monday morning.

Banking hours: Monday–Friday, 0900–1200 and 1400–1700.

Airport bus link: Findel Airport is 4 miles northeast of city. Buses depart Central Station every half hour. Fifteen minutes en route.

Munich Hotels (rates in Deutsche marks)

InterCity	Bahnhofspl. 2	Tel: (89)558571	Fax: (89)596229
4-Star	189–400 Located in station		Zip: D-8000
Drei Lowen	Schillerstr. 8	Tel: (89)551040	Fax: (89)55104905
4-Star	180–238		Zip: D-8000
Germania	Schwanthalerstr 28	Tel: (89)51680	Fax: (89)598491
4-Star	215–265		Zip: D-8000
Atrium	Landwehrstr. 59	Tel: (89)514190	Fax: (89)598491
4-Star	195–245		Zip: D-8000

To telephone or fax Munich hotels from the United States, dial 011–49, then the numbers as listed. Mailing address should include zip code and country: for example, D-8000 Munich, Germany.

Shopping hours: Monday–Friday, 0900–1830; Saturday, 0900–1400; first Saturday in every month open until 1600.

Banking hours: Monday–Friday, 0830–1300 and 1430–1600; Thursday until 1730.

Airport rail link: Connects from S–Bahn station in Hauptbahnhof to Reim station, 1 mile from Reim Airport.

Airport bus link: Direct airport bus service to Hauptbahnhof. Fare is 8 Deutsche marks.

Oslo Hotels (rates in Norwegian kroner)

Grand	Karl Johansgt. 31	Tel: (2)429390	Fax: (2)421225
4-Star	675–830		Zip: N-0159
Bondeheimen	Rosenkrantzgt. 8	Tel: (2)429530	Fax: (2)419437
3-Star	530–990		Zip: 0162
Hotel Nobel	Karl Johansgt. 33	Tel: (2)427480	Fax: (2)420519
4-Star	825–1,950		Zip: N-0106

To telephone or fax Oslo hotels from the United States, dial 011–47, then the numbers as listed. Mailing address should include: Oslo 1, Norway.

Shopping hours: Monday–Friday, 0900/1000–1700*; Thursday, 0900/1000–1800/1900; Saturday, 0900–1300.

Banking hours: Monday–Friday, 0815–1530, until 1700 on Thursday.

Airport bus links: Fornebu Airport, 5.5 miles southwest of Oslo. Bus departs from Oslo Sentral Station for airport every 20 minutes from 0606–2145 (departs from airport to Sentral Station 0720–2200); fare is 25 Norwegian kroner.

* During summer, stores close at 1600.

Paris Hotels (rates in French francs)

Ambassador Concorde	16, blvd Haussmann	Tel: (1)42469263	Fax: (1)40220874
3-Star	1,300–2,000		Zip: F-75009
Concorde St. Lazare	108, rue St. Lazare	Tel: (1)40084444	Fax: (1)42930120
3-Star	950–1,650		Zip: F-75008
Plaza Haussmann	177, blvd Haussmann	Tel: (1)45639383	Fax: (1)45611430
3-Star	650–770		Zip: F-75008
Elysées Maubourg	35, blvd de Latour	Tel: (1)45561078	Fax: (1)47056508
3-Star	560–1,100		Zip: F-75007
Lyon-Palace-Paris	11, rue de Lyon	Tel: (1)43072949	Fax: (1)46289155
3-Star	460–480		Zip: F-75012
Hotel Mansart	5, rue des Capucines	Tel: (1)42615028	Fax: (1)49279744
3-Star	465–565		Zip: F-75001

To telephone or fax the above-listed Paris hotels from the United States, dial 011–33, then the numbers as listed. Mailing address should include zip code and country: for example, F–75009 Paris, France.

Shopping hours: Monday–Saturday, 0930–1830; small shops closed Monday morning; open Monday afternoon until 1830.

Banking hours: Monday–Friday, 0900–1200 and 1400–1600.

Airport rail links: Roissy-Rail (railway services connecting Cité Universitaire, Denfert-Rochereau, Port Royal, Luxembourg, Saint-Michel

Châtelet, and Gare du Nord with Charles de Gaulle Airport), departs every 15 minutes from 0530–2330, 27.50 francs one way without extra métro. Orly-Rail (railway services connecting Boulevard Victor, Javel, Champ-de-Mars, Alma, Invalides, Orsay, Saint-Michel, and Austerlitz with Orly-South and Orly-West Airports), departs every 15 minutes from 0530 to 2045 and every 30 minutes from 2045 to 2245, 20.50 francs one way without extra métro.

Airport bus links: #350–Gare de l'Est/Gare du Nord to Charles de Gaulle Airport, 30 francs; Orlybus-Nation to Charles de Gaulle Airport, 30 francs; #215–Denfert-Rochereau to Orly-South and Orly-West Airports, 21 francs; #183A–Porte de Choisy to Orly-South Airport. Bus leaves from Arc de Triomphe every 15 minutes for Charles de Gaulle Airport, 39 francs. Bus for Orly leaves from Air France Terminal, 30 francs.

Stockholm Hotels (rates in Swedish kronor)

Sheraton	Tegelbacken 6, Box 289	Tel: 142600	Fax: (8)217026
4-Star	1,150–2,180		Zip: S-10123
Reso Continental	Vasagatan/Vattugrand 4	Tel: (8)244020	Fax: (8)113695
3-Star	745–1,875		Zip: S-10121
Terminus	Vasagatan 20	Tel: (8)222640	Fax: (8)248295
4-Star	525–1,320		Zip: S-10123

To telephone or fax the above-listed Stockholm hotels from the United States, dial 011–46, then the numbers as listed. Mailing address should include zip code and country: for example: S-10121 Stockholm, Sweden.

Shopping hours: Monday–Friday, 0900–1800; Saturday, 0930–1400.

Banking hours: Monday–Friday, 0930–1500; Thursday until 1730.

Airport bus link: Arlanda Airport, 24 miles northwest of Stockholm. Pickup points include the Sheraton Hotel and the Central Station. Trip takes 45 minutes; fare is 50 Swedish kronor. SAS limousine, 356 kronor; taxi approximately 400.

See page 613 for Silja Line Terminal information.

27   FERRY CROSSINGS

In addition to unlimited rail travel and other conveniences, a Eurailpass, Eurail Flexipass, or Eurail Youthpass provides holders with passage on ferries conveying train passengers within the Eurailpass countries. In some instances, passengers must detrain and board the ferries; but on most major rail lines, the passenger coaches are loaded directly onto the ferry. In either case, the ferries are equipped with amenities such as restaurants, bars, boutiques, and, when traveling between countries, money exchanges and tax-free shops.

Three major international ferry connections exist between Italy and Greece, Finland and Sweden, and France and Ireland. The distances are considerable and usually involve overnight travel. Details, including schedules and services available, appear on the following pages.

Other ferry crossings of international importance to Eurail travelers are those several connecting the Scandinavian countries of Denmark and Sweden plus the major rail route between Germany and Denmark. The latter lies between Puttgarden, Germany, and Rodby, Denmark. Passenger coaches are loaded on the ferries and the crossing takes a little more than an hour to complete, thereby presenting passengers with the decision either to eat or to shop—but not both. Tax-free liquor and tobaccos are available on this route (at considerable savings); so if your supply of these luxury items is low, we suggest that you shop first and then try the cafeteria line for a snack.

Three ferry crossings run between Denmark and Sweden. The crossings from Copenhagen to Malmö and, to the north of Copenhagen, between Helsingør (Denmark) and Helsingborg (Sweden) are of short duration with no tax-free facilities, but money-exchange services are available. You'll save time by using the bank aboard rather than standing in line at the railway station after disembarking.

The Copenhagen–Malmö crossing is by hydrofoil (Cook's Table 1215). Eurailpass holders get a 50 percent fare reduction. See page 184 of this edition for more details. Between Helsingør (Elsinore) and Helsingborg, passenger coaches are conveyed onto the ferry for the crossing.

The last of the three crossings is a three-hour cruise between Frederickshavn, on Denmark's Jutland Peninsula, and Goteborg, Sweden. Here, you leave the train and board the ferry (Cook's Table 1205). The crossing gives you ample time for shopping as well as eating—even a brief promenade on the deck may be made, weather permitting, of course.

BALTIC FERRY CROSSINGS

Silja Line Between Finland and Sweden

STOCKHOLM—HELSINKI V.V.

Stockholm	Depart daily	1800
Helsinki	Arrive following day	0830
Helsinki	Depart daily	1800
Stockholm	Arrive following day	0830

STOCKHOLM—TURKU V.V.

Depart Stockholm	Arrive Turku
0800	1900
2000	0800 following morning
Depart Turku	Arrive Stockholm
1000	1900
2000	0700 following morning

Reference: Thomas Cook European Timetable, Table 1250. Schedule is valid through 31 December 1995.

Eurailpass and Eurail Youthpass Bonus: Free deck passage on Silja Line day sailings between Stockholm and Turku/Helsinki (cabins extra).

Salmon and smoked reindeer, caviar and crayfish are just some of the local delicacies served while you watch the panoramic archipelago through your Silja Line ship's window. During your cruise, you'll experience the Baltic Sea's stunning beauty—thousands of islands form enchanting archipelagos, which are visible all day (and night) under the glow of Scandinavia's midnight sun.

Silja's luxurious ships have all types of accommodations from four-berth family cabins to luxury cabins and suites. There are facilities and activities to suit everyone's needs and desires. There are swimming pools and saunas, discos and night clubs, organized children's activities, shopping in Scandinavia's largest duty-free shop and more.

FINLAND–SWEDEN VIA EURAIL

The Silja Line has modern passenger terminals in Stockholm, Turku, Helsinki, Travemünde, and Malmö that rival any airport for convenience. Eurailpass holders are entitled to discounted rates on Silja Line and may use the food services and rest rooms aboard, but will not be provided with sleeping accommodations unless cabin space is reserved and paid for. Schedules are shown on the opposite page. Cabins may be reserved in advance by contacting Silja Line's U.S. agent:

> Bergen Line, Inc.
> 505 Fifth Avenue
> New York, NY 10017–4893
> Telephone: (800) 323–7436; (212) 986–2711
> Fax: (212) 983–1275

Crossing between Sweden and Finland, you may select between two routes: Stockholm-Helsinki direct, or Stockholm-Turku with train connections or the Silja Line express bus service between Turku and Helsinki. Our preference is the direct route between the two capital cities because it gives you a few more hours aboard ship to enjoy the scenery, which is spectacular. Both routes traverse the breathtaking archipelago between the two countries.

Although your Eurailpass entitles you to a discounted ticket issued by the Silja Line, you also need to obtain a boarding pass before embarking. If you need a ticket and a boarding pass, you should be at the ferry terminal one and one-half to two hours before ship departure; one-half hour is adequate if you already have your ticket. All terminals have cafeterias, waiting rooms, and baggage lockers.

Silja Terminal—Stockholm: Reached by underground line No. 13 or 14, both running from the city's Central Station to the end of the line—Ropsten. The fare is 12 Swedish kronor. Taxi fare from the train station to the Silja Line terminal is approximately 75 kronor and takes about 15 minutes.

Silja Terminal—Helsinki: Reached by tram No. 3T from the central railway station. Fare is 8.00 Finnish markkaa; journey takes 15 minutes. The taxi between the rail station and Silja terminal costs approximately 35 markkaa and takes 10 minutes.

Silja Terminal—Turku: Reached from Turku central station by train to harbor station (most through trains terminate at harbor). Taxi from central station costs about 30 markkaa and takes about 10 minutes.

MEDITERRANEAN FERRY CROSSING
Between Brindisi, Italy and Patras, Greece
Ferry Service Provided by
Adriatica di Navigazione or Hellenic Mediterranean Lines

DEPART BRINDISI	ARRIVE PATRAS	NOTES	DEPART PATRAS	ARRIVE BRINDISI	NOTES
2000	1330+1	(1)(2)	1700	0930+1	(4)
2200	1800+1	(3)			
2200	1700+1	(2)(3)	2100	1300+1	(6)

(1) Summer only, both lines	(4) Summer only, Hellenic
(2) Adriatica	(5) Summer only, Adriatica
(3) Hellenic	(6) Both lines

References: *Thomas Cook European Timetable*, Tables 1490 and 1525.

Arrivals and departures are shown in local times and are subject to cancellation or alteration without notice. Days of operation vary. Check with the Adriatica and Hellenic agents listed on page 615. For service between Brindisi and the Greek island of Corfu or Igoumenitsa, on the Greek mainland, telephone Extra Value Travel (813) 394–3384.

Reservation Fee: U.S. $3.00 (all year). Advance reservations recommended during July and August. During high season (June through September), a surcharge (U.S. $14.00) must be paid.

Before boarding, all passengers must check in at the pier office of the ferry line issuing the reservation.

Deck passage is free for Eurailpass holders. Meals and port charges are not included. "Deck passage" allows you to board the ferry. Aboard, you are limited to the public areas and facilities of the vessel unless you book accommodations.

RATES*
Reclining Seats and Cabin Rates
(Based on Eurailpass Credit)

Reclining Seats	Pullman Berths	3- & 4-Berth Cabins	2-Berth Cabins	Deluxe 2-Bed Cabins
$22	$31	$46	$90	$143

* Prices quoted at press time are per person, subject to change without notification.

Authors' suggestion: The port cities of Brindisi and Patras are interesting, charming, and steeped in history. Why not take a day to see them at a leisurely pace? Plan to arrive a day before your scheduled ferry departure. Ask your concierge to call ahead for a hotel reservation. Also ask him to check on your ferry reservation. The address and telephone numbers of the city tourist information offices are posted in the arrival halls of the rail stations.

GREECE–ITALY VIA EURAIL

Eurail covers travel via ferry facilities operated jointly by the Hellenic Mediterranean Lines and the Adriatica Line between Brindisi, Italy, and Patras, Greece. Departing either Greece or Italy, you must present your Eurailpass to the shipping-company office in the port and have a ticket and a boarding pass issued before boarding.

Eurailpass holders are granted free deck passage, but meals, reclining chairs, or sleeping accommodations are not included. (Reclining chairs, by the way, are similar to those found in commercial airlines and are a great bargain for the budget-minded traveler.) Reclining seats and cabin rates are shown on the opposite page. Reservations for departure dates and cabin accommodations may be reserved in advance by contacting:

Extra Value Travel, Inc. or All Leisure Travel
(agent for Adriatica) (agent for Hellenic)
683 South Collier Blvd. 1 Hallidie Plaza
Marco Island, FL 33937 San Francisco, CA 94102
Telephone: (813) 394–3384 Telephone: (415) 989–7434
Fax: (813) 394–4848 Fax: (415) 986–4037

Patras Ferry Terminal: To reach the office from the railway station, turn left as you exit the station. Walk along the street side of the quay approximately 300 yards to the office marked "Central Agency." Summer hours are 0900–2200 daily. Winter hours are 0900–1300 and 1700–2200. *Report on day of embarkation only.* No baggage checking is available. Useful telephone numbers for information: 429520 or 421614.

Brindisi Ferry Terminal: It's a 15-minute walk downhill to the Seno di Levante pier at the foot of Corso Umbert, Corso Garibaldi, and Via del Mera, the streets leading to the waterfront. The terminal is on the right, just before the pier. It opens daily 2 hours prior to departure times. With one peton (a telephone token) and a lot of patience, call ahead to the pier on 22861.

Attenzione (That's "attention" in Italian): From the time you arrive in Brindisi until you are safely aboard the ferry, beware of "entrepreneurs" approaching you with offers to help. Many are garbed in official-looking uniforms or are wearing "Official Guide" headgear. They bear alarming messages such as, "I have bad news. All of the deck space for tonight's sailing has been sold out." Then, he relates the good news: "You are fortunate in meeting me, for I can take you to an agency where a few cabins are still available." With that, he'll reach for your baggage unless, by now, you have interrupted his presentation with a firm, "No, thank you." If he insists, *Polizia* is another good word to inject into the conversation.

IRISH FERRY LINE FROM IRELAND TO FRANCE

	Day	Depart Ireland	Arrive Next Day France
Jan 1–Mar 28*			
Sep 28–Dec 31*			
Rosslare to Le Havre	Wed	1700	1500
	Sun	1700	1500
Rosslare to Cherbourg	Fri	2230	1730
Mar 29–Jun 1*			
Aug 31–Sep 9*			
Rosslare to Le Havre	Tu,We,Th,Fr,Sa	1700	1500
Rosslare to Cherbourg	Mon & Sun	1700	1100
Jun 2–Aug 30			
Rosslare to Le Havre	Tue & Thu	1700	1500
Rosslare to Cherbourg	Wed	1500	1300
	Mon	1430	0830
Cork to Le Havre	Sat	1700	1100
	Sun	1700	1530
Cork to Cherbourg	Fri	1430	0900
Sep 10–Sep 27*			
Rosslare to Le Havre	Wed & Sun	1700	1500
Rosslare to Cherbourg	Fri	1700	1100

FRANCE TO IRELAND

	Day	Depart France	Arrive Next Day Ireland
Jan 1–Mar 28*			
Sep 28–Dec 31*			
Le Havre to Rosslare	Tue	1800	1400
	Thu	2000	1600
Cherbourg to Rosslare	Sat	2030	1400
Mar 29–Jun 1*			
Aug 31–Sep 9*			
Le Havre to Rosslare	We,Th,Fr,Sa,Su	1800	1400**
Cherbourg to Rosslare	Mon & Tue	2030	1400**
Jun 2–Aug 30			
Le Havre to Rosslare	Mon,Wed,Fri	1800	1400
Cherbourg to Rosslare	Tue & Sun	1930	1130
Le Havre to Cork	Thu	1600	1230
Cherbourg to Cork	Sat	1930	1400
Sep 10–Sep 27*			
Le Havre to Rosslare	Tue & Thu	1800	1400
Cherbourg to Rosslare	Sat	2030	1400

* Departure dates for this period vary by week. Please ask for details or check Thomas Cook Timetable. Cherbourg/Cork service may operate. No sailing Dec 22–26.

** Vessel arrival 1 hour later Sep 29–Oct 22 inclusive.

IRELAND–FRANCE VIA EURAIL

Eurailpass holders may travel between the Continent and the Republic of Ireland aboard the vessels of the Irish Ferries line. Service from the French ports of Cherbourg and Le Havre to the Irish port of Rosslare is available year-round; service to the Irish port of Cork from Le Havre is also available from late June until late August. Ferry service is provided by the line's two ships, the *Saint Killian II* and the *Saint Patrick II*. The *Saint Killian* is a 10,256-ton vessel with a capacity of 2,000 passengers and 380 cars; the *Saint Patrick* can carry 1,630 passengers and 300 cars.

Eurailpass travelers are entitled to free deck passage (reservations are mandatory even for free deck space July and August), but meals and cabin accommodations are not included. For cabin rates, availability, and reservations, call or write: Lynott Tours, Inc. (agents for Irish Ferries), 350 Fifth Avenue, Suite 2619, New York, NY 10118. Telephone (212) 760–0101; toll free (800) 221–2474; or fax (212) 695–8347.

All passages are overnight. Cabin accommodations may also be booked at the ports when presenting your Eurailpass for a boarding pass. The check-in points are usually open 2 hours prior to sailing times. Passengers are requested to check in not less than 1 hour before the sailing time.

Rosslare Ferry Terminal: Trains from Dublin and Limerick connect with the Irish Continental ferries on the Rosslare harbor pier. There are no transfer costs.

Cork Ferry Terminal: Trains from the Heuston Station in Dublin connect with the Irish Ferries in Cork. A taxi from the station to the pier is recommended.

Le Havre Ferry Terminal: A bus transfer is available between the ferry terminal and the SNCF rail station. The cost of the transfer is 8 francs. The bus is available for connections with all principal trains to and from Paris.

Cherbourg Ferry Terminal: Bus transfer service from the SNCF rail station is not available. Alternatively, a taxi service is available for about 20 francs. Inquiries should be made because bus-transfer service may be implemented.

Connolly Station: Trains connecting Dublin with the Rosslare ferry terminal use this station. A sign directing visitors to the nearby tourist information office on O'Connell Street is located to the right of the station's cloakroom in the concourse. The train information office is just beyond the cloakroom on the right-hand side. Use the side escalator to the street exit. A taxi stand is located at the station front.

Heuston Station: Board any train outbound from Dublin to Cork but check to be certain that you are in a coach bound for Cork. Some trains serve both Cork and Limerick, splitting at Limerick Junction. Train information is available from any of the ticket windows alongside tracks 1 and 2.

Le Shuttle, which provides car, coach, and lorry (road freight) transportation through the Channel Tunnel, links Folkestone, England, with Calais, France, in just thirty-five minutes from platform to platform. Car passengers are free to walk around in the sound-proofed, air-conditioned environment. Each train can accommodate up to 180 cars or 120 cars and twelve coaches. (Photo courtesy of Eurotunnel.)

PICTOGRAPHS

. . . symbols used in and around European Rail
Facilities to direct and assist passengers

Rest rooms
Toilettes
Toiletten
Servicios
Toilette

Ladies' rest room
Toilettes (pour dames)
Toiletten (damen)
Senoras
Toilette-signore

Men's rest room
Toilettes (pour hommes)
Toiletten (herren)
Caballeros
Toilette-signori

Bath
Bains
Bader
Bano
Bagni

Shower
Douches
Dusche
Duchas
Docce

Telephone
Telephone public
Offentlicher fernsprecher
Telefono publico
Telefono pubblico

Telegram
Telegraphe
Telegrammannahme
Telegrafo
Telegrafo

Platform
Quai
Bahnsteig
Anden
Marciapiede

Call for porter
Porteur
Gepacktrager
Mozo de equipajes
Facchino

Taxi stand
Station de taxis
Taxistand
Parada de taxis
Posteggio taxi

Rent-a-car
Location de voitures sans chauffeur
Auto am bahnhof
Servicio "tren-auto"
Servizio "treno + auto"

Entrance
Entree
Eingang
Ingreso
Ingresso

Exit
Sortie
Ausgang
Salida
Uscita

INFORMATION

Information
Bureau de renseignements
Information Auskunft
Oficina de informacion
Ufficio informazioni

Tickets
Guichet des billets
Fahrkartenschalter
Taquilla de billetes
Sportello biglietti

RESERVATION

Reservation
Reservation des places
Platzreservierung
Reserva de plazas
Prenotazione dei posti

Luggage registration office
Enregistrement des bagages
Gepaeckannahme
Facturacion de equipajes
Registrazione dei bagagli

Baggage check room
Consigne des bagages
Gepackaufbewahrung
Consigna de equipajes
Deposito bagali

Locker
Consigne automatique
Gepack-schliessfach
Consigna automatica
Deposito bagali a cassette automatiche

Lost & Found
Bureau des objets perdus
Fundbiiro
Oficina de objetos perdidos
Ufficio oggetti smarriti

Customs
Bureau de douane
Zollamt
Despacho de aduanas
Ufficio doganale

Currency exchange
Bureau de change
Wechselstube
Oficina de cambio
Ufficio cambio

Waiting room
Salle d'attente
Wartesaal
Sala de espera
Sala di attesa

Barber—Beauty Parlor
Coiffeur
Friseur
Peluqueria
Parucchiere

Restaurant
Buffet (restaurant de gare)
Bahnhofswirtshaft
Fonda
Ristoratore

Do Not Drink Water
Eau non potable
Dies ist kein Trinkwasser
Agua no potable
Acqua nonpotabile

Drinking water
Eau potable
Trinkwasser
Agua potable
Acqua potabile

or

Post office
Bureau de poste
Postamt
Oficina de correos
Ufficio postale

Smoking permitted
Fumeurs
Raucher
Fumadores
Fumatori

No smoking
Non fumeurs
Nichtraucher
Prohibido fumar
Vietato fumare

Elevator
Ascenseur
Fahrstuhl
Ascensor
Ascensore

Escalator
Escalier roulant
Rolltreppe
Escalera mecanica
Scala mobile

Bus
Autobus
Autobus
Autobus
Autobus

Do Not Enter
Defense d'entrer
Zutritt verboten
Prohibido el paso
Ingresso vietato

24-HOUR TIME CONVERTER

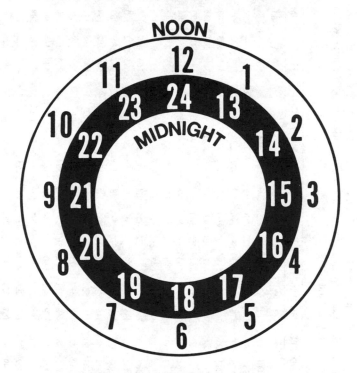

AN EASY GRAPHIC MEANS OF CONVERTING STANDARD 12-HOUR TIME TO 24-HOUR TIME AND VICE VERSA

Courtesy of Thomas Cook Ltd.
Thomas Cook International Timetable
Peterborough, England

RAIL FARES BETWEEN BASE CITIES

First Class one-way fares (*without* a Eurailpass) between base cities are listed in U.S. dollars, but do not include seat reservations fees or sleeping car accommodations charges. Rates applicable as of press time and subject to change without notice. Second Class fares are approximately one-third less than First Class.

	AMS	ATH	BAR	BER	BRN	BRU	BUD	CPH	DUB	HAM	HEL	LIS	LUX	LYN	MAD	MIL	MUC	NCE	OSL	PAR	ROM	STK	VEN
Amsterdam		618	233	142	290	47	354	200	343	111	363	318	81	202	258	289	255	246	340	100	363	325	313
Athens	618		462	535	393	574	440	697	714	600	843	584	475	390	524	317	391	361	800	471	270	797	398
Barcelona	233	462		437	187	237	331	433	376	338	604	122	218	91	62	172	240	102	573	133	182	558	265
Berlin	142	535	437		297	177	125	80	476	55	243	585	190	213	499	229	135	273	200	223	305	168	184
Berne	290	393	187	297		143	247	356	346	289	519	304	92	92	244	77	153	171	496	103	153	481	245
Brussels	47	574	237	177	143		301	248	346	159	411	321	43	112	261	212	127	203	388	302	199	529	294
Budapest	354	440	331	125	247	301		404	545	315	567	453	300	339	393	159	127	527	544	294	484	125	42
Copenhagen	200	697	433	80	356	248	404		537	97	163	565	261	448	505	289	418	527	140	243	467	643	362
Dublin	343	714	376	476	346	346	545	537		448	700	435	328	345	438	397	418	389	685	243	467	643	510
Hamburg	111	600	338	55	289	159	315	97	448		243	593	173	401	593	173	173	461	205	205	351	197	279
Helsinki	363	843	604	243	519	411	567	163	700	243		728	424	695	668	452	452	690	164	457	647	46	525
Lisbon	318	584	122	585	304	321	453	565	435	593	728		303	303	60	294	362	401	695	192	300	680	387
Luxembourg	81	475	218	190	92	43	300	261	328	173	424	303		78	243	244	173	339	588	134	253	578	234
Lyon	202	390	91	213	92	112	339	448	345	401	695	303	78		153	234	173	244	588	80	149	578	337
Madrid	258	524	62	499	244	261	393	505	438	593	668	60	243	153		234	302	164	635	195	240	620	327
Milan	289	317	172	229	77	212	159	289	397	173	452	294	244	234	234		94	44	554	154	76	535	92
Munich	255	391	240	135	153	127	127	418	418	173	452	362	173	173	302	94		138	448	175	140	311	92
Nice	246	361	102	273	171	203	527	527	389	461	690	401	339	244	164	44	138		586	146	96	657	163
Oslo	340	800	573	200	496	388	544	140	685	205	164	695	588	588	635	554	448	586		442	588	118	384
Paris	100	471	133	223	103	302	294	243	243	205	457	192	134	80	195	154	175	146	442		224	400	267
Rome	363	270	182	305	153	199	484	467	467	351	647	300	253	149	240	76	140	96	588	224		609	159
Stockholm	325	797	558	168	481	529	125	643	643	197	46	680	578	578	620	535	311	657	118	400	609		352
Vienna	313	398	265	184	245	294	42	362	510	279	525	387	234	337	327	92	92	163	384	267	159	352	

British & European Rail Passes
BRITRAIL PASS

(Prices applicable as of January 1, 1995, in U.S. Dollars)

BRITRAIL PASS* gives you unlimited rail travel in England, Scotland and Wales for periods ranging from 8 days to one month.

	First Class		Standard Class	
	Adult	Senior (60 & over)	Adult	Senior (60 & over)
8 days	$299	$279	$219	$199
15 days	$489	$455	$339	$305
22 days	$615	$555	$425	$379
1 month	$715	$645	$495	$445

BRITRAIL YOUTH PASS (ages 16-25, Standard Class only)

8 days	$179	22 days	$339
15 days	$269	1 month	$395

BRITRAIL FLEXIPASS* Travel by rail for any 4, 8 or 15 days within one month (within two months for Youth 15 day). Days of travel need not be consecutive.

		Adult	Senior	Youth
4 days/1 month	First Class	$249	$229	-
	Standard	$189	$169	$155
8 days/1 month	First Class	$389	$350	-
	Standard	$269	$245	$219
15 days/1 month	First Class	$575	$520	-
	Standard	$395	$355	-
15 days/2 months	Standard	-	-	$309

* Children under 5 travel free. Children 5 thru 15 years pay 1/2 adult fare for Britrail Pass and Flexipass. Youth = 16 thru 25 years, and Senior Citizen = 60 years and over.

LONDON VISITOR TRAVELCARD
Hop on and off of the subway and red double-decker buses in Central London. (Days of travel are consecutive).

	Adult	Child (5-15 years)
3 days	$25	$11
4 days	$32	$13
7 days	$49	$21

Call **1-800-722-7151** to order!

With your order, you receive a FREE timetable and fold-out rail map.

BRITFRANCE RAILPASS

Unlimited rail travel in Britain and France, plus one round-trip channel crossing by catamaran.

	Adult 1st Class	Adult Standard	Youth (12-25) Standard
5 days/15	$359	$259	$220
10 days/1 month	$539	$399	$340

Call about BritFrance Rail & Drive Passes. Children 4-11 pay 1/2 fare; under 4 travel free.

BRITIRELAND PASS

Unlimited rail travel in England, Scotland, Wales, Northern Ireland and the Republic of Ireland, and round-trip Sealink ferry service between Holyhead and Dun Laoghaire, Fishguard and Rosslare or Stranraer and Larne.

	First Class	Second Class
5 days in 15	$389	$269
10 days in 1 month	$599	$419

Children 5-15 pay half fare; under 5 travel free.

EURAIL PASS

(Prices applicable as of January 1, 1995, in U.S. Dollars)

EURAIL PASS*

is a convenient card for *unlimited 1st class rail travel* throughout 17 countries of Europe.

15 days	$498	2 months	$1,098
21 days	$648	3 months	$1,398
1 month	$798		

EURAIL SAVERPASS*

For three or more people traveling together. *Unlimited 1st class rail travel*. Same privileges as the regular Eurailpass, but requires that the group always travel together. (Saverpass for two people traveling together is valid between October 1 and March 31 only).

15 day Eurail Saverpass (price per person)	$430
21 day Eurail Saverpass (price per person)	$550
1 month Eurail Saverpass (price per person)	$678

EURAIL FLEXIPASS*

Unlimited 1st class rail travel for any 5, 10 or 15 days within a 2-month period with the same privileges as the regular Eurailpass.

Any 5 days within 2 months Flexipass	$348
Any 10 days within 2 months Flexipass	$560
Any 15 days within 2 months Flexipass	$740

Call 1-800-722-7151 to order!

With your order, you receive a FREE timetable and fold-out rail map.

EURAIL YOUTHPASS is designed only for people under 26 years of age. It entitles you to 15 days, 1 or 2 full months of *unlimited 2nd class rail travel* through 17 countries of Europe.

15 day Youthpass	$398
1 month Youthpass	$578
2 month Youthpass	$768

EURAIL YOUTH FLEXIPASS Designed only for people under 26 years of age, entitles you to *unlimited 2nd class rail travel* for any 5, 10 or 15 days within a 2-month period.

Any 5 days within 2 months	$255
Any 10 days within 2 months	$398
Any 15 days within 2 months	$540

EUROPASS Designed for travel in the five most frequently visited countries of Europe: France, Germany, Italy, Spain and Switzerland. You determine the number of countries visited based on the number of travel days purchases. Optional add-on countries: Austria, Belgium and Luxembourg (considered one country), and Portugal.

	Adult 1st Class	Youth* 2nd Class
3 COUNTRIES		
Any 5 days within 2 months	$280	$198
Any 6 days within 2 months	$318	$226
Any 7 days within 2 months	$356	$254
4 COUNTRIES		
Any 8 days within 2 months	$394	$282
Any 9 days within 2 months	$432	$310
Any 10 days within 2 months	$470	$338
5 COUNTRIES		
Any 11 days within 2 months	$508	$366
Any 12 days within 2 months	$546	$394
Any 13 days within 2 months	$584	$422
Any 14 days within 2 months	$622	$450
Any 15 days within 2 months	$660	$478
ASSOCIATE COUNTIRES		
Austria	$35	$25
Belgium & Luxembourg	$22	$16
Portugal	$22	$16

Associate countries extend the geographic area of the pass, they do not extend the pass' length in days.
*Youth pass for persons under 26 years.

Passes not refundable in case of loss, theft or once validated. An insurance option is available for $10 per pass, which refunds 100% of the unused portion of the pass in the event of loss or theft. Unused, unvalidated passes must be submitted to the issuing office within one year of issue date. Any refund is subject to a 15% cancellation charge. Please read the "Conditions of Use" on your pass. Prices applicable as of January 1, 1995. Children under 12 pay half price; under 4 travel free.

COUNTRY & REGIONAL PASSES

AUSTRIAN RABBIT CARD
Unlimited travel, for the 4 days you choose, on the entire Austrian rail network.

	First Class	Second Class
Any 4 days within 10	$153	$103
Junior* 4 days in 10	$95	$64

*Junior: Available only for passengers under 26 on their first date of travel. Children under 7 free.

BENELUX
Unlimited travel, for the days you choose, on the entire national rail networks of Belgium, the Netherlands and Luxembourg.

	First Class	Second Class
Any 5 days in 17	$185	$124
Junior* Any 5 days in 17	-	$92

*Junior: Available only for passengers under 26 on their first date of travel. Children under 4 free.

CENTRAL EUROPE
Unlimited travel, for the days you choose, on the entire national rail networks of Czech Republic, Germany, Poland and Slovakia.

	First Class
Any 10 days/1 month	$398

Children under 14 half adult fare; under 4 free.

GERMANY
Unlimited rail travel for any 5, 10 or 15 days within a 1-month period for the entire German Rail system.

	First Class		Second Class		
	1st Person	2nd Person Twinpass*	1st Person	2nd Person Twinpass*	Junior
5 days/1 month	$250	$200	$170	$130	$130
10 days/1 month	$390	$308	$268	$200	$178
15 days/1 month	$498	$400	$348	$250	$218

*Twinpass: Two people traveling together: 1st person pays normal German Railpass price (1st or 2nd Class). 2nd person pays Twinpass price in applicable class. Junior: Under 26 years of age.

ITALY
Unlimited travel, for the days you choose, on the national rail networks of Italy, including Intercity, Eurocity and Rapido trains with no surcharge. A supplementis required for TR450 trains.

ITALIAN RAIL PASS

	First Class	Second Class
8 days	$226	$152
15 days	$284	$190
21 days	$330	$220
30 days	$396	$264

ITALIAN FLEXI RAILCARD

4 days within 9 days	$170	$116
8 days within 21 days	$250	$164
12 days within 30 days	$314	$210

Children from 4-11 half adult fare; under 4 free.

PRAGUE EXCURSION Enjoy a side trip to the historic Czech capital. First class rail travel from any Czech border crossing to Prague and return.

	Adult	Youth (12-25)	Child (4-11)
7 days	$49	$39	$25

Children under 4 free.

SCANDINAVIA Unlimited travel, for the days you choose, on the national rail networks of Denmark, Finland, Norway and Sweden.

	First Class	Second Class
Any 4 days in 15	$189	$155
Any 9 days in 21	$325	$265
Any 14 days in 1 month	$475	$369

Children from 4-11 half adult fare; under 4 free.

Call about BritRail/Drive, Eurail/Drive, Europass/Drive, and German Rail/Drive Passes.

To order call:
RAIL PASS EXPRESS, INC.
2737 Sawbury Blvd., Columbus, OH 43235
Payment by Visa or MasterCard
1-800-722-7151
FAX: 1-614-764-0711
With your order, you receive a rail timetable and a fold-out rail map.

Pass availability and prices are subject to change.

PASSPORT OFFICES THROUGHOUT THE U.S.

You may apply for a passport at any passport agency and at many Clerks of Court Offices or Post Offices designated to accept passport applications. The regional offices are as follows:

Boston: Thomas P. O'Niell Federal Building, 10 Causeway Street, Suite 247, Boston, Massachusetts 02202-1094; (617) 565–6990.

Chicago: Kluczynski Office Building, 230 South Dearborn Street, Room 380, Chicago, Illinois 60604; (312) 353–7155.

Honolulu: New Federal Building, 300 Ala Moana Boulevard, Room C-106, P.O. Box 50815, Honolulu, Hawaii 96850-0001; (808) 541–1918.

Houston: Mickey Leland Federal Building, 1919 Smith Street, Suite 1100, Houston, Texas 77002-8049; (713) 653–3153.

Los Angeles: Federal Building, 11000 Wilshire Boulevard, Los Angeles, California 92061; (310) 575–7070.

Miami: Claude Pepper Federal Office Building, 51 Southwest First Avenue, Room 1616, Miami, Florida 33130-1680; (305) 536–4681.

New Orleans: 701 Loyal Avenue, Postal Services Building, T-12005, New Orleans, Louisiana 70113; (504) 589–6166.

New York: Rockefeller Center, International Building, 630 Fifth Avenue, Room 270, New York, New York 10020; (212) 541–7710 or (212) 399–5290.

Philadelphia: Federal Building, 600 Arch Street, Room 4426, Philadelphia, Pennsylvania 19106; (215) 597–7480.

San Francisco: Tishman Speyer Building, 525 Market Street, Room 200, San Francisco, California 94105; (415) 744–4010.

Seattle: Federal Building, 915 Second Avenue, Room 992, Seattle, Washington 98174; (206) 553–7745 or (206) 553–7747.

Stamford: One Landmark Square, Broad and Atlantic streets, Stamford, Connecticut 06901; (203) 325–3538.

Washington, D.C.: Room G62, 1425 K Street NW, Washington, D.C. 20522-1705; (202) 326–6060.

PASSPORT INFORMATION

Passport Services, located at the Bureau of Consular Affairs, Department of State, 2201 C Street NW, Room 5813, Washington, D.C. 20520, provides a recorded message at (202) 647–0518 that describes the documents you need and the application process for obtaining a passport as well as reporting the loss or theft of your passport. It also explains how you can obtain a copy of the report of a birth or death of a U.S. citizen abroad. The message will direct you to the proper agencies for information regarding naturalization, travel advisories, customs regulations, and shots required by various countries.

EUROPEAN TOURIST OFFICES IN NORTH AMERICA

AUSTRIAN NATIONAL TOURIST OFFICE

Chicago: 500 N. Michigan Avenue, Suite 1950, Chicago, Illinois 60611. Tel: (312) 644–8029. Fax: (312) 644–6526.

Houston: 1300 Post Oak Blvd., Suite 1700, Houston, Texas 77056. Tel: (713) 850–8888. Fax: (9001–713) 850–7857.

Los Angeles: P.O. Box 491938, Los Angeles, California 90049. Tel: (310) 477–3332. Fax: (310) 477–5141.

New York: P.O. Box 1142, New York, New York 10108-1142. Tel: (212) 944–6880. Fax: (212) 730–4568.

Montreal: Office National Autrichien du Tourisme, 1010 Quest Rue Sherbrooke, Suite 1410, Montreal, Quebec H3A 2R7, Canada. Tel: (514) 849–3709. Fax: (514) 849–9577.

Toronto: 2 Bloor Street East, Suite 3330, Toronto, Ontario M4W 1A8, Canada. Tel: (416) 967–3381. Fax: (416) 967–4101.

Vancouver: 200 Granville Street, Suite 1380, Granville Square, Vancouver, British Columbia V6C 1S4, Canada. Tel: (604) 683–5808. Fax: (604) 662–8528.

BELGIAN TOURIST OFFICE

New York: 780 Third Avenue, Suite 1501, New York, New York 10017-7076. Tel: (212) 758–8130. Fax: (212) 355–7675.

BRITISH TOURIST AUTHORITY

Atlanta: 2580 Cumberland Parkway, Suite 470, Atlanta, Georgia 30339–3909. Tel: (404) 432–9635.

Chicago: 625 N. Michigan Avenue, Suite 1510, Chicago, Illinois 60611. Tel: (312) 787–0490. Fax: (312) 787–7746.

Los Angeles: World Trade Center, 350 S. Figueroa Street, Suite 450, Los Angeles, California 90071. Tel: (213) 628–3525. Fax: (213) 687–6621.

New York: 551 Fifth Avenue, New York, New York 10176. Tel: (212) 986–2200. Fax: (212) 986–1188.

FRENCH GOVERNMENT TOURIST OFFICE

For information on France by telephone, dial 1–900–990–0040 in the U.S. (charge is 50 cents per minute).

Chicago: 645 N. Michigan Avenue, Suite 3360, Chicago, Illinois 60611. Tel: (312) 751–7800. Fax (312) 337–6339.

Los Angeles: 9454 Wilshire Blvd., Suite 303, Beverly Hills, California 90212. Tel: (310) 271–7838. Fax (310) 276–2835.

New York: 610 Fifth Avenue, Suite 516, New York, New York, 10020. Tel: (212) 757–1125. Fax (212) 247–6468.

Montreal: 1981 McGill College Avenue, Suite 490, Montreal, Quebec H3A 2W9, Canada. Tel: (514) 288–4264. Fax: (514) 845–4868.

Toronto: 30 St. Patrick Street, Suite 700, Toronto, Ontario M5T 3A3, Canada. Tel: (416) 593–4723. Fax: (416) 979–7587.

GERMAN NATIONAL TOURIST OFFICE

Los Angeles: 11766 Wilshire Boulevard, Suite 750, Los Angeles, California 90025. Tel: (310) 575–9799. Fax: (310) 575–1565.

New York: 122 E. 42nd Street, 52nd Floor, New York, New York 10168–0072. Tel: (212) 661–7200. Fax: (212) 661–7174.

Toronto: 175 Bloor Street, East, North Tower, Suite 604, Toronto, Ontario M4W 3R8, Canada. Tel: (416) 968–1570. Fax (416) 968–1986.

GREEK NATIONAL TOURIST ORGANIZATION

Chicago: 168 N. Michigan Avenue, Chicago, Illinois 60601. Tel: (312) 782–1084. Fax: (312) 782–1091.

Los Angeles: 611 West Sixth Street, Suite 2198, Los Angeles, California 90017. Tel: (213) 626–6696. Fax: (213) 489–9744.

New York: 645 Fifth Avenue, 5th Floor, New York, New York 10022. Tel: (212) 421–5777. Fax: (212) 826–6940.

Montreal: 1233 rue de la Montagne, Suite 101, Quebec H3G 1Z2, Canada. Tel: (514) 871–1535. Fax: (514) 871–1498.

Toronto: Upper Level, 1300 Bay Street, Toronto, Ontario M5R 3K8, Canada. Tel: (416) 968–2220. Fax: (416) 968–6533.

HUNGARY–IBUSZ HUNGARIAN TRAVEL COMPANY

Fort Lee: One Parker Plaza, Suite 1104, Fort Lee, New Jersey 07024. Tel: (201) 592–8585. Fax: (201) 592–8736.

IRISH TOURIST BOARD

New York: 345 Park Avenue, New York, New York 10156. Tel: (212) 418–0800, (800) 223–6470. Fax: (212) 371–9052.

Toronto: 160 Bloor Street, Suite 934, Toronto, Ontario M5C 1C3, Canada. Tel: (416) 929–2777. Fax: (416) 929–6783.

ITALIAN GOVERNMENT TRAVEL OFFICE

New York: 630 Fifth Avenue, Suite 1565, New York, New York 10111. Tel: (212) 245–4822. Fax: (212) 586–9249.

Los Angeles: 12400 Wilshire Boulevard, Suite 550, Los Angeles, California 90025. Tel: (310) 820–0098. Fax: (310) 820–6357.

Montreal: 1 Place Ville Marie, Suite 1914, Montreal, Quebec, H3B 3M9, Canada. Tel: (514) 866–7667. Fax (514) 392–1429.

LUXEMBOURG NATIONAL TOURIST OFFICE

New York: 17 Beekman Place, New York, New York 10022. Tel: (212) 935–8888. Fax: (212) 935–5896.

MALTA NATIONAL TOURIST OFFICE

New York: 249 East 35th Street, New York, New York 10016. Tel: (212) 213–6686. Fax: (212) 213–6689

MONACO GOVERNMENT TOURIST/CONVENTION BUREAU

New York: 845 Third Avenue, 19th Floor, New York, New York 10022. Tel: (212) 759–5227 or (800) 753–9696. Fax: (212) 754–9320.

Chicago: 542 S. Dearborn Street, Suite 550, Chicago, Illinois 60605. Tel: (312) 939–7863. Fax: (312) 939–8727

NETHERLANDS BOARD OF TOURISM

Chicago: 225 N. Michigan Avenue, Suite 326, Chicago, Illinois 60601. Tel: (312) 819–0300. Fax: (312) 819–1740.

New York: 355 Lexington Avenue, 21st Floor, New York, New York 10017.

Los Angeles: 9841 Airport Boulevard, Los Angeles, California 90045.

Toronto: 25 Adelaide Street, East, Suite 710, Toronto, Ontario M5C 1Y2, Canada. Tel: (416) 363–1577. Fax: (416) 363–1470.

PORTUGUESE NATIONAL TOURIST OFFICE

New York: 590 Fifth Avenue, 4th Floor, New York, New York 10036. Tel: (212) 354–4403. Fax: (212) 764–6137.

Toronto: 60 Bloor Street, Suite 1005, Toronto, Ontario M4W 3B8, Canada. Tel: (416) 921–7376. Fax: (416) 921–1353.

SCANDINAVIAN TOURIST BOARDS OF DENMARK, FINLAND, ICE-LAND, NORWAY, AND SWEDEN

New York: 655 Third Avenue, New York, New York 10017. Tel: (212) 949–2333. Fax: (212) 983–5260.

TOURIST OFFICE OF SPAIN

Chicago: 845 N. Michigan Avenue, Suite 915 E., Water Tower Place, Chicago, Illinois 60611. Tel: (312) 642–1992. Fax: (312) 642–9817.

Los Angeles: San Vicente Plaza Building, 8383 Wilshire Blvd., Suite 960, Beverly Hills, California 90211. Tel: (213) 658–7188. Fax: (213) 658–1061.

New York: 665 Fifth Avenue, New York, New York 10022. Tel: (212) 759–8822. Fax: (212) 980–1053.

Toronto: 102 Bloor Street W, 14th Floor, Toronto, Ontario M5S 1M8, Canada. Tel: (416) 961–3131.

Miami: 1221 Brickell Avenue, Miami, Florida 33131. Tel: (305) 358–1992. Fax: (305) 358–8223.

SWISS NATIONAL TOURIST OFFICE

Chicago: 150 North Michigan Avenue, Suite 2930, Chicago, Illinois 60601. Tel: (312) 630–5840. Fax: (312) 630–5848.

Los Angeles: 222 N. Sepulveda Blvd., Suite 1570, El Segundo, California 90245. Tel: (310) 335–5980. Fax: (310) 335–5982.

New York: 608 Fifth Avenue, New York, New York 10020. Tel: (212) 757–5944. Fax: (212) 262–6116.

Toronto: 154 University Avenue, Suite 610, Toronto, Ontario M5H 3Y4, Canada. Tel: (416) 971–9734. Fax: (416) 971–6425.

TOLL-FREE AIRLINE NUMBERS
(Dialing from U.S.)

Air Canada (AC) 800–776–3000
Air France (AF) 800–237–2747
American Airlines, Inc. (AA) ... 800–433–7300
Austrian Airlines (OS) 800–843–0002
British Airways (BA) 800–AIRWAYS
Continental Airlines (CO) 800–525–0280
Delta Air Lines, Inc. (DL) 800–221–1212
Finnair (AY) 800–950–5000
Icelandair 800–223–5500
KLM Royal Dutch
    Airlines (KL) 800–374–7747
Lufthansa German
    Airlines (LH) 800–645–3880
Northwest Airlines,
    Inc. (NW) 800–225–2525

Sabena Belgian World
    Airlines (SN) 800–955–2000
Scandinavian Airlines
    System (SK) 800–221–2350
Swissair (SR) 800–221–4750
TAP Air Portugal (TO) 800–221–7370
Trans World
    Airlines, Inc. (TWA) 800–221–2000
United Air Lines, Inc. (UA) 800–241–6522
USAir (US) 800–428–4322
Virgin Atlantic
    Airways Ltd. (US) 800–862–8621

TOLL-FREE HOTEL RESERVATIONS NUMBERS
(Dialing from U.S.)

Choice Hotels
    International, Inc. 800-4-CHOICE
Consort Hotels Ltd. 800-55-CONSORT
Forte Hotels, Inc. 800-225-5843
Golden Tulip International 800-344-1212
Hilton Reservations
    Worldwide 800-HILTONS
Holiday Inn Worldwide 800-HOLIDAY
Hyatt Worldwide Reservation
    Centres 800-233-1234
Inter-Continental Hotels Corp ... 800-327-0200
Inter-Europe Hotels 800-221-6509
ITT Sheraton Corporation 800-325-3535
Kempinski International 800-426-3135
Leading Hotels of the World 800-223-6800
Loews Representation
    International 800-223-0888

Marriott Corportation 800-228-9290
MinOtels Intl. 800-336-4668
Mount Charlotte Thistle Hotels . 800-847-4358
Movenpick Hotels
    International 800-34-HOTEL
Nikko Hotels International 800-645-5687
Preferred Hotels & Resorts
    Worldwide 800-323-7500
Radisson Hotels
    International, Inc. 800-333-3333
Ramada International
    Hotels & Resorts 800-854-7854
Romantik Hotels &
    Restaurants Intl. 800-826-0015
SRS Steigenberger Reservation
    Service 800-223-5652
Swissotel 800-63-SWISS

GEOGRAPHIC INDEX

All places that have a main entry appear in heavy type.

AUTHORS' NOTE

We take this opportunity to thank all of the European railroads, DER Tours, and the tourist offices for their cooperation. Thanks also to our European research teammates who are invaluable aids to us in our annual revisions: Elissa Austria, Major Robert S. Bean, Benoit and Simone Drillon, Margaret Keith, Matthew Palma, Shellie and Daniel Rubin, Andrea Simkins, and Dorothy and Emil Turansky.

Our well-trained rail-specialist colleagues at Rail Pass Express, Inc., deserve profuse praise as well. Mary Kish, general manager at Rail Pass Express, runs a tight ship—must be her Navy background. Mary's leadership and organizational skills coupled with her business and computer experience are incomparable. Like a talented orchestra leader, Mary keeps the music playing.

Our assistant editor, Christian Martin, helps keep us on the right track and up to date. Christian actually wears several hats. In addition to his research and editorial duties, he's also director of marketing for Rail Pass Express, Inc. Busy guy!

Ben Sehgal, Mary DiThomas, and Tonya Young specialize in rail schedules, itinerary planning, and rail reservations. Novices may become confused and frustrated when trying to decipher rail schedules or make seat reservations, but for Ben, Mary, and Tonya, it's elementary.

Holly Bovie, Emma-Jane Clowes, and Jill Schmid are very knowledgeable about all the different European rail passes available—and there are many of them! Gone are the days of the simple choice between one or two types of rail passes. Holly, Emma, and Jill's expertise can take the confusion out of deciding which rail pass best meets the needs of the traveler.

While handing out laudatory comments, we cannot forget our most capable editor, Mace Lewis, at The Globe Pequot Press. Thanks!

Most of all, we thank *you*, our readers. We enjoy hearing from you and receiving your helpful comments and suggestions. Things change rapidly—if you find that something is not the way we say it is, please let us know. We want to keep both *Europe by Eurail* and *Britain by Britrail* as current and accurate as possible. We try to acknowledge your letters personally, but because of our research trips schedule, we are sometimes unable to answer as soon as we (or you) would like. We appreciate your help.

George and LaVerne Ferguson
Rail Pass Express, Inc.
2737 Sawbury Boulevard
Columbus, OH 43235-4583
(800) 722-7151